Demetrius Charles de Kavanagh Boulger

A Short History of China

Being an Account for the General Reader of an Ancient Empire and People

Demetrius Charles de Kavanagh Boulger

A Short History of China
Being an Account for the General Reader of an Ancient Empire and People

ISBN/EAN: 9783337170301

Printed in Europe, USA, Canada, Australia, Japan

Cover: Foto ©ninafisch / pixelio.de

More available books at **www.hansebooks.com**

BEING AN ACCOUNT FOR THE GENERAL READER OF AN
ANCIENT EMPIRE AND PEOPLE

BY

DEMETRIUS CHARLES BOULGER

Author of the "History of China" "England and Russia in Central Asia" &c &c

LONDON

W H ALLEN & CO LIMITED

13 WATERLOO PLACE SW

Publishers to the India Office

1893

I DEDICATE THIS SHORT

HISTORY OF CHINA

TO

SIR HALLIDAY MACARTNEY, K.C.M.G.,

AS A SLIGHT TRIBUTE OF PERSONAL RESPECT AND ADMIRATION FOR ONE WHO HAS MAINTAINED THE RIGHT OF CHINA TO BE TREATED BY THE GOVERNMENTS OF EUROPE WITH THE DIGNITY AND CONSIDERATION THAT BECOME A

GREAT EMPIRE.

IF TO LORD MACARTNEY WE OWE THE FIRST SUCCESSFUL ATTEMPT TO OBTAIN AUDIENCE OF THE EMPEROR OF CHINA ON THE SAME CONDITIONS AS THOSE ON WHICH FOREIGN AMBASSADORS ARE RECEIVED AT EUROPEAN COURTS, TO

SIR HALLIDAY MACARTNEY,

A SCION OF THE SAME FAMILY,

CHINA

OWES MUCH OF THE SUCCESS THAT HAS ATTENDED HER DIPLOMACY IN FOREIGN COUNTRIES.

PREFACE.

As China has now fairly taken her place in the family of nations it is unnecessary to elaborate an argument in support of even the humblest attempt to elucidate her history. It is a subject to which we can no longer remain indifferent, because circumstances are bringing every day more clearly into view the important part China must play in the changes that have become imminent in Asia, and that will affect the security of our position and Empire in that continent. A good understanding with China should be the first article of our Eastern policy, for not only in Central Asia, but also in Indo-China where French ambition threatens to create a fresh Egypt, her interests coincide with ours and furnish the sound basis of a fruitful alliance.

This book, which I may be pardoned for saying is not an abridgment of my original work, but entirely re-written and re-arranged with the view of giving prominence to the modern history of the Chinese Empire, may appeal, although they generally treat Asiatic subjects with regrettable indifference, to that wider circle of English readers on whose opinion and efforts the development of our political and commercial relations with the greatest of Oriental States will mainly depend. To the strictly historical narrative I have, at the suggestion of several competent authorities, added, by the courteous permission of the *Times*, the description I wrote in 1889 for that paper of the mode in which China is Governed.

D. C BOULGER.

28th April, 1893.

CONTENTS.

CHAP.		PAGE
I.	THE EARLY AGES ...	1
II.	THE FIRST NATIONAL DYNASTY	10
III.	A LONG PERIOD OF DISUNION	21
IV.	THE SUNGS AND THE KINS...	35
V.	THE MONGOL CONQUEST OF CHINA ...	47
VI.	KUBLAI AND THE MONGOL DYNASTY ...	70
VII.	THE MING DYNASTY	81
VIII.	THE DECLINE OF THE MINGS	97
IX.	THE MANCHU CONQUEST OF CHINA ...	108
X.	THE FIRST MANCHU RULER	126
XI.	THE EMPEROR KANGHI	139
XII.	A SHORT REIGN AND THE BEGINNING OF A LONG ONE...	154
XIII.	KEEN LUNG'S WARS AND CONQUESTS	162
XIV.	THE COMMENCEMENT OF EUROPEAN INTERCOURSE	175
XV.	THE DECLINE OF THE MANCHUS	183
XVI.	THE EMPEROR TAOUKWANG..	196
XVII.	THE FIRST FOREIGN WAR	204
XVIII.	TAOUKWANG AND HIS SUCCESSOR ...	232
XIX.	THE SECOND FOREIGN WAR	247
XX.	THE TAEPING REBELLION	284
XXI.	THE REGENCY	307
XXII.	THE REIGN OF KWANGSU	334
	HOW CHINA IS GOVERNED	356
	CHRONOLOGICAL TABLE	375
	APPENDIX	383
	INDEX OF SUBJECTS	421

A SHORT
HISTORY OF CHINA.

CHAPTER I.

THE EARLY AGES.

THE Chinese are unquestionably the oldest nation in the world, and their history goes back to a period to which no prudent historian will attempt to give a precise date. They speak the language and observe the same social and political customs that they did several thousand years before the Christian era, and they are the only living representatives to-day of a people and government which were contemporary with the Egyptians, the Assyrians, and the Jews. So far as our knowledge enables us to speak, the Chinese of the present age are in all essential points identical with those of the time of Confucius, and there is no reason to doubt that before his time the Chinese national character had been thoroughly formed in its present mould. The limits of the Empire have varied from time to time under circumstances of triumph or disunion, but the Middle Kingdom, or China Proper, of the eighteen provinces has always possessed more or less of its existing proportions. Another striking and peculiar feature about China is the small amount of influence that the rest of the world has exercised upon it. In fact it is only during the present century that that influence can be said to have existed at all. Up to that point China had pursued a course of her own, carrying on her own struggles within a definite limit, and completely indifferent to, and ignorant of, the ceaseless competition and contests of mankind outside her orbit, which make up the history of the rest of the old world. The long struggles for supremacy in Western Asia between Assyrian, Babylonian, and Persian, the triumphs of the Greek, followed by the absorption of what remained of the Macedonian conquests in the Empire of Rome, even the appearance of Islam and the Mahomedan conquerors, who changed the face of Southern Asia from the Ganges to the Levant, and long threatened to overrun Europe, had no significance for the people of China, and reacted as little on their destiny as if they had happened in another planet. Whatever advantages the Chinese may have derived from this isolation, it has entailed the penalty that the early history of their country is devoid of interest for the rest of the world, and it is only when the long independent courses of China and Europe are brought into proximity by the Mongol conquests, the efforts of the mediæval travellers, the development of commerce, and the wars carried on for the purpose of obtaining a secure position for foreigners in China—four distinct phases covering the last seven centuries,—that any confidence can be felt in successfully attracting notice to the affairs of China. Yet, as a curiosity in human existence, the earlier history of that country may justly receive some notice. Even though the details are not recited the recollection of the antiquity of China's institutions must be ever present with the student, as affording an indispensable clue to the character of the Chinese people and the composition of their government.

The first Chinese are supposed to have been a nomad tribe in the province of Shensi which lies in the north-west of China, and among them at last appeared a ruler, Fohi, whose name at least has been preserved. His deeds and his person are mythical, but he is credited with having given his country its first regular institutions. One of his successors was Hwangti (which means Heavenly Emperor), who was the first to employ the imperial style of Emperor, the earlier rulers having been content with the inferior title of Wang, or prince. He adopted the convenient decimal division in his administration as well as his coinage. His dominions were divided into ten provinces, each of these into ten departments, these again into ten districts, each of which held ten towns. He regulated the calendar, originating the Chinese cycle of sixty years, and he encouraged commerce. He seems to have been a wise prince and to have been the first of the great Emperors. His grandson, who was also Emperor, continued his good work and earned the reputation of being "the restorer or even founder of true astronomy."

But the most famous of Hwangti's successors was his great grandson Yao, who is still one of the most revered of all Chinese rulers. He was "diligent, enlightened, polished, and prudent," and if his words reflected his actions he must have been most solicitous of the welfare of his people. He is specially remarkable for his anxiety to discover the best man to succeed him in the government, and during the last twenty-eight years of his reign he associated the minister Chun with him for that purpose. On his death he left the crown to him, and Chun, after some hesitation, accepted the charge, but he in turn hastened to secure the co-operation of another minister named Yu in the work of administration, just as he had been associated with Yao. The period covered by the rule of this triumvirate is considered one of the most brilliant and perfect in Chinese history, and it bears a resemblance to the age of the Antonines. These rulers seem to have passed their leisure from practical work in framing moral axioms, and in carrying out a model scheme of government based on the purest ethics. They considered that "a prince entrusted with the charge of a State has a heavy task. The happiness of his subjects absolutely depends upon him. To provide for everything is his duty; his ministers are only put in office to assist him," and also that "a prince who wishes to fulfil his obligations, and to long preserve his people in the ways of peace, ought to watch without ceasing that the laws are observed with exactitude." They were staunch upholders of temperance, and they banished the unlucky discoverer of the fact that an intoxicating drink could be obtained from rice. They also held fast to the theory that all government must be based on the popular will. In fact the reigns of Yao, Chun, and Yu are the ideal period of Chinese history when all questions were decided by moral right and justice, and even now Chinese philosophers are said to test their maxims of morality by the degree of agreement they may have with the conduct of those rulers.

With them passed away the practice of letting the most capable and experienced minister rule the State. Such an impartial and reasonable mode of selecting the head of a community can never be perpetuated. The rulers themselves may see its advantages and may endeavour as honestly as these three Chinese princes to carry out the arrangement, but the day must come when the family of the able ruler will assert its rights to the succession, and take advantage of its opportunities from its close connection with the government to carry out its ends. The Emperor Yu, true to the practice of his predecessors, nominated the President of the Council as his successor, but his son Tiki seized the throne, and became the founder of the first Chinese dynasty which was called the Hia from the name of the province first ruled by his father. This event is supposed to have taken place in the year 2197 B.C. and the Hia dynasty, of which there were seventeen Emperors, ruled down to the year 1776 B.C. These Hia princes present no features of interest, and the last of them, named Kia, was deposed by one of his principal nobles, Ching Tang, Prince of Chang.

This prince was the founder of the second dynasty, known as Chang, which held possession of the throne for 654 years, or down to 1122 B.C. With the exception of the founder, who seems to have been an able man, this dynasty of twenty-eight Emperors did nothing very noteworthy. The public morality deteriorated very much under this family, and it is said that when one of the Emperors wanted an honest man as minister he could only find one in the person of a common labourer. At last, in the 12th century before our era, the enormities of the Chang rulers reached a climax in the person of Chousin, who was deposed by a popular rising headed by Wou Wang, Prince of Chow.

This successful soldier, whose name signifies the Warrior King, founded the third Chinese dynasty of Chow, which governed the Empire for the long space of 867 years down to 255 B.C. During that protracted period there were necessarily good and bad Emperors, and the Chow dynasty was rendered specially illustrious by the appearance of the great social and religious reformers, Laoutse, Confucius, and Mencius during the existence of its power. The founder of the dynasty instituted the necessary reforms to prove that he was a national benefactor, and one of his successors, known as the Magnificent King, extended the authority of his family over some of the States of Turkestan. But on the whole the rulers of the Chow dynasty were not particularly distinguished, and one of them in the eighth century B.C. was weak enough to resign a portion of his sovereign rights to a powerful vassal, Siangkong the Prince of Tsin, in consideration of his undertaking the defence of the frontier against the Tartars. At this period the authority of the central government passed under a cloud. The Emperor's prerogative became the shadow of a name, and the last three centuries of the rule of this family would not call for notice but for the genius of Laoutse and Confucius, who were both great moral teachers and religious reformers.

Laoutse, the founder of Taouism, was the first in point of time, and in some respects he was the greatest, of these reformers. He found his countrymen sunk in a low state of moral indifference and religious infidelity which corresponded with the corruption of the times and the disunion in the kingdom. He at once set himself to work with energy and devotion to repair the evils of his day, and to raise before his countrymen a higher ideal of duty. He has been called the Chinese Pythagoras, the most erudite of sinologues have pronounced his text obscure, and the mysterious Taouism which he founded holds the smallest or the least assignable part in what passes for the religion of the Chinese. As a philosopher and minister Laoutse will always attract attention and excite speculation, but as a practical reformer and politician he was far surpassed by his younger and less theoretical contemporary Confucius.

Confucius was an official in the service of one of the great princes who divided the governing power of China among themselves during the whole of the seventh century before our era, which beheld the appearance of both of these religious teachers and leaders. He was a trained administrator with long experience when he urged upon his prince the necessity of reform, and advocated a policy of union throughout the States. His exhortations were in vain, and so far ill-timed that he was obliged to resign the service of one prince after another. In his day the authority of the Chow Emperor had been reduced to the lowest point. Each prince was unto himself the supreme authority. Yet one cardinal point of the policy of Confucius was submission to the Emperor, as implicit obedience to the head of the State throughout the country as was paid to the father of every Chinese household. Although he failed to find a prince after his own heart, his example and precepts were not thrown away, for in a later generation his reforms were executed, and down to the present day the best points in Chinese government are based on his recommendations. If "no intelligent monarch arose" in his time, the greatest Emperors have since sought to conform with his usages and to rule after the ideal of the great philosopher. His name and his teachings were perpetuated by a band of devoted disciples, and the book which contained the moral and philosophical axioms of Confucius passed into the classic literature of the country and stood in the place of a Bible for the Chinese. The list of the great Chinese reformers is completed by the name of Mencius, who, coming two centuries later, carried on with better opportunities the reforming work of Confucius, and left behind him in his Sheking the most popular book of Chinese poetry and a crowning tribute to the great Master.

From teachers we must again pass to the chronicle of kings, although few of the later Chow Emperors deserve their names to be rescued from oblivion. One Emperor suffered a severe defeat while attempting to establish his authority over the troublesome tribes beyond the frontier; of another it was written that "his good qualities merited a happier day," and the general character of the age may be inferred from its being designated by the native chroniclers "The warlike period." At last, after what seemed an interminable old age, marked by weakness and vice, the Chow dynasty came to an end in the person of Nan Wang, who, although he reigned for nearly sixty years, was deposed in ignominious fashion by one of his great vassals, and reduced to a humble position. His conqueror became the founder of the fourth Chinese dynasty.

During the period of internal strife which marked the last four centuries of the Chow dynasty, one family had steadily waxed stronger and stronger among the princes of China. The princes of Tsin, by a combination of prudence and daring, gradually made themselves supreme among their fellows. It was said of one of them that "like a wolf or a tiger he wished to draw all the other princes into his claws, so that he might devour them." Several of the later Tsin princes, and particularly one named Chow Siang Wang, showed great capacity, and carried out a systematic policy for their own aggrandisement. When Nan Wang was approaching the end of his career, the Tsin princes had obtained everything of the supreme power short of the name and the right to wear the Imperial yellow robes. Ching Wang, or to give him his later name as Emperor, Tsin Chi Hwangti, was the reputed great-grandson of Chow Siang Wang, and under him the fame and power of the Tsins reached their culminating point. This prince also proved himself one of the greatest rulers who ever sat on the Dragon Throne of China.

The country had been so long distracted by internal strife, and the authority of the Emperor had been reduced to such a shadow, that peace was welcome under any ruler, and the hope was indulged that the Tsin princes, who had succeeded in making themselves the most powerful feudatories of the Empire, might be able to restore to the central government something of its ancient power and splendour. Nor was the expectation unreasonable or ungratified. The Tsins had fairly earned by their ability the confidence of the Chinese nation, and their principal representative showed no diminution of energy on attaining the throne, and exhibited in a higher post, and on a wider field, the martial and statesman-like qualities his ancestors had displayed when building up the fabric of their power as princes of the Empire. Their supremacy was not acquiesced in by the other great feudatories without a struggle, and more than one campaign was fought before all rivals were removed from their path, and their authority passed unchallenged as occupants of the Imperial office.

It was in the middle of this final struggle, and when the result might still be held doubtful, that Tsin Chi Hwangti began his eventful reign. When he began to rule he was only thirteen years of age, but he quickly showed that he possessed the instinct of a statesman, and the courage of a born commander of armies. On the one hand he sowed dissension between the most formidable of his opponents, and brought about by a stratagem the disgrace of the ablest general in their service, and on the other he increased his army in numbers and efficiency, until it became unquestionably the most formidable fighting force in China. While he endeavoured thus to attain internal peace, he was also studious in providing for the general security of the Empire, and with this object he began the construction of a fortified wall across the northern frontier to serve as a defence against the troublesome Hiongnou tribes, who are identified with the Huns of Attila. This wall, which he began in the first years of his reign, was finished before his death, and still exists as the Great Wall of China, which has been considered one of the wonders of the world. He was careful in his many wars with the tribes of Mongolia not to allow himself to be drawn far from his own border, and at the close of a campaign he always withdrew his troops behind the Great Wall. Towards Central Asia he was more enterprising, and one of his best generals, Moungtien, crossed what is now the Gobi Desert, and made Hami the frontier fortress of the Empire.

In his civil administration Hwangti was aided by the minister Lisseh, who seems to have been a man of rare ability, and to have entered heartily into all his master's schemes for uniting the Empire. While Hwangti sat on the throne with a naked sword in his hand, as the emblem of his authority, dispensing justice, arranging the details of his many campaigns, and superintending the innumerable affairs of his government, his minister was equally active in reorganising the administration and in supporting his sovereign in his bitter struggle with the literary classes who advocated archaic principles, and whose animosity to the ruler was inflamed by the contempt, not unmixed with ferocity, with which he treated them. The Empire was divided into thirty-six provinces, and he impressed upon the governors the importance of improving communications within their jurisdiction. Not content with this general precept, he issued a special decree ordering that "roads shall be made in all directions throughout the Empire," and the origin of the main routes in China may be found with as much certainty in his reign as that of the roads of Europe in the days of Imperial Rome. When advised to assign some portion of his power to his relatives and high officials in the provinces he refused to repeat the blunders of his predecessors, and laid down the permanent truth that "good government is impossible under a multiplicity of masters." He centralised the power in his own hands, and he drew up an organisation for the civil service of the State which virtually exists at the present day. The two salient features in that organisation are the indisputable supremacy of the Emperor and the non-employment of the officials in their native provinces, and the experience of two thousand years has proved their practical value.

When he conquered his internal enemies he resolved to complete the pacification of his country by effecting a general disarmament, and he ordered that all weapons should be sent in to his capital at Hienyang. This "skilful disarming of the provinces added daily to the wealth and prosperity of the capital," which he proceeded to embellish. He built one palace within the walls, and the Hall of Audience was ornamented with twelve statues, each of which weighed twelve thousand pounds. But his principal residence, named the Palace of Delight, was without the walls, and there he laid out magnificent gardens, and added building to building. In one of the courts of this latter palace, it is said he could have drawn up 10,000 soldiers. This eye to military requirements in even the building of his residence, showed the temper of his mind, and, in his efforts to form a regular army, he had recourse to "those classes in the community who were without any fixed profession, and who were possessed of exceptional physical strength." He was thus the earliest possessor in China of what might be called a regular standing army. With this force he succeeded in establishing his power on a firm basis, and he may have hoped also to ensure permanence for his dynasty; but, alas! for the fallacy of human expectations, the structure he erected fell with him.

Great as an administrator, and successful as a soldier, Hwangti was unfortunate in one struggle that he provoked. At an early period of his career, when success seemed uncertain, he found that his bitterest opponents were men of letters, and that the literary class as a body was hostile to his interests and person. Instead of ignoring this opposition or seeking to overcome it by the same agency, Hwangti expressed his hatred and contempt, not only of the literary class, but of literature itself, and resorted to extreme measures of coercion. The writers took up the gage of battle thrown down by the Emperor, and Hwangti became the object of the wit and abuse of every literate who could use a pencil. His birth was aspersed. It was said that he was not a Tsin at all, that his origin was of the humblest, and that he was a substituted child foisted on the last of the Tsin princes. These personal attacks were accompanied by unfavourable criticism of all his measures, and by censure where he felt that he deserved praise. It would have been more prudent if he had shown greater indifference and patience, for although he had the satisfaction of triumphing by brute force over those who jeered at him, the triumph was accomplished by an act of Vandalism, with which his name will be quite as closely associated in history as any of the wise measures or great works that he carried out. His vanquished opponents left behind them a legacy of hostility and revenge of the whole literary class of China, which has found expression in all the national histories.

The struggle, which had been in progress for some years, reached its culminating point in the year 213 B.C., when a Grand Council of the Empire was summoned at Hienyang. At this council were present not only the Emperor's chief military and civil officers from the different provinces, but also the large literary class, composed of aspirants to office and the members of the academies and college of Censors. The opposing forces in China were thus drawn up face to face, and it would have been surprising if a collision had not occurred. On the one side were the supporters of the man who had made China again an Empire, believers in his person and sharers in his glory; on the other were those who had no admiration for this ruler, who detested his works, proclaimed his successes dangerous innovations, and questioned his right to bear the royal name. The purpose of the Emperor may be detected when he called upon speakers in this assembly of his friends and foes to express their opinions of his administration, and when a member of his household rose to extol his work and to declare that he had "surpassed the very greatest of his predecessors." This courtier-like declaration, which would have been excusable even if it had had a less basis of truth than it unquestionably possessed in the case of Hwangti, was received with murmurs and marks of dissent by the literati. One of them rose and denounced the speaker as "a vile flatterer," and proceeded to expatiate on the superior merit of several of the earlier rulers. Not content with this unseasonable eulogy, he advocated the restoration of the Empire to its old form of principalities, and the consequent undoing of all that Hwangti had accomplished. Hwangti interrupted this speaker and called upon his favourite minister Lisseh to reply to him and explain his policy. Lisseh began by stating what has often been said since, and in other countries, that " men of letters are, as a rule, very little acquainted with what concerns the government of a country, not that government of pure speculation which is nothing more than a phantom, vanishing the nearer we approached to it, but the practical government which consists in keeping men within the sphere of their proper duties." He then proceeded to denounce the literary class as being hostile to the State, and to recommend the destruction of their works, declaring that "now is the time or never to close the mouths of these secret enemies and to place a curb on their audacity." The Emperor at once from his throne ratified the policy and ordered that no time should be lost in executing the necessary measures. All books were proscribed, and orders were issued to burn every work except those relating to medicine, agriculture, and such science as then existed. The destruction of the national literature was carried out with terrible completeness, and such works as were preserved are not free from the suspicion of being garbled or incomplete versions of their original text. The burning of the books was accompanied by the execution of five hundred of the literati, and by the banishment of many thousands. By this sweeping measure, to which no parallel is to be found in the history of other countries, Hwangti silenced during the last few years of his life the criticisms of his chief enemies, but in revenge his memory has had to bear for two thousand years the sully of an inexcusable act of tyranny and narrow-mindedness. The price will be pronounced too heavy for what was a momentary gratification.

The reign of Hwangti was not prolonged many years after the burning of the books. In 210 B.C. he was seized with a serious illness, to which he succumbed, partly because he took no precautions, and partly, no doubt, through the incompetence of his physicians. His funeral was magnificent, and, like the Huns, his grave was dug in the bed of a river, and with him were buried his wives and his treasure. This great ruler left behind him an example of vigour such as is seldom found in the list of Chinese kings of effete physique and apathetic life. He is the only Chinese Emperor of whom it is said that his favourite exercise was walking, and his vigour was apparent in every department of State. On one occasion when he placed a large army of, it is said, 600,000 men at the disposal of one of his generals, the commander expressed some fear as to how this huge force was to be fed. Hwangti at once replied, "Leave it to me. I will provide for everything. There shall be want rather in my palace than in your camp." He does not seem to have been a great general himself, but he knew how to select the best commanders, and he was also so quick in discovering the merits of the generals opposed to him, that some of his most notable victories were obtained by his skill in detaching them from their service or by ruining their reputation by some intrigue more astute than honourable. Yet, all deductions made, Tsin Chi Hwangti stands forth as a great ruler and remarkable man.

The Tsin dynasty only survived its founder a few years. Hwangti's son Eulchi became Emperor, but he reigned no more than three years. He was foolish enough to get rid of the general Moungtien, who might have been the buttress of his throne; and the minister Lisseh was poisoned, either with or without his connivance. Eulchi himself shared the same fate, and his successor, Ing Wang, reigned only six weeks, committing suicide after losing a battle, and with him the Tsin dynasty came to an end. Its chief, nay its only claim to distinction, arises from its having produced the great ruler Hwangti, and its destiny was Napoleonic in its brilliance and evanescence.

Looking back at the long period which connects the mythical age with what may be considered the distinctly historical epoch of the Tsins, we find that by the close of the third century before the Christian era China possessed settled institutions, the most remarkable portion of its still existing literature, and mighty rulers. It is hardly open to doubt that the Chinese annalist finds in these remote ages as much interest and instruction as we should in the record of more recent times, and proof of this may be discovered in the fact that the history of the first four dynasties, which we must dismiss in these few pages, occupies as much space in the national history as the chronicle of events from Tsin Chi Hwangti to the end of the Ming dynasty in 1644, at which date the official history of China stops, because the history of the Manchu dynasty, which has occupied the throne ever since, will only be given to the world after it has ceased to rule. We must not be surprised at this discursiveness, because the teachings of human experience are as clearly marked in those early times as they have been since, and Chinese historians aim as much at establishing moral and philosophical truths as at giving a complete record of events. The consequences of human folly and incompetence are as patent and conspicuous in those days as they are now. The ruling power is lost by one family and transferred to another because the prince neglects his business, gives himself over to the indulgence of pleasure, or fails to see the signs of the times. Cowardice and corruption receive their due and inevitable punishment. The founders of the dynasties are all brave and successful warriors, who are superior to the cant of a hyper-civilised state of society, which covers declining vigour and marks the first phase of effeteness, and who see that as long as there are human passions they may be moulded by genius to make the many serve the few and to build up an autocracy. Nor are the lessons to be learnt from history applicable only to individuals. The faults of an Emperor are felt in every household of the community, and injure the State. Indifference and obtuseness at the capital entailed weakness on the frontier and in the provincial capitals. The barbarians grew defiant and aggressive, and defeated the Imperial forces. The provincial governors asserted their independence, and founded ruling families. The Empire became attenuated by external attack and internal division. But, to use the phrase of the Chinese historians, "after long abiding disunion, union revived." The strong and capable man always appears in one form or another, and the Chinese people, impressed with a belief in both the divine mission of their Emperor and also in the value of union, welcome with acclaim the advent of the prince who will restore their favourite and ideal system of one-man government. The time is still hidden in a far-distant and undiscoverable future when it will be otherwise, and when the Chinese will be drawn away from their consistent and ancient practice to pursue the *ignis fatuus* of European politics that seeks to combine human equality with good practical government and national security. The Chinese have another and more attainable ideal, nor is there any likelihood of their changing it. The fall of dynasties may, needs must, continue in the ordinary course of nature, but in China it will not pave the way to a Republic. The Imperial authority will rise triumphant after every struggle above the storm.

CHAPTER II.

THE FIRST NATIONAL DYNASTY.

As the Chinese are still proud to call themselves the sons of Han, it will be understood that the period covered by the Han rulers must be an important epoch in their history, and in more than one respect they were the first national dynasty. When the successors of Tsin Chi Hwangti proved unable to keep the throne, the victorious general who profited by their discomfiture was named Liu Pang. He had been a trusted official of the Emperor Hwangti, but on finding that his descendants could not bear the burden of government, he resolved to take his own measures, and he lost no time in collecting troops and in making a bid for popularity by endeavouring to save all the books that had not been burned. His career bears some resemblance to that of Macbeth, for a soothsayer meeting him on the road predicted, " by the expression of his features, that he was destined to become Emperor." He began his struggle for the throne by defeating another general named Pawang, who was also disposed to make a bid for supreme power. After this success Liu Pang was proclaimed Emperor as Kao Hwangti, meaning Lofty and August Emperor, which has been shortened into Kaotsou. He named his dynasty the Han, after the small state in which he was born.

Kaotsou began his reign by a public proclamation in favour of peace, and deploring the evils which follow in the train of war. He called upon his subjects to aid his efforts for their welfare by assisting in the execution of many works of public utility, among which roads and bridges occupied the foremost place. He removed his capital from Loyang in Honan to Singanfoo in Shensi, and as Singan was difficult of access in those days, he constructed a great high road from the centre of China to this somewhat remote spot on the western frontier. This road still exists, and has been described by several travellers in our time. It was constructed by the labour of 100,000 men through the most difficult country, crossing great mountain chains and broad rivers. The Chinese engineers employed on the making of this road, which has excited the admiration of all who have traversed it, first discovered and carried into execution the suspension bridge, which in Europe is quite a modern invention. One of these "flying bridges," as the Chinese called them, is 150 yards across a valley 500 feet below, and is still in use. At regular intervals along this road Kaotsou constructed rest-houses for travellers, and postal-stations for his couriers. No Chinese ruler has done anything more useful or remarkable than this admirable road from Loyang to Singanfoo. He embellished his new capital with many fine buildings, among which was a large palace, the grandeur of which was intended to correspond with the extent of his power.

The reign of Kaotsou was, however, far from being one of unchequered prosperity. Among his own subjects his popularity was great because he promoted commerce and improved the administration of justice. He also encouraged literature, and was the first ruler to recognise the claims of Confucius, at whose tomb he performed an elaborate ceremony. He thus acquired a reputation which induced the King of Nanhai—a state composed of the southern provinces of China with its capital at or near the modern Canton—to tender his allegiance. But he was destined to receive many slights and injuries at the hands of a foreign enemy who at this time began a course of active aggression that entailed serious consequences for both China and Europe.

Reference has been made to the Hiongnou or Hun tribes, against whom Tsin Hwangti built the Great Wall. In the interval between the death of that ruler and the consolidation of the power of Kaotsou, a remarkable chief named Meha, or Meta, had established his supremacy among the disunited clans of the Mongolian Desert, and had succeeded in combining for purposes of war the whole fighting force of what had been a disjointed and barbarous confederacy. The Chinese rulers had succeeded in keeping back this threatening torrent from overflowing the fertile plains of their country, as much by sowing dissension among these clans and by bribing one chief to fight another, as by superior arms. But Meha's success rendered this system of defence no longer possible, and the desert chieftain, realising the opportunity of spoil and conquest, determined to make his position secure by invading China. If the enterprise had failed, there would have been an end to the paramounce of Meha, but his rapid success convinced the Huns that their proper and most profitable policy was to carry on implacable war with their weak and wealthy neighbours. Meha's success was so great that in a single campaign he recovered all the districts taken from the Tartars by the general Moungtien. He turned the western angle of the Great Wall, and brought down his frontier to the river Hoangho. His light cavalry raided past the Chinese capital into the province of Szchuen, and returned laden with the spoil of countless cities. These successes were crowned by a signal victory over the Emperor in person. Kaotsou was drawn into an ambuscade in which his troops had no chance with their more active adversaries, and to save himself from capture, Kaotsou had no alternative but to take refuge in the town of Pingching, where he was closely beleaguered. It was impossible to defend the town for any length of time, and the capture of Kaotsou seemed inevitable, when recourse was had to a stratagem. The most beautiful Chinese maiden was sent as a present to propitiate the conqueror, and Meha, either mollified by the compliment, or deeming that nothing was to be gained by driving the Chinese to desperation, acquiesced in a convention which, while it sealed the ignominious defeat of the Chinese, rescued their sovereign from his predicament.

This disaster, and his narrow personal escape, seem to have unnerved Kaotsou, for when the Huns resumed their incursions in the very year following the Pingching convention, he took no steps to oppose them, and contented himself with denouncing in his palace Meha as "a wicked and faithless man, who had risen to power by the murder of his father, and one with whom oaths and treaties carried no weight." Notwithstanding this opinion, Kaotsou proceeded to negotiate with Meha as an equal, and gave this barbarian prince his own daughter in marriage as the price of his abstaining from further attacks on the Empire. Never, wrote a historian, "was so great a shame inflicted on the Middle Kingdom, which then lost its dignity and honour." Meha observed this peace during the life of Kaotsou, who found that his reputation was much diminished by his coming to terms with his uncivilised opponent, but although several of his generals rebelled, until it was said that "the very name of revolt inspired Kaotsou with apprehension," he succeeded in overcoming them all without serious difficulty. His troubles probably shortened his life, for he died when he was only fifty-three, leaving the crown to his son Hoeiti, and injunctions to his widow, Liuchi, as to the conduct of the administration.

The brief reign of Hoeiti is only remarkable for the rigour and terrible acts of his mother, the Empress Liuchi, who is the first woman mentioned in Chinese history as taking a supreme part in public affairs. Another of Kaotsou's widows aspired to the throne for her son, and the chief direction for herself. Liuchi nipped their plotting in the bud by poisoning both of them. She marked out those who differed from her, or who resented her taking the most prominent part in public ceremonies, as her enemies, to be removed from her path by any means. At a banquet she endeavoured to poison one of the greatest princes of the Empire, but her plot was detected and baffled by her son. It is, perhaps, not surprising that Hoeiti did not live long after this episode, and then Liuchi ruled in her own name, and without filling up the vacancy on the throne, until the public dissatisfaction warned her that she was going too far. She then adopted a supposititious child as her grandson, and governed as regent in his name. The mother of this youth seems to have made inconvenient demands on the Empress, who promptly put her out of the way, and when the son showed a disposition to resent this action, she caused him to be poisoned. She again ruled without a puppet Emperor, hoping to retain power by placing her relatives in the principal offices; but the dissatisfaction had now reached an acute point, and threatened to destroy her. It may be doubted whether she would have surmounted these difficulties and dangers, when death suddenly cut short her adventurous career. The popular legend is that this Chinese Lucrezia Borgia died of fright at seeing the apparitions of her many victims, and there can be no doubt that her crimes did not conduce to make woman government more popular in China.

It says much for the excellence of Kaotsou's work, and for the hold the Han family had obtained on the Chinese people, that when it became necessary to select an Emperor after the death of Liuchi the choice should have fallen unanimously on the Prince of Tai, who was the illegitimate son of Kaotsou. On mounting the throne, he took the name of Wenti. He began his reign by remitting taxes and by appointing able and honest governors and judges. He ordered that all old men should be provided with corn, meat, and wine, besides silk and cotton for their garments. At the suggestion of his ministers, who were alive to the dangers of a disputed succession, he proclaimed his eldest son heir to the throne. He purified the administration of justice by declaring that prince and peasant must be equally subject to the law; he abolished the too common punishment of mutilation, and had the satisfaction of seeing crime reduced to such low proportions in the Empire that the gaols contained only 400 prisoners. Wenti was a strong advocate of peace, which was, indeed, necessary to China, as it had not recovered from the effects of the last Hun invasion. He succeeded by diplomacy in inducing the Prince at Canton, who had shown a disposition to assert his independence, to recognise his authority, and thus averted a civil war. In his relations with the Huns, among whom the authority of Meha had passed to his son Lao Chang, he strove to preserve the peace, giving that chief one of his daughters in marriage, and showing moderation in face of much provocation. When war was forced upon him by their raids he did everything he could to mitigate its terrors, but the ill success of his troops in their encounters with the Tartars broke his confidence, and he died prematurely after a reign of twenty-three years, which was remarkable as witnessing the consolidation of the Hans. The good work of Wenti was continued during the peaceful reign of sixteen years of his son Kingti.

The next Emperor was Vouti, a younger son of Kingti, and one of his earliest conquests was to add the difficult and inaccessible province of Fuhkien to the Empire. He also endeavoured to propitiate the Huns by giving their chief one of the princesses of his family as a wife, but the opinion was gaining ground that it would be better to engage in a war for the overthrow of the national enemy than to purchase a hollow peace. Wang Kua, a general who had commanded on the frontier, and who knew the Hun mode of warfare, represented that success would be certain, and at last gained the Emperor's ear. Vouti decided on war, and raised a large army for the purpose. But the result was not auspicious. Wang Kua failed to bring the Huns to an engagement, and the campaign which was to produce such great results ended ingloriously. The unlucky general who had promised so much anticipated his master's displeasure by committing suicide. Unfortunatly for himself, his idea of engaging in a mortal struggle with the Tartars gained ground, and became in time the fixed policy of China. Notwithstanding this check, the authority of Vouti continued to expand. He annexed Szchuen, a province exceeding in size and population most European states, and he received from the ruler of Manchuria a formal tender of submission. In the last years of his reign the irrepressible Hun question again came up for discussion, and the episode of the flight of the Yuchi from Kansuh affords a break in the monotony of the struggle, and is the first instance of that western movement which brought the tribes of the Gobi desert into Europe. The Yuchi are believed to have been allied with the Jats of India, and there is little or no doubt that the Sacæ, or Scythians, were their descendants. They occupied a strip of territory in Kansuh from Shachow to Lanchefoo, and after suffering much at the hands of the Huns under Meha, they resolved to seek a fresh home in the unknown regions of Western Asia. The Emperor Vouti wished to bring them back, and he sent an envoy named Chang Keen to induce them to return. That officer discovered them in the Oxus region, but all his arguments failed to incline them to leave a quarter in which they had recovered power and prosperity. Powerless against the Huns, they had more than held their own against the Parthians and the Greek kingdom of Bactria. They retained their predominant position in what is now Bokhara and Balkh, until they were gathered up by the Huns in their western march, and hurled, in conjunction with them, on the borders of the Roman Empire.

Meantime, the war with the Huns themselves entered upon a new phase. A general named Wei Tsing obtained a signal victory over them, capturing 15,000 prisoners and the spoil of the Tartar camp. This success restored long-lost confidence to the Chinese troops, and it was followed by several other victories. One Chinese expedition, composed entirely of cavalry, marched through the Hun country to Soponomo on the Tian Shan, carrying everything before it and returning laden with spoil, including some of the golden images of the Hun religion. Encouraged by these successes, Vouti at last took the field in person, and sent a formal summons to the Tartar King to make his submission to China. His reply was to imprison the bearer of the message, and to defy the Emperor to do his worst. This boldness had the effect of deterring the Emperor from his enterprise. He employed his troops in conquering Yunnan and Leaoutung instead of in waging another war with the Huns. But he had only postponed, not abandoned, his intention of overthrowing, once and for all, this most troublesome and formidable national enemy. He raised an enormous force for the campaign, which might have proved successful but for the mistake of entrusting the command to an incompetent general. In an ill-advised moment, he gave his brother-in-law, Li Kwangli, the supreme direction of the war. His incompetence entailed a succession of disasters, and the only redeeming point amid them was that Li Kwangli was taken prisoner and rendered incapable of further mischief. Liling, the grandson of this general, was entrusted with a fresh army to retrieve the fortunes of the war; but, although successful at first, he was out-manœuvred, and reduced to the unpleasant pass of surrendering to the enemy. Both Li Kwangli and Liling adapted themselves to circumstances, and took service under the Tartar chief. As this conduct obtained the approval of the historian Ssematsien, it is clear that our views of such a proceeding would not be in harmony with the opinion in China of that day. The long war which Vouti waged with the Huns for half a century, and which was certainly carried on in a more honourable and successful manner than any previous portion of that historic struggle, closed with discomfiture and defeat, which dashed to the ground the Emperor's hopes of a complete triumph over the most formidable national enemy.

After a reign of fifty-four years, which must be pronounced glorious, Vouti died, amidst greater troubles and anxieties than any that had beset him during his long reign. He was unquestionably a great ruler. He added several provinces to his Empire, and the success he met with over the Huns was far from being inconsiderable. He was a Nimrod among the Chinese, and his principal enjoyment was to chase the wildest animals without any attendants. Like many other Chinese princes, Vouti was prone to believe in the possibility of prolonging human life, or, as the Chinese put it, in the draught of immortality. In connection with this weakness an anecdote is preserved that will bear telling. A magician offered the Emperor a glass containing the pretended elixir of eternal life, and Vouti was about to drink it when a courtier snatched it from his hand and drained the goblet. The enraged monarch ordered him to prepare for instant death, but the ready courtier at once replied, "How can I be executed, since I have drunk the draught of immortality?" To so convincing an argument no reply was possible, and Vouti lived to a considerable age without the aid of magicians or quack medicines. Of him also it may be said that he added to the stability of the Han dynasty, and he left the throne to Chaoti, the youngest of his sons, a child of eight, for whom he appointed his two most experienced ministers to act as governors. As these ministers were true to their duty, the interregnum did not affect the fortunes of the State adversely, and several claimants to the throne paid for their ambition with their lives. The reign of Chaoti was prosperous and successful, but, unfortunately, he died at the early age of thirty-one, and without leaving an heir.

After some hesitation, Chaoti's uncle Liucho was proclaimed Emperor, but he proved to be a boor with low tastes, whose sole idea of power was the license to indulge in coarse amusements. The chief minister, Ho Kwang, took upon himself the responsibility of deposing him, and also of placing on the throne Siuenti, who was the great-grandson, or, according to another account, the grandson, of Vouti. The choice was a fortunate one, and "Ho Kwang gave all his care to perfecting the new Emperor in the science of government." As a knowledge of his connection with the Imperial family had been carefully kept from him, Siuenti was brought from a very humble sphere to direct the destinies of the Chinese, and his greater energy and more practical disposition were probably due to his not having been bred in the enervating atmosphere of a palace. He, too, was brought at an early stage of his career face to face with the Tartar question, and he had what may be pronounced a unique experience in his wars with them. He sent several armies under commanders of reputation to wage war on them, and the generals duly returned, reporting decisive and easily obtained victories. The truth soon leaked out. The victories were quite imaginary. The generals had never ventured to face the Tartars, and they were given no option by their enraged and disappointed master but to poison themselves. Other generals were appointed, and the Tartars were induced to sue for peace, partly from fear of the Chinese, and partly because they were disunited among themselves. Such was the reputation of Siuenti for justice that several of the Tartar chiefs carried their grievances to the foot of his throne, and his army became known as "the troops of justice." It is said that all the tribes and countries of Central Asia as far west as the Caspian sent him tribute, and to celebrate the event he built a kilin or pavilion, in which he placed statues of all the generals who had contributed towards his triumph. Only one incident marred the tranquillity of Siuenti's reign. The great statesman, Ho Kwang, had sunk quietly into private life as soon as he found the Emperor capable of governing for himself, but his wife Hohien was more ambitious and less satisfied with her position, although she had effected a marriage between her daughter and Siuenti. This lady was only one of the queens of the ruler, and not the Empress. Hohien, to further her ends, determined to poison the Empress, and succeeded only too well. Her guilt would have been divulged by the doctor she employed, but that Ho Kwang, by an exercise of his authority, prevented the application of torture to him when thrown into prison. This narrow escape from detection did not keep Hohien from crime. She had the satisfaction of seeing her daughter proclaimed Empress, but her gratification was diminished by the son of the murdered Hiuchi being selected as heir to the throne. Hohien resolved to poison this prince, but her design was discovered, and she and all the members of her family were ordered to take poison. The minister, Ho Kwang, had taken no part in these plots, which, however, injured his reputation, and his statue in the Imperial pavilion was left without a name.

Siuenti did not long survive these events, and Yuenti, the son of Hiuchi, became Emperor. His reign of sixteen years presents no features of interest beyond the signal overthrow of the Tartar chief, Chichi, whose head was sent by the victorious general to be hung on the walls of Singan. Yuenti was succeeded by his son Chingti, who reigned twenty-six years, and who gained the reputation of a Chinese Vitellius. His nephew Gaiti, who was the next Emperor, showed himself an able and well-intentioned prince, but his reign of six years was too brief to allow of any permanent work being accomplished. One measure of his was not without its influence on the fate of his successors. He had disgraced and dismissed from the service an official named Wang Mang, who had attained great power and influence under Chingti. The ambition of this individual proved fatal to the dynasty. On Gaiti's death he emerged from his retirement, and in conjunction with that prince's mother, seized the government. They placed a child, grandson of Yuenti, on the throne, and they gave him the name of Pingti, or the Peaceful Emperor, but he never governed. Before Pingti was fourteen, Wang Mang resolved to get rid of him, and he gave him the poisoned cup with his own hands. This was not the only, or perhaps the worst, crime that Wang Mang perpetrated to gain the throne. Pressed for money to pay his troops, he committed the sacrilege of stripping the graves of the princes of the Han family of the jewels deposited in them. One more puppet prince was placed on the throne, but he was soon got rid of, and Wang Mang proclaimed himself Emperor. He also decreed that the Han dynasty was extinct, and that his family should be known as the Sin.

Wang Mang the usurper was certainly a capable administrator, but in seizing the throne he had attempted a task to which he was unequal. As long as he was minister or regent, respect and regard for the Han family prevented many from revolting against his tyranny, but when he seized the throne he became the mark of popular indignation and official jealousy. The Huns resumed their incursions, and, curiously enough, put forward a proclamation demanding the restoration of the Hans. Internal enemies sprang up on every side, and Wang Mang's attempt to terrify them by severity and wholesale executions only aggravated the situation. It became clear that the struggle was to be one to the death, but this fact did not assist Wang Mang, who saw his resources gradually reduced, and his enemies more confident as the contest continued. After twelve years' fighting, Wang Mang was besieged at Singan. The city was soon carried by storm, and Wang Mang retired to the palace to put an end to his existence. But his heart failed him, and he was cut down by the foe. His last exclamation and the dirge of his short-lived dynasty, which is denied a place in Chinese history, was, "If Heaven had given me courage, what could the family of the Hans have done?"

The eldest of the surviving Han princes, Liu Hiuen, was placed on the throne, and the capital was removed from Singan to Loyang, or Honan. Nothing could have been more popular among the Chinese people than the restoration of the Hans. It is said that the old men cried for joy when they saw the banner of the Hans again waving over the palace and in the field. But Liu Hiuen was not a good ruler, and there might have been reason to regret the change if he had not wisely left the conduct of affairs to his able cousin, Liu Sieou. At last the army declared that Liu Sieou should be Emperor, and when Liu Hiuen attempted to form a faction of his own he was murdered by Fanchong, the leader of a confederacy known as the Crimson Eyebrows, on whose co-operation he counted. The Crimson Eyebrows were so called from the distinguishing mark which they had adopted when first organised as a protest against the tyranny of Wang Mang. At first they were patriots, but they soon became brigands. After murdering the Emperor, Fanchong, their leader, threw off all disguise, and seizing Singan, gave it over to his followers to plunder. Liu Sieou, on becoming Emperor, took the style of Kwang Vouti, and his first task was to overthrow the Crimson Eyebrows, who had become a public enemy. He entrusted the command of the army he raised for this purpose to Fongy, who justified his reputation as the most skilful Chinese general of his day by gaining several victories over a more numerous adversary. Within two years Kwang Vouti had the satisfaction of breaking up the formidable faction known as the Crimson Eyebrows, and of holding its leader Fanchong as a prisoner in his capital.

Kwang Vouti was engaged for many more years in subduing the numerous potentates who had repudiated the Imperial authority. His efforts were invariably crowned with success, but he acquired so great a distaste for war that it is said when his son asked him to explain how an army was set in battle array he refused to reply. But the love of peace will not avert war when a State has turbulent or ambitious neighbours who are resolved to appeal to arms, and so Kwang Vouti was engaged in almost constant hostilities to the end of his days. Chingtse, the Queen of Kaochi, which may be identified with the modern Annam, defied the Chinese, and defeated the first army sent to bring her to reason. This reverse necessitated a still greater effort on the part of the Chinese ruler to bring his neighbour to her senses. The occupant of the Dragon Throne could not sit down tamely under a defeat inflicted by a woman, and an experienced general named Mayuen was sent to punish the Queen of Kaochi. The Boadicea of Annam made a valiant defence, but she was overthrown, and glad to purchase peace by making the humblest submission. The same general more than held his own on the northern and northwest frontiers. When Kwang Vouti died, in A.D. 57, after a brilliant reign of thirty-three years, he had firmly established the Han dynasty, and he left behind him the reputation of being both a brave and a just prince.

His son and successor, Mingti, was not unworthy of his father. His acts were characterised by wisdom and clemency, and the country enjoyed a large measure of peace through the policy of Mingti and his father. A general named Panchow, who was perhaps the greatest military commander China ever produced, began his long and remarkable career in this reign, and, without the semblance of an effort, kept the Huns in order, and maintained the Imperial authority over them. Among other great and important works, Mingti constructed a dyke, thirty miles long, for the relief of the Hoangho, and the French missionary and writer, Du Halde, states that so long as this was kept in repair there were no floods. The most remarkable event of Mingti's reign was undoubtedly the official introduction of Buddhism into China. Some knowledge of the great Indian religion and of the teacher Sakya Muni seems to have reached China through either Tibet, or, more probably, Burma, but it was not until Mingti, in consequence of a dream, sent envoys to India to study Buddhism, that its doctrine became known in China. Under the direct patronage of the Emperor it made rapid progress, and although never unreservedly popular, it has held its ground ever since its introduction in the first century of our era, and is now inextricably intertwined with the religion of the Chinese state and people. Mingti died after a successful reign of eighteen years in 75 A.D. His son, Changti, with the aid of his mother, Machi, the daughter of the general Mayuen, enjoyed a peaceful reign of thirteen years, and died at an early age lamented by his sorrowing people.

After Changti came his son Hoti, who was only ten at the time of his accession, and who reigned for seventeen years. He was a virtuous and well-intentioned prince, who instituted many internal reforms, and during his reign a new writing-paper was invented, which is supposed to have been identical with the papyrus of Egypt. But the reign of Hoti is rendered illustrious by the remarkable military achievements of Panchow. The success of that general in his operations with the Huns has already been referred to, and he at last formed a deliberate plan for driving them away from the Chinese frontier. Although he enjoyed the confidence of his successive sovereigns, the Imperial sanction was long withheld from this vast scheme, but during the life of Changti he began to put in operation measures for the realisation of this project that were only matured under Hoti. He raised and trained a special army for frontier war. He enlisted tribes who had never served the Emperor before, and who were specially qualified for desert warfare. He formed an alliance with the Sienpi tribes of Manchuria, who were probably the ancestors of the present Manchus, and thus arranged for a flank attack on the Huns. This systematic attack was crowned with success. The pressure brought against them compelled the Hiongnou to give way, and as they were ousted from their possessions, to seek fresh homes further west. In this they were no doubt stimulated by the example of their old opponents, the Yuchi, but Panchow's energy supplied a still more convincing argument. He pursued them wherever they went, across the Gobi desert and beyond the Tian Shan range, taking up a strong position at modern Kuldja and Kashgar, sending his expeditions on to the Pamir, and preparing to complete his triumph by the invasion of the countries of the Oxus and Jaxartes. When Hoti was still a youth, he completed this programme by overrunning the region as far as the Caspian, which was probably at that time connected with the Aral, and it may be supposed that Khiva marked the limit of the Chinese general's triumphant progress. It is affirmed with more or less show of truth that he came into contact with the Roman Empire or the great Thsin, as the Chinese called it, and that he wished to establish commercial relations with it. But however uncertain this may be, there can be no doubt that he inflicted a most material injury on Rome, for before his legions fled the Huns, who, less than four centuries later, debased the majesty of the Imperial City, and whose leader, Attila, may have been a descendant of that Meha, at whose hands the Chinese suffered so severely.

After this brilliant and memorable war, Panchow returned to China, where he died at the great age of eighty. With him disappeared the good fortune of the Han dynasty, and misfortunes fell rapidly on the family that had governed China so long and so well. Hoti's infant son lived only a few months, and then his brother Ganti became Emperor. The real power rested in the hands of the widow of Hoti, who was elevated to the post of Regent. Ganti was succeeded in A.D. 124 by his son Chunti, in whose time several rebellions occurred, threatening the extinction of the dynasty. Several children were then elevated to the throne, and at last an ambitious noble named Leangki, whose sister was one of the Empresses, acquired the supreme direction of affairs. He gave a great deal of trouble, but at last, finding that his ambitious schemes did not prosper, he took poison, thus anticipating a decree passed for his execution. Hwanti, the Emperor who had the courage to punish this powerful noble, was the last able ruler of the Hans. His reign was, on the whole, a brilliant one, and the Sienpi tribes, who had taken the place of the Hiognou, were, after one arduous campaign, defeated in a pitched battle. The Chinese were on the verge of defeat when their general, Twan Kang, rushed to the front, exclaiming: "Recall to your minds how often before you have beaten these same opponents, and teach them again to-day that in you they have their masters."

After Hwanti's death the decline of the Hans was rapid. They produced no other ruler worthy of the throne. In the palace the eunuchs, always numerous at the Chinese Court, obtained the upper hand, and appointed their own creatures to the great governing posts. Fortunately this dissension at the capital was not attended by weakness on the frontier, and the Sienpi were again defeated. The battle is chiefly memorable because the Sienpi endeavoured to frighten the Chinese general by threatening to kill his mother, who was a prisoner in their hands, if he attacked. Not deterred by this menace, Chow Pow attacked the enemy, and gained a decisive victory, but at the cost of his mother's life, which so affected him that he died of grief shortly afterwards. After some time dissensions rose in the Han family, and two half brothers claimed the throne. Pienti became Emperor by the skilful support of his uncle, General Hotsin, while his rival Hienti enjoyed the support of the eunuchs. A deadly feud ensued between the two parties, which was aggravated by the murder of Hotsin, who rashly entered the palace without an escort. His soldiers avenged his death, carrying the palace by storm, and putting 10,000 eunuchs to the sword. After this the last Emperors possessed only the name of Emperor. The practical authority was disputed among several generals, of whom Tsow Tsow was the most distinguished and successful; and he and his son Tsowpi founded a dynasty, of which more will be heard hereafter. In A.D. 220 Hienti, the last Han ruler, retired into private life as Prince of Chanyang, thus bringing to an end the famous Han dynasty, which had governed China for 450 years.

Among the families that have reigned in China none have obtained as high a place in popular esteem as the Hans. They rendered excellent work in consolidating the Empire and in carrying out what may be called the Imperial mission of China. Yunnan and Leaoutung were made provinces for the first time. Cochin China became a vassal state. The writ of the Emperor ran as far as the Pamir. The wealth and trade of the country increased with the progress of its armies. Some of the greatest public works, in the shape of roads, bridges, canals, and aqueducts, were constructed during this period, and still remain to testify to the glory of the Hans. As has been seen, the Hans produced several great rulers. Their fame was not the creation of one man alone, and as a consequence the dynasty enjoyed a lengthened existence equalled by few of its predecessors or successors. No ruling family was ever more popular with the Chinese than this, and it managed to retain the throne when less favoured rulers would have expiated their mistakes and shortcomings by the loss of the Empire. With the strong support of the people, the Hans overcame innumerable difficulties, and even the natural process of decay ; and when they made their final exit from history it was in a graceful manner, and without the execration of the masses, which generally attends the fall of greatness and the loss of sovereign authority. That this feeling retains its force is shown in the pride with which the Chinese still proclaim themselves to be the sons of Han.

CHAPTER III.

A LONG PERIOD OF DISUNION.

THE ignominious failure of the usurper Wang Mang to found a dynasty was too recent to encourage anyone to take upon himself the heavy charge of administering the whole of the Han Empire, and so the state was split up into three principalities, and the period is known from this fact as the Sankoue. One prince, a member of the late ruling family, held possession of Szchuen, which was called the principality of Chow. The southern provinces were governed by a general named Sunkiuen, and called Ou. The central and northern provinces, containing the greatest population and resources, formed the principality of Wei, subject to Tsowpi, the son of Tsow Tsow. A struggle for supremacy very soon began between these princes, and the balance of success gradually declared itself in favour of Wei. It would serve no useful purpose to enumerate the battles which marked this struggle, yet one deed of heroism deserves mention, the defence of Sinching by Changte, an officer of the Prince of Wei. The strength of the place was insignificant, and, after a siege of ninety days, several breaches had been made in the walls. In this strait Changte sent a message to the besieging general that he would surrender on the hundredth day if a cessation of hostilities were granted, "as it was a law among the princes of Wei that the governor of a place which held out for a hundred days and then surrendered, with no prospect of relief visible, should not be considered as guilty." The respite was short and it was granted. But the disappointment of the besieger, already counting on success, was great when a few days later he saw that the breaches had been repaired, that fresh defences had been improvised, and that Sinching was in better condition than ever to withstand a siege. On sending to inquire the meaning of these preparations, Changte gave the following reply: "I am preparing my tomb and to bury myself in the ruins of Sinching." Of such gallantry and resource the internecine strife of the Sankoue period presents few instances, but the progress of the struggle steadily pointed in the direction of the triumph of Wei.

The Chow dynasty of the Later Hans was the first to succumb to the Princes of Wei, and the combined resources of the two states were then directed against the southern principality of Ou. The supreme authority in Wei had before this passed from the family of Tsowpi to his best general, Ssemachow, who had the satisfaction of beginning his reign with the overthrow of the Chow dynasty. If he had carried out the wishes of his own commander, Tengai, by attacking Ou at once, and in the flush of his triumph over Chow, he might have completed his work at a stroke, for as Tengai wrote, "An army which has the reputation of victory flies from one success to another." But Ssemachow preferred a slower and surer mode of action, with the result that the conquest of Ou was put off for twenty years.

Ssemachow died in A.D. 265, and his son Ssemachu founded the new dynasty of the Latu Tsins under the name of Vouti, or the warrior prince.

The main object with Vouti was to add the Ou principality to his dominions, and the descendants of Sunkiuen thought it best to bend before the storm. They sent humble embassies to Loyang, expressing their loyalty and submission, but at the same time they made strenuous preparations to defend their independence. This double policy precipitated the collision it was intended to avert. Vouti paid more heed to the acts than the promises of his neighbour, and he ordered the invasion of his territory from two sides. He placed a large fleet of war junks on the Yangtsekiang to attack his opponent on the Tunting Lake. The campaign that ensued was decided before it began. The success of Vouti was morally certain from the beginning, and after his army had suffered several reverses Sunhow threw up the struggle and surrendered to his opponent. Thus was China again reunited for a short time under the dynasty of the Later Tsins. Having accomplished his main task, Vouti gave himself up to the pursuit of pleasure, and impaired the reputation he had gained among his somewhat severe fellow-countrymen by entertaining a theatrical company of 5,000 female comedians, and by allowing himself to be driven in a car drawn by sheep through the palace grounds. Vouti lived about ten years after the unity of the Empire was restored, and his son, Ssemachong, or Hweiti, became Emperor on his death in A.D. 290. One of the great works of his reign was the bridging of the Hoangho at Mongtsin, at a point much lower down its course than is bridged at the present time.

The reign of Hweiti was marred by the ambitious vindictiveness of his wife, Kiachi, who murdered the principal minister and imprisoned the widow of the Emperor Vouti. The only good service she rendered the state was to discern in one of the palace eunuchs named Mongkwan a great general, and his achievements bear a strong resemblance to those of Narses, who was the only other great commander of that unfortunate class mentioned in history. Wherever Mongkwan commanded in person victory attended his efforts, but the defeats of the other generals of the Tsins neutralised his success. At this moment there was a recrudescence of Tartar activity which proved more fatal to the Chinese ruler than his many domestic enemies. Some of the Hiongnou tribes had retired in an easterly direction towards Manchuria when Panchow drove the main body westwards, and among them, at the time of which we are speaking, a family named Lin had gained the foremost place. They possessed all the advantages of Chinese education, and had married several times into the Han family. Seeing the weakness of Hweiti these Lin chiefs took the title of Kings of Han, and wished to pose as the liberators of the country. Hweiti bent before the storm, and would have made an ignominious surrender but that death saved him the trouble.

His brother and successor, Hwaiti, fared somewhat better at first, but notwithstanding some flashes of success the Lin Tartars marched further and further into the country, capturing cities, defeating the best officers of the Tsins, and threatening the capital. In A.D. 310 Linsong, the Han chief, invaded China in force and with the full intention of ending the war at a blow. He succeeded in capturing Loyang, and carrying off Hwaiti as his prisoner. The capital was pillaged and the Prince Royal executed. Hwaiti is considered the first Chinese Emperor to have fallen into the hands of a foreign conqueror. Two years after his capture, Hwaiti was compelled to wait on his conqueror at a public banquet, and when it was over he was led out to execution. This foul murder illustrates the character of the new race and men who aspired to rule over China. The Tartar successes did not end here, for a few years later they made a fresh raid into China, capturing Hwaiti's brother and successor, Mingti, who was executed, twelve months after his capture, at Pingyang, the capital of the Tartar Hans.

After these reverses the enfeebled Tsin rulers removed their capital to Nankin, but this step alone would not have sufficed to prolong their existence had not the Lin princes themselves suffered from the evils of disunion and been compelled to remove their capital from Pingyang to Singan. Here they changed their name from Han to Chow, but the work of disintegration once begun proceeded rapidly, and in the course of a few years the Lin power crumbled completely away. Released from their most pressing danger by the fall of this family, the Tsin dynasty took a new lease of life, but it was unable to derive any permanent advantage from this fact. The last Emperors of this family were weak and incompetent princes, whose names need not be given outside of a chronological table. There would be nothing to say about them but that a humble individual named Linyu, who owed everything to himself, found in the weakness of the government and the confusion in the country the opportunity of distinction. He proved himself a good soldier and able leader against the successors of the Lin family on one side, and a formidable pirate named Sunghen on the other. Dissatisfied with his position, Linyu murdered one Emperor and placed another on the throne, and in two years he compelled his puppet, the last of the Later Tsins, to make a formal abdication in his favour. For a considerable portion of their rule they governed the whole of China, and it is absolutely true to say that they were the least worthy family ever intrusted with so great a charge. Of the fifteen Emperors who ruled for 155 years there is not more than the founder whose name calls for preservation on his own merits.

Although Linyu's success was complete as far as it went, his dynasty, to which he gave the name of Song, never possessed exclusive power among the Chinese. It was only one administration among many others, and during his brief reign of three years he could do nothing towards extending his power over his neighbours, although he may have established his own the more firmly by poisoning the miserable Tsin Emperor whom he deposed. His son and successor, Chowti, was deposed and murdered after a brief reign of one year. His brother Wenti succeeded him, and he was soon drawn into a struggle for power, if not existence, with his northern neighbour the King of Wei, who was one of the most powerful potentates in the Empire. The principal and immediate bone of contention between them was the great province of Honan, which had been overrun by the Wei ruler, but which Wenti was resolved to recover. As the Hoangho divides this province into two parts, it was extremely difficult for the Wei ruler to defend the portion south of it, and when Wenti sent him his declaration of war, he replied, "Even if your master succeeds in seizing this province I shall know how to retake it as soon as the waters of the Hoangho are frozen." Wenti succeeded in recovering Honan, but after a protracted campaign, during which the Wei troops crossed the river on the ice, his armies were again expelled from it, and the exhausted combatants found themselves at the close of the struggle in almost the same position they had held at the commencement. For a time both rulers devoted their attention to peaceful matters, although Topatao, King of Wei, varied them by a persecution of the Buddhists, and then the latter concentrated all his forces with the view of overwhelming the Song Emperor. When success seemed certain, victory was denied him, and the Wei forces suffered severely during their retreat to their own territory. This check to his triumphant career injured his reputation and encouraged his enemies. A short time after this campaign, Topatao was murdered by some discontented officers.

Nor was the Song ruler, Wenti, any more fortunate, as he was murdered by his son. The parricide was killed in turn by a brother who became the Emperor Vouti. This ruler was fond of the chase and a great eater, but on the whole he did no harm. The next two Emperors were cruel and bloodthirsty princes, and during their reigns the executioner was constantly employed. Two more princes, who were, however, not members of the Song family, but only adopted by the last ruler of that house, occupied the throne, but this weakness and unpopularity—for the Chinese, unlike the people of India, scout the idea of adoption and believe only in the rights of birth—administered the finishing stroke to the Songs, who now give place to the Tsi dynasty, which was founded by a general named Siaotaoching, who took the imperial name of Kaoti. The change did not bring any improvement in the conditions of China, and it was publicly said that the Tsi family had attained its pride of place "not by merit, but by force." The Tsi dynasty, after a brief and ignominious career, came to an end in the person of a youthful prince named Hoti. After his deposition, in A.D. 502, his successful enemies ironically sent him in prison a present of gold. He exclaimed, "What need have I of gold after my death? a few glasses of wine would be more valuable." They complied with his wish, and while he was drunk they strangled him with his own silken girdle.

After the Tsi came the Leang dynasty, another of those insignificant and unworthy families which occupy the stage of Chinese history during this long period of disunion. The new Emperor Vouti was soon brought into collision with the state of Wei, which during these years had regained all its power, and had felt strong enough to transfer its capital from the northern city of Pingching, to Honan while the Leang capital remained at Nankin. The progress of this contest was marked by the consistent success of Wei, and the prince of that kingdom seems to have been as superior in the capacity of his generals as in the resources of his state. One incident will be sufficient to show the devotion which he was able to inspire in his officers. During the absence of its governor, Vouti attempted to capture the town of Ginching, and he would certainly have succeeded in his object had not Mongchi, the wife of that officer, anticipating by many centuries the conduct of the Countess of Montfort and of the Countess of Derby, thrown herself into the breach, harangued the small garrison, and inspired it with her own indomitable spirit. Vouti was compelled to make an ignominious retreat from before Ginching, and his troops became so disheartened that they refused to engage the enemy, notwithstanding their taunts and their marching round the imperial camp with the head of a dead person decked out in a widow's cap and singing a doggrel ballad to the effect that none of Vouti's generals were to be feared. In the next campaign Vouti was able to restore his declining fortunes by the timely discovery of a skilful general in the person of

Weijoui, who, taking advantage of the division of the Wei army into two parts by a river, gained a decisive victory over each of them in turn. If Vouti had listened to his general's advice, and followed up this success, he might have achieved great and permanent results, but instead he preferred to rest content with his laurels, with the result that the Wei prince recovered his military power and confidence. The natural consequences of this was that the two neighbours once more resorted to a trial of strength, and, notwithstanding the valiant and successful defence of a fortress by another lady named Liuchi, the fortune of war declared in the main for Vouti. This may be considered one of the most remarkable periods for the display of female capacity in China, as the great state of Wei was governed by a Queen named Houchi, but the general condition of the country does not support an argument in favour of female government.

The tenure of power by Houchi was summarily cut short by the revolt of the Wei commander-in-chief, Erchu Jong, who got rid of his mistress by tying her up in a sack and throwing her into the Honugho. He then collected 2,000 of her chief advisers in a plain outside the capital, and there ordered his cavalry to cut them down. Erchu Jong then formed an ambitious project for reuniting the Empire, proclaiming to his followers his intention in this speech: "Wait a little while, and we shall assemble all the braves from out our western borders. We will then go and bring to reason the six departments of the north, and the following year we will cross the great Kiang, and place in chains Siaoyen, who calls himself Emperor." This scheme was nipped in the bud by the assassination of Erchu Jong. Although the death of its great general signified much loss to the Wei state, the Emperor Vouti experienced bitter disappointment and a rude awakening when he attempted to turn the event to his own advantage. His army was defeated in every battle, his authority was reduced to a shadow, and a mutinous officer completed in his palace the overthrow begun by his hereditary enemy. Vouti was now eighty years of age, and ill able to stand so rude a shock. On being deposed he exclaimed, "It was I who raised my family, and it was I who have destroyed it. I have no reason to complain"; and he died a few days later, from, it is said, a pain in his throat which his gaolors refused to alleviate with some honey. On the whole Vouti was a creditable ruler, although the Chinese annalists blame him for his superstition and denounce his partiality for Buddhism.

Vouti's prediction that his family was destroyed proved correct. He was succeeded in turn by three members of his family, but all of these died a violent death. A general named Chinpasien founded a fresh dynasty known as the Chin, but he died before he had enjoyed power many years. At this period also disappeared the Wei state, which was dissolved by the death of Erchu Jong, and now merged itself into that of Chow. The growth of this new power proved very rapid, and speedily extinguished that of the unfortunate Chins. The Chow ruler took the name of Kaotsou Wenti, and ruled over a great portion of China. He changed the name of his dynasty to the Soui, which, although it did not hold possession of the throne for long, vindicated its claim to supremacy by successful wars and admirable public works. This prince showed himself a very capable administrator, and his acts were marked by rare generosity and breadth of view. His son and successor, Yangti, although he reached the throne by the murder of a brother proved himself an intelligent ruler and a benefactor of his people. He transferred his capital from Nankin to Honan, which he resolved to make the most magnificent city in the world. It is declared that he employed 2,000,000 men in embellishing it, and that he caused 50,000 merchants to take up their residence there. But of all his works none will compare with the great system of canals which he constructed, and in connection with which his name will live for ever in history. Although he reigned no more than thirteen years, he completed nearly 5,000 miles of canals. Some of these, such as the Grand Canal from the Hoangho to the Yangtsekiang are splendid specimens of human labour, and could be made as useful to-day as they were when first constructed. The canal named is forty yards wide and is lined with solid stone. The banks are bordered with elms and willows. These works were constructed by a general *corvée* or levy *en masse*, each family being required to provide one able-bodied man, and the whole of the army was also employed on this public undertaking. It is in connection with it that Yangti's name will be preserved, as his wars, especially one with Corea, were not successful, and an ignominious end was put to his existence by a fanatic. His son and successor was also murdered when the Soui dynasty came to an end, and with it the magnificent and costly palace erected at Loyang, which was denounced as only calculated "to soften the heart of a prince and to foment his cupidity."

There now ensues a break in the long period of disunion which had prevailed in China, and for a time the supreme authority of the Emperor recovered the general respect and vigour which by right belonged to it. The deposer of the Souis was Liyuen, who some years before had been given the title of Prince of Tang. In the year A.D. 617 he proclaimed himself Emperor under the style of Kaotsou, and he began his reign in an auspicious manner by proclaiming an amnesty and by stating his "desire to found his Empire only on justice and humanity." While he devoted his attention to the reorganisation of the administration at Singan, which he chose for his capital, his second son, Lichimin, was entrusted with the command of the army in the field, to which was assigned the task of subjecting all the provinces. Lichimin proved himself a great commander, and his success was both rapid and unqualified. He was equally victorious over Chinese rebels and foreign enemies. His energy and skill were not more conspicuous than his courage. At the head of his chosen regiment of cuirassiers, carrying black tiger skins, he was to be found in the front of every battle, and victory was due as often to his personal intrepidity as to his tactical skill. Within a few years the task of Lichimin was brought to a glorious completion, and on his return to Singan he was able to assure his father that the Empire was pacified in a sense that had not been true for many centuries. His entry into Singan at the head of his victorious troops reminds the reader of a Roman triumph. Surrounded by his chosen bodyguard, and followed by 40,000 cavalry, Lichimin, wearing a breastplate of gold and accompanied by the most important of his captives, rode through the streets to make public offering of thanks for victory achieved at the Temple of his ancestors. His success was enhanced by his moderation, for he granted his prisoners their lives, and his reputation was not dimmed by any acts of cruelty or bloodshed.

The magnitude of Lichimin's success and his consequent popularity aroused the envy and hostility of his elder brother, who aspired to the throne. The intrigues against him were so far successful that he fell into disgrace with the Emperor, and for a time withdrew from the court. But his brother was not content with anything short of taking his life, and formed a conspiracy with his other brothers and some prominent officials to murder him. The plot was discovered, and recoiled upon its authors, who were promptly arrested and executed. Then Lichimin was formally proclaimed heir to the throne; but the event sinks into comparative insignificance beside the abdication of the throne by Kaotsou in the same year. The real cause of this step was probably not disconnected with the plot against Lichimin, but the official statement was that Kaotsou felt the weight of years, and that he wished to enjoy rest and the absence of responsibility during his last days. Kaotsou must be classed among the capable rulers of China, but his fame has been overshadowed by and merged in the greater splendour of his son. He survived his abdication nine years, dying in A.D. 635 at the age of seventy-one.

On ascending the throne, Lichimin took the name of Taitsong, and he is one of the few Chinese rulers to whom the epithet of Great may be given without fear of its being challenged. The noble task to which he at once set himself was to prove that the Chinese were one people, that the interests of all the provinces, as of all classes of the community, were the same, and that the pressing need of the hour was to revive the spirit of national unity and patriotism. Before he became ruler in his own name he had accomplished something towards this end by the successful campaigns he had conducted to ensure the recognition of his father's authority. But Taitsong saw that much more remained to be done, and the best way to do it seemed to him to be the prosecution of what might be called a national war against those enemies beyond the northern frontier, who were always troublesome, and who had occasionally founded governments within the limits of China like the Topa family of Wei. In order to achieve any great or lasting success in this enterprise, Taitsong saw that it was essential that he should possess a large and well-trained standing army, on which he could rely for efficient service beyond the frontier as well as in China itself. Before his time Chinese armies had been little better than a rude militia, and the military knowledge of the officers could only be described as contemptible. The soldiers were, for the most part, peasants, who knew nothing of discipline, and into whose hands weapons were put for the first time on the eve of a war. They were not of a martial temperament, and they went unwillingly to a campaign; and against such active opponents as the Tartars they would only engage when superiority of numbers promised success. They were easily seized with a panic, and the celerity and dash of Chinese troops only became perceptible when their backs were turned to the foe. So evident had these faults become that more than one Emperor had endeavoured to recruit from among the Tartar tribes, and to oppose the national enemy with troops not less brave or active than themselves. But the employment of mercenaries is always only a half remedy, and not free from the risk of aggravating the evil it is intended to cure. But Taitsong did not attempt any such palliation; he went to the root of the question, and determined to have a trained and efficient army of his own. He raised a standing army of 900,000 men, which he divided into three equal classes of regiments, one containing 1,200 men, another 1,000, and the third 800. The total number of regiments was 895, of which 634 were recruited for home service and 261 for foreign. By this plan he obtained the assured services of more than a quarter of a million of trained troops for operations beyond the frontier. Taitsong also improved the weapons and armament of his soldiers. He lengthened the pike and supplied a stronger bow. Many of his troops wore armour; and he relied on the co-operation of his cavalry, a branch of military power which has generally been much neglected in China. He took special pains to train a large body of officers, and he instituted a Tribunal of War, to which the supreme direction of military matters was entrusted. As these measures greatly shocked the civil mandarins, who regarded the Emperor's taking part in reviews and the physical exercises of the soldiers as "an impropriety," it will be allowed that Taitsong showed great moral courage and surmounted some peculiar difficulties in carrying out his scheme for forming a regular army. He overcame all obstacles, and gathered under his banner an army formidable by reason of its efficiency and equipment, as well as for its numerical strength.

Having acquired what he deemed the means to settle it, Taitsong resolved to grapple boldly with the ever-recurring danger from the Tartars. Under different names, but ever with the same object, the tribes of the vast region from Corea to Koko Nor had been a trouble to the Chinese agriculturist and government from time immemorial. Their sole ambition and object in life had been to harry the lands of the Chinese, and to bear back to their camps the spoils of cities. The Huns had disappeared, but in their place had sprung up the great power of the Toukinei or Turks, who were probably the ancestors of the Ottomans. With these turbulent neighbours, and with others of different race but of the same disposition on the southern frontier, Taitsong was engaged in a bitter and arduous struggle during the whole of his life; and there can be little or no doubt that he owed his success to the care he bestowed on his army. The Great Wall of Tsin Hwangti had been one barrier in the path of these enemies, but, held by a weak and cowardly garrison, it had proved inadequate for its purpose. Taitsong supplied another and a better defence in a consistent and energetic policy, and in the provision of a formidable and confident army.

The necessity for this military reform was clearly shown by the experience of his first campaign with these implacable enemies, when, in the year of his accession and before his organisation had been completed, a horde of these barbarians broke into the Empire and carried all before them, almost to the gates of the capital. On this occasion Taitsong resorted to diplomacy and remonstrance. He rode almost unattended to the Tartar camp, and reproached their chiefs with their breach of faith, reminding them that on his sending one of his sisters to be the bride of their chief they had sworn by a solemn oath to keep the peace. He asked: "Are these proceedings worthy, I will not say of princes, but of men possessing the least spark of honour? If they forget the benefits they have received from me, at the least they ought to be mindful of their oaths. I had sworn a peace with them; they are now violating it, and by that they place the justice of the question on my side." The Chinese chroniclers declare that the Tartars were so impressed by Taitsong's majestic air and remonstrances that they agreed to retire, and fresh vows of friendship and peace were sworn over the body of a white horse at a convention concluded on the Pienkiao bridge across the Weichoui river. The only safe deduction from this figurative narrative is that there was a Tartar incursion, and that the

Chinese army did not drive back the invaders. Their retreat was probably purchased, but it was the first and last occasion on which Taitsong stooped to such a measure.

The peace of Pienkiao was soon broken. The tribes again drew their forces to a head for the purpose of invading China, but before their plans were complete Taitsong anticipated them by marching into their territory at the head of a large army. Taken by surprise, the Tartars offered but a feeble resistance. Several of their khans surrendered, and at a general assembly Taitsong proclaimed his intention to govern them as Khan of their khans, or by the title of Tien Khan, which means Celestial Ruler. This was the first occasion on which a Chinese ruler formally took over the task of governing the nomad tribes and of treating their chiefs as his lieutenants. Down to the present day the Chinese Emperor continues to govern the Mongol and other nomadic tribes under this very title, which the Russians have rendered as Bogdo Khan. The success of this policy was complete, for not only did it give tranquillity to the Chinese borders, but it greatly extended Chinese authority. Kashgaria was then, for the first time, formed into a province under the name of Lonugsi, and Lichitsi, one of the Emperor's best generals, was appointed Warden of the Western Marches. Some of the most influential of Taitsong's advisers disapproved of this advanced policy, and attempted to thwart it, but in vain. Carried out with the vigour and consistency of Taitsong there cannot be two opinions about its wisdom and efficacy.

During this reign the relations between China and two of its neighbours, Tibet and Corea, were greatly developed, and the increased intercourse was largely brought about by the instrumentality of war. The first envoys from Tibet, or, as it was then called, Toufan or Toupo, are reported to have reached the Chinese capital in the year 634. At that time the people of Tibet were rude and unlettered, and their chiefs were little better than savages. Buddhism had not taken that firm hold on the popular mind which it at present possesses, and the power of the lamas had not arisen in what is now the most priest-ridden country in the world. A chief, named the Sanpou—which means the brave Lord—had, about the time of which we are speaking, made himself supreme throughout the country, and it was said that he had crossed the Himalaya and carried his victorious arms into Central India. Curiosity, or the desire to wed a Chinese princess, and thus to be placed on what may be termed a favoured footing, induced the Sanpou to send his embassy to Singan; but although the envoys returned laden with presents, Taitsong declined to trust a princess of his family in a strange country and among an unknown people. The Sanpou chose to interpret this refusal as an insult to his dignity, and he declared war with China. But success did not attend his enterprise, for he was defeated in the only battle of the war, and glad to purchase peace by paying 5,000 ounces of gold and acknowledging himself a Chinese vassal. The Sanpou also agreed to accept Chinese education, and as his reward Taitsong gave him one of his daughters as a wife. It is stated that one of his first reforms was to abolish the national practice of painting the face, and he also built a walled city to proclaim his glory as the son-in-law of the Emperor of China. During Taitsong's life there was no further trouble on the side of Tibet.

Taitsong was not so fortunate in his relations with Corea, where a stubborn people and an inaccessible country imposed a bar to his ambition. Attempts had been made at earlier periods to bring Corea under the influence of the Chinese ruler, and to treat it as a tributary state. A certain measure of success had occasionally attended these attempts, but on the whole Corea had preserved its independence. When Taitsong in the plentitude of his power called upon the King of Corea to pay tribute, and to return to his subordinate position, he received a defiant reply, and the Coreans began to encroach on Sinlo, a small state which threw itself on the protection of China. The name of Corea at this time was Kaoli, and the supreme direction of affairs at this period was held by a noble named Chuen Gaisoowun, who had murdered his own sovereign. Taitsong, irritated by his defiance, sent a large army to the frontier, and when Gaisoowun, alarmed by the storm he had raised, made a humble submission and sent the proper tribute, the Emperor gave expression to his displeasure and disapproval of the regicide's acts by rejecting his gifts and announcing his resolve to prosecute the war. It is never prudent to drive an opponent to desperation, and Gaisoowun, who might have been a good neighbour if Taitsong had accepted his offer, proved a bitter and determined antagonist. The first campaign was marked by the expected success of the Chinese army. The Coreans were defeated in several battles, several important towns were captured, but Taitsong had to admit that these successes were purchased at the heavy loss of 25,000 of his best troops. The second campaign resolved itself into the siege and defence of Anshu, an important town near the Yaloo river. Gaisoowun raised an enormous force with the view of effecting its relief, and he attempted to overwhelm the Chinese by superior numbers. But the better discipline and tactics of the Chinese turned the day, and the Corean army was driven in rout from the field. But this signal success did not entail the surrender of Anshu, which was gallantly defended. The scarcity of supplies and the approach of winter compelled the Chinese Emperor to raise the siege after he had remained before the place for several months, and it is stated that as the Chinese broke up their camp the commandant appeared on the walls and wished them "a pleasant journey." After this rebuff Taitsong did not renew his attempt to annex Corea, although to the end of his life he refused to hold any relations with Gaisoowun.

During the first portion of his reign Taitsong was greatly helped by the labours of his wife, the Empress Changsunchi, who was a woman of rare goodness and ability, and set a shining example to the whole of her court. She said many wise things, among which the most quotable was that "the practice of virtue conferred, however, upon men, especially on princes, and not the splendour of their appointments." She was a patron of letters, and an Imperial Library and College in the capital owed their origin to her. She was probably the best and most trustworthy adviser the Emperor had, and after her death the energy and good fortune of Taitsong seemed to decline. She no doubt contributed to the remarkable treatise on the art of government, called the "Golden Mirror," which bears the name of Taitsong as its author. Taitsong was an ardent admirer of Confucius, whom he exalted to the skies as the great sage of the world, declaring emphatically that "Confucius was for the Chinese what the water is for the fishes." The Chinese annalists tell many stories of Taitsong's personal courage. He was a great hunter, and in the pursuit of big game he necessarily had some narrow escapes, special mention being made of his slaying single-handed a savage boar. Another instance was his struggle with a Tartar attendant who attempted to murder him, and whom he killed in the encounter. He had a still narrower escape at the hands of his eldest son, who formed a plot to assassinate him which very nearly succeeded. The excessive anxiety of Prince Lichingkien to reach the crown cost him the succession, for on the discovery of his plot he was deposed from the position of heir-apparent and disappeared from the scene.

After a reign of twenty-three years, during which he accomplished a great deal more than other rulers had done in twice the time, Taitsong died in A.D. 649, leaving the undisturbed possession of the throne to his son known as the Emperor Kaotsong. There need be no hesitation in calling Taitsong one of the greatest rulers who ever sat on the Dragon Throne, and his death was received with extraordinary demonstrations of grief by the people he had ruled so well. Several of his generals wished to commit suicide on his bier, the representatives of the tributary nations at his capital cut off their hair or sprinkled his grave with their blood, and throughout the length and breadth of the land there was mourning and lamentation for a prince who had realised the ideal character of a Chinese Emperor. Nor does his claim to admiration and respect seem less after the lapse of so many centuries. His figure still stands out boldly as one of the ablest and most humane of all Chinese rulers. He not only re-united China, but he proved that union was for his country the only sure basis of prosperity and power.

Under Kaotsong the power of the Tangs showed for thirty years no diminution, and he triumphed in directions where his father had only pointed the way to victory. He began his reign with a somewhat risky act by marrying one of his father's widows, who then became the Empress Wou. She was perhaps the most remarkable woman in the whole range of Chinese history, acquiring such an ascendency over her husband that she practically ruled the state, and retained this power after his death. In order to succeed in so exceptional a task she had to show no excessive delicacy or scrupulousness, and she began by getting rid of the other wives, including the lawful Empress of Kaotsong in a summary fashion. It is stated that she cast them into a vase filled with wine, having previously cut off their hands and feet to prevent their extricating themselves. But on the whole her influence was exerted to promote the great schemes of her husband.

The Tibetan question was revived by the warlike proclivities of the new Sanpou, who, notwithstanding his blood relationship with the Chinese Emperor, sought to extend his dominion at his expense towards the north and the east. A desultory war ensued, in which the Chinese got the worst of it, and Kaotsong admitted that Tibet remained "a thorn in his side for years." A satisfactory termination was given to the struggle by the early death of the Sanpou, whose warlike character had been the main cause of the dispute. Strangely enough the arms of Kaotsong were more triumphant in the direction of Corea, where his father had failed. From 658 to 670 A.D. China was engaged in a bitter war on land and sea with the Coreans and their allies, the Japanese, who thus intervened for the first time in the affairs of the continent. Owing to the energy of the Empress Wou victory rested with the Chinese, and the Japanese navy of 400 junks was completely destroyed. The kingdom of Sinlo was made a Chinese province, and for sixty years the Coreans paid tribute and caused no trouble. In Central Asia also the Chinese power was maintained intact, and the extent of China's authority and reputation may be inferred from the King of Persia begging the Emperor's governor in Kashgar to come to his aid against the Arabs, who were then in the act of overrunning Western Asia in the name of the prophet. Kaotsong could not send aid to such a distance from his borders, but he granted shelter to several Persian princes, and on receiving an embassy from the Arabs, he impressed upon them the wisdom and magnanimity of being lenient to the conquered. Kaotsong died in 683, and the Empress Wou retained power until the year 704, when, at the age of eighty, she was compelled to abdicate. Her independent rule was marked by as much vigour and success as during the life of Kaotsong. She vanquished the Tibetans and a new Tartar race known as the Khitans, who appeared on the northern borders of Shensi. She placed her son in confinement and wore the robes assigned for an Emperor. The extent of her power may be inferred from her venturing to shock Chinese sentiment by offering the annual Imperial sacrifice to heaven and by her erecting temples to her ancestors. Yet it was not until she was broken down by age and illness that any of her foes were bold enough to encounter her. She survived her deposition one year, and her banished son Chongtsong was restored to the throne.

Chongtsong did not reign long, being poisoned by his wife, who did not reap the advantage of her crime. Several Emperors succeeded without doing anything to attract notice, and then Mingti brought both his own family and the Chinese Empire to the verge of ruin. Like other rulers, he began well, quoting the maxims of the "Golden Mirror" and proclaiming Confucius King of Literature. But defeats at the hands of the Khitans and Tibetans embittered his life and diminished his authority. A soldier of fortune, named Ganlochan, revolted and met with a rapid and unexpected success owing to "the people being unaccustomed, from the long peace, to the use of arms." He subdued all the northern provinces, established his capital at Loyang, and compelled Mingti to seek safety in Szchuen, when he abdicated in favour of his son. The misfortunes of Mingti, whose most memorable act was the founding of the celebrated Hanlin College and the institution of the "Pekin Gazette," the oldest periodical in the world, both of which exist at the present day, foretold the disruption of the Empire at no remote date. His son and successor Soutsong did something to retrieve the fortunes of his family, and he recovered Singan from Ganlochan. The Empire was then divided between the two rivals, and war continued unceasingly between them. The successful defence of Taiyuen, where artillery is said to have been used for the first time, A.D. 757, by a lieutenant of the Emperor Soutsong, consolidated his power, which was further increased by the murder of Ganlochan shortly afterwards. The struggle continued with varying fortune between the northern and southern powers during the rest of the reign of Soutsong, and also during that of his successor, Taitsong the Second. This ruler showed himself unworthy of his name, abandoning his capital with great pusillanimity when a small Tibetan army advanced upon it. The census returns threw an expressive light on the condition of the Empire during this period. Under Mingti the population was given at 52,000,000; in the time of the second Taitsong it had sunk to 17,000,000. A great general, named Kwo Tsey, who had driven back the Tibetan invaders, enabled Tetsong, the son and successor of Taitsong, to make a good start in the government of his dominion, which was sadly reduced in extent and prosperity. This great statesman induced Tetsong to issue an edict reproving the superstitions of the times, and the prevalent fashion of drawing auguries from dreams and accidents. The edict ran thus: "Peace and the general contentment of the people, the abundance of the harvest, skill and wisdom shown in the administration, these are prognostics which I hear of with pleasure; but 'extraordinary clouds,' 'rare animals,' 'plants before unknown,' 'monsters,' and other astonishing productions of nature, what good can any of these do men as auguries of the future? I forbid such things to be brought to my notice." The early death of Kwo Tsey deprived the youthful ruler of his best adviser and the mainstay of his power. He was a man of magnificent capacity and devotion to duty, and when it was suggested to him that he should not be content with any but the supreme place, he proudly replied that he was "a general of the Tangs." It seems from the inscription on the stone found at Singan that he was a patron of the Nestorian Christians, and his character and career have suggested a comparison with Belisarius.

Tetsong lived twenty-four years after the death of his champion, and these years can only be characterised as unfortunate. The great governors claimed and exacted the privilege that their dignities should be made hereditary, and this surrender of the Imperial prerogative entailed the usual deterioration of the central power which preceded a change of dynasty. Unpopularity was incurred by the imposition of taxes on the principal articles of production and consumption such as tea, and, worst symptom of all, the eunuchs again became supreme in the Palace. Although the dynasty survived for another century, it was clear that its knell was sounded before Tetsong died. Under his grandson Hientsong the mischief that had been done became more clearly apparent. Although he enjoyed some military successes, his reign on the whole was unfortunate, and he was poisoned by the chief of the eunuchs. His son and successor, Moutsong, from his indifference may be suspected of having been privy to the occurrence. At any rate, he only enjoyed power for a few years before he was got rid of in the same summary fashion. Several other nonentities came to the throne, until at last one ruler named Wentsong, whose intentions at least were stronger than those of his predecessors, attempted to grapple with the eunuchs and formed a plot for their extermination. His courage failed him and the plot miscarried. The eunuchs exacted a terrible revenge on their opponents, of whom they killed nearly 3,000, and Wentsong passed the last year of his life as a miserable puppet in their hands. He was not allowed even to name his successor. The eunuchs ignored his two sons, who were subsequently murdered, and placed his brother Voutsong on the throne. The only event of Voutsong's reign calling for mention was his persecution of the Buddhist priests, whom he ordered to join their families and abandon a life of celibacy.

The evils of the day became specially revealed during the reign of Ytsong, who was scarcely seated on the throne before his troops suffered several defeats at the hands of a rebel prince in Yunnan, who completely wrested that province from the Empire. He was as pronounced a patron of Buddhism as some of his predecessors had been oppressors, and he sent, at enormous expense, to India a mission to procure a bone of Buddha's body, and on its arrival he received the relic on bended knees before his whole court. His extravagance of living landed the Chinese government in fresh difficulties, and he brought the exchequer to the verge of bankruptcy. Nor was he a humane ruler. On one occasion he executed twenty doctors because they were unable to cure a favourite daughter of his. His son Hitsong came to the throne when he was a mere boy, and at once experienced the depth of misfortune to which his family had sunk. He was driven out of his capital by a rebel named Hwang Chao, and if he had not found an unexpected ally in the Turk chief Likeyong, there would then have been an end to the Tang dynasty. This chief of the Chato immigrants—a race supposed to be the ancestors of the Mahomedan Tungani of more recent times—at the head of 40,000 men of his own race, who, from the colour of their uniform, were named "The Black Crows," marched against Hwang Chao, and signally defeated him. The condition of the country at this time is painted in deplorable colours. The Emperor did not possess a palace, and all the great towns of Central China were in ruins. Likeyong took in the situation at a glance, when he said, "The ruin of the Tangs is not far distant." Likeyong, who was created Prince of Tsin, did his best to support the Emperor, but his power was inadequate for coping with another general named Chuwen, Prince of Leang, in whose hands the Emperor became a mere puppet. At the safe moment Chuwen murdered his sovereign, and added to this crime a massacre of all the Tang princes upon whom he could lay his hands. Chao Siuenti, the last of the Tangs, abdicated, and a few months later Chuwen, to make assurance doubly sure, assassinated him. Thus disappeared, after 289 years and after giving twenty rulers to the state, the great Tang dynasty which had restored the unity and the fame of China. It forms a separate chapter in the long period of disunion from the fall of the Hans to the rise of the Sungs.

After the Tangs came five ephemeral and insignificant dynasties, with the fate of which we need not long detain the reader. In less than sixty years they all vanished from the page of history. The struggle for power between Chuwen, the founder of the so-called Later Leang dynasty, and Likeyong was successfully continued by the latter's son, Litsunhiu, who proved himself a good soldier. He won a decisive victory at Houlieoupi, and extinguished the Leang dynasty by the capture of its capital and of Chuwen's son, who committed suicide. Litsunhiu ruled for a short time as Emperor of the Later Leangs, but he was killed during a mutiny of his turbulent soldiers. This dynasty had a very brief existence; the last ruler of the line, finding the game was up, retired with his family to a tower in his palace, which he set on fire, and perished, with his wives and children, in the flames. Then came the Later Tsins, who only held their authority on the sufferance of the powerful Khitan King, who reigned over Leaoutung and Manchuria. The fourth and fifth of these dynasties, named the Later Hans and Chows, ran their course in less than ten years; and when the last of these petty rulers was deposed by his prime minister a termination was at last reached to the long period of internal division and weakness which prevailed for more than 750 years. The student reaches at this point firmer ground in the history of China as an Empire, and his interest in the subject must assume a more definite form on coming to the beginning of that period of united government and settled authority which has been established for nearly 1,000 years, during which no more than four separate families have held possession of the throne.

CHAPTER IV.

THE SUNGS AND THE KINS.

One fact will have been noticed during the latter portion of the period that has now closed, and that is the increasing interest and participation in Chinese affairs of the races neighbouring to, but still outside, the Empire. A large number of the successful generals, and several of the princely families which attained independence, were of Tartar or Turk origin; but the founder of the new dynasty, which restored the unity of the Empire, was of pure Chinese race, although a native of the most northern province of the country. Chow Kwang Yn was born in Pechihli, at the small town of Yeoutou, on the site of which now stands the modern capital of Pekin. His family had provided the governor of this place for several generations, and Chow himself had seen a good deal of military service during the wars of the period. He is described as a man of powerful physique and majestic appearance, to whose courage and presence of mind the result of more than one great battle was due, and who had become in consequence the idol of the soldiery. The ingenuity of later historians rather than the credulity of his contemporaries, may have discovered the signs and portents which indicated that he was the chosen of Heaven; but his army had a simple and convincing method of deciding the destiny of the Empire. Like the legionaries of Rome, they exclaimed, "The Empire is without a master, and we wish to give it one. Who is more worthy of it than our General?" Thus did Chow Kwang Yn become the Emperor Taitsou and the founder of the Sung dynasty.

Taitsou began his reign by proclaiming a general amnesty, and he sent the proclamation of his pardon into provinces where he had not a shred of authority. The step was a politic one, for it informed the Chinese people that they again had an Emperor. At the same time he ordered that the gates and doors of his palace should always be left open, so that the humblest of his subjects might have access to him at any time. His own words were that "his house should resemble his heart, which was open to all his subjects." He also devoted his attention to the improvement of his army, and particularly to the training of his officers, who were called upon to pass an examination in professional subjects as well as physical exercises. A French writer said, forty years ago, that "The laws of military promotion in the states of Europe are far from being as rational and equitable as those introduced by this Chinese ruler." His solicitude for the welfare of his soldiers was evinced during a campaign when the winter was exceedingly severe. He took off his own fur coat, and sent it to the general in command, with a letter stating that he was sorry that he had not one to send to every soldier in the camp. A soldier himself, he knew how to win a soldier's heart, and the affection and devotion of his army never wavered nor declined. He had many opportunities of testing it. His first war was with the Prince of Han, aided by the King of Leaoutung, whom he speedily vanquished, and whose capacity for aggression was much curtailed by the loss of the frontier fortress of Loochow. His next contest was with an old comrade-in-arms named Li Chougsin, whom he had treated very well, but who was seized with a foolish desire to be greater than his ability or power warranted. The struggle was brief, and Li Chougsin felt he had no alternative save to commit suicide.

The tranquillity gained by these successes enabled Taitsou to institute a great reform in the civil administration of the Empire, and one which struck at the root of the evil arising from the excessive power and irresponsibility of the provincial governors. Up to this date the governors had possessed the power of life and death without reference to the capital. It had enabled them to become tyrants, and had simplified their path to complete independence. Taitsou resolved to deprive them of this prerogative and to retain it in his own hands, for, he said, "As life is the dearest thing men possess, should it be placed at the disposal of an official who is often unjust or wicked?" This radical reform greatly strengthened the Emperor's position, and weakened that of the provincial viceroys; and Taitsou thus inaugurated a rule which has prevailed in China down to the present day, where the life of no citizen can be taken without the express authority and order of the Emperor. Taitsou then devoted his attention to the subjugation of those governors who had either disregarded his administration or given it a grudging obedience. The first to feel the weight of his hand was the Viceroy of Honan, but his measures were so well taken and the military force he employed so overwhelming that he succeeded in dispossessing him and in appointing his own lieutenant without the loss of a single man. The Governor of Szchuen believing his power to be greater than it was, or trusting to the remoteness of his province, publicly defied Taitsou, and prepared to invade his dominions. The Emperor was too quick for him, and before his army was in the field 60,000 Imperial troops had crossed the frontier and had occupied the province. By these triumphs Taitsou acquired possession of some of the richest provinces and 40,000,000 of Chinese subjects.

Having composed these internal troubles with enemies of Chinese race, Taitsou resumed his military operations against his old opponents in Leaoutung. Both sides had been making preparations for a renewal of the struggle, and the fortress of Taiyuen, which had been specially equipped to withstand a long siege, was the object of the Emperor's first attack. The place was valiantly defended by a brave governor and a large garrison, and although Taitsou defeated two armies sent to relieve it, he was compelled to give up the hope of capturing Taiyuen on this occasion. Some consolation for this repulse was afforded by the capture of Canton and the districts dependent on that city. He next proceeded against the Governor of Kiangnan, the dual province of Anhui and Kiangsu, who had taken the title of Prince of Tang, and striven to propitiate the Emperor at the same time that he retained his own independence. The two things were, however, incompatible. Taitsou refused to receive the envoys of the Prince of Tang, and he ordered him to attend in person at the capital. With this the Tang prince would not comply, and an army was at once sent to invade and conquer Kiangnan. The campaign lasted one year, by which time the Tang power was shattered, and his territory resumed its old form as a province of China. With this considerable success Taitsou's career may be said to have terminated, for although he succeeded in detaching the Leaoutung ruler from the side of the Prince of Han, and was hastening at the head of his forces to crush his old enemy at Taiyuen, death cut short his career in a manner very closely resembling that of our Edward the First. Taitsou died in his camp, in the midst of his soldiers; and, acting on the advice of his mother, given on her death-bed a few years before, " that he should leave the throne to a relation of mature age," he appointed his brother his successor, and as his last exhortation to him said, " Bear yourself as becomes a brave prince, and govern well." Many pages might be filled with the recitation of Taitsou's great deeds and wise sayings; but his work in uniting China and in giving the larger part of his country tranquillity speaks for itself. His character as a ruler may be gathered from the following selection, taken from among his many speeches: " Do you think," he said, " that it is so easy for a sovereign to perform his duties? He does nothing that is without consequence. This morning the thought occurs to me that yesterday I decided a case in a wrong manner, and this memory robs me of all my joy."

The new Emperor took the style of Taitsong, and during his reign of twenty-three years the Sung dynasty may be fairly considered to have grown consolidated. One of his first measures was to restore the privileges of the descendant of Confucius, which included an hereditary title and exemption from taxation, and which are enjoyed to the present day. After three years' deliberation Taitsong determined to renew his brother's enterprise against Taiyuen, and as he had not assured the neutrality of the King of Leaoutung, his task was the more difficult. On the advance of the Chinese army, that ruler sent to demand the reason of the attack on his friend the Prince of Han, to which the only reply Taitsong gave was as follows: " The country of the Hans was one of the provinces of the Empire, and the prince having refused to obey my orders I am determined to punish him. If your prince stands aside, and does not meddle in this quarrel I am willing to continue to live at peace with him; if he does not care to do this we will fight him." On this the Leaou king declared war, but his troops were repulsed by the covering army sent forward by Taitsong, while he prosecuted the siege of Taiyuen in person. The fortress was well defended, but its doom was never in doubt. Taitsong moved by a feeling of humanity, offered the Prince of Han generous terms before delivering an assault which was, practically speaking, certain to succeed, and he had the good sense to accept them. The subjugation of Han completed the pacification of the Empire and the triumph of Taitsong; but when that ruler thought to add to this success the speedy overthrow of the Khitan power in Leaoutung he was destined to a rude awakening. His action was certainly precipitate, and marked by over-confidence, for the army of Leaoutung was composed of soldiers of a warlike race accustomed to victory. He advanced against it as if it were an army which would fly at the sight of his standard, but instead of this he discovered that it was superior to his own forces on the banks of the Kaoleang river, where he suffered a serious defeat. Taitsong was fortunate enough to retain his conquests over the southern Han states and to find in his new subjects in that quarter faithful and valiant soldiers. The success of the

Leaou army was also largely due to the tactical skill of its general, Yeliu Hiuco, who took a prominent part in the history of this period. When Taitsong endeavoured, some years later, to recover what he had lost by the aid of the Coreans, who, however, neglected to fulfil their part of the contract, he only invited fresh misfortunes. Yeliu Hiuco defeated his army in several pitched battles with immense loss; on one occasion it was said that the corpses of the slain checked the course of a river. The capture of Yangyeh, the old Han defender of Taiyuen, who died of his wounds, completed the triumph of the Leaou general, for it was said, "If Yangyeh cannot resist the Tartars they must be invincible." Taitsong's reign closed under the cloud of these reverses, but on the whole it was successful and creditable, marking an improvement in the condition of the country and the people, and the triumph of the Sungs over at least one of their natural enemies.

His son and successor, Chintsong, must be pronounced fortunate in that the first year of his reign witnessed the death of Yeliu Hiuco. The direct consequence of his death was that the Chinese were, for the first time, successful in their campaign against the Leaous. But this satisfactory state of things did not long continue, and the Leaous became so aggressive and successful that there was almost a panic among the Chinese, and the removal of the capital to a place of greater security was suggested. The firm counsel and the courageous demeanour of the minister Kaochun prevented this course being adopted. He figuratively described the evil consequences of retreat by saying, "Your Majesty can, without serious consequences, advance a foot farther than is absolutely necessary, but you cannot retire, even to the extent of an inch, without doing yourself much harm." Chintsong, fortunately for himself and his state, adopted this course; and the Tartars thought it best to come to terms, especially as the Chinese Emperor was willing to pay annually an allowance in silk and money as the reward of their respecting his frontier. The arrangement could not have been a bad one, as it gave the Empire eighteen years of peace. The country, no doubt, increased greatly in prosperity during this period; but the reputation of Chintsong steadily declined. He seems to have been naturally superstitious, and he gave himself up to fortune-tellers and soothsayers during the last years of his reign; and when he died, in A.D. 1022, he had impaired the position and power of the Imperial office. Yet, so far as can be judged, the people were contented, and the population rose to over 100,000,000.

Chintsong was succeeded by his sixth son, Jintsong, a boy of thirteen, for whom the government was carried on by his mother, a woman of capacity and good sense. She took off objectionable taxes on tea and salt—prime necessaries of life in China—and she instituted surer measures against the spiritualists and magicians who had flourished under her husband and acquired many administrative offices under his patronage. After ruling for ten peaceful years she died, and Jintsong assumed the personal direction of affairs. During the tranquillity that had now prevailed for more than a generation a new power had arisen on the Chinese frontier in the principality of Tangut or Hia. This state occupied the modern province of Kansuh, with some of the adjacent districts of Kokonor and the Gobi desert. Chao Yuen, the prince of this territory, was an ambitious warrior, who had drawn round his standard a force of 150,000 fighting men. With this he waged successful war upon the Tibetans and began a course of encroachments on Chinese territory which was not to be distinguished from open hostility. Chao Yuen was not content with the appellation of Prince, and "because he came of a family several of whose members had in times past borne the Imperial dignity," he adopted the title of Emperor. Having taken this step, Chao Yuen wrote to Jintsong expressing "the hope that there would be a constant and solid peace between the two Empires." The reply of the Chinese ruler to this insult, as he termed it, was to declare war and to offer a reward for the head of Chao Yuen.

It was soon made evident that Chao Yuen possessed the military power to support an Imperial dignity. He defeated the Emperor's army in two pitched battles at Sanchuen and Yang Moulong, and many years elapsed before the Sung rulers can be held to have recovered from the loss of their best armies. The Khitans of Leaoutung took advantage of these misfortunes to encroach, and as Jintsong had no army with which to oppose them, they captured ten cities with little or no resistance. The Chinese government was compelled to purchase them back by increasing the annual allowance it paid of gold and silk. A similar policy was resorted to in the case of Chao Yuen, who consented to a peace on receiving every year 100,000 pieces of silk and 30,000 lbs. of tea. Not content with this payment, Chao Yuen subsequently exacted the right to build fortresses along the Chinese frontier. Soon after this Chao Yuen was murdered by one of his sons, whose betrothed he had taken from him. If Jintsong was not fortunate in his wars he did much to promote education and to encourage literature. He restored the colleges founded by the Tangs, he built a school or academy in every town, he directed the public examinations to be held impartially and frequently, and he gave special prizes as a reward for elocution. Some of the greatest historians China has produced lived in his reign, and wrote their works under his patronage; of these Szemakwang was the most famous. His history of the Tangs is a masterpiece, and his "Garden of Szemakwang" an idyll. He was remarkable for his sound judgment as well as the elegance of his style, and during the short time he held the post of Prime Minister his administration was marked by ability and good sense. The character of Jintsong was, it will be seen, not without its good points, which gained for him the affection of his subjects despite his bad fortune against the national enemies, and his reign of thirty years was, generally speaking, prosperous and satisfactory. After the brief reign of his nephew, Yngtsong, that prince's son, Chintsong the Second, became Emperor.

The career of Wanganchi, an eccentric and socialistic statesman, who wished to pose as a great national reformer, and who long possessed the ear and favour of his sovereign, lends an interest to the reign of the second Chintsong. Wanganchi did not possess the confidence or the admiration of his brother officials, and subsequent writers have generally termed him an impostor and charlatan. But he may only have been a misguided enthusiast when he declared that "the State should take the entire management of commerce, industry, and agriculture into its own hands, with the view of succouring the working classes, and preventing their being ground to the dust by the rich." The advocacy of such a scheme is calculated to earn popularity, as few of those who are to benefit by it stop to examine its feasibility, and Wanganchi might have been remembered as an enlightened thinker and enthusiastic advocate of the rights of the masses if he had not been called upon to carry out his theories. But the proof of experience, like the touch of Ithuriel's spear, revealed the practical value of his suggestions, and dissolved the attractive vision raised by his perfervid eloquence and elevated enthusiasm. His honesty of purpose cannot, however, be disputed. On being appointed to the post of chief minister he took in hand the application of his own project. He exempted the poor from all taxation. He allotted lands, and he supplied the cultivators with seeds and implements. He also appointed local boards to superintend the efforts of the agricultural classes, and to give them assistance and advice. But this paternal government, this system of making the state do what the individual ought to do for himself, did not work as it was expected. Those who counted on the agricultural labourer working with as much intelligence and energy for himself as he had done under the direction of a master were doomed to disappointment. Want of skill, the fitfulness of the small holder, aggravated perhaps by national calamities, drought, flood, and pestilence, being felt more severely by labourers than by capitalists, led to a gradual shrinkage in the area of cultivated land, and at last to the suffering of the classes who were to specially benefit from the scheme of Wanganchi. The failure of his scheme, which, to use his own words, aimed at preventing there being any poor or over-rich persons in the state, entailed his disgrace and fall from power. But his work and his name have continued to excite interest and speculation among his countrymen down to the present day. His memory has been aspersed by the writers of China, who have generally denounced him as a free-thinker and a nihilist, and although, twenty years after his death, a tablet bearing his name was placed in the Hall of Confucius as the greatest Chinese thinker since Mencius, it was removed after a brief period, and since then both the name and the works of Wanganchi have been consigned to an oblivion from which only the curiosity of European writers has rescued them.

Chintsong's reign was peaceful, but he seems to have only avoided war by yielding to all the demands of the Tartars who encroached on the frontier and seized several Chinese cities. His son Chetsong was only ten when he became Emperor, and the administration was carried on by his mother, the Empress Tefei, another of the capable women of Chinese history. Her early death left Chetsong to rule as he listed, and his first acts of independent authority were not of happy augury for the future. He had not been on the throne many months before he divorced his principal wife without any apparent justification, and when remonstrated with he merely replied that he was imitating several of his predecessors. The censor's retort was, "You would do better to imitate their virtues, and not their faults." Chetsong did not have any long opportunity of doing either, for he died of grief at the loss of his favourite son, and it is recorded that, as "he did not expect to die so soon," he omitted the precaution of selecting an heir. Fortunately the mischief of a disputed succession was avoided by the unanimous selection of his brother Hoeitsong as the new Emperor. He proved himself a vain and superstitious ruler, placing his main faith in fortune tellers, and expecting his subjects to yield implicit obedience to his opinions as "the master of the law and the prince of doctrine." Among other fallacies, Hoeitsong cherished the belief that he was a great soldier, and he aspired to rank as the conqueror of the old successful enemy of China, the Khitans of Leaoutung. He had no army worthy of the name, and the southern Chinese who formed the mass of his subjects were averse to war, yet his personal vanity impelled him to rush into hostilities which promised to be the more serious because a new and formidable power had arisen on the northern frontier.

The Niuche or Chorcha Tartars, who had assumed a distinct name and place in the vicinity of the modern Kalgan, about the year 1000 A.D., had become subservient to the great Khitan chief Apaoki, and their seven hordes had remained faithful allies of his family and kingdom for many years after his death. But some of the clan had preferred independence to the maintenance of friendly relations with their greatest neighbour, and they had withdrawn northwards into Manchuria. For some unknown reason the Niuche became dissatisfied with their Khitan allies, and about the year 1100 A.D. they had all drawn their forces together as an independent confederacy under the leadership of a great chief named Akouta. The Niuche could only hope to establish their independence by offering a successful resistance to the King of Leaoutung, who naturally resented the defection of a tribe which had been his humble dependents. They succeeded in this task beyond all expectation, as Akouta inflicted a succession of defeats on the hitherto invincible army of Leaoutung. Then the Niuche conqueror resolved to pose as one of the arbiters of the empire's destiny, and to found a dynasty of his own. He collected his troops, and he addressed them in a speech reciting their deeds and his pretensions. "The Khitans," he said, "had in the earlier days of their success taken the name of Pintiei, meaning the iron of Pinchow, but although that iron may be excellent, it is liable to rust and can be eaten away. There is nothing save gold which is unchangeable and which does not destroy itself. Moreover, the family of Wangyen, with which I am connected through the chief Hanpou, had always a great fancy for glittering colours such as that of gold, and I am now resolved to take this name as that of my imperial family. I therefore give it the name of Kin, which signifies gold." This speech was made in the year 1115 A.D., and it was the historical introduction of the Kin dynasty, which so long rivalled the Sung, and which, although it attained only a brief lease of power on the occasion referred to, was remarkable as being the first appearance of the ancestors of the present reigning Manchus.

Like other conquerors who had appeared in the same quarter, the Kins, as we must now call them, owed their rise to their military qualifications and to their high spirit. Their tactics, although of a simpler kind, were as superior to those of the Leaous as the latter's were to the Chinese. Their army consisted exclusively of cavalry, and victory was generally obtained by its furious attacks delivered from several sides simultaneously. The following description taken from Mailla's translation of the Chinese official history, gives the best account of their army and mode of fighting

"At first the Niuche had only cavalry. For their sole distinction they made use of a small piece of braid on which they marked certain signs, and they attached this to both man and horse. Their companies were usually composed of only 50 men each, twenty of whom, clothed in strong cuirasses, and armed with swords and short pikes, were placed in the front, and behind those came the remaining thirty in less weighty armour, and with bows and arrows or javelins for weapons. When they encountered an enemy, two men from each company advanced as scouts, and then arranging their troops so as to attack from four sides, they approached the foe at a gentle trot until within a hundred yards of his line. Thereupon charging at full speed, they discharged their arrows and javelins, again retiring with the same celerity. This manœuvre they repeated several times until they threw the ranks into confusion, when they fell upon them with sword and pike so impetuously that they generally gained the victory."

The novelty, as well as the impetuosity of their attack, supplied the want of numbers and of weapons, and when the Khitans raised what seemed an overwhelming force to crush the new power that ventured to play the rival to theirs in Northern China, Akouta, confident in himself and his people, was not dismayed, and accepted the offer of battle. In two sanguinary battles he vanquished the Khitan armies, and threatened with early extinction the once famous dynasty of Leaoutung. When the Sung emperor heard of the defeats of his old opponents, he at once rushed to the conclusion that the appearance of this new power on the flank of Leaoutung must redound to his advantage, and, although warned by the King of Corea that "the Kins were worse than wolves and tigers," he sent an embassy to Akouta proposing a joint alliance against the Khitans. The negotiations were not at first successful. Akouta concluded a truce with Leaoutung, and took offence at the style of the emperor's letter. But the peace was soon broken by either the Kins or the Khitans, and Hoeitsong consented to address Akouta as the Great Emperor of the Kins. Then Akouta engaged to attack Leaoutung from the north, while the Chinese assailed it on the south, and a war began which promised a speedy termination. But the tardiness and inefficiency of the Chinese army prolonged the struggle, and covered the reputation of Hoeitsong and his troops with ignominy. It was compelled to beat a hasty and disastrous retreat, and the peasants of Leaoutung sang ballads about its cowardice and insufficiency,

But if it fared badly with the Chinese, the armies of Akouta continued to be victorious, and the Khitans fled not less precipitately before him than the Chinese did before them. Their best generals were unable to make the least stand against the Kin forces. Their capital was occupied by the conqueror, and the last descendant of the great Apaoki fled westwards to seek an asylum with the Prince of Hia or Tangut. He does not appear to have received the protection he claimed, for after a brief stay at the court of Hia, he made his way to the desert, where, after undergoing incredible hardships, he fell into the hands of his Kin pursuers. With his death soon afterwards the Khitan dynasty came to an end, after enjoying its power for 200 years, but some members of this race escaped across the Gobi desert, and founded the brief-lived dynasty of the Kara Khitay in Turkestan. Akouta died shortly before the final overthrow of the Leaoutung power, and his brother Oukimai ruled in his place.

The ill-success of Hoeitsong's army in its joint campaign against Leaoutung cost the emperor his share in the spoil. The Kins retained the whole of the conquered territory, and the Sung prince was the worse off, because he had a more powerful and aggressive neighbour. The ease of their conquest, and the evident weakness of the Chinese, raised the confidence of the Kins to such a high point, that they declared that the Sungs must surrender to them the whole of the territory north of the Hoangho, and they prepared to secure what they demanded by force of arms. The Chinese would neither acquiesce in the transfer of this region to the Kins nor take steps to defend it. They were driven out of that portion of the empire like sheep, and they even failed to make any stand at the passage of the Hoangho, where the Kin general declared that "there could not be a man left in China, for if 2,000 men had defended the passage of this river we should never have succeeded in crossing it." Hoeitsong quitted his capital Kaifong to seek shelter at Nankin, where he hoped to enjoy greater safety, and shortly afterwards he abdicated in favour of his son Kintsong. The siege of Kaifong which followed ended in a convention binding the Chinese to pay the Kins an enormous sum—ten millions of small gold nuggets, twenty millions of small silver nuggets, and ten million pieces of silk; but the Tartar soldiers soon realised that there was no likelihood of their ever receiving this fabulous spoil, and in their indignation they seized both Hoeitsong and Kintsong, as well as any other members of the royal family on whom they could lay their hands, and carried them off to Tartary, where both of the unfortunate Sung princes died as prisoners of the Kins.

Although the Kins wished to sweep the Sungs from the throne, and their general Walipou went so far as to proclaim the emperor of a new dynasty, whose name is forgotten, another of the sons of Hoeitsong, Prince Kang Wang, had no difficulty in establishing his own power and in preserving the Sung dynasty. He even succeeded in imparting a new vigour to it, for on the advice of his mother, who pointed out to him that "for nearly 200 years the nation appears to have forgotten the art of war," he devoted all his attention to the improvement of his army and the organisation of his military resources. Prince Kang Wang, on becoming emperor, took the name of Kaotsong, and finally removed the southern capital to Nankin. He was also driven by his financial necessities to largely increase the issue of paper money, which had been introduced under the Tangs. As both the Kins and the Mongols had recourse to the same expedient, it is not surprising that the Sungs should also have adopted the simplest mode of compensating for a depleted treasury. Considering the unexpected difficulties with which he had to cope, and the low ebb to which the fortunes of China had fallen, much might be forgiven to Kaotsong, who found a courageous counsellor in the Empress Mongchi, who is reported to have addressed him as follows: "Although the whole of your august family has been led captive into the countries of the north, none the less does China, which knows your wisdom and fine qualities, preserve towards the Sungs the same affection, fidelity, and zeal as in the past. She hopes and expects that you will prove for her what Kwang Vouti (their restorer, see *ante*, p. 17) was for the Hans." If Kaotsong did not attain the height of this success, he at least showed himself a far more capable prince than any of his immediate predecessors.

The successful employment of cavalry by the Kins naturally led the Chinese to think of employing the same arm against them, although the inhabitants of the eighteen provinces have never been good horsemen. Kaotsong also devoted his attention especially to the formation of a corps of charioteers. The chariots, four-wheeled, carried twenty-four combatants, and these vehicles drawn up in battle array not only presented a very formidable appearance, but afforded a very material shelter for the rest of the army. Kaotsong seems to have been better in imagining reforms than in the task of carrying them out. After he had originated much good work he allowed it to languish for want of definite support, and he quarrelled with and disgraced the minister chiefly responsible for these reforms. A short time after this the Kins again advanced southwards, but thanks to the improvement effected in the Chinese army, and to the skill and valour of Tsongtse, one of Kaotsong's lieutenants, they did not succeed in gaining any material advantage. Their efforts to capture Kaifong failed, and their general Niyamoho, recognising the improvement in the Chinese army, was content to withdraw his army with such spoil as it had been able to collect. Tsongtse followed up this good service against the enemy by bringing to their senses several rebellious officials who thought they saw a good opportunity of shaking off the Sung authority. At this stage of the war Tsongtse exhorted Kaotsong, who had quitted Nankin for Yangchow, to return to Kaifong to encourage his troops with his presence, especially as there never was such a favourable opportunity of delivering his august family out of the hands of the Kins. Tsongtse is reported to have sent as many as twenty formal petitions to his sovereign to do this, but Kaotsong was deaf to them all, and it is said that his obtuseness and want of nerve caused Tsongtse so much pain that he died of chagrin.

The death of Tsongtse induced the Kins to make a more strenuous effort to humiliate the Sungs, and a large army under the joint command of Akouta's son, Olito, and the general Niyamoho, advanced on the capital and captured Yangchow. Kaotsong, who saved his life by precipitate flight, then agreed to sign any treaty drawn up by his conqueror. In his letter to Niyamoho he said, "Why fatigue your troops with long and arduous marches when I will grant you of my own will whatever you demand." But the Kins were inexorable, and refused to grant any terms short of the unconditional surrender of Kaotsong, who fled to Canton, pursued both on land and sea. The Kin conquerors soon found that they had advanced too far, and the Chinese rallying their forces gained some advantage during their retreat. Some return of confidence followed this turn in the fortune of the war, and two Chinese generals, serving in the hard school of adversity, acquired a military knowledge and skill which made them formidable to even the best of the Kin commanders. The campaigns carried on between 1131 and 1134 differed from any that had preceded them in that the Kin forces steadily retired before Oukiai and Changtsiun, and victory, which had so long remained constant in their favour, finally deserted their arms. The death of the Kin emperor, Oukimai, who had upheld with no decline of lustre the dignity of his father Akouta, completed the discomfiture of the Kins, and contributed to the revival of Chinese power under the last emperor of the Sung dynasty. The reign of Oukimai marks the pinnacle of Kin power which under his cousin and successor Hola began steadily to decline.

The possession of Honan formed the principal bone of contention between the Kins and Sungs, but, after considerable negotiation and some fighting, Kaotsong agreed to leave it in the hands of the Kins, and also to pay them a large annual subsidy in silk and money. He also agreed to hold the remainder of his states as a gift at the hands of his northern neighbour, and thus, notwithstanding the very considerable successes gained by several of the Sung generals, Kaotsong had to undergo the mortification of signing a humiliating peace and retaining his authority only on sufferance. Fortunately for the independence of the Sungs, Hola was murdered by Ticounai, a grandson of Akouta, whose ferocious character and ill-formed projects for the subjugation of the whole of China furnished the Emperor Kaotsong with the opportunity of shaking off the control asserted over his actions and recovering his dignity. The extensive preparations of the Kin government for war warned the Sungs to lose no time in placing every man they could in the field, and when Ticounai rushed into the war, which was all of his own making, he found that the Sungs were quite ready to receive him and offer a strenuous resistance to his attack. A peace of twenty years' duration had allowed of their organising their forces and recovering from an unreasoning terror of the Kins. Moreover, there was a very general feeling among the inhabitants of both the north and the south that the war was an unjust one, and that Ticounai had embarked upon a course of lawless aggression which his tyrannical and cruel proceedings towards his own subjects served to inflame.

The war began in 1161, A.D., with an ominous defeat of the Kin navy, and when Kaotsong nerved himself for the crisis in his life and placed himself at the head of his troops, Ticounai must have felt less sanguine of the result than his confident declaration that he would end the war in a single campaign indicated. Before the two armies came into collision Ticounai learnt that a rebellion had broken out in his rear, and that his cousin Oulo challenged both his legitimacy and his authority. He believed, and perhaps wisely, that the only way to deal with this new danger was to press on, and by gaining a signal victory over the Sungs annihilate all his enemies at a blow. But the victory had to be gained, and he seems to have under-estimated his opponent. He reached the Yangtsekiang and the Sungs retired behind it. Ticounai had no means of crossing it, as his fleet had been destroyed and the Sung navy stood in his path. Such river junks as he possessed were annihilated in another encounter on the river. He offered sacrifices to heaven in order to obtain a safe passage, but the powers above were deaf to his prayers. Discontent and disorder broke out in his camp. The army that was to have carried all before it was stopped by a mere river, and Ticounai's reputation as a general was ruined before he had crossed swords with the enemy. In this dilemma his cruelty increased, and after he had sentenced many of his officers and soldiers to death he was murdered by those who found that they would have to share the same fate. After this tragic ending of a bad career, the Kin army retreated. They concluded a friendly convention with the Sungs, and Kaotsong, deeming his work done by the repulse of this grave peril, abdicated the throne, which had proved to him no bed of roses, in favour of his adopted heir Hiaotsong. Kaotsong ruled during the long period of thirty-six years, and when we consider the troubled time through which he passed and the many vicissitudes of fortune he underwent, he probably rejoiced at being able to spend the last twenty-five years of his life without the responsibility of governing the Empire, and free from the cares of sovereignty.

The new Kin ruler Oulo wished for peace, but a section of his turbulent subjects clamoured for a renewal of the expeditions into China, and he was compelled to bend to the storm. The Kin army, however, had no cause to rejoice in its bellicoseness, for the Chinese general, Changtsiun, defeated it in a battle the like of which had not been seen for ten years. After this a peace was concluded, which proved fairly durable, and the remainder of the reigns of both Oulo and Hiaotsong were peaceful and prosperous for northern and southern China. Both of these princes showed an aversion to war, and an appreciation of peace which was rare in their day. The Kin ruler is stated to have made this noble retort when he was solicited by a traitor from a neighbouring state to seize it: "You deceive yourself if you believe me to be capable of approving an act of treason whatever the presumed advantage it might procure me. I love all peoples of whatever nation they may be, and I wish to see them at peace with one another." It is not surprising to learn that a prince who was so thoroughly imbued with the spirit of civilisation should have caused the Chinese classics to be translated into the Kin language. Of all the Kin rulers he was the most intellectual, and the most anxious to elevate the standard of his people, who were far ruder than the inhabitants of southern China.

Hiaotsong was succeeded by his son Kwangtsong, and Oulo by his grandson Madacou, both of whom continued the policy of their predecessors. Kwangtsong was saved the trouble of ruling by his wife, the Empress Lichi, and after a very short space he resigned the empty title of emperor, which brought him neither satisfaction nor pleasure. Ningtsong, the son and successor of Kwangtsong, ventured on one war with the Kins in which he was worsted. This was the last of the Kin successes, for Madacou died soon afterwards, just on the eve of the advent of the Mongol peril, which threatened to sweep all before it, and which eventually buried both Kin and Sung in a common ruin. The long competition and the bitter contest between the Kins and Sungs had not resulted in the decisive success of either side. The Kins had been strong enough to found an administration in the north but not to conquer China. The Sungs very naturally represent in Chinese history the national dynasty, and their misfortunes rather than their successes appeal to the sentiment of the reader. They showed themselves greater in adversity than in prosperity, and when the Mongol tempest broke over China they proved the more doughty opponent, and the possessor of greater powers of resistance than their uniformly successful adversary the Kin or Golden Dynasty.

CHAPTER V.

THE MONGOL CONQUEST OF CHINA.

WHILE the Kins were absorbed in their contest with the Southern Chinese, they were oblivious of the growth of a new and formidable power on their own borders. The strength of the Mongols had acquired serious dimensions before the Kins realised that they would have to fight, not only for supremacy, but for their very existence. Before describing the long wars that resulted in the subjection of China by this northern race, we must consider the origin and the growth of the power of the Mongols, who were certainly the most remarkable race of conquerors Asia, or perhaps the whole world, ever produced.

The home of the Mongols, whose name signifies "brave men," was in the strip of territory between the Onon and Kerulon rivers, which are both tributaries or upper courses of the Amour. They first appeared as a separate clan or tribe in the ninth century, when they attracted special attention for their physical strength and courage during one of China's many wars with the children of the desert, and it was on that occasion they gained the appellation under which they became famous. The earlier history of the Mongol tribe is obscure, and baffles investigation, but there seems no reason to doubt their affinity to the Hiongnou, with whose royal house Genghis himself claimed blood relationship. If this claim be admitted, Genghis and Attila, who were the two specially typical Scourges of God, must be considered members of the same race, and the probability is certainly strengthened by the close resemblance in their methods of carrying on war. Budantsar is the first chief of the house of Genghis whose person and achievements are more than mythical. He selected as the abode of his race the territory between the Onon and the Kerulon, a region fertile in itself, and well protected by those rivers against attack. It was also so well placed as to be beyond the extreme limit of any triumphant progress of the armies of the Chinese emperor. If Budantsar had accomplished nothing more than this, he would still have done much to justify his memory being preserved among a free and independent people. But he seems to have incited his followers to pursue an active and temperate life, to remain warriors rather than to become rich and lazy citizens. He wrapped up this counsel in the exhortation, "What is the use of embarrassing ourselves with wealth? Is not the fate of men decreed by heaven?" He sowed the seed of future Mongol greatness, and the headship of his clan remained vested in his family.

In due order of succession the chiefship passed to Kabul Khan, who in the year 1135 began to encroach on the dominion of Hola, the Kin emperor. He seems to have been induced to commit this act of hostility by a prophecy, to the effect that his children should be emperors, and also by discourteous treatment received on the occasion of his visit to the court of Oukimai. Whatever the cause of umbrage Kabul Khan made the Kins pay dearly for their arrogance or short-sighted policy. Hola sent an army under one of his best generals, Hushahu, to bring the Mongol chief to reason, but the inaccessibility of his home stood him in good stead. The Kin army suffered greatly in its futile attempt to cross the desert, and during its retreat it was harassed by the pursuing Mongols. When the Kin army endeavoured to make a stand against its pursuers, it suffered a crushing overthrow in a battle at Hailing, and on the Kins sending a larger force against the Mongols in 1139, it had no better fortune. Kabul Khan, after this second success, caused himself to be proclaimed Great Emperor of the Mongols. His success in war, and his ambition, which rested satisfied with no secondary position, indicated the path on which the Mongols proceeded to the acquisition of supreme power and a paramount military influence whithersoever they carried their name and standards. The work begun by Kabul was well continued by his son Kutula, or Kublai. He, too, was a great warrior, whose deeds of prowess aroused as much enthusiasm among the Mongols as those of Cœur-de-Lion evoked in the days of the Plantagenets. The struggle with the Kins was rendered more bitter by the execution of several Mongols of importance, who happened to fall into the hands of the Kins. When Kutula died the chiefship passed to his nephew, Yissugei, who greatly extended the influence and power of his family among the tribes neighbouring to the Mongol home. Many of these, and even some Chinese, joined the military organisation of the dominant tribe, so that what was originally a small force of strictly limited numbers, became a vast and ever-increasing confederacy of the most warlike and aggressive races of the Chinese northern frontier. Important as Yissugei's work in the development of Mongol power undoubtedly was, his chief historical interest is derived from the fact that he was the father of Genghis Khan.

There are several interesting fables in connection with the birth of Genghis, which event may be safely assigned to the year 1162 A.D. One of these reads as follows:—"One day Yissugei was hunting in company with his brothers, and was following the tracks of a white hare in the snow. They struck upon the track of a waggon, and following it up came to a spot where a woman's yart was pitched. Then said Yissugei, 'This woman will bear a valiant son.' He discovered that she was the damsel Ogelen Eke (*i.e.*, the mother of nations), and that she was the wife of Yeke Yilatu, chief of a Tartar tribe. Yissugei carried her off and made her his wife." Immediately after his overthrow of Temujin, chief of one of the principal Tartar tribes, Yissugei learnt that the promised "valiant son" was about to be born, and in honour of his victory he gave him the name of Temujin, which was the proper name of the great Genghis. The village or encampment in which the future conqueror first saw the light of day still bears the old Mongol name, Dilun Boldak, on the banks of the Onon. When Yissugei died, Temujin, or Genghis, was only thirteen, and his clan of 40,000 families refused to recognise him as their leader. At a meeting of the tribe Genghis entreated them with tears in his eyes to stand by the son of their former chief, but the majority of them mocked at him, exclaiming, "The deepest wells are sometimes dry, and the hardest stone is sometimes broken, why should we cling to thee?" Genghis owed to the heroic attitude of his mother, who flung abroad the cow-tailed banner of his race, the acceptance of his authority by about half the warriors who had obeyed his father. The great advantage of this step was that it gave Genghis time to grow up to be a warrior as famous as any of his predecessors, and it certainly averted what might have easily become the irretrievable disintegration of the Mongol alliance.

The youth of Genghis was passed in one ceaseless struggle to regain the whole of his birthright. His most formidable enemy was Chamuka, chief of the Juriats, and for a long time he had all the worst of the struggle, being taken prisoner on one occasion, and undergoing the indignity of the cangue. On making his escape he rallied his remaining followers round him for a final effort, and on the advice of his mother Ogelen Eke, who was his principal adviser and staunchest supporter, he divided his forces into thirteen regiments of 1,000 men each, and confined his attention to the defence of his own territory. Chamuka, led away by what he deemed the weakness of his adversary, attacked him on the Onon with as he considered the overwhelming force of 30,000 men; but the result dispelled his hopes of conquest, for Genghis gained a decisive victory. Then was furnished a striking instance of the truth of the saying that "nothing succeeds like success." The despised Temujin, who was thought to be unworthy of the post of ruling the Mongols, was lauded to the skies, and the tribes declared with one voice, "Temujin alone is generous and worthy of ruling a great people." At this time also he began to show the qualities of a statesman and diplomatist. He formed in 1194 a temporary alliance with the Kin emperor, Madacou, and the richness of his reward seems to have excited his cupidity, while his experience of the Kin army went to prove that they were not so formidable as had been imagined. The discomfiture of Chamuka has been referred to, but he had not abandoned the hope of success, and when he succeeded in detaching the Kerait chief Wang Khan from the Mongols, to whom he was bound by ties of gratitude, he fancied that he again held victory in his grasp. But the intrigue did not realise his expectations. Wang Khan deserted Genghis while engaged in a joint campaign against the Naimans, but he was the principal sufferer by his treachery, for the enemy pursued his force, and inflicted a heavy defeat upon it. In fact, he was only rescued from destruction by the timely aid of the man he had betrayed.

But far from inspiring gratitude, this incident inflamed the resentment of Wang Khan, who, throwing off the cloak of simulated friendship, declared publicly that either the Kerait or the Mongol must be supreme on the great steppe, as there was not room for both. Such was the superiority in numbers of the Kerait, that in the first battle of this long and keenly-contested struggle, Wang Khan defeated Temujin near Ourga, where the mounds that cover the slain are still shown to the curious or sceptical visitor. After this serious, and in some degree unexpected reverse, the fortunes of Genghis sank to the lowest ebb. He was reduced to terrible straits, and had to move his camp rapidly from one spot to another. A small section of his followers, mindful of his past success and prowess, still clung to him, and by a sudden and daring coup he changed the whole aspect of the contest. He surprised Wang Khan in his camp at night, and overwhelmed him and his forces. Wang Khan escaped to his old foes, the Naimans, who, disregarding the laws of hospitality, put him to death. The death of Wang Khan signified nothing less than the wholesale defection of the Kerait tribe, which joined Genghis to the last man. Then Genghis turned westwards to settle the question of supremacy with the Naimans, who were both hostile and defiant. The Naiman chief shared the opinion of Wang Khan, that there could not be two masters on the Tian Shan, and with that vigorous illustration which has never been wanting to these illiterate tribes, he wrote, "There cannot be two suns in the sky, two swords in one sheath, two eyes in one eyepit, or two kings in one empire." Both sides made strenuous efforts for the fray, and brought every fighting man they could into the field. The decisive battle of the war was fought in the heart of Jungaria, and the star of Genghis rose in the ascendant. The Naimans fought long and well, but they were borne down by the heavier armed Mongols, and their desperate resistance only added to their loss. Their chief died of his wounds, and the triumph of Genghis was rendered complete by the capture of his old enemy, Chamuka. As Genghis had sworn the oath of friendship with Chamuka, he would not slay him, but he handed him over to a relative, who promptly exacted the rough revenge his past hostility and treachery seemed to call for. On his way back from this campaign the Mongol chief attacked the Prince of Hia, who reigned over Kansuh and Tangut, and thus began the third war he waged for the extension of his power. Before this assumed serious proportions he summoned a Grand Council or Kuriltai, at his camp on the Onon, and then erected outside his tent the royal Mongol banner of the nine white yak-tails. It was on this occasion that Temujin took, and was proclaimed among the Mongol chiefs by, the highly exalted name of Genghis Khan, which means Very Mighty Khan. The Chinese character for the name signifies "Perfect Warrior," and the earlier European writers affirm that it is supposed to represent the sound of "the bird of heaven." At this assemblage, which was the first of a long succession of Mongol councils summoned at the same place on critical occasions, it was proposed and agreed that the war should be carried on with the richer and less warlike races of the south. Among soldiers it is necessary to preserve the spirit of pre-eminence and warlike zeal by granting rewards and decorations. Genghis realised the importance of this matter, and instituted the order of Baturu or Bahadur, meaning warrior. He also made his two leading generals Muhula and Porshu princes, one to sit on his right hand and the other on his left. He addressed them before the council in the following words:—" It is to you that I owe my empire. You are and have been to me as the shafts of a carriage or the arms to a man's body." Seals of office were also granted to all the officials, so that their authority might be the more evident and the more honoured.

In A.D. 1207 Genghis began his war with the state of Hia, which he had determined to crush as the preliminary to an invasion of China. In that year he contented himself with the capture of Wuhlahai, one of the border fortresses of that principality, and in the following year he established his control over the tribes of the desert more fully, thus gaining many Kirghiz and Naiman auxiliaries. In 1209 he resumed the war with Hia in a determined spirit, and placed himself in person at the head of all his forces. Although the Hia ruler prepared as well as he could for the struggle, he was really unnerved by the magnitude of the danger he had to face. His army was overthrown, his best generals were taken prisoners, and he himself had no resource left but to throw himself on the consideration of Genghis. For good reasons the Mongol conqueror was lenient. He married one of the daughters of the king, and he took him into subsidiary alliance with himself. Thus did Genghis absorb the Hia power, which was very considerable, and prepared to enrol it with all his own resources against the Kin empire. If the causes of Mongol success on this occasion and afterwards are inquired for, I cannot do better than repeat what I previously wrote on this subject:—"The Mongols owed their military success to their admirable discipline and to their close study of the art of war. Their military supremacy arose from their superiority in all essentials as a fighting power to their neighbours. Much of their knowledge was borrowed from China, where the art of disciplining a large army and manœuvring it in the field had been brought to a high state of perfection many centuries before the time of Genghis. But the Mongols carried the teaching of the past to a further point than any of the former or contemporary Chinese commanders, indeed, than any in the whole world had done; and the revolution which they effected in tactics was not less remarkable in itself, and did not leave a smaller impression upon the age, than the improvements made in military science by Frederick the Great and Napoleon did in their day. The Mongol played in a large way in Asia the part which the Normans on a smaller scale played in Europe. Although the landmarks of their triumph have now almost wholly vanished, they were for two centuries the dominant caste in most of the states of Asia."

Having thus prepared the way for the larger enterprise, it only remained to find a plausible pretext for attacking the Kins. With or without a pretext Genghis would no doubt have made war, but even the ruthless Mongo. sometimes showed a regard for appearances. Many years before the Kins had sent as envoy to the Mongol encampment Chonghei, a member of their ruling house, and his mission had been not only unsuccessful, but had led to a personal antipathy between the two men. In the course of time Chonghei succeeded Madacou as emperor of the Kins, and when a Kin messenger brought intelligence of this event to Genghis, the Mongol ruler turned towards the south, spat upon the ground, and said, 'I thought that your sovereigns were of the race of the gods, but do you suppose that I am going to do homage to such an imbecile as that?' The affront rankled in the mind of Chonghei, and while Genghis was engaged with Hia, he sent troops to attack the Mongol outposts. Chonghei thus placed himself in the wrong, and gave Genghis justification for declaring that the Kins and not he began the war. The reputation of the Golden dynasty, although not as great as it once was, still stood sufficiently high to make the most adventurous of desert chiefs wary in attacking it. Genghis had already secured the co-operation of the ruler of Hia in his enterprise, and he next concluded an alliance with Yeliu Liuko, chief of the Khitans, who were again manifesting discontent with the Kins. Genghis finally circulated a proclamation among all the desert tribes, calling upon them to join him in his attack on the common enemy. This appeal was heartily and generally responded to, and it was at the head of an enormous force that Genghis set out in March, 1211, to effect the conquest of China. The Mongol army was led by Genghis in person, and under him his four sons and his most famous general, Chepe Noyan, held commands.

The plan of campaign of the Mongol ruler was as simple as it was bold, From his camp at Karakoram, on the Kerulon, he marched in a straight line through Kuku Khoten and the Ongut country to Taitong, securing an unopposed passage through the Great Wall, by the defection of the Ongut tribe. The Kins were unprepared for this sudden and vigorous assault directed on their weakest spot, and successfully executed before their army could reach the scene. During the two years that the forces of Genghis kept the field on this occasion, they devastated the greater portion of the three northern provinces of Shensi, Shansi, and Pechihli. But the border fortress of Taitong and the Kin capital, Tungking, successfully resisted all the assaults of the Mongols, and when Genghis received a serious wound at the former place, he reluctantly ordered the retreat of his army, laden with an immense quantity of spoil, but still little advanced in its main task of conquering China. The success of the Khitan Yeliu Liuko had not been less considerable, and he was proclaimed King of Leaou as a vassal of the Mongols. The planting of this ally on the very threshold of Chinese power facilitated the subsequent enterprises of the Mongols against the Kins, and represented the most important result of this war.

In 1213 Genghis again invaded the Kin dominions, but his success was not very striking, and in several engagements of no very great importance the Kin arms met with some success. The most important events of the year were, however, the deposition and murder of Chonghei, th murder of a Kin general, Hushahu, who had won a battle against the Mongols, and the proclamation of Utubu as emperor. The change of sovereign brought no change of fortune to the unlucky Kins. Utubu was only able to find safety behind the walls of his capital, and he was delighted when Genghis wrote him the following letter:—"Seeing your wretched condition and my exalted fortune, what may your opinion be now of the will of heaven with regard to myself? At this moment I am desirous to return to Tartary, but could you allow my soldiers to take their departure without appeasing their anger with presents?" In reply Utubu sent Genghis a princess of a family as a wife, and also "500 youths, the same number of girls, 3000 horses, and a vast quantity of precious articles." Then Genghis retired once more to Karakoram, but on his march he stained his reputation by massacring all his prisoners—the first gross act of inhumanity he committed during his Chinese wars.

When Utubu saw the Mongols retreating, he thought to provide against the most serious consequences of their return by removing his capital to a greater distance from the frontier, and with this object he transferred his residence to Kaifong. The majority of his advisers were against this change, as a retirement could not but shake public confidence. It had another consequence, which they may not have contemplated, and that was its providing Genghis with an excuse for renewing his attack on China. The Mongol at once complained that the action of the Kin emperor implied an unwarrantable suspicion of his intentions, and he sent his army across the frontier to recommence his humiliation. On this occasion a Kin general deserted to them, and thenceforward large bodies of the Chinese of the north attached themselves to the Mongols, who were steadily acquiring a unique reputation for power as well as military prowess. The great event of this war was the siege of Yenking—on the site of which now stands the capital Pekin—the defence of which had been entrusted to the Prince Imperial, but Utubu, more anxious for his son's safety than the interests of the state, ordered him to return to Kaifong. The governor of Yenking offered a stout resistance to the Mongols, and when he found that he could not hold out, he retired to the temple of the city and poisoned himself. His last act was to write a letter to Utubu begging him to listen no more to the pernicious advice of the man who had induced him to murder Hushahu.

The capture of Yenking, where Genghis obtained a large supply of war materials, as well as vast booty, opened the road to Central China. The Mongols advanced as far as the celebrated Tunkwan pass, which connects Shensi and Honan, but when their general, Samuka, saw how formidable it was, and how strong were the Kin defences and garrison, he declined to attack it, and, making a detour through very difficult country, he marched on Kaifong, where Utubu little expected him. The Mongols had to make their own road, and they crossed several ravines by improvised "bridges made of spears and the branches of trees bound together by strong chains." But the Mongol force was too small to accomplish any great result, and the impetuosity of Samuka was nearly leading to his destruction. A prompt retreat, and the fact that the Hoangho was frozen over, enabled him to extricate his army, after much fatigue and reduced in numbers, from its awkward position. The retreat of the Mongols inspired Utubu with sufficient confidence to induce him to attack Yeliu Liuko in Leaoutung, and the success of this enterprise imparted a gleam of sunshine and credit to the expiring cause of the Kins. Yeliu Liuko was driven from his newly-created kingdom, but Genghis hastened to the assistance of his ally by sending Muhula, the greatest of all his generals, at the head of a large army to recover Leaoutung. His success was rapid and remarkable. The Kins were speedily overthrown, Yeliu Liuko was restored to his authority, and the neighbouring King of Corea, impressed by the magnitude of the Mongol success, hastened to acknowledge himself the vassal of Genghis. The most important result of this campaign was that Genghis entrusted to Muhula the control of all military arrangements for the conquest of China. He is reported to have said to his lieutenant: "North of the Taihing mountains I am supreme, but all the regions to the south I commend to the care of Muhula," and he "also presented him with a chariot and a banner with nine scalops. As he handed him this last emblem of authority, he spoke to his generals, saying, 'Let this banner be an emblem of sovereignty, and let the orders issued from under it be obeyed as my own.'" The principal reason for entrusting the conquest of China to a special force and commander, was that Genghis wished to devote the whole of his personal attention to the prosecution of his new war with the King of Khwaresm and the other great rulers of Western Asia.

Muhula more than justified the selection and confidence of his sovereign. In the year 1218-19 he invaded Honan, defeated the best of the Kin commanders, and not merely overran, but retained possession of the places he occupied in the Kin dominions. The difficulties of Utubu were aggravated by an attack from Ningtsong the Sung emperor, who refused any longer to pay tribute to the Kins as they were evidently unable to enforce the claim, and the Kin armies were equally unfortunate against their southern opponents as their northern. Then Utubu endeavoured to negotiate terms with Muhula for the retreat of his army, but the only conditions the Mongol general would accept was the surrender of the Kin ruler and his resignation of the Imperial title in exchange for the principality of Honan. Utubu, low as he had sunk, declined to abase himself further and to purchase life at the loss of his dignity. The sudden death of Muhula gained a brief respite for the distressed Chinese potentate, but the advantage was not of any permanent significance, first of all because the Kins were too exhausted by their long struggle, and, secondly, because Genghis hastened to place himself at the head of his army. The news of the death of Muhula reached him when he was encamped on the frontier of India and preparing to add the conquest of that country to his many other triumphs in Central and Western Asia. He at once came to the conclusion that he must return to set his house in order at home, and to prevent all the results of Muhula's remarkable triumphs being lost. What was a disadvantage for China proved a benefit for India, and possibly for Europe, as there is no saying how much further the Mongol encroachment might have extended westward, if the direction of Genghis had not been withdrawn. While Genghis was hastening from the Cabul river to the Kerulon, across the Hindoo Koosh and Tian Shan ranges, Utubu died, and Ninkiassu reigned in his stead.

One of the first consequences of the death of Muhula was that the young king of Hia, believing that the fortunes of the Mongols would then wane, and that he might obtain a position of greater power and independence, threw off his allegiance, and adopted hostile measures against them. The prompt return of Genghis nipped this plan in the bud, but it was made quite evident that the conquest of Hia was essential to the success of any permanent annexation of Chinese territory, and as its prince could dispose of an army which he boasted numbered half-a-million of men, it is not surprising to find that he took a whole year in perfecting his arrangements for so grave a contest. The war began in 1225 and continued for two years. The success of the Mongol army was decisive, and unqualified. The Hias were defeated in several battles, and in one of them fought upon the frozen waters of the Hoangho, when Genghis broke the ice by means of his engines, the Hia army was almost annihilated. The king Leseen was deposed, and Hia became a Mongol province.

It was immediately after this successful war that Genghis was seized with his fatal illness. Signs had been seen in the heavens which the Mongol astrologers said indicated the near approach of his death. The five planets had appeared together in the south-west, and so much impressed was Genghis by this phenomenon that on his death-bed he expressed "the earnest desire that henceforth the lives of our enemies shall not be unnecessarily sacrificed." The expression of this wish undoubtedly tended to mitigate the terrors of war as carried on by the Mongols. The immediate successors of Genghis conducted their campaigns after a more humane fashion, and it was not until Timour revived the early Mongol massacres that their opponents felt there was no chance in appealing to the humanity of the Mongols. Various accounts have been published of the cause of his death, some authorities ascribing it to violence, either by an arrow, lightning, or drowning, and others to natural causes. The event seems to have unquestionably happened in his camp on the borders of Shansi, on 27th August, 1227, when he was about 65 years of age, during more than fifty of which he had enjoyed supreme command of his own tribe. With regard to his character and career I cannot do better than repeat what I have previously written on the subject in my larger work.

The area of the undertakings conducted under his eye was more vast and included a greater number of countries than was the case with any other conqueror. Not a country from the Euxine to the China Sea escaped the tramp of the Mongol horsemen, and if we include the achievements of his immediate successors, the conquest of Russia, Poland, and Hungary, the plundering of Bulgaria, Roumania, and Bosnia, the final subjection of China and its southern tributaries must be added to complete the tale of Mongol triumph. The sphere of Mongol influence extended beyond this large portion of the earth's surface, just as the consequence of an explosion cannot be restricted to the immediate scene of the disaster. If we may include the remarkable achievements of his descendant Baber, and of that prince's grandson Akbar, in India three centuries later, not a country in Asia enjoyed immunity from the effect of their successes. Perhaps the most important result of their great outpouring into Western Asia, which certainly was the arrest of the Mahomedan career in Central Asia, and the diversion of the current of the fanatical propagators of the Prophet's creed against Europe, is not yet as fully recognised as it should be. The doubt has been already expressed whether the Mongols would ever have risen to higher rank than that of a nomad tribe but for the appearance of Genghis. Leaving that supposition in the category of other interesting but problematical conjectures, it may be asserted that Genghis represented in their highest forms all the qualities which entitled his race to exercise governing authority. He was, moreover, a military genius of the very first order, and it may be questioned whether either Cæsar or Napoleon can as commanders be placed on a par with him. Even the Chinese said that he led his armies like a God. The manner in which he moved large bodies of men over vast distances without an apparent effort, the judgment he showed in the conduct of several wars in countries far apart from each other, his strategy in unknown regions, always on the alert, yet never allowing hesitation or over-caution to interfere with his enterprise, the sieges which he brought to a successful termination, his brilliant victories, a succession of 'suns of Austerlitz,' all combined make up the picture of a career to which Europe can offer nothing that will surpass, if indeed she has anything to bear comparison with it. After the lapse of centuries, and in spite of the indifference with which the great figures of Asiatic history have been treated, the name of Genghis preserves its magic spell. It is still a name to conjure with when recording the great revolutions of a period which beheld the death of the old system in China, and the advent in that country of a newer and more vigorous government which, slowly acquiring shape in the hands of Kublai and a more national form under the Mings, has attained the pinnacle of its utility and strength under the influence of the great emperors of the Manchu dynasty. But great as is the reputation Genghis has acquired it is probably short of his merits. He is remembered as a relentless and irresistible conqueror, a human scourge; but he was much more. He was one of the greatest instruments of destiny, one of the most remarkable moulders of the fate of nations to be met with in the history of the world. His name still overshadows Asia with its fame and the tribute of our admiration cannot be denied.

The death of Genghis did not seriously retard the progress of the war against the Kins. He expressed the wish that war should be carried on in a more humane and less vindictive manner, but he did not advocate there being no war or the abandonment of any of his enterprises. His son and successor Ogotai was indeed specially charged to bring the conquest of China to a speedy and victorious conclusion. The weakness of the Mongol confederacy was the delay connected with the proclamation of a new Khan and the necessity of summoning to a Grand Council all the princes and generals of the race, although it entailed the suspension and often the abandonment of great enterprises. The death of Genghis saved India but not China. Almost his last instructions were to draw up the plan for attacking and turning the great fortress of Tunkwan, which had provided such an efficient defence for Honan on the north, and in 1230, Ogotai who had already partitioned the territory taken from the Kins into ten departments, took the field in person, giving a joint command to his brother Tuli, under whom served the experienced generals Yeliu Chutsia, Antchar, and Subutai. At first the Mongols met with no great success, and the Kins, encouraged by a momentary gleam of victory, ventured to reject the terms offered by Ogotai and to insult his envoy. The only important fighting during the years 1230-1 occurred round Fongsian, which after a long siege surrendered to Antchar, and when the campaign closed the Kins presented a bold front to the Mongols and still hoped to retain their power and dominions.

In 1232 the Mongols increased their armies in the field, and attacked the Kins from two sides. Ogotai led the main force against Honan, while Tuli, marching through Shensi into Szchuen, assailed them on their western flank. The difficulties encountered by Tuli on this march, when he had to make his own roads, were such, that he entered the Kin territories with a much reduced and exhausted army. The Kin forces gained some advantage over it, but by either a feigned or a forced retreat, Tuli succeeded in baffling their pursuit, and in effecting a junction with his brother Ogotai, who had met with better fortune. Tuli destroyed everything along his line of march, and his massacres and sacks revived the worst traditions of Mongol ferocity. In these straits the Kins endeavoured to flood the country round their capital, to which the Mongols had now advanced, but the Mongols fell upon the workmen while engaged in the task, and slew 10,000 of them. When the main Kin army accepted battle before the town of Yuchow, it was signally defeated, with the loss of three of its principal generals, and Ninkiassu fled from Kaifong to a place more removed from the scene of war. The garrison and townspeople of Kaifong—an immense city with walls 36 miles in circumference, and a population during the siege it is said of 1,400,000 families, or nearly seven million people—offered a stubborn resistance to the Mongols, who entrusted the conduct of the attack to Subutai, the most daring of all their commanders. The Mongols employed their most formidable engines, catapults hurling immense stones, and mortars ejecting explosives and combustibles, but twelve months elapsed before the walls were shattered and the courage and provisions of the defenders exhausted. Then Kaifong surrendered at discretion, and Subutai wished to massacre the whole of the population. But fortunately for the Chinese Yeliu Chutsai was a more humane and a more influential general, and under his advice Ogotai rejected the cruel proposal.

At this moment, when it seemed impossible for fate to have any worse experience in store for the unfortunate Kins, their old enemies the Sungs, wishing to give them the *coup de grâce*, declared war upon them, and placed a large army in the field under their best general, Mongkong, of whom more will be heard. The relics of the Kin army under their sovereign Ninkiassu, took shelter in Tsaichau, where they were closely besieged by the Mongols on one side and the Sungs on the other. Driven thus into a corner, the Kins fought with the courage of despair, and long held out against the combined efforts of their enemies. At last Ninkiassu saw that the struggle could not be prolonged, and he prepared himself to end his life and career in a manner worthy of the race from which he sprang. When the enemy broke into the city, and he heard the stormers at the gate of his palace, he retired to an upper chamber and set fire to the building. Many of his generals, and even of his soldiers, followed his example, preferring to end their existence rather than to add to the triumph of their Mongol and Sung opponents. Thus came to an end in 1234 the famous dynasty of the Kins, who under nine emperors had ruled Northern China for 118 years, and whose power and military capacity may best be gauged by the fact that without a single ally they held out against the all-powerful Mongols for more than a quarter of a century. Ninkiassu, the last of their rulers, was not able to sustain the burden of their authority, but he at least showed himself equal to ending it in a worthy and appropriately dramatic manner.

The folly of the Sungs had completed the discomfiture of the Kins, and had brought to their own borders the terrible peril which had beset every other state in Asia, and which had in almost every case entailed destruction. How could the Sungs expect to avoid the same fate, or to propitiate the most implacable and insatiable of conquering races? They had done this to a large extent with their eyes open. More than once in the early stages of the struggle the Kin rulers had sent envoys to beg their alliance, and to warn them that if they did not help in keeping out the Mongols, their time would come to be assailed and to share in the common ruin. But Ningtsong did not pay heed to the warning, and scarcely concealed his gratification at the misfortunes of his old opponents. The nearer the Mongols came, and the worse the plight to which the Kins were reduced, the more did he rejoice. He forgave Tuli the violation of Sung territory, necessary for his flank attack on Honan, and when the knell of the Kins sounded at the fall of Kaifong, he hastened to help in striking the final blow at them, and to participate, as he hoped, in the distribution of the plunder. By this time Litsong had succeeded his cousin Ningtsong as ruler of the Sungs, and it is said that he received from Tsaichau the armour and personal spoils of Ninkiassu, which he had the satisfaction of offering up in the temple of his ancestors. But when he requested the Mongols to comply with the more important part of the convention, by which the Sung forces had joined the Mongols before Tsaichau, and to evacuate the province of Honan, he experienced a rude awakening from his dream that the overthrow of the Kins would redound to his advantage, and he soon realised what value the Mongols attached to his alliance. The military capacity of Mongkong inspired the Sung ruler with confidence, and he called upon the Mongols to execute their promises, or to prepare for war. The Mongol garrisons made no movement of retreat, and the utmost that Litsong was offered was a portion of Honan, if it could be practically divided. The proposition was probably meant ironically, but at all events Litsong rejected it, and sent Mongkong to take by force possession of the disputed province. The Mongol forces on the spot were fewer than the Chinese, and they met with some reverses. But the hope of the Sungs that the fortune of war would declare in their favour was soon destroyed by the vast preparations of the Mongols, who, at a special kuriltai, held at Karakoram, declared that the conquest of China was to be completed. Then Litsong's confidence left him, and he sent an appeal for peace to the Mongols, giving up all claim to Honan, and only asking to be left in undisturbed possession of his original dominions. It was too late. The Mongols had passed their decree, that the Sungs were to be treated like the Kins, and that the last Chinese government was to be destroyed.

In 1235, the year following the immolation of Ninkiassu, the Mongols placed half a million men in the field for the purpose of destroying the Sung power, and Ogotai divided them into three armies, which were to attack Litsong's kingdom from as many sides. The Mongol ruler entrusted the most difficult task to his son Kutan, who invaded the inaccessible and vast province of Szchuen, at the head of one of these armies. Notwithstanding its natural capacity for offering an advantageous defence, the Chinese turned their opportunities to poor account, and the Mongols succeeded in capturing all its frontier fortresses, with little or no resistance. The shortcomings of the defence can be inferred from the circumstances of the Chinese annalists making special mention of one governor having had the courage to die at his post. For some reason not clearly stated the Mongols did not attempt to retain possession of Szchuen on this occasion. They withdrew when they were in successful occupation of the northern half of the province, and when it seemed as if the other lay at their mercy. In the two dual provinces of Kiangnan and Houkwang, the other Mongol armies met with considerable success, which was dimmed, however, by the death of Kuchu, the son and proclaimed heir of Ogotai. This event, entailing no inconsiderable doubt and long-continued disputes as to the succession, was followed by the withdrawal of the Mongol forces from Sung territory, and during the last six years of his life Ogotai abstained from war, and gave himself up to the indulgence of his gluttony. He built a great palace at Karakoram, where his ancestors had been content to live in a tent, and he entrusted the government of the old Kin dominions to Yeliu Chutsai, who acquired great popularity among the Chinese for his clemency and regard for their customs. Yeliu Chutsai adopted the Chinese mode of taxation, and when Ogotai's widow, Turakina, who acted as Regent after her husband's death, ordered him to alter his system and to farm out the revenues, he sent in his resignation, and it is said, died of grief shortly afterwards. Ogotai was one of the most humane and amiable of all the Mongol rulers, and Yeliu Chutsai imitated his master. Of the latter the Chinese contemporary writers said "he was distinguished by a rare disinterestedness. Of a very broad intellect, he was able, without injustice and without wronging a single person, to amass vast treasures (D'Ohsson says only of books, maps, and pictures), and to enrich his family, but all his care and labours had for their sole object the advantage and glory of his masters. Wise and calculating in his plans, he did little of which he had any reason to repent."

During the five years following the death of Ogotai, the Mongols were absorbed in the question who should be their next Great Khan, and it was only after a warm and protracted discussion, which threatened to entail the disruption of Mongol power, and the revelation of many rivalries among the descendants of Genghis, that Kuyuk, the eldest son of Ogotai, was proclaimed emperor. At the kuriltai held for this purpose, all the great Mongol leaders were present, including Batu, the conqueror of Hungary, and after the Mongol chiefs had agreed as to their chief, the captive kings, Yaroslaf of Russia, and David of Georgia, paid homage to their conqueror. We owe to the monk Carpino, who was sent by the Pope to convert the Mongol, a graphic account of one of the most brilliant ceremonies to be met with in the whole course of Mongol history. The delay in selecting Kuyuk, whose principal act of sovereignty was to issue a seal having this inscription: "God in Heaven and Kuyuk on earth; by the power of God the ruler of all men," had given the Sungs one respite, and his early death procured them another. Kuyuk died in 1248, and his cousin Mangu, the son of Tuli, was appointed his successor. By this time the Mongol chiefs of the family of Genghis in Western Asia were practically independent of the nominal Great Khan, and governed their states in complete sovereignty, and waged war without reference to Karakoram. This change left the Mongols in their original home on the Amour absolutely free to devote all their attention to the final overthrow of the Sungs, and Mangu declared that he would know no rest until he had finally subjected the last of the Chinese ruling families. In this resolution Mangu received the hearty support of his younger, but more able brother, Kublai, to whom was entrusted the direction in the field of the armies sent to complete the conquest of China.

Kublai received this charge in 1251, so that the Sungs had enjoyed, first through the pacific disposition of Ogotai, and, secondly, from the family disputes following his death, peace for more than fifteen years. The advantage of this tranquillity was almost nullified by the death of Mongkong, a general whose reputation may have been easily gained, but who certainly enjoyed the confidence of his soldiers, and who was thought by his countrymen to be the best commander of his day. When the Chinese emperor Litsong saw the storm again approaching his northern frontier, he found that he had lost the main support of his power, and that his military resources were inferior to those of his enemy. He had allowed himself to be lulled into a false sense of security by the long inaction of the Mongols, and although he seems to have been an amiable prince, and a typical Chinese ruler, honouring the descendants of Confucius with the hereditary title of Duke, which still remains in that family, and is the only title of its kind in China, and encouraging the literary classes of his country, he was a bad sovereign to be entrusted with the task of defending his realm and people against a bold and determined enemy.

Kublai prepared the way for his campaigns in Southern China by following a very wise and moderate policy in Northern China similar to that begun by Muhula, and carried out with greater effect by Yeliu Chutsai. He had enjoyed the advantage of a Chinese education, imparted by an able tutor named Yaochu, who became the prince's private secretary and mentor in all Chinese matters. At his instigation, or, at least, with his co-operation, Kublai took in hand the restoration of the southern portion of Honan, which had been devastated during the wars, and he succeeded in bringing back its population and prosperity to that great province of Central China. He thus secured a base for his operations close to the Sung frontier, while he attached to his person a large section of the Chinese nation. There never was any concealment that this patronage of Chinese officials and these measures for the amelioration of many millions of Chinese subjects, were the well calculated preliminaries to the invasion of Southern China, and the extinction of the Sung dynasty.

If Kublai had succeeded in obtaining a wise adviser in Yaochu, he was not less fortunate in procuring a great general in the person of Uriangkadai, the son of Subutai, and his remarkable and unvarying successes were largely due to the efforts of those two men in the cabinet and the field. The plan of campaign, drawn up with great care and forethought by the prince and his lieutenant, had the double merit of being both bold and original. Its main purpose was not one that the Sung generals would be likely to divine. It was determined to make a flank march round the Sung dominions, and to occupy what is now the province of Yunnan, and by placing an army in the rear of their kingdom, to attack them eventually from two sides. At this time Yunnan formed an independent state, and its ruler, from his position behind the Sung territory, must have fancied himself secure against any attack by the Mongols. He was destined to a rude awakening. Kublai and Uriangkadai, marching across Szchuen and crossing the Kinchakiang, or "river of golden sand," which forms the upper course of the Great River, on rafts, burst into Yunnan, speedily vanquished the frontier garrisons, and laid siege to the capital, Talifoo. That town did not hold out long, and soon Kublai was in a position to return to his own state, leaving Uriangkadai with a considerable garrison in charge of Yunnan. That general, believing that his position would be improved by his resorting to an active offensive, carried the standard of his race against the many turbulent tribes in his neighbourhood, and invaded Burmah, whose king, after one campaign, was glad to recognise the supremacy of the Mongols. The success and the boldness, which may have been considered temerity, of this campaign, raised up enemies to Kublai at the court of Karakoram, and the mind of his brother Mangu was poisoned against him by many who declared that Kublai aspired to complete independence. These designs so far succeeded, that in 1257 Mangu finally deprived Kublai of all his commands, and ordered him to proceed to Karakoram. At this harsh and unmerited treatment Kublai showed himself inclined to rebel and dispute his brother's authority. If he had done this, although the provocation was great, he would have confirmed the charges of his accusers, and a war would have broken out among the Mongols, which would probably have rent their power in twain in Eastern Asia. But fortunately Yaochu was at hand to give prudent advice, and, after much hesitation, Kublai yielded to the impressive exhortations of his experienced and sagacious minister. He is reported to have addressed Kublai in the following terms:—"Prince! You are the brother of the emperor, but you are not the less his subject. You cannot, without committing a crime, question his decisions, and, moreover, if you were to do so, it would only result in placing you in a more dangerous predicament, out of which you could hardly succeed in extricating yourself, as you are so far distant from the capital where your enemies seek to injure you. My advice is that you should send your family to Mangu, and by this step you will justify yourself and remove any suspicions there may be."

Kublai adopted this wise course, and proceeded in person to Karakoram, where he succeeded in proving his innocence and in discomfiting his enemies. It is said that Mangu was so affected at the mere sight of his brother that he at once forgave him without waiting for an explanation and reinstated him in all his offices. To ratify this reconciliation Mangu proclaimed that he would take the field in person, and that Kublai should hold joint command with himself. When he formed this resolution to proceed to China in person, he appointed his next brother, Arikbuka, to act as his lieutenant in Mongolia. It is necessary to recollect this arrangement as Mangu died during the campaign, and it led to the separation of the Chinese empire and the Mongolian, which were divided after that event between Kublai and Arikbuka.

Mangu did not come to his resolution to prosecute the war with the Sungs any too soon, for Uriangkadai was beginning to find his isolated position not free from danger. Large as the army of that general was, and skilfully as he had endeavoured to improve his position by strengthening the fortresses and recruiting from the warlike tribes of Yunnan, Uriangkadai found himself threatened by the collected armies of the Sungs, who occupied Szchuen with a large garrison and menaced the daring Mongol general with the whole of their power. There seems every reason to believe that if the Sungs had acted with only ordinary promptitude they might have destroyed this Mongol army long before any aid could have reached it from the north. Once Mangu had formed his resolution the rapidity of his movements left the Sungs little or no chance of attacking Uriangkadai. This campaign began in the winter of 1257, when the troops were able to cross the frozen waters of the Hoangho, and the immense Mongol army was divided into three bodies, while Uriangkadai was ordered to march north and effect a junction with his old chief Kublai in Szchuen. The principal fighting of the first year occurred in this part of China, and Mangu hastened there with another of his armies. The Sung garrison was large, and showed great courage and fortitude. The difficulty of the country and the strength of several of their fortresses seconded their efforts, and after two years' fighting the Mongols felt so doubtful of success that they held a council of war to decide whether they should retreat or continue to prosecute the struggle. It has been said that councils of war do not come to bold resolutions, but this must have been an exception, as it decided not to retreat, and to make one more determined effort to overcome the Chinese. The campaign of 1259 began with the siege of Hochau, a strong fortress, held by a valiant garrison and commander, and to whose aid a Chinese army under Luwenti was hastening. The governor, Wangkien, offered a stout resistance, and Luwenti succeeded in harassing the besiegers, but the fall of the fortress appeared assured, when a new and more formidable defender arrived in the form of dysentery. The Mongol camp was ravaged by this foe, Mangu himself died of the disease, and those of the Mongols who escaped beat a hasty and disorderly retreat back to the north. Once more the Sungs obtained a brief respite.

The death of Mangu threatened fresh disputes and strife among the Mongol royal family. Kublai was his brother's lawful heir, but Arikbuka, the youngest of the brothers, was in possession of Karakoram, and supreme throughout Mongolia. He was hostile to Kublai, and disposed to assert all his rights and to make the most of his opportunities. No Great Khan could be proclaimed anywhere save at Karakoram, and Arikbuka would not allow his brother to gain that place, the cradle of their race and dynasty, unless he could do so by force of arms. Kublai attempted to solve the difficulty by holding a grand council near his favourite city of Cambaluc, the modern Pekin, and he sent forth his proclamation to the Mongols as their Khan. But they refused to recognise one who was not elected in the orthodox fashion at Karakoram; and Arikbuka not merely defied Kublai, but summoned his own kuriltai at Karakoram, where he was proclaimed Khakhan in the most formal manner and with all the accustomed ceremonies. Arikbuka was undoubtedly popular among the Mongols, while Kublai, who was regarded as half a Chinese on account of his education, had a far greater reputation south of the wall than north of it.

Kublai could not tolerate the open defiance of his authority, and the contempt shown for what was his birthright, by Arikbuka; and in 1261 he advanced upon Karakoram at the head of a large army. A single battle sufficed to dispose of Arikbuka's pretensions, and that prince was glad to find a place of refuge among the Kirghiz. Kublai proved himself a generous enemy. He sent Arikbuka his full pardon, he reinstated him in his rank of prince, and he left him virtually supreme amongst the Mongol tribes. He retraced his steps to Pekin, fully resolved to become Chinese emperor in reality, but prepared to waive his rights as Mongol Khan. Mangu Khan was the last of the Mongol rulers whose authority was recognised in both the east and the west, and his successor, Kublai, seeing that its old significance had departed, was fain to establish his on a new basis in the fertile, ancient, and wide-stretching dominions of China.

Before Kublai composed the difficulty with Arikbuka he had resumed his operations against the Sungs, and even before Mangu's death he had succeeded in establishing some posts south of the Yangtsekiang, in the impassability of which the Chinese fondly believed. During the year 1260 he laid siege to Wochow, the modern Wouchang, but he failed to make any impression on the fortress on this occasion, and he agreed to the truce which Litsong proposed. By the terms of this agreement Litsong acknowledged himself a Mongol vassal, just as his ancestors had subjected themselves to the Kins, paid a large tribute, and forbade his generals anywhere to attack the Mongols. The last stipulation was partly broken by an attack on the rear of Uriangkadai's corps, but no serious results followed, for Kublai was well satisfied with the manner in which the campaign terminated, as there is no doubt that his advance across the Yangtsekiang had been precipitate, and he may have thought himself lucky to escape with the appearance of success and the conclusion of a gratifying treaty. It was with the reputation gained by this nominal success, and by having made the Sungs his tributaries, that Kublai hastened northwards to settle his rivalry with Arikbuka. Having accomplished that object with complete success he decided to put an end to the Sung dynasty. The Chinese emperor, acting with strange fatuity, had given fresh cause of umbrage, and had provoked a war by many petty acts of discourtesy, culminating in the murder of the envoys of Kublai, sent to notify his proclamation as Great Khan of the Mongols. Probably the Sung ruler could not have averted war if he had shown the greatest forbearance and humility, but this cruel and inexcusable act precipitated the crisis and the extinction of his attenuated authority. If there was any delay in the movements of Kublai for the purpose of exacting reparation for this outrage, it was due to his first having to arrange a difficulty that had arisen in his relations with the King of Corea. That potentate had long preserved the peace with his Mongol neighbours, and perhaps he would have remained a friend without any interruption, had not the Mongols done something which was construed as an infraction of Corean liberty. The Corean love of independence took fire at the threatened diminution of their rights, they rose *en masse* in defence of their country, and even the king, Wangtien, who had been well disposed to the Mongol rulers, declared that he could not continue the alliance, and placed himself at the head of his people. Seeing himself thus menaced with a costly war in a difficult country on the eve of a more necessary and hopeful contest, Kublai resorted to diplomacy. He addressed Wangtien in complimentary terms and disclaimed all intention of injuring the Coreans with whom he wished to maintain friendly relations, but at the same time he pointed out the magnitude of his power and dilated on the extent of the Mongol conquests. Half by flattery and half by menace Kublai brought the Corean court to reason, and Wangtien again entered into bonds of alliance with Cambaluc and renewed his old oaths of friendship.

At this point of the long struggle with the Sungs it will be appropriate to consider what was the exact position of Kublai with regard to his own Chinese subjects, who now formed the backbone of his power. By this time Kublai had become to all practical intents and purposes a Chinese emperor. He had accepted all the traditional functions of the typical Hwangti, and the etiquette and splendour of his court rivalled that of the Sungs. He had not merely adopted the Chinese system of taxation and the form of administration to which the larger portion of his officials, being of Chinese race, had been accustomed, but he declared himself the patron of learning and of Buddhism, which had gained a hold on the minds of the Mongols that it has not lost to the present day. One of the most popular of his early measures had been the order to liberate all the literate class among his Chinese prisoners, and they had formed the nucleus of the civil service Kublai attached to his interests and utilised as his empire expanded. In his relations with Buddhism Kublai showed not less astuteness, and in realising that to attain durable success he must appeal to the religious side of human character, he showed that he had the true instincts of a statesman. At this time two facts were clearly apparent. The Chinese were sunk in a low state of religious disbelief, and the Sung rulers were not disposed to play the part of regenerators of their country. The second fact was that the only vigorous religion in China, or, indeed, in Eastern Asia, was Buddhism which, since the establishment of Brahmanism in India, had taken up its headquarters in Tibet, where, however, the supreme authority was still secular—that is to say, it was invested in the hands of a prince or king, and not in those of a priest or Grand Lama. It so happened that there was resident at Kublai's court a Tibetan priest, of the family which had always supplied the Sanpou with his minister, who gained the ear of Kublai, and convinced him how politic and advantageous to him personally it would be if he were to secure the co-operation and sympathy of his priestly order. Kublai fell in with his plans, and proclaimed his friend Pakba Lama, and sent him back to Tibet, there to establish the ecclesiastical authority, which still exists in that country, in intimate alliance and sympathy with the Chinese rulers. By this and other similar proceedings Kublai gained over to his side several influential classes among the Chinese people, and many reflecting persons thought they saw in him a true regenerator of the empire, and a worthy successor of their greatest rulers. It was, therefore, with a thoroughly pacified country, and to a great extent a contented people, that Kublai began his last war with the rulers of Southern China, and our account of this last campaign can have no better prelude than this extract from Kublai's letter to Wangtien, King of Corea:—

"The empire of the Mongols, founded by my grandsire of glorious memory, Genghis Khan, has been so widely extended under his successors, that it is composed of almost all the kingdoms enclosed between the four seas, and several even of our subjects possess the title of king, for themselves and their descendants, over vast extents of territory. Of all the countries of the earth there is only yours, besides that of the Sungs, which has refused to submit to us. The Chinese regarded their great river, the Kiang, as a barrier which we should never be able to face, and I have just shown that belief to be a vain hope. They thought that the valour of the troops of Szchuen and Houkwang, joined to their impassable mountains, would preserve those two provinces for them ; and behold, we have beaten them everywhere, and hold their strong places. They are at this moment like fish deprived of water, or as birds in the net."

In 1263 Kublai issued his proclamation of war, calling on his generals "to assemble their troops, to sharpen their swords and their pikes, and to prepare their bows and arrows," for he intended to attack the Sungs by land and sea. The treason of a Chinese general in his service named Litan served to delay the opening of the campaign for a few weeks, but this incident was of no importance, as Litan was soon overthrown and executed. Brief as was the interval, it was marked by one striking and important event—the death of Litsong, who was succeeded by his nephew, Chowki, called the Emperor Toutsong. Litsong was not a wise ruler, but compared with many of his successors, he might be more accurately styled unfortunate than incompetent. Toutsong, and his weak and arrogant minister, Kiassetao, hastened to show that there were greater heights of folly than any to which he had attained. Acting on the advice of a renegade Sung general, well acquainted with the defences of Southern China, Kublai altered his proposed attack, and prepared for crossing the Yangtsekiang by first making himself supreme on its tributary, the Han river. His earlier attack on Wouchang has been described, and his compulsory retirement from that place had taught him the evil of making a premature attack. His object remained the same, but instead of marching direct to it across the Yangtsekiang he took the advice of the Sung general, and attacked the fortress of Sianyang on the Han river, with the object of making himself supreme on that stream, and wresting from the Sungs the last first-class fortress they possessed in the north-west. By the time all these preliminaries were completed and the Mongol army had fairly taken the field it was 1268, and Kublai sent 60,000 of his best troops, with a large number of auxiliaries, to lay siege to Sianyang, which was held by a large garrison and a resolute governor. The Mongol lines were drawn up round the town, and also its neighbour of Fanching, situated on the opposite bank of the river, with which communication was maintained by several bridges, and the Mongols built a large fleet of fifty war junks, with which they closed the Han river and effectually prevented any aid being sent up it from Hankow or Wouchang. Liuwen Hoan, the commandant of Sianyang, was a brave man, and he commanded a numerous garrison and possessed supplies, as he said, to stand a ten years' siege. He repulsed all the assaults of the enemy, and, undaunted by his isolation, replied to the threats of the Mongols to give him no quarter if he persisted in holding out, by boasting that he would hang their traitor general in chains before his sovereign. The threats and vaunts of the combatants did not bring the siege any nearer to an end. The utmost that the Mongols could achieve was to prevent any provisions or reinforcements being thrown into the town. But on the fortress itself they made no impression. Things had gone on like this for three years, and the interest in the siege had begun to languish, when Kublai determined to make a supreme effort to carry the place, and at the same moment the Sung minister came to the conclusion to relieve it at all hazards.

The campaign of 1270 began with an heroic episode—the successful despatch of provisions into the besieged town, under the direction of two Chinese officers named Changkoua and Changchun, whose names deserve to be long remembered for their **heroism**. The flotilla **was** divided into two bodies, one composed of the fighting, the other of **the storeships**. The Mongols had made every preparation to blockade the river, **but the** suddenness and vigour of the Chinese attack surprised them, and, at **first,** the Chinese had the best of the day. But soon the Mongols recovered, **and** from their superior position threatened to overwhelm the assailing Chinese squadron. In this perilous **moment Changchun**, devoting himself to death **in the** interest of his country, **collected all his** war-junks, **and** making a desperate attack **on the** Mongols, **succeeded in** obtaining sufficient time to enable **the storeships** under Changkoua to pass safely **up to** Sianyang. The life **of so great a** hero as Changchun was, however, a heavy price to pay for the **temporary** relief of Sianyang, which was more closely besieged than ever **after the arrival** of Kublai **in person**. The heroic deed of Changchun roused a spirit of worthy emulation **in the** bosom of his comrade, Changkoua, who having thrown the needed supplies into Sianyang was no longer wanted in that beleagured city. He determined **to** cut his way back with such forces as he could collect, **and to take a part in the operations** in progress for the relief **of** the town. At the **head** of the **few** remaining war-junks he succeeded **in** breaking his way through the **chains** and other barriers by which the Mongols sought to close the river, and for a brief space it seemed as if he would evade **or** vanquish such of the Mongol ships as were on the alert. But the **Mongols** kept good watch, and as Changkoua refused to surrender he **and his** small band were destroyed to the last **man.** After the brief struggle was ended the Mongols sent the body of Changkoua into Sianyang, where **it was** received with loud lamentations, and buried **beside that of** Changchun, whose corpse had been rescued from the river. A Chinese historian might be pardoned for placing this episode **on a par** with Sir Richard Grenville's **defence** of the "Revenge."

After this affair the Mongols pushed the siege with greater vigour, **and** instead **of** concentrating their efforts on Sianyang they attacked both that fortress and Fanching from all sides. The Mongol commander, Alihaya, sent to Persia, where the Mongols were also supreme, for engineers trained in **the** working of mangonels or catapults, engines capable of throwing stones **of** 160-lbs. weight with precision for a considerable distance. By their aid the bridges across the river were first destroyed, and then the walls of Sianyang were so **severely** damaged that an assault appeared to be feasible. But Fanching had suffered still more from the Mongol bombardment, and Alihaya therefore attacked it first. The garrison offered a determined resistance, and the fighting was continued in the streets. Not a man of the garrison escaped, and when the slaughter **was over** the Mongols found that they had only acquired possession of a mass of ruins. But they had obtained the key to Sianyang, the weakest flank of which had been protected by Fanching, and the Chinese garrison was so discouraged that Liuwen Hoan, despairing of relief, agreed to accept the terms offered by Kublai. Those terms were expressed in the following noble letter from the Mongol emperor :—

"The generous defence you have **made** during **five** years covers you with **glory.** It is the duty of every faithful subject to serve his prince at the expense of his life, but in the straits to which you are reduced, your strength exhausted, deprived of succour and without hope of receiving any, would it be reasonable to sacrifice the lives of so many brave men out of sheer obstinacy? Submit in good faith to us and no harm shall come to you. We promise you still more; and that is to provide each and all of you with honourable employment. You shall have no grounds of discontent, for that we pledge you our Imperial word."

It will not excite surprise that Liuwen Hoan, who had been practically speaking deserted by his own sovereign, should have accepted the magnanimous terms of his conqueror, and become as loyal a lieutenant of Kublai as he had shown himself to be of the Sung Toutsong. The death of that ruler followed soon afterwards, but as the real power had been in the hands of the Minister Kiassetao, no change took place in the policy or fortunes of the Sung kingdom. At this moment Kublai succeeded in obtaining the services of Bayan, a Mongol general who had acquired a great reputation under Khulagu in Persia. Bayan, whose name signifies the noble or the brave, and who was popularly known as Bayan of the Hundred Eyes, because he was supposed to see everything, was one of the greatest military leaders of his age and race. He was entrusted with the command of the main army, and under him served, it is interesting to state, Liuwen Hoan. Several towns were captured after more or less resistance, and Bayan bore down with all his force on the triple cities of Hankow, Wouchang, and Hanyang. Bayan concentrated all his efforts on the capture of Hanyang, while the Mongol navy under Artchu compelled the Chinese fleet to take refuge under the walls of Wouchang. None of these towns offered a very stubborn resistance, and Bayan had the satisfaction of receiving their surrender one after another. Leaving Alihaya with 40,000 men to guard these places Bayan marched with the rest of his forces on the Sung capital, Lingan or Hangchow, the celebrated Kincsay of mediæval travellers. The retreating fleet and army of the Sungs carried with them fear of the Mongols, and the ever-increasing representation of their extraordinary power and irresistible arms. In this juncture public opinion compelled Kiassetao to take the lead, and he called upon all the subjects of the Sung to contribute arms and money for the purpose of national defence. But his own incompetence in directing this national movement deprived it of half its force and of its natural chances of success. Bayan's advance was rapid. Many towns opened their gates in terror or admiration of his name, and Liuwen Hoan was frequently present to assure them that Kublai was the most generous of masters, and that there was no wiser course than to surrender to his generals.

The Mongol forces at last reached the neighbourhood of the Sung capital where Kiassetao had succeeded in collecting an army of 130,000 men, but many of them were ill-trained, and the splendour of the camp provided a poor equivalent for the want of arms and discipline among the men. Kiassetao seems to have been ignorant of the danger of his position, for he sent an arrogant summons to the Mongols to retire, stating also that he would grant a peace based on the Yangtsekiang as a boundary. Bayan's simple reply to this notice was, "If you had really aimed at peace you would have made this proposition before we crossed the Kiang. Now that we are the masters of it, it is a little too late. Still if you sincerely desire it, come and see me in person, and we will discuss the necessary conditions." Very few of the Sung lieutenants offered a protracted resistance, and even the isolated cases of devotion were confined to the official class who were more loyal than the mass of the people. Chao Maofa and his wife Yongchi put an end to their existence sooner than give up their charge at Chichow, but the garrison accepted the terms of the Mongols without compunction, and without thinking of their duty. Kiassetao attempted to resist the Mongol advance at Kien Kang, the modern Nankin, but after an engagement on land and water the Sungs were driven back, and their fleet only escaped destruction by retiring precipitately to the sea. After this success Nankin surrendered without resistance, although its governor was a valiant and apparently a capable man. He committed suicide sooner than surrender, and among his papers was found a plan of campaign, after perusing which Bayan exclaimed, "Is it possible that the Sungs possessed a man capable of giving such prudent counsel? If they had paid heed to it should we ever have reached this spot?" After this success Bayan pressed on with increased rather than diminished energy, and the Sung emperor and his court fled from the capital. Kublai showed an inclination to temporise and to negotiate, but Bayan would not brook any delay. "To relax your grip even for a moment on an enemy whom you have held by the throat for a hundred years would only be to give him time to recover his breath, to restore his forces, and in the end to cause us an infinity of trouble."

The Sung fortunes showed some slight symptoms of improving when Kiassetao was disgraced, and a more competent general was found in the person of Chang Chikia. But the Mongols never abated the vigour of their attack or relaxed in their efforts to cut off all possibility of succour from the Sung capital. When Chang Chikia hoped to improve the position of his side by resuming the offensive he was destined to rude disappointment. Making an attack on the strong position of the Mongols at Nankin he was repulsed with heavy loss. The Sung fleet was almost annihilated and 700 war-junks were taken by the victors. After this the Chinese never dared to face the Mongols again on the water. This victory was due to the courage and capacity of Artchu. Bayan now returned from a campaign in Mongolia to resume the chief conduct of the war, and he signalised his return by the capture of Changchow. At this town he is said to have sanctioned a massacre of the Chinese troops, but the facts are enwrapped in uncertainty; and Marco Polo declares that this was only done after the Chinese had treacherously cut up the Mongol garrison. Alarmed by the fall of Changchow the Sung ministers again sued for peace, sending an imploring letter to this effect:—"Our ruler is young and cannot be held responsible for the differences that have arisen between the peoples. Kiassetao the guilty one has been punished; give us peace and we shall be better friends in the future." Bayan's reply was severe and uncompromising. "The age of your prince has nothing to do with the question between us. The war must go on to its legitimate end. Further argument is useless." The defences of the Sung capital were by this time removed, and the unfortunate upholders of that dynasty had no option save to come to terms with the Mongols. Marco Polo describes Kinesay as the most opulent city of the world, but it was in no position to stand a siege. The Empress-Regent acting for her son sent in her submission to Bayan, and agreed to proceed to the court of the conqueror. She abdicated for herself and family all the pretensions of their rank, and she accepted the favours of the Mongol with due humility, saying, "The Son of Heaven (thus giving Kublai the correct Imperial style) grants you the favour of sparing your life; it is just to thank him for it and to pay him homage." Bayan made a triumphal entry into the city, while the Emperor Kongtsong was sent off to Pekin. The majority of the Sung courtiers and soldiers came to terms with Bayan, but a few of the more desperate or faithful endeavoured to uphold the Sung cause in Southern China under the general, Chang Chikia. Two of the Sung princes were supported by this commander and one was proclaimed by the empty title of emperor. Capricious fortune rallied to their side for a brief space, and some of the Mongol detachments which had advanced too far or with undue precipitancy were cut up and destroyed.

The Mongols seem to have thought that the war was over, and the success of Chang Chikia's efforts may have been due to their negligence rather than to his vigour. As soon as they realised that there remained a flickering flame of opposition among the supporters of the Sungs they sent two armies, one into Kwantung and the other into Fuhkien, and their fleet against Chang Chikia. Desperate as was his position, that officer still exclaimed, " If heaven has not resolved to overthrow the Sungs, do you think that even now it cannot restore their ruined throne?" but his hopes were dashed to the ground by the capture of Canton, and the expulsion of all his forces from the mainland. One puppet emperor died and then Chang proclaimed another as Tiping. The last supporters of the cause took refuge on the island of Tai in the Canton estuary, where they hoped to maintain their position. The position was strong and the garrison was numerous; but the Mongols were not to be frightened by appearances. Their fleet bore down on the last Sung stronghold with absolute confidence, and, although the Chinese resisted for three days and showed great gallantry, they were overwhelmed by the superior engines as well as the numbers of the Mongols. Chang Chikia with a few ships succeeded in escaping from the fray, but the emperor's vessel was less fortunate, and finding that escape was impossible, Lousionfoo, one of the last Sung ministers, seized the emperor in his arms and jumped overboard with him. Thus died Tiping, the last Chinese emperor of the Sungs, and with him expired that ill-fated dynasty. Chang Chikia renewed the struggle with aid received from Tonquin, but when he was leading a forlorn hope against Canton he was caught in a typhoon and he and his ships were wrecked. His invocation to heaven, " I have done everything I could to sustain on the throne the Sung dynasty. When one prince died I caused another to be proclaimed emperor. He also has perished, and I still live! Oh, heaven, shall I be acting against thy desires if I sought to place a new prince of this family on the throne?" sounded the dirge of the race he had served so well.

Thus was the conquest of China by the Mongols completed. After half a century of warfare the kingdom of the Sungs shared the same fate as its old rival the Kin, and Kublai had the personal satisfaction of completing the work begun by his grandfather Genghis seventy years before. Of all the Mongol triumphs it was the longest in being attained. The Chinese of the north and of the south resisted with extraordinary powers of endurance the whole force of the greatest conquering race Asia had ever seen. They were not skilled in war and their generals were generally incompetent, but they held out with desperate courage and obstinacy long after other races would have given in. The student of history will not fail to see in these facts striking testimony of the extraordinary resources of China, and of the capacity of resistance to even a vigorous conqueror possessed by its inert masses. Even the Mongols did not conquer until they had obtained the aid of a large section of the Chinese nation, or before Kublai had shown that he intended to prove himself a worthy Emperor of China and not merely a great Khan of the Mongol Hordes.

CHAPTER VI.

KUBLAI AND THE MONGOL DYNASTY.

WHILE Bayan was winning victories for his master and driving the Chinese armies from the field, Kublai was engaged at Pekin in the difficult and necessary task of consolidating his authority. In 1271 he gave his dynasty the name of Yuen or Original, and he took for himself the Chinese title of Chitsou, although it will never supersede his Mongol name of Kublai. Summoning to his court the most experienced Chinese ministers, and aided by many foreigners, he succeeded in founding a government which was imposing by reason of its many-sidedness as well as its inherent strength. It satisfied the Chinese and it was gratifying to the Mongols, because they formed the buttress of one of the most imposing administrations in the world. All this was the distinct work of Kublai, who had enjoyed the special favour of Genghis, who had predicted of him that "one day he will sit in my seat and bring you good fortune such as you have had in my time." He resolved to make his court the most splendid in the world, and, if the testimony of Marco Polo may be accepted, he succeeded. His capital Cambaluc or Khanbalig—"the city of the Khan"—stood on or near the present site of Pekin, and the following description may be quoted :—

"Cambaluc was made for the first time capital of China by the Mongols. A city near or on its site had been the chief town of an independent kingdom on several occasions, e.g., of Yen, of the Khitans, and of the Kins. A long description is given by Marco Polo. There were, according to him, twelve gates, at each of which was stationed a guard of 1,000 men, and the streets were so straight and wide that you could see from one end to other, or from gate to gate. The extent given of the walls varies : according to the highest estimate they were twenty-seven miles round, according to the lowest eighteen. The Khan's palace at Chandu or Kaipingfoo, north of Pekin, where he built a magnificent summer palace, kept his stud of horses, and carried out his love of the chase in the immense park and preserves attached, may be considered the Windsor of this Chinese monarch. The position of Pekin had, and still has, much to recommend it as the site of a capital. The Mings, after proclaiming Nankin the capital, made scarcely less use of it, and Chuntche, the first of the Manchus, adopted it as his. It has since remained the sole metropolis of the Empire."

When Kublai permanently established himself at Pekin he drew up consistent lines of policy on all the great questions with which it was likely he would have to deal, and he always endeavoured to act upon these set principles. In framing this system of government he was greatly assisted by his old friend and tutor Yaochu as well as by other Chinese ministers.

He was thus able to deal wisely and also vigorously with a society with which he was only imperfectly acquainted; and the impartiality and insight into human character, which were his main characteristics, greatly simplified the difficult task before him. His impartiality was shown most clearly in his attitude on the question of religion; but it partook very largely of a hard materialism which concealed itself under a nominal indifference. At first he treated with equal consideration Buddhism, Mahomedanism, Christianity, and even Judaism, and he said that he treated them all with equal consideration because he hoped that the greatest among them would help him in Heaven. If some doubt may be felt as to the sincerity of this statement there can be none as to Kublai's effort to turn all religions to a political use, and to make them serve his turn. Some persons have thought he showed a predilection for Christianity, but his measures in support of Buddhism, and of his friend the Pakba Lama, are a truer indication of his feelings. But none were admitted into his private confidence, and his acts evinced a politic tolerance towards all creeds. But his religious tolerance or indifference did not extend to personal matters. He insisted on the proper prayers being offered to himself, and the extreme reverence of the kow-tow. Priests were appointed and specially enjoined to offer up prayers on his behalf before the people, who were required to attend these services and to join in the responses. Images of himself were also sent to all the provincial towns for reverence to be offered. He also followed the Chinese custom of erecting a temple to his ancestors, and the coins that passed current bore his effigy. Thus did Kublai more and more identify himself with his Chinese subjects, and as he found his measures crowned with success he became himself more wedded to Chinese views, less tolerant of adverse opinions, and more disposed to assert his sovereign majesty.

Having embellished his capital, it is not surprising to find that he drew up a strict court ceremonial, and that he prescribed gorgeous dresses for those who were to be allowed to approach him. The following picture has been drawn of his court. His courtiers were required to dress after a uniform fashion, and to appear in fixed apparel on all state occasions. His banquets were of the most sumptuous description. Strangers from foreign states were admitted to the presence, and dined at a table set apart for travellers, while the great king himself feasted in the full gaze of his people. His courtiers, guard, and ministers attended by a host of servitors, and protected from enemies by 20,000 guards, the flower of the Mongol army; the countless wealth seized in the capitals of numerous kingdoms; the brilliance of intellect among his chief adherents and supporters; the martial character of the race that lent itself almost as well to the pageantry of a court as to the stern reality of battle; and finally the majesty of the great king himself,—all combined to make Kublai's court and capital the most splendid, at that time, in the world. Although Kublai's instincts were martial, he gave up all idea of accompanying his armies in the field after his war with Arikbuka. As he was only forty-four when he formed this decision, it must be assumed that he came to it mainly because he had so many other matters to attend to, and also, no doubt, because he felt that he possessed in Bayan a worthy substitute. Marco Polo's description of his personal appearance will be read with interest as a conclusion to this record of his idiosyncrasies. "He is of a good stature, neither tall nor short, but of a middle height. He has a becoming amount of flesh, and is very shapely in all his limbs. His complexion is white and red, the eyes black and fine, the nose well formed and well set on."

The most fortunate and successful monarch rarely escapes without some misfortune, and Kublai was not destined to be an exception to the rule. The successes of the Mongol navy undoubtedly led Kublai to believe that his arms might be carried beyond the sea, and he formed the definite plan of subjecting Japan to his power. The ruling family in that kingdom was of Chinese descent, tracing back its origin to Taipe a fugitive Chinese prince of the twelfth century before our era. The Chinese in their usual way had asserted the superior position of a Suzerain and the Japanese had as consistently refused to recognise the claim, and had maintained their independence. As a rule the Japanese abstained from all interference in the affairs of the continent, and the only occasion on which they departed from this rule was when they aided Corea against China. In 1266 Kublai sent two ambassadors by way of Corea to Japan with a letter from himself complaining that the Japanese court had taken no notice of his accession to power, and treated him with indifference. The mission never had a chance of success, for the Coreans succeeded in frightening the Mongol envoys with the terrors of the sea, and by withholding their assistance prevented them reaching their destination. The envoys returned without having been able to deliver their letter. For some unknown reason Kublai decided that the Japanese were hostile to him, and he resolved to humble them. He called upon the King of Corea to raise an auxiliary force, and that prince promised to supply 1,000 ships and 10,000 men. In 1274 he sent a small force of 300 ships and 15,000 men to begin operations in the direction of Japan; but the Japanese navy came out to meet it, and attacking it off the island of Tsiusima, inflicted a crushing defeat. As this expedition was largely composed of the Corean contingent Kublai easily persuaded himself that this defeat did not indicate what would happen when he employed his own Mongol troops. He also succeeded in sending several envoys to Japan after his first abortive attempt, and they brought back consistent reports as to the hostility and defiance of the Japanese, who at last, to leave no further doubt on the subject, executed his envoy in 1280. For this outrage the haughty monarch swore he would exact a terrible revenge, and in 1280-1, when the last of his campaigns with the Sungs had been brought to a triumphant conclusion, he collected all his forces in the eastern part of the kingdom, and prepared to attack Japan with all his power.

For the purposes of this war he raised an army of over 100,000 men, of whom about one-third were Mongols; and a fleet large enough to carry this host and its supplies was gathered together with great difficulty in the harbours of Chekiang and Fuhkien. It would have been wiser if the expedition had started from Corea, as the sea voyage would have been greatly reduced; but the difficulty of getting his army to that country, and the greater difficulty of feeding it when it got there, induced him to make his own maritime possessions the base of his operations. From the beginning misfortunes fell thick upon it, and the Japanese, not less than the English, when assailed by the Spanish Armada and Boulogne invasions, owed much to the alliance of the sea. Kublai had felt bound to appoint a Chinese generalissimo as well as a Mongol to this host, but it did not work well. One general fell ill, and was superseded, another was lost in a storm, and there was a general want of harmony in the Mongol camp and fleet.

Still the fleet set sail, but the elements declared themselves against Kublai. His shattered fleet was compelled to take refuge off the islets to the north of Japan, where it attempted to refit, but the Japanese granted no respite, and assailed them both by land and sea. After protracted but unequal fighting the Mongol commander had no choice left but to surrender. The conquerors spared the Chinese and Coreans among their prisoners, but they put every Mongol to the sword. Only a stray junk or two escaped to tell Kublai the tale of the greatest defeat the Mongols had ever experienced. Thirty thousand of their best troops were slaughtered, and their newly-created fleet, on which they were founding such great expectations, was annihilated, while 70,000 Chinese and Coreans remained as prisoners in the hands of the victor. Kublai executed two of his generals who escaped, but it is clear no one was to blame. The Mongols were vanquished because they undertook a task beyond their power, and one with which their military experience did not fit them to cope. The most formidable portion of their army was cavalry, and they had no knowledge of the sea. Nor could their Chinese auxiliaries supply this deficiency; for, strange as it may appear, the Chinese, although many of them are good fishermen and sailors, have never been a powerful nation at sea. On the other hand, the Japanese have always been a bold and capable race of mariners. They have frequently proved that the sea is their natural element, and all the power and resources of Kublai availed not against the skill and courage of these hardy islanders. Kublai was reluctant to acquiesce in his defeat, and he endeavoured to form another expedition, but the Chinese sailors mutinied and refused to embark. They were supported by all the Chinese ministers at Pekin, who protested in the following language, and Kublai felt himself compelled to yield and abandon all designs of conquest beyond the sea:—" During the three or four years in which you have been engaged in wars in these foreign countries how many brave officers and soldiers have we not lost, and what advantages have been derived from them?—the people oppressed, and bands of vagabonds induced to levy on the country the enormous requisitions necessary for their sustenance; that is a true picture of the dire consequences of this expedition. However small the Kingdom of Kiaochi (Tonquin and Cochin China) may be, your Majesty ordered one of your sons to march for the purpose of subjecting it. He penetrated into it for considerable distance, but was obliged to beat a retreat without having accomplished anything, and after having lost the greater portion of his army and one of his best generals. Japan is separated from our Empire by a great sea, and we have nothing to fear from its enterprise. If, in the new expedition, over which you are meditating, a check similar to the last is experienced what a disappointment it will be to your Majesty, and how great the discontent must be among the people!"

The old success of the Mongols did not desert them on land, and Kublai received some consolation for his rude repulse by the Japanese in the triumph of his arms in Burmah. The conquest of Yunnan by Kublai at an early period of his career, and the subsequent successes of Uriangkadai have been described. The momentary submission of the King of Burmah, or Mien, as it was, and is still, called by the Chinese, had been followed by a fit of truculence and open hostility. This monarch had crossed over into Indian territory, and had assumed the title of King of Bengala in addition to his own. Emboldened by his success, he did not conceal his hostility to the Mongols, sent a defiant reply to all their representations, and even assumed the offensive with his frontier garrisons. He then declared open war. The Mongol General, Nasiuddin, collected all the forces he could, and when the Burmese ruler crossed the frontier at the head of an immense host of horse, foot, and elephants, he found the Mongol army drawn up on the plain of Yungchang. The Mongols numbered only 12,000 select troops, whereas the Burmese exceeded 80,000 men with a corps of elephants, estimated between 800 and 2,000, and an artillery force of 16 guns. Notwithstanding this numerical disadvantage the Mongols were in no way dismayed by their opponents' manifest superiority; but seldom has the struggle between disciplined and brute force proved closer or more keenly contested. At first the charge of the Burmese cavalry aided by the elephants and artillery, carried all before it. But Nasiuddin had provided for this contingency. He had dismounted all his cavalry, and had ordered them to fire their arrows exclusively against the elephant corps; and as the Mongols were then, not only the best archers in the world, but, used the strongest bows, the destruction they wrought was considerable, and soon threw the elephants into hopeless confusion. The crowd of elephants turned tail before this discharge of arrows, as did the elephants of Pyrrhus, and threw the whole Burmese army into confusion. The Mongols then mounting their horses, charged and completed the discomfiture of the Burmese, who were driven from the field with heavy loss and tarnished reputation. On this occasion the Mongols did not pursue the Burmese very far, and the King of Burmah lost little or no part of his dominions, but Nasiuddin reported to Pekin that it would be an easy matter to add the kingdom of Mien to the Mongol Empire. Kublai did not act on this advice until six years later, when he sent his kinsman Singtur with a large force to subdue Burmah. The king took shelter in Pegu, leaving his capital Amien at the mercy of the conqueror. The Mongol conquests were thus brought down to the very border of Assam. In Tonquin and Annam the arms of Kublai were not so successful. Reference is made in the memorial cited against the proposed second expedition to Japan, to the abortive campaign of Kublai's son Togan, in these regions. Whenever an open force had to be overcome, the Mongol army was successful, but when the Mongols encountered the difficulties of a damp and inclement climate, of the absence of road, and other disadvantages they were disheartened, and suffered heavily in men and morale. With the loss of his two generals, and the main portion of his army, Togan was lucky in himself escaping to China. Kublai wished to make another effort to subdue these inhospitable regions and their savage inhabitants, but Chinese public opinion proved too strong, and he had to yield to the representations of his ministers in this case as he did in that of Japan.

Kublai was the more compelled to sacrifice his feelings on this point, because there were not wanting indications that if he did not do so he would find a Chinese rebellion on his hands. Notwithstanding his many successes, and his evident desire to stand well with his Chinese subjects, it was already clear that they bore their new leader little love. Several of the principal provinces were in a state of veiled rebellion, showing that the first opportunity would be taken to shake off the Mongol yoke, and that Kublai's authority really rested on a quicksand. The predictions of a fanatic were sufficient to shake the emperor on his throne, and such was Kublai's apprehension that he banished all the remaining Sung prisoners to

Mongolia, and executed their last faithful minister, who went to the scaffold with a smile on his face, exclaiming, " I am content ; my wishes are about to be realised." It must not be supposed from this that Kublai's authority had vanished, or become effete. It was absolutely supreme over all declared enemies, but below the surface was seething an amount of popular hostility and discontent ominous to the longevity of the Mongol dynasty. The restless ambition of Kublai would not be satisfied with anything short of recognition, in some form or other, of his power by his neighbours, and he consequently sent envoys to all the kingdoms of Southern Asia to obtain, by lavish presents or persuasive language, that recognition of his authority on which he had set his heart. In most cases he was gratified, for there was not a power in Eastern Asia to compare with that of the Mongol prince seated on the Dragon Throne of China, and all were flattered to be brought into connection with it on any terms.

These successful and gratifying embassies had only one untoward result : they induced Kublai to revert to his idea of repairing the overthrow of his son Togan in Annam, and of finally subjugating that troublesome country. The intention was not wise, and it was rendered more imprudent by its execution being entrusted to Togan again. Another commander might have fared better, but great as was his initial success, he could not hope to permanently succeed. Togan began as he formerly commenced by carrying all before him. He won seventeen separate engagements, but the farther he advanced into the country the more evident did it appear that he only controlled the ground on which he stood. The King of Annam was a fugitive ; his capital was in the hands of the Mongols, and apparently nothing more remained to be done. Apachi, the most experienced of the Mongol commanders, then counselled a prompt retreat. Unfortunately the Mongol prince Togan would not take his advice, and the Annamites, gathering fresh forces on all sides, attacked the exhausted Mongols, and compelled them to beat a precipitate retreat from their country. All the fruits of early victory were lost, and Togan's disgrace was a poor consolation for the culminating discomfiture of Kublai's reign. The people of Annam then made good their independence, and they still enjoy it, so far as China is concerned, but I cannot help quoting what I wrote twelve years ago, when French projects were in embryo :—" If in the present age it is exposed to any immediate danger, it is at the hands of our gallant and courteous neighbours, the French, who only require the appearance of another Dupleix to carve out a fresh empire in the kingdoms of the Indo-Chinese peninsula, along the banks of the Mekong and the Songkoi, and on the shores of the Gulf of Tonquin." I will only add that Tonquin is now a French province, and Annam a dependency of the Republic. If there has not yet been a Dupleix, the French may be satisfied with the efforts of Riviere, Paul Bert, and de Lanessan.

We cannot doubt, and there is some evidence to support the opinion, that the failure of the emperor's endeavour to popularise his rule, was as largely due to the tyrannical acts and oppressive measures of some of his principal ministers as to unpopular and unsuccessful expeditions. Notwithstanding the popular dislike of the system, and Kublai's efforts to put it down, the Mongols resorted to the old plan of farming the revenue, and the extortion of those who purchased the right drove the Chinese to the verge of rebellion, and made the whole Mongol *régime* hateful. Several tax farmers were removed from their posts, and punished with death, but their successors carried on the same system. The financial straits of the time may be inferred from the fact that one of the Buddhist priests, who had gained the ear of Kublai, plundered the graves of the Sung emperors, and when arrested for the crime by a local official, the emperor not only ordered him to be released, but allowed him to retain possession of his ill-gotten plunder. The declining years of Kublai's reign were therefore marred by the growing discontent of his Chinese subjects, and by his inability or unwillingness to put down official extortion and mismanagement. But he had to cope with a still greater danger in the hostility of some members of his own family. The rivalry between himself and his brother Arikbuka formed one incident of his earlier career, the hostility of his cousin Kaidu proved a more serious peril when Kublai was stricken in years, and approaching the end of his long reign.

Kaidu was one of the sons of Ogotai, and consequently first cousin to Kublai. He held some high post in Mongolia, and he represented a reactionary party among the Mongols who wished the administration to be less Chinese, and who, perhaps, sighed for more worlds to conquer. But he hated Kublai, and was jealous of his pre-eminence, which was, perhaps, the only cause of his revolt. The hostility of Kaidu might have remained a personal grievance if he had not obtained the alliance of Nayan, a Mongol general of experience and ability, who had long been jealous of the superior reputation of Bayan. He was long engaged in raising an army, with which he might hope to make a bid for empire, but at last his preparations reached the ear of Kublai, who determined to crush him before his power had grown too great. Kublai marched against him at the head of 100,000 men, and all the troops Nayan could bring into the field were 40,000, while Kaidu, although hastily gathering his forces, was too far off to render any timely aid. Kublai commanded in person, and arranged his order of battle from a tower supported on the backs of four elephants chained together. Both armies showed great heroism and ferocity, but numbers carried the day, and Nayan's army was almost destroyed, while he himself fell into the hands of the victor. It was contrary to the practice of the Mongols to shed the blood of their own princes, so Kublai ordered Nayan to be sewn up in a sack, and then beaten to death. Meantime Kaidu had left Karakoram, and, undeterred by the fate of Nayan, was advancing by forced marches to again tempt the fortune of war. His confidence was raised by a victory he gained over Kanmala, Kublai's son, on the Selinga river, when Kanmala lost his army, and barely saved his own life, through the brave devotion of a Kipchak officer, named Tutuka, of whose action Kublai said, "The having delivered Prince Kanmala did him more honour than a victory." The war with Kaidu dragged on for many years, and there is no doubt that Kublai did not desire to push matters to an extremity with his cousin. Having restored the fortunes of the war by assuming the command in person, Kublai returned in a short time to Pekin, leaving his opponent, as he hoped, the proverbial golden bridge by which to retreat. But his lieutenant, Bayan, to whom he entrusted the conduct of the campaign, favoured more vigorous action, and was anxious to bring the struggle to a speedy and decisive termination. He had gained one remarkable victory under considerable disadvantage, when Kublai, either listening to his detractors or desirous of restraining his activity, dismissed him from his military posts and, summoning him to Pekin, gave him the uncongenial office of a minister of State. This happened in 1293, and in the following year Kublai, who was nearly eighty, and who had occupied the throne of China for thirty-five years, sickened and died, leaving behind him a great reputation which has survived the criticism of six centuries in both Europe and China.

With regard to the private character and domestic life of Kublai, we owe most of the details to that vivacious gossip and prince of travellers, Marco Polo. The accusation that this Mongol was destitute of natural affection, cannot be sustained in face of his unaffected grief at the death of his wife Honkilachi, and his eldest son, Chinkin, but there seems to be a better basis for the charges of avarice and gross superstition brought against him by the Chinese historians, who avenge themselves for the conquest of their country by disparaging the conqueror. His long reign marked the climax of the Mongol triumph which he had all the personal satisfaction of extending to China. Where Genghis failed, or attained only partial success, he succeeded to the fullest extent, thus verifying the prophecy of his grandfather. But although he conquered their country, he never vanquished the prejudices of the Chinese, and the Mongols, unlike the Manchus, failed completely to propitiate the good-will of the historiographers of the Hanlin. Of Kublai they take some recognition, as an enlightened and well-meaning prince, but for all the other Emperors of the Yuen line they have nothing good to say. Even Kublai himself could not assure the stability of his throne, and when he died it was at once clear that the Mongols could not long retain the supreme position in China.

But Kublai's authority was sufficiently established for it to be transmitted, without popular disturbance or any insurrection on the part of the Chinese, to his legal heir, who was his grandson. Such risk as presented itself to the succession arose from the dissensions among the Mongol princes themselves, but the prompt measures of Bayan arrested any trouble, and Prince Timour was proclaimed Emperor under the Chinese style of Chingtsong. A few months after this signal service to the ruling family Bayan died, leaving behind him the reputation of being one of the most capable of all the Mongol commanders. Whether because he could find no general worthy to fill Bayan's place, or because his temperament was naturally pacific, Timour carried on no military operations, and the thirteen years of his reign were marked by almost unbroken peace. But peace did not bring prosperity in its train, for a considerable part of China suffered from the ravages of famine, and the cravings of hunger drove many to become brigands. Timour's anxiety to alleviate the public suffering gained him some small measure of popularity, and he also endeavoured to limit the opportunities of the Mongol Governors to be tyrannical by taking away from them the power of life and death. Timour was compelled by the sustained hostility of Kaidu to continue the struggle with that prince, but he confined himself to the defensive, and the death of Kaidu, in A.D. 1301, deprived the contest of its extreme bitterness although it still continued.

Timour was, however, unfortunate in the one foreign enterprise which he undertook. The ease with which Burmah had been vanquished and reduced to a tributary state emboldened some of his officers on the southern frontier to attempt the conquest of Papesifu—a State which may be identified with the modern Laos. The enterprise, commenced in a thoughtless and light-hearted manner, revealed unexpected peril and proved disastrous. A large part of the Mongol army perished from the heat, and the survivors were only rescued from their perilous position, surrounded by the numerous enemies they had irritated, by a supreme effort on the part of Koko, the Viceroy of Yunnan, who was also Timour's uncle. The insurrectionary movement was not confined to the outlying districts of Annam and Burmah, but extended within the Chinese border, and several years elapsed before tranquillity was restored to the frontier provinces. Timour died in 1306 A.D. without leaving a direct legitimate heir, and his two nephews Haichan and Aiyuli Palipata were held to possess an equal claim to the throne. Haichan was absent in Mongolia when his uncle died, and a faction put forward the pretensions of Honanta, prince of Gansi, who seems to have been Timour's natural son, but Aiyuli Palipata, acting with great energy, arrested the pretender and proclaimed Haichan as Emperor. Haichan reigned five years, during which, the chief reputation he gained was as a glutton. When he died, in A.D. 1311, his brother Palipata was proclaimed Emperor, although Haichan left two sons. Palipata's reign of nine years was peaceful and uneventful, and his son Chutepala succeeded him. Chutepala was a young and inexperienced prince who owed such authority as he enjoyed to the courage of Baiju, a brave soldier, who was specially distinguished as the lineal descendant of the great general, Muhula. The plots and intrigues which compassed the ruin of the Yuen dynasty began during this reign, and both Chutepala and Baiju were murdered by conspirators. The next Emperor, Yesun Timour, was fortunate in a peaceful reign, but on his death, in 1328, the troubles of the dynasty accumulated, and its end came clearly into view. In little more than a year, three Emperors were proclaimed and died. Tou Timour, one of the sons of Haichan, who ruled before Palipata, was so far fortunate in reigning for a longer period, but the most interesting episode in his barren reign was the visit of the Grand Lama of Tibet to Pekin, where he was received with exceptional honour, but when Tou Timour attempted to compel his courtiers to pay the representative of Buddhism special obeisance he encountered the opposition of both Chinese and Mongols. The President of the Hanlin College, with that courage which has always been a conspicuous feature of the Chinese literary class, addressed the Lama thus, "You are the disciple of Fo and the master of all the bonzes; and I am the disciple of Confucius and the head of all the literati of this Empire. Confucius is not one whit less illustrious than Fo; therefore, there is no need for so many ceremonies between us." It is recorded that the Lama showed himself a man of tact, by agreeing with these remarks, and adapting his attitude to that of the Hanlin President.

After Tou Timour's death the Imperial title passed to Tohan Timour, who is best known by his Chinese title of Chunti. He found a champion in Bayan, a descendant of the general of that name, who successfully defended the Palace against the attack of a band of conspirators. In 1337 the first distinct rebellion on the part of the Chinese took place in the neighbourhood of Canton, and an order for the disarmament of the Chinese population aggravated the situation because it could not be effectually carried out. Bayan, after his defence of the palace, became the most powerful personage in the State, and to his arrogance was largely due the aggravation of the Mongol difficulties and the embittering of Chinese opinion. He murdered an Empress, tyrannised over the Chinese, and outshone the Emperor in his apparel and equipages, as if he were a Wolsey or a Buckingham. For the last offence Chunti could not forgive him, and Bayan was deposed and disgraced. While these dissensions were in progress at Pekin the Chinese were growing more daring and confident in their efforts to liberate themselves from the foreign yoke. They had adopted red bonnets as the mark of their patriotic league, and on the sea the piratical confederacy of Fangkue Chin vanquished and destroyed such navy as the Mongols ever possessed. But in open and regular fighting on land the supremacy of the Mongols was still incontestable, and a minister, named Toto, restored the sinking fortunes of Chunti until he fell the victim of a court intrigue—being poisoned by a rival named Hamar. With Toto disappeared the last possible champion of the Mongols, and the only thing needed to ensure their overthrow was the advent of a capable leader who could give coherence to the national cause, and such a leader was not long in making his appearance.

The deliverer of the Chinese from the Mongols was an individual named Choo Yuen Chang, who, being left an orphan, entered a monastery as the easiest way of gaining a livelihood. In the year 1345, when Chunti had been on the throne twelve years, Choo quitted his retreat and joined one of the bands of Chinese who had thrown off the authority of the Mongols. His physique and fine presence soon gained for him a place of authority, and when the chief of the band died he was chosen unanimously as his successor. He at once showed himself superior to the other popular leaders by his humanity, and by his wise efforts to convince the Chinese people that he had only their interests at heart. Other Chinese so called patriots thought mainly of plunder, and they were not less terrible to peaceful citizens than the most exacting Mongol commander or governor. But Choo strictly forbade plundering, and any of his band caught robbing or ill-using the people met with prompt and summary punishment. By this conduct he gained the confidence of the Chinese, and his standard among all the national leaders became the most popular and attracted the largest number of recruits. In 1356 he captured the city of Nankin which thereupon became the base of his operations as it was subsequently the capital of his dynasty. He then issued a proclamation declaring that his sole object was to expel the foreigners and to restore the national form of government. In this document he said, "It is the birthright of the Chinese to govern foreign peoples and not of these latter to rule in China. It used to be said that the Yuen or Mongols, who came from the regions of the north, conquered our Empire not so much by their courage and skill as by the aid of Heaven. And now it is sufficiently plain that Heaven itself wishes to deprive them of that Empire as some punishment for their crimes, and for not having acted according to the teaching of their forefathers. The time has now come to drive these foreigners out of China." While the Mongols were assailed in every province of the Empire by insurgents, Choo headed what was the only organised movement for their expulsion, and his alliance with the pirate, Fangkue Chin, added the command of the sea to the control he had himself acquired over some of the wealthiest and most populous provinces of Central China. The disunion among the Mongols contributed to their overthrow as much as the valour of the Chinese. The Emperor Chunti had quite given himself up to pleasure, and his debaucheries were the scandal of the day. The two principal generals Chahan Timour and Polo Timour hated each other, and refused to co-operate. Another general, Alouhiya, raised the standard of revolt in Mongolia, and, while he declared that his object was to regenerate his race, he, undoubtedly, aggravated the embarrassment of Chunti.

In 1366, Choo, having carefully made all the necessary preparations for war on a large scale, despatched from Nankin two large armies to conquer the provinces north of the Yangteskiang, which were all that remained in the possession of the Mongols. A third army was entrusted with the task of subjecting the provinces dependent on Canton, and this task was accomplished with rapidity and without a check. Such Mongol garrisons, as were stationed in this quarter, were annihilated. The main Chinese army of 250,000 men was entrusted to the command of Suta, Choo's principal lieutenant and best general, and advanced direct upon Pekin. In 1367 Suta had overcome all resistance south of the Hoangho, which river he crossed in the autumn of that year. The Mongols appeared demoralised, and attempted little or no resistance. Chunti fled from Pekin to Mongolia, where he died in 1370, and Suta carried the capital by storm from the small Mongol garrison which remained to defend it. Choo hastened to Pekin to receive the congratulations of his army, and to prove to the whole Chinese nation that the Yuen dynasty had ceased to rule. The resistance offered by the Mongols proved surprisingly slight, and, considering the value of the prize for which they were fighting, quite unworthy of their ancient renown. The real cause of their overthrow was that the Mongols never succeeded in propitiating the good opinion and moral support of the Chinese, who regarded them to the end as barbarians, and it must also be admitted that the main force of the Mongols had drifted to Western Asia, where the great Timour revived some of the traditions of Genghis. At the end of his career that mighy conqueror prepared to invade China, but he died shortly after he had begun a march that boded ill to the peace and welfare of China. Thus, with the flight of Chunti, the Mongol or Yuen dynasty came to an end, and the Mongols only reappear in Chinese history as the humble allies of the Manchus, when they undertook the conquest of China in the 17th century.

CHAPTER VII.

THE MING DYNASTY.

HAVING expelled the Mongols Choo assumed the style of Hongwou, and he gave his dynasty the name of Ming, which signifies "bright." He then rewarded his generals and officers with titles and pecuniary grants, and in 1369, the first year of his reign after the capture of Pekin, he erected a temple or hall in that city in honour of the generals who had been slain, while vacant places were left for the statues of those generals who still held command. But while he rewarded his army, Hongwou very carefully avoided giving his government a military character, knowing that the Chinese resent the superiority of military officials, and he devoted his main efforts to placing the civil administration on its old and national basis. In this he received the cordial support of the Chinese themselves, who had been kept in the background by their late conquerors, whose administration was essentially military. Hongwou also patronised literature, and endowed the celebrated Hanlin College, which was neglected after the death of Kublai. He at once provided a literary task of great magnitude in the history of the Yuen dynasty, which was entrusted to a commission of eighteen writers. But a still greater literary work was accomplished in the codified Book of Laws, which is known as the Pandects of Yunglo, and which not merely simplified the administration of the law, but also gave the people some idea of the laws under which they lived. He also passed a great measure of gratuitous national education, and, in order to carry out this reform in a thoroughly successful manner, he appointed all the masters himself. He also founded many public libraries, and he wished to establish one in every town, but this was beyond the extent of his power. Not content with providing for the minds of his subjects, Hongwou did his utmost to supply the needs of the aged. He cut down the court expenses and issued sumptuary laws, so that he might devote the sums thus economised to the support of the aged and sick. His last instructions to the new officials, on proceeding to their posts, were to "take particular care of the aged and the orphan." Thus did he show that the Chinese had found in him a ruler who would revive the ancient glories of the kingdom.

The frugality and modesty of his court have already been referred to. The later Mongols were fond of a lavish display, and expended large sums on banquets and amusements. At Pekin one of their emperors had erected in the grounds of the palace a lofty tower of porcelain, at enormous expense, and had arranged an ingenious contrivance at its base for denoting the time. Two statues sounded a bell and struck a drum at every hour. When Hongwou saw this edifice, he exclaimed, "How is it possible for men to neglect the most important affairs of life for the sole object of devoting their attention to useless buildings? If the Mongols in place of amusing themselves with these trifles had applied their energies to the task of contenting the people, would they not have preserved the sceptre in their family?" He then ordered that this building should be razed to the ground. Nor did this action stand alone. He reduced the size of the harem maintained by all the Chinese as well as the Mongol rulers, and he instituted a rigid economy in all matters of state ceremonial. Changtu, the Xanadu of Coleridge, the famous summer palace of Kublai had been destroyed during the campaigns with the Mongols, and Hongwou systematically discouraged any attempt to embellish the northern capital, Pekin, which, under the Kin and Yuen dynasties, had become identified with foreign rulers. Pekin, during the whole of the Ming dynasty, was only a second-rate city, and all the attention of the Ming rulers was given to the embellishment of Nankin, the truly national capital of China.

The expulsion of the Mongols beyond the Great Wall and the death of Chunti, the last of the Yuen emperors, by no means ended the struggle between the Chinese and their late northern conquerors. The whole of the reign of Hongwou was taken up with a war for the supremacy of his authority and the security of his frontiers, in which he, indeed, took little personal part, but which was carried on under his directions by his great generals, Suta and Fuyuta. The former of these generals was engaged for nearly twenty years, from A.D. 1368 to 1385, in constant war with the Mongols. His first campaign, fought when the Chinese were in the full flush of success, resulted in the brilliant and almost bloodless conquest of the province of Shansi. The neighbouring province of Shensi, which is separated from the other by the river Hoangho, was at the time held by a semi-independent Mongol governor named Lissechi, who believed that he could hold his ground against the Mings. The principal fact upon which this hope was based was the breadth and assumed impassability of that river. Lissechi believed that this natural advantage would enable him to hold out indefinitely against the superior numbers of the Chinese armies. But his hope was vain if not unreasonable. The Chinese crossed the Hoangho on a bridge of junks, and Tsin-yuen, which Lissechi had made his capital, surrendered without a blow. The population rose to welcome and assist the army of Suta, and the Mongols experienced the full force of the popular resentment aroused by their tyranny. Lissechi abandoned one fortress after another on the approach of Suta, thinking more of preserving his life than of maintaining his authority. Expelled from Shensi he hoped to find shelter and safety in the adjoining province of Kansuh, where he took up his residence at Lintao. For a moment the advance of the Chinese army was arrested while a great council of war was held to decide the further course of the campaign. The majority of the council favoured the suggestion that did not involve immediate action, and wished Suta to abandon the pursuit of Lissechi and complete the conquest of Shensi where several fortresses still held out. But Suta, fortunately, was of a more resolute temper, and resolved to ignore the decision of the council and to pursue Lissechi to Lintao. By the capture of that place he said, "we may expect to recruit our ranks from its population, and its resources would greatly contribute to our supplies. By pressing him with our main army, if he do not flee to the west, Lissechi will have forthwith to surrender without striking a blow. Lintao occupied, what will the neighbouring towns be able to do against us?" The vigour of

Suta's decision was matched by the rapidity of his march. Before Lissechi had made any arrangements to stand a siege he found himself surrounded at Lintao by the Ming army. In this plight he was obliged to throw himself on the mercy of the victor, who sent him to the capital, where Hongwou granted him his life and a small pension.

The overthrow of Lissechi prepared the way for the more formidable enterprise against Ninghia, where the Mongols had drawn their remaining power to a head. Ninghia, the old capital of Tangut, a principality mentioned at an earlier period of this history, is situated in the north of Kansuh, on the western bank of the Hoangho, and the Great Wall passes through it. Strongly fortified and admirably placed, the Mongols, so long as they possessed this town with its gates through the Great Wall, might hope to recover what they had lost, and to make a fresh bid for power in Northern China. North and west of Ninghia stretched the desert, but while it continued in their possession the Mongols remained on the threshold of China and held open a door through which their kinsmen from the Amour and Central Asia might yet re-enter to revive the feats of Genghis and Bayan. Suta determined to gain this place as speedily as possible, but he did not disguise from himself that it was a far more serious operation than the struggle with Lissechi. Midway between Lintao and Ninghia is the fortified town of Kingyang, which was held by a strong Mongol garrison. Suta laid close siege to this town, the governor of which had only time to send off a pressing appeal for aid to Kuku Timour, the governor at Ninghia, before he was shut in on all sides by the Ming army. Kuku Timour apparently did his best to aid his compatriot, but his forces were not sufficient to oppose those of Suta in the open field, and Kingyang was at last reduced to such straits that the garrison is said to have been compelled to use the slain as food. At last the place made an unconditional surrender, and the commandant was executed, not on account of his stubborn defence, but because at the beginning of the siege he had said he would surrender and had not kept his word. After the fall of Kingyang the Chinese troops were granted a well-earned rest, and Suta visited Nankin to describe the campaign to Hongwou.

The departure of Suta emboldened Kuku Timour so far as to lead him to take the field, and he hastened to attack the town of Lanchefoo, the capital of Kansuh, where there was only a small garrison. Notwithstanding this the place offered a stout resistance, but the Mongols gained a decisive success over a body of troops sent to its relief. This force was annihilated and its general taken prisoner. The Mongols thought to terrify the garrison by parading this general, whose name should be preserved, Yukwang, before the walls, but he baffled their purpose by shouting out, "Be of good courage, Suta is coming to your rescue." Yukwang was cut to pieces, but his timely and courageous exclamation, like that of D'Assas, saved his countrymen. Soon after this incident Suta reached the scene of action, and on his approach Kuku Timour broke up his camp and retired to Ninghia. The Chinese commander then hastened to occupy the towns of Souchow and Kia-yu-kwan, important as being the southern extremity of the Great Wall, and as isolating Ninghia on the west. Their loss was so serious that the Mongol chief felt compelled to risk a general engagement. The battle was keenly contested, and at one moment it seemed as if success was going to declare itself in favour of the Mongols. But Suta had sent a large part of his force to attack the Mongol rear, and when this movement was completely executed, he assailed the Mongol position at the head of all his troops. The struggle soon became a massacre, and it is said that as many as 80,000 Mongols were slain, while Kuku Timour, thinking Ninghia no longer safe, fled northwards to the Amour. How bitter the struggle had become may be judged from a single incident. When the Ming army reached the town of Hochow, they found that the Mongols had massacred all its inhabitants rather than allow them to again become Chinese subjects, and Suta's soldiers were so horrified at the spectacle that they were only induced with the greatest difficulty to occupy the town. The success of Suta was heightened and rendered complete by the capture of a large number of the ex-Mongol ruling family by Ly Wenchong, another of the principal generals of Hongwou. Among the prisoners was the eldest grandson of Chunti, and several of the ministers advised that he should be put to death. But Hongwou instead conferred on him a minor title of nobility, and expressed his policy in a speech equally creditable to his wisdom as a statesman and his heart as a man:—

"The last ruler of the Yuens took heed only of his pleasures. The great, profiting by his indolence, thought of nothing save of how to enrich themselves; the public treasures being exhausted by their malpractices, it needed only a few years of dearth to reduce the people to distress, and the excessive tyranny of those who governed them led to the forming of parties which disturbed the empire even to its foundations. Touched by the misfortunes with which I saw them oppressed, I took up arms, not so much against the Yuens as against the rebels who were engaged in war with them. It was over the same foe that I gained my first successes. And if the Yuen prince had not departed from the rules of wise government in order to give himself up to his pleasures, and had the magnates of his court performed their duty, would all honourable men have taken up arms as they did and declared against him? The misconduct of the race brought me a large number of partisans who were convinced of the rectitude of my intentions, and it was from their hands and not from those of the Yuens that I received the empire. If heaven had not favoured me, should I have succeeded in destroying with such ease those who withdrew into the desert of Shamo? We read in the Chiking that after the destruction of the Chang family there remained more than ten thousand of their descendants who submitted themselves to the Chow, because it was the will of heaven. Cannot men respect its decrees? Let them put in the public treasure-house all the spoil brought back from Tartary so that it may serve to alleviate the people's wants. And with regard to Maitilipala (Chunti's grandson), although former ages supply examples of similar sacrifice, did Wou Wang, I ask you, when exterminating the Chang family, resort to this barbarous policy? The Yuen princes were the masters of this empire for nearly one hundred years, and my forefathers were their subjects, and even although it were the constant practice to treat in this fashion the princes of a dynasty which has ceased to reign, yet could I not induce myself to adopt it."

These noble sentiments, to which there is nothing contradictory in the whole life of Hongwou, would alone place his reign high among the most civilising and humanly interesting epochs in Chinese history. To his people he appeared as a real benefactor as well as a just prince. He was ever studious of their interests, knowing that their happiness depended on what might seem trivial matters, as well as in showy feats of arms and high policy. He simplified the transit of salt, that essential article of life, to provinces where its production was scanty, and when dearth fell on the land he devoted all the resources of his treasury to its mitigation. His thoughtfulness for his soldiers was shown by sending fur coats to all the soldiers in garrison at Ninghia where the winter was exceptionally severe. A final instance of his justice and consideration may be cited in his ordering certain Mongol colonies established in Southern China, to whom the climate proved uncongenial, to be sent back at his expense to their northern homes, when his ministers exhorted him to proceed to extremities against them and to root them out by fire and sword.

The pacification of the northern borders was followed by the despatch of troops into the southern provinces of Szchuen and Yunnan, where officials appointed by the Mongols still exercised authority. One of these had incurred the wrath of Hongwou by assuming a royal style and proclaiming himself King of Hia. He was soon convinced of the folly of taking a title which he had not the power to maintain, and the conquest of Szchuen was so easily effected that it would not call for mention if it were not rendered interesting as providing Hongwou's other great general Fuyuta with the first opportunity of displaying his skill as a commander. The self-created King of Hia presented himself laden with chains at the Chinese camp and begged the favour of his life. The conquest of Szchuen was little more than completed when the attention of Hongwou was again directed to the north-west frontier, where Kuku Timour was making one more effort to recover the footing he had lost on the fringe of the Celestial Empire, and for a time fortune favoured his enterprise. Even when Suta arrived upon the scene and took the command of the Chinese forces in person, the Mongols more than held their own. Twice did Suta attack the strong position taken up by the Mongol chief in the desert, and twice was his assault repulsed with heavy loss. A detachment under one of his lieutenants was surprised in the desert and annihilated. Supplies were difficult to obtain, and discouraged by defeat and the scarcity of food the Chinese army was placed in an extremely dangerous position. Out of this dilemma it was rescued by the heroic Fuyuta, who, on the news of the Mongol recrudescence, had marched northwards at the head of the army with which he had conquered Szchuen. He advanced boldly into the desert, operated on the flank and in the rear of Kuku Timour, vanquished the Mongols in many engagements, and so monopolised their attention that Suta was able to retire in safety and without loss. The war terminated with the Chinese maintaining all their posts on the frontier, and the retreat of the Mongols, who had suffered too heavy a loss to feel elated at their repulse of Suta. At the same time no solid peace had been obtained, and the Mongols continued to harass the borders, and to exact blackmail from all who traversed the desert. When Hongwou endeavoured to attain a settlement by a stroke of policy his efforts were not more successful. His kind reception of the Mongol Prince Maitilipala has been referred to, and about the year 1374 he sent him back to Mongolia, in the hope that he would prove a friendly neighbour on his father's death. The gratitude of Maitilipala seems to have been unaffected, but although he was the legitimate heir the Mongols refused to recognise him as Khan on the death of his father. Gradually tranquillity settled down on those borders. The Chinese officials were content to leave the Mongols alone, and the Mongols abandoned their customary raids into Chinese territory. The death of Kuku Timour was followed by the abandonment of all ideas of reviving Mongol authority in China. Not long after that event died the great general, Suta, of whom the national historians give the following glowing description which merits preservation :—"Suta spoke little and was endowed with great penetration. He was always on good terms with the generals acting with him, sharing the good and bad fortune alike of his soldiers, of whom there was not one who touched by his kindness would not have done his duty to the death. He was not less pronounced in his modesty. He had conquered a capital, three provinces, several hundred towns, and on the very day of his return to court from these triumphs he went without show and without retinue to his own house, received there some learned professors and discussed various subjects with them. Throughout his life he was in the presence of the emperor respectful, and so reserved that one might have doubted his capacity to speak." Hongwou was in the habit of speaking thus in his praise:—"My orders received, he forthwith departed; his task accomplished, he returned without pride and without boasting. He loves not women, he does not amass wealth. A man of strict integrity, without the slightest stain, as pure and clear as the sun and moon, there is none like my first general Suta."

Hongwou had the satisfaction of restoring amicable relations with the King of Corea, a state in which the Chinese have always taken naturally enough a great interest from its proximity, as well as from an apprehension that the Japanese might make use of it as a vantage ground for the invasion of the continent. The King of Corea sent a formal embassy to Nankin, and when he died his son asked for and received investiture in his authority with the royal yellow robes at the hands of the Ming ruler. During this period it will be convenient here to note that the ruling power in Corea passed from the old royal family to the minister Li Chungwei, who was the ancestor of the present king. The last military episode of the reign of Hongwou was the conquest of Yunnan, which had been left over after the recovery of Szchuen, in consequence of the fresh outbreak of the Mongols in the north. This task was entrusted to Fuyuta who at the head of an army of 100,000 men, divided into two corps, invaded Yunnan. The prince of that state offered the utmost resistance he could, but in the one great battle of the war his army fighting bravely was overthrown, and he was compelled to abandon his capital. The Chinese conquest was speedily assured, but a large portion of the Yunnanese were so ill-advised as to revolt after all open resistance had been put down. Irritated by this useless outbreak the Ming generals punished the insurgents by massacring all who fell into their hands, and there is no doubt that many innocent and helpless persons shared the fate of those who had rebelled. The conquest of Yunnan completed the pacification of the empire, and the authority of Hongwou was unchallenged from the borders of Burmah, to the Great Wall and the Corean frontier. The population of the empire thus restored did not much exceed sixty millions. The last ten years of the reign of Hongwou were passed in tranquillity, marred by only one unpleasant incident, the mutiny of a portion of his army under an ambitious general. The plot was discovered in good time, but it is said that the emperor did not consider the exigencies of the case to be met until he had executed twenty thousand of the mutineers.

In 1398 Hongwou was attacked with the illness which ended his life.

He was then in his 71st year, and had reigned more than thirty years since his proclamation of the Ming dynasty at Nankin. The Emperor Keen Lung, in his history of the Mings, states that Hongwou possessed most of the virtues and few of the vices of mankind. He was brave, patient under suffering, far-seeing, studious of his people's welfare, and generous and forbearing towards his enemies. It is not surprising that he succeeded in establishing the Ming dynasty on a firm and popular basis, and that his family have been better beloved in China than any dynasty with the possible exception of the Hans. In his will, which is a remarkable document, he recites the principal events of his reign, how he had "pacified the empire and restored its ancient splendour." With the view of providing for the stability of his empire he chose as his successor his grandson Chuwen, because he had remarked in him much prudence, a gentle disposition, good intelligence, and a readiness to accept advice. He also selected him because he was the eldest son of his eldest son, and as his other sons might be disposed to dispute their nephew's authority he ordered them to remain at their posts, and not to come to the capital on his death. They were also enjoined to show the new emperor all the respect and docility owed by subjects to their sovereign. Through these timely precautions Chuwen, who was only sixteen years of age, was proclaimed emperor without any opposition, and took the title of Kien Wenti.

Hongwou had rightly divined that his sons might prove a thorn in the side of his successor, and his policy of employing them in posts at a distance from the capital was only half successful in attaining its object. If it kept them at a distance it also strengthened their feeling of independence, and enabled them to collect their forces without attracting much attention. Wenti, as it is most convenient to call the new Emperor, felt obliged to send formal invitations to his uncles to attend the obsequies of their father. Most of them had the tact to perceive that the invitation was dictated by regard for decency, and not by a wish that it should be accepted, and gave the simplest excuse for not attending the funeral. But Ty, Prince of Yen, the most powerful and ambitious of them all, declared that he accepted the Emperor's invitation. This decision raised quite a flutter of excitement, almost amounting to consternation, at Nankin, where the Prince of Yen was regarded as a bitter and vindictive enemy. The only way Wenti saw out of this dilemma was to send his uncle a special intimation that his presence at the capital would not be desirable. Before he had been many weeks on the throne Wenti was thus brought into open conflict with the most powerful and ambitious of all his relatives. He resolved, under the advice of his ministers, to treat all his uncles as his enemies, and he sent his officers with armies at their back to depose them, and bring them as prisoners to his court. Five of his uncles were thus summarily dealt with, one committed suicide, and the other four were degraded to the rank of the people. But the Prince of Yen was too formidable to be tackled in this fashion. Taking warning from the fate of his brothers, he collected all the troops he could, prepared to defend his position against the Emperor, and issued a proclamation stating that it was lawful for subjects to revolt for the purpose of removing the pernicious advisers of the sovereign. The last was he announced the cause of his taking up arms, and he disclaimed any motive of ambitious turbulence for raising his standard. He said, "I am endeavouring to avert the ruin of my family, and to maintain the Emperor on a throne which is placed in jeopardy by the acts of two traitors. My cause ought, therefore, to be that of all those who keep the blood of the great Hongwou now falsely aspersed in affectionate remembrance." A large number of the inhabitants of the northern provinces joined his side, and proclaimed him as "The Prince." Wenti had recourse to arms to bring his uncle back to his allegiance, and a civil war began, which was carried on, with exceptional bitterness, during five years. The resources of the Emperor, in men and money, were the superior, but he did not seem able to turn them to good account; and the prince's troops were generally victorious, and his power gradually increased. In the year 1401 both sides concentrated all their strength for deciding the contest by a single trial of arms. The two armies numbered several hundred thousand men, and it is stated that the imperial force alone mustered 600,000 strong. The battle, which was fought at Techow in Shantung, considering the numbers engaged, it is not surprising to learn, lasted several days, and its fortune alternated from one side to the other. At last victory declared for the prince, and the imperial army was driven in rout from the field with the loss of 100,000 men. Having gained this success, Yen followed it up by many other triumphs in the field, and the following incident will throw not merely a bright light on the customs of the age, but also indicate the further course of this struggle.

"The Prince of Yen, after these successes, laid siege to Tsinan, the governor of which place formed a plan to decide the war at a blow by the murder of the rebellious prince. Tsi Hiwen, such was his name, sent his assailant word that he desired to surrender, but requesting, as a favour, that he would only enter the town with a few troops. Yen did not suspect treachery, and readily assented to these terms which might be set down as either fanciful or politic. Tsi Hiwen had, however, placed iron harrows on the walls and in the towers of his fortress, and when Yen rode into the city these were dropped on the heads of himself and his party. Fortunately they were not directed with a sure aim, and although the prince's horse was killed and he himself thrown to the ground in the fall, he rose uninjured and escaped on the fleet steed of one of his companions. Of course he vowed and wished to take a summary vengeance; but Tsi Hiwen, fertile in resource, had still another device to make good the defence of Tsinan. He set all the artists in the place to work to paint as many portraits as they could of the Emperor Hongwou, and these, when completed, he caused to be hung from the ramparts, knowing that the prince would not dare, both out of respect to his father's memory and also for fear of offending public opinion, to order his troops to fire upon them. The ruse was completely successful, and Yen, although irritated at the result, was fain to admit that in Tsi Hiwen he was dealing with one more than his match in astuteness. The Chinese historians evidently consider that this and similar incidents which abound in their annals carry a significant lesson, for they show how great talent and powerful resources may, on occasions, be baffled by a little cunning."

The story gives a very fair illustration of the character of Chinese fighting. After his great victory at Techow the further progress of the prince was arrested by a capable general named Chinyong, who succeeded in gaining one great victory. If Wenti had known how to profit by this success he might have turned the course of the struggle permanently in his own favour. But instead of profiting by his good fortune, Wenti, believing that all danger from the prince was at an end, resumed his old practices and reinstated two of the most obnoxious of his ministers whom he had disgraced in a fit of apprehension. Undoubtedly this step raised against him a fresh storm of unpopularity, and at the same time brought many supporters to his uncle, who, even after the serious disaster described, found himself stronger than he had been before. The struggle must have shown little signs of a decisive issue, for in 1402 the prince made a voluntary offer of peace, with a view to putting an end to all strife and of giving the Empire peace ; but Wenti could not make up his mind to forgive him. The success of his generals in the earlier part of the struggle seemed to warrant the belief that there was no reason in prudence for coming to terms with his rebellious uncle, and that he would succeed in establishing his indisputable supremacy. The prince seemed, at this very moment, reduced to such straits that he had to give his army the option of retreat. Addressing his soldiers he said : "I know how to advance, but not to retreat ;" but his army decided to return to their homes in the north, when the extraordinary and unexpected retreat of the greater part of the army of Wenti revived their courage and induced them to follow their leader through one more encounter. Like Frederick the Great, the Prince of Yen was never greater than in defeat. He surprised the lately victorious army of Wenti, smashed it in pieces, and captured Tingan, the Emperor's best general. He heightened his reputation by treating that officer with due honour. " I am only here like an old bow which is broken and useless," said Tingan ; to which Yen replied, "The Emperor my father held bravery in honour, and I wish to imitate him." The occupation of Nankin and the abdication of Wenti followed this victory in rapid succession. Afraid to trust himself to the mercy of his relative he fled, disguised as a priest, to Yunnan, where he passed his life ignominiously for forty years, and his identity was only discovered after that lapse of time by his publishing, in his new character of a Buddhist priest, a poem reciting and lamenting the misfortunes of Wenti. Then he was removed to Pekin, where he died in honourable confinement. As a priest he seems to have been more fortunate than as a ruler, and history contains no more striking example of happiness being found in a private station when unattainable on a throne.

After some hesitation the Prince of Yen allowed himself to be proclaimed Emperor, and as such he is best known as Yonglo, a name signifying " Eternal Joy." Considering his many declarations that his only ambition was to reform and not to destroy the administration of his nephew, his first act obliterating the reign of Wenti from the records and constituting himself the immediate successor of Hongwou was not calculated to support his alleged indifference to power. He was scarcely seated on the throne before he was involved in serious troubles on both his northern and his southern frontiers. In Mongolia he attempted to assert a formal supremacy over the khans through the person of an adventurer named Kulitchi, but the agent was unable to fulfil his promises, and met with a speedy overthrow. In Tonquin an ambitious minister named Likimao deposed his master and established himself as ruler in his place. The Emperor sent an army to bring him to his senses, and it met with such rapid success that the Chinese were encouraged to annex Tonquin and convert it into a province of the Empire. When Yonglo's plans failed on the steppe he was drawn into a struggle with the Mongols, which necessitated annual expeditions until he died. During the last of these he advanced as far as the Kerulon, and on his return march he died in his camp at the age of 65. Although he bore arms so long against the head of the State there is no doubt that he greatly consolidated the power of the Mings, which he extended on one side to the Amour and on the other to the Songcoi. It was during his reign that Tamerlane contemplated the reconquest of China, and perhaps it was well for Yonglo that that great commander died when he had traversed only a few stages of his march to the Great Wall. One of his sons succeeded Yonglo as Emperor, but he only reigned under the style of Gintsong for a few months.

Then Suentsong, the son of Gintsong, occupied the throne, and during his reign a vital question affecting the constitution of the civil service, and through it the whole administration of the country, was brought forward, and fortunately settled without recourse to blows, as was at one time feared would be the case. Before his reign the public examinations had been open to candidates from all parts of the empire, and it had become noticeable that all the honours were being carried off by students from the southern provinces, who were of quicker intelligence than those of the north. It seemed as if in the course of a short time all the posts would be held by them, and that the natives of the provinces north of the Hoangho would be gradually driven out of the service. Naturally this marked tendency led to much agitation in the north, and a very bitter feeling was spreading when Suentsong and his minister took up the matter and proceeded to apply a sound practical remedy. After a commission of inquiry had certified to the reality of the evil, Suentsong decreed that all competitors for literary honours should be restricted to their native districts, and that for the purpose of the competitive examinations China should be divided into three separate divisions, one for the north, another for the centre, and the third for the south. The firmness shown by the Emperor Suentsong in this matter was equally conspicuous in his dealings with an uncle, who showed some inclination to revolt. He took the field in person, and before the country was generally aware of the revolt, Suentsong was conducting his relative to a state prison. Almost at the same time the Chinese were obliged by grave local disturbances to withdraw their garrison from Tonquin, and the emperor wisely decided to make no excessive sacrifice to maintain his authority over that region. Tonquin ceased in 1428 to be a Chinese province, and again sank into the doubtful category of a tribute-bearing nation. The rest of Suentsong's reign was peaceful and prosperous, and he left the crown to his son, Yngtsong, a child of eight years old.

During his minority the governing authority was exercised by his grandmother, the Empress Changchi, the mother of the Emperor Suentsong. At first it seemed as if there would be a struggle for power between her and the eunuch, Wangchin, who had gained the affections of the young Emperor, but after she had denounced him before the court and called for his execution, from which fate he was only rescued by the tears and supplications of the young sovereign, the feud was composed by Wangchin gaining such an ascendancy over the Empress that she made him her associate in the regency. Unfortunately Wangchin did not prove a wise or able administrator. He thought more of the sweets of office than of the duties of his lofty station. He appointed his relations and creatures to the highest civil and military posts without regard to their qualifications or ability. To his arrogance was directly due the commencement of a disastrous war with Yesien, the most powerful of the Mongol chiefs of the day. When that prince sent the usual presents to the Chinese capital, and made the customary request for a Chinese princess as wife, Wangchin appropriated the gifts for himself and sent back a haughty refusal to Yesien's petition, although it was both customary and rarely refused. Such a reception was tantamount to a declaration of war, and Yesien, who had already been tempted by the apparent weakness of the Chinese frontier to resume the raids which were so popular with the nomadic tribes of the desert, gathered his fighting men together and invaded China. Alarmed by the storm he had raised, Wangchin still endeavoured to meet it, and summoning all the garrisons in the north to his aid, he placed himself at the head of an army computed to number half a million of men. In the hope of inspiring his force with confidence he took the boy-Emperor, Yngtsong, with him, but his own incompetence nullified the value of numbers, and rendered the presence of the Emperor the cause of additional ignominy instead of the inspiration of invincible confidence. The vast and unwieldy Chinese army took up a false position at a place named Toumon, and it is affirmed that the position was so bad that Yesien feared that it must cover a ruse. He accordingly sent some of his officers to propose an armistice, but really to inspect the Chinese lines. They returned to say that there was no concealment, and that if an attack were made at once the Chinese army lay at his mercy. Yesien delayed not a moment in delivering his attack, and it was completely successful. The very numbers of the Chinese, in a confined position, added to their discomfiture, and after a few hours' fighting the battle became a massacre and a rout. Wangchin, the cause of all this ruin, was killed by Fanchong, the commander of the imperial guards, and the youthful ruler, Yngtsong, was taken prisoner. There has rarely been a more disastrous day in the long annals of the Chinese empire than the rout at Toumon.

Then Yesien returned to his camp on the Toula, taking his prisoner with him, and announcing that he would only restore him for a ransom of 100 taels of gold, 200 taels of silver, and 200 pieces of the finest silk. For some unknown reason the Empress Changchi did not feel disposed to pay this comparatively low ransom, and instead of reclaiming Yngtsong from his conqueror she placed his brother, Kingti, on the throne. The struggle with the Mongols under Yesien continued, but his attention was distracted from China by his desire to become the great Khan of the Mongols, a title still held by his brother-in-law, Thotho Timour, of the house of Genghis. Yesien suddenly released of his own accord Yngtsong, who returned to Pekin, and hastened to the Kerulon country, where he overthrew and assassinated Thotho Timour, and was in turn himself slain by another chieftain. While the Mongol was thus pursuing his own ambition, and reaching the violent death which forms so common a feature in the history of his family, the unfortunate Yngtsong returned to China, where, on the refusal of his brother Kingti to resign the throne, he sank quietly into private life. Kingti died seven years after his brother's return, and then, failing a better or nearer prince, Yngtsong was brought from his confinement and restored to the throne. He reigned eight years after his restoration, but he never possessed any real power, his authority being wielded by unscrupulous ministers, who stained his reign by the execution of Yukien, the most honest and capable general of the period. If his reign was not remarkable for political or military vigour, some useful reforms appear to have been instituted. Among others may be named the formation of state farms on waste or confiscated lands, the establishment of military schools for teaching archery and horsemanship, and the completion of some useful and elaborate educational works, of which a geography of China, in ninety volumes, is the most famous.

Yngtsong died in the year 1465, and was succeeded by his son, Hientsong, who began his reign with acts of filial devotion that attracted the sympathy of his subjects. He also rendered posthumous honours to the ill-used general, Yukien, and established his fame as a national benefactor. During the twenty-eight years that he occupied the throne he was engaged in a number of petty wars, none of which requires specific mention. The only unpopular measure associated with his name was the creation of a Grand Council of Eunuchs, to which was referred all questions of capital punishment, and this body soon acquired a power which made it resemble our own tyrannical and irresponsible Star Chamber. After five years this institution became so unpopular and was so deeply execrated by the nation that Hientsong, however reluctantly, had to abolish his own creation, and acquiesce in the execution of some of its most active members. A more important matter, and one that was pregnant with grave consequences in the more distant future, related to the land, and what may be termed the rights of feudalism. I have thus described it. The members of the reigning house, and all who had contributed to its elevation, naturally expected some reward for their position or their services; and it became their first ambition to obtain territorial grants from the sovereign, and to found an estate which could be handed down as a patrimony to their descendants. The feudal practice and system had died out in China many centuries before, and it was not to be supposed that a people like the Chinese, strongly imbued with the principles of equality, and only recognising as a superior class the representatives of officialism and letters, would look with much favour on any attempt to revive an order of territorial magnates with whom they had no sympathy. Hientsong himself felt no strong interest in the matter. He knew the people's mind on this subject, and he was aware that the authority of the king is rather diminished than enhanced by the presence of a powerful and warlike nobility, who have always been prone to see in the ruler the highest member of their order rather than the "divinely elected" guide of the people. On the other hand, he was not sufficiently cold to resist the importunities of his friends. In this matter, therefore, of making territorial grants to the more prominent of his supporters he vacillated between one side and the other. The representations of one of the censors led him to pass an edict against any territorial concessions, but within a very few weeks of this firm and wise decision he was so far influenced by his relations that he conferred several grants of land on members of his family. The rule once broken was seldom afterwards rigidly enforced, and gradually the scions of the Ming family became territorial magnates, much to the discontent of the people. It was in the eyes of the latter a flagrant interference with the laws of Providence to assign to one man a district which could supply the wants of a hundred families. The socialistic tendency of these theories is evident, but in China their evil has been arrested and corrected by the veneration of the people for the sovereign and by the natural conservatism of the masses.

During Hientsong's reign a systematic attempt was made to work the gold-mines reputed to exist in Central China, but although half a million men were employed upon them it is stated that the find did not exceed thirty ounces. More useful work was accomplished in the building of a canal from Pekin to the Peiho, which thus enabled grain junks to reach the northern capital by the Euho and Shaho canals from the Yangtsekiang. Another useful public work was the repairing of the Great Wall, effected along a considerable portion of its extent, by the efforts of 50,000 soldiers, which gave the Chinese a sense of increased security. In connection with this measure of defence, it may be stated that the Chinese advanced into Central Asia and occupied the town of Hami, which then and since has served them as a useful watch-tower in the direction of the west. The death of Hientsong occurred in 1487, at a moment when the success and prosperity of the country under the Mings may be described as having reached its height.

During the reign of his son and successor, Hiaotsong, matters progressed peacefully, for, although there was some fighting for the possession of Hami, which was coveted by several of the desert chiefs, but which remained during the whole of this reign subject to China, the Empire was not involved in any great war. An insurrection of the black aborigines of the island of Hainan was put down without any very serious difficulty. These events do not throw any very clear light on the character and personality of Hiaotsong, who died in 1505 at the early age of thirty-six; but his care for his people, and his desire to alleviate the misfortunes that might befall his subjects, was shown by his ordering every district composed of ten villages to send in annually to a State granary, a specified quantity of grain, until one hundred thousand bushels had been stored in every such building throughout the country. The idea was an excellent one; but it is to be feared that a large portion of this grain was diverted to the use of the peculating officials, whence arose the phrase, "The Emperor is full of pity, but the Court of Finance is like the never-dying worm which devours the richest crops." To Hiaotsong succeeded his son, Woutsong, during whose reign many misfortunes fell upon the land. A cabal was formed among the palace eunuchs to monopolise the governing power, and Liukin, the chief of them seems to have been instigated by the avarice as well as the ambition of a Wolsey. His schemes of self-aggrandisement were thwarted by a quarrel with some of his confederates, who then betrayed him, and the executioner ended his career. The Emperor's uncles also had designs on his authority, but these fell through and came to naught, rather through Woutsong's good fortune than the excellence of his arrangements. In Szchuen a peasant war threatened to assume the dimensions of a rebellion, and, in Pechihli, bands of mounted robbers, or Hiangmas, raided the open country. He succeeded in suppressing these revolts, but his indifference to the disturbed state of his realm was shown by his passing most of his time in hunting expeditions beyond the Great Wall. His successors were to reap the result of this neglect of business for the pursuit of pleasure; and, when he died, in 1519, without leaving an heir, the outlook was beginning to look serious for the Ming dynasty. One event, and, perhaps, the most important of Woutsong's reign, calls for special mention, and that is the arrival at Canton of the first native of Europe to reach China by sea. Of course it will be recollected that Marco Polo and others reached the Mongol Court by land, although the Venetian sailed from China on his embassy to southern India. In 1511, Raphael Perestralo sailed from Malacca to China, and in 1517 the Portuguese officer, Don Fernand Perez D'Andrade, arrived in the Canton river with a squadron, and was favourably received by the mandarins. D'Andrade visited Pekin, where he resided for some time as ambassador. The commencement of intercourse between Europeans and China was thus effected most auspiciously; and it might have continued so but that a second Portuguese fleet appeared in Chinese waters, and committed there numerous outrages and acts of piracy. Upon this D'Andrade was arrested by order of Woutsong, and after undergoing imprisonment, was executed by his successor in 1523. It was a bad beginning for a connection which, after nearly four hundred years, is neither as stable nor as general as the strivers after perfection could desire.

The death of Woutsong without children, or any recognised heir, threatened to involve the realm in serious dangers; but the occasion was so critical that the members of the Ming family braced themselves to it, and under the auspices of the Empress Changchi, the widow of the late ruler, a secret council was held, when the grandson of the Emperor Hientsong, a youth of fourteen, was placed on the throne under the name of Chitsong. It is said that his mother gave him good advice on being raised from a private station to the lofty eminence of Emperor, and that she told him that he was about to accept a heavy burden; but experience showed that he was unequal to it. Still, his shortcomings were preferable to a disputed succession. The earlier years of his reign were marked by some successes over the Tartars, and he received tribute from chiefs who had never paid it before. But Chitsong had little taste for the serious work of administration. He showed himself superstitious in matters of religion, and he cultivated poetry, and may even have persuaded himself that he was a poet. But he did not pay any heed to the advice of those among his ministers who urged him to take a serious view of his position, and to act in a manner worthy of his dignity. It is clear that his influence on the lot of his people, and even on the course of his country's history, was small, and such reigns as his inspire the regret expressed at there being no history of the Chinese people; but such a history is impossible, for reasons that I can but give by quoting my own words:—

"It might be more instructive to trace the growth of thought among the masses, or to indicate the progress of civil and political freedom; yet, not only do the materials not exist for such a task, but those we possess all tend to show that there has been no growth to describe, no progress to be indicated, during these comparatively recent centuries. It is the peculiar and distinguishing characteristic of Chinese history that the people and their institutions have remained practically unchanged, and the same from a very early period. Even the introduction of a foreign element has not tended to disturb the established order of things. The supreme ruler possesses the same attributes and discharges the same functions; the governing classes are chosen in the same manner; the people are bound in the same state of servitude, and enjoy the same practical liberty; all is now as it was. Neither under the Tangs nor the Sungs, under the Yuens nor the Mings, was there any change in national character or in political institutions to be noted or chronicled. The history of the Empire has always been the fortunes of the dynasty, which has depended, in the first place, on the passive content of the subjects, and, in the second, on the success or failure of its external and internal wars. This condition of things may be disappointing to those who pride themselves on tracing the origin of a constitution and the growth of civil rights, and also would have a history of China a history of the Chinese people; although the fact is undoubted that there is no history of the Chinese people apart from that of their country to be recorded. The national institutions and character were formed, and had attained in all essentials their present state more than two thousand years ago, or before the destruction of all trustworthy materials for the task by the burning of the ancient literature and chronicles of China. Without them we must fain content ourselves with the history of the country and the Empire."

Chitsong was engaged in three serious operations beyond his frontier, one with a Tartar chief named Yenta, another with the Japanese, and the third in Cochin China. Yenta was of Mongol extraction, and enjoyed supreme power on the borders of Shansi. His brother was chief of the Ordus tribe which dwells within the Chinese frontier. Changtu, the old residence of Kublai, was one of his camps, and it was said that he could bring a hundred thousand horsemen into the field. The success of his raids carried alarm through the province of Shansi, and during one of them he laid siege to the capital, Taiyuen. Then the emperor placed a reward on his head and offered an official post to the person who would rid him of his enemy by assassination. The offer failed to bring forward either a murderer or a patriot, and Yenta's hostility was increased by the personal nature of this attack, and perhaps by the apprehension of a sinister fate. He invaded China on a larger scale than ever, and carried his ravages to the southern extremity of Shansi, and returned laden with the spoil of forty districts, and bearing with him 200,000 prisoners to a northern captivity. After this success Yenta seems to have rested on his laurels, although he by no means gave up his raids, which, however, assumed more and more a local character. The Chinese annalists state that never was the frontier more disturbed, and even the establishment of horse fairs for the benefit of the Mongols failed to keep them quiet. In Cochin China the emperor gained some gratifying if not very important successes, and asserted his right as suzerain over several disobedient princes. But a more serious and less satisfactory question had to be settled on the side of Japan.

The Japanese had never forgiven the formidable and unprovoked invasion of their country by Kublai Khan. The Japanese are by nature a military nation, and the Chinese writers themselves describe them as "intrepid, inured to fatigue, despising life, and knowing well how to face death; although inferior in number a hundred of them would blush to flee before a thousand foreigners, and if they did they would not dare to return to their country. Sentiments such as these, which are instilled into them from their earliest childhood, render them terrible in battle." Emboldened by their success over the formidable Mongols the Japanese treated the Chinese with contempt, and fitted out piratical expeditions from time to time with the object of preying on the commerce and coasting towns of China. To guard against the descents of these enterprising islanders the Chinese had erected towers of defence along the coast, and had called out a militia which was more or less inefficient. On the main they did not so much as attempt to make a stand against their neighbours, whose war junks exercised undisputed authority on the Eastern Sea. While this strife continued a trade also sprang up between the two peoples, who share in an equal degree the commercial instinct, but as the Chinese Government only admitted Japanese goods when brought by the ambassador, who was sent every ten years from Japan, this trade could only be carried on by smuggling. A regular system was adopted to secure the greatest success and profit. The Japanese landed their goods on some island off the coast, whence the Chinese removed them at a safe and convenient moment to the mainland. The average value of the cargo of one of the small junks which carried on this trade is said to have been four thousand pounds of our money, so that it may be inferred that the profits were considerable. But the national antipathies would not be repressed by the profitable character of this trade, and the refusal of a Chinese merchant to give a Japanese the goods for which he had paid lit the embers of a war which went on for half a century, and which materially weakened the Ming power. During the last years of Chitsong's long reign of forty-five years this trouble showed signs of getting worse, although the Japanese confined their efforts to irregular and unexpected attacks on places on the coast, and did not attempt to wage a regular war. In the midst of these troubles and when it was hoped that the exhortation of his ministers would produce some effect, Chitsong died, leaving behind him a will or public proclamation to be issued after his death, and which reads like a long confession of fault. *Mea culpa*, exclaimed this Eastern ruler at the misfortunes of his people and the calamities of his realm, but he could not propound a remedy for them.

His third son succeeded him as the Emperor Moutsong, and the character and capacity of this prince gave promise that his reign would be satisfactory if not glorious. Unfortunately for his family, and perhaps for his country, the public expectations were dispelled in his case by an early death. The six years during which he reigned were rendered remarkable by the conclusion of a stable peace with the Tartar Yenta, who accepted the title of a Prince of the Empire. Moutsong when he found that he was dying grew apprehensive lest the youth of his son might not stir up dissension and provoke that internal strife which had so often proved the bane of the empire, and involved the wreck of many of its dynasties. He exhorted his ministers to stand by his son who was only a boy, to give him the best advice in their power, and to render him worthy of the throne. That the apprehensions of Moutsong were not without reason was clearly shown by the mishaps and calamities which occurred during the long reign of his son and successor Wanleh. With the death of Moutsong the period ends when it was possible to state that the majesty of the Mings remained undimmed, and that this truly national dynasty wielded with power and full authority the imperial mandate. When they had driven out the Mongol the Mings seem to have settled down into an ordinary and intensely national line of rulers. The successors of Hongwou did nothing great or noteworthy, but the Chinese acquiesced in their rule, and even showed that they possessed for it a special regard and affection.

CHAPTER VIII.

THE DECLINE OF THE MINGS.

THE reign of Wanleh covers the long and important epoch from 1573 to 1620, during which period occurred some very remarkable events in the history of the country, including the first movements of the Manchus with a view to the conquest of the Empire. The young prince was only six when he was placed on the throne, but he soon showed that he had been well-trained to play the part of ruler. At his first Court he singled out the chief of the ministers selected for him by his father, and thus addressed him: "My father used to regard you as the most zealous and faithful of his subjects; on succeeding to his crown I have inherited his sentiments. I do not doubt that you will anxiously instruct me as to my responsibilities and as to the manner in which I should bear myself." Thanks to the exertions and tact of his mother, the first year of Wanleh's reign was passed through without hitch or difficulty. The amiable character of the young Emperor made a favourable impression on all brought into contact with him, and it really seemed as if the virtues and success of Moutsong were to be emulated by his son. The best indication of the prosperity of the realm is furnished by the revenue, which steadily increased until it reached the great total in cash, excluding the grain receipts, of fifteen millions of our money. But a large revenue becomes of diminished value unless it is associated with sound finance. The public expenditure showed a steady increase; the Emperor and his advisers were incapable of checking the outlay, and extravagance, combined with improvidence, soon depleted the exchequer. Internal troubles occurred to further embarrass the executive, and the resources of the state were severely strained in coping with more than one serious rebellion, among which the most formidable was the mutiny of a mercenary force under the command of a Turk officer named Popai, who imagined that he was unjustly treated, and that the time was favourable to found an administration of his own. His early successes encouraged him to believe that he would succeed in his object; but when he found that all the disposable forces of the Empire were sent against him, he abandoned the field, and shut himself up in the fortress at Ninghia, where he hoped to hold out indefinitely. For many months he succeeded in baffling the attacks of Wanleh's general, and the siege might even have had to be raised if the latter had not conceived the idea of diverting the course of the river Hoangho, so that it might bear upon the walls of the fortress. Popai was unable to resist this form of attack, and when the Chinese stormers made their way through the breach thus caused, he attempted to commit suicide by setting fire to his residence. This satisfaction was denied him, for a Chinese officer dragged him from the flames, slew him, and sent his head to the general Li Jusong, who conducted the siege, and of whom we shall hear a great deal more.

The gratification caused by the overthrow of Popai had scarcely abated when the attention of the Chinese Government was drawn away from domestic enemies to a foreign assailant who threatened the most serious danger to China. Reference was made in the last chapter to the relations between the Chinese and the Japanese, and to the aggressions of the latter, increased, no doubt, by Chinese chicane and their own naval superiority and confidence. But nothing serious might have come out of these unneighbourly relations if they had not furnished an ambitious ruler with the opportunity of embarking on an enterprise which promised to increase his Empire and his glory. The old Japanese ruling family was descended, as already described, from a Chinese exile; but the hero of the sixteenth century could claim no relationship with the royal house, and owed none of his success to the accident of a noble birth. Fashiba, called by some English writers Hideyoshi; by the Chinese Pingsiuki; and by the Japanese, on his elevation to the dignity of Tycoon, Taiko Sama, was originally a slave; and it is said that he first attracted attention by refusing to make the prescribed obeisance to one of the daimios or lords. He was on the point of receiving condign punishment, when he pleaded his case with such ingenuity and courage that the daimio not only forgave him his offence, but gave him a post in his service. Having thus obtained honourable employment, Fashiba devoted all his energy and capacity to promoting the interests of his new master, knowing well that his position and opportunities must increase equally with them. In a short time he made his lord the most powerful daimio in the land, and on his death he stepped, naturally enough, into the position and power of his chief. How long he would have maintained himself thus in ordinary times may be matter of opinion, but he resolved to give stability to his position and a greater lustre to his name by undertaking an enterprise which should be popular with the people and profitable to the state. The Japanese had only attempted raids on the coast, and they had never thought of establishing themselves on the mainland. But Fashiba proposed the conquest of China, and he hoped to effect his purpose through the instrumentality of Corea. With this view he wrote the King of that country the following letter:—"I will assemble a mighty host, and, invading the country of the Great Ming, I will fill with hoar-frost from my sword the whole sky over the 400 provinces. Should I carry out this purpose, I hope that Corea will be my vanguard. Let her not fail to do so, for my friendship to your honourable country depends solely on your conduct when I lead my army against China."

Although Fashiba looked to the alliance of Corea to help him in his enterprise, he began it with an act of aggression at her expense, by seizing the important harbour of Fushan, over which Japan still claims a certain superiority and right of priority as to protection, as well as commerce. Having thus secured a foothold on the mainland and a gateway into the kingdom, Fashiba hastened to invade Corea at the head of a large army, and as neither the Corean king nor people seemed to care for his alliance or for his project of invading China, he treated them both as enemies and with marked brutality. The rude and untrained levies of the Corean monarch were vanquished in every encounter. His capital was sacked and the tombs of his ancestors desecrated, while Lipan himself fled to the

Chinese Court to implore the assistance of Wanleh. To such an appeal it is probable that the Chinese Government would, under any circumstances, have given a favourable reply, but the discomfiture of Corea entailed a contingent peril to China, and the ministers of Wanleh at once promised Lipan all the aid he demanded to expel the audacious islander from the Asiatic mainland. An army was hastily assembled and marched to arrest the progress of the Japanese invader, who had by this reached Pingyang, a town 400 miles north of Fushan. An action was fought outside this town, and, although the result could not be regarded as decisive, the advantage rested with the Japanese, who succeeded in destroying a Chinese regiment. After this a lull ensued in the campaign, and while some ineffectual attempts were made to conclude a peace, both sides brought up fresh forces. Fashiba came over from Japan with further supplies and troops to assist his general, Hingchang, while on the Chinese side, Li Jusong, the captor of Ninghia, was placed at the head of the Chinese army. A second battle was fought in the neighbourhood of Pingyang, and after some stubborn fighting the Japanese were driven out of that town. The remainder of the campaign was favourable to the Chinese arms, although the fruits of victory were nearly lost through the personal peril in which Li Jusong was placed. His own valour and the devotion of his body-guard alone saved him from falling a prisoner into the hands of the Japanese.

The second campaign was opened by a brilliant feat on the part of Li Jusong, who succeeded in surprising and destroying the granaries and storehouses constructed by the Japanese, near Seoul, the capital. The loss of their stores compelled the Japanese to retire on Fushan, but they did so with such boldness and confidence that the Chinese did not venture to attack them. A further attempt was made to settle the dispute in an amicable manner, and Fashiba was flattered and rendered disposed to come to terms by his recognition as sovereign of Japan. Presents were exchanged and envoys passed between the two camps, and all promised to end satisfactorily when Fashiba discovered that the Chinese official entrusted with the conclusion of the peace was of very inferior rank, and that the Chinese minister was endeavouring to propitiate him at the same time that he maintained the superior pretensions of his own sovereign. Fashiba broke off the peace negotiations, and, fitting out a fresh navy of over 200 vessels, prepared to prosecute the war with greater vigour and numbers. The war went on with undecided fortune, the jealousies of the Chinese commanders neutralised their superior numbers and the genius of Li Jusong, and the ultimate result of the struggle was still doubtful when the sudden death of Fashiba completely altered the complexion of the situation. The Japanese army then withdrew, taking with it a vast amount of booty and the ears of 10,000 Coreans. The Chinese troops also retired, leaving the Corean king at liberty to restore his disputed authority, and his kingdom once more sank into its primitive state of exclusion and semi-darkness. Unfortunately for their reputation, the Chinese stained their reputation by the murder of two Japanese officers, relatives of Fashiba, whom they described as a rebel instead of an independent prince. This act was an unwarrantable breach of the usages of war and the dictates of humanity. Fashiba had shown himself a formidable, but not the less an honourable, enemy, and the pretension of China to treat him as a rebellious vassal was on a par with the fiction which would have made the King of England the tributary of Pekin.

The seven years' war in Corea ended with this episode. The Chinese showed prudence and policy in defending it against the Japanese, but the successes of the early part of the campaign were not equalled in its subsequent stages, when doubtful engagements were converted into victories, and defeats were concealed under lying bulletins.

For the first time in Chinese history the relations between the Middle Kingdom and Europeans became of importance during the reign of Wanleh, which would alone give it a special distinction. The Portuguese led the way for European enterprise in China, and it was very unfortunate that they did so, for it was soon written of them that "the Portuguese have no other design than to come under the name of merchants to spy the country, that they may hereafter fall upon it with fire and sword." As early as the year 1560 they had obtained from the local officials the right to found a settlement and to erect sheds for their goods at a place which is now known as Macao. In a few years it became of so much importance that it was the annual resort of five or six hundred Portuguese merchants, and the Portuguese, by paying a yearly rent of 500 taels, secured the practical monopoly of the trade of the Canton river, which was then and long afterwards the only vent for the external trade of China. No doubt, the Portuguese had to supplement this nominal rent by judicious bribes to the leading mandarins. Next after the Portuguese came the Spaniards, who, instead of establishing themselves on the mainland, made their headquarters in the group of the Philippine Islands, which they still hold. Chinese traders also visited that archipelago, and Chinese settlers formed the bulk of its prosperous colonists. The Spaniards saw, in the vastly preponderating numbers of the Celestials, a danger to their own existence; and when they found that emissaries were passing to and fro, between the islanders and the mainland, they jumped to the conclusion that a plot was being formed to annihilate them. Quick in realising their danger, the Spaniards were not less quick in taking their measures to nip the danger in the bud, and they resolved, being only 800 to 20,000, to perpetrate a massacre on the lines of St. Bartholomew. Their plans, owing to the superiority of firearms, met with complete success, and during several months the unfortunate Chinese settlers were hunted down throughout the islands. The Chinese, however, returned in greater numbers, and the massacres were repeated on several occasions. It was not for half a century that the Spaniards acquired sufficient confidence in the security of their position to abstain from having recourse to that violent thinning of the population which seemed to them their only safeguard. The tradition of these massacres has not altogether passed away, for even in our time there has been more than one massacre of the natives that partook much of the same character. The promotion of European interests in China owed little or nothing to the forbearance and moderation of either the Spaniards or Portuguese. They tyrannised over the Chinese subject to their sway, and they employed all their resources in driving away other Europeans from what they chose to consider their special commercial preserves. Thus the Dutch were expelled from the south by the Portuguese, and compelled to take refuge in Formosa, while the English and French did not make their appearance, except by occasional visits, until a much later period, although it should be recorded that the English Captain Weddell was the first to discover the mouth of the Canton river, and to make his way up to that great city.

If, however, the acts of the principal representatives of the European trading nations were objectionable, and their policy calculated rather to confirm the exclusive spirit of the Chinese than to open their country to foreigners, there remain to the credit of European civilisation the noble devotion and the humanising efforts of the large band of missionaries sent out by the Church of Rome in the sixteenth and seventeenth centuries. Michel Roger and Matthew Ricci, two of the first in point of time, were exceptionally well qualified for their task. They were men of the world, skilful astrologers and mechanicians, looking to practical measures as much as to theological disquisitions to promote the cause of Christianity and the numbers of their Church. The Chinese were quick to see that they differed from the commercial classes, that their intellect and knowledge might be useful to the state, and that their services could be utilised without making any concession to their religion. One of their chief and most useful works was the reform of the Chinese calendar, and the correction of some astronomical errors. They were entrusted with this work by a Chinese official, Li Chitsao, or Petu, President of the Tribunal of Rites at Nankin, and the Imperial Observatory was placed under their charge. In return for these services they were granted free and secure residence, besides honourable rewards; but they made little progress in carrying out the Pope's mission, and their converts were few in number. As another missionary said, long afterwards, "it is a melancholy trait in the character of the Chinese people that Christian truth does but glide over its surface."

One of the principal troubles of the Emperor Wanleh arose from his having no legitimate heir, and his ministers impressed upon him, for many years, the disadvantage of this situation before he would undertake to select one of his children by the inferior members of the harem as his successor. And then he made what may be termed a divided selection. He proclaimed his eldest son heir-apparent, and declared the next brother to be in the direct order of succession, and conferred on him the title of Prince Fou Wang. The latter was his real favourite, and, encouraged by his father's preference, he formed a party to oust his elder brother and to gain the heritage before it was due. The intrigues in which he engaged long disturbed the Court and agitated the mind of the Emperor. Supported by his mother, Prince Fou Wang threatened the position and even the life of the heir-apparent, Prince Chu Changlo, but the plot was discovered and Fou Wang's rank would not have saved him from the executioner if it had not been for the special intercession of his proposed victim, Chu Changlo. In the midst of these family troubles, as well as those of the state, the Emperor Wanleh died, after a long reign, in 1620. The last years of his life were rendered unhappy and miserable by the reverses experienced at the hands of the new and formidable opponent who had suddenly appeared upon the northern frontier of the Empire.

Some detailed account of the Manchu race and of the progress of their arms before the death of Wanleh will form a fitting prelude to the description of the long wars which resulted in the conquest of China and in the placing of the present ruling family on the Dragon Throne. Their connection with the old Kin dynasty has been already referred to. After the Mongols overthrew that race the most active of its members retired to the then wild region north of Leaoutung, which is now known under the generic name of Manchuria. There they resumed the old tribal designation of the Niuche, and they became broken up into such small fragments that their national identity was almost lost, and they gave the border officers of the Empire little or no trouble. They never possessed the tendency and inclination of the Mongols to coalesce for purposes of rapine or conquest, and their rise to greatness was due rather to the genius of the chiefs of a special clan than to the warlike spirit of the whole race. This clan was the Manchu, meaning the "clear," which is also the translation of the Tsing, the name by which the present dynasty is distinguished, and it seems to have been located in a district thirty miles east of the present town of Moukden, and watered by the Soodsu stream, which is a tributary of the more important Hwun. The principal camp of the clan was situated in the valley of Hootooala, protected on three sides by water and on the fourth by a lofty mountain range. Naturally secure and fertile in its character, considering its northern latitude, this district was the appropriate home of a race destined to exercise its dominion over a great Empire. It bore a close resemblance to the home of the Mongols between the Onon and the Kerulon rivers, but it enjoyed the advantage of being much closer to the Chinese frontier, and of offering increased facilities of reaching the heart of that Empire.

The first chief of the Manchu clan was a mythical personage named Aisin Gioro, who flourished in the middle of the fourteenth century, while Hongwou, the founder of the Mings, was employed in the task of driving out the Mongols. Aisin Gioro is said to mean Golden Family Stem, and thus the connection with the Kin dynasty finds recognition at an early stage. His birth is described in mythical terms—it is said that a magpie dropped a red fruit into the lap of a maiden of the Niuche, who straightway ate it, and conceived a son. The sceptical have interpreted this as meaning that Aisin Gioro was a runaway Mongol, who was granted shelter by the Niuche of Hootooala. At all events he became lord of the valley, and five generations later, in the reign of Wanleh, his descendant, Huen, was head of the Manchus. His grandson, the great Noorhachu, was born in the year 1559, and his birth was attended by several miraculous circumstances. He is said "to have been a thirteen-months' child, to have had the dragon face and the phœnix eye, an enormous chest, large ears, and a voice like the tone of the largest bell." The reader must not take this description literally. Noorhachu was gifted with the most remarkable mental qualities, and it was only in consonance with the character of the time that he should be endowed with phenomenal and unnatural physical features. Noorhachu needed no adventitious characteristics to be considered famous. His physical strength was enormous, and his mental determination attracted notice at an early age. When he was only nineteen his step-mother, who did not appreciate his ability, gave him a small sum of money and sent him forth into the world to make his own fortune. When she heard of the many proofs he was giving of ability she repented of her harshness, and begged him to return to her house, but he refused to do so, or even to accept any assistance from her. In the meantime, a restless and energetic spirit had sprung up among the Niuche clans, and more than one chief entertained the idea that he might unite them in a single confederacy for purposes of military aggrandisement. In the stormy time which prevailed during the last years of the sixteenth century, Noorhachu saw and seized his opportunity.

A chief named Haida was the first to stir up the embers of internecine strife among the Niuche. To gratify his own ambition or to avenge some blood feuds, he obtained the assistance of one of the principal Chinese officers on the Leaoutung borders, and thus overran the territory of his neighbours. Encouraged by his first successes, Haida proceeded to attack the chief of Goolo, who was married to a cousin of Noorhachu, and who at once appealed to Hootooala for assistance. The whole Manchu clan marched to his rescue, and it was on this occasion that Noorhachu had his first experience of war on a large scale. The Manchus presented such a bold front that there is every reason to believe that Haida and his Chinese allies would have failed to conquer Goolo by force, but they resorted to fraud, which proved only too successful. Haida succeeded in enticing the old chief Huen and his son, the father of Noorhachu, into a conference, when he murdered them and many of their companions. The momentary success gained by this breach of faith was heavily paid for by the incentive it gave Noorhachu to exact revenge for the brutal and cowardly murder of his father and grandfather. It is said that he swore a terrible oath to immolate 200,000 Chinese to the *manes* of his sire. For a time the success of Haida seemed complete, and, notwithstanding the threats of Noorhachu, his authority extended and his power seemed to become more secure. So convinced were the Chinese that Haida must succeed that they ignored all the other princelets, and gave him a patent acknowledging his supremacy over all the Niuche tribes. But the pertinacity of Noorhachu proved too much for the strength of Haida and the patience of the Chinese. Haida constructed a fortified camp at Toolun, but he did not feel secure there against the open attacks of Noorhachu or the private plots he formed to gain possession of his person. Several times Haida fled from Toolun to Chinese territory, where he hoped to enjoy greater safety, until at last the Chinese became tired of giving him shelter and protecting one who could not support his own pretensions. Then, with strange inconstancy, they delivered him over into the hands of Noorhachu, who straightway killed him, thus carrying out the first portion of his vow to avenge the massacre at Goolo.

Then Noorhachu turned all his attention and devoted all his energy to the realisation of the project which Haida had conceived, the union of the Niuche clans; but whereas Haida had looked to Chinese support and patronage for the attainment of his object, Noorhachu resolved to achieve success as an enemy of China and by means of his own Manchu followers. His first measure was to carefully select a site for his capital on a plain well supplied with water, and then to fortify it by surrounding it with three walls. He then drew up simple regulations for the government of his people, and military rules imposing a severe discipline on his small army. The Chinese appear to have treated him with indifference, and they continued to pay him the sums of money and the honorary gifts which had been made to Haida. Several of the Niuche clans, won over by the success and reputation of Noorhachu, voluntarily associated themselves with him, and it was not until the year 1591 that the Manchu chief committed his first act of open aggression by invading the district of Yalookiang. That territory was soon overrun and annexed; but it roused such a fear among the other Niuche chiefs, lest their fate should be the same, that seven of them combined, under Boojai, to overthrow the upstart who aspired to play the part of a dictator. They brought into the field a force of 30,000 men, including, besides their own followers, a considerable contingent from the Mongols, and as Noorhachu's army numbered only 4,000 men, it seemed as if he must certainly be overwhelmed. But, small as was his force, it enjoyed the incalculable advantage of discipline ; and seldom has the superiority of trained troops over raw levies been more conspicuously illustrated than by this encounter between warriors of the same race. This battle was fought at Goolo Hill, and resulted in the decisive victory of Noorhachu. Boojai and 4,000 of his men were killed, a large number of his followers were taken prisoners and enrolled in the ranks of the victor, and the spoil included many suits of mail and arms of offence which improved the state of Noorhachu's arsenal. Several of the districts which had been subject to these confederated princes passed into the hands of the conqueror, and he carried his authority northwards up the Songari river over tribes who had never recognised any southern authority. These successes paved the way to an attack on Yeho, the principality of Boojai, which was reputed to be the most powerful of all the Niuche states ; and on this occasion it vindicated its reputation by repelling the attack of Noorhachu. Its success was not entirely due to its own strength, for the Chinese Governor of Leaoutung, roused at last to the danger from Noorhachu, sent money and arms to assist the Yeho people in their defence.

The significance of this repulse was diminished by other successes elsewhere, and Noorhachu devoted his main attention to disciplining the larger force he had acquired by his later conquests, and by raising its efficiency to the high point attained by the army with which he had gained his first triumphs. He also meditated a more daring and important enterprise than any struggle with his kinsfolk, for he came to the conclusion that it was essential to destroy the Chinese power in Leaoutung before he should undertake any further enterprise in Manchuria. His army had now been raised to an effective strength of 40,000 men, and the Manchu bowman, with his formidable bow, and the Manchu man-at-arms, in his cotton mail, proof to the arrow or spear, were as formidable warriors as then existed in the world. Confident in his military power, and thinking, no doubt, that a successful foreign enterprise was the best way to rally and confirm the allegiance of his race, Noorhachu invaded Leaoutung, and published a remarkable proclamation against the Chinese, which became known as the Seven Hates.

"(1). Though my ancestors never took a straw from, nor hurt an inch of earth within the Chinese boundary, the Chinese were unceasingly quarrelling with them, and without just cause abetting my neighbours to the great injury of my ancestors.

"(2). Notwithstanding such injuries, it was still my desire to be on friendly terms with the Chinese Emperor, and I therefore set up a stone slab on the border on which was engraved an oath that whoever, Manchu or Chinaman, should cross the frontier, must suffer instant death, and that if any man aided in sending back the trespasser he would himself suffer death instead. This oath was disregarded by the Chinese when soldiers crossed to aid Yeho.

"(3). At Nankiangan and Beihai, on the Ching-ho, the Chinese crossed the river every year, plundering all around, regardless of consequences. I carried out my oath to the letter, and slew as many as were seen on our side of the river. Thereupon the Chinese annulled the treaty between us, reproached me with murdering their people, and at our very border murdered my ambassador to Kwangning with his nine attendants.

"(4). The Chinese crossed the frontier to aid Yeho, and thus compelled men and women who were our subjects to return to Mongol allegiance.

"(5). For many generations we have tilled the lands along the Chai river and along the tripartite roads of Foongan mountain pass. The Chinese soldiers came and drove away the reapers when they went to gather in the harvest.

"(6). Though Yeho sinned against Heaven you continued to listen to their deceiving speech, and sent me a messenger with a letter upbraiding me, railing at and abusing me without restraint, causing me unspeakable shame.

"(7). Hada of old assisted Yeho in battling against me, who had only my resources on which to rely. Heaven gave me Hada. You of the Ming supported them, causing them to return to their own homes. But Hada was afterwards frequently attacked and robbed by this same Yeho. If these small kingdoms had obeyed the will of Heaven they could not but abide and prosper; disobeying the will of Heaven they must be broken and destroyed. Can you preserve in life those appointed to die? I took Hada's men; do you still desire to restore them? You are a prince of Heaven's appointment. You are the sole Emperor of all under Heaven; why do you envy me the possession of my small kingdom? When Hoolun kingdoms gathered against me to destroy me Heaven abandoned them and aided me, because they fought against me without a cause. At that time you aided Yeho against me, and thus ran counter to the will of Heaven, you reversed my right and his wrong, and thus divided an unjust judgment.

"For all these reasons I hate you with an intense hatred, and now make war upon you."

Significant as was this proclamation in its language, Noorhachu rendered it more significant by his mode of dealing with it. Instead of forwarding this document to the Chinese Court he burnt it in the presence of his army, so that Heaven itself might judge the justice of the cause between him and the Chinese. A comparison is suggested between the growth of the Manchus and that of Prussia in Europe. Noorhachu, not less than the rulers of Brandenburg, raised his people to greatness by thrift, in utilising to the utmost his limited resources, and by his admirable military organisation. Thus the invasion of China became possible by this insignificant northern tribe, notwithstanding its scanty resources and limited numbers; but there can be no doubt that, if the Ming rulers had awoke to their danger in good time, they should have easily triumphed over the Manchus. But they were blind to the danger until it had become formidable, and even when they realised their peril their measures were not as vigorous as they should have been. At the very moment that Noorhachu crossed the Leaoutung frontier, Wanleh was congratulating himself on some successes over the tribes of the south and on the complete security of his position.

It was in the year 1618 that Noorhachu invaded Leaoutung, and so surprised were the Chinese at his audacity that they offered little or no resistance. The town of Fooshun was captured and made the headquarters of the Manchu prince. From this place he sent a list of his requirements to the Governor of Leaoutung, and it is said that he offered, on the Chinese complying with his terms, to withdraw and desist from hostilities. But the Chinese did not appreciate the power of this new enemy. They treated his grievances with indifference and contempt, and they sent an army to drive him out of Leaoutung. The Chinese troops soon had a taste of the quality of the Manchu army. They were defeated in several encounters, and the best Chinese troops fled before the impetuous charge of the Manchu cavalry. Noorhachu then laid siege to the prefectural town of Tsingho, which he captured after a siege of some weeks, and where he massacred nearly 20,000 of the garrison and townspeople. He would have continued the campaign but that his followers demanded to be led back, stating that they feared for the safety of their homes at the hands of Yeho, still hostile and aggressive in their rear. The conquest of Leaoutung was therefore discontinued for the purpose of closing accounts with the last of the Niuche principalities; but enough had been accomplished to whet the appetite of the Manchu leader for more, and to show him how easy it was to vanquish the Chinese. On his return to his capital, Hingking, he prepared to invade Yeho, but his plans were undoubtedly delayed by the necessity of resting his troops and of allowing many of them to return to their homes. This delay, no doubt, induced the Chinese to make a supreme effort to avert the overthrow of Yeho, who had proved so useful an ally, and accordingly the Governor of Leaoutung advanced with one hundred thousand men into Manchuria. He sacrificed the advantage of superior numbers by dividing his army into four divisions, with very inadequate means of inter-communication. Noorhachu could only bring 60,000 men into the field; but, apart from their high training, they represented a compact body subject to the direction of Noorhachu alone. The Manchu leader at once perceived the faulty disposition of the Chinese army, and he resolved to attack and overwhelm each corps in detail before it could receive aid from the others. The strongest Chinese corps was that operating most to the west, and marching from Fooshun on Hingking; and Noorhachu perceived that if he could overthrow it the flank of the rest of the Chinese army would be exposed, and its line of retreat imperilled. The Chinese general in command of this corps was impetuous and anxious to distinguish himself. His courage might on another occasion have helped his country, but under the circumstances his very ardour served the purpose of Noorhachu. Tousong, such was his name, marched more rapidly than any of his comrades, and reached the Hwunho—the Tiber of the Manchus—behind which Noorhachu had, at a little distance, drawn up his army. Without pausing to reconnoitre, or to discover with what force he had to deal, Tousong threw himself across the river, and entrenched himself on Sarhoo Hill. His over-confidence was so extreme and fatuous that he weakened his army by sending a detachment to lay siege to the town of Jiefan. The Manchus had, however, well provided for the defence of that place, and while the Chinese detachment sent against it was being destroyed, Noorhachu attacked Tousong in his position on Sarhoo Hill with the whole of his army. The Chinese were overwhelmed, Tousong was slain, and the majority of those who escaped the fray perished in the waters of the Hwunho beneath the arrows and javelins of the pursuing Manchus

Then Noorhachu hastened to attack the second of the Chinese divisions under a capable officer named Malin, who selected a strong position with great care, and wished to stand on the defensive. His wings rested on two hills which he fortified, and he strengthened his centre in the intervening valley with a triple line of waggons. If he had only remained in this position he might have succeeded in keeping Noorhachu at bay until he could have been joined by the two remaining Chinese corps; but the impetuosity of his troops, or it may have been the artifice of the Manchu leader, drew him from his entrenchments. At first the Chinese seemed to have the best of the battle, but in a short time victory turned to the side of the Manchus, and Malin fled with the relics of his force back to Chinese territory. After these two successes Noorhachu proceeded to attack the third Chinese corps under Liuyen, who had acquired a cheap reputation by his success over the Miaotze. He had no better fortune than any of his colleagues, and his signal defeat completed the Manchu triumph over the Chinese army of invasion. The defeat of Liuyen was effected by a stratagem as much as by superior force. Noorhachu dressed some of his troops in the Chinese uniforms he had captured, and sent them among the Chinese, who received them as comrades until they discovered their mistake in the crisis of the battle. During this campaign it was computed that the total losses of the Chinese amounted to 310 general officers and 45,000 private soldiers. Among other immediate results of this success were the return of 20,000 Yeho troops to their homes, and the defection of 5,000 Coreans, who joined Noorhachu. Like all great commanders, Noorhachu gave his enemies no time to recover from their misfortunes. He pursued Malin to Kaiyuen, which he captured, with so many prisoners that it took three days to count them. He invaded Yeho, which recognised his authority without a blow, and gave him an additional 30,000 fighting men. All the Niuche clans thus became united under his banner, and adopted the name of Manchu. He had succeeded in the great object of his life, the union of his race, and he had well avenged the death of his father and grandfather; but his ambition was not satisfied with this success. It had rather grown with the widening horizon opened by the discomfiture of the Chinese, and with the sense of military superiority.

Amid these national disasters the long reign of Wanleh closed in the year 1620. That unhappy monarch lived long enough to see the establishment on his northern borders of the power which was to destroy his dynasty. In Noorhachu he could not help seeing a restless neighbour, and a powerful rival against whom even the superior wealth and population of China provided an inadequate or doubtful security. The very last act of his reign was, whether by accident or good judgment, the most calculated to prevent the Manchus overrunning the State, and that was the selection of a capable general in the person of Hiung Tingbi But the step was taken too late to benefit this unfortunate prince, and at the moment of his death Tingbi had had no opportunity of showing how well he deserved the confidence of his sovereign. With the death of Wanleh the decadence of Ming power became clearly marked, and the only question that remained was whether it could be arrested before it resulted in absolute ruin.

CHAPTER IX.

THE MANCHU CONQUEST OF CHINA.

TINGBI, with the wrecks of the Chinese armies, succeeded in doing more for the defence of his country than had been accomplished by any of his predecessors with undiminished resources. He built a chain of forts, he raised the garrison of Leaoutung to 180,000 men, and he spared no effort to place Leaouyang, the capital of that province, in a position to stand a protracted siege. If his counsels had been followed to the end, he might have succeeded in permanently arresting the flood of Manchu conquest; but at the very moment when his plans promised to give assured success, he fell into disgrace at the capital, and his career was summarily ended by the executioner. The greatest compliment to his ability was that Noorhachu remained quiescent as long as he was on the frontier, but as soon as he was removed he at once resumed his aggression on Chinese soil.

Meanwhile, Wanleh had been succeeded on the Chinese throne by his son, Chu Changlo, who took the name of Kwangtsong. He was an amiable and well-meaning prince, whose reign was unquestionably cut short by foul means. There is little doubt that he was poisoned by the mother of his half-brother, from a wish to secure the throne for her son; but if so she never gained the object that inspired her crime, for the princes of the family met in secret conclave, and selected Kwangtsong's son, a youth of sixteen, as his successor. The choice did not prove fortunate, as this prince became known as Tienki the Unhappy, whose reign witnessed the culmination of Ming misfortunes. One of his first acts was the removal of Tingbi from his command, and this error of judgment, aggravated by the ingratitude it implied to a faithful servant, fitly marked the commencement of a reign of incompetence and misfortune.

In 1621 the Manchu war reopened with an attack on Moukden or Fanyang, which Noorhachu had marked out as his next object. The garrison was numerous, and might have made a good defence, for the walls were strong; but the commandant was brave to the degree of temerity, and, leaving his fortress, marched out to meet the Manchus in the open. The result was a decisive overthrow, and the victors entered Moukden at the heels of the vanquished. The Chinese still resisted, and a terrible slaughter ensued, but the Manchus retained their conquest. At this juncture the Chinese were offered the assistance of the Portuguese at Macao, who sent a small body of 200 men, armed with arquebuses and with several cannon, to Pekin; but after some hesitation the Chinese, whether from pride or contempt of so small a force, declined to avail themselves of their service, and thus lost an auxiliary that might have turned the fortune of the war in their favour. The Portuguese were sent back to Macao, and, although the Chinese kept the cannon, and employed the Jesuit priests in casting others for them, nothing came of an incident which might have exercised a lasting influence not merely on the fortune of the war, but also on the relations between the Chinese and Europeans. The Chinese sent several armies to recover Moukden ; but, although they took these guns with them, they met with no success, and Noorhachu made it the base of his plan of attack on Leaouyang, the capital of the province. The defence of this important town was entrusted to Yuen Yingtai, the Court favourite and incompetent successor of Tingbi. That officer, unwarned by the past, and regardless of the experience of so many of his predecessors, weakened himself and invited defeat by attempting to oppose the Manchus in the open. He was defeated, losing some of his best soldiers, and compelled to shut himself up in the town with a disheartened garrison. The Manchus gave it no time to recover the confidence it had lost, and, by either treachery within the walls or skilful engineering, making a road across the moat, gained an entrance into the city. Then a terrible encounter took place. The garrison was massacred to a man, Yuen Yingtai, brave, if incapable, committed suicide, and those of the townspeople who wished to save their lives had to shave their heads in token of subjection. This is the first historical reference to a practice that is now universal throughout China, and that has become what may be called a national characteristic. The badge of conquest has changed to a mark of national pride; but it is strange to find that the Chinese themselves and the most patient inquirers among sinologues are unable to say what was the origin of the pig-tail. They cannot tell us whether shaving the head was the national custom of the Manchus, or whether Noorhachu only conceived this happy idea of distinguishing those who surrendered to his power among the countless millions of the long-haired people of China. It might be thought that, if the former were the case, it would have been the custom of the Kin rulers; but no record can be found of any such practice among the annals of that dynasty. This may be due to the fact that the Kins were not a literary race, and that the Chinese chroniclers, who alone recorded their history, had not the necessary information or interest in a foreign race to publish the details of their Court ceremonial and national customs: for it must be remembered that the Kins, although rulers of a great part of China, were not national or popular sovereigns like their contemporaries the Sungs. All that can be said of the origin of the pig-tail is that it was first enforced as a badge of subjugation by the Manchus at the siege of Leaouyang, and that thenceforward, until the whole of China was conquered, it was made the one condition of immunity from massacre.

The capture of Leaouyang signified the surrender of the remaining places in Leaoutung, which became a Manchu possession, and Noorhachu, to celebrate his triumph, and also to facilitate his plans for the further humiliation of the Chinese, transferred his capital from Moukden to Leaouyang. Misfortunes never come singly has been established as an undoubted truth by universal experience, and it was only natural that, while this heavy cloud from the Manchus was collecting on the northern frontier, other enemies of the Imperial House should have gathered strength and confidence to attack the Chinese officers, who might be generally embarrassed and weakened by the strain imposed on the resources of the government. In Szchuen the peril assumed a very definite and formidable character. A local chief had raised a force of 30,000 men for service on the frontier in the wars with the Manchus, and the Viceroy of the province not only declined to utilise their services, but dismissed them without reward or even recognition of their loyalty. These slighted and disbanded braves easily changed themselves into brigands, and as the government would not have them as supporters they determined to make it feel their enmity. Chet song Ming, the chief who had raised them, placed himself at their head, and attracted a large number of the inhabitants to his standard. The local garrisons were crushed, the Viceroy killed, and general disorder prevailed among the people of what was the most fertile and prosperous province of the Empire. Chetsong attempted to set up an administration, but he does not seem to have possessed the capacity or the knowledge to establish a regular government. While he headed the rebellious movement, a woman named Tsinleang, the hereditary chieftainess of a small district, placed herself at the head of the loyalists in the state, and, leading them herself, succeeded in recovering the principal cities and in driving Chetsong out of the province. She has been not inappropriately called by one of the missionary historians the Chinese Penthesilea. The success she met with in pacifying Szchuen after a two years' struggle was not attained in other directions without a greater effort, and at a still heavier cost. In Kweichow and Yunnan a rebel named Ganpangyen raised an insurrection on a large scale, and if his power had not been broken by the long siege of a strong fortress obstinately defended by a valiant governor, there is no telling to what success he might not have attained. But his followers were disheartened by the delay in carrying this place, and they abandoned him as soon as they found that he could not command success. In Shantung another rising occurred, but after two years' disturbance the rebel leader was captured and executed. These internal disorders, produced by the corruption and inertness of the officials as much as by a prevalent sense of the embarrassment of the Mings, distracted the attention of the central government from Manchuria, and weakened its preparations against Noorhachu.

For a time Noorhachu showed no disposition to cross the River Leaou, and confined his attention to consolidating his position in his new conquest. But it was clear that this lull would not long continue, and the Chinese Emperor, Tienki, endeavoured to meet the coming storm by once more entrusting the defence of the frontier to Tingbi. That general devised a simple and what might have proved an efficacious line of defence, but his colleague, with more powerful influence at Court, would have none of it, and insisted on his own plan being adopted. Noorhachu divined that the councils of the Chinese were divided, and that Tingbi was hampered. He promptly took advantage of the divergence of opinion, and, crossing the frontier, drove the Chinese behind the Great Wall. Even that barrier would not have arrested his progress but for the stubborn resistance offered by the fortress of Ningyuen—a town about seventy miles north-east of Shanhaikwan, once of great importance, but now, for many years past, in ruins. When he reached that place he found that Tingbi had fallen into disgrace and been executed, not for devising his own plan of campaign, but for animadverting on that of his colleague in satirical terms. The Chinese had made every preparation for the resolute defence of Ningyuen, and when Noorhachu sat down before it, its resolute defender, Chungwan, defied him to do his worst, although all the Chinese troops had been compelled to retreat, and there was no hope of reinforcement or rescue. At first Noorhachu did not conduct the siege of Ningyuen in person. It promised to be an affair of no great importance, and he entrusted it to his lieutenants, but he soon perceived that Chungwan was a resolute soldier, and that the possession of Ningyuen was essential to the realisation of his future plans. Therefore, he collected all his forces and sat down before Ningyuen with the full determination to capture it at all costs. But the garrison was resolute, its commander capable, and on the walls were arranged the cannon of European construction. Noorhachu led two assaults in person, both of which were repulsed, and it is said that this result was mainly due to the volleys of the European artillery. At last, Noorhachu was compelled to withdraw his troops, and although he obtained some successes in other parts of the country, he was so chagrined at this repulse that he fell ill and died some months later at Moukden in September, 1626. As to his career and position in Chinese history I must repeat my own words.

His descendants dated their dynasty from the year 1616, although the conquest of China had not then so much as commenced; and with the vanity of a new family they not merely assigned to their not very remote founder a semi-divine origin, but they gave to Noorhachu the posthumous and glorious title of Taitsou Hwangti. Although Noorhachu was very far indeed from enjoying the reputation which he sought to acquire as the Conqueror of China, yet there can be no doubt that he deserved all the respect and honour which his people and family could pay him. But for his energy and perseverance the small clan of which he was titular chief might never have risen to fame, and the titles of Manchu and Tatsing never been heard of or invented. In many respects he accomplished for the Manchus what Genghis did for the Mongols. It was not his fault if his sphere was a smaller one and more circumscribed. The credit of having emancipated himself from it may, indeed, have been all the more conspicuous, and it certainly seems that Noorhachu achieved a great exploit when he extended his sway from a small valley of a few square miles over a vast territory, including two Chinese or quasi-Chinese provinces, and stretching from the Great Wall to the Amour. If much of his extraordinary success must be attributed to the blunders and folly of his opponents, cannot almost the same be said of every conqueror from the days of Alexander to those of Napoleon? Noorhachu had the strength of will, seldom given to mortals, to know when to stop. His victories are not more remarkable than the vigour with which he made the most of their results, and with which he consolidated his authority in the new possessions that fell into his power. He built up the edifice of his Empire step by step, and his successors had to thank him that he sank its foundations very deep in the affections of his own people, and in the possession of a well-trained and valiant army.

Noorhachu was succeeded by his fourth son, the fourth Beira or Prince, known as Taitsong, who continued both his work and policy. The new ruler, following the prescribed form, wished to begin his rule with the exchange of compliments and the expressed desire for peace; but Chungwan saw through the hollowness of his protestations, and resented his employing the style of an equal with the Emperor. Then the true sentiments of the Manchu became revealed, and he wrote, "If your kingdom and ours have been so long at war the cause must be attributed to the insufferable pride of the mandarins who have governed Leaoutung. They regard their sovereign as a being raised above the heavens, and they consider themselves men very superior to everybody else, despising all neighbouring princes to whom Providence has entrusted the care of peoples, and not hesitating to commit against them the worst outrages. Heaven considers only the justice of a cause, without reference to the vastness or the smallness of kingdoms. That is the reason why it has protected us and allowed us to take vengeance for the injustice of your master and his officers. Our grievances are well known."

Chungwan replied to this letter in terms that showed him to be an able debater as well as a brave soldier.

"I see with satisfaction that you are disposed to keep due respect towards this Empire and to abstain from further hostilities, with the view of binding your neighbours to permit your subjects to enjoy all the advantages of peace. This is a proof that you attach value to men's lives, and that you do not desire to shed their blood. Heaven cannot fail to reward you for it by making your states to flourish. As to your grievances against us, permit me, Emperor of the Manchus, to express some doubt as to their being as serious as you make them out to be. I think not only that the Emperor, my master, is unaware of them, but that you would do well to bury them in an eternal oblivion. You pass over in silence the ten years of constant war during which you have caused blood to flow in streams, and during which a vast extent of territory, before thickly populated, has been devastated. Are your wrongs to be compared with so many ravages? Your people, both of the north and of the south, of the east and of the west, have lost no more than ten men; and of all those who inhabited the borders of Leaoutung and Chinyang there remains but one old woman whom you have spared. If your wish for peace is sincere evacuate the towns which you have taken from us, restore the mandarins and the other subjects of the Empire whom you have captured; and then you will convince us of the uprightness of your intentions and of your respect towards Heaven."

This correspondence could not blind people to the real state of the relations between the Manchus and China. The truce between them was a hollow one, and Taitsong was as determined to humiliate the Mings as his father had been. He commenced his offensive measures by an attack on Corea, which he speedily reduced to such a pass that it accepted his authority and transferred its allegiance from the Mings to the Manchus. This was an important success, as it secured his eastern flank and deprived the Chinese of a useful ally in the Forbidden Kingdom. It encouraged Taitsong to think that the time was once more ripe for attacking Ningyuen, and he laid siege to that fortress at the head of a large army, including the flower of his troops. Notwithstanding the energy of his attack, Chungwan, the former bold defender of the place, had again the satisfaction of seeing the Manchus repulsed, and compelled to admit that the ramparts of Ningyuen presented a serious if not insuperable obstacle to their progress. Almost at the very moment of this success the Emperor Tienki died, and was succeeded, in 1627, by his younger brother, Tsongching, who was destined to be the last of the Ming rulers.

The repulse of Taitsong before Ningyuen might have been fatal if he had not been a man of great ability and resource. The occasion called for some special effort, and Taitsong proved himself equal to it by a stroke of genius that showed he was the worthy inheritor of the mission of Noorhachu. Without taking anybody into his confidence he ordered his army and his allies, the Kortsin Mongols, to assemble in the country west of Ningyuen, and when he had thus collected over a hundred thousand men, he announced his intention of ignoring Ningyuen, and marching direct on Pekin. At this juncture Taitsong divided his army into eight banners, which still remain the national divisions of the Manchu race. The Manchus seem to have been a little alarmed by the boldness of Taitsong's scheme, and they might have hesitated to follow him if he had given them any time for reflection, but his plans were not fully known until his forces were through the Dangan Pass on the march to the capital. The Chinese relying altogether on Ningyuen as a defence had made no preparation to hold their ground on this side, and Taitsong encountered no opposition until he reached Kichow. Then Chungwan realising that he had been out-manoeuvred, and that the defences of Ningyuen had been turned, hastened back by forced marches to defend Pekin. Owing to his road being the better of the two he gained the capital in time, and succeeded in throwing himself and his troops into it in order to defend it against the assault of the Manchus. After Taitsong sat down before Pekin he issued a proclamation to the Chinese nation reciting his wrongs, and denouncing the incompetence of the Mings. He concluded by asking the question, "Whether it was not possible that Heaven had chosen him to be the master of the Empire, and to succeed the Mings." Taitsong thus began to coquet with Chinese public opinion at the same time that he invested rather than laid close siege to the northern capital. He was quite content to establish himself in pleasant quarters at Haidsu, a Ming palace and hunting box near Pekin, and to engage in an intrigue for the ruin of Chungwan, whose disgrace would be equivalent to a great victory. The method is not to be approved on general grounds, but Taitsong conceived that he was justified in bribing persons in Pekin to discredit Chungwan and compass his ruin. The emperor was persuaded that Chungwan was too powerful a subject to be absolutely loyal, and it was asserted that he was in communication with the enemy. The charge exposed itself, but it answered its purpose. The irate monarch ordered the arrest of the faithful general, and the heroic Chungwan, who had been so long the buttress of the kingdom, was secretly arrested and thrown into a prison from which he never issued. The disappearance of Chungwan was as valuable to Taitsong as a great victory, and he made his final preparations for assaulting Pekin, but either the want of supplies or the occurrence of some disturbance in his rear prevented the execution of his plan. He drew off his forces and retired behind the Great Wall at the very moment when Pekin seemed at his mercy.

Taitsong's first attack on Pekin was by nature of an experiment. He followed it up by endeavouring to pose more and more as the friend of the Chinese people. In his proclamations he dwelt on their injuries and wrongs, and on his desire to see them righted. He established schools in which Chinese was taught, and he instituted public examinations for appointments in the public service on the lines laid down by Confucius. All his proclamations were framed with the end of propitiating opinion in China, and he devised a list of military and civil dignities for those Chinese who attached themselves to his fortunes. He also adopted the astute plan of conferring on those who joined him a step higher in rank, so that it is not surprising that the desertions from the sinking side of the Mings to the rising one of the Manchus were not few or unfrequent. But more important than the accession of numbers was the impression produced that Taitsong aspired to be a model prince after the pattern of the greatest rulers of China. If the results of this policy were not at once apparent, there can be no doubt that it facilitated the Manchu conquest some years later when Taitsong had established himself in the heart of China, and when it became a practical question for the Chinese to consider whether they would not do wiser to accept the inevitable than to prolong a hopeless struggle. During four years of more or less tranquillity Taitsong confined his attention to these political designs, and to training a corps of artillery, and then he resumed his main project of the conquest of China. Instead of availing themselves of the lull thus afforded to improve their position, the Chinese ministers seemed to believe that the danger from the Manchus had passed away, and they treated all the communications from Taitsong with imprudent and unnecessary disdain. Their attention was also distracted by many internal troubles, produced by their own folly, as well as by the perils of the time.

The most serious of these was the mutiny of the troops in garrison in the northern provinces. These had not been paid for some time, and it was said that their pay had been appropriated by one of the officials at Court. The charge was in all probability true, and the consequences to the State were undoubtedly serious. The insurrection spread. A Viceroy was murdered, his successor shared the same fate, and the resources of the Empire had to be strained to restore tranquillity. This was at last effected, but the leader, Kongyuta, made his escape to Taitsong's Court, and became in due course one of his most trusted lieutenants. The welcome given to Kongyuta was, no doubt, enhanced by the number of adherents he brought to the Manchus. He was accompanied by 100,000 persons, and he brought with him no inconsiderable amount of arms, provisions, and jewels. Taitsong received him with the following address:—" No thought of regret should enter your heart at entering my service. With the help of God I hope to procure for us all a great Empire, and if I succeed there are no honours or riches to which you cannot look forward if you serve me faithfully." Encouraged, no doubt, by this accession of strength, and also seeing that the times were propitious, Taitsong, in 1634, resumed his operations in China, and on this occasion he invaded the province of Shansi, at the head of an army composed largely of Mongols as well as of Manchus. Although the people of Shansi had not had any practical experience of Manchu prowess, and notwithstanding that their frontier was exceedingly strong by nature, Taitsong met with little or no resistance from either the local garrisons or the people themselves. One Chinese governor, it is said, ventured to publish a boastful report of an imaginary victory over the Manchus, and to send a copy of it to Pekin. Taitsong, however, intercepted the letter, and at once sent the officer a challenge, matching 1,000 of his men against 10,000 of the Chinese. That the offer was not accepted is the best proof of the superiority of the Manchu army.

It was at the close of this successful campaign in Shansi, that Taitsong, in the year 1635, assumed, for the first time, amongst any of the Manchu rulers the style of Emperor of China. Events had long been moving in this direction, but an accident is said to have determined Taitsong to take this final measure. The jade seal of the old Mongol rulers was suddenly discovered, and placed in the hands of Taitsong. When the Mongols heard of this, forty-nine of their chiefs hastened to tender their allegiance to Taitsong, and the only condition made was that the King of Corea should be compelled to do so likewise. Taitsong, nothing loth, at once sent off letters to the Corean Court announcing the adhesion of the Mongols, and calling upon the king of that state to recognise his supremacy. But the Corean ruler had got wind of the contents of these letters and declined to open them, thus hoping to get out of his difficulty without offending his old friends the Chinese. But Taitsong was not to be put off in this fashion. He sent an army to inflict chastisement on his neighbour, and its mission was successfully discharged. The king and his family were taken prisoners, although they had fled to the island of Gangwa for safety, and Corea became a Manchu possession. The last years of Taitsong's life were spent in conducting repeated expeditions into the provinces of Shansi and Pechihli, but the strength of the fortresses of Ningyuen and Shanhaikwan on the Great Wall effectually prevented his renewing his attempt on Pekin. These two places, with the minor forts of Kingchow and Songshan formed a quadrilateral that effectually secured Pekin on its northern side, and being entrusted to the defence of Wou Sankwei, a general of great capacity, of whom much more will be heard, all Taitsong's ability and resources were taxed to overcome those obstacles to his progress south of the Great Wall. He succeeded after great loss, and at the end of several campaigns, in taking Kingchow and Songshan, but these were his last successes, for in the year 1643 he was seized with a fatal illness at Moukden, which terminated his career at the comparatively early age of fifty-two.

Although Taitsong had achieved many remarkable military successes, and inflicted an incalculable amount of injury and humiliation on China, he made little or no progress in the main object of his life, which was the conquest of that country. If he had lived there is no doubt that he would have succeeded in his project, although the chances of the Chinese seemed as good of maintaining their independence at the moment of his death as his of subduing them. But he would, unquestionably, have known how to turn the events which destroyed the Mings, and exalted the Manchus to as good account as any of his successors. Of the ability and great sovereign qualities of Taitsong there can be no doubt. He was as good a soldier, and as capable a general as Noorhachu, but he was far the more skilful administrator, and he set himself the task of elevating the Manchu regime and customs. He was the civiliser of his race, and he strove to convince the Chinese that he was worthy of being their ruler. His fame spread much farther than his authority. He added little to the extent of territory transmitted to him by his father, but his reputation stood highest among all the rulers of Eastern Asia. Even the Chinese recognised his merit, and compared his rule favourably with that of their own Ming princes. Taitsong's premature death due, in all probability, to the incompetence of his physicians, cut short a career that had not reached its prime, and retarded the conquest of China, for the supreme authority among the Manchus then passed from a skilful and experienced ruler into the hands of a child.

The possession of a well-trained army, the production of two great leaders of admitted superiority, and forty years of almost continuously successful war, had not availed to bring the authority of the Manchus in any permanent form south of the Great Wall. The barrier of Tsin Che Hwangti still kept out the most formidable adversary who had ever borne down upon it, and the independence of China seemed far removed from serious jeopardy. At this juncture events occurred that altered the whole situation, and the internal divisions of the Chinese proved more serious, and entailed a more rapid collapse than all the efforts of the Manchus. Some description has already been given of the risings in different parts of the realm which hampered the Ming executive during the earlier campaigns with the Manchus, but they did not entail any very serious consequences, and were gradually one and all suppressed. But the public dissatisfaction continued to spread, and the demand was increasing every day for the Mings to reform, or to be got rid of. The time was auspicious for a genuine patriot, and also for unscrupulous adventurers. China failed to find the former, but the production of the latter was abundant, and one of these completed the ruin of his country, and paved the way for the triumph of the Manchus.

The arch rebel Li Tseching, who proved more formidable to the Ming ruler than his Manchu opponent, was the son of a peasant in the province of Shansi, and at an early age he attached himself to the profession of arms, and became well known as a skilful archer and horseman. In 1629, he first appears on the scene as member of a band of robbers, who were, however, destroyed by a rare display of energy on the part of one of the Emperor's lieutenants. Li was one of the few who were fortunate enough to escape with their lives and liberty. He soon gathered round him another band, and under his successful and courageous leading it shortly acquired the size of an army. One reason of his success was his forming an alliance with the Mahomedan settlers in Kansuh who were already known as Tungani or "Colonists." But the principal cause of his success was his skill and promptitude in coming to terms with the Imperial authorities whenever they became too strong for him, and he often purchased a truce when, if the officials had pushed home their advantage, he must have been destroyed. His power thus grew to a high point, while that of other robber chiefs only waxed to wane and disappear ; and about the year 1640, when it was said that his followers numbered half a million of men, he began to think seriously of displacing the Ming and placing himself on the throne of China. With this object in view he laid siege to the town of Honan, the capital of the province of the same name. At first the resolution of the governor baffled his attempt, but treachery succeeded when force failed. A traitor opened a gate for a sum of money which he was never paid, and Li's army burst into the city. The garrison was put to the sword, and horrible outrages were perpetrated on the townspeople. From Honan Li marched on Kaifong, which he besieged for seven days, but he did not possess the necessary engines to attack a place of any strength, and Kaifong was reputed to be the strongest fortress in China, and he was obliged to beat a hasty retreat, pursued by an army that the Imperial authorities had hurriedly collected. There is reason to think his retreat was a skilful movement to the rear in order to draw the Emperor's troops after him. Certain it is that they pursued him in four separate corps, and that he turned upon them and beat them one after the other. When he had vanquished these armies in four separate encounters he again laid siege to Kaifong, and it was thought that he would have taken it when Li was wounded by an arrow, and called off his troops in consequence. Several times afterwards he resumed the attempt, but with no better fortune, until an accident accomplished what all his power had failed to do. The governor had among other precautions flooded the moat from the Hoangho, and this extra barrier of defence had undoubtedly done much towards discomfiting the besiegers. But in the end it proved fatal to the besieged, for the Hoangho, at all times capricious in its movements, and the source of as much trouble as benefit to the provinces it waters, rose suddenly to the dimensions of a flood, and overflowing its banks spread over the country. Many of Li's soldiers were drowned, and his camp was flooded, but the most serious loss befel the Imperialists in Kaifong. The waters of the river swept away the walls and flooded the town. Thousands perished at the time, and those who attempted to escape were cut down by the rebels outside. Kaifong itself was destroyed and has never recovered its ancient importance, being now a town of only the third or fourth rank. This great success established the reputation of Li Tseching on a firm basis, and constituted him one of the arbiters of his country's destiny.

The capture of Kaifong was followed at a very brief interval by the attack on, and acquisition of, Tunkwan, the famous fortress between Honan and Shansi, which generally carried with it the supremacy of the northwest. He owed his speedy capture of that place to his good fortune in being able to make his way into the city with the relics of an army he had beaten in the field, so that its formidable walls and towers were never called into play. The severity of Li's measures towards the vanquished spread the terror of his name among the Chinese masses, and when he appeared before the town of Singan, the metropolis of the west, the townspeople refused to allow any defence to be made, and when the garrison showed signs of insisting on holding out they rose up and massacred their own troops and opened their gates to Li Tseching. Thus rapidly did the authority of this truculent chieftain spread throughout north-west China, and as soon as he found himself master of one-third of the state he proclaimed himself Emperor of China, under the style of Yongchang, and he gave his dynasty the name of Tachun. Having taken this step of open defiance to the Ming government, Li invaded Shansi, which he reduced to subjection with little difficulty or bloodshed. An officer, named Likintai, was sent to organise some measures of defence, but, on arrival, he found the province in the hands of the rebel, and he had no choice save to beat a discreet and rapid retreat. The success of Li continued unchecked. Important places like Taiyuen and Taitong surrendered to him after a merely nominal resistance, and when they fell there was no further impediment in the way of his marching on Pekin.

At the very moment when the danger from the Manchus under Taitsong seemed most formidable, a fresh and more pressing peril presented itself to the Ming ruler in the person of the rebel, Li Tseching. It was a singular situation that the Mings should feel safe against the Manchus who had been gaining victory after victory for forty years, and that they should at once begin to despair when a native rebel, such as Li, threatened them in their capital. Yet before Li had finally subjected Shansi the Ming Emperor, Tsongching, summoned his ministers and officers to a conference to decide how the Empire might be saved. Likintai, still endeavouring to keep the semblance of an army in the field, advised that the emperor should retire to Nankin and gather the forces of southern China for the defence of the Empire. But his advice, the best as it was, was not taken, and it was decided that the Emperor should hold on to Pekin and make the best stand there that he could. Tsongching, seeing the weakness and indecision of those around him, knew what this meant, and exclaimed with prophetic accuracy, "I now perceive that I am only the emperor of a dynasty which is about to end.

My chief grief is to see in you so much lukewarmness towards your master. Where are the zeal and fidelity which you owe him?" No preparations had been made to defend Pekin. The defences were weak, the garrison insufficient, as all the best troops were on the frontier, and the citizens disposed to come to terms with the assailant rather than to die in the breach for their sovereign. When Li pitched his tent outside the western gate of the capital, and sent a haughty demand to the Emperor to abdicate his throne, he knew that he was master of the situation; but Tsongching, ignorant of his own impotence, defied and upbraided his opponent as a rebel. His indignation was turned to despair when he learnt that the troops had abandoned his cause, that the people were crying out for Li Tseching, and that that leader's followers were rapidly approaching his palace. Then his thoughts turned to personal security rather than to making a dignified historical exit as the representative of the great Hongwou. He summoned round him in the palace the members of his family and the most faithful of his adherents, and in the old fashion he toasted them in the wine of the country, assuming in the supreme hour of his fate a dignity that might have augured a better demeanour when fortune and victory were not altogether lost. He turned to his attendants and entrusted to them the persons of his children, whom he hoped they would convey in safety to their mother's kinsmen. He then addressed his wife and said, "All is lost for us," and she, equal to the occasion, retired to her apartment and hung herself. Finally he said to his daughter, "Why were you born of a father so unfortunate as I?" and struck her to the ground with his sword. She recovered to marry the next year a magnate of the court whom she had long loved, so that her ending was not unhappy; while Tsongching, having ordered all his wives, princesses and women of the palace to be slain to save their honour, hastily quitted his apartment in which this dread decision was come to, to make one more effort to prolong his own miserable existence. From one gate he sped to another, but at all points he encountered the troops of the besiegers, and he was obliged to again seek shelter in his palace. When he sounded the gong for his courtiers none replied, for all had fled to seek shelter. Then he realised that he was abandoned, and he retired to the Wansin Hill, a favourite spot in the palace grounds, where he drew up his last protest against the bad advice of his ministers, and the iniquity of fortune. It said as follows:—

"Seventeen years have I occupied the throne, and rebellious subjects are come to insult me even in my capital; and that which is happening to me is evidently a punishment sent by Heaven. I am not the only one who is guilty; all my ministers are so in a worse degree than myself. They have ruined me by concealing from me the exact position of affairs. With what countenance shall I, after death, be able to appear before my ancestors? You who reduce me to this unhappy pass, take my body if you will, and hack it to pieces. I shall make no protest. But spare my people, and refrain from doing them injury."

Then Tsongching strangled himself with his girdle, but only one officer was found devoted enough to share his fate. Although Tsongching had some nominal successors, he was strictly speaking the last of the Ming Emperors, and with him the great dynasty founded by Hongwou came to an end. The many disasters that preceded its fall rendered the loss of the imperial station less of a blow to the individual, and the last of the Ming rulers seems to have even experienced relief on reaching the term of his anxieties. The episode of the faithful officer, Li Kweiching, concludes the dramatic events accompanying the capture of Pekin and the fall of the dynasty. After the death of his sovereign he attempted to defend the capital; but overpowered by numbers he surrendered to the victor, who offered him an honourable command in his service. Li Kweiching accepted the offer on the stipulation that he should be allowed to give the Emperor Tsongching honourable burial, and that the surviving members of the Ming family should be spared. These conditions, so creditable to Li Kweiching, were granted: but, at the funeral of his late sovereign, grief or a spirit of duty so overcame him that he committed suicide on the grave of Tsongching. Li Tseching, who had counted on valuable assistance from this officer, became furious at this occurrence. He plundered and destroyed the ancestral temple of the Mings, and he caused every member of the imperial family on whom he could lay hands to be executed. Thus terminated the events at Pekin in the absolute and complete triumph of the rebel Li Tseching, and the panic produced by his success and severity blinded observers to the hollowness of his power, and to the want of solidity in his administration. Yet it seemed for a time as if he were left the virtual master of China.

While the Ming power was collapsing before the onset of Li Tseching, there still remained the large and well-trained Ming army in garrison on the Manchu frontier, under the command of the able general, Wou Sankwei. At the eleventh hour the Emperor Tsongching had sent a message to Wou Sankwei, begging him to come in all haste to save the capital; and that general, evacuating Ningyuen, and leaving a small garrison at Shanhaikwan, had begun his march for Pekin, when he learnt that it had fallen, and that the Ming dynasty had ceased to be. Placed in this dilemma, between the advancing Manchus, who immediately occupied Ningyuen on his evacuation of it, and the large rebel force in possession of Pekin, Wou Sankwei had no choice between coming to terms with one or other of them. Li Tseching offered him liberal rewards and a high command, but in vain, for Wou Sankwei decided that it would be better to invite the Manchus to enter the country, and to assist them to conquer it. There can be no doubt that this course was both the wiser and the more patriotic, for Li Tseching was nothing more than a successful brigand on a large scale; whereas the Manchu government was a respectable one, and well organized, and aspired to revive the best traditions of the Chinese. Having come to a prompt decision, Wou Sankwei lost no time in promptly carrying it out. He wrote a letter to the Manchus, asking them to send an army to co-operate with his in driving Li Tseching out of Pekin; and the Manchus, at once realising that the moment had arrived for conquering China, acquiesced promptly in his plans, sent forward their advanced corps, and ordered a *levée en masse* of the nation for the conquest of China. Assured of his rear, and also of speedy reinforcement, Wou Sankwei did not delay a day in marching on Pekin. Li Tseching sent out a portion of his army to oppose the advance of Wou Sankwei; but the officer's instructions were rather to negotiate than to fight, for to the last Li Tseching expected that Wou Sankwei would come over to his side. He was already beginning to feel doubtful as to the security of his position; and his fears were increased by his superstition, for, when on entering Pekin, he passed under a gate above which was written the character "joong" (middle), he exclaimed, drawing his bow at the same time, "If I hit this joong in the middle, it is a sign I have gained the whole empire, as the empire is joong, the middle kingdom." His arrow missed its mark. The apprehensions of Li Tseching were soon confirmed, for Wou Sankwei defeated the first army he had sent out with a loss of 20,000 men. Li does not seem to have known of the alliance between that officer and the Manchus, for he marched at the head of 60,000 men to encounter him. He took with him the aged father of Wou Sankwei and two Ming princes, who had survived the massacre of their family, with a view to appealing to the affection and loyalty of that commander; but these devices proved vain.

Wou Sankwei drew up his forces at Yungping in a strong position near the scene of his recent victory; his front seems to have been protected by the river Zanho, and he calmly awaited the attack of Li Tseching, whose army far outnumbered his. Up to this point Wou Sankwei had not been joined by any of the Manchus, but a body was known to be approaching, and he was anxious to put off the battle until they arrived. For the same reason Li Tseching was as anxious to begin the attack, and, notwithstanding the strength of Wou Sankwei's position, he ordered his troops to engage without delay. Adopting the orthodox Chinese mode of attack of forming his army in a crescent, so that the extreme wings should overlap and gradually encompass those of the enemy, Li trusted to his numerical superiority to give him the victory. At one moment it seemed as if his expectation would be justified, for, bravely as Wou Sankwei and his army fought, the weight of numbers was telling its inevitable tale when a Manchu corps opportunely arrived, and attacking the Chinese with great impetuosity, changed the fortune of the day and put the army of Li Tseching to the rout. Thirty thousand men are said to have fallen on the field, and Li himself escaped from the carnage with only a few hundred horsemen. He fled back to Pekin but he quickly realised that he could not hold out there, for the Manchu troops were now crossing the frontier in great numbers, and hastening to the front. The Manchus very astutely left the chief command in the hands of Wou Sankwei, who had shown himself so worthy of the trust, and a few weeks after the battle of Yungping he sat down before Pekin at the head of a large army of Manchus as well as his own Chinese. Li Tseching once more endeavoured to detach Wou Sankwei from the new allegiance he had formed, but when he found that all his overtures were treated with silent contempt he took his revenge by executing his father, and the first sight that greeted Wou Sankwei on sitting down before the town was his father's head dangling on the eastern gate. This outrage converted the struggle into one of war to the knife, but Li Tseching had no hope of being able to hold out in Pekin. His efforts were devoted to making good his escape from that place with as much of its vast booty as he could collect. In this object he was fairly successful, for, although he lost ten thousand men and part of his plunder in a battle at the Palikao Bridge, he made his way back to Shansi gathering up *en route* the garrisons he had left in different towns of Pechihli. Encouraged by these reinforcements he thought once more of tempting fortune, and with that view he took up a strong position at Chingting. He was the more induced to come to this decision because the character of his army was such that a persistent retreat would have led to its voluntary dispersal, as each individual was more of a robber than a soldier. Wou Sankwei, in close pursuit, at the head of an army of nearly 200,000 men, of whom half were Manchus, was delighted to find that Li Tseching was resolved to again appeal to the god of battles. A desperate and sanguinary encounter ensued, and after a whole day's fighting the result seemed indecisive, but Li had lost 40,000 men and he had no alternative but to beat a hasty retreat during the night, leaving his camp with much spoil in the hands of the victor. After this Li met with disaster after disaster. He was driven out of Shansi into Honan, and from Honan into Shensi. Wou Sankwei took Tunkwan without firing a shot, and when Li attempted to defend Singan he found that his soldiers would not obey his orders, and wished only to come to terms with Wou Sankwei. Expelled from the last of his towns he took refuge in the hills, but the necessity of obtaining provisions compelled him now and then to descend into the plains, and on one of these occasions he was surprised in a village and killed. His head was placed in triumph over the nearest prefecture, and thus ended the most remarkable career of a princely robber chieftain to be found in Chinese annals. At one time it seemed as if Li Tseching would be the founder of a dynasty, but his meteor-like career ended not less suddenly than his rise to supreme power was rapid. Extraordinary as was his success, Wou Sankwei had rightly gauged its nature when he declared that it had no solid basis.

The overthrow of Li Tseching paved the way for a fresh difficulty. It had been achieved to a large extent by the military genius of Wou Sankwei and by the exertions of his Chinese army. That officer had invited the Manchus into the country, but when victory was achieved he showed some anxiety for their departure. This was no part of the compact, nor did it coincide with the ambition of the Manchus. They determined to retain the territory they had conquered, at the same time that they endeavoured to propitiate Wou Sankwei and to retain the command of his useful services. He was given the high sounding title of Ping-si Wang, or Prince Pacifier of the West, and many other honours. Gratified by these rewards and unable to discover any person who could govern China, Wou Sankwei gradually reconciled himself to the situation, and performed his duty faithfully as the most powerful lieutenant of the young Manchu ruler, Chuntche, the son of Taitsong, who, after the fall of Li Tseching, removed his capital to Pekin, and assumed the style and ceremony of a Chinese Emperor. The active administration was entrusted to Prince Dorgun, brother of Taitsong, who now became known as Ama Wang, the Father Prince, and who acted as regent during the long minority of his nephew. The new dynasty was inaugurated at Pekin with a grand ceremony and court, at which Chuntche, although a mere child, delivered the following spirited address:—

"Princes, my uncles, and you illustrious generals of my armies, you have seen me ascend, with a tranquil and firm step, the throne to which you have elevated me. Do I derive that sense of security, that degree of assurance which I have exhibited from my own virtue, from my own capacity, or from my own talents? I am only a child, and your suffrages alone have constituted me your master. Too young to have yet had an opportunity to justify your choice by some exploit worthy of you, I still feel myself superior to the weakness of my age when I perceive so many heroes assembled round my throne. By your valour and wisdom you have raised our nation from obscurity to the height of power which all the kings, our neighbours, admire, and to crown the glory you have placed the Empire of China at the disposal of my family. Hence comes the confidence which you yourselves are, perhaps, surprised to find in a child. What may I no expect from your courage and experience? Already I can see myself master of all the provinces of this great Empire. Do not think that I am ambitious solely for my own ends to possess those vast estates. I desire them only in order to give peace to the many peoples who have suffered much during these later years, and also to reward your zeal and services."

After this formal and solemn assumption of the governing power in China by the young Manchu prince, the activity of the Manchus increased, and several armies were sent south to subject the provinces, and to bring the whole Chinese race under his authority. For some time no serious opposition was encountered, as the disruption of Li's forces entailed the surrender of all the territory north of the Hoangho. But at Nankin, and in the provinces south of the Yangtsekiang, an attempt had been made, and not unsuccessfully, to set up a fresh administration under one of the members of the prolific Ming family. Fou Wang, a grandson of Wanleh, was placed on the Dragon throne of southern China in this hope, but his character did not justify the faith reposed in him. He thought nothing of the serious responsibility he had accepted, but showed that he regarded his high station merely as an opportunity for gratifying his own pleasures. There is little or no doubt that if he had shown himself worthy of his station he might have rallied to his side the mass of the Chinese nation, and Wou Sankwei, who had shown some signs of chafing at Manchu authority, might have been won back by a capable and sympathetic sovereign. But notwithstanding the ability of Fou Wang's minister, Shu Kofa, who strove to repair the errors of his master, the new Ming power at Nankin did not prosper. Wou Sankwei cautious not to commit himself, rejected the patent of a duke, and the money gifts sent him by Shu Kofa, while Ama Wang, on his side, sought to gain over Shu Kofa by making him the most lavish promises of reward. But that minister proved as true to his sovereign as Wou Sankwei did to the Manchu. The result of the long correspondence between them was *nil*, but it showed the leaders of the Manchus in very favourable colours, as wishing to avert the horrors of war, and to simplify the surrender of provinces which could not be held against them. When Ama Wang discovered that there was no hope of gaining over Shu Kofa, and thus paving his way to the disintegration of the Nankin power, he decided to prosecute the war against the surviving Ming administration with the greatest activity.

While these preparations were being made to extend the Manchu conquest over central China, all was confusion at Nankin. Jealousies between the commanders, none of whom possessed much merit or experience, bickerings among the ministers, apathy on the part of the ruler, and bitter disappointment and disgust in the ranks of the people, all combined to precipitate the overthrow of the ephemeral throne that had been erected in the Southern capital. Ama Wang waited patiently to allow these causes of disintegration time to develop their full force, and to contribute to the ruin of the Mings, but in the winter of 1644-5 he decided that the right moment to strike had come. Shu Kofa made some effort to oppose the Manchu armies, and even assumed the command in person, although he was only a civilian, but his troops had no heart to oppose the Manchus, and the devices to which he resorted to make his military power appear more formidable were both puerile and ineffective. Yet one passage may be quoted to his credit if it gave his opponent an advantage. It is affirmed on good authority that he could have obtained a material advantage if he would only have flooded the country, but he "refused to do so on the ground that more civilians would perish than Manchus, and he said, 'First the people, next the dynasty.'" The sentiment was a noble one, but it was too severe a crisis to admit of any sentiment, especially when fighting an up-hill battle, and Shu Kofa, soon realising that he was not qualified to play the part of a great soldier, resolved to end his existence. He took shelter with a small force in the town of Yangchow, and when he heard that the Manchus were entering the gate, he and his officers committed suicide. The Chinese lamented and were crushed by his death. In him they saw the last of their great men, and, no doubt, they credited him with a higher capacity even than he possessed. Only a military genius of the first rank could have saved the Mings, and Shu Kofa was nothing more than a conscientious and capable civil mandarin, ignorant of war. His fortitude could only be measured by his indifference to life, and by his resolve to anticipate the fall of his sovereign as soon as he saw it to be inevitable.

Fou Wang speedily followed the fate of his faithful minister, for when the Manchus marched on Nankin, he abandoned his capital, and sought safety in flight. But one of his officers, anxious to make favourable terms for himself with the conqueror, undertook his capture, and coming up with him when on the point of entering a junk to put to sea, Fou Wang had no alternative left between an ignominious surrender and suicide. He chose the latter course, and throwing himself into the river was drowned, thus ending his own career, and the Ming dynasty in its southern capital of Nankin. The Manchus established themselves in that city, and reinstated all the Chinese officials, who agreed to shave their heads and recognise the Tartar authority. This was now obligatory on all, and even the great Wou Sankwei, who had invited the Manchus into China, had to submit to this operation. Hangchow shared the same fate as Nankin, but the Manchus sullied their success there by executing a Ming prince with whom they had negotiated for the peaceful surrender of the place. After establishing themselves on the Great River, the Manchus encountered little or no serious opposition in subduing the provinces south of it. In Fuhkien one scion of the Ming family attempted to make a stand, and, aided by a piratical chieftain, named Ching Chelong, he was not altogether unsuccessful, at least wherever it was possible to employ his ships. But the military success of the Manchus continued unchecked in the thickly populated provinces of Kiangsi, Kiangsu and Chekiang. The army of the Fuhkien confederacy was routed in the one battle it ventured to engage in, and the Manchu cavalry, operating in small bodies, occupied towns at a considerable distance from the main army, and compelled the Chinese to shave their heads in token of surrender. At Soochow, a place with a large population, a thousand Manchu horse were threatened by a large Chinese force, and as the town had not surrendered, the Tartars seemed placed at a great disadvantage, when their commander, coming to a prompt resolution, ordered every Chinaman in the place to shave his head, or lose it without an hour's delay. Cowed by this act of resolution, neither the Chinese citizens nor the Chinese force outside ventured on any further hostilities.

Meantime dissension further weakened the already discouraged Chinese forces. The pirate Ching Chelong, who was the mainstay of the Ming cause, cherished the hope that he might place his own family on the throne and he endeavoured to induce the Ming prince to recognise his son, Koshinga, as his heir. Low as he had fallen, it is to the credit of this prince that he refused to sign away the birthright of his family. Ching was bitterly chagrined at this refusal, and after detaching his forces from the other Chinese he at last came to the resolution to throw in his lot with the Manchus. He was promised honourable terms, but the Tartars seem to have had no intention of complying with them, so far at least as allowing him to retain his liberty.' For they sent him off to Pekin, where he was kept in honourable confinement, notwithstanding his protests and promises, and the defiant threats of his son Koshinga. In preserving his life he was more fortunate than the members of the Ming family, who were hunted down in a remorseless manner and executed with all their relations on capture. The only place that offered any resistance to the Manchus was the town of Kanchow, on the Kan river, in Kiangsi. The garrison defended themselves with desperate valour during two months, and a council of war was held amid much anxiety, to consider whether the siege should be abandoned. Bold counsels prevailed, and the Manchu chiefs exclaimed, "Up to this our arms have been uniformly victorious, but if we fail before this place the courage of the Chinese will revive, and the reputation which we have gained by so many glorious expeditions will be diminished. We shall have to take care also that something does not happen beyond the failure of the matter we have immediately in hand. Let us, therefore, rather ask for fresh troops to replace those we have lost, and let us collect cannon of a larger calibre than those we have hitherto employed in this siege. We shall then very soon see success crown our perseverance in having refused to abandon an enterprise which it is necessary for the glory of our nation to sustain, if we do not wish to lose in a moment the fruit of our success and the honour of our arms." The Manchus returned to the attack, and had the satisfaction of carrying the town by assault, when the garrison were put to the sword.

The relics of the Chinese armies gathered for a final stand in the city of Canton, but unfortunately for them the leaders were still divided by petty jealousies. One Ming prince proclaimed himself Emperor at Canton, and another in the adjoining province of Kwangsi. Although the Manchus were gathering their forces to overwhelm the Chinese in their last retreat, they could not lay aside their divisions and petty ambitions in order to combine against the national enemy, but must needs assail one another to decide which should have the empty title of Ming Emperor. The Manchus had the satisfaction of seeing the two rivals break their strength against each other, and then they advanced to crush the victor at Canton. Strong as the place was said to be, it offered no serious resistance, and the great commercial city of the south passed into the hands of the race who had subdued the whole country from Pekin to the Tonquin frontier. At this moment the fortune of the Manchus underwent a sudden and inexplicable change. Two repulses before a fortress south-west of Canton, and the disaffection of a large part of their Chinese auxiliaries, who clamoured for their pay, seem to have broken the strength of the advanced Manchu army. A wave of national antipathy drove the Tartars out of Canton and the southern provinces, but it soon broke its force, and the Manchus returning with fresh troops speedily recovered all they had lost, and by placing stronger garrisons in the places they occupied consolidated their hold on southern China. Although the struggle between the Manchus and their new subjects was far from concluded, the conquest of China as such may be said to have reached its end at this stage, and we may fitly conclude by reproducing what was formerly written as to its significance and causes. How a small Tartar tribe succeeded after fifty years of war in imposing its yoke on the sceptical, freedom-loving, and intensely national millions of China will always remain one of the enigmas of history. We have traced the course of these campaigns, but even while venturing to indicate some of the causes of their success, we must still come to the conclusion that the result has exceeded what would at any time during the struggle have been thought to be credible. The military genius of Wou Sankwei, the widely prevalent dissensions among the people, and the effeteness of the reigning house on the one hand, and the superior discipline, sagacity, and political knowledge of the Tartars on the other, are some of the principal causes of the Manchu success that at once suggest themselves to the mind. But in no other case has a people, boldly resisting to the end and cheered by occasional flashes of victory, been subjected after more than a whole generation of war, with a despised and truly insignificant enemy in the durable form in which the Manchus trod the Chinese under their heel, and secured for themselves all the perquisites and honour accruing to the governing class in one of the richest and largest empires under the sun. The Chinese were made to feel all the bitterness of subjection by the imposition of a hated badge of servitude, and that they proved unable to succeed under this aggravation of circumstances, greatly increases the wonder with which the Manchu conquest must ever be regarded. But the most significant feature of the Manchu conquest is that it provides a durable proof of the possibility of China being conquered by a small but determined body of men. Once Wou Sankwei had opened the door to the foreigner, the end proved easy, and was never in doubt. The Chinese were subjugated with extraordinary ease, and the only testimony to their undiminished vitality has been the quiet and silent process by which the conquerors have been compelled to assimilate themselves to the conquered.

CHAPTER X.

THE FIRST MANCHU RULER.

WHILE the Manchu generals and armies were establishing their power in southern China the young Emperor Chuntche, under the direction of his prudent uncle, the regent Ama Wang, was setting up at Pekin the central power of a ruling dynasty. In doing so little or no opposition was experienced at the hands of the Chinese, who showed that they longed once more for a settled government; and this acquiescence on the part of the Chinese people in their authority no doubt induced the Manchu leaders to adopt a far more conciliatory and lenient policy towards the Chinese than would otherwise have been the case. Ama Wang gave special orders that the lives and property of all who surrendered to his lieutenants should be scrupulously respected. This moderation was only departed from in the case of some rebels in Shensi, who, after accepting, repudiated the Manchu authority, and laid close siege to the chief town of Singan, which held a garrison of only 3,000 Manchus. The commandant wished to make his position secure by massacring the Chinese of the town, but he was deterred from taking this extreme step by the representations of a Chinese officer, who, binding himself for the good faith of his countrymen, induced him to enrol them in the ranks of the garrison. They proved faithful and rendered excellent service in the siege; and when a relieving Manchu army came from Pekin the rebels were quickly scattered and pursued with unflagging bitterness to their remotest hiding places.

In the adjoining province of Shansi another insurrection temporarily upset Manchu authority, but it was brought about by an outrage of a Manchu prince. In 1649 Ama Wang sent an embassy to the principal khan of the Mongols, with whom it was the first object of the Manchus to maintain the closest friendly relations, in order to arrange a marriage between Chuntche and a Mongol princess. The mission was entrusted to a Manchu prince, who took up his residence at Taitong, in Shansi, a place still held by a Chinese garrison under an officer named Kiangtsai. The Manchu prince and his attendants behaved in a most arrogant and overbearing manner, and at last their conduct culminated in an outrage which roused the indignation of the Chinese populace, and converted a loyal city into a hostile centre. The daughter of one of the most influential citizens of Taitong was being led through the streets in honour of her wedding day when several of the ambassador's associates broke into the procession and carried off the bride. The Chinese were shocked at this outrage, and clamoured for the prompt punishment of its perpetrators. The governor, Kiangtsai, supported the demand of the citizens, but, unfortunately, the Manchu prince was indifferent to the Chinese indignation, and made light of his comrades' conduct. Then the Chinese resolved to enact a terrible vengeance, and Kiangtsai organised a movement to massacre every Manchu in the place. He carried out his intention to the letter, and the Manchu prince was the only one to escape, thanks to the swiftness of his horse. The inevitable consequence of this act was that Kiangtsai passed from a loyal servant into a rebel. Ama Wang might have condoned his offence out of consideration for the provocation, but Kiangtsai, thinking of his own safety, decided that there was no course open to him save to pose as the enemy of the Manchu. He seems to have done everything that prudence suggested to strengthen his position, and he showed the grasp of a statesman when he turned to the Mongols and sought to obtain their alliance by begging them to restore the Empire, and to assert their national superiority over the Manchus. His policy at first promised to be signally successful, as the Mongol chief entered into his plans and promised to render him all the aid in his power. But his hopes on this score proved short-lived, for Ama Wang, realising the situation at a glance, nipped the alliance between Kiangtsai and the Mongols in the bud by sending a special embassy with exceptionally costly gifts to the Mongol camp. The cupidity of the Mongols prevailed, and they repudiated with scant ceremony the convention they had just concluded with Kiangtsai. Then the Manchus bore down from all sides on Kiangtsai, who had assumed the title of Prince of Han. He had gathered round him such a considerable force that he did not hesitate to march out to meet the Manchus, and he trusted for victory to a skilfully devised artifice as much as to superior numbers. He sent forward, under a small guard, a number of waggons containing canisters of gunpowder, and when the Tartar cavalry saw this baggage train approaching they at once concluded that it was a valuable prize, and pounced down upon it. The Chinese guard having fired the train took to flight, and the Manchus lost many men in the ensuing explosion, but the most serious consequence was that it threw the whole Manchu army into confusion, and thus enabled Kiangtsai to attack it at a disadvantage, and to overthrow it with a loss of 15,000 men. In a second battle he confirmed the verdict of the first, and it is almost unnecessary to add that the reputation of Kiangtsai was raised to a high point, and that the Manchus trembled on the throne. If the Mongols had only joined him it is impossible to say what might not have happened.

So grave did the possible consequences of these defeats appear that Ama Wang decided to take the field in person, and to proceed against Kiangtsai with the very best troops he could collect. Matters had reached such a pass that, if a general insurrection were to be averted, the Taitong rising would have to be put down without delay. Ama Wang resolved to strike promptly, yet he had the prudence to adopt Fabian tactics in front of an opponent whose confidence had been raised by two successes in the field. The opposing armies each exceeded 100,000 men, and Kiangtsai was as eager to force on a battle as Ama Wang was to avoid it. During two months there was much manœuvring and counter manœuvring, and at last Kiangtsai, apprehensive of losing Taitong by a *coup de main*, and finding his supplies failing, retired into that place, flattering himself that an enemy who feared to attack him in the open would never venture to assail him in a fortress. But the object of Ama Wang was accomplished, and he proceeded to invest the place on all sides. Then Kiangtsai realised his error, and saw that he had no alternative between fighting at a disadvantage to cut his way out and remaining besieged until the want of supplies should compel him to surrender. He chose the more valiant course, and haranguing his men in the following words he led them out to assault the Manchu lines. "I will not lose a moment in exposing to you the danger which threatens us, it must be evident to yourselves. Your valour alone can avail to secure safety for us all. Success is not impossible, but it will require a great effort of valour on your part. Who have we to fight after all? Men already weakened and discouraged by two defeats, and who so much feared a third battle that all our efforts to bring them to an engagement failed. The part which alone remains for us is not doubtful. If we must perish let it be with arms in our hands. Is it not better to sell our lives like brave men than to fall ingloriously under the steel of the Tartars?" Such was the impetuosity of the Chinese onslaught that after four hours' fighting the Manchus were driven from their first entrenchments. The Chinese were as much elated as their adversaries were depressed by this initial success, and counted on victory. A single incident served to change the fortune of the day. Kiangtsai placed himself at the head of his men to lead them to the attack of the remaining Manchu positions when he was struck in the head by an arrow. The death of their leader created a panic among the Chinese troops, who, abandoning all they had won, fled in irretrievable confusion back to Taitong, where they were more closely beleaguered than before by the Manchus. The discouraged and disorganised Chinese offered but a feeble resistance, and in a very short time the Manchus were masters of Taitong; and the most formidable Chinese gathering which had, up to that time, threatened the new dynasty was broken up. The Taitong insurgents acquired all their strength from the personal genius and ascendancy of Kiangtsai, and with his death they collapsed.

In the province of Szchuen a Chinese leader of very different character and capacity from Kiangtsai, set up an administration. He distinguished himself by his brutality, and although he proclaimed himself Si Wang, or King of the West, he was execrated by those who were nominally his subjects. Among the most heinous of his crimes was his invitation to literary men to come to his capital for employment, and when they had assembled to the number of 30,000, to order them to be massacred. He dealt in a similar manner with 3,000 of his courtiers, because one of them happened to omit a portion of his full titles. His excesses culminated in the massacre of Chentu, when 600,000 innocent persons are said to have perished. Even allowing for the Eastern exaggeration of numbers, the crimes of this inhuman monster have rarely, if ever, been surpassed. His rage or appetite for destruction was not appeased by human sacrifices. He made equal war on the objects of nature and the works of man. He destroyed cities, levelled forests, and overthrew all the public monuments that embellished his province. In the midst of his excesses he was told that a Manchu army had crossed the frontier, but he resolved to crown his inhuman career by a deed unparalleled in the records of history, and what is more extraordinary, he succeeded in inducing his followers to execute his commands. His project was to massacre all the women in attendance on his army, and his motives can only be described in his own words.

"The province of Szchuen is no more than a mass of ruins and a vast desert. I have wished to signalise my vengeance, and at the same time to detach you from the wealth which it offered, in order that your ardour for the conquest of the Empire, which I have still every hope of attaining, should not flag. The execution of my project is easy, but one obstacle which might prevent or delay the conquest I meditate disturbs my mind. An effeminate heart is not well suited to great enterprises; the only passion heroes should cherish is that of glory. All of you have wives, and the greater number of you have several in your company. These women can only prove a source of embarrassment in camp, and especially during marches or other expeditions demanding celerity of movement. Have you any apprehension lest you should not find elsewhere wives as charming and as accomplished? In a very short time I promise you others who will give us every reason to congratulate ourselves for having made the sacrifice which I propose to you. Let us, therefore, get rid of the embarrassment which these women cause us. I feel that the only way for me to persuade you in this matter is by setting you an example. Tomorrow, without further delay, I will lead my wives to the public parade. See that you are all present, and cause to be published, under most severe penalties, the order to all your soldiers to assemble there at the same time, each accompanied by his wives. The treatment I accord to mine shall be the general law."

When the assembly took place Si Wang slew his wives *coram populo*, and his followers, seized with an extreme frenzy, followed his example. It is said that as many as 400,000 women were slain that day, and Si Wang, intoxicated by his success in inducing his followers to execute his inhuman behests, believed that he had nothing to fear at the hands of the Manchus. But he was soon undeceived, for in one of the earliest affairs at the outposts he was killed by an arrow. His power at once crumbled away, and Szchuen passed under the authority of the Manchus. The conquest of Szchuen paved the way for the recovery of the position that had been lost in Southern China, and close siege was laid to the city of Canton, where the Chinese leaders had collected all their forces. The Manchus adopted the astute course of giving the highest nominal commands to Chinese, and consequently many of their countrymen surrendered to them more readily than if they had been foreigners. One officer, named Kiuchessa, who is said to have been a Christian, remained faithful to the Ming prince of Southern China until his execution, and he refused to accept a pardon as the price of his apostacy. Outside Canton the Manchus carried everything before them, and that city itself at last was captured, after what passed for a stubborn resistance. Canton was given over to pillage, and the sack continued for ten days. The Ming pretender fled to Yunnan, and afterwards into Burmah, where he enjoyed shelter for seven years. At this moment of success Ama Wang, the wise regent, died. His last years had been full of anxiety from the dangers that had arisen in the path of the Manchus, but he lived long enough to see it much allayed, and the most serious perils removed. He gave all his time and energy to improving his nephew in the work of government, and to looking after his interests. Towards the Chinese he assumed an attitude of moderation, and even of studied conciliation, which produced a beneficial effect on the public mind. To this attitude, as well as to the successful measures of his government, must be attributed the success he experienced in tranquillising the country. He was not the first nor the last of the great rulers and statesmen which the present imperial family of China has produced in the last three centuries.

Some of the elder princes of the Manchu family attempted to succeed

K

to his position, but the principal ministers and courtiers combined together and insisted that the Emperor Chuntche was old enough to rule for himself, and that they would not recognise any other master. This extreme step settled the question, and Chuntche assumed the reins of government. He at once devoted his attention to administrative reforms. It is said that corruption had begun to sway the public examinations, and that Chuntche issued a special edict, enjoining the examiners to give fair awards and to maintain the purity of the service. But several examiners had to be executed and others banished beyond the Wall before matters were placed on a satisfactory basis. He also adopted the astronomical system in force in Europe, and he appointed the priest Adam Schaal head of the Mathematical Board at Pekin. But his most important work was the institution of the Grand Council, which still exists, and which is the supreme power under the Emperor in the country. It is composed of only four members—two Manchus and two Chinese—who alone possess the privilege of personal audience with the Emperor whenever they may demand it. They are far higher in rank than any member of the Six Tribunals or the Board of Censors, whose wide liberty of expression is limited to written memorials. As this act gave the Chinese an equal place with the Manchus in the highest body of the Empire it was exceedingly welcome, and explains, among other causes, the popularity and stability of the Manchu dynasty. When allotting Chuntche his place among the founders of Manchu greatness allowance must be made for this wise and far-reaching measure, the consequences of which cannot be accurately gauged.

Another interesting event in the reign of Chuntche, was the arrival at Pekin of more than one embassy from European States. The Dutch and the Russians can equally claim the honour of having had an envoy resident in the Chinese capital during the year 1656, but in neither case could the result be described as altogether satisfactory. After some delay and difficulty and on making the required concessions to the dignity of the Emperor—which means the performance of the Kotao, or making the prostration by beating the ground with the forehead—the Dutch merchants, who were sent as envoys, were admitted to audience, but although they bribed freely, the only favour they obtained was the right to present tribute at stated intervals, which was a doubtful gain. The Emperor restricted their visit to once in every eight years, and then they were not to exceed one hundred persons, of whom only twenty might proceed to the capital. The most interesting circumstance in connection with this embassy is that it provided Nieuhoff, the *maître d'hôtel* to the envoys, with the material for a description of Pekin at a time when it had not recovered from the effects of the wars we have described. The conquest of Siberia by the Cossack Irmak had brought the Russians into immediate contact with the Chinese, and it was held desirable to establish some sort of diplomatic relations with them. An officer was accordingly sent from Siberia to Pekin, but as he persistently refused to perform the Kotao, he was denied audience, and returned without having accomplished anything. The commencement of diplomatic relations between Russia and China was therefore postponed to a later day. With Tibet Chuntche succeeded in establishing relations of a specially cordial nature, which preserve their force to the present time. In 1653 he received a visit from the Grand Lama of Lhasa, and he conferred upon him the title of Dalai, or Ocean Lama, because his knowledge was as deep and profound as the ocean. It says much for the influence of China, and the durability of the tie thus established, that the supreme Lama of Lhasa has been generally known by this title ever since its being conferred on him.

During the last years of the reign of Chuntche, the growth of the naval power of Koshinga, son of Ching Chelong, attracted considerable attention. When Canton fell, many Chinese escaped in their junks, and as the Manchus had no fleet they were unable to follow the fugitives, and the Chinese derived fresh confidence from this security at sea. The daring and activity of Koshinga became the solace and admiration of his countrymen. He first established his headquarters on the island of Tsong-ming, at the mouth of the river Yangtsekiang, and had he been content with operations along the sea-coast, he might have enjoyed immunity from attack, and an indefinite scope for plunder for many years. But his ambition led him to take an exaggerated view of his power, and, by attempting too much, he jeopardised all he had gained, and finally curtailed his sphere of enterprise. In 1656, he sailed up the river to attack Nankin, and his enterprise was so far well-timed that the Manchu garrison was then very weak, and that the chances of a popular rising in his favour were also at their highest point. But he seems to have relied for success mainly on the latter contingency, and in the desire to spare his men, he postponed his attack until the favourable opportunity had passed away, and the Manchu garrison being strongly reinforced, the townspeople were both afraid to revolt, and Koshinga to deliver his attack. When at last he nerved himself to assault the place, the Manchus anticipated his intention by delivering a night attack upon his camp, which was completely successful. Three thousand of his best men were slain, and Koshinga and the remainder were only too glad to seek shelter in their ships. The repulse at Nankin destroyed all Koshinga's dreams of posing as a national deliverer. After this episode he could only hope to be powerful as a rover of the sea, and the head of a piratical confederacy.

In 1661, the health of Chuntche became so bad that it was evident to his courtiers that his end was drawing near, although he was little more than thirty years of age. Authorities differ as to the precise cause of his death. Philippe Couplet says that it was small-pox, but the more general version was that it was grief at the death of his favourite wife and infant son. Probably his domestic affliction aggravated his malady, and nullified the efforts of his physicians. On his death-bed he selected as his successor the second of his sons, who afterwards became famous as the Emperor Kanghi, and the choice proved an exceedingly fortunate one. The reign of Chuntche was specially remarkable as witnessing the consolidation of Manchu authority, the introduction of the Chinese to a share in the administration, and the adoption of a policy of increased moderation towards the subject people.

When Kanghi was placed on the throne he was only eight years old, and the administration was consequently entrusted to four of the chief and most experienced officials. These co-regents devoted themselves to their duty with energy and intelligence. Their first act was to impeach the principal eunuchs who had acquired power under Chuntche, and to issue a decree prohibiting the employment of any of that unfortunate class in the public service. This law was engraved on iron tablets weighing more than 1,000 pounds, and the Manchu rulers have ever since remained faithful to the pledge taken by these Manchu regents in the name of the young Emperor

Kanghi. The very first year of Kanghi's reign witnessed the zenith and the fall of the power of Koshinga. After the failure of his attack on Nankin, Koshinga fixed his designs on the island of Formosa, which offered, as it seemed, the best vantage ground for a naval confederacy such as he controlled. In order to carry out this plan, Koshinga had to oust, not the aboriginal tribes who held most of the interior of the island, but the Dutch traders who had seized most of the ports and had fortified them. Koshinga found willing allies in the Chinese emigrants who had fled from the mainland to Formosa. They rose up against the Dutch, and before they were subdued the warlike aboriginal tribes had to be recruited against them. But the Dutch, who had been on the island for 35 years, flattered themselves that they could hold their own, and that it might not be impossible to live on friendly terms with Koshinga. They themselves had acquired their place in Formosa by the retirement of the Japanese from Taiwan, in 1624, when the Dutch, driven away by the Portuguese from Macao, sought a fresh site for their proposed settlement in the Pescadore group, and eventually established themselves at Fort Zealand. The Dutch seem to have been lulled into a sense of false security by their success over the Chinese settlers, and to have believed that Koshinga was not as formidable as he was considered to be. Koshinga did not strike until all his plans were completed, and then he laid siege to Fort Zealand. The Dutch fought well, but they were overpowered, and lost their possessions, which passed to the Chinese adventurer. Koshinga assumed the style of King of Formosa, but he did not long survive this triumph. In the year after this conquest he died of a malady which was aggravated by resentment at the insubordination of his eldest son, and thus terminated his remarkable career when he was no more than 38. The Chinese province of Formosa endured for another twenty years, but its spirit and formidableness departed with Koshinga. In his relations with the English and Dutch merchants he showed all the prejudice and narrow-mindedness of his countrymen.

One of the earliest incidents in the reign of Kanghi was an agitation got up by some of the most bigoted courtiers, and fanned by popular ignorance and fanaticism, against the Christian priests, who, as has been mentioned, had obtained various posts under the Chinese government. They had not been very successful as the propagators of religion, but they had undoubtedly rendered the Chinese valuable service as mathematicians and men of science. The Emperor Chuntche had treated them with marked consideration, and there was little to cause surprise in this favour being resented by the Chinese officials, and in their intriguing to discredit and injure the foreigners whose knowledge was declared to be superior to their own. They formulated a charge against them of "propagating a false and monstrous religion," which was easily understood and difficult to refute. The Abbé Schaal was deposed from the Presidentship of the Mathematical Board, and cast into prison. The other Europeans were also incarcerated. They were all tried on a common charge, and, the case being taken as proved, all condemned to a common death. The only respite granted between sentence and execution was for the purpose of discovering some specially cruel mode of execution that might be commensurate to the offence, not merely of being a Christian, but of holding offices that were the prescriptive right of the followers of Confucius. The delay thus obtained enabled one of the regents, named Sony, and a man of an en-

lightened and noble mind, to take steps to save these victims of ignorance.
Supported by the mother of Kanghi, he succeeded in gaining his point,
and in obtaining a reversal of the iniquitous sentence of ignorant jealousy,
but the reprieve came too late to save the life of the Abbé Schaal, who
escaped the public executioner, only to perish from the consequences of
his sufferings in prison. Unfortunately, Sony did not live long after this for
his country to profit by his clemency, or to display it in other acts of the
government. It was during these incidents that the young Emperor Kanghi
gave the first indication of his capacity to judge important matters for
himself, by deciding after personal examination that the astronomical system of Europe was superior to that of China, and by appointing Father
Verbiest to succeed the Abbé Schaal.

The death of the regent Sony threatened not merely disorders within
the supreme administration, but an interruption of the good work of the
government itself. Kanghi, with no doubt the support of his mother,
solved the difficulty by assuming the personal direction of affairs, although he
was then only fourteen years of age. Such a bold step undoubtedly betokened
no ordinary vigour on the part of a youth, and its complete success reflected
still further credit upon him. He seems to have been specially impelled to
take this step by his disapproval of the tyrannical and overbearing conduct
of another of his regents, Baturu Kong, who had only been kept in check
by the equal influence of Sony, and who promised himself on his rival's
death a course of unbridled power. Baturu Kong had taken the most
prominent part in the agitation against the Christians, and the success of
his schemes would have signified the undoing of much of the good work
accomplished during the first twenty years of Manchu power. The
vigilance and resolution of the young Emperor thwarted his plans. By an
imperial decree the regency was dissolved, and Kong was indicted on
twelve separate charges, each sufficient to receive the punishment of death.
A verdict of guilty was returned, and he and his family suffered the
supreme punishment for treason. This act of vigour inaugurated the reign
of Kanghi, and the same resolution and courage characterised it to the
end. In this early assertion of sovereign power, as in much else, it will be
seen that Kanghi bore a striking resemblance to his great contemporary,
Louis the Fourteenth of France.

The interest of the period now passes from the scenes at Court to the
camp of Wou Sankwei, who, twenty years earlier, had introduced the
Manchus into China. During the Manchu campaign in Southern China
he had kept peace on the western frontier, gradually extending his authority
from Shensi into Szchuen and thence over Yunnan. When the Ming
prince, Kwei Wang, who had fled into Burmah, returned with the support of
the King of that country to make another bid for the throne, he found himself confronted by all the power and resources of Wou Sankwei, who was
still as loyal a servant of the Manchu Emperor as when he carried his
ensigns against Li Tseching. Kwei Wang does not appear to have expected
opposition from Wou Sankwei, and in the first encounter he was overthrown and taken prisoner. The conqueror, who was already under suspicion at the Manchu Court, and whom every Chinese rebel persisted in
regarding as a natural ally, now hesitated as to how he should treat these
important prisoners. Kwei Wang and his son—the last of the Mings—
were eventually led forth to execution, although it should be stated that a less
authentic report affirms they were allowed to strangle themselves. Having

made use of Wou Sankwei, and obtained as they thought the full value of his services, the Manchus sought to treat him with indifference and to throw him into the shade. But the splendour of his work was such that they had to confer on him the title of Prince, and to make him Viceroy of Yunnan and the adjacent territories. He exerted such an extraordinary influence over the Chinese subjects that they speedily settled down under his authority; revenue and trade increased, and the Manchu authority was maintained without a Tartar garrison, for Wou Sankwei's army was composed exclusively of Chinese, and its nucleus was formed by his old garrison of Ningyuen and Shanhaikwan. There is no certain reason for saying that Wou Sankwei nursed any scheme of personal aggrandisement, but the measures he took and the reforms he instituted were calculated to make his authority become gradually independent of Manchu control. For a time the Manchu Government suppressed its apprehensions on account of this powerful satrap, by the argument that in a few years his death in the course of nature must relieve it from this peril, but Wou Sankwei lived on and showed no signs of paying the common debt of humanity. Then it seemed to Kanghi that Wou Sankwei was gradually establishing the solid foundation of a formidable and independent power. The Manchu generals and ministers had always been jealous of the greater fame of Wou Sankwei. When they saw that Kanghi wanted an excuse to fall foul of him, they carried every tale of alleged self-assertion on the part of the Chinese Viceroy to the Imperial ears, and represented that his power dwarfed the dignity of the Manchu throne and threatened its stability.

At last Kanghi resolved to take some decisive step to bring the question to a climax, and he accordingly sent Wou Sankwei an invitation to visit him at Pekin. This was in 1671, when Kanghi had reached the age of eighteen. There was nothing unreasonable in this request, for Wou Sankwei had not visited Pekin since the accession of Kanghi, and any tender of allegiance had been made by deputy. It was the practice of the time that all the great governors should have a son or other near relative at the Manchu Court as a hostage for their good conduct, and a son of Wou Sankwei resided in this character at Pekin. He had been treated with special honour by the Manchu rulers, and was married to a half sister of the Emperor Kanghi. He received the title of a Royal Duke, and was admitted into the intimate life of the Palace. When he heard of the invitation to his father he sent off a message to him, warning him of the disfavour into which he had fallen, and advising him not to come to Pekin. The advice, although prompted by affection, was not good, but Wou Sankwei took it, and excused himself from going to Court on the ground that he was very old, and that his only wish was to end his days in peace. He also deputed his son to tender his allegiance to the Emperor and to perform the Kotao in his name. But Kanghi was not to be put off in this way, and he sent two trusted officials to Wou Sankwei to represent that he must comply with the exact terms of his command, and to point out the grave consequences of his refusing. There is no doubt that they were also instructed to observe how far Wou Sankwei was borne down by age, and what was the extent of his military power. The envoys were received with every courtesy and befitting honour, but when they repeated Kanghi's categorical demand to come to Pekin on penalty of being otherwise treated as a rebel, he broke loose from the restraint he had long placed upon himself, and there and then repudiated the Manchu authority in the most indignant and irrevocable terms, which at least exposed the hollowness of his statement that he felt the weight of years and thought only of making a peaceful end. His reply to the envoys of Kanghi was as follows :—" Do they think at the Court that I am so blind as not to see the motive in this order of summons? I shall, indeed, present myself there if you continue to press me, but it will be at the head of twice forty thousand men. You may go on before, but I hope to follow you very shortly with such a force as will speedily remind those in power of the debt they owe me." Thus did the great Wou Sankwei cast off his allegiance to the Manchus, and enter upon a war which aimed at the subversion of their authority. Such was the reputation of this great commander, to whose ability and military prowess the Manchus unquestionably were indebted for their conquest of the empire, that a large part of southern China at once admitted his authority, and from Szchuen to the warlike province of Hunan his lieutenants were able to collect all the fighting resources of the State, and to array the levies of those provinces in the field for the approaching contest with Kanghi.

While Wou Sankwei was making these extensive preparations in the south, his son at Pekin had devised an ingenious and daring plot for the massacre of the Manchus and the destruction of the dynasty. He engaged in his scheme the large body of Chinese slaves who had been placed in servitude under their Tartar conquerors, and these, incited by the hope of liberty, proved very ready tools to his designs. They bound themselves together by a solemn oath to be true to one another, and all the preparations were made to massacre the Manchus on the occasion of the New Year's Festival. This is the grand religious and social ceremony of the Chinese. It takes place on the first day of the first moon, which falls in our month of February. All business is stopped, the tribunals are closed for ten days, and a state of high festival resembling the Carnival prevails. The conspirators resolved to take advantage of this public holiday, and of the excitement accompanying it to carry out their scheme, and the Manchus appear to have been in total ignorance until the eleventh hour of the plot for their destruction. The discovery of the conspiracy bears a close resemblance to that of the Gunpowder Plot. A Chinese slave, wishing to save his master, gave him notice of the danger, and this Manchu officer at once informed Kanghi of the conspiracy. The son of Wou Sankwei and the other conspirators were immediately arrested and executed without delay. The Manchus thus escaped by the merest accident from a danger which threatened them with annihilation, and Kanghi, having succeeded in getting rid of the son, concentrated his power and attention on the more difficult task of grappling with the father.

But the power and reputation of Wou Sankwei were so formidable that Kanghi resolved to proceed with great caution, and the Emperor began his measures of offence by issuing an edict ordering the disbandment of all the native armies maintained by the Chinese Viceroys, besides Wou Sankwei. The object of this edict was to make all the governors of Chinese race to show their hands, and Kanghi learnt the full measure of the hostility he had to cope with by every governor from the sea coast of Fuhkien to Canton defying him, and throwing in their lot with Wou Sankwei. The piratical confederacy of Formosa, where Ching, the son of Koshinga, had succeeded to his authority, also joined in with what may be called the national party, but its alliance proved of little value, as Ching, at an early period, took umbrage at his reception by a Chinese official, and returned to his island home. But the most formidable danger to the young Manchu ruler came from an unexpected quarter. The Mongols, seeing his embarrassment, and believing that the hours of the dynasty were numbered, resolved to take advantage of the occasion to push their claims. Satchar, chief of one of the Banners, issued a proclamation, calling his race to his side, and declaring his intention to invade China at the head of 100,000 men. It seemed hardly possible for Kanghi to extricate himself from his many dangers. With great quickness of perception Kanghi saw that the most pressing danger was that from the Mongols, and he sent the whole of his northern garrisons to attack Satchar before the Mongol clans could have gathered to his assistance. The Manchu cavalry, by a rapid march, surprised Satchar in his camp, and carried him and his family off as prisoners to Pekin. The capture of their chief discouraged the Mongols and interrupted their plans for invading China. Kanghi thus obtained a respite from what seemed his greatest peril. Then he turned his attention to dealing with Wou Sankwei, and the first effort of his armies resulted in the recovery of Fuhkien, where the governor and Ching had reduced themselves to a state of exhaustion by a contest inspired by personal jealousy, not patriotism. From Fuhkien his successful lieutenants passed into Kwantung, and the Chinese, seeing that the Manchus were not sunk as low as had been thought, abandoned all resistance, and again recognised the Tartar authority. The Manchus did not dare to punish the rebels except in rare instances, and, therefore, the recovery of Canton was unaccompanied by any scenes of blood. But a garrison of Manchus was placed in each town of importance, and it was by Kanghi's order that a walled town, or "Tartar city," was built within each city for the accommodation and security of the dominant race.

But nothwithstanding these successes Kanghi made little or no progress against the main force of Wou Sankwei, whose supremacy was undisputed throughout the whole of south-west China. It was not until 1677 that Kanghi ventured to move his armies against Wou Sankwei in person. Although he obtained no signal success in the field the divisions among the Chinese commanders were such that he had the satisfaction of compelling them to evacuate Hunan, and when Wou Sankwei took his first step backwards the sun of his fortunes began to set. Calamity rapidly followed calamity. Wou Sankwei had not known the meaning of defeat in his long career of fifty years, but now, in his old age, he saw his affairs in inextricable confusion. His adherents deserted him, many rebel officers sought to come to terms with the Manchus, and Kanghi's armies gradually converged on Wou Sankwei from the east and the north. Driven out of Szchuen Wou Sankwei endeavoured to make a stand in Yunnan. He certainly succeeded in prolonging the struggle down to the year 1679, when his death put a sudden end to the contest, and relieved Kanghi from much anxiety, for although the success of the Manchus was no longer uncertain, the military skill of the old Chinese warrior might have indefinitely prolonged the war. Wou Sankwei was one of the most conspicuous, and attractive figures to be met with in the long course of Chinese history, and his career covered one of the most critical periods in the modern existence of that empire. From the time of his first distinguishing himself in the defence of Ningyuen until he died, half a century later, as Prince of Yunnan, he occupied the very foremost place in the minds of his fellow-countrymen. The part he had taken, first in keeping out the Manchus, and then in introducing them into the State, reflected equal credit on his ability and his patriotism. In requesting the Manchus to crush the robber Li and to take the throne which the fall of the Mings had rendered vacant, he was actuated by the purest motives. There was only a choice of evils, and he selected that which seemed the less. He gave the empire to a foreign ruler of intelligence, but he saved it from an unscrupulous robber. He played the part of king-maker to the family of Noorhachu, and the magnitude of their obligations to him could not be denied. They were not as grateful as he may have expected, and they looked askance at his military power and influence over his countrymen. Probably he felt that he had not been well treated, and chagrin undoubtedly induced him to reject Kanghi's request to proceed to Pekin. If he had only acceded to that arrangement he would have left a name for conspicuous loyalty and political consistency in the service of the great race, which he had been mainly instrumental in placing over China. But even as events turned out he was one of the most remarkable personages the Chinese race ever produced, and his military career shows that they are capable of producing great generals and brave soldiers.

The death of Wou Sankwei signified the overthrow of the Chinese uprising which had threatened to extinguish the still growing power of the Manchu under its youthful Emperor Kanghi. Wou Shufan the grandson of that prince endeavoured to carry on the task of holding Yunnan as an independent territory, but by the year 1681 his possessions were reduced to the town of Yunnanfoo, where he was closely besieged by the Manchu forces. Although the Chinese fought valiantly, they were soon reduced to extremities, and the Manchus carried the place by storm. The garrison were massacred to the last man, and Wou Shufan only avoided a worse fate by committing suicide. The Manchus not satisfied with his death, sent his head to Pekin to be placed on its principal gate in triumph, and the body of Wou Sankwei himself was exhumed so that his ashes might be scattered in each of the eighteen provinces of China as a warning to traitors. Having crushed their most redoubtable antagonist, the Manchus resorted to more severe measures against those who had surrendered in Fuhkien and Kwantung, and many insurgent chiefs who had surrendered, and enjoyed a brief respite, ended their lives under the knife of the executioner. The Manchu soldiers are said to have been given spoil to the extent of nearly two millions sterling, and the war which witnessed the final assertion of Manchu power over the Chinese was essentially popular with the soldiers who carried it on to a victorious conclusion. A very short time after the final overthrow of Wou Sankwei and his family, the Chinese *régime* in Formosa was brought to an end. Kanghi, having collected a fleet, and concluded a convention with the Dutch, determined on the invasion and conquest of Formosa. In the midst of these preparations Ching, the son of Koshinga died, and, no doubt, the plans of Kanghi were facilitated by the confusion that followed. The Manchu fleet seized Ponghu, the principal island of the Pescadore group and thence the Manchus threw a force into Formosa. It is said that they were helped by a high tide, and by the superstition of the islanders, who exclaimed, "The first Wang (Koshinga), got possession of Taiwan by a high tide. The fleet now comes in the same manner. It is the will of Heaven." Formosa accepted the supremacy of the Manchus without further ado. Those of the islanders who had ever recognised the authority of any government, accepted that of the Emperor

Kanghi, shaved their heads in token of submission, and became so far as in them lay respectable citizens.

The overthrow of Wou Sankwei and the conquest of Formosa completed what may be called the pacification of China by the Manchus. From that period to the Taeping rebellion, or for nearly 200 years, there was no internal insurrection on a large scale. On the whole the Manchus stained their conclusive triumph by few excesses, and Kanghi's moderation was scarcely inferior to that of his father, Chuntche. The family of Wou Sankwei seems to have been rooted out more for the personal attempt of the son at Pekin than for the bold ambition of the potentate himself. The family of Koshinga was spared, and its principal representative received the patent of an earl. Thus, by a policy judiciously combined of severity and moderation, did Kanghi make himself supreme, and complete the work of his race. Whatever troubles may have beset the government in the last 220 years it will be justifiable to speak of the Manchus and the Tatsing dynasty as the legitimate authorities in China, and instead of foreign adventurers, as the national and recognised rulers of the Middle Kingdom.

CHAPTER XI.

THE EMPEROR KANGHI.

The overthrow of Wou Sankwei and the pacification of Southern China did not terminate the anxiety Kanghi felt as to the security of his position, and, indeed, he was engaged until the end of his long reign in unceasing efforts to confirm the stability of the dynasty and to impress upon his subjects and neighbours that the Chinese Empire could best be controlled and held together by a Manchu ruler. Kanghi was the first Chinese ruler in modern times to define a policy for dealing with the ever-recurring danger from the tribes and warlike races of Central Asia; and as his policy has been consistently carried on by his successors it claims careful consideration. The attention of Kanghi seems to have been first attracted to the gravity of the question by the outbreak of Satchar, whose project threatened the very existence of the Manchu Government. That danger was averted by the promptitude of the Emperor's measures; but Kanghi, seeing that it might at any time recur, resolved to take steps to provide against it, even though the decision compelled him to interfere in the affairs of the more remote States of Central Asia. It was only by a policy of vigour and constant attention that he could hope to maintain control over the innumerable tribes beyond the Wall, who had looked upon China from time immemorial as their legitimate prey. Even the Mongols, who had been the allies of the Manchus in their invasions of China, could not be kept true to their allegiance—such, at least, was the teaching of Satchar's revolt—and of the other tribes who had never held any relations with the Manchus, it would have been absurd to expect anything but the indulgence of their natural predatory instincts.

Among the Mongol tribes the noblest at this period were the Khalkas. They prided themselves on being the descendants of the house of Genghis, the representatives of the special clan of the great conqueror, and the occupants of the original home in the valleys of the Onon and Kerulon. Although their military power was slight, the name of the Khalka princes stood high among the Mongol tribes, and they exercised an influence far in excess of their numbers or capacity as a fighting force. Kanghi determined to establish friendly relations with this clan, and by the despatch of friendly letters and costly presents he succeeded in inducing the Khalka chiefs to enter into formal alliance with himself, and to conclude a treaty of amity with China, which be it noted they faithfully observed. Kanghi's efforts in this direction, which may have been dictated by apprehension at the movements of his new neighbours, the Russians, were thus crowned with success, and the adhesion of the Khalkas signified that the great majority of the Mongols would thenceforth abstain from acts of unprovoked aggression on the Chinese frontier. But the advance of China and her influence, even in the form of paying homage to the Emperor as the Bogdo Khan, or the Celestial Ruler, so far west as the upper course of the Amour, involved the Pekin Government in fresh complications by bringing it into contact with tribes and peoples of whom it had no cognizance. Beyond the Khalkas were the Eleuths, supreme in Ili and Kashgaria, and divided into four hordes, who obeyed as many chiefs. They had had some relations with the Khalkas, but of China they knew nothing more than the greatness of her name. When the surrender of the Khalka princes became known the Eleuth chiefs held a grand assembly or kuriltai, and at this it was finally, and, indeed, ostentatiously, decided not to yield Kanghi his demands. Important as this decision was, it derived increased weight from the character of the man who was mainly instrumental in inducing the Eleuths to take it.

Much has been written of the desert chiefs from Yenta to Yakoob Beg, but none of these showed greater ability or attained more conspicuous success than Galdan, who strained the power of China, and fought for many years on equal terms with the Emperor Kanghi. Galdan was the younger son of the most powerful chief of the Eleuths; but his ambition chafed at the inferior position assigned him by his birth. He slew his elder brother, and fled the paternal encampment, but he still preserved his original hope of being supreme over the whole Eleuth confederacy. He fled to Tibet, where he showed a wish to enter a lamasery, but the Dalai Lama refused to admit a murderer whose hands were still red with the blood of a brother. After a brief stay at Lhasa, Galdan determined to return to his own people, and to risk the revenge or justice that might await him for having slain his brother. But on his arrival he was pleasantly surprised to find that his absence had cast his crime into oblivion, and that such was the reputation of the Dalai Lama that the mere fact of his having lived in his presence sufficed to expiate his offence. There is no doubt that Galdan and the Dalai Lama established a close political alliance, for the latter induced the Eleuth chief to take up the cause of a particular prince in Kashgaria, and to place him in possession of that country. This was after Galdan had asserted his supreme authority over the Eleuths by massacring all the members of his family whom he thought he had any reason for deeming his enemies. After this extreme step the Eleuths recognised the supremacy of Galdan without further demur. One of Galdan's first steps after the recognition of his authority was to send a mission to the Chinese court, nominally of congratulation, but really of enquiry. It arrived when the rebellion of Wou Sankwei was in progress, and when the resources of the Emperor seemed over-taxed. There is nothing unlikely in Galdan's envoys having brought him back word that Kanghi was scarcely able to hold his own in China, and that there was no danger from this quarter. He had been meditating over the two policies, of being the friend and ally of China, or of being its foe; and this mission had the effect of determining him to take the final and irrevocable step of declaring war on China, and of endeavouring to reassert the natural privilege of a desert chief to harry the borders of the great Chinese Empire.

Having once decided upon his course, Galdan lost no time in putting his army in the field. He determined that the easiest and most advantageous beginning for his enterprise would be to attack his neighbours the

Khalkas, who, by accepting Kanghi's offers, had made themselves the advanced guard of China in Central Asia. He began a systematic encroachment into their lands in the year 1679, but at the same time he resorted to every device to screen his movements from the Chinese Court, and such was the delay in receiving intelligence, and the ignorance of the situation beyond the border, that in the very year of his beginning to attack the Khalkas, his envoy at Pekin received a flattering reception at the hands of Kanghi, still hopeful of a peaceful settlement, and returned with the seal and patent of a Khan. Events had not reached a state of open hostility three years later, when Kanghi sent special envoys to the camp of Galdan, as well as to the Khalkas. They were instructed to promise and pay much, but to rest content with nothing short of the formal acceptance by all the chiefs of the supremacy of China. Galdan, bound by the laws of hospitality, nowhere more sacred than in the East, gave them an honourable reception, and lavished upon them the poor resources he commanded. In hyperbolic terms he declared that the arrival of an embassy from the rich and powerful Chinese Emperor in his poor State would be handed down as the most glorious event of his reign. But he refused to make any tender of allegiance, or to subscribe himself as a Chinese vassal. The dissensions among the Khalka princes assisted the development of Galdan's ambition, and added to the anxiety of the Chinese ruler. Kanghi admonished them to heal their differences and to abstain from an internecine strife, which would only facilitate their conquest by Galdan and he succeeded so far that he induced them to swear a peace among themselves before an image of Buddha.

At this juncture the Chinese came into collision with the Russians on the Amour, and a brief account must be given of so interesting an incident. The Russians had built a fort at Albazin, on the upper course of that river, and the Chinese army located in the Khalka country, considering its proximity a menace to their own security, attacked it in overwhelming force. Albazin was taken, and those of the garrison who fell into the hands of the Chinese were carried off to Pekin, where, strangely enough, their descendants still reside as a distinct Russian colony. But when the Chinese evacuated Albazin the Russians returned there with characteristic obstinacy, and Kanghi, becoming anxious at the increasing activity of Galdan, accepted the overtures of the Russian authorities in Siberia, who, in 1688, sent the son of the Governor-General of Eastern Siberia to Pekin to negotiate a peace. After twelve months' negotiation, protracted by the outbreak of war with Galdan, the Treaty of Nerchinsk, the first concluded between China and any European Power, was signed, and the brief and only war between Russia and China was thus brought to a speedy and satisfactory termination. The Russians agreed to the destruction of Fort Albazin, but they were allowed to build another at Nerchinsk.

There is reason to believe that Galdan thought that he might derive some advantage from the complications with Russia, for his military movements were hastened when he heard that the two Powers were embroiled on the Amour, and he proclaimed his intention of invading the Khalka region, because some of their people had murdered his kinsmen. There does not seem to have been much truth in the allegation, but it served its purpose as a justification for the declaration of war. Galdan had long fixed on the Khalkas as the object through whom he could best injure Kanghi, and from this point of view one excuse for invading their territory was as good as another. Even then the Chinese seem to have remained in strange and inexplicable ignorance of Galdan's plans. Chepsuntanpa, one of the leading Khalka princes, upon whom Kanghi had conferred the title of Kutuktoo, was the first to send the Chinese certain intelligence of Galdan's advance. He wrote that Galdan had marched at the head of 30,000 men, and that unless assistance were promptly sent it would be impossible to escape the yoke of the Eleuths. Kanghi, fully aroused to the situation, ordered eight of the Mongol Banners to take the field with all their contingents, and at the same time he moved westwards part of the Leaoutung garrison and some of his own chosen Manchu troops. But time was an essential element in the situation, and the distance from Pekin to Ourga, which was the centre of the threatened territory, is vast. Galdan soon proved himself the most active of enemies. Never throwing away a chance, Galdan endeavoured, and not unsuccessfully, to enlist the support of the Dalai Lama of Tibet, by piquing his vanity at the patronage extended by the Emperor Kanghi to the Kutuktoo of Ourga, who was already becoming known as the Taranath Lama of the Mongols. The Dalai Lama went so far as to send an envoy to Pekin, advising the Emperor to come to terms with Galdan, by throwing over the Kutuktoo, and allowing the Eleuth prince to wreak his vengeance on him. But Kanghi turned aside these specious representations by merely remarking that it was not worthy of a great prince to abandon the unfortunate. He offered all Khalka fugitives free lands and shelter within the Kirong boundary, pending his preparations to carry the war into Central Asia. With a view to giving his authority greater consistency, and also to strengthening the position of the Khalkas themselves, he decreed that there should only be two chiefs over the whole of the Khalka tribes, and that they should be appointed by himself.

At this moment, when fortune seemed to promise Galdan a complete and unqualified triumph, the unexpected attack of his own nephew effected a diversion in his rear which interrupted the progress of his career. Galdan had begun his career with the murder of his brother Tsenka, and Tsenka's son, Tse Wang Rabdan, devoted himself to the avengement of his father's death. He was the more incited to this course because Galdan had carried off his affianced bride; and his victory in 1689 over the troops of the Eleuth prince was the first act in the working out of a drama of family vengeance. This reverse did not induce Galdan to seriously modify his policy, for in 1690 he seized the Chinese envoys resident at his Court as hostages, and at last convinced Kanghi that there was no possibility of maintaining any pacific relations with him. In a final letter of remonstrance the Chinese ruler, after expatiating on his efforts to preserve the peace, said: "If you compel me to draw the sword from the scabbard I shall not sheathe it again until I have exacted vengeance for the contempt with which you have treated my advice." The remonstrances of the Emperor produced no effect, and he accordingly placed three armies in the field, and ordered them to march with all despatch into the Khalka country. Galdan, expert in desert warfare, succeeded in evading their pursuit but his position was rendered insecure by the menacing attitude of his nephew Tse Wang Rabdan. In this position Galdan endeavoured to conclude an alliance with the Russians, who sent an officer to his camp; but they soon came to the determination that it would be more advantageous to keep on friendly terms with the Chinese than to embark on a hazardous adventure with the chief of an Asiatic horde. The mere rumour of a possible alliance between Galdan and the Russians roused Kanghi to increased activity, and all the picked troops of the Eight Manchu Banners, the Forty-nine Mongol Banners, and the Chinese auxiliaries, were despatched across the steppe to bring the Napoleon of Central Asia to reason. In face of this formidable danger Galdan showed undiminished courage and energy. Realising the peril of inaction, he did not hesitate to assume the offensive, and the war began with a victory he gained over a general named Horni, within the limits of Chinese territory. The moral of this success was that it showed that Kanghi had not decided a moment too soon in resorting to extreme measures against the ambitious potentate who found the Gobi desert and the surrounding region too circumscribed for his ambition.

Kanghi entrusted the chief command of his armies to his brother, Yu Tsing Wang, who justified his appointment by bringing the Eleuth forces speedily to an engagement, and by gaining a more or less decisive victory over them at Oulan Poutong. The loss was considerable on both sides, among the imperial officers killed being an uncle of the Emperor, but Galdan's forces suffered a great deal more during the retreat than they had done in the action. After this disaster Galdan signed a treaty with the Chinese commander, Yu Tsing Wang. At first he attempted to gain an advantage by excluding his personal enemies, the Khalkas, from it, but the Chinese were not to be entrapped into any such arrangement, and, standing up for their dependents, the provisions of the treaty provided equally for their safety, and for the acceptance by Galdan of the supremacy of China. This new arrangement or treaty was concluded in 1690, but Kanghi himself seems to have placed no great faith in the sincerity of Galdan, and to have regarded it merely as a truce. This view was soon found to be correct, for neither side laid aside their arms, and the unusual vigilance of the Chinese gave Galdan additional cause for umbrage. Kanghi showed that he was resolved not to let the terms, to which Galdan had subscribed, become a dead letter. He summoned a great assemblage of the Khalka tribes on the plain of Dolonor—the Seven Springs near Changtu—and he attended it in person, bestowing gifts and titles with a lavish hand. Kanghi was thus able to convince himself that, so far as the Mongol tribes were concerned, he might count on their loyalty and support. He then began to establish an understanding with Tse Wang Rabdan, and thus obtain an ally in the rear of Galdan. This latter circumstance was the direct cause of the second war with Galdan, for Kanghi's ambassador was waylaid and murdered in the neighbourhood of Hami. The outrage for which, whether he inspired it or not, Galdan was held blameworthy, aroused the strongest resentment and anger of Kanghi, who addressed him in the following terms:—

"I learnt that, notwithstanding your oaths, you and Tse Wang Rabdan cannot live at peace with one another; the instant I was informed of your disagreements, I took steps to remove them. I sent one of the officers of my tribunal to be the bearer of words of peace, and your people, like mere savages, have committed the inhuman act of massacreing him! I call upon you to judge whether an act so atrocious does not demand vengeance, and whether it can be approved of by a prince who ought to set his subjects an example of morality. The letter which my envoy, Mati, was bearing to Tse Wang Rabdan has, without doubt, fallen into your hands; with what shame ought you not to have been overwhelmed when you read it? You have violated with effrontery the rights of mankind. The ambassadors of princes, even though they may be at open war, are among all nations regarded as sacred persons. After the battle of Oulan Poutong, how did I act towards your envoys? Have you the slightest ground for complaint at the manner in which I treated them? . . . You ask me to send back the Khalkas to their ancient home! What? You demand that I should again place them at the mercy of an implacable enemy? What opinion would you have of my humanity? Recall the oath with which you sealed our last treaty of peace. Would you then refuse to recognize myself as your sovereign, and the Dalai Lama as your spiritual head? You no longer respect either his counsel or my commands. What ought I to think of conduct which proclaims you false to both your oath and your allegiance? I now desire to finally warn you that unless your repentance follows close upon your fault, I shall come with arms in my hands to exact from you the fullest reparation for so many outrages."

The reference in Kanghi's letter to the vain admonitions of the Dalai Lama is explained by the quarrel between Galdan and that saintly personage whom Kanghi had satisfied on the subject of his patronage of the Kutuktoo. When Galdan found that the High Priest of Tibet would not be subservient to his policy, he determined to repudiate his authority and to change his religion. At that time the Mahomedan Church had made many converts among the tribes on the western borders of China and even within its limits, and the whole of Central Asia was occupied by warlike races, who were among the most energetic propagators of Islam. Galdan, believing that he would thereby obtain useful and powerful allies, proclaimed himself a Mahomedan, and endeavoured to impart a religious character to his war with China. This fresh move filled the Chinese monarch with considerable apprehension, and while he denounced Galdan as having "made ambition his only god, sacrificing to it even the religion of his fathers," he drew up a plan of campaign which, he trusted, would bring Galdan within reach of his power. In 1695 Kanghi, taking the Kortsin Mongols into his confidence, proposed to them that they should pretend to come to a secret understanding with Galdan, and in an interview with their chiefs he thus unfolded his design.

"Galdan, you are well aware, has long trampled on all the laws of honour and of honesty; wicked, deceitful, and turbulent of character we could never hope for tranquillity so long as he survives. I have sworn his ruin; I owe it both to my glory, and also to my people whom he has annoyed and oppressed. This is the object of the great war preparations which at present occupy me. I know that the news will no sooner have reached him than he will seek to escape us by flight, and that he will only await the withdrawal of my troops to recommence his hostilities. And here is the plan which, after the experience I have had of his conduct, I have resolved upon, in order to circumvent this wicked man. I have learnt that Galdan has solicited your alliance: you must assume the appearance of complying with his request; write and tell him that you are at his disposal with your ten banners, and that on his approaching the frontiers of the Empire you will pass over to his side. I have no doubt that he will fall into the trap, when, suddenly attacking him, with all our troops, we shall indubitably take him prisoner."

Kanghi made extraordinary preparations for this campaign. He placed four armies in the field numbering about 150,000 combatants, and it has been computed that with non-combatants, the total of men employed did not fall short of a million. The first of these armies numbered 35,600 men, and was entrusted to Feyanku, the Ney of the Manchu army. Kanghi took personal command of the second, and its strength is given at 37,700 men; and the third army, 35,400 men, was placed under the orders of Sapsu. The fourth army of unstated but greatest numerical strength of all acted as the reserve force for the others, and did not, properly speaking, come into action at all. In order to render the war popular Kanghi offered special pay to the soldiers, and undertook to provide for the widows and orphans of those slain. At the same time Kanghi neglected no precaution to ensure the success of his arms. He provided cotton armour which was proof to the bullet for his cavalry and part of his infantry, and he organised a corps of artillerists mounted on camels, which also carried the light pieces, and rendered good service as "flying artillery." Before setting out for the campaign, the Emperor reviewed his army, and he chose for the occasion the date of the popular Feast of Lanterns, when all China takes a holiday. After the inspection of the numerous, and well equipped army, an impressive ceremony took place. Feyanku approached his sovereign, and received at his hands a cup of wine which the general took whilst on his knees, and which, on descending from the steps of the throne, he quaffed in full view of the spectators. Each of his assistant generals, and the subordinate officers in groups of ten went through the same ceremony, and the ruin of Galdan was anticipated in the libations of his conquerors. While Feyanku marched to encounter Galdan wherever he should find him, the ministers and courtiers at Pekin made a strenuous effort to prevent Kanghi taking the field in person, expatiating on the dangers of a war in the desert, and of the loss to the Empire if anything happened to him. But Kanghi, while thanking them for their solicitude, was not to be deterred from his purpose. He led his army by a parallel route to that pursued by Feyanku across the Gobi desert to Kobdo, where Galdan had established his headquarters. The details of the march are fully described by the Roman Catholic priest, Gerbillon in his interesting narrative. They reveal the difficulties of the enterprise as well as its success. Some detachments of the Chinese army were compelled to beat a retreat, but the main body succeeded in making its way to the valley of the Kerulon where some supplies could be obtained. Feyanku's corps, when it reached the neighbourhood of the modern Ourga, was reduced to an effective strength of 10,000 men, and of Sapsu's army only 2,000 ever reached the scene of operations, and they formed a junction with the force under Feyanku. But Galdan did not possess the military strength to take any advantage of the enfeebled state in which the Chinese armies reached his neighbourhood. He abandoned camp after camp, and sought to make good his position by establishing an empty alliance with the Russians in Siberia, from whom he asked 60,000 troops to consummate the conquest of China. Such visionary projects as this provided a poor defence against the active operations of a Chinese army in his own country. In a fit bordering on desperation Galdan suddenly determined to risk an attack on the camp of Feyanku at Chowmodo. That general less fortunate than his sovereign had been reduced to the verge of distress by the exhaustion of his supplies, and was even meditating a retreat back to China, when the action of Galdan relieved him from his dilemma. The exact course of the battle at Chowmodo is not described in any authentic document. During three hours Feyanku stood on the defensive, but when he gave the order for attack, the Eleuths broke in confusion before the charge of his

L

cavalry. Two thousand of their best warriors were slain, their organisation was shattered, and Galdan became a fugitive in the region where he had posed as undisputed master. This victory undoubtedly relieved the Chinese from serious embarrassment, and Kanghi felt able to return to Pekin leaving the further conduct of the war, and the pursuit of Galdan, in the hands of Feyanku. Formidable enemy as Galdan had proved himself, the defeat at Chowmodo put an end to his career, and destroyed all his schemes of greatness. The Chinese pursued him with great persistence, and at last he died in 1697, either of his deprivations or by the act of his own hand. With Galdan disappeared one of the most remarkable of the desert chiefs, but, although Kanghi flattered himself that such would be the case, peace did not settle down on Central Asia as the consequence of the death of his active and enterprising antagonist. The Chinese armies were recalled for this occasion, and the only force left on the remote frontier was a small one under the command of the gallant Feyanku.

The overthrow and death of Galdan brought Tse Wang Rabdan into direct contact with the Chinese. He had from his hostile relations with Galdan—the murderer of his father Tsenka—acted as the ally of Kanghi, but when he became the chief of the Eleuths on the death of his uncle, his ideas underwent a change, and he thought more of his dignity and independence. No rupture might have taken place, but that the Chinese in their implacable resolve to exterminate the family of their enemy Galdan demanded from Tse Wang Rabdan not only the bones of that chieftain, but also the persons of his son and daughter, who had taken refuge with him. Tse Wang Rabdan resented both the demand itself, and the language in which it was expressed. He evaded the requests sent by Feyanku, and he addressed a letter of remonstrance to Kanghi in the course of which he said, "The war being now concluded, past injuries ought to be buried in oblivion. Pity should be shown to the vanquished, and it would be barbarous to think of nothing but of how to overwhelm them. It is the first law inspired by humanity, and one which custom has consecrated from the earliest period among us who are Eleuths." Kanghi, undeterred by this homily, continued to press his demand, and sent several missions to the Eleuth camp to obtain the surrender of Galdan's remains and relations. His pertinacity was at last rewarded, and the bones of his old opponent were surrendered to be scattered as those of a traitor throughout China, and his son was sent to Pekin, where, however, he received an honourable appointment in lieu of being handed over to the public executioner. Although Tse Wang Rabdan at last conceded to Kanghi what he demanded, his general action soon marked him out as the antagonist of the Chinese in Central Asia. He first vanquished in battle, and then established an alliance with the Kirghiz, and thus his military forces were recruited from the whole of the vast territory from Hami on the east to Khokand on the west.

The main object of his policy was to assert his influence and authority in Tibet, and to make the ruling lama at Lhasa accept whatever course he might dictate for him. Galdan had at one time entertained the same idea; but probably because he had not as good means of access into the country as Tse Wang Rabdan had on account of his possession of Khoten, it lay dormant until it was dispelled by the rupture after his adoption of Mahomedanism. Up to this time China had been content with a very shadowy hold on Tibet, and she had no resident representative at Lhasa. But Kanghi convinced of the importance of maintaining his supremacy in Tibet, took energetic measures to counteract the Eleuth intrigues, and for a time there was a keen diplomatic struggle between the contending potentates. From an early period the supremacy in the Tibetan administration had been disputed between two different classes, the one which represented the military body making use of religious matters to forward its designs, the other being an order of priests supported by the unquestioning faith and confidence of the mass of the people. The former became known as Red Caps and the latter as Yellow Caps. The rivalry between these classes had been keen before, and was still bitterly contested when Chuntche first ascended the throne; but victory had finally inclined to the side of the Yellow Caps before the fall of Galdan. The Dalai Lama was their great spiritual head, and his triumph had been assisted by the intervention and influence of the Manchu Emperor. The Red Caps were driven out of the country into Bhutan, where they still hold sway. After this success a new functionary with both civil and military authority was appointed to carry on the administration, under the orders of the Dalai Lama, who was supposed to be lost in his spiritual speculations and religious devotions. This functionary received the name of the Tipa, and, encouraged by the little control exercised over his acts, he soon began to carry on intrigues for the elevation of his own power at the expense of that of his priestly superiors. The ambition of one Tipa led to his fall and execution, but the offence was attributed to the individual, and a new one was appointed. This second Tipa was the reputed son of a Dalai Lama, and when his father died in 1682 he kept the fact of his death secret, giving out that he had only retired into the recesses of the palace, and ruled the state in his name for the space of sixteen years. The Tipa well knew that he could not hope to obtain the approval of Kanghi for what he had done, and he had made overtures to the princes of Jungaria for protection, whenever he might require it against the Chinese Emperor. At last the truth was divulged, and Kanghi was most indignant at having been duped, and threatened to send an army to punish the Tipa for his crime. Then the Tipa selected a new Dalai Lama, and endeavoured to appease Kanghi, but his choice proved unfortunate because it did not satisfy the Tibetans. His own general Latsan Khan made himself the executor of public opinion. The Tipa was slain with most of his supporters, and the boy Dalai Lama shared the same fate. These occurrences did not ensure the tranquillity of the state, for when another Dalai Lama was found, the selection was not agreeable to Latsan Khan, and his friends had to convey the youth for safety to Sining, in China.

It was at this moment that Tse Wang Rabdan determined to interfere in Tibet, and, strangely enough, instead of attempting to make Latsan Khan his friend, he at once resolved to treat him as an enemy, throwing his son, who happened to be at Ili, into prison. He then despatched an army into Tibet to crush Latsan Khan, and at the same time he sent a force against Sining in the hope of gaining possession of the person of the young Dalai Lama. The Eleuth army quitted the banks of the Ili in 1700, under the command of Zeren Donduk, and having crossed Eastern Turkestan appeared in due course before Lhasa. It met with little or no resistance. Latsan Khan was slain, and the Eleuth army collected an incalculable quantity of spoil, with which it returned to the banks of the Ili. The expedition against Sining failed, and the rapid advance of a Chinese army compelled the retreat of Zeren Donduk without having attained any permanent success. As the Eleuth army had evacuated Tibet there was no object in sending Chinese troops into that state, and Kanghi's generals were instructed to march westwards from Hami to Turfan. But their movements were marked by carelessness or over-confidence, and the Eleuths surprised their camp, and inflicted such loss upon Kanghi's commanders that they had even to evacuate Hami. But this was only a temporary reverse. A fresh Manchu army soon retrieved it, and Hami again became the bulwark of the Chinese frontier. At the same time Kanghi sent a garrison to Tibet, and appointed resident ambans at Lhasa, which officials China has retained there ever since. The war with Tse Wang Rabdan was not ended by these successes, for he resorted to the hereditary tactics of his family, retiring when the Chinese appeared in force, and then advancing on their retreat. As Kanghi wrote, they are "like wolves who, at the sight of the huntsmen, scatter to their dens, and at the withdrawal of danger assemble again round the prey they have abandoned with regret. Such was the policy of these desert robbers." The last year of Kanghi's reign was illustrated by a more than usually decisive victory over the forces of Tse Wang Rabdan, which a courtier declared to be "equivalent to the conquest of Tibet"; but on the whole the utmost success that can be claimed for Kanghi's policy was that it repelled the chronic danger from the desert chiefs and their turbulent followers to a greater distance from the immediate frontier of the Empire than had been the case for many centuries. He left the task of breaking the Eleuth power to his grandson, Keen Lung.

Although every year of Kanghi's reign was marked by the conduct of extensive and hazardous campaigns on the western borders, they did not affect the general work of administration or the progress of the country. There can be no doubt of the prosperity and contentment of the people during the forty years that followed the suppression of Wou Sankwei's revolt, and the best proof that can be furnished of this is the cessation of all further attempt on the part of the Chinese to shake off the rule of their Manchu conquerors. They acquiesced in their lot, and the Tatsing dynasty took its place in the popular mind among the families appointed by Heaven to rule over the Middle Kingdom. During this reign the question of intercourse with the different nations of Europe first became a matter of marked importance, and Kanghi gave several definitions of China's best policy in the matter, not always consistent with each other, that claim our careful consideration, if the subsequent events leading down for a century and a half to the wars of the last fifty years are to be rightly appreciated. Kanghi, personally by association and education, was well disposed towards those Europeans with whom he had been brought in contact. They were without exception missionary priests of the Church of Rome, carefully selected for their high attainments and animated by a lofty purpose. The Emperor Kanghi had to a great extent received his education at their hands, and he became well acquainted with the learning as well as the politics of Europe. He appreciated and he utilised in his government the services which they were able to render, and the missionaries were consequently employed in various high and responsible posts. Kanghi compelled them, as the condition on which he would alone permit them to remain in China, to give a promise that they would never think of returning to Europe; and these high-minded men devoted their lives and their energies to the stupendous task of making some impression on the religious apathy and indifference of the Chinese masses. But the sight of their employment and the preference shown for their mathematical and astronomical systems were most galling and offensive to the Chinese officials, who took advantage of popular prejudice and every passing whim of the Emperor to inveigh against foreigners, and to protest against both the justice and the policy of employing them. But the philosophical calmness and political sagacity of Kanghi led him to tolerate the presence of men whose ethics he could appreciate with an academic pleasure, and whose practical services he recognised as invaluable. He employed them as envoys, geographers, doctors, and astronomers. Their maps brought under his eye the extent and the form of the territories he ruled, their artillery sometimes turned the tide of battle in his favour, their medicines more than once saved him from illness, and perhaps from death.

They were given permission to remain in China on account of their practical knowledge and usefulness, but for many years they were denied leave to publicly practise their religion, and this point they fought for with equal tact and pertinacity. They were willing to give up all thought of returning to Europe, but they would not make this great sacrifice, if they were forbidden to follow their religion in the church they had built with their own money at Pekin. The question was discussed and contested for many years; but at last, in 1692, the Tribunal of Rites passed a decision in favour of the foreigners. This order of the Tribunal of Rites has been very appropriately called the Great Charter of Christianity in China, and it so happened that in the very year of its being sanctioned, the French missionaries saved the life of Kanghi, after his own doctors had given up all hope. Some years later Kanghi showed his gratitude for this signal service by presenting them with the site for a church next his own palace and a large sum of money towards the building. This exceptionally favourable treatment was entirely due to the sagacity and magnanimity of Kanghi; but unfortunately the Jesuits thought that it signified that the Chinese were ripe for conversion, and came to China in ever-increasing numbers. There was no employment for these persons, and the more they came the greater did the national and official antipathy to them grow. When they travelled into the provinces and attempted to build new churches, their project was opposed on the ground that the edict of 1692 only referred to Christianity being preached in churches already existing; but Kanghi again came to their assistance, and declared that "they have never been the cause of any trouble to the Empire, nor ever committed any reprehensible act, and that their doctrine is not bad." He even went further, and gave them the following testimonial in a public address :—" Europeans whom I employ, even in the interior of my palace, you have always served me with zeal and affection without anyone having been able to cast the slightest reproach upon you. There are many Chinese who distrust you; but as for myself—and I have carefully observed the whole of your conduct, in which I never found anything irregular— I am so fully convinced of your uprightness and good faith that I publicly declare that you are deserving of every trust and confidence." Unfortunately, it was becoming too evident that the Christians only enjoyed their position by the favour of an enlightened ruler, and not from the regard of the people or the intelligence of the ministers; and their increasing numbers rather weakened this favour, for even Kanghi had never advocated that the Chinese should adopt the

Christian religion. As missionaries, the Jesuits were complete failures, as representatives of European knowledge and culture they were conspicuously successful, and maintained the high standard of Western knowledge and probity.

At this time also the question of the residence of Europeans and of the relations with them was complicated by the increasing activity of foreign traders at Canton and generally along the southern coasts of China. Kanghi was well disposed towards the French and other priests at Pekin, but he was not inclined to favour the European traders; and his view was strengthened by the priests declaring that they had nothing in common with the Dutch or the English, not even religion. Thus the very influence obtained by some Europeans at Pekin tended to retard the promotion of trade with China and the free intercourse of Europeans with that country. They were not far-sighted enough to see that the success of their mission and the triumphant introduction of Christianity into China depended, not on the privileges enjoyed by a few men at Pekin, but on the pursuit of an enlightened policy towards all outside nations by the Chinese government. We must make allowance for facts and prejudices; but the missionaries at the Chinese capital hoped to keep official and religious China as much a close preserve for their own advantage as the Portuguese did commercial China from Macao. The Chinese never acquiesced in the smallest degree in either of these arrangements. The "men from over the sea" were equally obnoxious to them in either guise, and it was only the superior intelligence of Kanghi that gained for them a more privileged position. Towards the end of his reign there was also some abatement in his favour. As the great ruler grew more feeble from age and ill-health the fanatical opposition of the Chinese officials increased, and his patronage showed some decline, for in 1718 he sanctioned measures placing some restriction on the construction of churches, and thus arrested the propagation of Christianity. Almost at the same time he interdicted the export of rice to the Philippines and the despatch of any Chinese junk to those islands, thus breaking off all intercourse with the outside world.

The close of Kanghi's reign witnessed a decline in the interest he took in the representatives of Europe, and this was not revived by the splendour of the embassy which Peter the Great sent to Pekin in 1719. The embassy consisted of the ambassador himself, M. Ismaloff; his secretary, M. de Lange; the English traveller, Mr. Bell, and a considerable suite. Kanghi so far went out of his way to overrule the prejudices of his Court that he insisted on an honourable reception being given to this mission, and that the kotao ceremony should be waived. A house was set apart for the use of its members, and they lived as the honoured guests of the Emperor. He received in the most gracious manner the letter which Peter addressed to him in the following terms: "To the Emperor of the vast countries of Asia, to the Sovereign Monarch of Bogdo, to the Supreme Majesty of Khitay, friendship and greeting. With the design I possess of holding and increasing the friendship and close relations long established between your Majesty and my predecessors and myself, I have thought it right to send to your Court, in the capacity of ambassador-extraordinary, Leon Ismaloff, captain in my Guards. I beg you will receive him in a manner suitable to the character in which he comes, to have regard and to attach as much faith to what he may say on the subject of our mutual affairs as if I were speaking to you myself, and also to permit his residing at your

Court of Pekin until I recall him. Allow me to sign myself your Majesty's good friend, Peter." Kanghi gave the Russian envoy a very honourable reception. A house was set apart for his accommodation, and when the difficulties raised by the mandarins on the question of the kotao ceremony at the audience threatened to bring the embassy to an abortive end, Kanghi himself intervened with a suggestion that solved the difficulty. He arranged that his principal minister should perform the kotao to the letter of the Russian Emperor, while the Russian envoy rendered him the same obeisance. The audience then took place without further delay, and it was allowed on all hands that no foreign embassy had ever been received with greater honour in China than this. Ismaloff returned to his master with the most roseate account of his reception and of the opening in China for Russian trade. A large and rich caravan was accordingly fitted out by Peter, to proceed to Pekin; but when it arrived it found a very different state of affairs from what Ismaloff had pictured. Kanghi lay on his death-bed, the anti-foreign ministers were supreme, declaring that "trade was a matter of little consequence, and regarded by them with contempt," and the Russians were ignominiously sent back to Siberia with the final declaration that such intercourse as was unavoidable must be restricted to the frontier. Thus summarily was ended Peter's dream of tapping the wealth of China.

Although Kanghi was not altogether free from domestic trouble, through the ambition of his many sons to succeed him, his life must on the whole be said to have passed along tranquilly enough apart from his cares of state. The public acts and magnificent exploits of his reign prove him to have been wise, courageous, and magnanimous, and his private life will bear the most searching examination, and only render his virtue the more conspicuous. He always showed a tender solicitude for the interests of his people, which was proved, among other things, by his giving up his annual tours through his dominions on account of the expense thrown on his subjects by the inevitable size of his retinue. His active habits as a hunter, a rider, and even as a pedestrian, were subjects of admiring comment on the part of the Chinese people, and he was one of their few rulers who made it a habit to walk through the streets of his capital. He was also conspicuous as the patron of learning. His support of the foreign missionaries as geographers and cartographers has been dwelt upon. He was also the consistent and energetic supporter of the celebrated Hanlin College, and, as he was no ordinary *litterateur* himself, this is not surprising. His own works filled a hundred volumes, prominent among which were his Sixteen Maxims on the Art of Government, and it is believed that he took a large part in bringing out the Imperial Dictionary of the Hanlin College. His writings were marked by a high code of morality as well as by the lofty ideas of a broad-minded statesman. His enemies have imputed to him an excessive vanity and avarice; but the whole tenour of his life disproves the former statement, and, whatever foundation in fact the latter may have had, he never carried it to any greater length than mere prudence and consideration for the wants of his people demanded. We know that he resorted to gentle pressure to attain his ends rather than to tyrannical force. When he wished to levy a heavy contribution from a too rich subject he had recourse to what may be styled a mild joke, sooner than to threats and corporal punishment. The following incident has been quoted in this connection: One day Kanghi made an official, who had grown very wealthy, lead him, riding on an ass, round his gardens. As recompense the Emperor gave him a tael. Then he himself led the mandarin in similar fashion. At the end of the tour he asked how much greater he was than his minister? "The comparison is impossible," said the ready courtier. "Then I must make the estimate myself," replied Kanghi. "I am 20,000 times as great, therefore you will pay me 20,000 taels." His reign was singularly free from the executions so common under even the best of Chinese rulers; and, whenever possible, he always tempered justice with mercy.

Notwithstanding his enfeebled health and the many illnesses from which he had suffered in later life, he persisted in following his usual sporting amusements, and he passed the winter of 1722 at his hunting-box at Haidsu. He seems to have caught a chill, and after a brief illness he died on the 20th December in that year. From his earliest youth Kanghi had given abundant promise of his future greatness, and one story which is preserved of him, when about to succeed to the crown, is indicative of his ample confidence in himself and his destiny. It is said that when Chuntche lay on his death-bed he summoned his children into his presence and asked, "Which of you feels that he possesses the ability and strength to retain a crown that has been won only so short a time?" All pleaded youth and inexperience except Kanghi, the youngest, in whose vigorous instincts there dwelt the full assurance of success. The result more than justified his confidence in himself. The death of Kanghi called forth from all sides, and very different persons, unanimous testimony as to his ability and worth. The European missionaries who had benefited by his patronage were equally eloquent and emphatic in his praise. One priest wrote of him: "This prince was one of those extraordinary men who are only met with once in the course of several centuries. He placed no limits to his desire for knowledge, and of all the princes of Asia there never was one with so great a taste for the arts and sciences. This prince was not put out by the expression of an opinion different from his own—rare as it is for princes of his rank to tolerate contradiction." Of his personal appearance another priest speaks not less favourably than of his moral and intellectual character: "There is nothing in his appearance which is not worthy of the throne he occupies. His air is majestic, his figure is excellently proportioned and above the middle height; all the features of the countenance are regular; his eyes bright and larger than is usual with his nation; the nose slightly curved and drooping at the point; and the few marks left by the small-pox detract nothing from the charm which is conspicuous throughout his person." But the greatest tribute of all comes from Mailla, the laborious historian, or rather the translator of Chinese histories from the earliest times to the death of Kanghi. He writes of this prince, in concluding his great work, "Just posterity will beyond doubt assign to this prince a distinguished place among the greatest monarchs. Fully occupied between affairs of state, military achievements, and the study of liberal pursuits; beneficent, brave, generous, wise, active and vigilant in policy, of profound and extended genius, having nothing of the pomp or indolence of Asiatic Courts, although his power and wealth were both immense; the one thing alone wanting to this prince, according to the desire of the missionaries who have become the exponents of his eminent qualities, was to crown them all with the adoption of the Christianity of which he knew the principles, and of which he valued the morality and the maxims, but which policy and the human passions prevented his openly embracing." With regard to Kanghi's services and place among the rulers of China, we must repeat what we have already written. Of the magnitude of Kanghi's services to both China and his own race there can be no question. They were conspicuous and incontestable. He had ascended the throne at a time when it seemed that the Manchu conquest, far from giving China the assurance of a settled and peaceful rule, would prove in its main result the perpetuation of internal dissension and sanguinary strife. The presence of the able and powerful feudatory Wou Sankwei strengthened that conviction, and none dared think, when the crisis reached the stage of open war, that the youthful prince would more than hold his own, and eventually triumph over the veteran general whose military skill and consistent good fortune had been the theme of admiration with his countrymen for more than a generation.

The place of Kanghi among Chinese sovereigns is clearly defined. He ranks on almost equal terms with the two greatest of them all—Taitsong and his own grandson, Keen Lung—and it would be ungracious, if not impossible, to say in what respect he falls short of complete equality with either, so numerous and conspicuous were his talents and his virtues. His long friendship and high consideration for the Christian missionaries have no doubt contributed to bring his name and the events of his reign more prominently before Europe than was the case with any other Chinese ruler. But, although this predilection for European practices may have had the effect of strengthening his claims to precede every other of his country's rulers, it can add but little to the impression produced on even the most cursory reader by the remarkable achievements in peace and war accomplished by this gifted Emperor. Kanghi's genius dominates one of the most critical periods in Chinese history, of which the narrative should form neither an uninteresting nor an uninstructive theme. Celebrated as the consolidator and completer of the Manchu conquest, Kanghi's virtue and moderation have gained him permanent fame as a wise, just, and beneficent national sovereign in the hearts of the Chinese people.

CHAPTER XII.

A SHORT REIGN AND THE BEGINNING OF A LONG ONE.

IMMEDIATELY after the death of Kanghi, his fourth son, who had long been designated as his heir, was proclaimed Emperor, under the style of Yung Ching, which name means "the indissoluble concord or stable peace." The late Emperor had always favoured this prince, and in his will he publicly proclaimed that he bore much resemblance to himself, and that he was a man of rare and precious character. His first acts indicated considerable vigour and decision of mind. In the edict announcing the death of his father and his own accession he said that on the advice of his ministers he had entered upon the discharge of his Imperial duties, without giving up precious time to the indulgence of his natural grief, which would be gratifying to his feelings, but injurious to the public interests. As Yung Ching was of the mature age of 45, and as he had enjoyed the confidence of his predecessor, he was fully qualified to carry on the administration. He declared that his main purpose was to continue his father's work, and that he would tread as closely as he could in Kanghi's footsteps. While Yung Ching took these prompt steps to secure himself on the throne, some of his brothers assumed an attitude of menacing hostility towards him, and all his energy and vigilance were required to counteract their designs. A very little time was needed, however, to show that Kanghi had selected his worthiest son as his successor, and that China would have no reason to fear under Yung Ching the loss of any of the benefits conferred on the nation by Kanghi. His fine presence, and frank, open manner, secured for him the sympathy and applause of the public, and in a very short time he also gained their respect and admiration by his wisdom and justice.

The most important and formidable of his brothers was the fourteenth son of Kanghi, by the same mother, however, as that of Yung Ching. He and his son Poki had been regarded with no inconsiderable favour by Kanghi, and at one time it was thought that he would have chosen them as his successors; but these expectations were disappointed. He was sent instead to hold the chief command against the Eleuths on the western borders. Yung Ching determined to remove him from this post, in which he might have opportunities of asserting his independence, and for a moment it seemed as if he might disobey. But more prudent counsels prevailed, and he returned to Pekin, where he was placed in honourable confinement, and retained there during the whole of Yung Ching's reign. He and his son owed their release thirteen years later to the greater clemency or self-confidence of Keen Lung. Another brother, named Sessaka, also fell under suspicion, and he was arrested, and his estates confiscated. He was then so far forgiven that a small military command was given him in the provinces. Others of more importance were involved in his affairs. Lessihin, son of Prince Sourniama, an elder brother of Kanghi, was denounced as a sympathiser and supporter of Sessaka. The charge seems to have been based on slender evidence, but it sufficed to cause the banishment of this personage and all his family to Sining. It appears as if they were specially punished for having become Christians, and there is no doubt that their conversion embittered the Emperor's mind against the Christian missionaries and their religion. It enabled him to say, or at least induced him to accept the statement, that the Christians meddled and took a side in the internal politics of the country. Yung Ching saw and seized his opportunity. His measures of repression against the recalcitrant party in his own family culminated in the summary exile of Sourniama and all his descendants down to the fourth generation. Sourniama vainly endeavoured to establish his innocence, and he sent three of his sons, laden with chains, to the palace, to protest his innocence and devotion. But they were refused audience, and Sourniama and his family sank into oblivion and wretchedness on the outskirts of the Empire.

Having thus settled the difficulties within his own family, Yung Ching next turned his attention to humbling the bold band of foreigners who had established themselves in the capital and throughout the country, as much by their own persistency and indifference to slight as by the acquiescence of the Chinese government, and who, after they had reached some of the highest official posts, continued to preach and propagate their gospel of a supreme power and mercy beyond the control of kings, a gospel which was simply destructive of the paternal and sacred claims on which a Chinese Emperor based his authority as superior to all earthly interference, and as transmitted to him direct from Heaven. The official classes confirmed the Emperor's suspicions, and encouraged him to proceed to extreme lengths. On all sides offences were freely laid at the doors of the missionaries. It was said of them that "their doctrine sows trouble among the people, and makes them doubt the goodness of our laws." In the province of Fuhkien their eighteen churches were closed, and the priests were summarily ordered to return to Macao. At Pekin itself the Jesuits lost all their influence. Those who had been well-disposed towards them were either banished or cowed into silence. The Emperor turned his back on them and refused to see them, and they could only wait with their usual fortitude until the period of Imperial displeasure had passed over. When they endeavoured to enlist in their support the sympathy and influence of the Emperor's brother— the thirteenth prince—who in Kanghi's time had been considered their friend, they met with a rebuff not unnatural or unreasonable when the mishaps to his relations for their Christian proclivities are borne in mind. This prince said, in words which have often been repeated since by Chinese ministers and political writers, "What would you say if our people were to go to Europe and wished to change there the laws and customs established by your ancient sages? The Emperor, my brother, wishes to put an end to all this in an effectual manner. I have seen the accusation of the Tsongtou of Fuhkien. It is undoubtedly strong, and your disputes about our customs have greatly injured you. What would you say if we were to transport ourselves to Europe and to act there as you have done here? Would you stand it for a moment? In the course of time I shall master this business, but I declare to you that China will want for nothing when you cease to live in it, and that your absence will not cause it any loss.

Here nobody is retained by force, and nobody also will be suffered to break the laws or to make light of our customs."

The final expression of Chinese policy with regard to the Christians was given, however, by the Emperor himself, when at last he agreed to receive the missionaries in audience, but refused to allow them to say a word when he delivered his ultimatum in the following carefully-prepared speech:—

"The late Emperor, my father, after having instructed me during forty years, chose me in preference to any of my brothers to succeed him on the throne. I make it one of my first objects to imitate him, and to depart in nothing from his manner of government Some Europeans in the province of Fuhkien have shown a wish to destroy our laws, and they have been a cause of trouble to our people. The high officials of that province have duly apprised me of these facts. It is my duty to provide a remedy for the disorder. That is a matter for the government with which I am charged. I could not and ought not to act now as I used to do when I was only a simple prince. You tell me that your law is not a false one. I believe you; if I thought that it was false, what would prevent me from destroying your churches, and from driving you out of the country? False laws are those which, under the pretext of spreading virtue, rouse a spirit of revolt. But what would you say if I were to send a troop of bonzes and lamas into your country in order to preach their doctrines? How would you receive them? Ricci came to China in the first year of Wanleh. I will not touch upon what the Chinese did at that time, as I am in no way responsible for it. But then you were very few in numbers. In fact there were only one or two of you, and you had not your people and churches in every province. It was only in my father's reign that these churches were raised on all sides, and that your doctrines spread with rapidity. We then saw these things clearly enough, and we dared say nothing on the subject. But if you knew how to beguile my father, do not hope to be able to deceive me in the same manner. You wish that all the Chinese should become Christians, and indeed your creed demands it. I am well aware of this, but in that event what would become of us? Should we not soon be merely the subjects of your kings? The converts you have made already recognise nobody but you, and in a time of trouble they would listen to no other voice than yours. I know, as a matter of fact, that we have nothing now to fear, but when the foreign vessels shall come in their thousands and tens of thousands, then it may be that some disaster will ensue. China has in the north the Empire of the Russians, which is not to be despised; on the south there are the Europeans and their kingdoms, which are still more considerable; and on the west there is Tse Wang Rabdan, whom I wish to keep back within his borders, lest he should enter China, and cause us trouble. The Czar's ambassador solicited that permission should be given the Russians to establish factories for commerce in all the provinces. His request was refused, and trade was only allowed at Pekin or at Kiachta, on the frontier of the Kalka country. I permit you to reside here, and at Canton, as long as you give no cause for complaint; but if any should arise I will not allow you to remain either here or at Canton. I will have none of you in the provinces. The Emperor, my father, suffered much in reputation among the *literati* by the condescension with which he allowed you to establish yourselves. He could not himself make any changes in the laws of our sages, and I will not suffer that in the least degree there shall be cause to reproach my reign on this score. When my sons and grandsons are on the throne they may do as shall seem good to them. It matters not to me in the smallest what Wanleh did on your account. Do not imagine, in conclusion, that I have nothing against you, or on the other hand that I wish to oppress you. You are aware how I used to act in your behalf when I was only a Regulo. What I do now I do in my character of Emperor. My sole care is to govern the Empire well. To that I apply myself from morning to evening. I do not see even my children or the Empress, but only those who are engaged in the public administration. This will continue as long as the time of mourning, which is for three years. When that is over I shall perhaps then be able to see you more often."

The importance of this speech, and indeed the influence of Yung Ching on the development of the important foreign question, was that it arrested the ambition and sanguine flight of the imagination of the Roman Catholic missionaries who, rendered over-confident by their success under Kanghi, believed that they held the future of China in their own hands, and that persistency alone was needed to secure the adhesion of that country to the Christian Church. Yung Ching dispelled these illusions, and so far as they were illusions, which nearly two subsequent centuries have proved them to be, it was well that they should be so dispelled. He asserted himself in very unequivocal terms as an Emperor of China, and as resolute in maintaining his sovereign position outside the control of any religious potentate or creed. The progress of the Christian religion of the Roman Catholic Church in China was quite incompatible with the supposed celestial origin of the Emperor, who was alleged to receive his authority direct from Heaven. It is not surprising that Yung Ching, at the earliest possible moment, decided to blight these hopes, and to assert the natural and inherited prerogative of a Chinese Emperor. There is no room to doubt that the Catholic priests had drawn a too hasty and too favourable deduction from the favour of Kanghi. They confounded their practical utility with the intrinsic merit and persuasive force of Christianity. An enlightened ruler had recognised the former, but a sceptical people showed themselves singularly obdurate to the latter. The persecution of the Christians, of which the letters from the missionaries at Pekin at this time are so full, did not go beyond the placing of some restraint on the preaching of their religion. No wholesale executions or sweeping decrees passed against their persons attended its course or marked its development. Yung Ching simply showed by his conduct that they must count no longer on the favour of the Emperor in the carrying out of their designs. The difficulties inherent in the task they had undertaken stood for the first time fully revealed, and having been denounced as a source of possible danger to the stability of the Empire, they became an object of suspicion even to those who had sympathised with them personally, if not with their creed.

The early years of the reign of Yung Ching were marked by extraordinary public misfortunes. The flooding of the Hoangho entailed a famine, which spread such desolation throughout the northern provinces that it is affirmed, on credible authority, that 40,000 persons were fed at the state expense in Pekin alone for a period of four months. The taxes in some of the most important cities and wealthiest districts had to be greatly reduced, and the resources of the Exchequer were severely strained. But the loss and suffering caused by the famine were speedily cast into the shade by a terrible and sudden visitation which carried desolation and destruction throughout the whole of the metropolitan province of Pechihli.

The northern districts of China have for many centuries been liable to the frequent recurrence of earthquakes on a terribly vast and disastrous scale, but none of them equalled in its terrific proportions that of the year 1730. It came without warning, but the shocks continued for ten days. Over one hundred thousand persons were overwhelmed in a moment at Pekin, the suburbs were laid in ruins, the Imperial palace was destroyed, the summer residence at Yuen Ming Yuen, on which Yung Ching had lavished his taste and his treasure, suffered in scarcely a less degree. The Emperor and the inhabitants fled from the city, and took shelter without the walls, where they encamped. The loss was incalculable, and it has been stated that Yung Ching expended fifteen millions sterling in repairing the damage and allaying the public misfortune. Notwithstanding these national calamities the population increased, and in some provinces threatened to outgrow the production of rice. Various devices were resorted to check the growth of the population; but they were all of a simple and harmless character, such as the issue of rewards to widows who did not marry again and to bachelors who preserved their state.

The military events of Yung Ching's reign were confined to the side of Central Asia, where Tse Wang Rabdan emulated with more than ordinary success the example of his predecessors, and where he transmitted his power and authority to his son, Galdan Chereng, on his death in 1727. He established his sovereignty over the whole of Kashgaria, which he ruled through a prince named Daniel, and he established relations with the Russians, which at one time promised to attain a cordial character, but which were suddenly converted into hostility by the Russian belief that the Upper Urtish lay in a gold region which they resolved to conquer. Instead of an ally they then found in Tse Wang Rabdan the successful defender of that region. But the wars of Central Asia had no interest for Yung Ching. He was one of the Chinese rulers who thought that he should regard these matters as outside his concern, and the experience of Kanghi's wars had divided Chinese statesmen into two clearly-defined parties: those who held that China should conquer Central Asia up to the Pamir, and those who thought that the Great Wall was the best practical limit for the exercise of Chinese authority. Yung Ching belonged to the latter school, and, instead of despatching fresh armies into the Gobi region to complete the triumph of his father, he withdrew those that were there, and publicly proclaimed that the aggressive chiefs and turbulent tribes of that region might fight out their own quarrels, and indulge their own petty ambitions as best they felt disposed. The success of this policy would have been incontestable if it had been reflected in the conduct of the Central Asian princelets, who, however, seemed to see in the moderation and inaction of the Chinese ruler only a fresh incentive to aggression and turbulence. Yung Ching himself died too soon to appreciate the shortcomings of his own policy.

In the midst of his active labours as a beneficent ruler the life of Yung Ching was cut short. On the 7th October, 1735, he gave audience to the high officials of his Court in accordance with his usual custom; but feeling indisposed he was compelled to break off the interview in a sudden manner. His indisposition at once assumed a grave form, and in a few hours he had ceased to live. The loss of this Emperor does not seem to have caused any profound or widespread sentiment of grief among the masses, although the more intelligent recognised in him one of those wise and prudent rulers whose tenure of power makes their people's happiness. Rumours were spread about to his disadvantage and to the detriment of his private character; but an impartial consideration of his reign shows them to have possessed little or no foundation in fact. During the thirteen years that he ruled we find him ever anxious to promote the public weal and to alleviate the sufferings of his people. Whether it was in matters of state or of his private conduct he seemed equally mindful of the dignity of his position and of the fame of his family. Without aspiring to the eminence of his father he left a name for justice and public spirit that entitles him to rank high among those sovereigns of China who have deserved well of their country. Even his attitude towards the Christians was dictated by a firm belief in the necessity of limiting the intercourse of his people with the Europeans, and of curtailing the growing influence of the latter. Yung Ching always placed the public interests in the forefront of his conduct, and whether rearranging the order of the official classes or compiling the history of his family, or providing for the wants of his people, we find him equally true to his principles, and not less ardent than consistent in carrying out the dictates of his conscience. He will not rank with either his father or his son, but nevertheless he may be termed a highly-creditable ruler, equal to his office and worthy of his race.

Yung Ching died so suddenly that he had not nominated his heir. He left three sons, and, after brief consideration, the eldest of these—to whom was given the name of Keen Lung—was placed upon the throne. The choice was justified by the result, although the chroniclers declare that it came as a surprise to the recipient of the honour, as he had passed his life in the pursuit of literary studies rather than in practical administrative work. His skill and proficiency in the field of letters had already been proved before his father's death; but of public affairs and the government of a vast Empire he knew little or nothing. He was a student of books rather than of men, and he had to undergo a preliminary course of training in the art of government before he felt himself capable of assuming the reins of power. Moreover, Keen Lung, although the eldest son, was not the offspring of the Empress, and the custom of succession in the Imperial family was too uncertain to allow anyone in his position to feel absolute confidence as to his claims securing the recognition they might seem to warrant. His admission of his being unequal to the duties of his lofty position, notwithstanding that he was 25 years of age, was thoroughly characteristic of the man, and augured well for the future of his reign. He appointed four regents, whose special task was to show him how to rule; but in the edict delegating his authority to them he expressly limited its application to the period of mourning, covering a space of four years; and as a measure of precaution against any undue ambition he made the office terminable at his discretion.

Keen Lung began his reign with acts of clemency which seldom fail to add a special lustre to a sovereign's assumption of power. His father had punished with rigour some of the first princes of the court simply because they were his relations, and there is some ground for thinking that he had put forward antipathy to the foreign heresy of the Christians as a cloak to conceal his private animosities and personal apprehensions. Keen Lung at once resolved to reverse the acts of his predecessor, and to offer such reparation as he could to those who had suffered for no sufficient offence. The sons of Kanghi and their children who had fallen under the suspicion of Yung Ching were released from their confinement, and restored to their rank and privileges. They showed their gratitude to their benefactor by sustained loyalty and practical service that contributed to the splendour of his long reign. The impression thus produced on the public mind was also most favourable, and already the people were beginning to declare that they had found a worthy successor to the great Kanghi.

There is nothing surprising to learn that in consequence of the pardon and restitution of the men who had nominally suffered for their Christian proclivities, the foreign missionaries began to hope and to agitate for an improvement in their lot and condition. They somewhat hastily assumed that the evil days of persecution were over, and that Keen Lung would accord them the same honourable positions as they had enjoyed under his grandfather, Kanghi. These expectations were destined to a rude disappointment, as the party hostile to the Christians remained as strong as ever at Court, and the regents were not less prejudiced against them than the ministers of Yung Ching had been. The Emperor's own opinion does not appear to have been very strong one way or the other, but it seems probable that he was slightly prejudiced against the foreigners. He certainly assented to an order prohibiting the practice of Christianity by any of his subjects, and ordaining the punishment of those who should obstinately adhere to it. At the same time the foreign missionaries were ordered to confine their labours to the secular functions in which they were useful, and to give up all attempts to propagate their creed. Still some slight abatement in practice was procured of these rigid measures through the mediation of the painter Castiglione, who, while taking a portrait of the Emperor, pleaded, and not ineffectually, the cause of his countrymen. There was one distinct persecution on a large scale in the province of Fuhkien, where several Spanish missionaries were tortured, their chief native supporters strangled, and Keen Lung himself sent the order to execute the missionaries in retaliation for the massacre of Chinese subjects by the Spaniards in the Philippines. After he had been on the throne fifteen years Keen Lung began to unbend towards the foreigners, and to avail himself of their services in the same manner as his grandfather had done. The artists Castiglione and Attiret were constantly employed in the palace, painting his portrait and other pictures. Keen Lung is said to have been so pleased with that drawn by Attiret that he wished to make him a mandarin. The French in particular strove to amuse the great monarch, and to enable him to wile away his leisure with ingeniously constructed automatons worked by clockwork machinery. He also learned from them much about the politics and material condition of Europe, and it is not surprising that he became imbued with the idea that France was the greatest and most powerful state in that continent. Almost insensibly Keen Lung entertained a more favourable opinion of the foreigners, and extended to them his protection with other privileges that had long been withheld. But this policy was attributable to practical considerations and not to religious belief.

Very little detailed information is obtainable about the inner working of the government and the annual course of events, owing to the practice of not giving the official history of the dynasty publicity until after it has ceased to reign; and all that can be said with any confidence of the first fifteen years of Keen Lung's reign, is that they were marked by great internal prosperity arising from the tranquillity of the realm, and the content of the people. Any misfortunes that befell the realm were of personal importance to the sovereign rather than of national significance, although some of the foreign priests affected to see in them the retribution of Providence for the apathy and tyranny of the Chinese rulers. In 1751 Keen Lung lost both his principal wife, the Empress, and his eldest son. His disagreements with his ministers also proved many and serious, and the letters from Pekin note, with more than a gleam of satisfaction, that those who were most prominent as Anti-Christians suffered most heavily. Keen Lung suffered from physical weakness, and a susceptibility to bodily ailments, that detracted during the first few years of his reign from his capacity to discharge all the duties of his position, and more than their usual share of power consequently fell into the hands of the great tribunals of the State. When Keen Lung resolutely devoted himself to the task of supervising the acts of the official world the evils became less perceptible, and gradually the provincial governors found it to be their best and wisest course to obey and faithfully execute the behests of their sovereign. For a brief space Keen Lung seemed likely to prove more indifferent to the duties of his rank than either of his predecessors; but after a few years' practice he hastened to devote himself to his work with an energy which neither Kanghi nor Yung Ching had surpassed.

Keen Lung seems to have passed his time between his palace at Pekin, and his hunting box at Jehol, a small town beyond the Wall. The latter, perhaps, was his favourite residence, because he enjoyed the quiet of the country, and the purer and more invigorating air of the northern region agreed with his constitution. Here he varied the monotony of rural pursuits —for he never became as keen a hunter as Kanghi—with grand ceremonies which he employed the foreigners in painting. It was at Jehol that he planned most of his military campaigns, and those conquests which carried his banners to the Pamir and the Himalaya. If the earlier period of Keen Lung's reign was tranquil and undisturbed by war, the last forty years made up for it by their sustained military excitement and achievement. As soon as Keen Lung grasped the situation and found that the administration of the country was working in perfect order, he resolved to attain a complete settlement of the questions pending in Central Asia, which his father had shirked. Up to this time Keen Lung had been generally set down as a literary student, and as a man more of thought than of action. But his reading had taught him one thing, and that was that the danger to China from the side of Central Asia was one that went back to remote ages, that it had never been allayed, save for brief intervals, and then only by establishing Chinese authority on either side of the Tian Shan. His studies showed Keen Lung what ought to be done, and the aggressions of his neighbours soon gave him the opportunity of carrying out the policy that he felt to be the best.

CHAPTER XIII.

KEEN LUNG'S WARS AND CONQUESTS.

IF there is room for difference of opinion as to whether Keen Lung was as great a sovereign as Kanghi, there is no doubt that he was the greater conqueror of the two, and this is the more remarkable as, unlike his grandfather, he never attempted to lead an army in the field, or to figure as a great general. It was his boast that he never entered upon a war without concluding it with the humiliation of his enemy, and the conquest of his country. Neither the power nor the numbers of his antagonists prevented his attaining complete success, and the persistency with which he pursued his enemies, and his purpose has never been surpassed. Nor were the obstacles of nature any bar to the triumphant progress of his arms. His soldiers crossed the Himalaya, and penetrated into the recesses of the Pamirs, establishing over that inaccessible region a sovereignty which remains a living force to this day. He solved the troublesome and ever-recurring Central Asian question in the only way in which it could be settled for the dignity and security of China, by establishing his authority over all the tribes and races who had ever menaced them, and if his successors had only maintained the efficiency of the administration in Kuldja and Kashgaria, there is no reason to doubt that his solution would have proved permanent.

Keen Lung did not act in the matter with undue precipitation; for immediately after his succession he was brought face to face with the fact that Galdan Chereng claimed and exercised an independent state. The military reverses of the last year of Kanghi's reign, and the sustained apathy of Yung Ching encouraged and left undisturbed this assertion of independence. Galdan Chereng before his death had set up in Kashgaria a form of administration in dependence upon himself. He divided it between the four sons of one of its old chiefs, and as long as he lived he retained sufficient control over their acts, to prevent the outbreak of civil strife or a contest for power. But on his death in 1745, the old dissensions which had been so common a feature in the history of these states, broke out again and threatened to involve the border districts of the Empire as well, principally because the Chinese had withdrawn from Hami and Turfan. Even in Jungaria the death of Galdan Chereng proved the signal for the outbreak of rivalries and contentions. And among those of his relatives who succeeded in establishing their authority, none rose higher than the representative of the collateral branch of Ta Chereng. The son of Galdan Chereng, after enjoying a brief term of power, was deposed by an elder but half-brother, who usurped his place and ruled for several years, chiefly by the support of the Lamas, as monarch of Jungaria, under the style of

Dardsha. This insurrection and the violent scenes by which it was accompanied carried confusion throughout the tribes forming the confederacy. Dardsha was opposed by the faction headed by Davatsi, grandson of Ta Chereng, whose strength was derived solely from the support of a chief named Amursana. At first Dardsha was successful, but he soon experienced a reversal of fortune. He was slain in battle, and Davatsi recovered the undisputed sovereignty of Jungaria. But this triumph did not end the strife, for Amursana set himself up as an independent prince, and having played the part of king-maker, aspired to all the rank and power of King. He failed to make good these pretensions, and after a brief struggle with Davatsi he was compelled to flee for safety to China, and bore to the foot of Keen Lung's throne the tale of his wrongs, and his suggestions as to how he might recover his position for the advantage of the Chinese ruler.

It was the arrival of Amursana at his court that first led Keen Lung to seriously entertain the idea of advancing into Central Asia. Keen Lung saw that a period of serious trouble was approaching in that quarter, that the Jungarian monarchy was an ephemeral creation, and that Davatsi, having got rid of his rival, was likely to combine his forces for an attack on Chinese territory. Keen Lung has himself instructed posterity as to the motives which induced him to take up the cause of Amursana. With some delicacy he suggests that he inherited this difficulty from his father whose vacillating policy and half-hearted measures had failed to provide a remedy for the evil, or in any degree to curb the aggressiveness of his neighbours. Keen Lung's policy was to be of an entirely different sort, but while formulating a bold and energetic policy, he also indicated that his success should be tempered with moderation. "If I draw the sword," he said, "it is that I may use it, but it shall be replaced in the scabbard when my object has been attained." When Keen Lung first ascended the throne he was resolved to pursue a pacific policy, and to leave the Eleuths to govern themselves—at least such was his declaration in his history of his relations with those people. But the restlessness of the Eleuths soon showed him that a stable peace was impossible, and that he must adopt sharp measures against them. Even then he declared that "his first intention was not to enter upon a war." It is uncertain what the result would have been if the arrogance and defiant attitude of Davatsi had not come to the aid of the arguments of Amursana. With the intention of exalting himself among his neighbours, he gave himself the airs of an equal to the Chinese ruler, and he sent an embassy to China, as if that country and his were completely on a par. The style of this mission and the language of the letter it bore roused the wrath of Keen Lung, who denounced Davatsi as a "traitor and usurper, who, full of a stupid pride, has dared to address me in his letter as he would his equal."

Having determined on the Central Asian campaign, Keen Lung's military preparations were commensurate with the importance and magnitude of the undertaking. He collected an army of 150,000 men, including the picked Manchu Banners and the celebrated Solon contingent, each of whom was said to be worth ten other soldiers. The command of this army was given to Panti, the best of the Manchu generals, and Amursana, who accompanied it, received a seal and the honorary title of Great General. But Keen Lung superintended all the operations of the war, and took credit to himself for its successful issue. On this point his own words should be read, "Although on account of the very great distance separating this place from the seat of war, I have not found it possible to take the field in person, I can say, nevertheless, that I have taken part in this campaign. I have been, as it were, at a game of chess; I have arranged all the pieces, and I have caused them to be moved as was most appropriate." Within the short period of five months this large army had crossed the desert, and penetrated into the recesses of the Ili region, where Davatsi indulged a belief as to his own security. Once that belief was broken he abandoned the hope of resistance. His power crumbled away at the first contact with the Manchu legions, and Davatsi himself was conveyed as a prisoner to Pekin. Keen Lung himself said of his army that, "confident of marching to victory they break cheerfully through every obstacle; they arrive, terror had gone before them. Scarcely have they time to bend a bow or draw an arrow, when everything submits to them. They give the law, Davatsi is a prisoner, he is sent into my presence." Thus, by the aid of a Chinese army, Amursana recovered what he represented, though with doubtful accuracy, to be his birthright, but on finding himself in possession of the privileges which he claimed he gave reins to his ambition and again allowed his thoughts to run on the idea of independence to which he had aspired as the rival of Davatsi. A personal significance was given to these sentiments by the favourable reception accorded by Keen Lung to Davatsi, who was granted titles and a pension, and whom the impatient disposition of Amursana magnified into a rival that Chinese policy might some day play off against himself.

The triumph of Amursana, by the aid of the Chinese, did not bring tranquillity to Central Asia. He was not contented with the position to which the friendship of Keen Lung had raised him, and placing too high an estimate on his own ability and resources he was inclined to dispute the accepted opinion that all his success was due to the Chinese army. On the termination of the campaign the major portion of that army returned to China, but Panti was left with a select contingent, partly to support Amursana, and partly to secure the restoration of China's authority. Amursana, however, considered that the presence of this force detracted from the dignity of his position. Having risen to the greatness he coveted, Amursana meditated casting aside the prop by which he had risen, but before he took an irretraceable step he resolved to make use of the Chinese forces for extending his authority south of the Tian Shan range into Kashgaria. With some hesitation Panti lent him 500 Chinese soldiers, and with their aid the Eleuth prince captured the cities of Kashgar and Yarkand, and set up a chief named Barhanuddin Khoja as his nominee. This success confirmed Amursana in his good opinion of himself and his resources, and when Keen Lung, who had grown mistrustful of his good faith, summoned him to Pekin he resolved to throw off the mask and his allegiance to China. At this supreme moment of his fate not the least thought of gratitude to the Chinese Emperor, who had made him what he was, seems to have entered his mind. He determined not merely to disregard the summons to Pekin and to proclaim his independence, but also to show the extent of his hostility by adding to his defiance an act of treachery. Before he fully revealed his plans he surprised the Chinese garrison and massacred it to the last man; the valiant Panti, who had gained his victories for him, being executed by the public executioner. As the dependent of Keen Lung, not less than as the ally of Davatsi, Amursana allowed his overweening pretensions to lead him into an erroneous path, in which, when **trying** to **attain** the highest **summit of** ambition, he failed to preserve the very solid and gratifying position **he had** acquired **as the friend of the** Eleuth Chief, or the representative of the great Chinese **ruler.** The fruits of Keen Lung's sacrifices and policy were thus as **rapidly destroyed as they** had been acquired. The first half of the year 1755 **had** sufficed **to give tranquillity to** Central Asia, and **to** replace a hostile poten**tate** with **a friendly, and the next** half **saw this peace** upset, and the **old sense of insecurity and uncertainty revived by an** ambitious prince who thought nothing **of the claims of humanity or of a** superficial gratitude. The massacre **of** Panti and his soldiers seemed to signify **a** triumph in **the eyes of** Amursana, **whereas that act of black and** inexcusable treachery really heralded his **overthrow and ruin.**

The impression **produced by this event** was profound, and when Amursana followed up **the blow by spreading abroad rumours** of the magnitude of his designs they obtained **some** credence even among the Mongols. **Encouraged by this success he** sought **to rally those tribes to** his side **by imputing sinister intentions to** Keen Lung. **His** emissaries declared **that Keen Lung wished to deprive** them all **of their** rank **and** authority, **and that he had summoned** Amursana to Pekin **only for the purpose of** deposing him. They also represented that their master, **Amursana, like a** true desert chief, preferred **his** liberty to everything else, and **sooner than trust himself within the toils of the** Emperor had bidden **him defiance, and raised between them an** inexpiable cause **of** hostility. **To complete the quarrel, Amursana** declared himself King **of the Eleuths, and absolutely indepen**dent **of** China. **But the energy and indignation of Keen Lung soon ex**posed the hollowness **of these designs, and the inadequacy of** Amursana's power and capacity **to make** good **his pretensions. He was proved to be a very unworthy** successor of **the Great Galdan. Some of his** ministers wished Keen Lung **to accept the overthrow of his plans, to** condone **the murder of Panti, and to have done with a "useless and disastrous war:" but** Keen **Lung did not allow himself to be swayed by their advice. The blood** of **his slaughtered soldiers called for a complete revenge, the objects of his** policy **demanded that Amursana should be** deposed **from the posi**tion **of defiance and independence which he had** assumed, **and the** reputation and fair **fame of China rendered it absolutely** imperative **that a** reverse **suffered in the field should be as openly and as** signally retrieved. For each and **all of** these **reasons Keen Lung** rejected the counsels **of the timid as** advice unworthy **of their race and country, and collected another army larger** than that which **had placed him on his throne, to hurl Amursana from the** supremacy **which had not satisfied him and which he had grossly abused.** The armies **of Keen Lung traversed the Gobi** desert **and arrived in** Central Asia, **but the incapacity of his generals** prevented **the campaigns** having those **decisive results which he expected.** The **autocratic Chinese ruler** treated **his generals who failed like the** fickle **French Republic. The** penalty **of failure was a public** execution. Keen **Lung would accept nothing** short **of the capture of** Amursana **as evidence of his victory, and** Amursana **escaped to the Kirghiz. His celerity** or **ingenuity cost the lives of four respectable** Chinese generals, **two of whom were executed at Pekin and two were slain** by brigands **on** their way there **to share the same fate.** Emboldened **by the inability of** the Chinese to **capture him,** Amursana again assembled **an army and pursued the retiring Chinese across the desert, where he succeeded** in inflicting **no** inconsiderable loss upon them. In fact, it appears that the whole Chinese army was only saved from destruction by one brigade, under an heroic commander, devoting itself to destruction.

Yet, not for such disappointments and disasters as these did Keen Lung give up his policy or alter the line of action, in the wisdom of which he fully believed. The failure of his plans was due to the incompetence of his generals, and not to any flaw in his policy. He was engaged in the search for a new commander when fortune so far declared itself in his favour that one of his officers revealed the possession of exceptional capacity, and of a courage out of the common mould. When the Chinese army retired before Amursana one corps maintained its position and successfully defied him, thanks to the capacity of its commander, Tchaohoei. Tchaohoei not merely held his ground, but drew up a scheme for regaining all that had been lost in Central Asia, and Keen Lung was so impressed by it that he at once resolved to entrust the execution of his policy to the only officer who had shown any military capacity. Two fresh armies were sent to the Ili, and placed, on their arrival there, under the command of Tchaohoei, who was exhorted, above all things, to capture Amursana, dead or alive. Tchaohoei at once assumed the offensive, and as Amursana was abandoned by his followers as soon as they saw that China was putting forth the whole of her strength, he had no alternative but once more to flee for shelter to the Kirghiz. But the conditions imposed by Keen Lung were so rigorous that Tchaohoei realised that the capture of Amursana was essential to his gaining the confidence and gratitude of his master. He, therefore, sent his best lieutenant, Fouta, to pursue the Eleuth prince. Fouta pursued Amursana with the energy of one who has to gain his spurs, and he almost succeeded in effecting his capture, but Amursana just made his escape in time across the frontier into Russian territory. But Keen Lung was not satisfied with this result, and he sent both to Fouta and Tchaohoei to rest satisfied with nothing short of the capture of Amursana. The close of that unfortunate prince's career was near at hand, although it was not ended by the act of the Chinese officers. As Keen Lung himself wrote, it was due to natural causes, for "an irritated heaven hastened the time of its vengeance, and a pestilent malady slit the black thread of his life." Amursana died in Russian territory of a fever, and when the Chinese demanded of their neighbours that his body should be surrendered they refused, on the ground that enmity should cease with death, but Fouta was able to report to his sovereign that he had seen with his own eyes the mortal remains of the Eleuth chief who had first been the humble friend and then the bitter foe of the Manchu ruler.

Notwithstanding the completeness of Tchaohoei's success from a military point of view, the peace party at Pekin again urged on Keen Lung the advisability of abandoning the whole enterprise and withdrawing from Central Asia. They said that "the kingdom of the Eleuths is too remote from the centre of our authority for us to be able to long govern it. Let us therefore abandon it to the care of whoever wishes to take it. What matters it to the glory of the Middle Kingdom these uncultivated lands and a people more than half savage?" But the advice of these timid counsellors carried no weight with Keen Lung, who described them as "sunk in the bosom of repose, to whom indolence and ease supply the place of all the virtues, and of whose absurd representations I made as little count as they deserved." Keen Lung decided to administer the country which he had conquered. At first he endeavoured to do this through the native chiefs, to whom he gave patents as khans. This may be described as the system on which Mongolia was and is still governed, but it did not work well in Jungaria, where the petty chiefs still aspired to independence. A succession of risings, or, more accurately, of acts of insubordination, led to severe reprisals on the part of the Chinese, and at last it was resolved to take over the whole administration and to place Chinese officials in all the civil posts. But another step was seen to be necessary to give stability to the Chinese administration, and that was the annexation of Kashgaria. The overthrow of Amursana had led to the conquest of only Jungaria and the Ili region. The great region of Little Bokhara or Eastern Turkestan, known to us now under the more convenient form of Kashgaria, was still ruled by the Khoja Barhanuddin, who had been placed in power by Amursana, and it afforded a shelter for all the disaffected, and a base of hostility against the Chinese. Barhanuddin himself showed no disposition to make his submission to the Chinese, or to offer to Keen Lung that formal tender of submission which was expected and which would have been becoming. For the Chinese ruler held that the conquest of the kingdom of the Eleuths carried with it the proper subordination, if not the open surrender, to him of the territory of its vassals. Even if Tchaohoei had not reported that the possession of Kashgaria was essential to the military security of Jungaria, there is no doubt that sooner or later Keen Lung would have proceeded to extreme lengths with regard to Barhanuddin. The Chinese even went so far as to accuse the Khoja of ingratitude to them, but there seems little or no justification for their contention that they had placed him on the throne. They were fully warranted, however, in treating him as an enemy when he seized an envoy sent to his capital by Tchaohoei and executed him and his escort. This outrage precluded all possibility of an amicable arrangement, and the Chinese prepared their fighting men for the invasion and conquest of Kashgaria. "March," wrote Keen Lung, "against the perfidious Mahomedans who have so insolently abused my favours ; avenge your companions who have been the unhappy victims of their barbarous fury."

The details of this campaign have been preserved with greater accuracy and verisimilitude than is customary in Chinese wars. The Chinese crossed the frontier in two bodies, one under the command of Tchaohoei, the other under that of Fouta. Any resistance that Barhanuddin and his brother attempted was speedily overcome; the principal cities, Kashgar and Yarkand, were occupied, and the ill-advised princes, lately rejoicing in all the conviction of security, were compelled to seek their personal safety by a precipitate flight. The two brothers fled over the Pamir to Badakshan, but the chief of that country caused them to be slain, and sent their heads as a peace offering to the Chinese. Fouta pursued the relics of the Khoja force wherever they were to be encountered, and it is said that the only member of the ruling family to escape was a boy named Sarimsak, who was the ancestor of the Khoja adventurers who at different times during the present century put forward their pretensions to the throne of Kashgar. The conquest and annexation of Kashgaria completed the task with which Tchaohoei was charged, and it also realised Keen Lung's main idea by setting up his authority in the midst of the turbulent tribes who had long disturbed the Empire, and who first learnt peaceful pursuits as his subjects. The Chinese commanders followed up this decided success by the despatch of several expeditions into the adjoining states, of which the precise course has not been preserved, but which must at least have been attended with success, as they gave rise to the superstition among the Mahomedans that "the Chinese conquest of the whole world would one day herald its destruction." The ruler of Khokand was either so much impressed by his neighbour's prowess, or, as there is much reason to believe, experienced himself the weight of their power by the occupation of his principal cities, Tashkent and Khokand, that he hastened to recognise the authority of the Emperor and to enrol himself among the tributaries of the Son of Heaven. The tribute he bound himself to pay was sent without a break for a period of half a century. The Kirghiz chiefs of low and high degree imitated his example, and a firm peace was thus established from one end of Central Asia to the other. The administration was divided between Chinese and native officials, and if there was tyranny, the people suffered rather from that of the Mahomedan Hakim Beg than that of the Confucian Amban.

With one other striking incident this description of the conquest of Central Asia may be ended. When Tse Wang Rabdan was at the height of his fame he formed a design to seize the territory of the Tourguts, but their chief, Ayouka, foiled his plan by fleeing with his tribe into Russian territory, where, after many wanderings, they were assigned a home in the Government of Orenburg, between the Yaik and the Volga. They had resided there more than half a century when Keen Lung's lieutenants appeared in Central Asia as conquerors. A report of the Chinese victories seems to have reached them in their new home on the Caspian, and to have revived the memory of their birthplace. At the same time Keen Lung caused the intimation to be conveyed to them that he would be glad to welcome them back to their own country. Nothing might have come of these representations but that the exactions of the Russian tax-gatherers happened at the moment to be particularly excessive, and an official insult offered their chief, Oubacha, the great-grandson of Ayouka, added fuel to the smouldering flame of their dissatisfaction with their lot as Russian subjects. Then they came to a mighty resolution to return to their original home and to claim the protection of the Chinese ruler. Towards the close of the year 1770 they gathered in their flocks, collected their belongings, and set out to the number of several hundred thousand for their original home. The journey from the Yaik to the Ili occupied eight months, but it was unopposed, as the Russian forces were too few and scattered. The Tourguts again became the faithful subjects or dependents of the Bogdo Khan, the name given the Emperor of China by the Calmucks or the Russians.

The return of the Tourguts, ten years after the close of active campaigning in Kashgaria, came as if to ratify the wisdom of Keen Lung's Central Asian policy. The sneers and doubts of the timid or the incapable had been silenced long before by the prowess and success of Tchaohoei, but, ten years of peace and prosperity had placed in still clearer light than military triumphs the advantages of the able and far-seeing policy of Keen Lung. A strong frontier had been secured; the hostile and semi-hostile peoples and tribes of Mahomedan Turkestan had been overawed and converted into peaceful subjects; the reputation of China had been extended to the furthest bounds of the Asiatic continent; and the monarch who had conceived the grand scheme of conquest and seen how to carry it out, had crowned the glory and durability of his achievements by showing that he knew when and where to stop. Keen Lung himself said, "There is no cause to blush when we know how to be contented, nor is anything to be feared when we can desist from a course at the proper moment." In the boundless wastes and intricate passages of the Pamir, in the dizzy heights and impracticable passes of the Hindoo Koosh and the Kara Tau, he had found the perfection of a frontier. His own immediate territory, the rich provinces of China, was rendered secure against aggression by the strong position he occupied on either side of the Tian Shan in the remote Central Asian region, three thousand miles distant from his capital. His policy was vindicated by results. He could say that he had effected a complete and durable remedy of an evil that up to his time had been dealt with for many centuries only by half-measures and by compromise.

Keen Lung was engaged in many more wars than those in Central Asia. On the side of Burmah he found his borders disturbed by nomad and predatory tribes not less than in the region of Gobi. These clans had long been a source of annoyance and anxiety to the Viceroy of Yunnan, but the weakness of the courts of Ava and Pegu, who stood behind these frontagers, had prevented the local grievance becoming a national danger. But the triumph of the remarkable Alompra, who united Pegu and Burmah into a single state, and who controlled an army with which he effected many triumphs, showed that this state of things might not always continue, and that the day would come when China might be exposed to a grave peril from this side. The successors of Alompra inherited his pretensions if not his ability, and when the Chinese called upon them to keep the borders in better order or to punish some evildoers, they sent back a haughty and unsatisfactory reply. Sembuen, the grandson of Alompra, was king when Keen Lung ordered, in the year 1768, his generals to invade Burmah, and the conduct of the war was entrusted to an officer in high favour at Court, named Count Alikouen, instead of to Fouta, the hero of the Central Asian war, who had fallen under the Emperor's grave displeasure for what, after all, appears to have been a trifling offence. The course of the campaign is difficult to follow, for both the Chinese and the Burmese claim the same battles as victories, but this will not surprise those who remember that the Burmese Court chroniclers described all the encounters with the English forces in the wars of 1829 and 1853 as having been victorious. The advance of the Chinese army, estimated to exceed 200,000 men, from Bhamo to Ava shows clearly enough the true course of the war, and that the Chinese were able to carry all before them up to the gates of the capital. Count Alikouen did not display any striking military capacity, but by retaining possession of the country above Ava for three years he at last compelled the Burmese to sue for peace on humiliating terms. The King of Burmah is said to have been so irritated by the poltroonery of his general in concluding this ignominious, but probably inevitable, treaty, that he sent him a woman's dress. But he did not dare to repudiate the arrangement, and the Chinese army only retired after having obtained the amplest reparation for the wrong originally inflicted on a Chinese subject, and a formal recognition on the part of the ruler of Ava of the supremacy of the Emperor of China. Thus was Burmah added to the long list of the tribute bearers to Pekin, and though the tie has been denied in our time on the strength of the Court annals of Burmah, there is no doubt that it existed, and in a certain form it has been perpetuated under the clauses of the Convention of Pekin of 1886.

The savage and independent Miaotze tribes of the provinces of Kweichow and Szchuen were the next to incur the imperial wrath, and as these people formed and still form an *imperium in imperio*, it is clear that the great Chinese ruler did not coerce them in the same complete manner as he did his other opponents. Yet, after a hard and dubious struggle, he obtained over them a more signal success than had been gained by any of his predecessors. The Miaotze were by nature averse to agricultural pursuits and chafed at the restraints of a settled life. Their courage and rude capacity for war enabled them to hold and maintain a position of isolation and independence during those critical periods which had witnessed the disintegration of the empire and the transfer of power from one race to another. Each successive conquest had passed over the face of the country without disturbing their equanimity or interfering with their lot. The Miaotze remained a barbarous people, living within the limits of the Empire but outside its civilisation, and the representatives of some pre-historic race of China. Their turbulence was, moreover, generally provoked by some exceptionally tyrannical act on the part of the Chinese mandarins with whom they were brought into contact. In the year 1771, immediately on the close of the Burmese war, the Miaotze broke forth from their mountain fastnesses and committed many acts of hostility within Chinese territory. The local Chinese forces were unable to cope with these highlanders, and their successes compelled the Emperor to take up the subject in a serious manner, and to send a large army to bring them to reason. The Miaotze of Szchuen formed the principal object of Keen Lung's resentment. They occupied two large settlements known from the names of streams as the Great and Little Golden River districts, and a large army was collected for the express purpose of conquering this region, and placed under the command of Akoui, one of the noblest members of the Manchu race. When Akoui reached the scene of war, he found that the rashness of a Chinese officer had involved the destruction of a brigade, and he at once devoted himself to preparing for a difficult campaign in such a way that the result could not be rendered doubtful. Having collected the necessary supplies, Akoui delivered his attack on the Little Golden River district, which he occupied after inflicting no slight loss on the Miaotze. He made his new possession the base for an attack on the more important Great Golden River district, which proved a far more arduous undertaking. Sonom, the chief of the Miaotze, had made the most strenuous preparations for defence, and refused to listen to any terms of peace, and even the women took up arms and became combatants. The campaign proved slow, although the result was never in doubt. The narrowness of the few passes, the natural strength of fortresses built on the summit of mountains and protected on several sides by precipices, and the impossibility of effectually utilising their superior numbers, all contributed to retard a decisive result; but notwithstanding all these obstacles, the Chinese steadily approached Sonom's chief stronghold of Karai. At this place the whole Miaotze population had collected, but when Sonom saw that resistance was impossible he offered to surrender on the condition that all lives were spared. Akoui replied that he had no authority to grant such terms, and as Sonom would not trust the clemency of the Emperor, the siege went on. When Keen Lung heard of this he sent orders that all lives might be spared, and thereupon Sonom surrendered, and the Great Golden river passed into the imperial possession. The Miaotze of Kweichow, who are still more or less independent, awed by the fate of their kinsmen, gave hostages for their good conduct and no longer disturbed the Chinese in their possessions. Unfortunately for his reputation, Keen Lung marred his victory by a gross breach of faith. The brave Sonom and his family were executed within the palace at Pekin, and the other Miaotze prisoners were exiled to Ili. The reasons for this breach of faith, the only one alleged against Keen Lung, are unknown, but charity would induce us to say that they must have been weighty, although the only ground alleged is that the Chinese regarded the Miaotze as only half human. Honours were showered on Akoui, who was raised from the Red Girdle to the imperial Yellow Girdle, and Fouta, the hero of the Pamir, was disgraced for disparaging the new commander-in-chief, under whom, however, he had served in a subordinate capacity. For some unknown reason Keen Lung was not sympathetic to this officer, who, for what seems a trifling fault, was publicly executed, thus ending a career that promised to be of the most glorious.

In previous chapters the growth of China's relations with Tibet has been traced, and especially under the Manchu dynasty. The control established by Kanghi after the retirement of the Jungarian army was maintained by both his successors, and for fifty years Tibet had that perfect tranquillity which is conveyed by the expression that it had no history. The young Dalai Lama, who fled to Sining to escape from Latsan Khan, was restored, and under the name of Lobsang Kalsang pursued a subservient policy to China for half-a-century. In the year 1749 an unpleasant incident took place through a collision between the Chinese ambans and the Civil Regent or Gyalpo, who administered the secular affairs of the Dalai Lama. The former acted in a high-handed and arbitrary manner, and put the Gyalpo to death. But in this they went too far, for both the lamas and the people strongly resented it, and revolted against the Chinese, whom they massacred to the last man. For a time it looked as if the matter might have a very serious ending, but Keen Lung contented himself with sending fresh ambans and an escort to Tibet, and enjoining them to abstain from undue interference with the Tibetans. But at the same time that they showed this moderation the Chinese took a very astute measure to render their position stronger than ever. They asserted their right to have the supreme voice in nominating the Gyalpo, and they soon reduced that high official, the Prime Minister of Tibet, to the position of a creature of their own. The policy was both astute and successful. The Tibetans had welcomed the Chinese originally because they saved them from the Eleuth army, and provided a guarantee against a fresh invasion. But the long peace and the destruction of the Eleuth power had led the Tibetans to think less of the advantage of Chinese protection, and to pine for complete independence. The lamas also bitterly resented the assumption by the ambans of all practical authority. How long these feelings could have continued without an open outbreak must remain a matter of opinion; but an unexpected event brought into evidence the unwarlike character of the Tibetans, and showed that their country was exposed to many dangers from which only China's protection could preserve them. In Kanghi's time the danger had come from Ili; in the reign of Keen Lung it came from the side of Nepaul.

As a general rule the mighty chain of the Himalaya has effectually separated the peoples living north and south of it, and the instances in history are rare of any collision between them. Of all such collisions the most important was that which has now to be described as the main cause of the tightening of the hold of China upon Tibet. The mountain kingdom of Nepaul was equally independent of the British and the Mogul Empire of Delhi. It was ruled by three separate kings, until in the year 1769 the Goorkha chief Prithi Narayan established the supremacy of that warlike race. The Goorkhas cared nothing for trade, and their exactions resulted in the cessation of the commercial intercourse which had existed under the Nepaulese kings between India and Tibet. Their martial instincts led them to carry on raids into both Tibet and India. The Tibetans were unequal to the task of punishing or restraining them, and at last the Goorkhas were inspired with such confidence that they undertook the invasion of their country. It is said that the Goorkhas were encouraged to take this step by the belief that the Chinese would not interfere, and that the lamaseries contained an incalculable amount of treasure. The Goorkhas invaded Tibet in 1791 with an army of less than 20,000 men, and, advancing through the Kirong and Kuti passes, overcame the frontier guards, and carried all before them up to the town of Degarchi, where they plundered the famous lamasery of Teshu Lumbo, the residence of the Teshu Lama. Having achieved this success and gratified their desire for plunder, the Goorkhas remained inactive for some weeks, and wasted much precious time. The Tibetans did not attempt a resistance, which their want of military skill and their natural cowardice would have rendered futile, but they sent express messengers to Pekin entreating the Chinese Emperor to send an army to their assistance. Keen Lung had not sent troops to put a stop to the raids committed on the frontier by the Goorkhas; but when he heard that a portion of his dominions was invaded, and that the predominance of his country in the holy land of Buddhism was in danger, he at once ordered his generals to collect all the forces they could and to march without delay to expel the foreign invader. He may have been urged to increased activity by the knowledge that the Tibetans had also appealed for aid to the British, and by his being ignorant what steps the Indian Government would take. Within a very short time of the receipt of the appeal for assistance a Chinese army of 70,000 men was despatched into Tibet, and the Goorkhas, awed by this much larger force, began their retreat to their own country. Their march was delayed by the magnitude of their spoil, and before they had reached the passes through the Himalaya the Chinese army had caught them up. In the hope of securing a safe retreat for his baggage and booty, the Goorkha commander drew up his force in battle array on the plain of Tengri Maidan, outside the northern entrance of the Kirong pass, and the Chinese general, Sund Fo, made his dispositions to attack the Goorkhas; but before delivering his attack he sent a letter reciting the outrages committed, and the terms on which his imperial master would grant peace. Among these were the restitution of the plunder and the surrender of the renegade lama, whose tales were said to have whetted the cupidity of the Goorkhas. A haughty reply was sent back, and the Chinese were told to do their worst.

In the desperately-contested battle which ensued it is impossible to doubt that the valiant hillmen showed their usual courage. They were fighting for their lives and the safety of the spoil, which represented the reward of their Tibetan inroad. But notwithstanding these incentives they were unable to hold their ground, and the beaten Goorkha army fled through the Kirong pass, leaving most of its booty in the hands of the victor. The Chinese commander followed up his success with admirable quickness, and the Goorkhas suffered heavily during their flight. The forts guarding the mountain defiles were captured one after the other. At Kassoa, half-way between Kirong and Daibung, the Goorkhas defended the passage over a chasm for three days, but they were driven from their position with much loss. The Chinese had also suffered heavily; but, when he reached the neighbourhood of Khatmandu, Sund Fo was still at the head of 40,000 confident troops. The Goorkha ruler drew up his remaining forces near the village of Nayakot on the Tadi stream, and in the hope of saving his capital again accepted battle. The position chosen was a strong one, within twenty miles of Khatmandu, and it reflected much credit on the fortitude of the Goorkhas that after so many defeats they were able to make another stand against their relentless and persistent antagonist. The details of this last and most bitterly contested battle of the war have been better preserved than those of any of its predecessors. The Goorkhas fought with the fury of despair, and after some time the Chinese troops hesitated to renew the attack; but Sund Fo was equal to the emergency, and, turning his guns on his own men, drove them forward to assault the Goorkha position. It is said that he kept up the fire after the two armies had become mixed, and that he thus swept a large number of Goorkhas and many of his own soldiers over a precipice. However obtained the victory was decisive, and the Goorkha King at once sued for peace, which was readily granted, as the Chinese had attained all their objects, and Sund Fo was beginning to be anxious about his retreat owing to the approach of winter. When, therefore, the Goorkha embassy entered his camp Sund Fo granted terms which, although humiliating, were as favourable as a defeated people could expect. The Goorkhas took an oath to keep the peace towards their Tibetan neighbours, to acknowledge themselves the vassals of the Chinese Emperor, to send a quinquennial embassy to China with the required tribute, and, lastly, to restore all the plunder that had been carried off from Teshu Lumbo. The exact language of this treaty has never been published, but its provisions have been faithfully kept. The Goorkhas still pay tribute to China; they have kept the peace with one insignificant exception ever since on the Tibetan border; and they are correctly included among the vassals of Pekin at the present time. The gratitude of the Tibetans, as well as the increased numbers of the Chinese garrison, ensured the security of China's position in Tibet, and, as both the Tibetans and the Goorkhas considered that the English deserted them in their hour of need, for the latter when hard pressed also appealed to us for assistance, China has had no difficulty in effectually closing Tibet to Indian trade. China closed all the passes on the Nepaul frontier, and only allowed the quinquennial mission to enter by the Kirong pass. Among all the military feats of China none is more remarkable or creditable than the overthrow of the Goorkhas, who are among the bravest of Indian races, and who, only twenty years after their crushing defeats by Sund Fo, gave the Anglo-Indian army and one of its best commanders, Sir David Ochterloney, an infinity of trouble in two doubtful and keenly-contested campaigns.

Keen Lung's war in Formosa calls for only brief notice; but, in concluding our notice of his many military conquests and campaigns, some description must be given of the great rising in an island which Chinese writers have styled "the natural home of sedition and disaffection." In the year 1786 the islanders rose, slaughtered the Tartar garrisons, and completely subverted the Emperor's authority. The revolt was one, not on the part of the savage islanders themselves, but of the Chinese colonists, who were goaded into insurrection by the tyranny of the Manchu officials. At first it did not assume serious dimensions, and it seemed as if it would pass over without any general rising, when the orders of the Viceroy of Fuhkien, to which Formosa was dependent until made a separate province a few years ago, fanned the fuel of disaffection to a flame. The popular leader Ling organised the best government he could, and, when Keen Lung offered to negotiate, laid down three conditions as the basis of negotiation. They were that "the mandarin who had ordered the cruel measures of repression should be executed," that "Ling personally should never be required to go to Pekin," and, thirdly, that "the mandarins should abandon their old tyrannical ways." Keen Lung's terms were an unconditional surrender and trust in his clemency, which Ling, with perhaps the Miaotze incident fresh in his mind, refused. At first Keen Lung sent numerous but detached expeditions to reassert his power; but these were attacked in detail, and overwhelmed by Ling. Keen Lung said that "his heart was in suspense both by night and by day as to the issue of the war in Formosa"; but, undismayed by his reverses, the Emperor sent 100,000 men under the command of a member of his family to crush the insurrection. Complete success was attained by weight of numbers, and Formosa was restored to its proper position in the Empire. Its pacification is still only partial, as a large portion of its surface is held by aboriginal tribes who absolutely defy the Chinese authority.

A rising in Szchuen, which may be considered from some of its features the precursor of the Taeping rebellion, and the first outbreak of the Tungan Mahomedans in the north-west, whom Keen Lung wished to massacre, marked the close of this long reign, which was rendered remarkable by so many military triumphs. The reputation of the Chinese Empire was raised to the highest point, and maintained there by the capacity and energy of this ruler. Within its borders the commands of the central government were ungrudgingly obeyed, and beyond them foreign peoples and states respected the rights of a country that had shown itself so well able to exact obedience from its dependents and to preserve the very letter of its rights. The military fame of the Chinese, which had always been great among Asiatics, attained its highest point in consequence of these numerous and rapidly-succeeding campaigns. The evidences of military proficiency, of irresistible determination, and of personal valour not easily surpassed, were too many and too apparent to justify any in ignoring the solid claims of China to rank as the first military country in Asia—a position which, despite the appearance of England and Russia in that continent, she still retains, and which must eventually enable her to exercise a superior voice in the arrangement of its affairs to that of either of her great and at present more powerful and better-prepared neighbours.

CHAPTER XIV.

THE COMMENCEMENT OF EUROPEAN INTERCOURSE.

IF the reign of Keen Lung was remarkable for its conquests and successful administration it was a not less important epoch in Chinese history as marking the commencement of European intercourse on what may be called a regular basis, and with it of that foreign question which has exercised so powerful an influence on the destiny of China herself, and which is still, after three wars and many treaties, wrapped in uncertainty, if not unsettled. Before his reign there had been what may be called surreptitious visits of foreign envoys to the capital; the Portuguese, the Dutch, and the English had been allowed to found trading settlements on the coast, and there had been one formal treaty with a foreign Power—that of Nerchins with Russia. But Keen Lung was the first Manchu prince to receive formal embassies from the sovereigns of Europe, and to become an object of solicitude and even of political calculation in the great capitals of this continent. It will be appropriate at this stage to carefully review the relations that had subsisted between China and the different countries of Europe.

Among these the Portuguese were the first in point of time, although they never attained the advantage derivable from that priority; and indeed the important period of their connection with China may be said to have terminated before the Manchus had established their authority. Still, as the tenants of Macao, the oldest European settlement in China for more than three centuries and a half, their connection with the Chinese government must always possess some features of interest and originality. The Portuguese paid their rent to and carried on all their business with the mandarins at Canton, who lost no opportunity of squeezing large sums out of the foreigners, as they were absolutely in their power. The Portuguese could only pay with good or bad grace the bribes and extra duty demanded as the price of their being allowed to trade at all. The power of China seemed so overwhelming that they never attempted to make any stand against its arbitrary decrees, and the only mode they could think of for getting an alleviation of the hardships inflicted by the Canton authorities was to send costly embassies to the Chinese capital. These, however, failed to produce any tangible result. Their gifts were accepted, and their representatives were accorded a more or less gratifying reception; but there was no mitigation of the severity shown by the local mandarins, and, for all practical purposes, the money expended on these missions was as good as thrown away. The Portuguese succeeded in obtaining an improvement in their lot only by combining their naval forces with those of the Chinese in punishing and checking the raids of the pirates, who infested the estuary of the Canton river known as the Bogue. But they never succeeded in emancipating themselves from that position of inferiority in which the Chinese have always striven to keep all foreigners; and if the battle of European enterprise against Chinese exclusiveness had been carried on and fought by the Portuguese it would have resulted in the discomfiture of Western progress and enlightenment.

Nor would the result have been any different if our champions had been either the Dutch or the Spaniards, both of which nations were among the first to establish relations with China. The former, indeed, sent an embassy to Pekin in 1795, but it was treated with such contumely that it does not reflect much credit on those who sent it. The reception has been compared to a masquerade; the envoy was rudely hustled, and lost his hat; and the Chinese even now turn this embassy into ridicule. The Spaniards never held any relations with the central government, all their business being conducted with the Viceroy of Fuhkien; and the successive massacres of Manila completely excluded them from any good understanding with the Pekin government. With Russia, China's relations have always been different from those with the other Powers, and this is explained partly by the fact of neighbourship, and partly by Russia seeking only her own ends, and not advantages for the benefit of every other foreign nation. The first collision on the Amour in the days of Kanghi had been brought to a speedy and amicable end by the Treaty of Nerchinsk, and such incidents as the surrender of Amursana's body, and the flight of the Tourguts, had not sufficed to seriously ruffle the relations of the two countries. The Empress Catherine, anxious to continue and complete the work of her great predecessor, Peter, in this as in other matters sought to establish cordial relations with Pekin, and even went so far as to suggest to the Emperor Keen Lung the desirability of his sending a resident agent to her Court. The Emperor seems so far to have felt the suggestion as a slight that he refused to receive the envoy who bore it, and when a dispute arose as to the surrender of some criminals on the frontier he wrote a letter of remonstrance to the Empress, and threatened to close the trade viâ Kiachta unless certain escaped criminals were extradited. He wrote, he said, in the character of "an elder brother"; but his eloquence did not effect a settlement of the question, nor did the pressure of his other engagements allow him to seriously attempt to put down the caravan trade viâ Kiachta, which steadily assumed increased dimensions, and was long the most active and flourishing outlet of Chinese trade. Whatever the slights and injuries inflicted, they were confined to the frontier, and the remoteness of the point of contact from the capitals of both Empires served to blunt the edge of these wrongs and to avert the hostile collision which seemed repeatedly inevitable. From that time down to the second foreign war the relations between Russia and China preserved their generally cordial character, and there were far fewer cases of friction or disagreement between them than with any other foreign Power.

With France, the relations of China, owing to a great extent to the efforts and influence of the missionaries, had always been marked with considerable sympathy and even cordiality. The French monarchs had from time to time turned their attention to promoting trade with China and the Far East. Henry the Fourth sanctioned a scheme with this object, but it came to nothing; and Colbert only succeeded in obtaining the right for his countrymen to land their goods at Whampoa, the river port of Canton.

But French commerce never flourished in China, and a bold, but somewhat Quixotic attempt to establish a trade between that country and the French settlements on the Mississippi, failed to achieve anything practical. But what the French were unable to attain in the domain of commerce they succeeded in accomplishing in the region of literature. They were the first to devote themselves to the study of the Chinese literature and language, and what we know of the history of China down to the last century is exclusively due to their laborious research and painstaking translations of Chinese histories and annals. They made China known to the polite as well as the political world of Europe. Keen Lung himself appreciated and was flattered by these efforts. His poetry, notably his odes on "Tea," and the "Eulogy of Moukden" as the cradle of his race, was translated by Père Amiot, and attracted the attention of Voltaire, who addressed to the Emperor an epistolary poem on the requirements and difficulties of Chinese versification. The French thus rendered a material service in making China better known to Europe and Europe better known in China, which, although it may be hard to gauge precisely, entitles them still to rank among those who have opened up China to Europeans. The history of China, down to the 18th century at least, could not have been written but for the labours of the French, of Mailla, Du Halde, Amiot, and many others.

There remains only to summarise the relations with the English, who early in the 17th century, and before the Manchus had established their supremacy, possessed factories at Amoy and on the island of Chusan. But their trade, hampered by official exactions, and also by the jealousy of the Portuguese and Dutch, proved a slow growth; and at Canton, which they soon discovered to be the best and most convenient outlet for the State, they were more hampered than anywhere else, chiefly through the hostile representations of the Portuguese, who bribed the mandarins to exclude all other foreigners. The English merchants, like the Portuguese, believed that the only way to obtain a remedy for their grievances was by approaching the Imperial Court and obtaining an audience with the Emperor; but they were wise in not attempting to send delegates of their own. They saw that if an impression was to be created at Pekin the ambassador must come fully accredited by the British government, and not merely as the representative of a body of merchants who were suppliants for commercial privileges. The war with the Goorkhas had made the Chinese authorities acquainted with the fact that the English, who were only humble suitors for trade on the coast, were a great power in India. The knowledge of this fact undoubtedly created a certain amount of curiosity in the mind of Keen Lung, and when he heard that the King of England contemplated sending an embassy to his Court he gave every encouragement to the suggestion, and promised it a welcome and honourable reception. Permission was given it to proceed to Pekin, and thus was a commencement made in the long story of diplomatic relations between England and China, which have at length acquired a cordial character. As great importance was attached to this embassy, every care was bestowed on fitting it out in a worthy manner. Colonel Cathcart was selected as the envoy, but died on the eve of his departure, and a successor was found in the person of Lord Macartney, a nobleman of considerable attainments, who had been Governor of Madras two years before. Sir George Staunton, one of the few English sinologues, was appointed secretary, and several interpreters were sought for and obtained, not without difficulty. The presents were many and valuable, chosen with the double object of gratifying the Emperor and impressing him with the wealth and magnificence of the English sovereign. In September, 1792—the same month that witnessed the overthrow of the Goorkhas at Nayakot—the embassy sailed from Portsmouth, but it did not reach the Peiho, on which Pekin is inaccurately said to stand, until the following August.

An honourable and exceedingly gratifying reception awaited it. The ambassador and his suite, on landing from the man-of-war, were conducted with all ceremony and courtesy up the Peiho to Tientsin, where they received what was called the unusual honour of a military salute. Visits were exchanged with the Viceroy of Pechihli and some of the other high officials, and news came down from Pekin that "the Emperor had shown some marks of great satisfaction at the news of the arrival of the English ambassador." Keen Lung happened to be residing at his summer palace at Jehol beyond the Wall, but he sent peremptory instructions that there was to be no delay in sending the English up to Pekin. Up to this point all had gone well, but the anti-foreign party began to raise obstructions, and, headed by Sund Fo, the conqueror of the Goorkhas, to advise the Emperor not to receive the ambassador, and to reject all his propositions. Whether to strengthen his case, or because he believed it to be the fact, Sund Fo declared that the English had helped "the Goorkha robbers," and that he had found among them "men with hats," *i.e.* Europeans, as well as "men with turbans." As Sund Fo was the hero of the day, and also the Viceroy of the Canton province, his views carried great weight, and they were also of unfavourable omen for the future of foreign relations. But for this occasion the inquisitiveness of the aged Emperor prevailed over the views of the majority in his council and also over popular prejudice. When the embassy had been detained some time at Pekin, and after it looked as if a period of vexatious delay was to herald the discomfiture of the mission, such positive orders were sent by Keen Lung for the embassy to proceed to Jehol that no one dared to disobey him. Lord Macartney proceeded to Jehol with his suite and a Chinese guard of honour, and he accomplished the journey, about one hundred miles, in an English carriage. The details of the journey and reception are given in Sir George Staunton's excellent narrative; but here it may be said that the Emperor twice received the British ambassador in personal audience in a tent specially erected for the ceremony in the gardens of the palace. The embassy then returned to Pekin, and, as the Gulf of Pechihli was frozen, it was escorted by the land route to Canton. On this journey Lord Macartney and his party suffered considerable inconvenience and annoyance from the spite and animosity of the Chinese inferior officials; but nothing serious occurred to mar what was on the whole a successful mission. Keen Lung is said to have wished to go further, but his official utterance was limited to the reciprocation of "the friendly sentiments of His Britannic Majesty." His advanced age and his abdication already contemplated left him neither the inclination nor the power to go very closely into the question of the policy of cultivating closer relations with the foreign people who asserted their supremacy on the sea and who had already subjugated one great Asiatic Empire. But it may at least be said that he did nothing to make the ultimate solution of the question more difficult, and his flattering reception of Lord Macartney's embassy was an important and encouraging precedent for English diplomacy with China.

The events of internal interest in the history of the country during the last twenty years of this reign call for some brief notice, although they relate to comparatively few matters that can be disentangled from the Court chronicles and official gazettes of the period. The great floods of the Hoangho and the destruction caused thereby had been a national calamity from the earliest period. Keen Lung, filled with the desire to crown his reign by overcoming it, entrusted the task of dealing with this difficulty to Count Akoui, whose laurels over the Miaotze had raised him to the highest position in public popularity and his sovereign's confidence. Keen Lung issued his personal instructions on the subject in unequivocal language. He said in his edict, "My intention is that this work should be unceasingly carried on, in order to secure for the people a solid advantage both for the present and in the time to come. Share my views, and in order to accomplish them, forget nothing in the carrying out of your project, which I regard as my own, since I entirely approve of it, and the idea which originated it was mine. For the rest, it is at my own charge, and not at the cost of the province, that I wish all this to be done. Let expenses not be stinted. I take upon myself the consequences whatever they may be." Akoui threw himself into his great task with energy, and it is said that he succeeded in no small degree in controlling the waters and restricting their ravages. We are ignorant of the details of his work, but it may certainly be said that the Hoangho has done less damage since Akoui carried out his scheme than it had effected before. The question is still unsolved, and probably there is no undertaking in which China would benefit more from the engineering science of Europe than this, if the Chinese government were to seriously devote its attention to a matter that affects many millions of people and some of the most important provinces of the Empire.

A great famine about the same period is chiefly remarkable for the persecution it entailed on the Christian missionaries and those among the Chinese themselves professing the foreign religion. The cause of this scarcity was mainly due to the extraordinary growth of the population, which had certainly doubled in fifty years, and which, according to the official censuses, had risen from sixty millions in 1735 to three hundred millions in 1792. Of course the larger part of this increase was due to the expansion of the Empire and the consolidation of the Manchu authority. So great was the national suffering that the gratuitous distribution of grain and other supplies at the cost of the state provided but a very partial remedy for the evil, which was aggravated by the peculation of the mandarins, and the evidence of the few European witnesses shows that the horrors of this famine have seldom been surpassed. The famine was laid to the charge of the Christians, and a commission of mandarins drew up a formal indictment of Christianity, which has stood its ground ever since as the text of the argument of the anti-foreign school. It read as follows : "We have examined into the European religion (or the doctrine) of the Lord of Heaven, and although it ought not to be compared with other different sects, which are absolutely wicked, yet, and that is what we lay to its blame, it has had the audacity to introduce itself, to promulgate itself, and to establish itself in secret. No permission has ever been given to the people of this country to embrace it. Nay, the laws have absolutely long forbidden its adoption. And now all these criminals have had the boldness to come, all of a sudden, into our kingdom, to establish their bishops and priests in order to seduce the people ! This is why it is necessary to extinguish this religion by degrees and to prevent its multiplying its votaries." The fury of the Chinese, fortunately, soon exhausted itself, and although many Europeans were injured none lost their lives, but several thousand native converts were branded on the face and sent to colonise the Ili valley.

While Lord Macartney was at Pekin it was known that the Emperor contemplated abdicating when he had completed the sixtieth year of his reign —the cycle of Chinese chronology—because he did not desire his reign to be of greater length than that of his illustrious grandfather, Kanghi. This date was reached in 1796, when on New Year's-day (6th February) of the Chinese calendar, he publicly abdicated, and assigned the Imperial functions to his son, Kiaking. He survived this event three years, and during that period he exercised, like Charles the Fifth of Germany, a controlling influence over his son's administration; and he endeavoured to inculcate in him the right principles of sound government. But in China, where those principles have been expressed in the noblest language, their practical application is difficult, because the official classes are underpaid and because the law of self-preservation, as well as custom, compels them to pay themselves at the equal expense of the subjects and the Government. Even Keen Lung had been unable to grapple with this difficulty of the Chinese Civil Service, which is as formidable at the present time as ever. One of the ablest and most honest of Keen Lung's ministers, when questioned on the subject, said that there was no remedy. "It is impossible, the Emperor himself cannot do it, the evil is too widespread. He will, no doubt, send to the scene of these disorders mandarins, clothed with all his authority, but they will only commit still greater exactions, and the inferior mandarins, in order to be left undisturbed, will offer them presents. The Emperor will be told that all is well, while everything is really wrong, and while the poor people are being oppressed." And so the vicious circle has gone on to the present day, with serious injury to the state and the people. When Keen Lung had the chance of bringing matters under his own personal control he did not hesitate to exercise his right and power, and all capital punishments were carried out at the capital only after he had examined into each case. It is declared that he always tempered justice with mercy, and that none but the worst offenders suffered death. Transportation to Ili, which he wished to develop, was his favourite form of punishment.

To the end of his life Keen Lung retained the active habits which had characterised his youth. Much of his official work was carried on at an early hour of the morning, and it surprised many Europeans to find the aged ruler so keen and eager for business at these early conferences. His vigour was attributed by competent observers to the active life and physical exercises common among the Tartars. It will be proper to give a description of the personal appearance of this great prince. A missionary thus described him: "He is tall and well built. He has a very gracious countenance, but capable at the same time of inspiring respect. If in regard to his subjects he employs a great severity, I believe it is less from the promptings of his character than from the necessity which would otherwise not render him capable of keeping within the bounds of dependence and duty two empires so vast as China and Tartary. Therefore the greatest tremble in his presence. On all the occasions when he has done me the honour to address me it has been with a gracious air that inspired me with the courage to appeal to him in behalf of our religion. . . .

He is a truly great prince, doing and seeing everything for himself." Keen Lung survived his abdication about three years, dying on the 8th February, 1799—which also happened to be the Chinese New Year's-day—and as to the character and historical importance of his reign, I may be permitted to repeat the language I formerly employed on this subject.

It formed the most important epoch in modern Chinese history, for it marked what was long thought to be the zenith of Manchu power, and it certainly beheld the thorough and complete establishment of that authority. The exceptional brilliance of this reign was enhanced and rendered the more conspicuous by not only a succession of unsurpassed military exploits, but also by a series of literary and administrative achievements unequalled in Tartar if not in Chinese history. Keen Lung's attention to his people's wants, and his zeal in promoting what he thought were their best interests, showed that he desired to appear in their eyes as the paternal ruler, which is the salient characteristic of a Chinese Emperor. That he was almost completely successful in realising his objects there can be little doubt, and it was by general consent, more than by palace flattery, that the title of Magnificent was attached to his name. Taking his reign in conjunction with that of his grandfather, Kanghi, whose work he carried on and completed, the period was one of almost unexampled achievement in the annals of any country. The authority of the Manchus, which appeared likely to be overthrown and obliterated before the vigorous onslaught of the Chinese commander, Wou Sankwei, was triumphantly asserted, and the sovereignty of the Empire was established and made good over remote tributary kingdoms and recalcitrant vassals. The Emperor Kanghi accomplished a great deal, but he left much undone, or half done, for those who came after him to complete. Keen Lung, on the other hand, succeeded in everything he undertook, and his success was never partial, but always complete and decided. Those who followed him on the Dragon Throne had but to retain what he had won, to maintain intact the authority he exercised, to be able to boast with truth that they swayed the destinies of the most remarkable empire of a homogeneous race since the time of Rome.

When Keen Lung released his hold upon the sceptre the Manchu power had reached its pinnacle. A warrior race, supported by the indomitable courage of a great people, and by the unlimited resources of a most favourably situated country, had been able to set up its unquestioned authority throughout the Middle Kingdom and the dependencies which, from a remote period, had been included under the vague and uncertain term of tributaries. From that post of vantage, and by means of those powerful elements of support, it had succeeded in establishing its undisputed supremacy throughout Eastern Asia from Siam to Siberia, and from Nepaul to Corea. There remained no military feat for the loftiest ambition to accomplish when the aged Keen Lung retired into private life, leaving the responsibilities and anxieties of power to his sons and their descendants. Well for those later rulers of the Manchu race would it have been if they could have retained peaceful and undisturbed possession of the great empire to which they succeeded. But a long period of decadence was to follow this century and a half of unexampled vigour and capacity. With the disappearance of the great Keen Lung the stern qualities necessary to the preservation of a widely extended sway also take for a time their departure from the region of Chinese history. Often it was thought that they had departed altogether, and that the long period of decay and disunion would terminate in complete disruption and disaster. Within a quite recent time the character of the people reasserted itself under trying circumstances, and the evil day for them has again been postponed, if not finally put off. But before that reassertion of natural strength takes place a period of internal trouble and external weakness has to be gone through and described. With the death of Keen Lung the vigour of China reached a term, and just as the progress had been consistent and rapid during the space of 150 years, so now will its downward course be not less marked or swift, until, in the very hour of apparent dissolution, the Empire will find safety in the valour and probity of an English officer, and in the ability and resolution of the Empress-Regents and their two great soldier-statesmen, Li Hung Chang and Tso Tsung Tang.

CHAPTER XV.

THE DECLINE OF THE MANCHUS.

ALTHOUGH it is usual and historically accurate to date the decline of Manchu power from the accession of Kiaking, it must not be supposed that it crumbled rapidly away, or that either Chinese statesmen or their European critics were aware that a great change had taken place, and that the power of the Government had been seriously diminished. On the contrary, the great achievements of Keen Lung left a profound impression after his death, assuring tranquillity against internal rebels, and deterring external enemies from attacking his State. Even to the eyes of Europeans China appeared a mighty and formidable empire nearly twenty years after the death of Keen Lung. Mr. Henry Ellis, one of the British Commissioners in 1816, and a man well acquainted with European courts and countries, said, "However absurd the pretensions of the Emperor of China may be to universal supremacy, it is impossible to travel through his dominions without feeling that he has the finest country within an Imperial ring-fence in the world." And if this was the opinion of a competent observer, there is no doubt that the general view of the exalted character of the Chinese autocrat and the extent of his power was still more pronounced. The merchants and factors of the East India Company, which retained the monopoly of the Chinese trade down to the year 1834, spread about their view of the magnificence of the Chinese Court and of the resources of the country, and only harsh experience could show how far this appearance of strength was delusive, and how far Manchu authority rested on an insecure foundation.

The favourable opinion which his father had held of him does not seem to have been shared by all the ministers of Kiaking. The most prominent of them all, Hokwan, who held to Keen Lung the relation that Wolsey held to Henry the Eighth, soon fell under the displeasure of the new Emperor, and was called upon to account for his charge of the finances. The favour and the age of Keen Lung had left Hokwan absolutely without control, and the minister turned his opportunities to such account that he amassed a private fortune of eighty million taels, or more than twenty-five millions of our money. He was indicted for peculation shortly after the death of the great Emperor, and without any friends he succumbed to the attack of his many enemies incited to attack him by the greed of Kiaking. But the amount of his peculations amply justified his punishment, and Kiaking in signing his death warrant could not be accused of harshness or injustice. The execution of Hokwan restored some of his ill-gotten wealth to the State, and served as a warning to other officials, but as none could hope to enjoy his opportunities, it did not act as a serious deterrent upon the mass of the Chinese Civil Service. If arraigned, they might have justified their conduct by the example of their sovereign, who, instead of devoting the millions of Hokwan to the necessities of the State, employed them on his own pleasure, and in a lavish palace expenditure.

Several independent circumstances served to direct attention to the question of the foreign relations of China in the first years of the new reign. The increased import of opium entailing the increased export of silver became for the first time a matter of apprehension in the official world; and in the year 1800, the Hoppo, or Farmer of the Customs, at Canton, the only port where foreign trade was nominally tolerated, issued an edict denouncing the use of opium as a "growing evil," blaming the foreigners for importing it, and employing all sorts of threats against those indulging in or facilitating the practice. As the Hoppo could have stopped the import of opium if he had been so minded at this period, there is no doubt, and, indeed, the fact was notorious, that he did not share the sentiments expressed in the edict which bore his name. The suppression of the opium trade would have deprived his office of the pecuniary advantages which alone rendered it attractive, and enabled him to pay the large sum required for the appointment. The edict was drawn up by the Board of Censors at Pekin and published by Imperial command; but its enactments never possessed any force, and the Hoppo and his satellites, as well as the foreign merchants, treated it as a dead letter. In another matter the Chinese acted with greater energy and determination, and as it throws considerable light on the views prevailing at the time both in China and about China, and as it also forms what may be called the first scene of the drama for the effectual opening of Canton to foreigners, which was not closed for another half-century, it calls for detailed description.

The Portuguese were the tenants, as has previously been stated, of Macao, for which they paid an annual rent to the Chinese; but the nature of their tenure was not understood in Europe, where Macao was considered a Portuguese possession. During the progress of the great European struggle, the French, as part of one of their latest schemes for regaining their position in the East, conceived the idea of taking possession of Macao; but while they were contemplating the enterprise, an English squadron had accomplished it, and during the year 1802 Macao was garrisoned by an English force. The Treaty of Amiens provided for its restoration to Portugal, and the incident closed, chiefly because the period of occupation was brief, without the Chinese being drawn into the matter, or without the true nature of the Portuguese hold on Macao being explained. The exigences of war unfortunately compelled the re-occupation of Macao six years later, when the indignation of the Chinese authorities at the violation of their territory fully revealed itself. Peremptory orders were sent to the Canton authorities from Pekin to expel the foreigners at all costs. The Government of India was responsible for what was a distinct blunder in our political relations with China. In 1808, when alarm at Napoleon's schemes was at its height, it sent Admiral Drury and a considerable naval force to occupy Macao. The Chinese at once protested, withheld supplies, refused to hold any intercourse with that commander, and threatened the English merchants at Lintin with the complete suspension of the trade. In his letter of rebuke the chief mandarin at Canton declared that, "as long as there remained a single soldier at Macao," he would not allow any trade to be carried on, and threatened to "block up the entrance to Macao, cut off your provisions, and send an army to surround you, when repentance would be too late." The English merchants were in favour of compliance with the Chinese demands, but Admiral Drury held a very exalted opinion of his own power and a corresponding contempt for the Chinese. He declared that, as "there was nothing in his instructions to prevent his going to war with the Emperor of China," he would bring the Canton officials to reason by force. He accordingly assembled all his available forces, and proceeded up the river at the head of a strong squadron of boats with the avowed intention of forcing his way up to the provincial capital. On their side the Chinese made every preparation to defend the passage, and they blocked the navigation of the river with a double line of junks, while the Bogue forts were manned by all the troops of the province. When Admiral Drury came in sight of these defences, which must have appeared formidable to him, he hesitated, and instead of delivering his attack, he sent a letter requesting an interview with the mandarin, again threatening to force his way up to Canton. But the Chinese had by this time taken the measure of the English commander, and they did not even condescend to send him a reply; when Admiral Drury, submitting to their insult, hastily beat a retreat. On several subsequent occasions he renewed his threats, and even sailed up the Bogue, but always retreated without firing a shot. It is not surprising that the Chinese were inflated with pride and confidence by the pusillanimous conduct of the English officer, or that they should erect a pagoda at Canton in honour of the defeat of the English fleet. After these inglorious incidents Admiral Drury evacuated Macao and sailed for India, leaving the English merchants to extricate themselves as well as they could from the embarrassing situation in which his hasty and blundering action had placed them. If the officials at Canton had not been as anxious for their own selfish ends that the trade should go on as the foreign merchants themselves, there is no doubt that the views of the ultra school at Pekin who wished all intercourse with foreigners interdicted, and who caused Père Amiot, notwithstanding his signal services under Keen Lung, to be expelled from the country, would have prevailed. But the Hoppo and his associates were the real friends of the foreigner, and opened the back door to foreign commerce at the very moment that they were signing edicts denouncing it as a national evil and misfortune.

If Admiral Drury was weak, it is gratifying to find that, in a matter affecting the national honour and the first principles of justice, other English officers were resolute and consistent. The Chinese authorities on the Canton river, who were good enough to allow the foreigners to dispose of their useful articles in the profit of which they shared, advanced on behalf of their sovereign the judicial authority over the persons of foreigners, which is admitted without dispute among nations on an equal footing in laws and civilisation. For offences committed within Chinese territory, or more explicitly on Chinese subjects, they claimed to possess the same power of punishing an European as a Chinese, and for a time they not merely claimed but exercised that power. One tragic incident in 1784 had brought into prominence the full extent of the Chinese pretension, and the gross injustice it entailed when carried out, as Chinese judges would execute it without regard for circumstances or qualifications. When firing a salute the gun of a sailor on board an English merchantman happened to be loaded with ball, and to hit and kill a Chinese sailor. Although the affair was quite accidental, the Chinese authorities demanded the surrender of the culprit, and after long discussion the culprit was surrendered under the threat of the suspension of the trade, and in the belief that whatever punishment was inflicted, it would stop short of death. The Chinese did not condescend to any form of trial. They had obtained an European victim, and on the retaliatory principle of a life for a life they ordered him at once to be strangled. The Chinese obtained a momentary triumph, but they had effectually over-reached themselves, for after such an inhuman act it was impossible to again give way to their demands. Many subsequent cases of manslaughter occurred on the crowded river and in brawls on shore, but in no instance were Englishmen handed over to the cruel mercy of a Chinese judge. For whatever offences they had committed they were tried and punished in accordance with the practice of their own country and with due allowance for the provocation received. Long before the signature of any treaty the English asserted and maintained to the full extent of their power the principle of ex-territoriality.

The Macartney mission had attracted what may be called the official attention of the British Government to the Chinese question, and the East India Company, anxious to acquire fresh privileges to render that trade more valuable, exercised all its influence to sustain that attention. On its representations a costly present was sent to Sung Tajin, one of the ablest and most enlightened of all the Chinese officials who had shown cordiality to Lord Macartney, but the step was ill-advised and had unfortunate consequences. The present, on reaching Pekin, was returned to Canton with a haughty message that a minister of the Emperor dare not even see a present from a foreign ruler. The publicity of the act rather than the offer of a present must be deemed the true cause of this unqualified rejection, but the return of the present was not, unfortunately, the worst part of the matter. The Emperor Kiaking sent a letter couched in lofty language to George the Third, declaring that he had taken such British subjects as were in China under his protection, and that there was "no occasion for the exertions of your Majesty's Government." The advice of the Minister Sung, who was suspected of sympathy with the foreigners, was much discredited, and from a position of power and influence he gradually sank into one of obscurity and impotence. This was especially unfortuate at a moment when several foreign powers were endeavouring to obtain a footing at Pekin. The Russian Emperor, wishing no doubt to emulate the English, sent, in 1805, an imposing embassy under Count Goloyken to the Chinese capital. The presents were rich and numerous, for the express purpose of impressing the Chinese ruler with the superior wealth and power of Russia over other European states, and great hopes were entertained that Count Goloyken would establish a secure diplomatic base at Pekin. The embassy reached Kalgan on the Great Wall in safety, but there it was detained until reference had been made to the capital. The instructions came back that the Russian envoy would only be received in audience provided he would perform the kotow, or prostration ceremony, and that if he would not promise to do this he was not to be allowed through the Wall. Count Goloyken firmly refused to give this promise, and among other arguments, he cited the exemption accorded to Lord Macartney. The Chinese remained firm in their purpose, Count Goloyken was informed that his visit had been prolonged too far, and the most brilliant of all Russian embassies to China had to retrace its steps without accomplishing any of its objects. This was not the only rebuff Russia experienced at this time. The naval officer Krusenstern conceived the idea that it would be possible to attain all the objects of his sovereign, and to open up a new channel for a profitable trade by establishing communications by sea with Canton, where the Russian flag had never been seen. The Russian Government fitted out two ships for him, and he safely arrived at Canton, where he disposed of their cargoes. When it became known at Pekin that a new race of foreigners had presented themselves at Canton, a special edict was issued ordering that "all vessels belonging to any other nation than those which have been in the habit of visiting this port shall on no account whatever be permitted to trade, but merely suffered to remain in port until every circumstance is reported to us and our pleasure made known." Thus in its first attempt to add to its possession of a land trade, via Kiachta and the Mongol steppe, a share in the sea trade with Canton, Russia experienced a rude and discouraging rebuff.

The unsatisfactory state of our relations with the Chinese Government which was brought home to the British authorities by the difficulty our ships of war experienced in obtaining water and other necessary supplies on the China coast, which had generally to be obtained by force, led to the decision that another embassy should be sent to Pekin, for the purpose of effecting a better understanding. The reasoning which led to this conclusion was natural but fallacious. The home Government was much swayed in its judgment by the experience it had acquired in other Asiatic countries, especially Persia, where the rulers thought it derogatory to treat with ambassadors of a lower rank than from a sovereign. Unfortunately the Chinese reasoned in a totally different fashion. They would much rather have dealt with the East India Company's agents at Canton, as they could treat them as mere merchants who were quite content so long as they were on amicable terms with the Hoppo. They felt a very different arrangement and mode of treatment were required when they had to deal with the spokesmen of powerful and independent Empires. The pretension of foreigners that their sovereigns were on a perfect equality with the ruler of the Middle Kingdom was both inconvenient and dangerous. Embassies from States of undoubted inferiority, which were not offended at being styled tributary nations, were welcome at Pekin, but those from nations asserting a position of equality were quite beyond the comprehension of the Chinese, and as such to be deprecated and absolutely forbidden. The experience of official treatment in China was also very much against any sanguine view as to the benefits that might accrue from another mission to the capital. In favour of it there was only the reception accorded to Lord Macartney by the Emperor Keen Lung, who was a ruler of exceptional breadth of view and independence of judgment, and even that audience had produced little or no practical result. On the other hand, many circumstances forbade a too hopeful view of the case. The rejection of the present to Sung Tajin, the arrogant tone of the Emperor's letters, the assertion of China's sovereign rights at Macao, and the failure of the Russian embassy under Count Goloyken, all pointed to the conclusion that the Emperor Kiaking would give any envoy to his Court a very different reception from what his father did. But in face of these unfavourable facts the decision to send a second embassy to Pekin was formed and persisted in. By a strange coincidence the second embassy, like the first, was contemporaneous with a disturbed condition of things in Nepaul. When Lord Macartney went to

Pekin the Chinese had just completed their successful invasion of Nepaul, and when Lord Amherst followed in his steps we were bringing to a victorious conclusion a long and arduous war in the same country. The Goorkhas, when hard pressed, had applied to the Chinese for aid, concluding their letter with the remark, "Consider, if you abandon your dependents, that the English will soon be masters of Lhasa"; but they received no comfort from the Chinese authorities, who told them that they "were a race of robbers, who richly deserved whatever punishment they received." Notwithstanding this, the probability remains that events in the Himalayan region led the Chinese government to doubt the wisdom of cultivating close relations with the power which was supreme in India.

Lord Amherst, who was specially selected for the mission on account of his diplomatic experience, reached the mouth of the Peiho in August, 1816. Among the members of his staff was Sir George Staunton, one of the earliest of English sinologues, and he seems to have formed the conclusion immediately on reaching Tientsin that the mission had arrived at the wrong moment to do any good. However, Lord Amherst, relying on his pacific and friendly intentions, as expressed in the phrase "conciliation and compliment," remained hopeful long after his experienced secretary had made up his mind that the mission would prove abortive, and the permission to proceed to Pekin seemed to warrant the belief that something, after all, might be accomplished. The preliminary discussions at Tientsin had related to the question of the ceremony to be observed during an audience with the Emperor, and as to whether the prostration ceremony of the kotow should be performed or not. They had led to no final decision, and the point remained in abeyance until the embassy reached Pekin, whither it was sent more from the desire of the Tientsin officials to shift on to other shoulders the settlement of a delicate point than by the express order of the Emperor. At the time it was thought differently, and Lord Amherst naturally supposed that he had been summoned to Pekin by the Emperor; and as some assurance had been given that the kotow would be waived, he thought at least that he might count on an audience. But the circumstances of the journey were little calculated to inspire confidence as to the good results likely to ensue from even an audience with the Emperor. The mission was hurried along at a rapid rate over bad roads in uncomfortable vehicles without any time for rest or refreshment, and on reaching Pekin it was led by a circuitous route outside the walls to the palace of Yuen-min-yuen. Immediately on arrival Lord Amherst was informed that the Emperor was willing to grant him audience, and that he then and there awaited him. It is not surprising that Lord Amherst should have considered this sudden summons, following on the discourteous treatment he had received during the hurried journey from Tientsin to Pekin, as part of a plan to humiliate and throw discredit on the British mission. In begging to be excused from this hasty and unprepared-for interview, Lord Amherst pleaded the fatigue of himself and his party, the absence of their uniforms and of the presents for the Emperor, which were in the heavy baggage in the rear, and it was obvious that the suggestion violated every point of diplomatic punctilio. Lord Amherst was supported in his refusal by both his Assistant-commissioners, Sir George Staunton and Mr. Henry Ellis; and it is not surprising that they should all have come to the same conclusion, that behind this proposal for an immediate reception there lurked an intention to cast a stigma on the majesty of the sovereign of Great Britain. The positive and repeated assurance that the kotow would be waived, and that everything should be done in accordance with the English ceremony, did not avail to induce the envoy to alter his decision.

However natural the views of Lord Amherst were,—and it would be absurd for anyone to attempt to censure his action,—there can be no doubt, from the information subsequently obtained, that the proposal for an immediate audience was made in good faith, and with the most friendly intentions. The Emperor Kiaking had not been acquainted with the departure of the mission from Tientsin, and he appears only to have been apprised of its arrival at Pekin when it entered the palace of Yuen-min-yuen. Then his curiosity to see the foreigners overcame his political resolutions, and with the natural resolve of an irresponsible despot to gratify his wish without regard to the convenience of others, he determined to see them at once, and ordered that Lord Amherst and his companions should be brought forthwith into his presence. This sudden decision was most disconcerting to his own ministers, who had practically decided that no audience should be granted unless Lord Amherst performed the kotow, and especially to his brother-in-law Ho Koong Yay, who, at the Emperor's repeated wish to see the English representatives, was compelled to abandon his own schemes and to remove all restrictions to the audience. The firmness of Lord Amherst was unexpected and misunderstood. Ho Koong Yay repeated his invitation several times, and even resorted to entreaty; but when the Chinese found that nothing was to be gained they changed their tone, and the infuriated Kiaking ordered that the ambassador and his suite should not be allowed to remain at Yuen-min-yuen, and that they should be sent back to the coast without a moment's delay. Mr. Henry Ellis, in his account of the embassy, writes as follows on this incident: "The house of Sung Tajin, selected for our residence, was extremely commodious and pleasantly situated, with flowers and trees near the principal apartments. Its aspect was so agreeable that we could not but look forward with some satisfaction to remaining there a few days. Such, however, was not to be our fate; before two hours had elapsed a report was brought that opposition was made by the Chinese to unloading the carts; and soon after the mandarins announced that the Emperor, incensed by the ambassador's refusal to attend him according to his commands, had given orders for our immediate departure. The order was so peremptory that no alteration was proposed; in vain was the fatigue of every individual of the embassy pleaded; no consideration was allowed to weigh against the positive commands of the Emperor." Thus ignominiously ended the Amherst mission, which was summarily dismissed, and hurried back to the coast in a highly-inconvenient and inglorious manner. In a letter to the Prince Regent, Kiaking suggested that it would not be necessary for the British government to send another embassy to China. He took some personal satisfaction out of his disappointment by depriving Ho Koong Yay of all his offices, and mulcting him in five years of his pay as an Imperial Duke. The cause of his disgrace was expressly stated to be the mismanagement of the relations with the English ambassador and the suppression of material facts from the Emperor's knowledge. Sung Tajin, who had been specially recalled from his governorship in Ili to take part in the reception of the Europeans, and whose sympathy for them was well known, was also disgraced, and did not recover his position until after the death of Kiaking. The failure of the Amherst mission put an end to all schemes for diplomatic intercourse with Pekin until another generation had passed away; but the facts of the case show that its failure was not altogether due to the hostility of the Chinese Emperor. No practical results, in all probability, would have followed; but if Lord Amherst had gone somewhat out of his way to humour the Chinese autocrat, there is no doubt that he would have been received in audience without any humiliating conditions.

Long before the Amherst mission reached China evidence had been afforded that there were many elements of disorder in that country, and that a dangerous feeling of dissatisfaction was seething below the surface. The Manchus, even in their moments of greatest confidence, had always distrusted the loyalty of their Chinese subjects, and there is no dispute that one of their chief reasons for pursuing an excluding policy towards Europeans was the fear that they might tamper with the mass of their countrymen. What had been merely a sentiment under the great rulers of the 18th century became an absolute conviction when Kiaking found himself the mark of conspirators and assassins. The first of the plots to which he nearly fell a victim occurred at such an early period of his reign that it could not be attributed to popular discontent at his misgovernment. In 1803, only four years after the death of Keen Lung, Kiaking, while passing through the streets of his capital in his chair, carried by coolie bearers, was attacked by a party of conspirators, members of one of the secret societies, and narrowly escaped with his life. His eunuch attendants showed considerable devotion and courage, and in the struggle several were killed; but they succeeded in driving off the would-be assassins. The incident caused great excitement, and much consternation in the Imperial palace, where it was noted that out of the crowds in the streets only six persons came forward to help the sovereign in the moment of danger. After this the Emperor gave up his practice of visiting the outer city of Pekin, and confined himself to the Imperial city, and still more to the Forbidden palace which is situated within it. But even here he could not enjoy the sense of perfect security, for the discovery was made that this attempted assassination was part of an extensive plot with ramifications into the Imperial family itself. Inquisitorial inquiries were made, which resulted in the disgrace and punishment of many of the Emperor's relatives, and thus engendered an amount of suspicion and a sense of insecurity that retained unabated force as long as Kiaking filled the throne. That there was ample justification for this apprehension the second attempt on the person of the Emperor clearly revealed. Whatever dangers the Emperor might be exposed to in the streets of Pekin, where the members of the hated and dreaded secret societies had as free access as himself, it was thought that he could feel safe in the interior of the Forbidden city—a palace-fortress within the Tartar quarter garrisoned by a large force, and to which admission was only permitted to a privileged few. Strict as the regulations were at all times, the attempt on Kiaking and the rumours of sedition led undoubtedly to their being enforced with greater rigour, and it seemed incredible for any attempt to be made on the person of the Emperor except by the mutiny of his Guards or an open rebellion. Yet it was precisely at this moment that an attack was made on the Emperor in his own private apartments which nearly proved successful, and which he himself described as an attack under the elbow. In the year 1813 a band of conspirators, some two hundred in number, made their way into the Palace either by forcing one of the gates, or, more probably, by climbing the walls at an unguarded spot, and, overpowering the few Guards they met, some of them forced their way into the presence of the Emperor. There is not the least doubt that Kiaking would then have fallen but for the unexpected valour of his son Prince Meenning, afterwards the Emperor Taoukwang, who, snatching up a gun, shot two of the intruders. This prince had been set down as a harmless, inoffensive student, but his prompt action on this occasion excited general admiration, and Kiaking, grateful for his life, at once proclaimed him his heir.

Towards the close of his reign, and very soon after the departure of Lord Amherst, Kiaking was brought face to face with a very serious conspiracy, or what he thought to be such, among the princes of the Manchu Imperial family. By an ordinance passed by Chuntche all the descendants of that prince's father were declared entitled to wear a yellow girdle and to receive a pension from the state; while, with a view to prevent their becoming a danger to the dynasty, they were excluded from civil or military employment, and assigned to a life of idleness. This Imperial colony was, and is still, one of the most peculiar and least understood of the departments of the Tartar government; and although it has served its purpose in preventing dynastic squabbles, there must always remain the doubt as to how far the dynasty has been injured by the loss of the services of so many of its members who might have possessed useful capacity. They purchased the right to an easy and unlaborious existence, with free quarters and a small income guaranteed, at the heavy price of exclusion from the public service. No matter how great their ambition or natural capability, they had no prospect of emancipating themselves from the dull sphere of inaction to which custom relegated them. Towards the close of Kiaking's reign the number of these useless Yellow Girdles had risen to several thousand, and the Emperor, alarmed by the previous attacks, or having some reason to fear a fresh plot, adopted strenuous measures against them. Whether the Emperor's apprehensions overcame his reason, or whether there were among his kinsmen some men of more than average ability, it is certain that the princes of the Manchu family were goaded or incited into what amounted to rebellion. The exact particulars remain unknown until the dynastic history sees the light of day; but it is known that many of them were executed, and that many hundreds of them were banished to Manchuria, where they were given employment in taking care of the ancestral tombs of the ruling family.

Special significance was given to these intrigues and palace plots by the remarkable increase in the number and the confidence of the secret societies which, in some form or other, have been a feature of Chinese public life from an early period. Had they not furnished evidence by their increased numbers and daring of the dissatisfaction prevalent among the Chinese masses, whether on account of the hardships of their lot, or from hatred of their Tartar lords, they would scarcely have created so much apprehension in the bosom of the Emperor Kiaking, whose authority met with no open opposition, and whose reign was nominally one of both internal and external peace. These secret societies have always been, in the form of fraternal confederacies and associations, a feature in Chinese life; but during the present century they have acquired an importance they could never previously claim, both in China and among Chinese colonies abroad.

The first secret society to become famous was that of the Water-Lily, or Pe-leen-keaou, which association chose as its emblem and title the most popular of all plants in China. "The poets have celebrated the water-lily in their verses on account of the beauty of its flowers; the doctors of reason have placed it among the ingredients for the elixir of immortality; and the economists have extolled it for its utility." Although the most famous of the societies, and the one which is regarded as the parent of all that have come after it, the Water-Lily had, as a distinct organisation, a very brief existence. Its organisers seem to have dropped the name, or to have allowed it to sink into disuse in consequence of the strenuous official measures taken against the society by the government for the attempt, in 1803, on Kiaking's life in the streets of Pekin. They merged themselves into the widely-extended confederacy of the Society of Celestial Reason— the Theen-te-Hwuy—which became better known by the title given to it by Europeans of the Triads, from their advocacy of the union between Heaven, earth, and man. The Water-Lily Society, before it was dissolved, caused serious disturbances in both Shantung and Szchuen, and especially in the latter province, where the disbanded army that had rescued Tibet and punished the Goorkhas furnished the material for sedition. With more or less difficulty, and at a certain expense of life, these risings were suppressed, and Kiaking's authority was rendered secure against these assailants, while for his successors was left the penalty of feeling the full force of the national indignation of which their acts were the expression.

With regard to the organisation of these secret societies, which probably remain unchanged to the present day, China had nothing to learn from Europe either as to the objects to be obtained in this way or as to how men are to be bound together by solemn vows for the attainment of illegal ends. In China, where the ordinary affairs of life are always wrapped up in some high moral sentiment, or in some accepted axiom of wisdom enunciated by one of the early sages, the objects of a political association borrow their force from this national peculiarity. Men were brought together, not to oust the Manchus or reform society, but with the object of attaining some ideal perfection in morality, such as "uniting Heaven and earth," or "spreading the worship of the Queen of Heaven, the mother and nurse of all things." In China the precaution has even been taken of further masking the projected scope of operations by the assumption of a title of not merely inappropriate meaning, but occasionally of absolutely no meaning at all. By this device not only has the suspicion of the executive been often allayed, but the curiosity of the public—that powerful agent and frequently very useful ally—has been enlisted in behalf of its objects, without knowing whither they tended. The first principle of a secret society is equality. Each assumes the same risk, and fidelity to the common bond can only be assured by all being pledged to mutual support in both danger and necessity. Such conditions formed the basis of membership in those political and socialistic clubs which became so numerous during Kiaking's reign. In a couplet wherein was supposed to be expressed the guiding maxim of one of the most important of these societies, it was said that "the blessing and the woe should be reciprocally borne and shared." In the machinery of government drawn up for the guidance of its members the ingenuity of the people revealed itself; and the Nihilistic associations of Russia could not find much to improve upon in the regulations of these Chinese confederacies, which, after thirty years of silent intrigue, succeeded in plunging the Empire into a state of insurrection, from the effects of which it has only recently recovered. The principles of Freemasonry were adopted, and all the members were called brothers. The chosen leaders were, in addition, styled Elders; but few reached this superior rank, and those only after a long and trying probation. Bound together by laws of which the full nature has never been revealed or discovered, treachery or want of the necessary zeal in carrying out the behests of the Order was punished by death, inflicted by a chosen delegate, or more than one, as representative of the injured brotherhood. Various ceremonies of as impressive a character as the human mind can conceive were drawn up to mark the entrance of a new member. The night was selected as the appropriate hour for so grave an undertaking, and the members assembled from far and near to take part in an office which enhanced their individual importance while it added to their collective strength. When thirty-six oaths had been sworn to advance the cause and to stand by the Order to the last extremity, and when a present of money had been made to show that the candidate placed his worldly goods at the service of the common fund, the most important part of the ceremony was next performed. This was called "Crossing the bridge." The candidate stood underneath two drawn swords, held over his head by two members, while the Elder brother heard him affirm his undeviating fidelity to the cause; and, when this was finished, the new member cut off the head of a cock, with the exclamation, "Thus may I perish if the secret I divulge!" To meetings such as these, held in retired woods, lonely houses, or in the deserted burial-places of the ancient rulers, did Kiaking's enemies flock, and they returned from them to their daily avocations with thoughts in their minds and pledges on their consciences that could only bode ill for the tranquillity of the realm and the peace of mind of the sovereign. By signs known only to themselves, and by pass-words, these sworn conspirators could recognise their members in the crowded streets, and could communicate with each other without exciting suspicion as to their being traitors at heart. In its endeavours to cope with this formidable and widespread organisation under different names, Kiaking's government found itself placed at a serious disadvantage. Without an exact knowledge of the intentions or resources of its secret enemies it failed to grapple with them, and, as its sole remedy, it could only decree that proof of membership carried with it the penalty of death.

During the last years of the reign of Kiaking the secret societies rather threatened future trouble than constituted a positive danger to the state. They were compelled to keep quiet and to confine their attention to increasing their numbers rather than to realising their programme. The Emperor was consequently able to pass the last four years of his life with some degree of personal tranquillity, and in full indulgence of his palace pleasures, which seem at this period to have mainly consisted of a theatrical troupe which accompanied him even when he went to offer sacrifice in the temples. His excessive devotion to pleasure did not add to his reputation with his people, and it is recorded that one of the chief causes of the Minister Sung's disgrace and banishment to Ili was his making a protest against the Emperor's proceedings. Some time before his death Kiaking drew up his will, and on account of his great virtues he specially selected as his successor his second son, Prince Meenning, who had saved his life from the assassins in the attack on the palace. Kiaking died on

2nd September, 1820, in the 61st year of his age, leaving to his successor a diminished authority, an enfeebled power and a discontented people. Some mitigating circumstance may generally be pleaded against the adverse verdict of history in its estimation of a public character. The difficulties with which the individual had to contend may have been exceptional and unexpected, the measures which he adopted may have had untoward and unnatural results, and the crisis of the hour may have called for genius of a transcendent order. But in the case of Kiaking not one of these extenuating facts can be pleaded. His path had been smoothed for him by his predecessor, his difficulties were raised by his own indifference, and the consequences of his spasmodic and ill-directed energy were scarcely less unfortunate than those of his habitual apathy. So much easier is the work of destruction than the labour of construction, that Kiaking in twenty-five years had done almost as much harm to the constitution of his country and to the fortunes of his dynasty as Keen Lung had conferred solid advantages on the state in his brilliant reign of sixty years.

It must not be supposed that because the available records of Kiaking's reign are few, and refer to detached events rather than to the daily life and continuous political existence of the country, the Chinese people had no thoughts save for the foibles of their ruler, and for the numerous efforts made by Europeans to establish with them relations of intimacy and equality. The means of describing it do not exist, but the life of the nation went on less disturbed than would be supposed by the disquieting events of Kiaking's reign, and the people were as ever resolutely bent on performing their mundane duties according to the fashion and precepts of their forefathers. The effect of the secret societies on public opinion was unquestionably great, and the people, fond of the mysterious and ingrained with superstition, turned with as much eagerness to the latest social or political propagandum as they did to the predictions of the village soothsayer. Had these societies continued secret and peaceful there is no saying how far their numbers might not have increased, but the instant their hostility to the state and dynasty became revealed the natural caution of the Chinese made them draw away from an enterprise that assumed the gravity of an insurrection. The instant the Water-Lily sect threw off the mask and resorted to acts of violence, a different condition of things came into force, and the majority of the people held aloof from open rebellion. In no country in Asia, and perhaps in the world, do the people themselves form the national strength more incontestably than in China. It is not a question of one class or of one race, but of the whole body of the inhabitants. The governing orders are recruited from and composed of men who, in the strictest sense of the phrase, owe everything to themselves and nothing to birth. They gain admission into the public service by passing a series of examinations of more or less difficulty, and having entered the venerable portals of the most ancient civil service in the world, there is no office beyond the reach of the humblest—even though it be to wield almost despotic power in a great province, or to stand among the chosen ministers round the Dragon Throne. The interest of every family in the government of the kingdom is a personal concern. There is a sure element of stability in such an arrangement as this. A people does not quarrel with its institutions when the best brains in the land form the pillars by which they are supported. Kiaking's errors were a source of grief and anxiety to his experienced ministers, who knew how easily the provincial officials neglected their duties when they perceived apathy at the centre of government; but they interfered in a very slight degree with the daily life of the nation at large. The people were not altogether contented, but still they were able to obtain their own subsistence, and thus absorbed in the struggle of existence they felt no inclination to disturb the tranquillity of the country by denouncing the shortcomings of the executive, or by attempting to change the form of government. What had happened showed that there were dangers ahead, and that some strong disaffection or race antipathy was seething below the surface among the Chinese masses; but on the whole it seems as if the material prosperity of the people was never greater than during the reign of Kiaking. The population by the census of 1812 is said to have exceeded 360 millions, and the revenue never showed a more flourishing return on paper. To the external view all was still fair and prosperous when Kiaking died; under his successor, who was in every sense a worthier prince, the canker and decay were to be clearly revealed.

CHAPTER XVI.

THE EMPEROR TAOUKWANG.

THE early years of the new reign were marked by a number of events unconnected with each other but all contributing to the important incidents of the later period which must be described, although they cannot be separated. The name of Taoukwang, which Prince Meenning took on ascending the throne, means Reason's Light, and there were many who thought it was especially appropriate for a prince who was more qualified for a college than a palace. Most of the chroniclers of the period gave an unfavourable picture of the new ruler, who was described as "thin and toothless," and as "lank in figure, low of stature, with a haggard face, a reserved look, and a quiet exterior." He was superior to his external aspect, for it may be truly said that although he had to deal with new conditions he evinced under critical circumstances a dignity of demeanour and a certain royal patience which entitled him to the respect of his opponents.

As he owed his elevation to the favour of his father—for he was a younger son, although the best information disproves the statement that he was the son of a mere concubine—there seemed for a brief space a probability of a struggle for power between him and his eldest brother, Hwuy Wang, whose mother was the principal surviving widow of Kiaking. It was believed that she had poisoned Taoukwang's mother, and before he was proclaimed heir-apparent she had made him suffer many indignities, but, fortunately for the peace of the realm, she decided to silence her personal feelings and to acquiesce in Kiaking's choice. Public spirit overcame private animosity, and the Empress-mother and her son, Hwuy Wang, were the most forward in recognising the new Emperor. A few words will throw light on the personal character of this prince. His early training had not been of a nature to bring out his good points or to quicken whatever warm sympathies and natural talent he may have possessed. Brought up in a licentious Court, and surrounded by ministers of pleasure, with whom, unquestionably, he had not the least fellow-feeling, he had always lived a retired life, as far aloof from the pursuits of the Court as was possible. He had thus obtained a reputation for reserve, if not for stupidity, that secured him against the antipathy of many, if it prevented his obtaining the friendship of more than a few chosen companions. His life had been neither very pleasant nor very happy. He had had to show great self-restraint, and the leisure which he had passed in reflection seems to have increased his natural irresolution and to have rendered him still more unfitted to assume that active part in the guidance of affairs which the condition of China so imperatively demanded.

Yet Taoukwang began his reign in every way in a creditable manner. While professing in his proclamations the greatest admiration for his father, his first acts reversed his policy and aimed at undoing the mischief he had accomplished. He released all the political prisoners who had been consigned to gaol by the suspicious fear of Kiaking, and many of the banished Manchu princes were allowed to return to Pekin. He made many public declarations of his intention to govern his people after a model and conscientious fashion, and his subsequent acts showed that he was at least sincere in his intentions, if an accumulation of troubles prevented his attaining all the objects he set before himself when he first took the government in hand. Nothing showed his integrity more clearly than his restoration of the minister Sung to the favour and offices of which he had been dispossessed. The vicissitudes of fortune passed through by this official have been more than once referred to, and his restoration to power was a practical proof of the new ruler's good resolutions, and meant more than all the virtuous platitudes expressed in vermilion edicts. Sung had gained a popularity that far exceeded that of the Emperor, through the lavish way in which he distributed his wealth, consistently refusing to accumulate money for the benefit of himself or his family. But his independent spirit rendered him an unpleasant monitor for princes who were either negligent of their duty or sensitive of criticism, and even Taoukwang appears to have dreaded, in anticipation, the impartial and fearless criticism of the minister whom he restored to favour. Sung was employed in two of the highest possible posts, Viceroy of Pechihli and President of the Board of Censors, and until his death he succeeded in maintaining his position in face of his enemies, and notwithstanding his excessive candour. One of the first reforms instituted by the Emperor Taoukwang was to cut down the enormous palace expenses, which his father had allowed to increase to a high point, and to banish from the Imperial city all persons who could not give some valid justification for their being allowed to remain. The troupes of actors and buffoons were expelled, and the harem was reduced to modest dimensions. Taoukwang declared himself to be a monogamist, and proclaimed his one wife Empress. He also put a stop to the annual visits to Jehol and to the costly hunting establishment there, which entailed a great waste of public funds. The money thus saved was much wanted for various national requirements, and the sufferings caused by flood and famine were alleviated out of these palace savings. How great the national suffering had become was shown by the marked increase of crime, especially all forms of theft and the coining of false money, for which new and severe penalties were ordained without greatly mitigating the evil. During all these troubles and trials Taoukwang endeavoured to play the part of a beneficent and merciful sovereign, tempering the severity of the laws by acts of clemency, and personally superintending every department of the administration. He seems thus to have gained a reputation among his subjects which he never lost, and the blame for any unpopular measures was always assigned to his ministers. But although he endeavoured to play the part of an autocrat, there is every ground for saying that he failed to realise the character, and that he was swayed more than most rulers by the advice of his ministers.

A brief sketch of the principal of these ministers will elucidate the policy of the Chinese government during the critical period we have now reached. The four principal officials after Sung, whose death occurred at an early date after Taoukwang's accession, were Hengan, Elepoo, Keying, and Keshen. Taking them in the order named, Hengan was the most ambitious and daring of them all, and from his connection with the Emperor, who had married his sister, he enjoyed a personal influence to which none of the others could make any pretension. He seems to have been a man of considerable energy and capacity, for exhibiting which he obtained a favourable opportunity during the Miaotze war, which he conducted to a successful end. Elepoo owed his high position in the Imperial Council to his honesty, which was, perhaps, the rarest quality at Pekin. Keying was a far more remarkable personage than either of those named. A Manchu of the purest race, and one of the noblest among the Bannermen, he added extraordinary personal ability to the advantages and influence he enjoyed from his birth. He was also very rich, having amassed a large fortune as collector of custom at Shanhaikwan, the most eastern extremity of the Great Wall, and the place through which trade passed between Manchuria and China. His literary attainments were also of the highest class, and quite unusual for a Tartar. His ascendancy at Court was long indisputable, and he was probably the greatest of all Taoukwang's advisers. Keshen, the last of this group, was also a remarkable man, who played a great part throughout the whole of this reign. He was of Mongol descent, being a member of the Banner which was formed out of those Mongols who had joined Noorhachu on the eve of his invasion of China, and who had been assigned a place of special favour. But his character resembled the Chinese rather than the children of the desert. The fascination of his manner, the clearness of his understanding, the subtlety of his intellect, and the infinity of his resource gave him an exceptional position at Court, and when the policy of others had failed Keshen was always employed to effect the most graceful exit from a dilemma, or to smooth over the painful admission of discomfiture and the necessity of concession.

The first ten years of Taoukwang's reign have been termed prosperous, because they have left so little to record, but this application of the theory that "the country is happy which has no history," does not seem borne out by such facts as have come to our knowledge. There is no doubt that there was a great amount of public suffering, and that the prosperity of the nation declined from the high point it had reached under Kiaking. Scarcity of food and want of work increased the growing discontent, which did not require even secret societies to give it point and expression, and as far as could be judged it was worse than when the Water-Lily Society inspired Kiaking with most apprehension. Kiaking, as has been observed, escaped the most serious consequences of his own acts. There was much popular discontent, but there was no open rebellion. Taoukwang had not been on the throne many years before he was brought face to face with rebels who openly disputed his authority, and, strangely enough, his troubles began in Central Asia, where peace had been undisturbed for half a century.

The conquest of Central Asia had been among the most brilliant and remarkable of the feats of the great Keen Lung. Peace had been preserved there as much by the extraordinary prestige or reputation of China as by the skill of the administration or the soundness of the policy of the governing power, which left a large share of the work to the subject races. Outside each of the principal towns the Chinese built a fort or gulbagh, in which their garrison resided, and military officers or ambans were appointed to every district. The Mahomedan officials were held responsible for the good conduct of the people and the due collection of the taxes, and as long as the Chinese garrison was maintained in strength and efficiency, they discharged their duties with the requisite good faith. The lapse of time and the embarrassment of the government at home led to the neglect of the force in Central Asia, which had once been an efficient army. The Chinese garrison, ill-paid and unrecruited, gradually lost the semblance of a military force, and was not to be distinguished from the rest of the civil population. The difference of religion was the only unequivocal mark of distinction between the rulers and the ruled, and it furnished an ever-present cause of enmity and dislike, although apart from this the Mahomedans accepted the Chinese rule as not bad in itself, and even praised it. The Chinese might have continued to govern Ili and Kashgar indefinitely, notwithstanding the weakness and decay of their garrison, but for the ambition of a neighbour. The Chinese are to blame, however, not merely for having ignored the obvious aggressiveness of that neighbour, but for having provided it with facilities for carrying out its plans. The Khanate of Khokand, the next-door state in Central Asia, had been intimately connected with Kashgar from ancient times, both in politics and trade. The Chinese armies in the 18th century had advanced into Khokand, humbled its Khan, and reduced him to a state of vassalage. For more than fifty years the Khan sent tribute to China, and was the humble neighbour of the Chinese. He gave, however, a place of refuge and a pension to Sarimsak, the last representative of the old Khoja family of Kashgar, and thus retained a hold on the legitimate ruler of that state. Sarimsak had as a child escaped from the pursuit of Fouta and the massacre of his relations by the chief of Badakshan, but he was content to remain a pensioner at Khokand to the end of his days, and he left the assertion of what he considered his rights to his children. His three sons were named, in the order of their age, Yusuf, Barhanuddin, and Jehangir, and each of them attempted at different times to dispossess the Chinese in Kashgar. In the year 1812, when Kiaking's weakness was beginning to be apparent, the Khan of Khokand, a chief of more than usual ability, named Mahomed Ali, refused to send tribute any more to China, and the Viceroy of Ili, having no force at his disposal, acquiesced in the change with good grace, and no hostilities ensued. The first concession was soon followed by others. The Khan obtained the right to levy a tax on all Mahomedan merchandise sold in the bazaars of Kashgar and Yarkand, and deputed consuls or aksakals for the purpose of collecting the duties. These aksakals naturally became the centre of all the intrigue and disaffection prevailing in the state against the Chinese, and they considered it to be as much their duty to provoke political discontent as to supervise the customs placed under their charge. Before the aksakals appeared on the scene the Chinese ruled a peaceful territory, but after the advent of these foreign officials trouble soon ensued.

Ten years after his refusal to pay tribute the Khan of Khokand decided to support the Khoja pretenders who enjoyed his hospitality, and in 1822 Jehangir was provided with money and arms to make an attempt on the Chinese position in Kashgaria. Although the youngest, Jehangir seems to have been the most energetic of the Khoja princes; and having obtained the alliance of the Kirghiz, he attempted, by a rapid movement, to surprise the Chinese in the town of Kashgar. In this attempt he was disappointed, for the Chinese kept better guard than he expected, and he was compelled to make an ignominious retreat. The Khan of Khokand, disappointed at the result and apprehensive of counter action on the part of the Chinese, repudiated all participation in the matter, and forbade Jehangir to return to his country. That adventurer then fled to Lake Issik Kul, whither the Chinese pursued him; but when his fortunes seemed to have reached their lowest ebb a revulsion suddenly took place, and by the surprise and annihilation of a Chinese force he was again able to pose as an arbiter of affairs in Central Asia. The fortitude of Jehangir confirmed the attachment of his friends, and the Khokandian ruler, encouraged by the defeat of the Chinese, again took up his cause and sent him troops and a general for a fresh descent on Kashgaria. The Khan had his own ends in view quite as much as to support the Khoja pretender; but his support encouraged Jehangir to leave his mountain retreat and to cross the Tian Shan into Kashgaria. This happened in the year 1826, and the Chinese garrison of Kashgar very unwisely quitted the shelter of its citadel and went out to meet the invaders. The combat is said to have been fiercely contested, but nothing is known about it except that the Chinese were signally defeated. This overthrow was the signal for a general insurrection throughout the country, and the Chinese garrisons, after more or less resistance, were annihilated. An attempt was then made to restore the old Mahomedan administration, and Jehangir was proclaimed by the style of the Seyyid Jehangir Sultan. One of his first acts was to dismiss the Khokandian contingent, and to inform his ally or patron, Mahomed Ali, that he no longer required his assistance. His confidence received a rude check when he learnt a short time afterwards that the Chinese were making extraordinary preparations to recover their lost province, and that they had collected an immense army in Ili for the purpose. Then he wished his Khokandian allies back again; but he still resolved to make as good a fight as he could for the throne he had acquired; and when the Chinese general Chang marched on Kashgar, Jehangir took up his position at Yangabad and accepted battle. He was totally defeated; the capture of Kashgar followed, and Jehangir himself fell into the hands of the victors. The Khoja was sent to Pekin, where, after many indignities, he was executed and quartered as a traitor. The Chinese punished all open rebels with death, and as a precaution against the recurrence of rebellion they removed 12,000 Mahomedan families from Kashgar to Ili, where they became known as the Tarantchis, or toilers. They also took the very wise step of prohibiting all intercourse with Khokand, and if they had adhered to this resolution they would have saved themselves much serious trouble. But Mahomed Ali was determined to make an effort to retain so valuable a perquisite as his trade relations with Kashgar, and as soon as the Chinese had withdrawn the main portion of their force he hastened to assail Kashgar at the head of his army, and put forward Yusuf as a successor to Jehangir. Only desultory fighting ensued, but his operations were so far successful that the Chinese agreed to resort to the previous arrangement, and Mahomed Ali promised to restrain the Khojas. Fourteen years of peace and prosperity followed this new convention.

Serious disorders also broke out in the islands of Formosa and Hainan. In the former the rebellion was only put down by a judicious manipulation of the divisions of the insurgent tribes; but the settlement attained must be pronounced so far satisfactory that the peace of the island has not been

seriously disturbed from that time to the present day. In Hainan, an
island of extraordinary fertility and natural wealth, which must some day
be developed, the aboriginal tribes revolted against Chinese authority, and
massacred many of the Chinese settlers, who had begun to encroach on the
possessions of the natives. Troops had to be sent from Canton before the
disorders were suppressed, and then Hainan reverted to its tranquil state,
from which only the threat of a French occupation during the Tonquin war
roused it. These disorders in different parts of the Empire were matched
by troubles of a more domestic character within the palace. In 1831
Taoukwang's only son, a young man of 20, whose character was not of
the best, gave him some cause of offence, and he struck him. The young
prince died of the blow, and the Emperor was left for the moment without
a child. His grief was soon assuaged by the news that two of his favourite
concubines had borne him sons, one of whom became long afterwards the
Emperor Hienfung. At this critical moment Taoukwang was seized with
a severe illness, and his elder brother, Hwuy Wang, whose pretensions had
threatened the succession, thinking his chance had at last come, took steps
to seize the throne. But Taoukwang recovered, and those who had made
premature arrangements in filling the throne were severely punished. These
minor troubles culminated in the Miaotze rebellion, the most formidable
internal war which the Chinese government had to deal with between
that of Wou Sankwei and the Taepings. From an early period the
Miaotze had been a source of trouble to the executive, and the relations
between them and the officials had been anything but harmonious. The
Manchu rulers had only succeeded in keeping them in order by stopping
their supply of salt on the smallest provocation; and in the belief that they
possessed an absolutely certain mode of coercing them, the Chinese mandarins assumed an arrogant and dictatorial tone towards their rude and
unreclaimed neighbours. In 1832 the Miaotze, irritated past endurance,
broke out in rebellion, and their principal chief caused himself to be
proclaimed Emperor. Their main force was assembled at Lienchow, in
the north-west corner of the Canton province, and their leader assumed
the suggestive title of the Golden Dragon, and called upon the Chinese
people to redress their wrongs by joining his standard. But the Chinese,
who regarded the Miaotze as an inferior and barbarian race, refused to combine with them against the most extortionate of officials or the most
unpopular of governments. Although they could not enlist the support of
any section of the Chinese people, the Miaotze, by their valour and the
military skill of their leader, made so good a stand against the forces sent
against them by the Canton Viceroy that the whole episode is redeemed
from oblivion, and may be considered a romantic incident in modern
Chinese history. The Miaotze gained the first successes of the war, and
for a time it seemed as if the Chinese authorities would be able to effect
nothing against them. The Canton Viceroy fared so badly that Hengan
was sent from Pekin to take the command, and the chosen braves of
Hoonan were sent to attack the Miaotze in the rear. The latter gained a
decisive victory at Pingtseuen, where the Golden Dragon and several
thousand of his followers were slain. But, although vanquished in one
quarter, the Miaotze continued to show great activity and confidence in
another, and when the Canton Viceroy made a fresh attack on them they
repulsed him with heavy loss. The disgrace of this officer followed, and
his fall was hastened by the suppression of the full extent of his losses,

which excited the indignation of his own troops, who said, "There is no use in our sacrificing our lives in secret; if our toils are concealed from the Emperor neither we nor our posterity will be rewarded." This unlucky commander was banished to Central Asia, and after his supersession Hengan had the satisfaction of bringing the war to a satisfactory end within ten days. Some of the leaders were executed, the others swore to keep the peace, and a glowing account of the pacification of the Miaotze region was sent to Pekin. Some severe critics suggested that the whole arrangement was a farce, and that Hengan's triumph was only on paper. But the lapse of time has shown this scepticism to be unjustified, as the Miaotze have remained tranquil ever since, and the formidable Yaoujin, or Wolfmen, as they are called, have observed the promises given to Hengan, which would not have been the case unless they had been enforced by military success. Should they ever break out again, the government would possess the means, from their command of money and modern arms, of repressing their lawlessness with unprecedented thoroughness, and of absolutely subjecting their hitherto inaccessible districts.

If the first ten or twelve years of the reign of the Emperor Taoukwang were marked by these troubles on a minor scale, an undue importance should not be attached to them, for they did not seriously affect the stability of the government or the authority of the Emperor. It is true that they caused a decline in the revenue and an increase in the expenditure, which resulted in the year 1834 in an admitted deficit of ten millions sterling, and no state could be considered in a flourishing condition with the public Exchequer in such a condition. But this large deficit must be regarded rather as a floating debt than an annual occurrence. It showed that the Pekin government had had to draw on its resources, but it scarcely signified that the national wealth had been seriously diminished. The real significance of these local disturbances and of the embarrassment they caused the Emperor lay in the fact that they encouraged a seditious movement on the part of more formidable disturbers of the peace, and that they distracted some of the government's attention from the foreign problem, which was now entering upon its most important phase. The Chinese authorities continued to hinder and protest against the foreign trade and intercourse between their subjects and the merchants of Europe as much as ever; but their opposition was mainly confined to edicts and proclamations. When Commissioner Lin resorted to force and violence some years later the auspicious moment for expelling all foreigners had passed away, and the weakness of the government contributed in no small degree to this result. Taoukwang, although his claims as occupant of the Dragon Throne were unabated, could not pretend to the power of a great ruler like Keen Lung, who would have known how to enforce his will. Nor was it possible after 1834 to continue the policy of uncompromising hostility to all foreign nations whose governments had become directly interested in, and to a certain extent responsible to, their respective peoples, for the opening of the Chinese Empire to civilised intercourse and commerce. Up to this point Taoukwang's only experience of the pretensions of the foreign Powers had been the Amherst mission, in the time of his father, which had ended so ignominiously, and the Russian mission which arrived at Pekin every ten years to recruit the Russian college there, and to pay the descendants of the garrison of Albazin the sum allotted by the Czar for their support. This latter mission was of a very humble and unpretending kind, not venturing to approach the Court, and accepting whatever treatment the minor officials cared to extend to it. Its unpretentiousness served to save it from the insults and opposition offered to more imposing missions. But from these trifling matters Taoukwang's attention was suddenly and completely distracted to the important situation at Canton and on the coast, the settlement of the questions arising out of which filled the remainder of his reign.

CHAPTER XVII.

THE FIRST FOREIGN WAR.

At the very time that the Emperor Taoukwang, by the dismissal of the Portuguese astronomers at Pekin and by his general indifference to the foreign question, was showing that no concessions were to be expected from him, an unknown legislature at a remote distance from his capital was decreeing, in complete indifference to the susceptibilities of the occupant of the Dragon Throne, that trade with China might be pursued by any English subject. Up to the year 1834 trade with China had, by the Royal charter, remained the monopoly of the East India Company; but when the charter was renewed in that year for a further period of twenty years, it was shorn of the last of its commercial privileges, and an immediate change became perceptible in the situation at Canton, which was the principal seat of the foreign trade. The withdrawal of the monopoly was dictated solely by English, and not Chinese, considerations. Far from facilitating trade with the Chinese, it tended to hinder and prevent its developing, for the Chinese officials had no objection to foreigners coming to Canton, and buying or selling articles of commerce, so long as they derived personal profit from the trade, and so long as the laws of the Empire were not disputed or violated. The servants of the East India Company were content to adapt themselves to this view, and they might have carried on relations with the Hong merchants for an indefinite period, and without any more serious collision than occasional interruptions. Had the monopoly been renewed things would have been left in precisely the same position as when intercourse was first established, and trade might have continued within its old restricted limits. But the abolition of the monopoly and the opening of the trade created quite a new situation, and by intensifying the opposition of the Chinese government, paved the way to the only practicable solution of the question of foreign intercourse with China, which was that, however reluctantly, she should consent to take her place in the family of nations.

The Chinese were not left long in doubt as to the significance of this change. In December, 1833, a Royal Commission was issued appointing Lord Napier Chief Superintendent of Trade with China, and two assistants under him, of whom one was Sir John Davis. The Chinese had to some extent contributed to this appointment, for the Hoppo at Canton had written that "in case of the dissolution of the Company it was incumbent on the British government to appoint a chief to come to Canton for the general management of commercial dealings, and to prevent affairs from going to confusion." But in this message the Hoppo seems to have expressed his own view rather than that of the Pekin government or the

Canton Viceroy; and certainly none of the Chinese were prepared to find substituted for "a chief of commercial dealings," an important commissioner clothed with all the authority of the British ruler. How very different was the idea formed of this functionary by the Chinese and English may be gathered from their official views of his work. What the Chinese thought has been told in the words of Hoppo. Lord Palmerston was more precise from his point of view. His instruction to Lord Napier read, "Your Lordship will announce your arrival at Canton by letter to the Viceroy. In addition to the duty of protecting and fostering the trade at Canton, it will be one of your principal objects to ascertain whether it may not be practicable to extend that trade to other parts of the Chinese dominions. It is obvious that, with a view to the attainment of this object, the establishment of direct communication with the Imperial Court at Pekin would be most desirable." The two points of radical disagreement between these views were that the Chinese wished to deal with an official who thought exclusively of trade, whereas Lord Napier's task was not less diplomatic than commercial; and, secondly, that they expected him to carry on his business with the Hoppo, as the Company's agents had done, while Lord Napier was specially instructed to communicate with the Viceroy, whom those agents had never dared to approach.

If it was thought that the Chinese would not realise all the significance of the change, those who held so slight an opinion of their clear-headedness were quickly undeceived. Lord Napier reached the Canton river in July, 1834, and he at once addressed a letter of courtesy to the Viceroy announcing his arrival. The Chinese officers, after perusing it, refused to forward it to the Viceroy, and returned it to Lord Napier. Such was the inauspicious commencement of the assumption of responsibility by the Crown in China. The Chinese refused to have anything to do with Lord Napier, whom they described as "a barbarian eye," and they threatened the merchants with the immediate suspension of the trade. The Viceroy issued an order forbidding the new Superintendent to proceed to Canton, and commanding him to stay at Macao until he had applied in the prescribed form for permission to proceed up the river. But Lord Napier did not listen to these representations, nor did he condescend to delay his progress a moment at Macao. He proceeded up the river to Canton, but, although he succeeded in making his way to the English factory, it was only to find himself isolated, and that, in accordance with the Viceroy's order, the Hoppo had interdicted all intercourse with the English. The Chinese declared that the national dignity was at stake, and so thoroughly did both officials and merchants harmonise that the English factory was at once deserted by all Chinese subjects, and even the servants left their employment. On his arrival at Canton Lord Napier found himself confronted with the position that the Chinese authorities refused to have anything to do with him, and that his presence effectually debarred his countrymen from carrying on the trade, which it was his first duty to promote. At this conjuncture it happened that the Chinese had discovered what they thought to be a new grievance against the foreign traders in the steady efflux of silver as the natural consequence of the balance of trade being against China. In a report to the Throne in 1833 it was stated that as much as 60,000,000 taels of silver, or £20,000,000 sterling, had been exported from China in the previous eleven years, and, as the Chinese of course made no allowance for the equivalent value imported into their country, this total seemed in their eyes an incredibly large sum to be lost from the national treasure. It will be easily understood that at this particular moment the foreign trade appeared to possess few advantages, and found few patrons among the Chinese people.

In meeting this opposition Lord Napier endeavoured to combine courtesy and firmness. He wrote courteous and argumentative letters to the mandarins, combating their views, and insisting on his rights as a diplomatist to be received by the officials of the Empire; and at the same time he issued a notice to the Chinese merchants which was full of threats and defiance. "The merchants of Great Britain," he said, "wish to trade with all China on principles of mutual benefit; they will never relax in their exertions till they gain a point of equal importance to both countries, and the Viceroy will find it as easy to stop the current of the Canton river as to carry into effect the insane determinations of the Hong." This notice was naturally enough interpreted as a defiance by the Viceroy, who placed the most severe restrictions he could on the trade, sent his troops into the foreign settlements to remove all Chinese servants, and ordered the Bogue forts to fire on any English ship that attempted to pass. The English merchants, alarmed at the situation, petitioned Lord Napier to allay the storm he had raised by retiring from Canton to Macao, and, harassed in mind and enfeebled in body, Lord Napier acquiesced in an arrangement that stultified all his former proceedings. The Chinese were naturally intoxicated by their triumph, which vindicated their principle that no English merchant or emissary should be allowed to come to Canton except by the Viceroy's permit, granted only to the petition and on the guarantee of the Hong merchants. The Viceroy had also carried his point of holding no intercourse with the English envoy, to whom he had written that "the great ministers of the Celestial Empire, unless with regard to affairs of going to Court and carrying tribute, or in consequence of Imperial commands, are not permitted to have interviews with outside barbarians." While the Chinese officials had been both consistent and successful, the new English Superintendent of Trade had been both inconsistent and discomfited. He had attempted to carry matters with a high hand and to coerce the mandarins, and he was compelled to show in the most public manner that he had failed by his retirement to Macao. He had even imperilled the continuance of the trade which he had come specially to promote, and all he could do to show his indignation was to make a futile protest against "this act of unprecedented tyranny and injustice." Very soon after Lord Napier's return to Macao he died, leaving to other hands the settlement of the difficult affair which neither his acts nor his language had simplified.

On Lord Napier's departure from Canton the restrictions placed on trade were removed, and the intercourse between the English and Chinese merchants of the Hong was resumed. But even then the mandarins refused to recognise the trade superintendents, and after a short time they issued certain regulations which had been specially submitted to and approved by the Emperor Taoukwang as the basis on which trade was to be conducted. These Regulations, eight in number, forbade foreign men-of-war to enter the inner seas, and enforced the old practice that all requests on the part of Europeans should be addressed through the Hong in the form of a petition. It therefore looked as if the Chinese had completely triumphed in carrying out their views, that the transfer of authority from the East India Company to the British Crown, with the so-called opening of the trade, had effected no change in the situation, and that such commerce as was carried on should be as the Chinese dictated, and in accordance with their main idea, which was to "prevent the English establishing themselves permanently at Canton." The death of the Viceroy Loo and the familiarity resulting from increased intercourse resulted in some relaxation of these severe regulations, and at last, in March, 1837, nearly three years after Lord Napier's arrival in the Bogue, the new Superintendent of Trade, Captain Elliot, received, at his own request, permission through the Hong to proceed to Canton. The Emperor passed a special edict authorising Captain Elliot to reside in the factory at Canton, where he was to "control the merchants and seamen"; but it was also stipulated that he was to strictly abide by the old regulations and not to rank above a supercargo. As Captain Elliot was the representative of a government not less proud or exacting than that of China, it was clear that these conditions could not be permanently enforced; and although he endeavoured for a period to conciliate the Chinese and to obtain more favourable terms by concessions, there came a time when it was impossible to assent to the arrogant demands of the mandarins, and when resort became necessary to the *ultima ratio regum*. But for the first two critical years Captain Elliot pursued the same policy as Lord Napier, alternating concessions with threats, and, while vaunting the majesty of his sovereign, yielding to demands which were unreasonable and not to be endured.

At this juncture it happened that all the vague and innate objections of the Chinese government to an extensive intercourse with foreigners who refused to be classed among tributary nations took a more definite and pronounced cause for specific reasons. In the first place, the old Manchu dread of Europeans working on the latent feelings of hostility with which they believed that their Chinese subjects regarded them had become intensified by the seditious movements throughout the Empire during Taoukwang's reign. In the second place, the drain of silver, as a necessary accompaniment of the foreign trade, had spread the liveliest alarm in official circles, which was not wholly unreasonable, seeing that the annual export was admitted to be three millions sterling. These facts were more alarming to the government than to the Chinese merchants, who showed an increasing eagerness to engage in what was undoubtedly the profitable foreign trade. With the view of arresting this tendency and inciting the public mind to make some demonstration against the trade with foreigners, it became necessary to denounce some special branch of that trade, and to introduce that moral aspect into the question which plays so large a part in Chinese life and politics. These considerations led to the first serious denunciation of the opium traffic. The balance of trade against China was the principal cause of the export of silver, and the balance of trade was only against China through the increasing import of opium. Without acquiescing in the least with the strong allegations of the anti-opium party, there is no reason to doubt that the excessive use of opium, especially in a crowded city like Canton, was attended with sufficient mischief to justify its official denunciation. The Pekin Government may be so far credited with the honest intention to reduce the mischief and to prevent a bad habit from becoming more and more of a national vice, when they determined for far other reasons to place it in the front of their tirade against foreign trade generally. They soon found that it would be more convenient and more plausible to substitute the moral opposition to the opium traffic for the political disinclination to foreign intercourse in any form. They scarcely expected that in this project they would receive the assistance and co-operation of many of the Europeans themselves, who shared with them the opinion that opium was detestable, and its use or sale a mark of depravity.

The Board of Censors and the learned doctors of the Hanlin, representing the keenest and most highly-trained intelligence in China, exercised their minds in drawing up the most plausible and convincing indictment they could conceive against the use of opium. Their labours showed that their uppermost thought was how to arrest the export of silver rather than to put down the use of opium. The first censor to memorialise the throne openly advocated the legalisation of opium for the double reason that the government would then draw a large revenue from it, and that the more severe the penalties passed against it the more general had its use become. The views of the memorialist, although expressed with great ability, did not find favour, and in the controversy that followed the opponents of legalisation were in an overwhelming majority. The one remedy received with unquestioning favour was to expel the foreigner and to destroy all the stores of opium on which the authorities could lay their hands. But the practical execution of this policy was attended with much difficulty, for the mandarins were freely addicted to the use of opium, and always appropriated for their own use the greater part of the quantities ordered to be destroyed. So far, however, as the government could arrest an evil by interdicting it, the official proclamations forbade, and ordained special punishments for, the use of opium. The cruel penalty of cutting out the upper lip was devised for the express purpose of putting down the practice; but as the officials charged with the execution of these laws were those most addicted to the practice of opium smoking, it is not surprising to learn that they were carried out in a very perfunctory manner, and that only those suffered at the hands of the law who were least capable of defending themselves. There is no reason to question the sincerity of Taoukwang and his immediate advisers; but their efforts were rendered nugatory by the corruption and want of zeal of the minor officials entrusted with the execution of their policy and orders. Matters might have gone on in this way indefinitely but for the appearance on the scene of one of the most remarkable men China has produced in the present century. The Pekin executive had at last found in one of its officers an active and conscientious agent to carry out the policy on which it had resolved. In January, 1839, Taoukwang ordered Lin Tsihseu, Viceroy of the double province of Houkwang and an official of high reputation, to proceed to Canton as Special Commissioner to report on the situation, and to propound the best remedy for the opium evil. At this moment the anti-opium party was supreme in the Imperial council, and three Manchu princes were disgraced and banished from Pekin for indulging in the practice. The peremptory instructions given to Commissioner Lin, as he is historically known, were "to cut off the fountain of evil, and, if necessary for the attainment of his object, to sink his ships and break his cauldrons, for the indignation of the great Emperor has been fairly aroused at these wicked practices—of buying and selling and using opium—and that the hourly thought of his heart is to do away with them for ever."

Before Lin reached Canton there had been frequent friction between Captain Elliot and the local mandarins, and more than one interruption of the trade. Less than six months after his installation at Canton his official relations were broken off, and he wrote home to his government a despatch complaining of the difficulty of conducting any sort of amicable relations with the local mandarins, and endorsing the growing demand for the right of dealing direct with the Pekin government. Captain Elliot hauled down his flag at Canton and returned to Macao, thus showing for a second time that the attempt to conduct diplomatic relations on a basis of trade involved circumstances that were incompatible with each other and that no ingenuity could reconcile. Several men-of-war were sent from Europe or the Indian seas to the Canton river, and towards the end of 1838 Captain Elliot returned to that city and rehoisted his flag. The Bogue forts fired on one of the vessels, and instituted a search before they allowed it to pass; but still the English ships made their way to Canton, where for a time it seemed as if the second arrival of Captain Elliot would entail open hostilities. When the situation looked most critical an amicable arrangement was patched up until the arrival of Commissioner Lin introduced a fresh and more critical phase of the whole question. When the officials at Canton realised that their own government was in earnest in its proceedings against opium they felt bound to do something to exhibit their energy and zeal, and they came down on the Hong merchants, who endeavoured to prove themselves patriots by demolishing the factory of an English merchant who was erroneously supposed to be an opium dealer. The officials themselves, whenever they had any criminal to execute, brought him down to the square in front of the foreign residences for his punishment, so that it might be thought that the foreigners were in some degree participators in the crime of the victim. An end was put to these proceedings by the English merchants combining in the form of a volunteer force and clearing the square on the occasion of an execution which assumed a more than usually offensive character. A more serious collision was then narrowly averted, and the latent antipathy smouldering on both sides threatened to find a vent before long.

At this critical moment Captain Elliot, acting under instructions from home, issued a public notice warning all English subjects to discontinue the illicit opium trade, and stating that "Her Majesty's government would not in any way interfere if the Chinese government should think fit to seize and confiscate the same." After so formal a repudiation of all sympathy and connection with the illicit opium trade on the part of the representative of the English government, it became essentially a question for the Chinese authorities to deal with as they felt able and thought fit. One of the first consequences, therefore, of the cessation of the Company's monopoly was that the Crown declined to sanction the most important branch of the Indian trade which the Company had sought to foster and extend. This repudiation of sympathy as well as participation in the opium traffic on the part of the British government was necessarily followed by increased activity on the side of the mandarins, who, not unnaturally, came to the conclusion that their proceedings against the opium traffic would have the passive support at least of the English Superintendent of Trade. In this opinion they trusted too much to the personal and, as it proved, irresponsible utterance of the British official. It is just possible, however, that if the Chinese government had devoted its attention exclusively to rooting up the opium traffic it would have obtained the sympathy and co-operation of the British government, which was very

P

much disposed to agree on moral grounds with the Chinese executive in its denunciation of opium. But at this juncture Commissioner Lin, whose fervour and energy carried him away, appeared upon the scene, and, whereas a less capable or honest man would have come to an arrangement with Captain Elliot, his very ability and enthusiasm tended to complicate the situation and render a pacific solution unattainable.

Commissioner Lin, on taking up his post, lost no time in showing that he was terribly in earnest; but both his language and his acts proved that he had a very much larger programme than was included in his propaganda against the opium traffic. He wished to achieve the complete humiliation of the foreigners, and nothing less would satisfy him. Within a week of his arrival at Canton he issued an edict denouncing the opium trade; throwing all the blame for it on the English, and asserting what was absolutely untrue, viz.—that "the laws of England prohibited the smoking of opium, and adjudged the user to death." The language of the edict was unfriendly and offensive. The Europeans were stigmatised as a barbarous people, who thought only of trade and of making their way by stealth into the Flowery Land. At the same time that he issued this edict he gave peremptory orders that no foreigner was to leave Canton or Macao until the opium question had been settled to his satisfaction. Even then English merchants and officials, who felt no great sympathy with the opium traffic, saw that these proceedings indicated an intention to put down the trade in other articles, and to render the position of foreigners untenable. Lin's demands culminated in the request for all stores of opium to be surrendered to him within three days. By the efforts of some of the merchants about a thousand chests were collected and handed over to the Chinese for destruction; but this did not satisfy Lin, who collected a large rabble force, encamped it outside the settlement and threatened to carry the place by storm. In this crisis Captain Elliot, who had declared that his confidence in the justice and good faith of the provincial government was destroyed, and who had even drawn up a scheme for concentrating all his forces at Hongkong, called upon all the English merchants to surrender to him, for paramount considerations of the lives and property of everyone concerned, all the stores of opium in their possession. More than 20,000 chests, of an estimated value of two millions sterling, were placed at his disposal, and in due course handed over by him to Commissioner Lin for destruction. This task was performed at Chuenpee, when the opium was placed in trenches, then mixed with salt and lime, and finally poured off into the sea. After this very considerable triumph, Lin wrote a letter to Queen Victoria—whose reign has witnessed the most critical periods of the China question and its satisfactory settlement—calling upon Her Majesty to interdict the trade in opium for ever. The letter was as offensive in its tone as it was weak in argument, and no answer was vouchsafed to it. Before any reply could be given the situation, moreover, had developed into one of open hostilities.

But great as were the concessions made by Captain Elliot, in consequence of the threatening attitude of Commissioner Lin, the Chinese were not satisfied, and made fresh and more exacting demands of those who had been weak enough to make any concession at all. They reasserted their old pretension that Europeans in China must be subject to her laws, and as the sale of opium was a penal offence they claimed the right to punish those Englishmen who had been connected with the traffic. They accordingly drew up a list of sixteen of the principal merchants, some of whom had never had anything to do with opium, and they announced their intention to arrest them and to punish them with death. Not only did Commissioner Lin and the Canton authorities claim the right to condemn and punish British subjects, but they showed in the most insolent manner that they would take away their liberty and lives on the flimsiest and falsest pretext. Captain Elliot, weak and yielding as he was on many points, declared that "this law is incompatible with safe or honourable continuance at Canton." Apparently the Chinese authorities acted on the assumption that so long as there remained even one offending European the mass of his countrymen ought to be hindered in their avocations, and consequently petty restrictions and provocations continued to be enforced. Then Captain Elliot, seeing that the situation was hopeless and that there was no sign of improvement, took the bold, or at least the pronounced, step of ordering all British subjects to leave Canton or to stay at their own peril. It was on this occasion that he explained away, or put a new interpretation on, his action with regard to the opium surrendered for destruction, which most of the merchants thought represented an irrecoverable loss. It will be best to give the precise words used in his notice of 22nd May, 1839. "Acting on behalf of Her Majesty's government in a momentous emergency, he has, in the first place, to signify that the demand he recently made to Her Majesty's subjects for the surrender of British owned opium under their control had no special reference to the circumstances of that property; but (beyond the actual pressure of necessity) that demand was founded on the principle that these violent compulsory measures being utterly unjust *per se* and of general application for the enforced surrender of any other property, or of human life, or for the constraint of any unsuitable terms or concessions, it became highly necessary to vest and leave the right of exacting effectual security and full indemnity for every loss directly in the Queen." Unfortunately, Captain Elliot's language at the time of the surrender of opium had undoubtedly led to the conclusion that he sympathised with Commissioner Lin, and that he took the same view as the Chinese officials of the moral iniquity of selling or using opium. The whole mercantile community adopted Captain Elliot's counsel, and the English factory at Canton, which had existed for nearly two hundred years, was abandoned. At the same time a memorial was sent home begging the government to protect the English merchants in China against "a capricious and corrupt government," and demanding compensation for the two millions' worth of opium destroyed by Commissioner Lin. Pending the reply of the home government to that appeal, nothing could be more complete than the triumph of Commissioner Lin. The Emperor Taoukwang rewarded him with the important viceroyship of the Two Kiang, the seat of which administration is at Nankin

But the limit of endurance had been reached, and the British government was on the point of taking decisive action at the very moment when the Chinese triumph seemed most complete and unthreatened. Even before the action of the home authorities was known in the Bogue the situation had become critical, and the sailors in particular had thrown off all restraint. Frequent collisions occurred between them and the foreigners, and in one of them a Chinaman was killed. Commissioner Lin characterised this act as "going to the extreme of disobedience to the laws," and demanded the surrender of the sailor who committed the act, so that a life might be given for a life. This demand was flatly refused, and in consequence of the measures taken by the Chinese at Lin's direction to prevent all supplies reaching the English, Captain Elliot felt bound to remove his residence from Macao to Hongkong. The Chinese called out all their armed forces, and incited their people along the Canton river to attack the foreigners wherever found. An official notice said, "Produce arms and weapons; join together the stoutest of your villagers, and thus be prepared to defend yourselves. If any of the said foreigners be found going on shore to cause trouble, all and every of the people are permitted to fire upon them, to withstand and drive them back, or to make prisoners of them." This appeal to a force which the Chinese did not possess was an act of indiscretion that betrayed an overweaning confidence or a singular depth of ignorance. When the mandarins refused to supply the ships with water and other necessaries they carried their animosity to a length which the English naval officers at once defined as a declaration of open hostilities. They retaliated by ordering their men to seize by force whatever was necessary, and thus began a state of things which may be termed one of absolute warfare. The two men-of-war on the station had several encounters with the forts in the Bogue, and on 3rd November, 1839, they fought a regular engagement with a Chinese fleet of twenty-nine junks, off Chuenpee. The Chinese showed more courage than skill, and four of their junks were sunk. It is worth noting that the English sailors pronounced both their guns and their powder to be excellent. While this action deterred the Chinese fleet from coming to close quarters, it also embittered the contest, and there was no longer room to doubt that if the Chinese were to be brought to take a more reasonable view of foreign trade, it would have to be by the disagreeable lesson of force. And at the end of 1839 the Chinese were fully convinced that they had the power to carry out their will and to keep the European nations out of their country by the strong hand.

A short time after the action at Chuenpee an Englishman named Mr. Gribble was seized by the Canton officials and thrown into prison. The English men-of-war went up the river as far as the Bogue forts, which they threatened to bombard unless he was released; and, after considerable discussion, Mr. Gribble was set free, mainly because the Chinese heard of the large force that was on its way from England. Before that armament arrived the Emperor Taoukwang had committed himself still further to a policy of hostility. A report of the fight at Chuenpee was duly submitted to him, but the affair was represented as a very creditable one for his commander, and as a Chinese victory. The misled monarch at once conferred a high honour on his admiral, and commanded his officers at Canton "to at once put a stop to the trade of the English nation." This had, practically speaking, been already accomplished, and the English merchants had taken refuge at Macao or in their ships anchored at Hongkong.

Before describing the military operations now about to take place, a survey may conveniently be taken of events since the abolition of the monopoly, and it may be pardonable to employ the language formerly used. From an impartial review of the facts, and divesting our minds, so far as is humanly possible, of the prejudice of accepted political opinions, and of conviction as to the hurtful or innocent character of opium in the mixture as smoked by the Chinese, it cannot be contended that the course pursued by Lord Napier and Captain Elliot, and particularly by the latter, was either prudent in itself or calculated to promote the advantage and reputation of England. Captain Elliot's proceedings were marked by the inconsistency that springs from ignorance. The more influential English merchants, touched by the appeal to their moral sentiment, or impressed by the depravity of large classes of the Canton population, of which the practice of opium-smoking was rather the mark than the cause, set their faces against the traffic in this article, and repudiated all sympathy and participation in it. The various foreign publications, whether they received their inspirations from Mr. Gutzlaff or not matters little, differed on most points, but were agreed on this, that the trade in opium was morally indefensible, and that we were bound, not only by our own interests, but in virtue of the common obligations of humanity, to cease to hold all connection with it. Those who had surrendered their stores of opium at the request of Captain Elliot held that their claim for compensation was valid, in the first place, against the English government alone. They had given them up for the service of the country at the request of the Queen's representative, and, considering the line which Captain Elliot had taken, many believed that it would be quite impossible for the English government to put forward any demand upon the government of China. The two millions sterling, according to these large-hearted and unreflecting moralists, would have to be sacrificed by the people of England in the cause of humanity, to which they had given so much by emancipating the slaves, and the revenue of India should, for the future, be poorer by the amount that used to pay the dividend of the great Company! The Chinese authorities could not help being encouraged in their opinions and course of proceeding by the attitude of the English. Their most sweeping denunciations of the iniquity of the opium traffic elicited a murmur of approval from the most influential among the foreigners. No European stood up to say that their allegations as to the evil of using opium were baseless and absurd. What is more, no one thought it. Had the Chinese made sufficient use of this identity of views, and showed a desire to facilitate trade in the so-called innocent and legitimate articles, there is little doubt that the opium traffic would have been reduced to very small dimensions, because there would have been no rupture. But the action of Commissioner Lin revealed the truth that the Chinese were not to be satisfied with a single triumph. The more easily they obtained their objects in the opium matter the more anxious did they become to impress the foreigners with a sense of their inferiority, and to force them to accept the most onerous and unjust conditions for the sake of a continuance of the trade. None the less, Captain Elliot went out of his way to tie his own hands, and to bind his own government, so far as he could, to co-operate with the Emperor's officials in the suppression of the opium traffic. That this is no random assertion may be judged from the following official notice, issued several months after the surrender of the stores of opium. In this Captain Elliot announced that " Her Majesty's flag does not fly in the protection of a traffic declared illegal by the Emperor, and, therefore, whenever a vessel is suspected of having opium on board Captain Elliot will take care that the officers of his establishment shall accompany the Chinese officers in their search, and that if, after strict investigation, opium shall be found, he will offer no objection to the seizure and confiscation of the cargo."

A new phase in the development of the Chinese question is reached with the decision to employ force to bring the Pekin government to reason, and to obtain for English merchants the right to trade in security. The Queen's speech at the opening of Parliament for the session of 1840 states, with studied moderation, the ground of offence. "Events have happened in China which have occasioned an interruption of the commercial intercourse of my subjects with that country. I have given, and shall continue to give, the most serious attention to a matter so deeply affecting the interests of my subjects and the dignity of my crown." Lord John Russell defined the scope of the expedition as "obtaining reparation for the insults and injuries offered to Her Majesty's Superintendent and Her Majesty's subjects by the Chinese government; and, in the second place, it was to obtain for the merchants trading in China an indemnification for the loss of their property incurred by threats of violence offered by persons under the direction of the Chinese government; and, in the last place, it was to obtain a certain security, that persons and property in future trading with China shall be protected from insult or injury, and that their trade and commerce be maintained upon a proper footing." The arrival of an English expedition did not strike the Chinese with terror. The Chinese believed, not merely that they were secure against invasion, but that they could give a good account of any assailant, and the smallness of the English force tended to increase their confidence, for they had no knowledge of the superiority arising from discipline and good weapons. The Chinese have never admitted the superiority of Europeans, which most other Asiatics, whether they acknowledge it or not, feel; and at this moment nothing had occurred to make them do so. The prestige of the Emperor was intact, and no Chinese subject doubted that the Imperial resources were equal to the maintenance of his extreme pretensions.

The British expedition arrived at the mouth of the Canton river in the month of June, 1840. It consisted of 4,000 troops on board twenty-five transports, with a convoy of fifteen men-of-war. If it was thought that this considerable force would attain its objects without fighting and merely by making a demonstration, the expectation was rudely disappointed. The reply of Commissioner Lin was to place a reward on the person of all Englishmen, and to offer twenty thousand dollars for the destruction of an English man-of-war. The English fleet replied to this hostile step by instituting a close blockade at the mouth of the river, which was not an ineffectual retort. Sir Gordon Bremer, the commander of the first part of the expedition, came promptly to the decision that it would be well to extend the sphere of his operations, and he accordingly sailed northwards with a portion of his force to occupy the island of Chusan, which had witnessed some of the earliest operations of the East India Company two centuries before. The capture of Chusan presented no difficulties to a well-equipped force, yet the fidelity of its garrison and inhabitants calls for notice as a striking instance of patriotism. The officials at Tinghai, the capital of Chusan, refused to surrender, as their duty to their Emperor would not admit of their giving up one of his possessions. It was their duty to fight, and although they admitted resistance to be useless, they refused to yield, save to force. The English commander reluctantly ordered a bombardment, and after a few hours the Chinese defences were demolished, and Tinghai was occupied. Chusan remained in our possession as a base of operations during the greater part of the war, but its insalubrity rather dissipated the reputation it had acquired as an advantageous and well-placed station for operations on the coast of China. Almost at the same time as the attack on Chusan, hostilities were recommenced against the Chinese on the Canton river in consequence of the carrying off of a British subject, Mr. Vincent Stanton, from Macao. The barrier forts were attacked by two English men-of-war and two smaller vessels. After a heavy bombardment, a force of marines and blue-jackets was landed, and the Chinese positions carried. The forts and barracks were destroyed, and Mr. Stanton released. Then it was said that "China must either bend or break," for the hour of English forbearance had passed away, and unless China could vindicate her policy by force of arms there was no longer any doubt that she would have to give way.

While these preliminary military events were occurring, the diplomatic side of the question was also in evidence. Lord Palmerston had written a letter stating in categorical language what he expected at the hands of the Chinese government, and he had directed that it should be delivered into nobody else's hands but the responsible ministers of the Emperor Taoukwang. The primary task of the English expedition was to give this despatch to some high Chinese official who seemed competent to convey it to Pekin. This task proved one of unexpected difficulty, for the mandarins, basing their refusal on the strict letter of their duty, which forbade them to hold any intercourse with foreigners, returned the document, and declared that they could not receive it. This happened at Amoy and again at Ningpo, and the occupation of Chusan did not bring our authorities any nearer to realising their mission. Baffled in these attempts, the fleet sailed north for the mouth of the Peiho, when at last Lord Palmerston's letter was accepted by Keshen, the Viceroy of the Province, and duly forwarded by him to Pekin. The arrival of the English fleet awoke the Chinese Court for the time being from its indifference, and Taoukwang not merely ordered that the fleet should be provided with all the supplies it needed, but appointed Keshen High Commissioner for the conclusion of an amicable arrangement. The difficulty thus seemed in a fair way towards settlement, but as a matter of fact it was only at its commencement, for the wiles of Chinese diplomacy are infinite, and were then only partially understood. Keshen was remarkable for his astuteness and for the yielding exterior which covered a purpose of iron, and in the English political officer, the Captain Elliot of Canton, he did not find an opponent worthy of his steel. Although experience had shown how great were the delays of negotiation at Canton, and how inaccessible were the local officials, Captain Elliot allowed himself to be persuaded that the best place to carry on negotiations was at that city, and after a brief delay the fleet was withdrawn from the Peiho and all the advantages of the alarm created by its presence at Pekin were surrendered. Relieved by the departure of the foreign ships, Taoukwang sent orders for the despatch of forces from the inland provinces, so that he might be able to resume the struggle with the English under more favourable conditions, and at the same time he hastened to relieve his over-charged feelings by punishing the man whom he regarded as responsible for his misfortunes and humiliation. The full weight of the Imperial wrath fell on Commissioner Lin, who from the position of the foremost official in China fell at a stroke of the vermilion pencil to a public criminal arraigned before the Board of Punishments to receive his deserts. He was stripped of all his offices, and ordered to proceed with "the speed of flames" to Pekin, where, however, his life was spared.

Keshen arrived at Canton on 29th November, 1840, but his despatch to the Emperor explaining the position he found there shows that his view of the situation did not differ materially from that of Lin. "Night and day I have considered and examined the state of our relations with the English. At first moved by the benevolence of His Majesty and the severity of the laws, they surrendered the opium. Commissioner Lin commanded them to give bonds that they would never more deal in opium—a most excellent plan for securing future good conduct. This the English refused to give, and then they trifled with the laws, and so obstinate were their dispositions that they could not be made to submit. Hence it becomes necessary to soothe and admonish them with sound instruction, so as to cause them to change their mien and purify their hearts, after which it will not be too late to renew their commerce. It behoves me to instruct and persuade them so that their good consciences may be restored, and they reduced to submission." The language of this document showed that the highest Chinese officers still believed that the English would accept trade facilities as a favour, that they would be treated *de haut en bas*, and that China possessed the power to make good her lofty pretensions. China had learnt nothing from her military mishaps at Canton, Amoy, and Chusan, and from the appearance of an English fleet in the Gulf of Pechihli. Keshen had gained a breathing space by procrastination in the north, and he resorted to the same tactics at Canton. Days expanded into weeks, and at last orders were issued for an advance up the Canton river, as it had become evident that the Chinese were not only bent on an obstructive policy, but were making energetic efforts to assemble a large army. On 7th January, 1841, orders were consequently issued for an immediate attack on the Bogue forts, which had been placed in a state of defence, and which were manned by large numbers of Chinese. Fortunately for us, the Chinese possessed a very rudimentary knowledge of the art of war, and showed no capacity to take advantage of the strength of their position and forts, or even of their excellent guns. The troops were landed on the coast in the early morning to operate on the flank and rear of the forts at Chuenpee. The advance squadron, under Captain, afterwards Sir Thomas, Herbert, was to engage the same forts in front, while the remainder of the fleet proceeded to attack the stockades on the adjoining island of Taikok. The land force of 1,500 men and three guns had not proceeded far along the coast before it came across a strongly entrenched camp in addition to the Chuenpee forts, with several thousand troops and many guns in position. After a sharp cannonade the forts were carried at a rush, and a formidable army was driven ignominiously out of its entrenchments with hardly any loss to the assailants. The forts at Taikok were destroyed by the fire of the ships, and their guns spiked and garrisons routed by storming parties. In all, the Chinese lost five hundred killed, besides an incalculable number of wounded, and many junks. The Chinese showed some courage as well as incompetence, and the English officers described their defence as "obstinate and honourable."

The capture of the Bogue forts produced immediate and important consequences. Keshen at once begged a cessation of hostilities, and offered terms which conceded everything we had demanded. These were the payment of a large indemnity, the cession of Hongkong, and the right to hold official communication with the central government. In accordance with these preliminary articles, Hongkong was proclaimed, on 29 January,

1841, a British possession, and the troops evacuated Chusan to garrison the new station. It was not considered at the time that the acquisition was of much importance, and no one would have predicted for it the brilliant and prosperous position it has since attained. But the promises given by Keshen were merely to gain time and to extricate him from a very embarrassing situation. The morrow of what seemed a signal reverse was marked by the issue of an imperial notice, breathing a more defiant tone than ever. Taoukwang declared, in this edict, that he was resolved "to destroy and wash the foreigners away without remorse," and he denounced the English by name as "staying themselves upon their pride of power and fierce strength." He, therefore, called upon his officers to proceed with courage and energy, so that "the rebellious foreigners might give up their ringleaders, to be sent encaged to Pekin, to receive the utmost retribution of the laws." So long as the sovereign held such opinions as these, it was evident that no arrangement could endure. The Chinese did not admit the principle of equality in their dealings with the English, and this was the main point in contention, far more than the alleged evils of the opium traffic. So long as Taoukwang and his ministers held the opinions which they did not hesitate to express, a friendly intercourse was impossible. There was no practical alternative between withdrawing from the country altogether, leaving the Chinese in undisturbed seclusion, and forcing their government to recognise a common humanity and an equality in national privileges.

It is not surprising that under these circumstances the suspension of hostilities proved of brief duration. The conflict was hastened by the removal of Keshen from his post, in consequence of his having reported that he considered the Chinese forces unequal to the task of opposing the English. His candour in recognising facts did him credit, while it cost him his position; and his successor, Eleang, was compelled to take an opposite view, and to attempt something to justify it. Eleang refused to ratify the convention signed by Keshen, and, on 25th February, the English commander ordered an attack on the inner line of forts which guarded the approaches to Canton. After a brief engagement, the really formidable lines of Anunghoy, with 200 guns in position, were carried at a nominal loss. The many other positions of the Chinese, up to Whampoa, were occupied in succession; and, on 1st March, the English squadron drew up off Howqua's Folly, in Whampoa Reach, at the very gateway of Canton. On the following day the dashing Sir Hugh Gough arrived to take the supreme direction of the English forces. After these further reverses, the Chinese again begged a suspension of hostilities, and an armistice for a few days was granted. The local authorities were on the horns of a dilemma. They saw the futility of a struggle with the English, and the Cantonese had to bear all the suffering for the obstinacy of the Pekin government; but, on the other hand, no one dared to propose concession to Taoukwang, who, confident of his power, and ignorant of the extent of his misfortunes, breathed nothing but defiance. After a few days' delay, it became clear that the Cantonese had neither the will nor the power to conclude a definite arrangement, and consequently their city was attacked with as much forbearance as possible. The fort called Dutch Folly was captured, and the outer line of defences was taken possession of, but no attempt was made to occupy the city itself. Sir Hugh Gough stated, in a public notice, that the city was spared because the Queen had desired that all peaceful people should be tenderly considered. The first English successes had entailed the disgrace of Lin, the second were not less fatal to Keshen. Keshen was arraigned before the Board at Pekin, his valuable property was escheated to the Crown, and he himself sentenced to decapitation, which was commuted to banishment to Tibet, where he succeeded in amassing a fresh fortune. The success of the English was proclaimed by the merchants reoccupying their factories on 18th March, 1841, exactly two years after Lin's first fiery edict against opium. It was a strange feature in this struggle that the instant they did so, the Chinese merchants resumed trade with undiminished ardour and cordiality. The officials even showed an inclination to follow their example, when they learnt that Taoukwang refused to listen to any conclusive peace, and that his policy was still one of expelling the foreigners. To carry out his views, the Emperor sent a new commission of three members to Canton, and it was their studious avoidance of all communication with the English authorities that again aroused suspicion as to the Chinese not being sincere in their assent to the convention which had saved Canton from an English occupation. Taoukwang was ignorant of the success of his enemy, and his commissioners, sent to achieve what Lin and Keshen had failed to do, were fully resolved not to recognise the position which the English had obtained by force of arms, or to admit that it was likely to prove enduring. This confidence was increased by the continuous arrival of fresh troops, until at last there were 50,000 men in the neighbourhood of Canton, and all seemed ready to tempt the fortune of war again, and to make another effort to expel the hated foreigner. The measure of Taoukwang's animosity may be taken by his threatening to punish with death anyone who suggested making peace with the barbarians.

While the merchants were actively engaged in their commercial operations, and the English officers in conducting negotiations with a functionary who had no authority, and who was only put forward to amuse them, the Chinese were busily employed in completing their warlike preparations, which at the same time they kept as secret as possible, in the hope of taking the English by surprise. But it was impossible for such extensive preparations to be made without their creating some stir, and the standing aloof of the commissioners was in itself ground of suspicion. Suspicion became certainty when, on Captain Elliot paying a visit to the prefect in the city, he was received in a disrespectful manner by the mandarins, and insulted in the streets by the crowd. He at once acquainted Sir Hugh Gough, who was at Hongkong, with the occurrence, and issued a notice, on 21st May, 1841, advising all foreigners to leave Canton that day. This notice was not a day too soon, for, during the night, the Chinese made a desperate attempt to carry out their scheme. The batteries which they had secretly erected at various points in the city and along the riverbanks, began to bombard the factories and the ships at the same time that fire-rafts were sent against the latter in the hope of causing a conflagration. Fortunately the Chinese were completely baffled, with heavy loss to themselves and none to the English; and during the following day the English assumed the offensive, and with such effect that all the Chinese batteries were destroyed, together with forty war-junks. The only exploit on which the Chinese could compliment themselves was that they had sacked and gutted the English factory. This incident made it clearer than ever that the Chinese government would only be amenable to force, and that it was absolutely necessary to inflict some weighty punishment on the Chinese leaders at Canton, who had made so bad a return for the moderation shown them and their city, and who had evidently no intention of complying with the arrangement to which they had been a party.

Sir Hugh Gough arrived at Canton with all his forces on 24th May, and on the following morning the attack commenced with the advance of the fleet up the Macao passage, and with the landing of bodies of troops at different points which appeared well suited for turning the Chinese position and attacking the gates of Canton. The Chinese did not molest the troops in landing, which was fortunate, as the operation proved exceedingly difficult, and occupied more than a whole day. The Chinese had taken up a strong position on the hills lying north of the city, and they showed considerable judgment in their selection, and no small skill in strengthening their ground by a line of forts. The Chinese were said to be full of confidence in their ability to reverse the previous fortune of the war, and they fought with considerable confidence, while the turbulent Cantonese populace waited impatiently on the walls to take advantage of the first symptoms of defeat among the English troops. The English army, divided into two columns of nearly 2,000 men each, with a strong artillery force of 7 guns, 4 howitzers, 5 mortars, and 52 rockets, advanced on the Chinese entrenchments across paddy fields, rendered more difficult of passage by numerous burial-grounds. The obstacles were considerable and the progress was slow, but the Chinese did not attempt any opposition. Then the battle began with the bombardment of the Chinese lines, and after an hour it seemed as if the Chinese had had enough of this and were preparing for flight, when a general advance was ordered. But the Chinese thought better of their intention or their movement was misunderstood, for when the English streamed up the hill to attack them they stood to their guns and presented a brave front. Three of their forts were carried with little or no loss, but at the fourth they offered a stubborn if ill-directed resistance. Even then the engagement was not over, for the Chinese rallied in an entrenched camp one mile in the rear of the forts, and, rendered confident by their numbers, they resolved to make a fresh stand, and hurled defiance at the foreigners. The English troops never halted in their advance, and, led by the 18th or Royal Irish—one of the most distinguished regiments in the service—they carried the entrenchment at a rush and put the whole Chinese army to flight. The English lost seventy killed and wounded, the Chinese losses were never accurately known. It was arranged that Canton was to be stormed on the following day, but a terrific hurricane and deluge of rain prevented all military movements on 26th May, and, as it proved, saved the city from attack. Once more Chinese diplomacy came to the relief of Chinese arms. To save Canton the mandarins were quite prepared to make every concession, if they only attached a temporary significance to their language, and they employed the whole of that lucky wet day in getting round Captain Elliot, who once more allowed himself to place faith in the promises of the Chinese. The result of this was seen on the 27th, when, just as Sir Hugh Gough was giving orders for the assault, he received a message from Captain Elliot stating that the Chinese had come to terms and that all hostilities were to be suspended. The terms the Chinese had agreed to in a few hours were that the Commissioners and all the troops should retire to a distance of sixty miles from Canton, and that six million dollars should be paid "for the use of the English Crown."

There can be no doubt that these terms were inadequate in themselves, and that they afforded no guarantee of any improvement in the future relations of the two peoples. Nor were they deemed suitable for the occasion by Sir Hugh Gough and the other military leaders, who rightly held that the occupation of Canton was necessary to convince the Chinese of the magnitude of their defeat and the hopelessness of continuing the struggle.

The accuracy of these views was soon confirmed, and if there was ever any doubt as to the opposite counsels that swayed the action of the Chinese it was removed by their extraordinary proceedings on this occasion. Five of the six million dollars had been handed over to Captain Elliot, and amicable relations had been established with the city authorities, when the Imperial Commissioners, either alarmed at the penalties their failure entailed, or encouraged to believe in the renewed chances of success from the impotence into which the English troops might have sunk, made a sudden attempt to surprise Sir Hugh Gough's camp and to retrieve a succession of disasters at a single stroke. The project was not without a chance of success, but it required prompt action and no hesitation in coming to close quarters—the two qualifications in which the Chinese were most deficient. So it was on this occasion. Ten or fifteen thousand Chinese braves suddenly appeared on the hills about two miles north of the English camp, but instead of seizing the opportunity created by the surprise at their sudden appearance and at the breach of armistice and delivering home their attack, they merely waved their banners and uttered threats of defiance. They stood their ground for some time in face of the rifle and artillery fire opened upon them, and then they kept up a sort of running fight for three miles as they were pursued by the English. They did not suffer any serious loss, and when the English troops retired in consequence of a heavy storm they became in turn the pursuers and inflicted a few casualties. The advantages they obtained were due to the terrific weather more than to their courage, but one party of Madras sepoys lost its way, and was surrounded by so overwhelming a number of Chinese that they would have been annihilated but that their absence was fortunately discovered and a rescuing party of marines, armed with the new percussion gun, which was to a great degree secure against the weather, went out to their assistance. They found the sepoys, under their two English officers, drawn up in a square firing as best they could and presenting a bold front to the foe—"many of the sepoys, after extracting the wet cartridge very deliberately, tore their pocket handkerchiefs or lining from their turbans, and baling water with their hands into the barrel of their pieces, washed and dried them, thus enabling them to fire an occasional volley." Out of sixty sepoys one was killed and fourteen wounded. After this Sir Hugh Gough threatened to bombard Canton if there were any more attacks on his camp, and they at once ceased, and when the whole of the indemnity was paid the English troops were withdrawn, leaving Canton as it was, for a second time "a record of British magnanimity and forbearance."

After this trade reverted to its former footing, and by the Canton convention, signed by the Imperial Commissioners in July, 1841, the English obtained all the privileges they could hope for from the local authorities. But it was essentially a truce, not a treaty, and the great point of direct intercourse with the central Government was no nearer settlement than ever. At this moment Sir Henry Pottinger arrived as Plenipotentiary from

England, and he at once set himself to obtaining a formal recognition from the Pekin executive of his position and the admission of his right to address them on diplomatic business. With the view of pressing this matter on the attention of Taoukwang, who personally had not deviated from his original attitude of emphatic hostility, Sir Henry Pottinger sailed northwards with the fleet and a large portion of the land forces about the end of August. The important seaport of Amoy was attacked and taken after what was called "a short but animated resistance." This town is situated on an island, the largest of a group lying at the entrance to the estuary of Lungkiang, and it has long been famous as a convenient port and flourishing place of trade. On the eastern side of the harbour is the large but flat island of Quemoy, with abundant rice-fields and a toiling population, and on the western is the barren and elevated islet of Kulangsu. On the former the Chinese had raised a rampart of 1,100 yards in length, and this they had armed with ninety guns, while a battery of forty-two guns protected its flank. Kulangsu was also fortified, and the Chinese had placed in all 500 guns in position. They believed in the impregnability of Amoy, and it was allowed that no inconsiderable skill as well as great expense had been devoted to the strengthening of the place. When the English fleet arrived off the port the Chinese sent a flag of truce to demand what it wanted, and they were informed the surrender of the town. The necessity for this measure would be hard to justify, especially as we were nominally at peace with China, for the people of Amoy had inflicted no injury on our trade, and their chastisement would not bring us any nearer to Pekin. Nor was the occupation of Amoy necessary on military grounds. It was strong only for itself, and its capture had no important consequences. As the Chinese determined to resist the English, the fleet engaged the batteries, and the Chinese, standing to their guns "right manfully," only abandoned their position when they found their rear threatened by a landing party. Then, after a faint resistance, the Chinese sought safety in flight, but some of their officers, preferring death to dishonour, committed suicide, one of them being seen to walk calmly into the sea and drown himself in face of both armies. The capture of Amoy followed, but it is instructive to cull the following from the opinions expressed by different English officers at the attack. "The batteries were admirably constructed, and manned by Europeans no force could have stood before them"; again, "The batteries were never completely silenced by the ships' guns, and it is believed they never would have been"; and again, "Let the Chinese be trained and well found with European implements and munitions of war, and depend upon it they will prove themselves no contemptible foe."

As the authorities at Amoy refused to hold any intercourse with the English, the achievement remained barren of any useful consequence, and after leaving a small garrison on Kulangsu, and three war-ships in the roadstead, the English expedition continued its northern course. After being scattered by a storm in the perilous Formosa channel, the fleet reunited off Ningpo, whence it proceeded to attack Chusan for a second time. The Chinese defended Tinghai, the capital, with great resolution, an officer who was present giving the following description of the affair: "Many of the Chinese seeing our men advance into the battery, quickly turned, and a very smart affair followed. They assembled in great numbers close to some brass guns, and then fought like Turks; in their haste, however, they fired too high to do much injury, and some of the advance saved their lives by making good use of their pistols. At this place General Keo, the chief naval and military commander, was killed, and all his officers, sticking to him to the last, also fell with him. Their conduct in fact was noble; nothing could have surpassed it." On the re-occupation of Chusan, which it was decided to retain until a formal treaty had been concluded with the Emperor, Sir Henry Pottinger issued a proclamation to the effect that years might elapse before that place would be restored to the Emperor's authority, and many persons wished that it should be permanently annexed as the best base for commercial operations in China. A garrison of 400 men was left at Tinghai, and then the expedition proceeded to attack Chinhai on the mainland, where the Chinese had made every preparation to offer a strenuous resistance. Sir Hugh Gough divided his small force into three columns, the two outside of which were ordered to outflank the Chinese position. This they succeeded in doing with extraordinary success owing to some inequalities in the ground, and the Chinese suffered the most signal defeat and the greatest loss they had yet incurred during the war. Hundreds fell at the point of the bayonet, hundreds more were drowned in the river, and the overthrow of the Chinese army was unqualified and complete. The victory at Chinhai was followed by the unopposed occupation of the important city of Ningpo, where the inhabitants shut themselves up in their houses, and wrote on their doors "Submissive People." Ningpo was put to ransom and the authorities informed that unless they paid the sum within a certain time their city would be handed over to pillage and destruction. This harsh declaration was, it is said, made not with the intention of literally carrying it out, but of impressing the Chinese with our resolute determination to stand no prevarication. As the Pekin government had made no sign of giving in, it was felt that no occasion ought to be lost of overawing the Chinese, and compelling them to admit that any further prolongation of the struggle would be hopeless. The arrival of further troops and warships from Europe enabled the English commanders to adopt a more determined and uncompromising attitude, and the capture of Ningpo would have been followed up at once but for the disastrous events in Afghanistan, which distracted attention from the Chinese question, and delayed its settlement. It was hoped, however, that the continued occupation of Amoy, Chusan, and Ningpo would cause sufficient pressure on the Pekin government to induce it to yield all that was demanded.

These anticipations were not fulfilled, for neither the swift-recurring visitation of disaster nor the waning resources of the Imperial government in both men and treasure could shake the fixed hostility of Taoukwang, or induce him to abate his proud pretensions. Minister after minister passed into disgrace and exile. Misfortune shared the same fate as incompetence, and the more the embarrassments of the state increased the heavier fell the hand of the ruler and the verdict of the Board of Punishments upon beaten generals and unsuccessful statesmen. The period of inaction which followed the occupation of Ningpo no doubt encouraged the Emperor to think that the foreigners were exhausted, or that they had reached the end of their successes, and he ordered increased efforts to be made to bring up troops, and to strengthen the approaches to Pekin. He was also informed by his defeated generals that although they had been worsted they had succeeded in inflicting heavy losses on the English. The first proof of his returning spirit was shown in March, 1842, when the Chinese attempted to seize Ningpo by a *coup de main*. Suddenly, and without warning, a force of between ten and twelve thousand men appeared at daybreak outside the south and west gates of Ningpo, and many of them succeeded in making their way over the walls and gaining the centre of the town; but, instead of proving the path to victory, this advance resulted in the complete overthrow of the Chinese. Attacked by artillery and foot in the market place they were almost annihilated, and the great Chinese attack on Ningpo resulted in a fiasco. Similar but less vigorous attacks were made about the same time on Chinhai and Chusan, but they were both repulsed with heavy loss to the Chinese. In consequence of these attacks and the improved position in Afghanistan it was decided to again assume the offensive, and to break up the hostile army at Hangchow, of which the body that attacked Ningpo was the advanced guard. Sir Hugh Gough commanded the operations in person, and he had the co-operation of a naval force under Sir William Parker. The first action took place outside Tszeki, a small place ten miles from Ningpo, where the Chinese fancied they occupied an exceedingly strong position. But careful inspection showed it to be radically faulty. Their lines covered part of the Segaou Hills, but their left was commanded by some higher hills on the right of the English position, and the Chinese left again commanded their own right. It was evident, therefore, that the capture of the left wing of the Chinese encampment would entail the surrender or evacuation of the rest. The difficulties of the ground caused a greater delay in the advance than had been expected, and the assault had to be delivered along the whole line, as it was becoming obvious that the Chinese were growing more confident, and, consequently, more to be feared from the delay in attacking them. The assault was made with the impetuosity good troops always show in attacking inferior ones, no matter how great the disparity of numbers, and here the Chinese were driven out of their position, although they stood their ground in a creditable manner, and chased over the hills down to the rice-fields below. The Chinese loss was over a thousand killed, including many of the Imperial Guard, of whom 500 were present, and whom Sir Hugh Gough described as "remarkably fine men," while the English had six killed and thirty-seven wounded. For the moment it was intended to follow up this victory by an attack on the City of Hangchow, the famous Kinesay of mediæval travellers; but the arrival of fresh instructions gave a complete turn to the whole war.

The reader will have perceived how very little permanent good had been effected by these successful operations on the coast, and that Taoukwang was still as resolute as ever in his hostility; nor is there any reason to suppose that the capture of Hangchow, or any other of the coast towns, would have caused a material change in the situation. The credit of initiating the policy which brought the Chinese government to its knees belongs exclusively to that much-maligned statesman Lord Ellenborough, then Governor-General of India. He detected the futility of operations along the coast, and he suggested that the great waterway of the Yangtsekiang, perfectly navigable for war-ships up to the immediate neighbourhood of Nankin, provided the means of coercing the Chinese, and effecting the objects which the English government had in view. The English expedition, strongly reinforced from India, then abandoned Ningpo and Chinhai, and, proceeding north, began the final operations of the war with an attack on Chapoo, where the Chinese had made extensive measures of defence. Chapoo was the port appointed for trade with Japan, and the Chinese had collected there a very considerable force from the levies of Chekiang, which ex-Commissioner Lin had been largely instrumental in raising. Sir Hugh Gough attacked Chapoo with 2,000 men, and the main body of the Chinese was routed without much difficulty, but 300 desperate men shut themselves up in a walled enclosure, and made an obstinate resistance. They held out until three-fourths of them were slain, when the survivors, fifty wounded men, accepted the quarters offered them from the first. The English lost ten killed, and fifty-five wounded, and the Chinese more than a thousand. After this the expedition proceeded northwards for the Great River, and it was found necessary to attack Woosung, the port of Shanghai, *en route*. This place was also strongly fortified with as many as 175 guns in position, but the chief difficulty in attacking it lay in that of approach, as the channel had first to be sounded, and then the sailing-ships towed into position by the steamers. Twelve vessels were in this manner placed broadside to the batteries on land, a position which obviously they could not have maintained against a force of anything like equal strength; but they succeeded in silencing the Chinese batteries with comparatively little loss, and then the English army was landed without opposition. Shanghai is situated sixteen miles up the Woosung river, and while part of the force proceeded up the river another marched overland. Both columns arrived together, and the disheartened Chinese evacuated Shanghai after firing one or two random shots. No attempt was made to retain Shanghai, and the expedition re-embarked, and proceeded to attack Chankiang or Chinkiangfoo, a town on the southern bank of the Yangtsekiang, and at the northern entrance of the southern branch of the Great Canal. This town has always been a place of great celebrity, both strategically and commercially, for not merely does it hold a very strong position with regard to the Canal, but it forms, with the Golden and Silver Islands, the principal barrier in the path of those attempting to reach Nankin. At this point Sir Hugh Gough was reinforced by the 98th Regiment, under Colonel Colin Campbell, afterwards Lord Clyde. The difficulties of navigation and the size of the fleet, which now reached seventy vessels, caused a delay in the operations, and it was not until the latter end of July, or more than a month after the occupation of Shanghai, that the English reached Chinkiangfoo, where, strangely enough, there seemed to be no military preparations whatever. The inquisitive townspeople assembled on the walls to look at the foreign ships and soldiers rather as some interesting spectacle than as the evidence of a hostile invasion. A careful reconnaissance revealed the presence of three strong encampments at some distance from the town, and the first operation was to carry them, and to prevent their garrisons joining such forces as might still remain in the city. This attack was entrusted to Lord Saltoun's brigade, which was composed of two Scotch regiments—the 26th and 98th—and portions of two native regiments, with only three guns. The opposition was almost insignificant, and the three camps were carried with comparatively little loss, and their garrisons scattered in all directions. At the same time as Lord Saltoun's brigade attacked the camps the remainder of the force assaulted the city, which was surrounded by a high wall and a deep moat. Some delay was caused by these obstacles, but at last the western gate was blown in by Captain Pears, of the Engineers, and at the same moment the walls were escaladed at two different points, and the

English troops, streaming in on three sides, fairly surrounded a considerable portion of the garrison, who retired into a detached work, where they perished to the last man either by our fire or in the flames of the houses which were ignited partly by themselves and partly by the fire of our soldiers. The resistance did not stop here, for the Tartar or inner city was resolutely defended by the Manchus, and owing to the intense heat the Europeans would have been glad of a rest; but, as the Manchus kept up a galling fire, Sir Hugh Gough felt bound to order an immediate assault before the enemy grew too daring. The fight was renewed, and the Tartars were driven back at all points; but the English troops were so exhausted that they could not press home this advantage. The interval thus gained was employed by the Manchus, not in making good their escape, but in securing their military honour by first massacreing their women and children and then committing suicide. It must be remembered that these were not Chinese, but Manchu Tartars of the dominant race; and this unique scene in the annals of war can best be described in Sir Hugh Gough's own words:—

"The Tartar General's house was burnt; that of the Lieutenant-General Hailing, it appears, had been set on fire by his own orders, and he was destroyed in it; his secretary, who was found the next morning by Mr. Morrison, related this event, and pointed out the body of his unfortunate chief. Finding dead bodies of Tartars in every house he entered—principally women and children—thrown into wells, or otherwise murdered by their own people, I was glad to withdraw the troops from this frightful scene of destruction. A great number of those who escaped our fire committed suicide after destroying their families; the loss of life has been therefore appalling, and it may be said that the Manchu race in the city is extinct."

The losses of the English army at this battle—40 killed, and 130 wounded—were heavy, and they were increased by several deaths caused by the heat and exhaustion of the day. The Chinese, or rather the Tartars, never fought better, and it appears from a document discovered afterwards that if Hailing's recommendations had been followed, and if he had been properly supported, the capture of Chinkiangfoo would have been even more difficult and costly than it proved.

Some delay at Chinkiang was rendered necessary by the exhaustion of the troops and by the number of sick and wounded; but a week after the capture of that place in the manner described the arrangements for the further advance on Nankin were completed. A small garrison was left in an encampment on a height commanding the entrance to the canal; but there was little reason to apprehend any fresh attack, as the lesson of Chinkiangfoo had been a terrible one. That city lay beneath the English camp like a vast charnel house, its half-burnt buildings filled with the self-immolated Tartars who had preferred honour to life, and so thickly strewn were these and so intense the heat that the days passed away without the ability to give them burial, until at last it became absolutely impossible to render the last kind office to a gallant foe. Despite the greatest precautions of the English authorities, Chinkiangfoo became the source of pestilence, and an outbreak of cholera caused more serious loss in the English camp than befell the main force entrusted with the capture of Nankin. Many a brave soldier who had led the charge up to the very line of the Manchu spears without receiving a scratch succumbed to the fell disease which originated from the self-slaughtered defenders of their hearths and homes, and the vindicators of the national honour. Contrary winds delayed the progress of the English fleet, and it was not until the fifth of August, more than a fortnight after the battle at Chinkiangfoo, that it appeared off Nankin, the second city in reputation and historical importance of the Empire, with one million inhabitants and a garrison of 15,000 men, of whom two-thirds were Manchus. The walls were twenty miles in length, and hindered, more than they promoted, an efficient defence; and the difficulties of the surrounding country, covered with the *débris* of the buildings which constituted the larger cities of Nankin at an earlier period of history, helped the assailing party more than they did the defenders. Sir Hugh Gough drew up an admirable plan for capturing this vast and not defenceless city with his force of 5,000 men, and there is no reason to doubt that he would have been completely successful; but by this the backbone of the Chinese government had been broken, and even the proud and obstinate Taoukwang was compelled to admit that it was imperative to come to terms with the English, and to make some concessions in order to get rid of them.

Before considering the final negotiations and the terms of the peace which adjusted, however temporarily, the international difficulty, a few concluding words may be said on the conduct of the war, which n one form or another had gone on for more than two years. At first conducted without any system and in a desultory manner, and prosecuted in its larger phases almost with reluctance, the military operations had gone to prove that neither the courage nor the craft of the Chinese could compensate them for the want of proper weapons, and of the discipline and experience in war which made the armies of Europe victorious. Although the English did not enjoy the same superiority in scientific and mechanical resources as they did in the second war seventeen years later, yet they possessed so many advantages over Taoukwang's levies that the result of an encounter was never in doubt, even although the Chinese possessed a strong position and an overwhelming preponderance in numbers. The war of 1839-42 demonstrated that the British soldier who had vanquished the most warlike races of India was also incomparably the superior of the Chinese on such conditions as those prevailing forty years ago. But to the intelligent it conveyed a lesson of a different significance. The Chinese were the worst equipped and the most innocent of military knowledge in the long list of Asiatic foes with whom we had come into contact. Often they were no better than a badly-armed mob, and even the Manchus had no more formidable weapons than their bows and spears. Yet not once did these badly armed and ignorant men evince cowardice. The English commanders always testified to their gallantry, even when hopeless, and to their devotion to duty when most other people would have thought only of their personal safety. Their defeat under all the circumstances was inevitable; but they knew how to save their reputation for courage, and to prove beyond the shadow of a doubt that men who could fight so manfully when victory was practically impossible could never be permanently conquered, and only needed the proper arms and knowledge to hold their own against Europeans.

The minister Elepoo, who once enjoyed the closest intimacy with Taoukwang, and who was the leader of the Peace party, which desired the cessation of an unequal struggle, had begun informal negotiations several months before they proved successful at Nankin. He omitted no opportunity of learning the views of the English officers, and what was the minimum of concession on which a stable peace could be based. He had endeavoured also to give something of a generous character to the struggle, and he had more than once proved himself a courteous as well as a gallant foe. After the capture of Chapoo and Woosung he sent back several officers and men who had at different times been taken prisoners by the Chinese, and he expressed at the same time the desire that the war should end. Sir Henry Pottinger's reply to this letter was to inquire if he was empowered by the Emperor to negotiate. If he had received this authority the English plenipotentiary would be very happy to discuss any matter with him, but if not the operations of war must proceed. At that moment Elepoo had not the requisite authority to negotiate, and the war went on until the victorious English troops were beneath the walls of Nankin. At the same time as these pourparlers were held with Elepoo at Woosung, Sir Henry Pottinger issued a proclamation to the Chinese stating what the British government required to be done. In this document the equality of all nations as members of the same human family was pointed out, and the right to hold friendly intercourse insisted on as a matter of duty and common obligation. Sir Henry said that "England, coming from the utmost west, has held intercourse with China in this utmost east for more than two centuries past, and during this time the English have suffered ill-treatment from the Chinese officials, who, regarding themselves as powerful and us as weak, have thus dared to commit injustice." Then followed a list of the many highhanded acts of Commissioner Lin and his successors. The Chinese, plainly speaking, had sought to maintain their exclusiveness and to live outside the comity of nations, and they had not the power to attain their wish. Therefore they were compelled to listen to and to accept the terms of the English plenipotentiary, which were as follows:—The Emperor was first of all to appoint a high officer with full powers to negotiate and conclude arrangements on his own responsibility, when hostilities would be suspended. The three principal points on which these negotiations were to be based were compensation for losses and expenses, a friendly and becoming intercourse on terms of equality between officers of the two countries, and the cession of insular territory for commerce and for the residence of merchants, and as a security and guarantee against the future renewal of offensive acts. The first step towards the acceptance of these terms was taken when an Imperial Commission was formed of three members, Keying, Elepoo, and Niu Kien, Viceroy of the Two Kiang; and to the last-named, as governor of the provinces most affected, fell the task of writing the first diplomatic communication of a satisfactory character from the Chinese government to the English plenipotentiary. This letter was important for more reasons than its being of a conciliatory nature. It held out to a certain extent a hand of friendship, and it also sought to assign an origin to the conflict, and Niu Kien could find nothing more handy or convenient than opium, which thus came to give its name to the whole war. With regard to the Chinese reverses, Niu Kien, while admitting them, explained that "as the central nation had enjoyed peace for a long time the Chinese were not prepared for attacking and fighting, which has led to this accumulation of insult and disgrace." In a later communication Niu Kien admitted that "the English at Canton had been exposed to insults and extortions for a series of years, and that steps should be taken to ensure in future that the people of your honourable nation might carry on their commerce to advantage, and not receive injury thereby." These documents showed that the Chinese were at last willing to abandon the old and impossible principle of superiority over other nations, for which they had so long contended; and with the withdrawal of this pretension negotiations for the conclusion of a stable peace became at once possible and of hopeful augury.

The first step of the Chinese Commissioners was to draw up a memorial for presentation to the Emperor, asking his sanction of the arrangement they suggested. In this document they covered the whole ground of the dispute, and stated in clear and unmistakable language what the English demanded, and they did not shrink from recommending compliance with their terms. Keying and his colleagues put the only two alternatives with great cogency. Which will be the heavier calamity, they said, to pay the English the sum of money they demand (21,000,000 dollars, made up as follows: 6,000,000 for the destroyed opium, 3,000,000 for the debts of the Hong merchants, and 12,000,000 for the expenses of the war), or that they should continue those military operations which seemed irresistible, and from which China had suffered so grievously? Even if the latter alternative were faced and the war continued, the evil day would only be put off. The army expenses would be very great, the indemnity would be increased in amount, and after all there would be only "the name of fighting without the hope of victory." Similar arguments were used with regard to the cession of Hongkong, and the right of trading at five of the principal ports. The English no doubt demanded more than they ought, but what was the use of arguing with them, as they were masters of the situation? Moreover, some solace might be gathered in the midst of affliction from the fact that the English were willing to pay certain duties on their commerce which would in the end repay the war indemnity, and contribute to "the expenditure of the Imperial family." With regard to the question of ceremonial intercourse on a footing of equality, they declared that it might be "unreservedly granted." The reply of Taoukwang to this memorial was given in an edict of considerable length, and he therein assented to all the views and suggestions of the Commissioners, while he imposed on Keying alone the responsibility of making all the arrangements for paying the large indemnity. All the preliminaries for signing a treaty of peace had therefore been arranged before the English forces reached Nankin, and as the Chinese Commissioners were sincere in their desire for peace, and as the Emperor had sanctioned all the necessary arrangements, there was no reason to apprehend any delay, and much less a breakdown of the negotiations.

It was arranged that the treaty should be signed on board a British man-of-war, and the Chinese Commissioners were invited to pay a visit for the purpose to the *Cornwallis*, the flagship of the admiral. The event came off on the 20th of August, 1842, and the scene was sufficiently interesting, if not imposing. The long line of English war-ships and transports, drawn up opposite to and within short range of the lofty walls of Nankin; the land forces so disposed on the raised causeways on shore as to give them every facility of approach to the city gates, while leaving it doubtful to the last which gate would be the real object of attack; and then the six small Chinese boats, gaily decorated with flags, bearing the Imperial Commissioners and their attendants, to sign for the first time in history a treaty of defeat with a foreign power. The Commissioners were dressed in their plainest clothes, as they explained, because Imperial commissioners are supposed to proceed in haste about their business, and have no time to waste on their persons, but there is reason to believe that they thought such clothing best consorted with the inauspicious character for China of the occasion. The ceremony passed off without a hitch, and four days later Sir Henry Pottinger paid the Chinese officers a return visit, when he was received by them in a temple outside the city walls. A third and more formal reception was held on the 26th of August in the College Hall, in the centre of Nankin, when Sir Henry Pottinger, twenty officers, and an escort of native cavalry rode through the streets of one of the most famous cities of China. It was noted at the time that on this date an event of great importance had happened in each of the three previous years. On the 26th August, 1839, Lin had expelled the English from Macao, in 1840 the British fleet anchored off the Peiho, and in 1841 Amoy was captured. Three days after this reception the treaty itself was signed on board the *Cornwallis*, when Keying and his colleagues again attended for the purpose. The act of signing was celebrated by a Royal salute of twenty-one guns, and the hoisting of the standards of England and China at the mast-head of the man-of-war. The Emperor Taoukwang ratified the treaty with commendable despatch, and the only incident to mar the cordiality of the last scene in this part of the story of Anglo-Chinese relations was the barbarous and inexcusable injury inflicted by a party of English officers and soldiers on the famous Porcelain Tower, which was one of the finest specimens of Chinese art, having been built 400 years before at great expense and the labour of twenty years.

The ports in addition to Canton to be opened to trade were Shanghai, Ningpo, Amoy, and Foochow, but these were not to be opened until a tariff had been drawn up and consular officers appointed. As the instalments of the indemnity were paid the troops and fleet were withdrawn, but a garrison was left for some time in Chusan and Kulangsu, the island off Amoy. The attack and massacre of some shipwrecked crews on the coast of Formosa gave the Chinese government an occasion of showing how marked a change had come over its policy. An investigation was at once ordered, the guilty officials were punished, and the Emperor declared, " We will not allow that, because the representation came from outside foreigners, it should be carelessly cast aside without investigation. Our own subjects and foreigners, ministers and people, should all alike understand that it is our high desire to act with even-handed and perfect justice." Sir Henry Pottinger's task was only half performed until he had drawn up the tariff and installed consular officers in the new treaty ports. Elepoo was appointed to represent China in the tariff negotiations, and Canton was selected as the most convenient place for discussing the matter. Within two months of the resumption of negotiations they seemed on the point of a satisfactory termination, when the death of Elepoo, the most sincere and straightforward of all the Chinese officials, caused a delay in the matter. Elepoo was a member of the Manchu Imperial family, being descended from one of the brothers of Yung Ching, who had been banished by that ruler and reinstated by Keen Lung. That the Pekin government did not wish to make his death an excuse for backing out of the arrangement was shown by the prompt appointment of Keying as his successor. At this stage of the question the opium difficulty again rose up as of the first importance in reference to the settlement of the commercial tariff. The main point was whether opium was to appear in the tariff at all or to be relegated to the category of contraband articles. Sir Henry Pottinger disclaimed all sympathy with the traffic, and was quite willing that it should be declared illicit, but at the same time he stated that the responsibility of putting it down must rest with the Chinese themselves. The Chinese were not willing to accept this responsibility, and said that "if the supervision of the English representatives was not perfect, there will be less or more of smuggling." Keying paid Sir Henry Pottinger a ceremonious visit at Hongkong on the 26th of June, 1843, and within one month of that day the commercial treaty was signed. Sir Henry issued a public proclamation calling upon British subjects to faithfully conform with its provisions, and stating that he would adopt the most stringent and decided measures against any offending persons. On his side Keying published a notification that "trade at the five treaty ports was open to the men from afar." The only weak point in the commercial treaty was that it contained no reference to opium. Sir Henry Pottinger failed to obtain the assent of the Chinese government to its legalisation, and he refused to undertake the responsibility of a preventive service in China, but at the same time he publicly stated that the "traffic in opium was illegal and contraband by the laws and imperial edicts of China." Those who looked farther ahead realised that the treaty of Nankin, by leaving unsettled the main point in the controversy and the primary cause of difference, could not be considered a final solution of the problem of foreign intercourse with China. The opium question remained over to again disturb the harmony of our relations.

As has been said before, it would be taking a narrow view of the question to affirm that opium was the principal object at stake during this war. The real point was whether the Chinese government could be allowed the possession of rights which were unrecognised in the law of nations and which rendered the continuance of intercourse with foreigners an impossibility. What China sought to retain was never claimed by any other nation, and could only have been established by extraordinary military power. When people talk, therefore, of the injustice of this war as another instance of the triumph of might over right, they should recollect that China in the first place was wrong in claiming an impossible position in the family of nations. We cannot doubt that if the acts of Commissioner Lin had been condoned the lives of all Europeans would have been at the mercy of a system which recognises no gradation in crime, which affords many facilities for the manufacture of false evidence, and which inflicts punishment altogether in excess of the fault. It is gratifying to find that many unprejudiced persons declared at the time that the war which resulted in the Nankin treaty was a just one, and so eminent an authority on international law as John Quincy Adams drew up an elaborate treatise to show that "Britain had the righteous cause against China." We may leave the scene of contest and turn from the record of an unequal war with the reflection that the results of the struggle were to be good. However inadequately the work of far-seeing statesmanship may have been performed in 1842, enough was done to make present friendship possible and a better understanding between two great governing peoples a matter of hope and not desponding expectancy. The Treaty of Nankin did not place the English representatives on that footing of dignity which the equality of their sovereign with the Chinese Emperor demanded. The commercial arrangement at Canton ignored the opium trade—according to some, the main cause of the war. The Chinese government showed no desire to establish relations with the European capitals, even with the view of learning something of the kingdom which had sent strong fleets and brave armies to the lands of the far East. So long as this was the case it was impossible to feel any real belief in the cordiality of the friendship. The utmost that could be said was that certain guarantees had been procured. The English government had obtained a material guarantee in the cession of Hongkong, the English merchant had acquired fresh opportunities of trade by the opening of four new ports, and by the abolition of the Hong monopoly, and Englishmen generally were to enjoy increased security, if not perfect safety, by the vindication of British power. If these advantages were not everything, if they were not even enough to stifle the pride and dispel all the pretensions of China, they were still no small result for an expedition which had not approached the capital and which was conducted under extreme difficulties of distance and ignorance of China and her idiosyncrasies. That the war accomplished as much as it did must always be held creditable to those who had the conduct of it, and the Treaty of Nankin will remain one of the principal charters of the presence of Europeans in China.

CHAPTER XVIII.

TAOUKWANG AND HIS SUCCESSOR.

The progress and temporary settlement of the foreign question so completely overshadows every other event during Taoukwang's reign that it is difficult to extract anything of interest from the records of the government of the country, although the difficult and multifarious task of ruling three hundred millions of people had to be performed. Judged by the standard of a Chinese ruler, this Emperor undoubtedly came up to the requirements of his exalted office in his sense of how much his subjects required of him, and also in his manner of giving expression to their wishes. But his want of energy, or perhaps of the necessary knowledge, rendered him unable to properly supervise his own orders, or to sufficiently impress on his officers that they must be carried out without subterfuge. More than one fact went to show that the bonds of constituted authority were loosened in China, and that men paid only a qualified respect to the Imperial edict. Bands of robbers prowled about the country, and even the capital was not free from their presence. While one band made its headquarters within the Imperial city, another established itself in a fortified position in the central provinces of China, whence it dominated a vast region. The police were helpless, and such military forces as existed were unable to make any serious attempt to crush an opponent who was stronger than themselves. The foreign war had led to the recruiting of a large number of braves, and the peace to their sudden disbandment, so that the country was covered with a large number of desperate and penniless men, who were not particular as to what they did for a livelihood. It is not surprising that the secret societies began to look up again with so promising a field to work in, and a new association, known as the Green Water Lily, became extremely formidable among the truculent braves of Hoonan. But none of these troubles assumed the extreme form of danger in open rebellion, and there was still wanting the man to weld all these hostile and dangerous elements into a national party of insurgents against Manchu authority, and so it remained until Taoukwang had given up his throne to his successor.

In Yunnan there occurred, about the year 1846, the first simmerings of disaffection among the Mahomedans, which many years later developed into the Panthay rebellion, but on that occasion the vigour of the Viceroy nipped the danger in the bud. In Central Asia there was a revival of activity on the part of the Khoja exiles, who fancied that the discomfiture of the Chinese by the English and the internal disorders, of which rumour had no doubt carried an exaggerated account into Turkestan, would entail a very much diminished authority in Kashgar. As it happened, the Chinese authority in that region had been consolidated and extended by the energy and ability of a Mahomedan official named Zuhuruddin. He had risen to power by the thoroughness with which he had carried out the severe repressive measures sanctioned after the abortive invasion of Jehangir, and during fifteen years he increased the revenue and trade of the great province entrusted to his care. His loyalty to the Chinese government seems to have been unimpeachable, and the only point he seems to have erred in was an over-confident belief in the strength of his position. He based this opinion chiefly on the fact of his having constructed strong new forts, or yangyshahr, outside the principal towns. But a new element of danger had in the meantime been introduced into the situation in Kashgar by the appointment of Khokandian consuls, who were empowered to raise custom dues on all Mahomedan goods. These officials became the centre of intrigue against the Chinese authorities, and whenever the Khan of Khokand determined to take up the cause of the Khojas he found the ground prepared for him by these emissaries.

In 1842 Mahomed Ali Khan of Khokand, a chief of considerable ability and character, died, and his authority passed, after some confusion, to his kinsman, Khudayar, who was a man of little capacity, and indisposed to meddle with the affairs of his neighbours. But the Khokandian chiefs were loth to forego the turbulent adventures to which they were addicted for the personal feelings of their nominal head, and they thought that a descent upon Kashgar offered the best chance of glory and booty. Therefore they went to the seven sons of Jehangir and, inciting them by the memory of their father's death as well as the hope of a profitable adventure, to make another attempt to drive the Chinese out of Central Asia, succeeded in inducing them to unfurl once more the standard of the Khojas. The seven Khojas—Haft Khojagan—issued their proclamation in the winter of 1845-6, rallied all their adherents to their side, and made allies of the Kirghiz tribes. They did not at once resort to vigorous action, but hung on the frontier during the winter, and when they did not advance Zuhuruddin seems to have thought that they and their forces would melt away with the snows of the Pamir. The Khoja forces were, moreover, not a very formidable-looking body; but on the other hand, the Chinese garrison was very weak, and distributed over a wide area. The Khokandian agents reported that the people of Kashgar were ripe for revolt, and the inaction of Zuhuruddin even raised a suspicion of his fidelity. The chances of success were not as unequal as they appeared on the surface to be, and only the miserable incapacity of the Khojas prevented their attaining a greater success than they did. When the Mahomedan forces left the hills they advanced with extreme rapidity on Kashgar, to which they laid siege. After a siege of a fortnight they obtained possession of the town through the treachery of some of the inhabitants, but the citadel or yangyshahr continued to hold out, and their excesses in the town so alienated the sympathy of the Kashgarians, that no popular rising took place, and the Chinese were able to collect all their garrisons to expel the invaders. The Khojas were defeated in a battle at Kok Robat, near Yarkand, and driven out of the country. The affair of the seven Khojas, which at one time threatened the Chinese with the gravest danger, thus ended in a collapse, and it is remarkable as being the only invasion in which the Mahomedan subjects of China did not fraternise with her enemies. Notwithstanding the magnitude of his services as an administrator, Zuhuruddin was disgraced and dismissed from his post for what seemed his culpable apathy at the beginning of the campaign.

Another indication of the weakness of the Chinese executive was furnished in the piratical confederacy which established itself at the entrance of the Canton river, and defied all the efforts of the mandarins until they enlisted in their behalf the powerful co-operation of the English navy. The Bogue had never been completely free from those lawless persons who are willing to commit any outrage if it holds out a certain prospect of gain with a minimum amount of danger, and the peace had thrown many desperate men out of employment who thought they could find in piracy a mode of showing their patriotism as well as of profiting themselves. These turbulent and dangerous individuals gathered round a leader named Shapuntsai, and in the year of which we are speaking, 1849, they controlled a large fleet and a well-equipped force, which levied blackmail from Foochow to the Gulf of Tonquin, and attacked every trading ship, European or Chinese, which did not appear capable of defending itself. If they had confined their attacks to their own countrymen, it is impossible to say how long they might have gone on in impunity, for the Empire possessed no naval power; but, unfortunately for them, and fortunately for China, they seized some English vessels and murdered some English subjects. One man-of-war under Captain Hay was employed in operations against them, and in the course of six months fifty-seven piratical vessels were destroyed, and a thousand of their crews either slain or taken prisoners. Captain Hay, on being joined by another man-of-war, had the satisfaction of destroying the remaining junks and the depôts in the Canton river, whereupon he sailed to attack the headquarters of Shapuntsai in the Gulf of Tonquin. After some search the piratical fleet was discovered off an island which still bears the name of the Pirates' hold, and after a protracted engagement it was annihilated. Sixty junks were destroyed, and Shapuntsai was compelled to escape to Cochin China, where it is believed that he was executed by order of the King. The dispersion of this powerful confederacy was a timely service to the Chinese, who were informed that the English government would be at all times happy to afford similar aid at their request. Even at this comparatively early stage of the intercourse it was apparent that the long-despised foreigners would be able to render valuable service of a practical kind to the Pekin executive, and that if the Manchus wished to assert their power more effectually over their Chinese subjects they would be compelled to have recourse to European weapons and military and scientific knowledge. The suppression of the piratical confederacy of the Bogue was the first occasion of that employment of European force, which was carried to a much more advanced stage during the Taeping rebellion, and of which we have certainly not seen the last development.

One of the last acts of Taoukwang's reign showed to what a depth of mental hesitation and misery he had sunk. It seems that the Chinese New-year's day—12th February, 1850—was to be marked by an eclipse of the sun, which was considered very inauspicious, and as the Emperor was especially susceptible to superstitious influences, he sought to get out of the difficulty and to avert any evil consequences by decreeing that the new year should begin on the previous day. But all-powerful as a Chinese Emperor is, there are some things he cannot do, and the good sense of the Chinese revolted against this attempt to alter the course of nature. The

Imperial decree was completely disregarded, and received with expressions of derision, and in several towns the placards were torn down and defaced. Notwithstanding the eclipse, the Chinese year began at its appointed time. Some excuse might be made for Taoukwang on the ground of ill health, for he was then suffering from the illness which carried him off a few weeks later. His health had long been precarious, the troubles of his reign had prematurely aged him, and he had experienced a rude shock from the death, at the end of 1849, of his adopted mother, towards whom he seems to have preserved the most affectionate feelings. From the first day of his illness its gravity seems to have been appreciated, and an unfavourable issue expected. On 25th February, a grand council was held in the Emperor's bedchamber, and the Emperor wrote in his bed the following Vermilion Edict, proclaiming his fourth son his heir and chosen successor "Let Yihchoo, the Imperial fourth son, be set forth as the Imperial Heir Apparent. You princes and high officers, why wait for our words? Assist and support him with united hearts, and do you all regard whatever pertains to the concerns of the country and the public as of high importance, without sympathy for aught else." Taoukwang survived this important act only a very short time, but the exact date of his death is uncertain. There is some reason for thinking that his end was hastened by the outbreak of a fire within the Imperial City, which threatened it with destruction. The event was duly notified to the Chinese people in a proclamation by his successor, in which he dilated on the virtues of his predecessor, and expressed the stereotyped wish that he could have lived a hundred years.

Taoukwang was in his sixty-ninth year, having been born on 12th September, 1781, and the thirty years over which his reign had nearly extended were among the most eventful, and in some respects the most unfortunate, in the annals of his country. When he was a young man, the power of his grandfather, Keen Lung, was at its pinnacle, but the misfortunes of his father's reign had prepared him for the greater misfortunes of his own, and the school of adversity in which he had passed the greater portion of his life had imbued him only with the disposition to bear calamity, and not the vigour to grapple with it. Yet Taoukwang was not without many good points, and he seems to have realised the extent of the national trouble, and to have felt acutely his inability to retrieve what had been lost. He was also averse to all unnecessary display, and his expenditure on the Court and himself was less than that of any of his predecessors or successors. He never wasted the public money on his own person, and that was a great matter. His habits were simple and manly. As a young man he had given himself up to military exercises, and even after he became Emperor, he pursued his old partiality for active exercises, such as archery and riding. To preserve his physical vigour he took "strengthening pills," composed probably of the famous gensing, which is sent annually to the capital from Manchuria, but their only apparent effect was to destroy his teeth, and thus greatly detract from his personal appearance. Although Taoukwang's reign had been marked by unqualified misfortune, he seems to have derived consolation from the belief that the worst was over, and that as his authority had recovered from such rude shocks, it was not likely to experience anything worse. He had managed to extricate himself from a foreign war, which was attended with an actual invasion of a most alarming character, without any diminution of his authority. The symptoms of internal rebellion which had revealed themselves in more than one quarter of the Empire had not attained any formidable dimensions, and seemed likely to pass away without endangering the Chinese constitution. Taoukwang may have hoped that while he had suffered much he had saved his family and dynasty from more serious calamities, and that on him alone had fallen the resentment of an offended Heaven. The experience of the next fifteen years was to show how inaccurately he had measured the situation, and how far the troubles of the fifteen years following his death were to exceed those of his reign, for just as he had inherited from his father, Kiaking, a legacy of trouble, so did he pass on to his son an inheritance of misfortune and difficulty, rendered all the more onerous by the pretension of supreme power without the means to support it.

The accession of Prince Yihchoo—who took the name of Hienfung, which means "great abundance," or "complete prosperity"—to the throne threatened for a moment to be disturbed by the ambition of his uncle, Hwuy Wang, who, it will be remembered, had attempted to seize the throne from his brother Taoukwang. This prince had lived in retirement during the last years of his brother's reign, and the circumstances which emboldened him to again put forward his pretensions will not be known until the state history of the Manchu dynasty is published. His attempt signally failed, but Hienfung spared his life, while he punished the ministers, Keying and Muchangah, for their supposed apathy, or secret sympathy with the aspirant to the Imperial office by dismissing them from their posts. When Hienfung became Emperor he was less than twenty years of age, and one of his first acts was to confer the title of Prince on his four younger brothers, and to associate them in the administration with himself. This was a new departure in the Manchu policy, as all the previous Emperors had systematically kept their brothers in the background. Hienfung's brothers became known in order of their ages as Princes Kung, Shun, Chun, and Fu, and as Hienfung was the fourth son of Taoukwang, they were also distinguished numerically as the Fifth, Sixth, Seventh, and Eighth princes. Although Hienfung became Emperor at a time of great national distress, he was so far fortunate that an abundant harvest, in the year 1850, tended to mitigate it, and by having recourse to the common Chinese practice of "voluntary contributions," a sufficiently large sum was raised to remove the worst features of the prevailing scarcity and suffering. But these temporary and local measures could not improve a situation that was radically bad, or allay a volume of popular discontent that was rapidly developing into unconcealed rebellion.

An imperial proclamation was drawn up by the Hanlin College in which Hienfung took upon himself the whole blame of the national misfortunes, but the crisis had got far beyond a remedy of words. The corruption of the public service had gradually alienated the sympathies of the people. Justice and probity had for a time been banished from the civil service of China. The example of the few men of honour and capacity served but to bring into more prominent relief the faults of the whole class. Justice was nowhere to be found; the verdict was sold to the highest bidder. The guilty, if well provided in worldly goods, escaped scot-free; the poor suffered for their own frailties as well as the crimes of wealthier offenders. There was seen the far from uncommon case of individuals sentenced to death obtaining substitutes for the capital punishment. Offices were sold to men who had never passed an examination, and who were wholly illiterate, and the sole value of office was as the means of extortion. The nation was heavily taxed, but the taxes to the state were only the smaller part of the sums wrung from the people of the Middle Kingdom. How was honour, or a sense of duty, to be expected from men who knew that their term of office must be short, and who had to receive their purchase money and the anticipated profit before their post was sold again to some fresh and possibly higher bidder? The officials waxed rich on ill-gotten wealth, and a few individuals accumulated enormous fortunes, while the government sank lower and lower in the estimation of the people. It lost also in efficiency and striking power. A corrupt and effeminate body of officers and administrators can serve but as poor defenders for an embarrassed prince and an assailed government against even enemies who are in themselves insignificant and not free from the vices of a corrupt society and a decaying age, and it was only on such that Hienfung had in the first place to lean against his opponents. Even his own Manchus, the warlike Tartars, who, despite the smallness of their numbers, had conquered the whole of China, had lost their primitive virtue and warlike efficiency in the southern climes which they had made their home. To them the opulent cities of the Chinese had proved as fatal as Capua to the army of the Carthaginian, and, as the self-immolations of Chapoo and Chinkiang proved to have no successors, they showed themselves unworthy of the Empire won by their ancestors. For the first time since the revolt of Wou Sankwei, the Manchus were brought face to face with a danger threatening their right of conquest, yet on the eve of the Taeping rebellion all Hienfung could think of to oppose his foes with was fine words as to his shortcomings and lavish promises of amendment.

Among the secret societies the Triads were the first to give a political and dynastic significance to their propaganda. The opening sentence of the oath of membership read as follows: "We combine everywhere to recall the Ming and exterminate the barbarians, cut off the Tsing and await the right prince." But as there were none of the Mings left, and as their name had lost whatever hold it may have possessed on the minds of the Chinese people, this proclaimed object tended rather to deter than to invite recruits to the society. Yet if any secret society shared in the origination of the Taeping rebellion that credit belongs to the Triads, whose anti-Manchu literature enjoyed a wide circulation throughout southern China, and they may have had a large share in drafting the programme that the Taeping leader, Tien Wang, attempted to carry out.

The individual on whom that exalted title was subsequently bestowed had a very common origin, and sprang from an inferior race. Hung-tsiuen, such was his own name, was the son of a small farmer near Canton, and he was a *hakka*, a despised race of tramps who bear some resemblance to our gipsies. He was born in the year 1813, and he seems to have passed all his examinations with special credit; but the prejudice on account of his birth prevented his obtaining any employment in the civil service of his country. He was therefore a disappointed aspirant to office, and at such a period it was not surprising that he should have become an enemy of the constituted authorities and the government. As he could not be the servant of the state he set himself the ambitious task of being its master, and with this object in view he resorted to religious practices in order to acquire a popular reputation, and a following among the masses.

He took up his residence in a Buddhist monastery; and the ascetic deprivations, the loud prayers and invocations, the supernatural counsels and meetings, were the course of training which every religious devotee adopts as the proper novitiate for those honours based on the superstitious reverence of mankind which are sometimes no inadequate substitute for temporal power and influence, even when they fail to pave the way to their attainment. He left his place of seclusion to place himself at the head of the largest party of rebels, who had made their headquarters in the remote province of Kwangsi, and he there proclaimed himself as Tien Wang, which means the Heavenly Prince, and as an aspirant to the Imperial dignity. Gradually the rebels acquired possession of the whole of the territory south of the Canton river, and when they captured the strong and important military station at Nanning the Emperor sent three Commissioners, one of them being his principal minister Saichangah, to bring them to reason, but the result was not encouraging, and although the Taepings were repulsed in their attempt on Kweiling, they remained masters of the open part of the province. One of the Chinese officers had the courage to write and tell the Emperor that "the outlaws were neither exterminated nor made prisoners." Notwithstanding the enormous expenditure on the war and the collection of a large body of troops, the Imperial forces made no real progress in crushing the rebels. Fear or inexperience prevented them from coming at once to close quarters with the Taepings, when their superior numbers must have decided the struggle in their favour and nipped a most formidable rebellion in the bud. That some of Hienfung's officers realised the position can be gathered from the following letter, written at this period by a Chinese mandarin: "The whole country swarms with rebels. Our funds are nearly at an end, and our troops few; our officers disagree, and the power is not concentrated. The commander of the forces wants to extinguish a burning waggon-load of faggots with a cupful of water. I fear we shall hereafter have some serious affair—that the great body will rise against us, and our own people leave us." The military operations in Kwangsi languished during two years, although the tide of war declared itself, on the whole, against the Imperialists; but the rebels themselves were exposed to this danger—that they were exclusively dependent on the resources of the province, and that these being exhausted they were in danger of being compelled to retire into Tonquin. It was at this exceedingly critical moment that Tien Wang showed himself an able leader of men by coming to the momentous decision to march out of Kwangsi, and invade the vast and yet untouched provinces of central China. If the step was more the pressure of dire need than the inspiration of genius, it none the less forms the real turning-point in the rebellion.

Tien Wang announced his decision by issuing a proclamation, in the course of which he declared that he had received "the Divine commission to exterminate the Manchus, and to possess the Empire as its true sovereign"; and, as it was also at this time that his followers became commonly known as Taepings, it may be noted that the origin of this name is somewhat obscure. According to the most plausible explanation it is derived from the small town of that name, situated in the south-west corner of the province of Kwangsi, where the rebel movement seems to have commenced. Another derivation gives it as the style of the dynasty which Tien Wang hoped to found, and its meaning as "Universal peace." Having called in all his outlying detachments, and proclaimed his five principal lieutenants by titles which have been rendered as the northern, southern, eastern, western and assistant kings, Tien Wang began his northern march in April, 1852. At the town of Yungan, on the eastern borders of the province of Kwangsi, where he seems to have hesitated between an attack on Canton and the invasion of Hoonan, an event occurred which threatened to break up his force. The Triad chiefs, who had allied themselves with Tien Wang, were superior in knowledge and station to the immediate followers of the Taeping leader, and they took offence at the arrogance of his lieutenants after they had been elevated to the rank of kings. These officers, who possessed no claim to the dignity they had received, assumed the yellow dress and insignia of Chinese royalty, and looked down on all their comrades, especially the Triad organisers, who thought themselves the true originators of the rebellion. Irritated by this treatment, the Triads took their sudden and secret departure from the Taeping camp, and hastened to make their peace with the Imperialists. Of these Triads one chief, named Chang Kwoliang, received an important command, and played a considerable part in the later stages of the struggle.

The defection of the Triads put an end to the idea of attacking Canton, and the Taepings marched to attack Kweiling, where the Imperial Commissioners still remained. Tien Wang's assault was repulsed with some loss, and, afraid of discouraging his troops by any further attempt to seize so strong a place, he marched into Hoonan. Had the Imperial commanders, who had shown no inconsiderable capacity in defence, exhibited as much energy in offensive measures, they might then and there have annihilated the power of the Taepings. Had they pursued the Taeping army they might have harassed its rear, delayed its progress, and eventually brought it to a decisive engagement at the most favourable moment. But the Imperial Commissioners did nothing, being apparently well satisfied with having rid themselves of such troublesome neighbours. The advance of the Taepings across the vast province of Hoonan was almost unopposed. The towns were unprepared to resist an assailant, and it was not until Tien Wang reached the provincial capital, Changsha, that he encountered any resistance worthy of the name. Some vigorous preparations had been made here to resist the rebels. Not merely was there a garrison in the place, but it so happened that Tseng Kwofan, a man of considerable ability and an influential family, was residing near the town. Tseng had held several offices in the public service, and, as a member of the Hanlin, enjoyed a high position and reputation: but he happened to be at his own home in retirement in consequence of the death of a near relation when tidings of the approaching Taepings reached him, and he at once made himself responsible for the defence of Changsha. He threw himself with all the forces his influence or resources enabled him to collect into that town, and at the same time he ordered all the militia of the province to collect and harass the enemy. He called upon all those who had the means to show their duty to the state and Sovereign by raising recruits or by promising rewards to those volunteers who would serve in the army against the rebels. Had the example of Tseng Kwofan been generally followed, it is not too much to say that the Taepings would never have got to Nankin. When the rebels reached Changsha therefore, they found the gates closed, the walls manned, and the town victualled for a siege. They attempted to starve the place into surrender, and to frighten the garrison into yielding by threats of extermination; but when these efforts failed they delivered three separate assaults, all of which were repulsed. After a siege of eighty days, and having suffered very considerable losses, the Taepings abandoned the attack, and on 1st December resumed their march northwards, which, if information could have been rapidly transmitted, would have soon resulted in their overthrow. On breaking up from before Changsha they succeeded in seizing a sufficient number of junks and boats to cross the great inland lake of Tungting, and on reaching the Yangtsekiang at Yochow they found that the Imperial garrison had fled at the mere mention of their approach. The capture of Yochow was important, because the Taepings acquired there an important arsenal of much-needed weapons and a large supply of gunpowder, which was said to have been the property of Wou Sankwei. Thus, well equipped and supplying their other deficiencies by celerity of movement, they attacked the important city of Hankow, which surrendered without a blow. The scarcely less important town of Wouchang, on the southern and opposite bank of the river, was then attacked, and carried after a siege of a fortnight. The third town of Hanyang, which forms, with the others, the most important industrial and commercial hive in central China, also surrendered without any attempt at resistance, and this striking success at once restored the sinking courage of the Taepings, and made the danger from them to the dynasty again wear an aspect of the most pressing importance.

It would be difficult to exaggerate the effect of this success on the spirits of the Taepings, who had been seriously discouraged before they achieved this gratifying result. The capture of these towns removed all their most serious causes of doubt, and enabled them to repay themselves for the losses and hardships they had undergone, while it also showed that the enterprise they had in hand was not likely to prove unprofitable. After one month's rest at Hankow, and having been joined by many thousands of new followers, the Taepings resolved to pursue their onward course. To tell the truth, they were still apprehensive of pursuit from Tseng Kwofan, who had been joined by the Triad leader, Chang Kwoliang; but there was no ground for the fear, as these officials considered themselves tied to their own province, and unfortunately the report of the success of the Imperialists in Hoonan blinded people to the danger in the Yangtse valley from the Taepings. The Taepings resumed active operations with the capture of Kiukiang and Ganking, and in March, 1853, they sat down before Nankin. The siege continued for a fortnight, but notwithstanding that there was a large Manchu force in the Tartar city, which might easily have been defended against an enemy without artillery, the resistance offered was singularly and unexpectedly faint-hearted. The Taepings succeeded in blowing in one of the gates, the townspeople fraternised with the assailants, and the very Manchus who had defied Sir Hugh Gough in 1842 surrendered their lives and their honour to a force which was nothing more than an armed rabble. The Tartar colony at Nankin, numbering 4,000 families, had evidently lost the courage and discipline which could alone enable them to maintain their position in China. Instead of dying at their posts they threw themselves on the mercy of the Taeping leader, imploring him for pity and for their lives when the gate was blown in by Tien Wang's soldiery. Their cowardice helped them not; of 20,000 Manchus not one hundred escaped. The tale rests on undoubted evidence. A Taeping who took part in the massacre said, "We killed them all, to the infant in arms; we left not a root to sprout from, and the bodies of the slain we cast into the Yangtse."

The acquisition of Nankin at once made the Taepings a formidable rival to the Manchus, and Tien Wang a contestant with Hienfung for imperial honours. The possession of the second city in the Empire gave them the complete control of the navigation of the Yangtsekiang, and thus enabled them to cut off communications between the north and the south of China. To attain this object in a still more perfect manner they occupied Chinkiangfoo at the entrance to the Grand Canal. They also seized Yangchow on the northern bank of the river immediately opposite the place where Sir Hugh Gough had gained his decisive victory in 1842. Such was the terror of the Taepings that the Imperial garrisons did not attempt the least resistance, and town after town was evacuated at their approach. Tien Wang, encouraged by his success, transferred his headquarters from Hankow to Nankin, and proclaimed the old Ming city his capital. By rapidity and an extraordinary combination of fortunate circumstances, the Taepings had advanced from the remote province of Kwangsi into the heart of the empire, but it was clear that unless they could follow up their success by some blow to the central government they would lose all they had gained as soon as the Manchus recovered their confidence. At a council of war at Nankin it was decided to send an army against Pekin as soon as Nankin had been placed in a proper state to undergo a protracted siege. Provisions were collected to stand a siege for six or seven years, the walls were repaired and fresh batteries erected. By the end of May, 1853, these preparations were completed, and as the Taeping army had then been raised to a total of 80,000 men, it was decided that a large part of it could be spared for operations north of the Yangtsekiang. That army was increased to a very large total by volunteers who thought an expedition to humble the Manchus at the capital promised much glory and spoil. The progress of this northern army very closely resembled that of the Taepings from Kwangsi to Nankin. They overran the open country, and none of the Imperial troops ventured to oppose them, but when any Manchu officer showed valour in defending a walled city they were fain to admit their inadequate engineering skill and military capacity. They attacked Kaifong, the capital of Honan, but were repulsed, and pursuing their former tactics continued their march on Pekin. Having crossed the Hoangho they attacked Hwaiking, where, after being delayed two months, they met with as signal a repulse as at Kaifong. Notwithstanding this further reverse, the Taepings pressed on, and defeating a Manchu force in the Lin Limming Pass, they entered the metropolitan province of Pechihli in September, 1853. The object of their march was plain. Not only did they mystify the Emperor's generals, but they passed through an untouched country where supplies were abundant, and they thus succeeded in coming within striking distance of Pekin in almost as fresh a state as when they left Nankin. Such was the effect produced by their capture of the Limming Pass that none of the towns in the southern part of the province attempted any resistance, and they reached Tsing, only twenty miles south of Tientsin, and less than a hundred from Pekin, before the end of October. This place marked the northern limit of Taeping progress, and a reflex wave of Manchu energy bore back the rebels to the Yangtse.

The forcing of the Limming Pass carried confusion and terror into the Imperial palace and capital. The fate of the dynasty seemed to tremble

R

in the balance at the hands of a ruthless and determined enemy. There happened to be very few troops in Pekin at the time, and levies had to be hastily summoned from Mongolia. If the Taepings had only shown the same enterprise and rapidity of movement that they had exhibited up to this point there is no saying that the central government would not have been subverted and the Manchu family extinguished as completely as the Mings. But fortunately for Hienfung, an unusual apathy fell upon the Taepings, who remained halted at Tsing until the Mongol levies had arrived, under their great chief, Sankolinsin. They seem to have been quite exhausted by their efforts, and after one reverse in the open field they retired to their fortified camp at Tsinghai, and sent messengers to Tien Wang for succour. In this camp they were closely beleaguered by Sankolinsin from October, 1853, to March, 1854, when their provisions being exhausted they cut their way out and began their retreat in a southerly direction. They would undoubtedly have been exterminated but for the timely arrival of a relieving army from Nankin. The Taepings then captured Lintsing, which remained their headquarters for some months, but during the remainder of the year 1854, their successes were few and unimportant. They were vigilantly watched by the Imperial troops, which had expelled them from the whole of the province of Shantung before March, 1855. Their numbers were thinned by disease as well as loss in battle, and of the two armies sent to capture Pekin only a small fragment ever regained Nankin. While these events were in progress in the region north of Nankin, the Taepings had been carrying their arms up the Yangtsekiang as far as Ichang, and eastwards from Nankin to the sea. These efforts were not always successful, and Tien Wang's arms experienced as many reverses as successes. The important city of Kanchang, the capital of the province of Kiangsi, was besieged by them for four months, and after many attempts to carry it by storm, the Taepings were compelled to abandon the task. They were more successful at Hankow, which they recovered after a siege of eighty days. They again evacuated this town, and yet once again, in 1855, wrested it from an Imperial garrison.

The establishment of Taeping power at Nankin and the rumour of its rapid extension in every direction had drawn the attention of Europeans to the new situation thus created in China, and had aroused opposite opinions in different sections of the foreign community. While the missionaries were disposed to regard the Taepings as the regenerators of China, and as the champions of Christianity, the merchants only saw in them the disturbers of peace and the enemies of commerce. To such an extent did the latter anticipate the ruin of their trade that they petitioned the consuls to suspend, if not withhold, the payment of the stipulated customs to the Chinese authorities. This proposed breach of treaty was emphatically rejected, and the consuls enjoined the absolute necessity of preserving a strict neutrality between the Taepings and the Imperial forces. But at the same time it became necessary to acquaint the Taeping ruler with the fact that he would be expected to observe the provisions of the Treaty of Nankin as scrupulously as if he were sovereign of China or a Manchu Viceroy. Sir George Bonham, the Superintendent of Trade and the Governor of Hongkong, determined to proceed in person to Nankin, in order to acquaint the Taepings with what would be expected from them, and also to gain necessary information as to their strength and importance by personal observation. But unfortunately this step of Sir George Bonham tended to help the Taepings by increasing their importance and spreading about the belief that the Europeans recognised in them the future ruling power of China. It was not intended to be, but it was none the less, an unfriendly act to the Pekin government, and as it produced absolutely no practical result with the Taepings themselves, it was distinctly a mistaken measure. Its only excuse was that the Imperial authorities were manifesting an increasing inclination to enlist the support of Europeans against the rebels, and it was desirable that accurate information should be obtained beforehand. The Taotai of Shanghai even presented a request for the loan of the man of war at that port, and when he was informed that we intended to remain strictly neutral, the decision was also come to to inform the Taepings of this fact. Therefore in April, 1853, before the army had left for the northern campaign, Sir George Bonham sailed for Nankin in the *Hermes* man-of-war. On the twenty-seventh of that month the vessel anchored off Nankin, and several interviews were held with the Taeping Wangs, of whom the Northern King was at this time the most influential. The negotiations lasted a week, and they had no result. It was soon made apparent that the Taepings were as exclusive and impracticable as the worst Manchu mandarin, and that they regarded the Europeans as an inferior and subject people. Sir George Bonham failed to establish any direct communication with Tien Wang, who had by this retired into private life, and while it was given out that he was preparing sacred books he was really abandoning himself to the pursuit of profligacy. There is nothing to cause surprise in the fact that the apathy of Tien Wang led to attempts to supersede him in his authority. The Eastern King in particular posed as the delegate of Heaven. He declared that he had interviews with the celestial powers when in a trance, he assumed the title of the Holy Ghost or the Comforter, and he censured Tien Wang for his shortcomings, and even inflicted personal chastisement upon him. If he had had a following he might have become the despot of the Taepings, but as he offended all alike his career was cut short by a conspiracy among the other Wangs, who, notwithstanding his heavenly conferences, murdered him.

At this period one of the most brilliant military exploits of the Taepings was performed, and as it served to introduce the real hero of the whole movement, it may be described in more detail than the other operations, which were conducted in a desultory manner, and which were unredeemed by any exhibition of courage or military capacity. The government had succeeded in placing two considerable armies in the field. One numbering 40,000 men, under the command of Hochun and the ex-Triad Chang Kwoliang, watched Nankin, while the other, commanded by a Manchu general, laid close siege to Chinkiang, which seemed on the point of surrender. The Taepings at Nankin determined to effect its relief, and a large force was placed under the orders of an officer named Li, but whom it will be more convenient to designate by the title subsequently conferred on him of Chung Wang, or the Faithful King. His energy and courage had already attracted favourable notice, and the manner in which he executed the difficult operation entrusted to him fully established his reputation. By a concerted movement with the Taeping commandant of Chinkiang, he attacked the Imperialist lines at the same time as the garrison made a sortie, and the result was a decisive victory. Sixteen stockades were carried by assault, and the Manchu army was driven away from the town which seemed to lie at its mercy. But this success promised only to be momentary, for the Imperialist forces, collecting from all sides, barred the way back to Nankin, while the other Manchu army drew nearer to that city, and its general seemed to meditate attacking Tien Wang in his capital. An imperative summons was sent to Chung Wang to return to Nankin. As the Imperialist forces were for the most part on the southern side of the river, Chung Wang crossed to the northern bank and began his march to Nankin. He had not proceeded far when he found that the Imperialists had also crossed over to meet him, and that his progress was arrested by their main army under Chang Kwoliang. With characteristic decision and rapidity he then regained the southern bank, and falling on the weakened Imperialists gained so considerable a victory that the Manchu commander felt bound to commit suicide. After some further fighting he made good his way back to Nankin. But when he arrived there the tyrant Tung Wang refused to admit him into the city until he had driven away the main Imperialist army, which had been placed under the command of Hienfung's generalissimo, Heang Yung, and which had actually seized one of the gates of the city. Although Chung Wang's troops were exhausted they attacked the government troops with great spirit, and drove them back as far as Tanyang, where, however, they succeeded in holding their ground, notwithstanding his repeated efforts to dislodge them. Heang Yung, taking his misfortune too deeply to heart, committed suicide, and thus deprived the Emperor of at least a brave officer. But with this success the Taeping tide of victory reached its end, for Chang Kwoliang arriving with the other Imperialist army, the whole force fell upon Chung Wang and drove him back into the city with the loss of 700 of his best men, so that the result left of Chung Wang's campaign was the relief of Chinkiang and the return to the *status quo* at Nankin. It was immediately after these events that Tung Wang was assassinated, and scenes of blood followed, which resulted in the massacre of 20,000 persons and the disappearance of all, except one, of the Wangs whom Tien Wang had created on the eve of his enterprise. Chung Wang seems to have had no part in these intrigues and massacres, and there is little doubt that if the Imperialist commanders had taken prompt advantage of them the Taepings might have been crushed at that moment, or ten years earlier than proved to be the case.

While the main Taeping force was thus causing serious danger to the existing government of China, its offshoots or imitators were emulating its example in the principal treaty ports which brought the rebels into contact with the Europeans. The Chinese officials, without any military power on which they could rely, had endeavoured to maintain order among the turbulent classes of the population by declaring that the English were the allies of the Emperor, and that they would come to his aid with their formidable engines of war if there were any necessity. Undoubtedly this threat served its turn and kept the turbulent quiet for a certain period; but when it could no longer be concealed that the English were determined to take no part in the struggle, the position of the government was weakened by the oft-repeated declaration that they mainly relied on the support of the foreigners. The first outbreak occurred at Amoy in May, 1853, when some thousand marauders, under an individual named Magay, seized the town and held it until the following November. The Imperialists returned in sufficient force in that month and regained possession of the town, when, unfortunately for their reputation, they avenged their expulsion in a particularly cruel and undiscriminating fashion. Many thousand citizens were executed without any form of trial, and the arrest of the slaughter was entirely due to the intervention of the English naval officer at Amoy. The rising at Shanghai was of a more serious character, and took a much longer time to suppress. As the European settlement there was threatened with a far more imminent danger than anywhere else, preparations to defend it began in April, 1853, and under the auspices of the Consul, Mr. Rutherford Alcock, the residents were formed into a volunteer corps, and the men-of-war drawn up so as to effectually cover the whole settlement. These precautions were taken in good time, for nothing happened to disturb the peace until the following September. The Triads were undoubtedly the sole instigators of the rising, and the Taepings of Nankin were in no sense responsible for, or participators in it. They seized the Taotai's official residence, and as his guard deserted him, that officer barely escaped with his life. Other officials were not so fortunate, but on the whole Shanghai was acquired by the rebels with very little bloodshed. In a few hours this important Chinese city passed into the hands of a lawless and refractory mob, who lived on the plunder of the townspeople, and who were ripe for any mischief. The European settlement was placed meantime in a position of efficient defence, and although the Triads wished to have the spoil of its rich factories, they very soon decided that the enterprise would be too risky, if not impossible.

After some weeks' inaction the Imperialist forces, gathering from all quarters, proceeded to invest the marauders in Shanghai, and had the attack been conducted with any degree of military skill and vigour, they must have succumbed at the first onset. But, owing to the pusillanimity of the Emperor's officers and their total ignorance of the military art, the siege went on for an indefinite period, and twelve months after it began seemed as far off conclusion as ever. While the Imperialists laboriously constructed their lines and batteries they never ceased to importune the Europeans for assistance, and as it became clearer that the persons in possession of Shanghai were a mob rather than a power, the desire increased among the foreigners generally to put an end to what was an intolerable position. On this occasion the French took an initiative which had previously been left to the English. The French settlement at Shanghai consisted at this time of a consulate, a cathedral, and one house, but as it was situated nearest the walls of the Chinese city it was most exposed to the fire of the besiegers and besieged. In consequence of this the French admiral, Laguerre, determined to take a part in the struggle, and erecting a battery in the French settlement, proceeded to bombard the rebels on one side of the city while the Imperialists attacked it on another. Although the bombardment was vigorous and effective, the loss inflicted on the insurgents was inconsiderable, because they had erected an earthwork behind the main wall of the place, and every day the Triads challenged the French to come on to the assault. At last a breach was declared to be practicable, and 400 French sailors and marines were landed to carry it, while the Imperialists, wearing blue sashes to distinguish them from the rebels, escaladed the walls at another point. But the assault was premature, for, although the assailants gained the inside of the fortification, they could not advance. The insurgents fought desperately behind the earthworks and in the streets, and after four hours' fighting they put the whole Imperialist force to flight. The French were carried along by their disheartened allies, who, allowing race hatred to overcome a temporary arrangement, even fired on them, and when Admiral Laguerre reckoned up the cost of his intervention he found it amounted to four officers and sixty men killed and wounded. Such was the result of the French attack on Shanghai, and it taught the lesson that even good European troops cannot ignore the recognised rules and precautions of war. After this engagement the siege languished, and the French abstained from taking any further part in it. But the Imperialists continued their attack in their own bungling but persistent fashion, and at last the insurgents, having failed to obtain the favourable terms they demanded, made a desperate sortie, when a few made their way to the foreign settlement, where they found safety, but by far the greater number perished by the sword of the Imperialists. More than 1,500 insurgents were captured and executed along the high roads, but the two leaders of the movement escaped, one of them to attain great fortune as a merchant in Siam. The Imperialists unfortunately sullied their success by grave excesses and by the cruel treatment of the unoffending townspeople, who were made to suffer for the original incapacity and cowardice of the officials themselves. At Canton, which was also visited by the Triads in June, 1854, matters took a different course. The Chinese merchants and shopkeepers combined and raised a force for their own protection, and these well-paid braves effectually kept the insurgents out of Canton. They, however, seized the neighbouring town of Fatshan, where the manufacturing element was in strong force, and but for the unexpected energy of the Cantonese they would undoubtedly have seized the larger city too, as the government authorities were not less apathetic here than at Shanghai. The disturbed condition of things continued until February, 1855, when the wholesale executions by which its suppression was marked, and during which a hundred thousand persons, most of whom were innocent, are said to have perished, ceased.

The events have now been passed in review which marked the beginning and growth of the Taeping rebellion, from the time of its being a local rising in the province of Kwangsi to the hour of its leader being installed as a ruling prince in the ancient city of Nankin. The success was more striking than thorough. The Taepings had lost quite as many battles as they had gained, and if they had not succeeded in seizing Nankin and thus obtaining the control of the Yangtsekiang, they would scarcely ever have emerged from the rank of insignificant disturbers of the internal tranquillity of China. Had the government possessed a really capable lieutenant, or been able to engage the services of an English officer ten years earlier than it did, they would have stamped out the rebellion without an effort, so far superior were its numbers and resources. But its measures were characterised by the usual dilatoriness and sluggishness, and the insurrection, which another government would have suppressed in a few months, was allowed to develop until it became a national calamity, and its suppression the task of years. But from the growing Taeping rebellion, which we have now followed down to the year 1856, our attention must be directed to the more serious and important foreign question which had again reached a crisis, and which would not wait on the convenience of the Celestial Emperor and his advisers. It is surprising to find that the grave peril in which the Pekin government stood from its domestic enemies failed to arouse it to the danger of again provoking the Europeans, and that it invited perils which the most elementary knowledge and common sense would have led it to avoid. By its own folly the crisis was provoked which, if the English government had not shown great moderation, might have entailed the disintegration of China.

CHAPTER XIX.

THE SECOND FOREIGN WAR.

The events which caused the second foreign war began to come into evidence immediately after the close of the first, and for the sake of clearness and brevity they have been left for consideration to the same chapter, although they happened while Taoukwang was Emperor. After the departure of Sir Henry Pottinger, who was succeeded by Sir John Davis, and the arrival of the representatives of the other European Powers who hastened to claim the same rights and privileges as had been accorded to England, the main task to be accomplished was to practically assert the rights that had been theoretically secured, and to place the relations of the two nations on what may be called a working basis. The consulates were duly appointed, the necessary land for the foreign settlements was acquired, and the war indemnity being honourably discharged, Chusan was restored to the Chinese. With regard to the last matter there was some manœuvring of a not altogether creditable nature, and although the Chinese paid the last instalment punctually to date, Chusan and Kulangsu were not evacuated for some months after the stipulated time. It was said that our hesitation in the former case was largely due to the fear that France would seize it, but this has been permanently removed by the expressed assertion of our prior right to occupy it. A far more gratifying subject is suggested by the harmony of the relations which were established in Chusan between the garrison under Sir Colin Campbell and the islanders, who expressed deep regret at the departure of the English troops. The first members of the consular staff in China were as follows: Mr. G. T. Lay was consul at Canton, Captain George Balfour at Shanghai (where, however, he was soon succeeded by Sir Rutherford Alcock), Mr. Henry Gribble at Amoy, and Mr. Robert Thom at Ningpo. Among the interpreters were the future Sir Thomas Wade and Sir Harry Parkes. Various difficulties presented themselves with regard to the foreign settlements, and the island of Kulangsu at Amoy had to be evacuated because its name was not mentioned in the treaty. At Canton also an attempt was made to extend the boundaries of the foreign settlement by taking advantage of a great conflagration, but in this attempt the Europeans were baffled by the superior quickness of the Chinese, who constructed their new houses in a single night. These incidents showed that the sharpness was not all on one side, and that if the Chinese were backward in conceding what might be legitimately demanded, the Europeans were not averse to snatching an advantage if they saw the chance.

The turbulence of the Canton populace, over whom the officials possessed but a nominal control, was a constant cause of disagreement and trouble.

In the spring of 1846 a riot was got up by the mob on the excuse that a vane erected on the top of the flagstaff over the American Consulate interfered with the Fung Shui, or spirits of earth and air; and although it was removed to allay the excitement of the superstitious, the disturbance continued, and several personal encounters took place, in one of which a Chinese was killed. The Chinese mandarins, incited by the mob, demanded the surrender of the man who fired the shot; and that they should have made such a demand after they had formally accepted and recognised the jurisdiction of consular courts furnished strong evidence that they had not mastered the lessons of the late war or reconciled themselves to the provisions of the Treaty of Nankin. The fortunate arrival of Keying to "amicably regulate the commerce with foreign countries" smoothed over this difficulty, and the excitement of the Canton mob was allayed without any surrender. It was almost at this precise moment, too, that Taoukwang made the memorable admission that the Christian religion might be tolerated as one inculcating the principles of virtue. But the two pressing and practical difficulties in the foreign question were the opening of the gates of Canton and the right of foreigners to proceed beyond the limits of their factories and compounds. The Chinese wished for many reasons, perhaps even for the safety of the foreigners, to confine them to their settlements, and it might be plausibly argued that the treaty supported this construction. Of course such confinement was intolerable, and English merchants and others would not be prevented from making boating or shooting excursions in the neighbourhood of the settlements. The Chinese authorities opposed these excursions, and before long a collision occurred with serious consequences. In March, 1847, a small party of Englishmen proceeded in a boat to Fatshan, a manufacturing town near Canton which has been called the Chinese Birmingham. On reaching the place symptoms of hostility were at once manifested, and the Europeans withdrew for safety to the yamen of the chief magistrate, who happened unfortunately to be away. By this time the populace had got very excited, and the Englishmen were with difficulty escorted in safety to their boat. The Chinese, however, pelted them with stones, notwithstanding the efforts of the chief officer, who had by this time returned and taken the foreigners under his protection. It was due to his great heroism that they escaped with their lives and without any serious injury.

The incident, unpleasant in itself, might have been explained away and closed without untoward consequences if Sir John Davis had not seized, as he thought, a good opportunity of procuring greater liberty and security for Englishmen at Canton. He refused to see in this affair an accident, but denounced it as an outrage, and proclaimed "that he would exact and require from the Chinese government that British subjects should be as free from molestation and insult in China as they would be in England." This demand was both unreasonable and unjust. It was impossible that the hated foreigner, or "foreign devil" as he was called, could wander about the country in absolute security when the treaty wrung from the Emperor as the result of an arduous war confined him to five ports, and limited the Emperor's capacity to extend protection to those places. But Sir John Davis determined to take this occasion of forcing events, so that he might compel the Chinese to afford greater liberty to his countrymen, and thus hasten the arrival of the day for the opening of the gates of Canton. On the 1st April all the available troops at Hongkong were warned for immediate service, and on the following day the two regiments in garrison left in three steamers and escorted by one man-of-war to attack Canton. They landed at the Bogue forts, seized the batteries without opposition, and spiked the guns. The Chinese troops, whether surprised or acting under orders from Keying, made no attempt at resistance. Not a shot was fired, not a man was injured among the assailants. The forts near Canton, the very batteries on the island opposite the city, were captured without a blow, and on the 3rd April, 1847, Canton again lay at the mercy of an English force. Sir John Davis then published another notice, stating that "he felt that the moderation and justice of all his former dealings with the government of China lend a perfect sanction to measures which he has been reluctantly compelled to adopt after a long course of misinterpreted forbearance," and made certain demands of the Chinese authorities which may be epitomised as follows: The City of Canton to be opened at two years' date from 6th April, 1847; Englishmen to be at liberty to roam for exercise or amusement in the neighbourhood of the city on the one condition that they returned the same day; and some minor conditions, to which no exception could be taken. After brief consideration, and notwithstanding the clamour of the Cantonese to be led against the foreigners, Keying agreed to the English demands, although he delivered a side-thrust at the high-handed proceedings of the English officer when he said, " If a mutual tranquillity is to subsist between the Chinese and foreigners, the common feelings of mankind, as well as the just principles of Heaven, must be considered and conformed with." Although successful, there can scarcely be two opinions that the action of Sir John Davis was both unnecessary and imprudent. The employment of so small a force might well have encouraged the Chinese to offer resistance, when the outbreak of a fresh war between the two nations as the consequence of a holiday trip on the part of some English merchants could not have been avoided. The home government strongly condemned the whole affair, and Lord Grey peremptorily forbade any further military enterprise, stating that "another appeal to arms should only be made after due preparation and with the employment of such an amount of force as may afford just grounds for expecting that the objects which may be proposed by such a measure will be effectually accomplished without unnecessary loss." There were one or two other collisions between Chinese and Europeans at the other treaty ports similar to that at Fatshan, but they produced no serious consequences, and the situation generally settled down on the basis that Englishmen might visit the country round the ports on the understanding that they returned within twenty-four hours.

Keying, by the terms of his convention with Sir John Davis, had agreed that the gates of Canton were to be opened on 6th April, 1849, but the nearer that day approached the more doubtful did it appear whether the promise would be complied with, and whether, in the event of refusal, it would be wise to have recourse to compulsion. The officials on both sides were unfeignedly anxious for a pacific solution, but trade was greatly depressed in consequence of the threatening demeanour of the Canton populace. There was scarcely any doubt that the Chinese authorities did not possess the power to compel obedience on the part of the Cantonese to an order to admit Europeans into their city, and on the question being referred to Taoukwang he made an oracular reply which was interpreted as favouring the popular will. "That," he said, "to which the hearts of the people incline is that on which the decree of Heaven rests. Now the people of Kwantung are unanimous and determined that they will not have foreigners enter the city; and how can I post up everywhere my Imperial order and force an opposite course on the people?" The English government was disposed to show great forbearance, and refrained from opposing Taoukwang's views. But although the matter was allowed to drop the right acquired by the convention with Keying was not surrendered; and, as Taoukwang had never formally ratified the promise of that minister, it was considered that there had been no distinct breach of faith on the part of the Chinese government. The Chinese continued to cling tenaciously to their rights, and to contest inch by inch every concession demanded by the Europeans, and sometimes they were within their written warrant in doing so. Such a case happened at Foochow shortly after the accession of Hienfung, when an attempt was made to prevent foreigners residing in that town, and after a long correspondence it was discovered that the Chinese were so far right, as the treaty specified as the place of foreign residence the *kiangkan* or mart at the mouth of the river, and not the *ching* or town itself. It was at this critical moment that the Chinese were attracted in large numbers by the discovery of gold in California and Australia to emigrate from China, and they showed themselves well capable by their trade organisation and close union of obtaining full justice for themselves and an ample recognition of all their rights in foreign countries. The effect of this emigration on Chinese public opinion was much less than might have been expected, and the settlement of the foreign question was in no way simplified or expedited by their influence.

The position of affairs at Canton could not, by the greatest stretch of language, be pronounced satisfactory. The populace was unequivocally hostile; the officials had the greatest difficulty in making their authority respected, and the English government was divided between the desire to enforce the stipulation as to the opening of the Canton gates, and the fear lest insistence might result in a fresh and serious rupture. Sir George Bonham, who succeeded Sir John Davis, gave counsels of moderation, and when he found that some practical propositions which he made for improved intercourse were rejected he became more convinced that the question must wait for solution for a more convenient and promising occasion. His views found the following expression in an official despatch to Lord Palmerston: "If the gates of Canton can only be opened by the force of arms the consequences of such a step become a matter for deep consideration. I am thoroughly persuaded that the populace and 'braves' of the adjacent country will join heartily in resisting our approach, and the result will be that we should require a very respectable force to gain our point, for the opposition will be infinitely greater than it was in 1841, when the troops and mandarins were in the first instance its only defenders. A military operation of this nature would, under the most favourable circumstances, not only for the time put a stop to all trade, but it would furthermore require a very long period to elapse before confidence would be restored. This would cause much loss to the native, as well as to our own merchants, and operate most detrimentally on our revenues at home." Lord Palmerston took very much the same view, stating, in his reply, that "the entrance into Canton was a privilege which we have indeed a right to demand, but which we could scarcely enjoy with security or advantage if we were to succeed in enforcing it by arms. It may be true that the Chinese might be encouraged by their success in evading compliance with their engagements in this matter to attempt to violate other engagements, but this consideration does not seem to me to be sufficient to determine Her Majesty's government to put the issue of peace and war upon this particular point." From these considerations the English government assented to the putting-off of the execution of Keying's agreement until a more favourable opportunity; but, unfortunately, the Chinese only interpreted this forbearance as a sign of weakness, and as signifying that our claim was waived and withdrawn. The consideration of these early and preliminary disputes is necessary for the elucidation of the graver difficulties which broke out between the English and Chinese authorities shortly after the accession of Hienfung. These disputes did not arise out of one single occurrence, but from a succession of events, of antagonistic views and opposite readings of accepted obligations, which followed the Viceroy's refusal, in 1849, to fulfil Keying's promise to open the gates of Canton.

In 1852 Sir George Bonham returned to England on leave, and his place was taken by Dr. John Bowring, who had officiated for a short period as consul at Canton. His instructions were of a simple and positive character. They were "to avoid all irritating discussions with the authorities of China." He was also directed to avoid pushing arguments on doubtful points in a manner that would fetter the free action of the government; but he was, at the same time, to recollect that it was his duty to carefully watch over and insist upon the performance by the Chinese authorities of their engagements. The proper fulfilment of the latter duty necessarily involved some infringement of the former recommendation; and, while the paramount consideration with the Foreign Office was to keep things quiet, it was natural that the official on the spot should think a great deal, if not altogether, of how best to obtain compliance to the fullest extent with the pledges given in the treaty and the subsequent conventions. Dr. Bowring was not an official to be deterred from expressing his opinions by fear of headquarters. He sent home his view of the situation, expressed in very clear and intelligible language. "The Pottinger treaties," he said, "inflicted a deep wound upon the pride, but by no means altered the policy, of the Chinese government. . . . Their purpose is now, as it ever was, not to invite, not to facilitate, but to impede and resist the access of foreigners. It must, then, ever be borne in mind, in considering the state of our relations with these regions, that the two governments have objects at heart which are diametrically opposed, except in so far that both earnestly desire to avoid all hostile action, and to make its own policy, as far as possible, subordinate to that desire." At this point a Liberal administration gave place to a Conservative; but Lord Malmesbury reiterated in stronger language the instructions of Lord Granville. "All irritating discussions with the Chinese should be avoided, and the existing good understanding must in no way be imperilled." One of Dr. Bowring's first acts was to write a letter to the Viceroy expressing a desire for an interview, with the object of suggesting a settlement of pending difficulties; but the Viceroy made his excuses. The meeting did not take place, and the whole question remained dormant for two years, by which time not only had Sir John Bowring been knighted and confirmed in the post of Governor, but the Viceroy had been superseded by the subsequently notorious Commissioner

Yeh. Up to this point all Sir John Bowring's suggestions with regard to the settlement of the questions pending with the Chinese had been received with the official reply that he was to abstain from all action, and that he was not to press himself on the Canton authorities. But, in the beginning of 1854, his instructions were so far modified that Lord Clarendon wrote admitting the desirability of "free and unrestricted intercourse with the Chinese officials," and of "admission into some of the cities of China, especially Canton."

Encouraged by these admissions in favour of the views he had been advancing for some time, Sir John Bowring wrote an official letter to Commissioner Yeh inviting him to an early interview, but stating that the interview must be held within the city of Canton at the Viceroy's yamen. It will be noted that what Sir John asked fell short of what Keying had promised. The opening of the gates of Canton was to have been to all Englishmen, but the English government would at this point have been satisfied if its representative had been granted admission for the purpose of direct negotiation with the Chinese authorities. To the plain question put to him Yeh returned an evasive answer. All his time was taken up with the military affairs of the province, and he absolutely ignored the proposal for holding an interview within the city. The matter had gone too far to be put on one side in this manner, and Sir John Bowring sent his secretary to overcome, if possible, the repugnance of Commissioner Yeh to the interview, and in any case to gain some information as to his objections. As the secretary could only see mandarins of very inferior rank he returned to Hongkong without acquiring any very definite information, but he learnt enough to say that Yeh denied that Keying's arrangement possessed any validity. The Chinese case was that it had been allowed to drop on both sides, and the utmost concession Yeh would make was to agree to an interview at the Jinsin Packhouse outside the city walls. This proposition was declared to be inadmissible, when Yeh ironically remarked that he must consequently assume that "Sir John Bowring did not wish for an interview." It was hoped to overcome Chinese finesse with counter finesse, and Sir John Bowring hastened to Shanghai with the object of establishing direct relations with the Viceroy of the Two Kiang. After complaining of the want of courtesy evinced by Yeh throughout his correspondence, he expressed the wish to negotiate with any of the other high officials of the Empire. The reply of Eleang, who held this post, and who was believed to be well disposed to Europeans did not advance matters. He had no authority, he said, in the matter, and could not interfere in what was not his concern. Commissioner Yeh was the official appointed by the Emperor to conduct relations with the foreigners, and no other official could assume his functions. Sir John Bowring therefore returned to Hongkong without having effected anything by his visit to Shanghai, but at this moment the advance of the rebels to the neighbourhood of Canton seemed likely to effect a diversion that might have important consequences. In a state of apprehension as to the safety of the town, Yeh applied to Sir John Bowring for assistance against the rebels, but this could not be granted, and Sir John Bowring only proceeded to Canton to superintend the preparations made for the defence of the English settlement at that place. All the consuls issued a joint proclamation declaring their intention to remain neutral. The prompt suppression of the rebellion, so far as any danger to Canton went, restored the confidence of the Chinese authorities, and they reverted to their old position on the question of the opening of the gates of Canton.

In June, 1855, Sir John Bowring returned to the subject of official interviews, and made an explicit demand for the reception if not of himself, then at least of the Consul at Canton. Yeh took his time before he made any reply, and when he did send one it was to the effect that there was no precedent for an interview with a consul, and that as Sir John had refused to meet him outside the city, there was an end of the matter. In face of the obstinate attitude of the Chinese, Sir John wrote home to his government that "until the city question at Canton is settled, there is little hope of our relations being placed on anything like a satisfactory foundation." That the situation was aggravated by the personal character of Yeh does not admit of question, and only the occurrence of the Crimean War caused the postponement of the application of the extreme remedy of all. Mr. Harry Parkes succeeded Mr. Alcock as consul at Canton, and no inconsiderable amount of tact was required to carry on relations with officials who refused to show themselves. But the evil day of open collision could not be averted, and the antagonism caused by clashing views and interests at last broke forth on a point which would have been promptly settled, had there been direct intercourse between the English and Chinese officials. The event which provoked the crisis calls for description in calm and dispassionate language, more especially as it has been made the subject of much heated controversy.

On 8th October, 1856, Mr. Parkes reported to Sir John Bowring at Hongkong the particulars of an affair which had occurred on a British-owned lorcha at Canton. The lorcha *Arrow*, employed in the iron trade between Canton and the mouth of the river, commanded by an English captain, and flying the English flag, had been boarded by a party of mandarins and their followers while at anchor near the Dutch Folly. The lorcha—a Portuguese name for a fast sailing-boat—had been duly registered in the office at Hongkong, and although not entitled at that precise moment to British protection, through the careless neglect to renew the license, this fact was only discovered subsequently, and was not put forward by the Chinese in justification of their action. The gravity of the affair was increased by the fact that the English flag was conspicuously displayed, and that, notwithstanding the remonstrances of the master, it was ostentatiously hauled down. The crew were carried off prisoners with the exception of two men, left at their own request to take charge of the vessel. Mr. Parkes at once sent a letter to Yeh on the subject of this "very grave insult," requesting that the captured crew of the *Arrow* should be returned to that vessel without delay, and that any charges made against them should be then examined into at the English Consulate. In his reply Commissioner Yeh justified and upheld the act of his subordinates. Of the twelve men seized, he returned nine, but with regard to the three whom he detained, he declared one to be a criminal, and the others important witnesses. Not merely would he not release them, but he proceeded to justify their apprehension, while he did not condescend to so much as notice the points of the insult to the English flag, and of his having violated treaty obligations. Yeh did not attempt to offer any excuse for the proceedings taken in his name. He asserted certain things as facts which in his opinion it was sufficient for him to accept that they should pass current. But the evidence on which they were based was not sufficient to obtain credence in the laxest court of justice; but even if it had been conclusive it would not have justified the removal of the crew from the *Arrow* when the British flag was flying conspicuously at her mast. What, in brief, was the Chinese case? It was that one of the crew had been recognised by a man passing in a boat as one of a band of pirates who had attacked, ill-used, and plundered him several weeks before. He had forthwith gone to the Taotai of Canton, presented a demand for redress, and that officer had at once given the order for the arrest of the offender, with the result described. There is no necessity to impugn the veracity of the Chinaman's story, but it did not justify the breach of "the ex territorial rights of preliminary consular investigation before trial" granted to all under the protection of the English flag. The plea of delay did not possess any force either, for the man could have been arrested just as well by the English consul as by the mandarins, but it would have involved a damaging admission of European authority in the matter of a Chinese subject, and the mandarins thought there was no necessity to curtail their claim to jurisdiction. Commissioner Yeh did not attempt any excuses, and he even declared that "the *Arrow* is not a foreign lorcha, and, therefore," he said, "there is no use to enter into any discussion about her."

The question of the nationality of the *Arrow* was complicated by the fact that its registry had expired ten days before its seizure. The master explained that this omission was due to the vessel having been at sea, and that it was to have been rectified as soon as he returned to Hongkong. As Lord Clarendon pointed out, this fact was not merely unknown to the Chinese, but it was also "a matter of British regulation which would not justify seizure by the Chinese. No British lorcha would be safe if her crew were liable to seizure on these grounds." The history of the lorcha *Arrow* was officially proved to be as follows: "The *Arrow* was heretofore employed in trading on the coast, and while so employed was taken by pirates. By them she was fitted out and employed on the Canton river during the disturbances between the Imperialists and the insurgents. While on this service she was captured by the braves of one of the loyalist associations organised by the mandarins for the support of the government. By this association she was publicly sold, and was purchased by a Chinchew Hong, a respectable firm at Canton, which also laid out a considerable sum in repairing her and otherwise fitting her out. She arrived at Hongkong about the month of June, 1855, at which time a treaty was on foot (which ended in a bargain) between Fong Aming, Messrs. T. Burd & Co.'s comprador, and Lei-yeong-heen, one of the partners in the Chin-chew Hong, for the purchase of the lorcha by the former. Shortly after the arrival of the vessel at Hongkong she was claimed by one Quantai, of Macao, who asserted that she had been his property before she was seized by the pirates. Of course, the then owner disputed his claim; upon which he commenced a suit in the Vice-Admiralty Court. After a short time, by consent of the parties, the question was referred to arbitration, but the arbitrators could not agree and an umpire was appointed, who awarded that the ownership of the lorcha should continue undisturbed. The ownership of the vessel was then transferred to Fong Aming, and in his name she is registered. These are the simple facts connected with the purchase of the lorcha by a resident of the colony at Hongkong and her registry as a British vessel, and it is from these facts that the Imperial

Commissioner Yeh has arrived at an erroneous conclusion as to the ownership of the boat." As the first step towards obtaining the necessary reparation, a junk, which was supposed to be an Imperial war vessel, was seized as a hostage, and Mr. Parkes addressed another letter to Yeh reminding him that "the matter which has compelled this menace still remains unsettled."

Six years before Sir George Bonham had written the prophetic words in reference to the gates of Canton: "Let the Chinese government well consider these things and whatever may happen in future between the two countries that may be disagreeable to China, let the Chinese government remember that the fault thereof will be upon them." Had there been that convenient mode of communication between the Governor of Hongkong and the Chinese officials at Canton which was provided for by the Nankin Treaty and the Keying Convention, the *Arrow* complication would, in all probability, never have arisen, and it is also scarcely less certain that it would not have produced such serious consequences as it did but for the arrogance of Yeh. He never showed in any of his letters the least trace of regret at what had occurred. Even after the capture of the junk, which he explained with ill concealed gratification was not a war junk, he repeated that the English had no right to interfere in the matter as the lorcha was a Chinese vessel and the criminal a native of the Middle Kingdom. He even attempted to deny that the *Arrow* carried the English flag, but this was so clearly proved to be a fact by both English and Chinese witnesses that it ceased to hold a place in the Chinese case. As it was clear that Commissioner Yeh would not give way, and as delay would only encourage him, the Admiral on the station, Sir Michael Seymour, received instructions to attack the four forts of the Barrier, and he captured them without loss. Thus, after an interval of fourteen years, was the first blow struck in what may be called the third act of Anglo-Chinese relations, but it would be a mistake to suppose that the *Arrow* case was the sole cause of this appeal to arms. A blue book, bearing the significant title of "Insults to Foreigners," gives a list and narrative of the many outrages and indignities inflicted on Europeans between 1842 and 1856, and should be read by all who doubt the justice of our second war with China. The evidence contained therein justifies the statement that the position of Europeans in China had again become most unsafe and intolerable. Those who persist in regarding the *Arrow* affair as the only cause of the war, and treat with indifference the events that led up to it, may delude themselves into believing that the Chinese were not the most blameworthy parties in the quarrel; but no one who seeks the truth and reads all the evidence will doubt that if there had been no *Arrow* case there would still have been a rupture between the two countries. The Chinese officials, headed by Yeh, had fully persuaded themselves that, as the English had put up with so much, and had acquiesced in the continued closing of the gates of Canton, they were not likely to make the *Arrow* affair a *casus belli*. Even the capture of the Barrier forts did not bring home to their minds the gravity of the situation.

After dismantling these forts, Sir Michael Seymour proceeded up the river, capturing the fort in Macao Passage, and arriving before Canton on the same day. An ultimatum was at once addressed to Yeh, stating that unless he at once complied with all the English demands the Admiral would "proceed with the destruction of all the defences and public buildings of this city and of the government vessels in the river." This threat brought no satisfactory answer, and the Canton forts were seized, their guns spiked and the men-of-war placed with their broadsides opposite the city. Then Yeh, far from being cowed, uttered louder defiance than ever. He incited the population to make a stubborn resistance; he placed a reward of thirty dollars on the head of every Englishman slain or captured, and he publicly proclaimed that there was no alternative but war. He seems to have been driven to these extremities by a fear for his own personal safety and official position. He had no warrant from his Imperial master to commit China to such a dangerous course as another war with the English, and he knew that the only way to vindicate his proceedings was to obtain some success gratifying to national vanity. While Yeh was counting on the support of the people, the English Admiral began the bombardment of the city, directing his fire principally against Yeh's yamen and a part of the wall, which was breached in two days. After some resistance the breach was carried; a gate was occupied, and Sir Michael Seymour and Mr. Parkes proceeded to the yamen of the Viceroy, but as it was thought dangerous to occupy so large a city with so small a force the positions seized were abandoned, although still commanded by the fire of the fleet. After a few days' rest active operations were resumed against the French Folly fort and a large fleet of war junks which had collected up the river. After a warm engagement the vessels were destroyed and the fort captured, and when the Chinese attempted to retrieve the fortunes of war by sending down a number of fire-ships the attempt, although made with a certain amount of skill, miscarried. Undaunted by these successive reverses, Yeh still breathed nothing but defiance. He refused to make the least concession, and he proclaimed that he had "assembled a very large force and decided in his own mind as to the course he was to pursue." There remained no alternative but to prosecute hostilities with renewed vigour. On 12th and 13th November, Sir Michael attacked the Bogue forts on both sides of the river and captured them with little loss. These forts mounted 400 guns but only contained 1,000 men, and the commandant, replying to the English Admiral's suggestion that he should not attempt a hopeless resistance, made the despairing reply of a brave soldier, that he knew he could not defend the forts, but that his duty to his sovereign precluded his surrendering them.

Notwithstanding these continuous reverses, the Chinese remained defiant and energetic. As soon as the English Admiral left Canton to attack the Bogue forts the Chinese hastened to re-occupy all their positions and to repair the breaches. They succeeded in setting fire to and thus destroying the whole foreign settlement, and they carried off several Europeans, all of whom were put to death and some of them tortured. The heads of these Europeans, treacherously seized and barbarously murdered, were paraded throughout the villages of Kwantung, in order to stimulate recruiting and to raise national enthusiasm to a high pitch. Notwithstanding their reverses whenever it became a question of open fighting, the Chinese, by their obstinacy and numbers, at last succeeded in convincing Sir Michael Seymour that his force was too small to achieve any decisive result, and he accordingly withdrew from his positions in front of the city, and sent home a request for a force of 5,000 troops. How bitter the struggle had now become may be inferred from an attempt to poison the whole white population of Hongkong by the Chinese bakers putting arsenic in the bread.

The attempt was fortunately discovered by an excessive amount of arsenic being used; but, although strongly suspected of having instigated this infamous plot, Yeh emphatically denied all knowledge of it, and the truth was never ascertained. Meantime the Chinese were much encouraged by the lull in hostilities, and for the time being Yeh himself was not dissatisfied with the result. The Cantonese saw in the destruction of the foreign settlement and the withdrawal of the English fleet some promise of future victory, and at all events sufficient reason for the continued confidence of the patriot Yeh. Curiously enough, there was peace and ostensible goodwill along the coast and at the other treaty ports, while war and national animosity were in the ascendant at Canton. The Governor-Generals of the Two Kiang and Fuhkien declared over and over again that they wished to abide by the Treaty of Nankin, and they threw upon Yeh the responsibility of his acts. Even Hienfung refrained from showing any unequivocal support of his truculent lieutenant, although there is no doubt that he was impressed by the reports of many victories over the English barbarians with which Yeh supplied him. As long as Yeh was able to keep the quarrel a local one, and to thus shield the central government from any sense of personal danger, he enjoyed the good wishes, if not the active support, of his sovereign. But, unfortunately for the success of his schemes, only the most energetic support of the Pekin government in money and men could have enabled him to hold his own; and as he did nothing but report victories in order to gain a hearing for his policy, he could not grumble when he was not sent the material aid of which he stood most in need. His unreasonable action had done much to unite all foreign nations against China. French, American, and Spanish subjects had been the victims of Chinese ignorance and cruelty, as well as English, and they all saw that the success of Yeh's policy would render their position untenable. Dr. Parker, the United States representative, wrote as follows to Yeh: "The fountain of all difficulties between China and foreign nations is the unwillingness of China to acknowledge England, France, America, and other great nations of the West as her equals and true friends, and to treat them accordingly. So far as respects this grave matter the American government is sensible that the English are in the right, and does choose to co-operate with them." It is a pity that before denouncing the action taken upon the *Arrow* affair as unjustifiable the home critics did not first make themselves acquainted with the facts of the case and the opinions formed by the most competent foreign observers on the spot.

On the receipt of Sir Michael Seymour's request for a force of 5,000 men, it was at once perceived in London that the question of our relations with China had again entered a most important and critical phase. It was at once decided to send the force for which the Admiral asked; and, while 1,500 men were sent from England and a regiment from the Mauritius, the remainder was to be drawn from the Madras army. At the same time it was considered necessary to send an ambassador of high rank to acquaint the Pekin authorities that, while such acts as those of Yeh would not be tolerated, there was no desire to press too harshly on a country which was only gradually shaking off its exclusive prejudices. Lord Elgin was selected for the difficult mission, and his instructions contained the following five categorical demands, the fourth of which was the most important in its consequences:—

Those instructions were conveyed in two despatches of the same date, 20th April, 1857. (See Blue Book on Lord Elgin's Mission, 1857-9.) We quote the following as the more important passages: "The demands which you are instructed to make will be (1), for reparation of injuries to British subjects, and, if the French officers should co-operate with you, for those to French subjects also; (2) for the complete execution at Canton, as well as at the other ports, of the stipulations of the several treaties; (3) compensation to British subjects, and persons entitled to British protection, for losses incurred in consequence of the late disturbances; (4) the assent of the Chinese government to the residence at Pekin, or to the occasional visit to that capital, at the option of the British government, of a minister duly accredited by the Queen to the Emperor of China, and the recognition of the right of the British Plenipotentiary and Chief Superintendent of Trade to communicate directly in writing with the high officers at the Chinese capital, and to send his communications by messengers of his own selection, such arrangements affording the best means of ensuring the due execution of the existing treaties, and of preventing future misunderstandings; (5) a revision of the treaties with China with a view to obtaining increased facilities for commerce, such as access to cities on the great rivers as well as to Chapoo and to other ports on the coast, and also permission for Chinese vessels to resort to Hongkong for purposes of trade from all ports of the Chinese Empire without distinction." These were the demands formulated by the English government for the consent of China, and seven proposals were made as to how they were to be obtained should coercion become necessary. It was also stated that "it is not the intention of Her Majesty's government to undertake any land operations in the interior of the country."

There is no doubt that the arrival of this force in China in the summer of 1857 would have attained a speedy and satisfactory solution of the Chinese difficulty, so far as the position at Canton went; but unfortunately for the rapid settlement of the dispute with Commissioner Yeh an event of superior, and, indeed, supreme, importance occurred to arrest the movement of the expedition to Canton, and to compel the concentration of all our power to overcome an unexpected danger. There can be do doubt that the delay encouraged the Chinese generally, brought the Pekin government over to the views of its enterprising representative at Canton, and rendered the task to be achieved infinitely more arduous. When Lord Elgin reached Singapore, on 3rd June, 1857, he found a letter waiting for him from Lord Canning, then Governor-General of India, informing him of the outbreak of the Indian Mutiny, and imploring him to send all his troops to Calcutta in order to avert the overthrow of our authority in the valley of the Ganges, where, "for a length of 750 miles, there were barely 1,000 European soldiers." To such an urgent appeal there could only be one answer, and the men who were to have chastised Commissioner Yeh followed Havelock to Cawnpore and Lucknow. But while Lord Elgin sent his main force to Calcutta he himself proceeded to Hongkong, where he arrived in the first week of July, and found that hostilities had proceeded to a still more advanced stage than when Sir Michael Seymour wrote for reinforcements. The Chinese had become so confident during the winter that that officer felt bound to resume offensive measures against them, and having been joined by a few more men-of-war, and having also armed some merchant ships of light draught, he attacked a main portion of the Chinese fleet occupying a very strong position in Escape creek. The attack was entrusted to Commodore Elliott, who, with five gunboats and the galleys of the larger men-of-war, carried out with complete success and little loss the orders of his superior officer. Twenty-seven armed junks were destroyed, and the thirteen that escaped were burnt the next day. It was then determined to follow up this success by attacking the headquarters of Yeh's army at Fatshan, the place already referred to as being some distance from Canton. By road it is six and by water twelve miles from that city. The remainder of the Chinese fleet was drawn up in Fatshan channel, and the Chinese had made such extensive preparations for its defence, both on land and on the river, that they were convinced of the impregnability of its position. But they did not yet realise the intrepidity and dash of the English sailor.

The Chinese position was unusually strong, and had been selected with considerable judgment. An island named after the hyacinth lies in midstream two miles from the entrance to the Fatshan channel, which joins the main course of the Sikiang a few miles above the town of that name. The island is flat, and presents no special advantages for defence, but it enabled the Chinese to draw up a line of junks across the two channels of the river, and to place on it a battery of six guns, thus connecting their two squadrons. The 72 junks were drawn up with their sterns facing down stream, and their largest gun bearing on any assailant proceeding up it. On the left bank of the river an elevated and precipitous hill had been occupied in force, and crowned with a battery of 19 guns, and other batteries had been erected at different points along the river. There seems no reason to question the accuracy of the estimate that more than 300 pieces of artillery and 10,000 men were holding this position, which had been admirably chosen and carefully strengthened. The force which Sir Michael Seymour had available to attack this formidable position slightly exceeded 2,000 men, conveyed to the attack in six gunboats and a large flotilla of boats. The English advance was soon known to the Chinese, who began firing from their junks and batteries as soon as they came within range. Three hundred marines were landed to attack the battery on the hill, which was found not to be so strong as it appeared; for on the most precipitous side the Chinese, believing it to be unscalable, had placed no guns, and those in position could not be moved to bear on the assailants in that quarter. The marines gained the top with scarcely any loss, and as they charged over the side the Chinese retired "sulkily," it is said by an eyewitness, and with little loss, owing to the ill-directed fire of the marines.

Meantime the sailors had attacked the Chinese position on the river, and begun a day's fighting which is still unsurpassed for gallantry in the glorious annals of the English navy. The tide was at low water, and the Chinese had barred the channel with a row of sunken junks, leaving a narrow passage known only to themselves. The leading English boat struck on the hidden barrier, but the passage being discovered the other vessels got through. Those boats which ran aground were gradually floated, one after the other, by the rising tide, and at last the flotilla, with little damage, reached the line of stakes which the Chinese had placed to mark the range of the guns in their junks. At once the fire from the 72 junks and the battery on Hyacinth Island became so furious and well-directed that it was matter of astonishment how the English boats passed through it; and only the impetuosity of the attack carried them across the zone of fire where the least hesitation would have meant destruction. They reached and pierced the line of junks, of which one after another was given to the flames. Much of the success of the attack was due to the heroic example of Commodore Harry Keppel, who led the advance party of 500 cutlasses, and who, shouting to his men "Never wait, lads!" gave the Chinese no time to rest or rally. Having broken the line of junks, he took up the pursuit in his seven boats, having determined that the only proof of success could be the capture of Fatshan, and after four miles' hard rowing he came in sight of the elaborate defences drawn up by the Chinese for the security of that place. At the short range of a quarter of a mile the fire of the Chinese guns was tremendous and destructive. Keppel's own boat was reduced to a sinking state, and had to be abandoned. Some of his principal officers were killed, three of his boats ran aground, and things looked black for the small English force. At this critical moment, the Chinese, thinking that they had checked the English attack, and hearing of the magnitude of their reverse down stream, thought their best course would be to retire. Then the few English boats resumed the attack, and hung on to the retreating junks like bulldogs. Many junks were given to the flames, and five were carried off under the teeth of the Fatshan populace; but Keppel's force was too small to hold that town and put it to the ransom, so the worn-out, but still enthusiastic, force retired to join the main body under Sir Michael Seymour, who was satisfied that he had achieved all that was necessary or prudent with his squadron. In these encounters thirteen men were killed and forty wounded, of whom several succumbed to their wounds, for it was noticed that the Chinese shot inflicted cruel injuries. The destruction of the Chinese fleet on the Canton river could not be considered heavily purchased at the cost, and the extent of the trepidation caused by Commodore Keppel's intrepidity could not be accurately measured.

Lord Elgin reached Hongkong very soon after this event, and, although he brought no soldiers with him, he found English opinion at Hongkong very pronounced in favour of an attack on Canton with the view of reopening that city to trade. But the necessary force was not available, and Lord Elgin refused to commit himself to this risky course. Sir Michael Seymour said the attack would require 5,000 troops, and General Ashburnham thought it could be done with 4,000 men if all were effective, while the whole Hongkong garrison numbered only 1,500, and of these one-sixth were invalided. But at the same time Lord Elgin felt bound to do something, and as the fleet was fairly strong, and the time of year as favourable for sea operations as it was the reverse for those on land, he announced his intention of sailing to the Peiho in the hope of bringing the central government to reason. Many persons at Hongkong disapproved of the course. They argued that the crisis arose from a personal quarrel with Yeh, and that it should be arranged at Canton. Trade had continued uninterrupted at the other treaty ports; but if the Pekin authorities were drawn into the discussion it was inevitable that there would be a general suspension of trade on their taking up the same attitude as Yeh's, of which there was already some evidence. Great stress was laid on the uncertainty of the success of such an expedition, and after Lord Elgin had written home asking for official approval of an operation upon which he had decided in the face of local opinion, he allowed himself to be over-persuaded by that opinion and to abandon the scheme, on which his official superiors in Downing Street hastened to compliment him. Instead of sailing for the

Peiho, Lord Elgin decided to go to Calcutta, and ascertain when Lord Canning would be able to spare him the troops necessary to bring China to reason. A plausible case can be made out for this change of plans as for any other, but the conviction cannot be easily repressed that the arrival of an ambassador from the Queen of England on an ostentatiously portentous errand, only to be followed in a few weeks by his precipitate departure, was calculated to increase the confidence of the Chinese and to render the task of coming to an arrangement with them more difficult. The Chinese at Hongkong drew their own inference from these proceedings, and expressed their belief in the security of Canton in the following graphic sentence of pigeon-English. "Inglishmen too much brave in devilship, but no too much large heart catchee that city."

Lord Elgin returned to Hongkong on 20th September, and he found matters very much as he had left them, and all the English force was capable of was to blockade the river. To supplement the weakness of the garrison a coolie corps of 750 Chinese was organised, and proved very efficient, and towards the end of November troops, chiefly marines, began at last to arrive from England. A fleet of useful gunboats of small draught, under Captain Sherard Osborn, arrived for the purpose of operating against the junks in shallow creeks and rivers. At the same time, too, came the French ambassador, Baron Gros, charged with a similar mission to Lord Elgin, and bent on proving once for all that the pretensions of China to superiority over other nations were absurd and untenable. On 12th December Lord Elgin sent Yeh a note apprising him of his arrival as plenipotentiary from Queen Victoria, and pointing out the repeated insults and injuries inflicted on Englishmen, culminating in the outrage to their flag and the repeated refusal to grant any reparation for their wrongs. But Lord Elgin went on to say that even at this eleventh hour there was time to stay the progress of hostilities by making prompt redress. The terms were plain and simple, and the English demands were confined to two points—the complete execution at Canton of all treaty engagements, including the free admission of British subjects to the city, and compensation to British subjects and persons entitled to British protection for losses incurred in consequence of the late disturbances. To this categorical demand Yeh made a long reply, going over the ground of controversy, reasserting what he wished to believe were the facts, and curtly concluding that the trade might continue on the old conditions, and that each side should pay its own losses. Mr. Wade said that his language might bear the construction that the English consul, Mr. Harry Parkes, should pay all the cost himself. If Commissioner Yeh was a humorist he chose a bad time for indulging his proclivities, and, a sufficient force being available, orders were at once given to attack Canton. On 15th December Honan was occupied, and ten days were passed in bringing up the troops and the necessary stores, when, all being in readiness, an ultimatum was sent to Yeh that if he would not give way within forty-eight hours the attack would commence. At the same time every effort was made to warn the unoffending townspeople, so that they might remove to a place of safety. The attacking force numbered about 5,000 English, 1,000 French, and 750 of the Chinese coolie corps, and it was agreed that the most vulnerable point in the Chinese position was Lin's fort, on the eastern side of the city. When the attack began, on 28th December, this fort was captured in half an hour, and the Chinese retired to the northern hills, which they had made their chief position in 1842. The destruction of Lin's fort by the accidental explosion of the magazine somewhat neutralised the advantage of its capture. On the following day the order was given to assault the city by escalade, and three separate parties advanced on the eastern wall. The Chinese kept up a good fire until the troops were within a short distance, but before the ladders were placed against the wall they abandoned their defences and fled. The English troops re-formed on the wide rampart of the wall and pursued the Chinese to the north gate, where, being joined by some Manchu troops, the latter turned and charged up to the bayonets of an English regiment. But they were repulsed and driven out of the city, and simultaneously with this success the fort on Magazine Hill, commanding both the city and the Chinese position on the northern hills, was captured without loss. In less than two hours the great city of Canton was in the possession of the allies, and the Chinese resistance was far less vigorous and worse directed than on any occasion of equal importance. Still, the English loss was fourteen killed and eighty-three wounded, while the French casualties numbered thirty-four. The Chinese had, however, to abandon their positions north of the city, and their elaborate fortifications were blown up.

Although all regular resistance had been overcome the greater part of the city remained in possession of the Chinese and of Yeh in person. That official, although in the lowest straits, had lost neither his fortitude nor his ferocity. He made not the least sign of surrender, and his last act of authority was to order the execution of 400 citizens, whom he denounced as traitors to their country. From his yamen in the interior of the city, when he found that the English hesitated to advance beyond the walls, he incited the populace to fresh efforts of hostility, and, in order to check their increasing audacity, it was resolved to send a force into the city to effect the capture of Yeh. On 5th January, 1858, three detachments were sent into the native city, and they advanced at once upon the official residences of Yeh and Pihkwei, the governor. The Chinese were quite unprepared for this move, and being taken unawares they offered scarcely any resistance. The yamen was occupied and the treasury captured, while Pihkwei was made prisoner in his own house. The French at the same time attacked and occupied the Tartar city—a vast stone-built suburb which had been long allowed to fall into decay, and which, instead of being occupied, as was believed, by 7,000 Manchu warriors, was the residence of bats and nauseous creatures. But the great object of the attack was unattained, for Yeh still remained at large, and no one seemed to know where he ought to be sought, for all the official buildings had been searched in vain. But Mr. Parkes, by indefatigable inquiry, at last gained a clue from a poor scholar whom he found poring over an ancient classic at the library, undisturbed in the midst of the turmoil. From him he learnt that Yeh would probably be found in a yamen situated in the south west quarter of the city. Mr. Parkes hastened thither with Captain (afterwards Admiral) Cooper Key and a party of sailors. They arrived just in time, for all the preparations for flight had been made, and Captain Key caught Yeh with his own hand as he was escaping over the wall. One of his assistants came forward with praiseworthy devotion and declared himself to be Yeh, in the hope of saving his superior; but the deception was at once detected by Mr. Parkes, who assured Yeh that no harm would be done him. The capture of Yeh completed the effect of the occupation of Canton, and the disappearance of the most fanatical opponent of the foreigners ensured the tranquillity of the Canton region, which had been the main seat of disorder, during the remainder of the war. The government of Canton was then entrusted to Pihkwei and a commission of one Frenchman and two Englishmen, and the Chinese admitted it had never been better governed. Yeh himself was sent to Calcutta, where he died two years later, and, considering the abundant evidence of his cruel treatment of defenceless prisoners, he had every reason to consider his punishment lenient.

Having thus settled the difficulty at Canton it remained for Lord Elgin to carry out the other part of his task, and place diplomatic relations between England and China on a satisfactory basis by obtaining the right of direct communication with Pekin. A letter dated 11th February, 1858, was sent to the senior Secretary of State at Pekin describing what had occurred in the south, and summarising what would be required from the Chinese government. The English and French plenipotentiaries also notified that they would proceed to Shanghai for the purpose of conducting the further negotiations. This letter was duly forwarded to Pekin by the Governor of Kiangsu, and when Lord Elgin reached Shanghai on 30th March he found the reply of Yuching, the chief adviser of Hienfung, waiting for him. Yuching's letter was extremely unsatisfactory. It was arrogant in its terms and impracticable as to its proposals. Lord Elgin was told that "no Imperial Commissioner ever conducts business at Shanghai," and that it behoved the English minister to wait at Canton until the arrival of a new Imperial Commissioner from Pekin. The only concession the Chinese made was to dismiss Yeh from his posts, and as he was a prisoner in the hands of the English this did not mean much. Lord Elgin's reply to this communication was to announce his intention of proceeding to the Peiho and there negotiating direct with the Imperial government. Lord Elgin reached the Gulf of Pechihli about the middle of April, and he again addressed Yuching in the hope of an amicable settlement, and requested that the Emperor would appoint some official to act as his plenipotentiary. Three minor officials were appointed, more out of curiosity than from a desire to promote business, but on Lord Elgin discovering that they were of inferior rank and that their powers were inadequate, he declined to see them. But Yuching refused to appoint any others; stating curtly that their powers were ample for the adjustment of affairs, and then Lord Elgin announced that he would proceed up the Peiho to Tientsin. Some delay was caused by the non-arrival of the fleet, which was not assembled in the Gulf of Pechihli, through different causes of delay, until the end of May, or about three weeks after Lord Elgin announced his intention of forcing his way up to Tientsin. There is no doubt that Sir Michael Seymour was in no sense to blame for this delay, but unfortunately it aroused considerable irritation in the mind of Lord Elgin, who sent home a despatch, without informing his colleague, stating that the delay was "a most grievous disappointment," and attributing it to the supineness of the Admiral.

On 19th May the allied fleet proceeded to the mouth of the river, and summoned the Commandant to surrender the Taku forts on the following morning. No reply being received the attack commenced, and after the bombardment had gone on at short range for an hour and a quarter the Chinese gunners were driven from their batteries, and the troops landed, occupying the whole line of forts and entrenched camps. An attempt to injure our fleet by fire-ships miscarried, and considering that the Chinese had some of their best troops present, including a portion of the Imperial Guard, their resistance was not as great as might have been expected. Their general committed suicide, and the Chinese lost the best part of their artillery, which had been removed from Pekin and Tientsin for the defence of the entrance to the Peiho. The fleet proceeded up the river to Tientsin, and Lord Elgin took up his quarters in that city. The Chinese government was brought to reason by this striking success, and, with his capital menaced, the Emperor hastened to delegate full powers to two high Commissioners, Kweiliang and Hwashana, both Manchus and dignitaries of the highest birth and rank. Their powers were superior to those granted to Keying at the time of the old war, and they were commanded with affectionate earnestness to show the foreigners that they were competent and willing to grant anything not injurious to China. Nothing could be more satisfactory than the proposals of the new Chinese representatives, and they were anxious to settle everything with the least possible delay. At this point there reappeared upon the scene a man whose previous experience and high position entitled him to some consideration. Less than a week after his first interview with the Imperial representatives, Lord Elgin received a letter from Keying, who, it was soon found, had come on a self-appointed mission to induce the English by artifice and plausible representation to withdraw their fleet from the river. His zeal was increased by the knowledge that the penalty of failure would be death, and as his reputation had been very great among Europeans there is no saying but that he might have succeeded had there not been discovered in Yeh's yamen at Canton some of his papers, which showed that he had played a double part throughout, and that at heart he was bitterly anti-foreign. When he found that the English possessed this information he hastened back to Pekin, where he was at once summoned before the Board of Punishment for immediate judgment, and, being found guilty, it was ordered that as he had acted "with stupidity and precipitancy" he should be strangled forthwith. As an act of extreme grace the Emperor allowed him to put an end to his existence in consideration of his being a member of the Imperial family.

After the departure of Keying, negotiations proceeded very satisfactorily with Kweiliang and Hwashana, and all the points were practically agreed upon, excepting the right to have a resident minister at Pekin. This claim was opposed on several grounds. It was not merely something that had never been heard of, but it would probably be attended with peril to the envoy as well as to the Chinese government. Then the Commissioners wanted to know if he would wear the Chinese dress, if all the Powers would have only one minister, and if he would make the kotow? Finding such arguments fail they asked that the visit of an English ambassador to Pekin should be postponed till a more favourable occasion. They made the admission that "there is properly no objection to the permanent residence at Pekin of a Plenipotentiary Minister of Her Britannic Majesty," and they even spoke of sending a return mission to London; but they deprecated the proposal as novel and as specially risky at this moment in consequence of the formidable Taeping rebellion. These representations did not fail to produce their effect, for it was not to the interest of Europeans generally that the Emperor's authority should be subverted on the morrow of his signing a treaty with us. In consequence of these feelings, and with a wish to reciprocate the generally-conciliatory attitude of the Chinese officials, Kweiliang and Hwashana were informed that the right would be waived for the present, except that it would be necessary for the English minister to visit Pekin twelve months later, on the occasion of exchanging the ratifications of the treaty; and so the matter was left pending the arrival of that occasion. While the Treaty of Tientsin provided for the conclusion of a peace that promised to be enduring, and arranged for the future diplomatic relations of the two countries, Commissioners were duly appointed to meet at Shanghai and draw up a tariff. But at Tientsin the great crux in the commercial relations between us and the Chinese had been settled by the legalisation of opium. It was agreed that opium might be imported into China on payment of thirty taels, or about ten pounds, per chest. Experience had shown that leaving the most largely-imported article into China contraband had been both futile and inconvenient, while the Chinese government was a direct loser by not enjoying a legitimate source of revenue. How general the view had become that the evils of the use of opium were exaggerated, and, even admitting them, that there was no better way of diminishing their effect than by legalising the import of opium, can be judged by the ready acquiescence of the Chinese Commissioners; and here, from many other matured opinions, we may quote the final and deliberate conviction of Sir Henry Pottinger:—

"I take this opportunity to advert to one important topic on which I have hitherto considered it right to preserve a rigid silence—I allude to the trade in opium; and I now unhesitatingly declare in this public manner that after the most unbiassed and careful observations I have become convinced during my stay in China that the alleged demoralising and debasing evils of opium have been and are vastly exaggerated. Like all other indulgences, excesses in its use are bad and reprehensible; but I have neither myself seen such vicious consequences as are frequently ascribed to it, nor have I been able to obtain authentic proofs or information of their existence. The great, and perhaps I might say sole, objection to the trade, looking at it morally and abstractedly, that I have discovered is that it is at present contraband and prohibited by the laws of China, and therefore to be regretted and disavowed; but I have striven—and I hope with some prospect of eventual success—to bring about its legalisation; and were that point once effected, I am of opinion that its most objectionable feature would be altogether removed. Even as it now exists it appears to me to be unattended with a hundredth part of the debasement and misery which may be seen in our native country from the lamentable abuse of ardent spirits, and those who so sweepingly condemn the opium trade on that principle need not, I think, leave the shores of England to find a far greater and besetting evil."

The ink on the Tientsin treaty was scarcely dry before reasons began to be furnished against the sincerity of the Emperor and his desire for peace. Before the fleet left the Peiho workmen were already engaged repairing and re-arming the Taku forts, and the morrow of Lord Elgin's departure from Hongkong witnessed the revival of disturbances round Canton, where the new Imperial Commissioner Hwang, instead of seeking to restore harmony, had devoted himself to inciting the population to patriotic deeds in emulation of Commissioner Yeh. It was found necessary to take strenuous measures against the turbulent patriots of Kwantung, and to break up their main force in their strong and well-chosen position at Shektsin, which was accomplished by a vigorous attack both on land and water. The suspicion that the Chinese were not absolutely straightforward in their latest dealings with us was confirmed by the discovery at Shektsin of secret Imperial edicts, breathing defiance to the foreigners and inciting the people to resistance. These and other facts warned the European authorities on the spot that there was no certainty that the Treaty of Tientsin would be ratified, or that a British envoy would be admitted into the capital for even the temporary business of a diplomatic ceremony. While people in Europe were assuming that the Chinese question might be dismissed for twenty years, the English consuls and commanders in the treaty ports were preparing themselves for a fresh and more vigorous demonstration of Chinese hostility and animosity. The matter that was to prove the sincerity and good faith of the Chinese government was the reception at Pekin of the English officer entrusted with the duty of exchanging the ratified copies of the treaty. If he were allowed to proceed to Pekin there would be reason for accepting the assurances of the Emperor that a permanent arrangement should be effected later on, when it would not injure his dignity or authority.

Mr. Frederick Bruce, who had been secretary to his brother, Lord Elgin, and who had previously served at Hongkong, was appointed Her Majesty's representative for the purpose of exchanging the ratification of the treaty. He was instructed to inform the Chinese officials that, while the British government would not renounce the right of having a permanent resident minister at Pekin, they were prepared to waive it for a time by allowing diplomatic intercourse to be carried on at Shanghai. But no deviation was to be permitted from the arrangement that the ratifications were to be exchanged at Pekin, and Lord Malmesbury warned the new envoy that "all the arts at which the Chinese are such adepts will be put in practice to dissuade you from repairing to the capital." Mr. Bruce received his instructions on 1st March, 1859, and the exchange of ratifications had to be effected before the 26th June. Mr. Bruce reached Hongkong in April, and he found the air full of unsatisfactory rumours; and when he reached Shanghai the uncertainty was intensified by the presence of Kweiliang and Hwashana, who seemed to think that everything might be settled without a journey to Pekin. They endeavoured to get up a discussion on some unsettled details of minor importance, in the hope that the period for the ratification of the treaty might be allowed to expire. Mr. Bruce announced his imminent departure for the Peiho to Kweiliang, and expressed the hope that arrangements would be made for his safe conveyance to and appropriate accommodation at Pekin. Neither Mr. Bruce's instructions nor his own opinion justified any delay in proceeding to the north, and the fleet sent on in advance under the command of Admiral Hope reached the mouth of the Peiho on the 17th June, three days before Mr. Bruce. The Admiral on arrival sent a notification to the Chinese officers in command of the forts that the English envoy was coming. But the reception given to the officers who conveyed this intimation was distinctly unfavourable and even hostile. The two boats sent ashore found that the entrance to the river was effectually barred by a row of iron stakes and by an inner boom, and that a large and excited crowd forbade them to land. A vague promise was given that an opening would be made in the obstructions to admit the passage of the English ships; but on the boats repeating their visit on the succeeding day they found that the small passages had been more effectually secured, and that there could no longer be any doubt that the Chinese did not intend to admit the English envoy. It was therefore determined to make a demonstration with the fleet, and if necessary to resort to force, which it was never doubted would be attended with little risk and crowned with complete success.

On 25th June the attack on the Taku forts began with the removal of the iron stakes forming the outer barrier by the steamer *Opossum*, and this part of the operations was performed without a shot being fired. When, however, the eleven ships forming the English fleet reached the inner boom all the Chinese forts and batteries began to fire with an accuracy which showed that the guns had been trained to bear on this precise spot. The result of this unexpectedly vigorous bombardment was soon shown in the damaged condition of our ships. Two gunboats were sunk, all the vessels were more or less damaged, and when, after three hours' cannonade, it was sought to retrieve the doubtful fortune of the day by a land attack, the result only went to accentuate the ill results of the naval engagement. The attack was entrusted to the marines and engineers, and the men on landing found that they had to cross for 500 yards a mud-bank, in which they sank ankle deep, and some of the men either lost or injured their weapons. They advanced under a heavy fire, and before they reached the edge of the ditch all the ladders and portable bridges were destroyed, and it was clear that the attack must fail. In this disastrous affair more than 300 men were killed and wounded, which, added to the loss of three gunboats, represented a very serious disaster. But the worst of it was that it convinced the Emperor and his advisers that they could hold their own against Europeans, and that it placed the extreme party once more in the ascendant at Pekin. Sankolinsin, the Mongol prince who had checked the advance of the Taepings, became master of the situation, and declared that there was nothing to fear from an enemy who had been repulsed by the raw levies of the province while he held the flat country between the Peiho and Pekin with the flower of the Banner army. The success of the Chinese at Taku obliterated the memory of all their previous defeats, and, as Mr. Bruce very truly said, it became impossible to carry out the provisions of the Treaty of Tientsin until we had recovered our superiority in the eyes of the Chinese. Mr. Bruce returned to Shanghai, the fleet to Hongkong, and the matter remained suspended until fresh instructions and troops could be received from Europe.

After some hesitation and delay, a plan of joint action was agreed upon in November, 1859, between France and England, and it was hoped that the whole expeditionary force would have reached its destination by April, 1860. Pending its arrival Mr. Bruce was instructed to present an ultimatum with thirty days' grace demanding an immediate apology, the payment of a large indemnity amounting to £2,400,000 to both England and France, and the ratification of the Treaty of Tientsin. The minister, Pang Wanching, replied, categorically refusing all these requests; and, as neither indemnity nor apology was offered, there remained no alternative but the inevitable and supreme appeal to arms.

The troops which were to form the expedition* were mainly drawn from India, and Sir Hope Grant, who had not merely distinguished himself during the Mutiny, but who had served in the first English war with China during the operations round Canton, was appointed to the command of the

---

* As it would be impossible to describe the operations of this campaign in a different manner from my larger History, it is deemed proper to use the same language, with, however, some slight but necessary abbreviation.

army; while Admiral Hope, strongly reinforced in ships, retained the command of the naval forces. A force of five batteries of artillery, six regiments of infantry, two squadrons of cavalry, together with a body of horse and foot from the native army of India, amounting in all to about 10,000 men, was placed at the General's disposal in addition to the troops already in China. The French government agreed to send another army of about two-thirds this strength to co-operate on the Peiho, and General Montauban was named for the command. The collection of this large expedition brought into prominence the necessity of employing as ambassador a diplomatist of higher rank than Mr. Bruce; and accordingly, in February Lord Elgin and Baron Gros were commissioned to again proceed to China for the purpose of securing the ratification of their own treaty. Sir Hope Grant reached Hongkong in March, 1860, and by his recommendation a stronger native contingent (one Sikh regiment, four Punjab regiments, two Bombay regiments, one Madras regiment of foot, and two irregular regiments of Sikh cavalry, known as Fane's and Probyn's Horse. Sir John Michel and Sir Robert Napier commanded divisions under Sir Hope Grant) was added, raising the English force in the field to more than 13,000 men. A lease was obtained in perpetuity, through the skilful negotiation of Mr. Parkes, of Kowlun and Stonecutter Island, where, from their salubrious position, it was proposed to place the troops on their arrival from India or England. Chusan was occupied the following month without opposition by an English brigade of 2,000 men.

The summer had commenced before the whole of the expedition assembled at Hongkong, whence it was moved northwards to Shanghai about a year after the failure of the attack on the forts on the Peiho. A further delay was caused by the tardiness of the French, and July had begun before the expedition reached the Gulf of Pechihli. Then opposite opinions led to different suggestions, and while the English advocated proceeding to attack Pehtang, General Montauban drew up another plan of action. But the exigencies of the alliance compelled the English, who were ready, to wait for the French, who were not, in order that the assault might be made simultaneously. Before that time arrived the French commander had been brought round to the view that the proper plan of campaign was that suggested by the English commander—viz., to attack and capture Pehtang, whence the Taku forts might be taken in the rear. It is somewhat remarkable to observe that no one suggested a second time endeavouring to carry by a front attack these forts, which had in the interval since Admiral Hope's failure been rendered more formidable.

At Pehtang the Chinese had made few preparations for defence, and nothing of the same formidable character as at Taku. The forts on both sides of the river were neither extensive nor well-armed. The garrison consisted largely of Tartar cavalry, more useful for watching the movements of the foreigners than for working artillery when exposed to the fire of the new Armstrong guns of the English. The attacking force landed in boats and by wading, Sir Hope Grant setting his men the example. No engagement took place on the night of disembarkation, and the advanced force slept on an elevated causeway bordered on both sides by the sea, which had flooded a considerable extent of the country. When morning broke, a suspicious silence in the enemy's quarters strengthened the belief that Pehtang would not be defended; and Mr. Parkes, ever to the front when information was wanted, soon confirmed the impression. While the garrison had resolved not to resist an attack, they had contemplated causing their enemy as much loss as if he had been obliged to carry the place by storm by placing shells in the magazine which would be exploded by the moving of some gunlocks put in a spot where they could not fail to be trodden upon. This plot, which was thoroughly in accordance with the practices of Chinese warfare, was fortunately divulged by a native more humane than patriotic, and Pehtang was captured and occupied without the loss of a single man. This success at the commencement enabled the whole of the expedition to land without further delay or difficulty. Three days after the capture of Pehtang, reconnoitring parties were sent out to ascertain what the Chinese were doing, and whether they had made any preparations to oppose an advance towards Taku or Tientsin. Four miles from Pehtang they came in sight of a strongly-entrenched camp, where several thousand men opened fire upon the reconnoitring parties with their gingalls, and several men were wounded. The object being only to find out what the Celestial army was doing, and where it was, the Europeans withdrew on discovering the proximity of so strong a force. The great difficulty was to discover a way of getting from Pehtang on to some of the main roads leading to the Peiho ; for the whole of the surrounding country had been under water, and was more or less impassable. In fact, the region round Pehtang consisted of nothing but mud, while the one road, an elevated causeway, was blocked by the fortified camp just mentioned as having been discovered by the reconnoitring party. A subsequent reconnaissance, conducted by Colonel (now Lord) Wolseley, revealed the presence of a cart-track which might prove available for the march of troops. This track was turned to advantage for the purpose of taking the Chinese position in flank, and to Sir Robert Napier's division was assigned this, as it proved, difficult operation. When the manœuvre of out-flanking had been satisfactorily accomplished, the attack was commenced in front. Here the Chinese stood to their position, but only for a brief time, as the fire from eighteen guns, including some 40-pounders, soon silenced their gingalls, and they precipitately abandoned their entrenchments. While the engagement in front had reached this favourable termination Sir Robert Napier had been engaged on the right hand with a strong body of Tartar cavalry, which attacked with considerable valour, and with what seemed a possibility of success, until the guns opening upon them and the Sikh cavalry charging them dispelled their momentary dream of victory. The prize of this battle was the village of Sinho with its line of earthworks, one mile north of the Peiho, and about seven miles in the rear of the Taku forts.

The next day was occupied in examining the Chinese position and in discovering, what was more difficult than its capture, how it might be approached. It was found that the village, which formed a fortified square protected by batteries, could be best approached by the river-bank, and the only obstacle in this quarter was that represented by the fire of the guns of two junks, supported by a battery on the opposite side of the river. These, however, were soon silenced by the superior fire directed upon them, and the guns were spiked by Captain Willis and a few sailors, who crossed the river for the purpose. The flank of the advance being thus protected, the attack on Tangku itself began with a cannonade from thirty-six pieces of the best artillery of that age. The Chinese fire was soon rendered innocuous, and their walls and forts were battered down. Even then, however, the garrison gave no signs of retreat, and it was not until the Armstrongs had been dragged within a very short distance of the walls, and the foot-soldiers had absolutely effected an entrance, that the garrison thought of their personal safety and turned in flight. The following description by an eye-witness of how the Chinese fought at a great disadvantage will be interesting :—" The Tartars really for a time fought nobly. I saw one man, stripped to his loins, fighting his gun single-handed after every bit of parapet near him had been knocked away and our shot was crashing in all around him. . . . Having seen that one brave man, the survivor of all the gun detachment, working his gun alone, loading and firing among the corpses of his fellows, with no one near at hand to applaud him nor witness his fall, working away, whatever his motive might be, until he fell like his comrades, I could not but picture to myself in all those grim groups of eight or ten perhaps at a gun, how one by one they had fallen, and yet the survivors disdained to fly."

Some days before the battle and capture of Tangku, Lord Elgin received several communications from Hang, the Governor-General of Pechihli, requesting a cessation of hostilities, and announcing the approach of two Imperial Commissioners appointed for the express purpose of ratifying the Treaty of Tientsin. But Lord Elgin very wisely perceived that it would be impossible to negotiate on fair terms unless the Taku forts were in his possession. The capture of Tangku placed the allied forces in the rear of the northern forts on the Peiho; and those forts once occupied, the others on the southern side would be practically untenable and obliged to surrender at discretion. Several days were passed in preliminary observations and skirmishing. On the one side the whole of the Tartar cavalry was removed to the southern bank; on the other, a bridge of boats was thrown across the Peiho, and the approach to the northern fort carefully examined up to 600 yards from the wall. At this point the views of the allied generals agained clashed. General Montauban wished to attack the southern forts. Sir Hope Grant was determined to begin by carrying the northern. The attack on the chief northern fort commenced on the morning of the 21st of August with a heavy cannonade; the Chinese, anticipating the plans of the English, were the first to fire. The Chinese fought their guns with extraordinary courage. A shell exploded their principal magazine, which blew up with a terrible report; but as soon as the smoke cleared off they recommenced their fire with fresh ardour. Although even this fort had not been constructed with the same strength in the rear as they all presented in the front, the resistance was most vigorous. A premature attempt to throw a pontoon across the ditch was defeated with the loss of sixteen men. The Coolie Corps here came to the front, and rushing into the water, held up the pontoons while the French and some English troops dashed across. But all their efforts to scale the wall were baffled, and it seemed as if they had only gone to self-destruction. While the battle was thus doubtfully contested, Major Anson, who had shown the greatest intrepidity on several occasions, succeeded in cutting the ropes that held up a drawbridge, and an entrance was soon effected within the body of the works. The Chinese still resisted nobly, and it was computed that out of a garrison of 500 men but 100 escaped. The English loss was 22 killed, and 179, including 21 officers, were wounded. To these figures must be added the French loss.

There still remained four more forts on the northern side of the river, and it seemed as if these would offer further resistance, as the garrisons uttered threats of defiance to a summons to surrender. But appearances were deceptive, and for the good reason that all of these forts were only protected in the rear by a slight wall. The French rushed impetuously to the attack, only to find that the garrison had given up the defence, while a large number had actually retired. Two thousand prisoners were made, and the fall of the forts on the northern bank was followed by an immediate summons to those on the southern to surrender; and as they were commanded by the guns in the former they yielded with as good a grace as they could muster. The following day formal occupation was made, and the spoil included more than 600 cannon of various sizes and degrees of efficiency. On that day also the fleet, which had during these operations been riding at anchor off the mouth of the river, proceeded across the bar, removed the different obstacles that had been intended to hinder its approach, and Admiral Hope anchored in security off those very forts which had repulsed him in the previous year, and which would in all probability have continued to defy any direct attack from the sea. Let it not be said, therefore, that Sir Hope Grant's capture of the Taku forts reflected in any way on the courage or capacity of Admiral Hope for the failure in 1859.

By this decisive success, which fully justified the foresight of the English general, the road to Tientsin was opened both by land and by the river. The fleet of gun-boats, which had participated as far as they could without incurring any undue danger in the attack on the forts, were ordered up the Peiho; and the English ambassador, escorted by a strong naval and military force, proceeded to Tientsin, where it would be possible, without any loss of dignity, to resume negotiations with the Pekin government. The advanced gun-boats arrived at Tientsing on the 23rd of August, and three days later the greater portion of the expedition had entered that city. No resistance was attempted, although several batteries and entrenched camps were passed on the way. Precautions were at once taken to make the position of the troops as secure as possible in the midst of a very large and presumably hostile population. The people showed, according to the ideas of Europe, an extraordinary want of patriotic fervour, and were soon engaged on the most amicable terms, in conducting a brisk trade with the invaders of their country; but there was never any doubt that on the first sign of a reverse they would have turned upon the foreign troops, and completed by all the means in their power their discomfiture. Several communications passed between the opposite camps during these days; and when Hang announced the withdrawal of all Chinese troops from Tientsin he expressed a wish that the English ambassador would not bring many vessels of war with him. But such requests were made more with the desire to save appearances than from any hope that they would be granted. The reality of their fears, and of their consequent desire to negotiate, was shown by the appointment of Kweiliang, who had arranged the Treaty of Tientsin, as High Commissioner to provide for the necessary ceremonies in connection with its ratification. Kweiliang apparently possessed powers of the most extensive character; and he hastened to inform Lord Elgin, who had taken up his residence in a beautiful yamen in Tientsin, that he had received the Emperor's authority to discuss and decide everything. In response to this notification the reply was sent that the three conditions of peace were an apology for the attack on the English flag at Peiho, the payment of an indemnity, including the costs of the war, and, thirdly, the ratification and execution of the Treaty of Tientsin, including, of course, the reception at Pekin of the representative of the Queen of England on honourable terms adequate to the dignity of that great sovereign. To none of these was Kweiliang himself disposed to raise any objection. Only in connection with the details of the last-named point was there likely that any difference of opinion would arise; and that difference of opinion speedily revealed itself when it became known that the English insisted on the advance of their army to the town of Tungchow, only twelve miles distant from the walls of Pekin. To the Chinese ministers this simple precaution seemed like exacting the extreme rights of the conqueror, before, too, the act of conquest had been consummated; for already fresh troops were arriving from Mongolia and Manchuria, and the valour of Sankolinsin was beginning to revive. That the Chinese government had under the hard taskmaster, necessity, made great progress in its views on foreign matters was not to be denied, but somehow or other its movements always lagged behind the requirements of the hour, and the demands of the English were again ahead of what it was disposed to yield.

If the Chinese government had promptly accepted the inevitable, and if Kweiliang had negotiated with as much celerity as he pretended to be his desire, peace might have been concluded and the Chinese saved some further ignominy. But it soon became clear that all the Chinese were thinking about was to gain time, and as the months available for active campaigning were rapidly disappearing, it was imperative that not the least delay should be sanctioned. On the 8th of September, Lord Elgin and Sir Hope Grant left Tientsin with an advance force of about 1,500 men; and marching by the high road, reached the pretty village of Hosiwu, half-way between that town and the capital. A few days later this force was increased by the remainder of one division, while to Sir Robert Napier was left the task of guarding with the other Tientsin and the communications with the sea. At Hosiwu negotiations were resumed by Tsai, Prince of I, a nephew of the Emperor, who declared that he had received authority to conclude all arrangements; but he was curtly informed that no treaty could be concluded save at Tungchow, and the army resumed its advance beyond Hosiwu. The march was continued without molestation to a point beyond the village of Matow, but when Sir Hope Grant approached a place called Chan-chia-wan he found himself in presence of a large army. This was the first sign of any resolve to offer military opposition to the invaders since the capture of the Taku forts, and it came to a great extent in the manner of a surprise, for by a special agreement with Mr. Parkes the settlement of the difficulty was to be concluded at Chan-chia-wan in an amicable manner. Instead, however, of the Emperor's delegates, the English commander found Sankolinsin and the latest troops drawn from Pekin and beyond the Wall in battle array, and occupying the very ground which had been assigned for the English encampment.

The day before the English commander perceived that he was in face of a strong force Mr. Parkes and some other officers and civilians* had been

---

* The party consisted, besides Mr. Parkes, of Mr. Henry Loch, Mr. De Normann, and Mr. Bowlby, the Special Correspondent of the "Times." The escort was composed of six English dragoons and twenty sowars of Fane's Horse, under the command of Lieutenant Anderson. Colonel Walker and Mr. Thompson, of the Commissariat, also accompanied the party for a portion of the way (Loch's narrative). They were subsequently joined on their return by the French commissioner, Comte d'Escayrac de Lauture, who prepared an exhaustive memoir on the condition of the Chinese Empire in six volumes.

sent ahead with an escort of Sikh cavalry to arrange the final preliminaries with the Imperial Commissioners at Tungchow, both as to where the camp was to be pitched and also as to the interview between the respective plenipotentiaries of the opposing Powers. This party proceeded to Tungchow without encountering any opposition or perceiving any exceptional military precautions. Troops were indeed observed at several points, and officers in command of pickets demanded the nature of their business and where they were going, but the reply "To the Commissioners" at once satisfied all enquiries and opened every barrier. The one incident that happened was of happy augury for a satisfactory issue if the result went to prove the fallaciousness of human expectations. A change had in the meanwhile come over the minds of the Imperial Commissioners, whether in accordance with the working of a deep and long-arranged policy, or from the confidence created by the sight of the numerous warriors drawn from the cradle of the Manchu race for the defence of the capital and dynasty, can never be ascertained with any degree of certainty. Their tone suddenly assumed greater boldness and arrogance. To some of the Englishmen it appeared "almost offensive," and it was only after five hours' discussion between Mr. Parkes and the Commissioners at Tungchow that some sign was given of a more yielding disposition. The final arrangements were hastily concluded in the evening of the 17th of September for the arrival of the troops at the proposed camping-ground on the morrow, and for the interview that was to follow as soon after as possible. While Mr. Parkes and some of his companions were to ride forward in the morning to apprise Sir Hope Grant of what had been agreed upon, and to point out the site for his camp, the others were to remain in Tungchow with the greater part of the Sikh escort.*

On their return towards the advancing English army in the early morning of the following day, Mr. Parkes and his party met with frequent signs of military movement in the country between Tungchow and Chanchia-wan. Large bodies of infantry and gingall-men were seen marching from all quarters to the town. At Chan-chia-wan itself still more emphatic tokens were visible of a coming battle. Cavalry were drawn up in dense bodies, but under shelter. In a nullah one regiment of a thousand sabres was stationed with the men standing at their horses' heads ready for instant action. At another point a number of men were busily engaged in constructing a battery, and in placing twelve guns in position. When the Englishmen gained the plain they found the proposed site of the English camp in the actual possession of a Chinese army, and a strong force of Tartar cavalry, alone reckoned to number six or seven thousand men, scouring the plain. To all enquiries as to what these warlike arrangements betokened no reply was made by the soldiers, and when the whereabouts of the responsible general was asked there came the stereotyped answer that "he was many li away." To the most obtuse mind these arrangements could convey but one meaning. They indicated that the Chinese government had resolved to make another endeavour to avert the concessions demanded from them by the English and their allies, and to appeal once more to the God of Battles ere they accepted the inevitable. When the whole truth flashed across the mind of Mr. Parkes, the army of Sir Hope

---

* Mr. Parkes, Colonel Walker, Mr. Loch, Mr. Thompson, the Dragoons and three Sikhs formed the first party. De Normann, Bowlby, and Anderson remained at Tungchow with seventeen Sikhs.

Grant might be, and indeed was, marching into the trap prepared for it, with such military precautions perhaps as a wise general never neglected, but still wholly unprepared for the extensive and well-arranged opposition planned for its reception by a numerous army established in a strong position of its own choosing. It became, therefore, of the greatest importance to communicate the actual state of affairs to him, and to place at his disposal the invaluable information which the Englishmen returning from Tungchow had in their possession. But Mr. Parkes had still more to do. It was his duty to bring before the Chinese Imperial Commissioners at the earliest possible moment the knowledge of this flagrant breach of the convention he had concluded the day before, to demand its meaning, and to point out the grave consequences that must ensue from such treacherous hostility ; and in that supreme moment, as he had done on the many other critical occasions of his career in China—at Canton and Taku in particular —the one thought in the mind of Mr. Parkes was how best to perform his duty. He did not forget also that, while he was almost in a place of safety near the limits of the Chinese pickets, and not far distant from the advancing columns of Sir Hope Grant, there were other Englishmen in his rear possibly in imminent peril of their lives amid the Celestials at Tungchow.

Mr. Parkes rode back, therefore, to that town, and with him went one English dragoon, named Phipps, and one Sikh sowar carrying a flag of truce on his spear-point. We must leave them for the moment to follow the movements of the others. To Mr. Loch was entrusted the task of communicating with Sir Hope Grant ; while the remainder of the party were to remain stationary, in order to show the Chinese that they did not suspect anything, and that they were full of confidence. Mr. Loch, accompanied by two Sikhs, rode at a hard canter away from the Chinese lines. He passed through one body of Tartar cavalry without opposition, and reached the advanced guard of the English force in safety. To tell his news was but the work of a minute. It confirmed the suspicions which General Grant had begun to feel at the movements of some bodies of cavalry on the flank of his line of march. Mr. Loch had performed his share of the arrangement. He had warned Sir Hope Grant. But to the chivalrous mind duty is but half-performed if aid is withheld from those engaged in fulfilling theirs. What he had done had proved unexpectedly easy ; it remained for him to assist those whose share was more arduous and perilous. So Mr. Loch rode back to the Chinese lines, Captain Brabazon insisting on following him, again accompanied by two Sikhs, but not the same who had ridden with him before. Sir Hope Grant had given him the assurance that unless absolutely forced to engage he would postpone the action for two hours. This small party of four men rode without hesitation, and at a rapid pace, through the skirmishers of the Chinese army. The rapidity of their movements disconcerted the Chinese, who allowed them to pass without opposition and almost without notice. They rode through the streets of Chan-chia-wan without meeting with any molestation, although they were crowded with the mustering men of the Imperial army. They gained Tungchow without let or hindrance, after having passed through probably not less than thirty thousand men about to do battle with the long hated and now feared foreigners. It may have been, as suggested, they they owed their safety to a belief that they were the bearers of their army's surrender ! Arrived at Tungchow, Mr. Loch found the Sikh escort at the temple outside the gates unaware of any danger—all the Englishmen being absent in the town, where they were shopping—and a letter left by Mr. Parkes warning them on return to prepare for instant flight, and saying that he was off in search of Prince Tsai. In that search he was at last successful. He found the High Commissioner, he asked the meaning of the change that had taken place, and was told in curt and defiant tones that "there could be no peace, there must be war."

The last chance of averting hostilities was thus shown to be in vain. Prince Tsai endorsed the action of Sankolinsin. Mr. Parkes had only the personal satisfaction of knowing that he had done everything he could to prove that the English did not wish to press their military superiority over an antagonist whose knowledge of war was slight and out of date. He had done this at the greatest personal peril. It only remained to secure his own safety and that of his companions. By this time the whole party of Englishmen had re-assembled in the temple; and Mr. Loch, anxious for Mr. Parkes, had gone into the city and met him galloping away from the yamen of the Commissioner. There was no longer reason for delay. Not an Englishman had yet been touched, but between this small band and safety lay the road back through the ranks of Sankolinsin's warriors. From Tungchow to the advanced post of Sir Hope Grant's army was a ten mile ride; and most of the two hours' grace had already expired. Could it be done? By this time most of the Chinese troops had reached Chanchia-wan, where they had been drawn up in battle array among the maize-fields and in the nullahs as already described. From Tungchow to that place the country was almost deserted; and the fugitives proceeded unmolested along the road till they reached that town. The streets were crowded partly with armed citizens and peasants, but chiefly with panic-stricken householders; and by this time the horses were blown, and some of them almost exhausted. Through this crowd the seven Englishmen and twenty Sikhs walked their horses, and met not the least opposition. They reached the eastern side without insult or injury, passed through the gates, and descending the declivity found themselves in the rear of the whole Chinese army. The dangers through which they had passed were as nothing compared with those they had now to encounter. A shell burst in the air at this moment, followed by the discharge of the batteries on both sides. The battle had begun. The promised two hours had expired. The fugitives were some ten minutes too late.

The position of this small band in the midst of an Asiatic army actually engaged in mortal combat with their kinsmen may be better imagined than described. They were riding down the road which passed through the centre of the Chinese position, and the banks on each side of them were lined with matchlock-men, among whom the shells of the English guns were already bursting. Parties of cavalry were not wanting here, but out in the plain where the Tartar horsemen swarmed in thousands the greatest danger of all awaited them. Their movements were slow, painfully slow, and the progress was delayed by the necessity of waiting for those who were the worst mounted; but they were "all in the same boat, and like Englishmen would sink or swim together." In the accumulation of difficulties that stared them in the face not the least seemed to be that they were advancing in the teeth of their own countrymen's fire, which was growing fiercer every minute. In this critical moment men turned to Mr. Parkes, and Captain Brabazon expressed the belief of those present in a cool brave man in arduous extremity when he cried out "I vote Parkes decides what is to be done." To follow the main road seemed to be certain destruction and death without the power of resisting; for even assuming that some of them could have cut their way through the Tartar cavalry, and escaped from the English shell, they could hardly have avoided being shot down by the long lines of matchlock-men who were ready to fire on them the instant they saw their backs. There was only one possible avenue of escape, and that was to gain the right flank of the army, and endeavour to make their way by a detour round to the English lines. Assuredly this was not a very promising mode of escape, but it seemed to have the greatest chances of success. But when the Chinese, who had up to this regarded their movements without interfering, saw this change in their course, they at once took measures to stop it. A military mandarin said if they persisted in their attempt they would be treated as enemies and fired upon; but that he was willing to respect their flag of truce, and that if they would accompany him to the general's presence he would obtain a safe conduct for them. The offer was accepted, partly no doubt because it could not be refused, but still also on its own merits. Safe conducts during the heat of battle, even with civilised European peoples, are, however, not such easy things either to grant or to carry out. Mr. Parkes accepted his offer, therefore, and he, Mr. Loch, and the Sikh trooper Nalsing, bearing a flag of truce, rode off with the mandarin in search of the general, while the five other Europeans and the Sikh escort remained on the road awaiting their return. They proceeded to the left, where it was understood that Sankolinsin commanded in person. They met with some adventures even on this short journey. Coming suddenly upon a large body of infantry, they were almost pulled from their horses, and would have been killed but for the mandarin rushing between them and shouting to the men "not to fire." A short distance beyond this they halted, when the approach of Sankolinsin was announced by loud shouts of his name from the soldiery. Mr. Parkes at once addressed him, saying that they had come under a flag of truce, and that they wished to regain their army. The Chinese commander replied to his remarks on the usages of war in true Tartar fashion—with laughter and abuse. The soldiers pressed round the unfortunate Englishmen and placed their matchlocks against their bodies. Escape was hopeless, and death seemed inevitable. But insult was more the object of the Mongol general than their death. They were dragged before him and forced to press the ground with their heads at the feet of Sankolinsin. They were subjected to numerous other indignities, and at last, when it became evident that the battle was going against the Chinese, they were placed in one of the country carts and sent off to Pekin. While Mr. Parkes and Mr. Loch were thus ill-used, their comrades waiting on the road had fared no better. Shortly after their departure the Chinese soldiers begun to hustle and jeer at the Englishmen and their native escort, and as the firing increased and some of the Chinese were hit, they grew more violent. When the news was received of what had happened to Mr. Parkes, and of how Sankolinsin had laughed to scorn their claim to protection, the soldiers could no longer be restrained. The Englishmen and the natives were dragged from their horses, cruelly bound, and hurried to the rear, whence they followed at no great distance their companions in misfortune. While the greater portion of these events had been in progress, Colonel Walker, Mr. Thompson, and the men of the King's Dragoon

Guards, had been steadily pacing up and down on the embankment as arranged, in order to show the Chinese that they suspected no treachery and had no fears. They continued doing this until a French officer joined them, but on his getting into a dispute with some of the Chinese about his mule, he drew his pistol and fired at them. He was immediately killed. There was then no longer the least hope of restraining the Chinese, so the whole of the party spurred their horses and escaped to the English army under a heavy but ineffectual fire from matchlocks and gingalls. Their flight was the signal for the commencement of the battle, although at that very moment, had they only known it, the chief party of Englishmen had gained the road east of Chan-chia-wan, and, if the battle had only been delayed a quarter of an hour, they might all have escaped.

But the two hours of grace were up, and Sir Hope Grant saw no further use in delay. General Montauban was still more impatient, and the men were eager to engage. They had to win their camping ground that night, and the day was already far advanced. The French occupied the right wing, that is the position opposite the spot where we have seen Sankolinsin commanding in person, and a squadron of Fane's Horse had been lent them to supply their want of cavalry The battle began with the fire of their batteries, which galled the Chinese so much that the Tartar cavalry were ordered up to charge the guns, and right gallantly they did so. A battery was almost in their hands, its officers had to use their revolvers, when the Sikhs and a few French dragoons, led by Colonel Foley, the English Commissioner with the French force, gallantly charged them in turn, and compelled them to withdraw. Neither side derived much advantage from this portion of the contest, but the repulse of the Tartar cavalry enabled the French guns to renew their fire with great effect on the line of Chinese infantry. While the French were thus engaged on the right, the English troops had begun a vigorous attack on both the centre and their left. The Chinese appeared in such dense masses, and maintained so vigorous, but fortunately so ill-directed, a fire, that the English force made but little progress at either point. The action might have been indefinitely prolonged and left undecided, had not Sir Hope Grant suddenly resolved to reinforce his left with a portion of his centre, and to assail the enemy's right vigorously. This latter part of the battle began with a charge of some squadrons of Probyn's Horse against the bodies of mounted Tartars moving in the plain, whom they, with their gallant leader at their head, routed in the sight of the two armies. This overthrow of their chosen fighting-men greatly discouraged the rest of the Chinese soldiers, and when the infantry advanced with the Sikhs in front they slowly began to give ground. But even then there were none of the usual symptoms of a decisive victory. The French were so exhausted by their efforts that they had been compelled to halt, and General Montauban was obliged to curb his natural impetuosity, and to admit that he could take no part in the final attack on Chan-chia-wan. Sir Hope Grant, however, pressed on and occupied the town. He did not call in his men until they had seized without resistance a large camp about one mile west of the town, where they captured several guns. Thus ended the battle of Chan-chia-wan with the defeat and retreat of the strong army which Sankolinsin had raised in order to drive the barbarians into the sea, and which, as English witnesses stated, had occupied in the morning a position of very considerable strength in front of that town.

Although the battle was won, Sir Hope Grant, measuring the resistance with the eye of an experienced soldier, came to the conclusion that his force was not sufficiently strong to overawe so obstinate a foe; and accordingly ordered Sir Robert Napier to join him with as many troops as he could spare from the Tientsin garrison. Having thus provided for the arrival of reinforcements at an early date, he was willing to resume his onward march for Tungchow, where it was hoped some tidings would be obtained of the missing officers and men. Two days intervened before any decisive move was made, but Mr. Wade was sent under a flag of truce into Tungchow to collect information. But he failed to learn anything more about Mr. Parkes, than that he had quitted the town in safety after his final interview with Prince Tsai. Lord Elgin now hastened up from Hosiwu to join the military headquarters, and on the 21st September, the French having been joined by another brigade, offensive operations were recommenced. The delay had encouraged the Chinese to make another stand, and they had collected in considerable force for the defence of the Palikao bridge, which affords the means of crossing the Peiho west of Tungchow. Here again the battle commenced with a cavalry charge which, despite an accident that might have had more serious results, was completely successful. This achievement was followed up by the attack on several fortified positions which were not defended with any great amount of resolution, and while these matters were in progress on the side where the English were engaged, the French had carried the bridge with its twenty-five guns in position in very gallant style. The capture of this bridge and the dispersion of the troops, including the Imperial Guard, which had been entrusted with its defence, completed the discomfiture of the Chinese. Pekin itself lay almost at the mercy of the invader, and, unless diplomacy could succeed better than arms, nothing would prevent the hated foreigners violating its privacy not merely with their presence, but in the most unpalatable guise of armed victors.

The day after the battle at the Palikao bridge came a letter from Prince Kung, the Emperor's next brother, stating that Prince Tsai and his colleagues had not managed matters satisfactorily, and that he had been appointed with plenipotentiary powers for the discussion and decision of the peace question. But the prince went on to request a temporary suspension of hostilities—a demand with which no general or ambassador could have complied so long as officers were detained who had been seized in violation of the usages of war. Lord Elgin replied in the clearest terms that there could be no negotiations for peace until these prisoners were restored, and that if they were not sent back in safety the consequences would be most serious for the Chinese government. But even at this supreme moment of doubt and danger, the subtlety of Chinese diplomacy would have free play. Prince Kung was young in years and experience, but his finesse would have done credit to a grey-haired statesman. Unfortunately for him, the question had got beyond the stage for discussion: the English ambassador had stated the one condition on which negotiations would be renewed, and until that had been complied with there was no need to give ear to the threats, promises, and entreaties even of Prince Kung. As the prince gave no sign of yielding this point during the week's delay in bringing up the second division from Tientsin, Lord Elgin requested Sir Hope Grant to resume his march on Pekin, from which the advanced guard of the allied forces was distant little more than ten miles. The cavalry had reconnoitred almost up to the gates, and had returned with the report that the walls were strong and in good condition. The danger to a small army of attempting to occupy a great city of the size and population of Pekin is almost obvious; and, moreover, the consistent policy of the English authorities had been to cause the Chinese people as little injury and suffering as possible. Should an attack on the city become unavoidable, it was decided that the point attacked should be the Tartar quarter, including the palace, which occupied the northern half of the city. By this time it had become known that Parkes and Loch were living, that they were confined in the Kaou Meaou Temple, near the Tehshun Gate, and that latterly they had been fairly well treated.

In execution of the plan of attack that had been agreed upon, the allied forces marched round Pekin to the north-west corner of the walls, having as their object the Summer Palace of the Emperor at Yuen Min Yuen, not quite four miles distant from the city.

On the approach of the foreign army, Hienfung fled in terror from his palace, and sought shelter at Jehol, the hunting residence of the Emperors beyond the Wall. His flight was most precipitate; and the treasures of the Summer Palace were left at the mercy of the Western spoilers. The French soldiers had made the most of the start they had obtained, and left comparatively little for their English comrades, who, moreover, were restrained by the bonds of a stricter discipline. But the amount of prize property that remained was still considerable, and, by agreement between the two generals, it was divided in equal shares between the armies. The capture and occupation of the Summer Palace completed the European triumph, and obliged Prince Kung to promptly acquiesce in Lord Elgin's demand for the immediate surrender of the prisoners if he wished to avoid the far greater calamity of a foreign occupation of the Tartar quarter of Pekin and the appropriation of its vaster collection of treasures.

On the 6th of October Mr. Parkes wrote from his place of confinement that the French and English detained were to be returned on the 8th of the month, and that the Imperial commanders had been ordered at the same time to retire for a considerable distance from Pekin. These promises were carried out. Prince Kung was at last resolved to make all the concessions requisite to ensure the speedy conclusion of peace. The restoration of these captives removed what was thought to be the one obstacle to Lord Elgin's discussing the terms on which the invading force would retire and to the respective governments resuming diplomatic relations. It was fortunate for China that the exact fate of the other prisoners was unknown, and that Lord Elgin felt able, in consequence of the more friendly proceedings of Prince Kung, to overlook the earlier treatment of those now returned to him, for the narrative of Mr. Parkes and his fellow prisoners was one that tended to heighten the feeling of indignation at the original breach of faith. To say that they were barbarously ill-used is to employ a phrase conveying a very inadequate idea of the numerous indignities and the cruel personal treatment to which they were subjected. Under these great trials neither of these intrepid Englishmen wavered in their refusal to furnish any information or to make any concession compromising their country. Mr. Loch's part was in one sense the more easy, as his ignorance of the language prevented his replying, but in bodily suffering he had to pay a proportionately greater penalty. The incidents of their imprisonment afford the most creditable testimony to the superiority which the pride of race as well as "the equal mind in arduous circumstance" gives weak humanity over physical suffering. They are never likely to pass out of the public memory; and those who remember the daring and the chivalry which had inspired Mr. Parkes and Mr. Loch on the day when Prince Tsai's treachery and Sankolinsin's mastery were revealed, will not be disposed to consider it exaggerated praise to say that, for an adventure so honourably conceived and so nobly carried out, where the risk was never reckoned and where the penalty was so patiently borne, the pages of history may be searched almost in vain for an event that, in the dramatic elements of courage and suffering, presents such a complete and consistent record of human gallantry and devotion as the capture and subsequent captivity of these English gentlemen and their Sikh companion.

The further conditions as preliminary to the ratification of the Treaty of Tientsin were gradually, if reluctantly, complied with. On the 13th of October the north-east gate was handed over to the allied troops, but not before Sir Hope Grant had threatened to open fire on the walls. At the same time Prince Kung returned eight sowars of Fane's horse and one Frenchman, all the survivors, besides those already surrendered, of the small band which had ridden from Tungchow nearly a month before. The Chinese Prince stated in explanation that "a certain number were missing after the fight, or have died of their wounds or of sickness." But the narrative of the Sikhs was decisive as to the fate of the five Englishmen and their own comrades. They had been brutally bound with ropes which, although drawn as tight as human force could draw them, were tightened still more by cold water being poured upon the bands, and they had been maltreated in every form by a cruel enemy, and provided only with food of the most loathsome kind. Some of the prisoners were placed in cages. Lieutenant Anderson, a gallant young officer for whom future renown had been predicted, became delirious and died on the ninth day of his confinement. Mr. De Normann died a week later. What fate befell Captain Brabazon and his French companion the Abbé de Luc is uncertain, but the evidence on the subject inclines us to accept as accurate the statement that the Chinese commander in the fight at Palikao, enraged at his defeat, caused them to be executed on the bridge. The soldier Phipps endured for a longer time than Mr. Bowlby the taunts and ill-usage of their gaolers, but they at last shared the same fate, dying from the effects of their ill-treatment. The bodies of all the Englishmen, with the exception of Captain Brabazon, were restored, and of most of the Sikhs also. The Chinese officials were more barbarous in their cruelty than even the worst scum among their malefactors; for the prisoners in the gaols, far from adding to the tortures of the unfortunate Europeans, did everything in their power to mitigate their sufferings, alleviate their pains, and supply their wants.

The details of these cruel deeds raised a feeling of great horror in men's minds, and, although the desire to arrange the question of peace without delay was uppermost with Lord Elgin, still it was felt that some grave step was necessary to express the abhorrence with which England regarded this cruel and senseless outrage, and to bring home to the Chinese people and Government the fact that Englishmen could not be murdered with impunity. Lord Elgin refused to hold any further intercourse with the Chinese government until this great crime had been purged by some signal punishment. Sir Hope Grant and he had little difficulty in arriving at the decision that the best mode of expiation was to destroy the Summer Palace. The French commander refused to participate in the act which carried a permanent lesson of political necessity to the heart of the Pekin government, and which did more than any other incident of the campaign to show Hienfung that the hour had gone by for trifling. On the 18th of October the threat was carried into execution. The Summer Palace was destroyed by fire, and the sum of £100,000 was demanded and obtained from the Chinese as some compensation for the families of the murdered men. The palace of Yuen Min Yuen had been the scene of some of the worst sufferings of the English prisoners. From its apartments the high mandarins and the immediate courtiers of the Emperor had gloated over and enjoyed the spectacle of their foreign prisoners' agony. The whole of Pekin witnessed in return the destruction wrought to the Sovereign's abode by the indignant English, and the clouds of smoke hung for days like a vast black pall over the city.

That act of severe but just vengeance consummated, the negotiations for the ratification of the treaty were resumed, and, not unexpectedly, proceeded with the greater despatch because of the more abundant testimony provided that the English were in earnest. Mr. Parkes and Mr Loch were specially chosen to select an appropriate building within the city for the ratification of the treaty, and they rode through the streets at the head of an escort of English and Sikh cavalry. The same populace which a few weeks before had regarded their entry as the first symptom of a coming national triumph, now watched them with perhaps a closer scrutiny in anticipation of further barbarian exactions. The Hall of Ceremonies was selected as the place in which the ratifying act should be performed, while, as some punishment for the hostile part he had played, the palace of Prince Tsai was appropriated as the temporary official residence of Lord Elgin and Baron Gros. Both these buildings were situate in the Tartar quarter, but near the boundary wall of the Chinese city. The formal act of ratification was performed in this building on the 24th of October. Lord Elgin proceeded in a chair of state accompanied by his suite, and also by Sir Hope Grant with an escort of 100 officers and 500 troops, through the streets from the Anting Gate to the Hall of Ceremonies. Prince Kung, attended by a large body of civil and military mandarins, was there in readiness to produce the Imperial edict authorising him to attach the Emperor's seal to the treaty, and to accept the responsibility for his country of conforming with its terms and carrying out its stipulations. Some further delay was caused by the necessity of waiting until the edict should be received from the Emperor at Jehol authorising the publication of the treaty, not the least important point in connection with its conclusion if the millions of China were to understand and perform what their rulers had promised for them. That closing act was successfully achieved, and more rapidly than had been expected. The Pekinese beheld English troops and officers in residence in their midst for the first time, and when the army was withdrawn and the Plenipotentiary, Lord Elgin, transferred to his brother, Mr. Frederick Bruce, the charge of affairs in China as Resident Minister, the ice had been broken in the relations between the officials of the two countries, and the greatest, if not the last, barrier of Chinese exclusiveness had been removed. The last of the allied troops turned their backs upon Pekin on the 9th of November, and the greater portion of the expedition departed for India and Europe just before the cold weather set in A few days later the rivers were frozen and navigation had become impossible, which showed how narrow was the margin left for the completion of the operations of war.

The object which the more far-seeing of the English residents had from the first hour of difficulty stated to be necessary for satisfactory relations—direct intercourse with the Pekin Government—was thus obtained after a keen and bitter struggle for thirty years. The first war, closing with the treaty of Nankin, had contributed little more to the solution of the question than to place a few additional facilities in the way of trade. The provisions which might perhaps have possessed greater importance were never enforced, and were tacitly allowed to drop. A single disastrous war had not sufficed to bring the Pekin Government to reason or to wean it from traditions always remembered with feelings of pride. The years following the signature of that treaty were not without their clouds and causes of anxiety. The refusal alone to open the gates of Canton was a most serious breach of treaty. It was followed, as we have seen, by many acts of hostility, and by a general line of policy quite incompatible with friendship. The appointment of Yeh was made for very much the same reason as that of Lin had been—to humiliate the foreigner. It had been followed by an increased tension in the relations between the Canton yamen and the English authorities. The too much debated *Arrow* case came as the last of a long series of deeds in which all diplomatic courtesy was laid aside; and when once the English government resorted to force, it was compelled to continue it until satisfactory results were produced and its objects attained. Success at first seemed to come for the asking. Sir Michael Seymour's victorious operations round Canton and at the mouth of the Peiho simplified the task of diplomacy; and Lord Elgin, despite the original disadvantage under which he laboured from the outbreak of the Indian Mutiny and the diversion of the China Expedition, was enabled by the success of the admiral to conclude a favourable treaty at Tientsin. With the attempt twelve months later to obtain its ratification, the whole complication was suddenly revived. Admission to the Peiho was refused, and when an English squadron attempted to carry its way by force, it was repulsed with heavy loss. The defeat was the more important inasmuch as it was admittedly due, not to any mistake or rashness on the part of the admiral, but to the strength of the defences which the Chinese had erected in less than a year. Another twelvemonth was employed in the fitting out and despatch of an expedition of 20,000 men to bring the Court of Pekin to a more reasonable frame of mind, and Lord Elgin was again sent to China to complete the work he had half accomplished. We have seen how these purposes were effected, and how the superiority of European arms and discipline was again established over another brave but ill-prepared antagonist. Although vanquished, the Chinese may be said to have come out of this war with an increased military reputation. The war closed with a treaty enforcing all the concessions made by its predecessor. The right to station an ambassador in Pekin signified that the great barrier of all had been broken down. The old school of politicians were put completely out of court, and a young and intelligent prince, closely connected with the Emperor, assumed the personal charge of the foreign relations of the country. As one who had seen with his own eyes the misfortunes of his countrymen, Prince Kung was the more disposed to adhere to what he had promised to perform. Under his direction the ratified treaty of Tientsin became a bond of union instead of an element of discord between the cabinets of London and Pekin; and a termination was put, by an arrangement carried at the point of the sword, to the constant friction and recrimination which had been the prevailing characteristics of the intercourse for a whole generation. The Chinese had been subjected to a long and bitter lesson. They had at last learnt the virtue of submitting to necessity; but although they have profited to some extent both in peace and war by their experience, it requires some assurance to declare that they have even now accepted the inevitable. That remains the problem of the future; but in 1860 Prince Kung came to the sensible conclusion that for that period, and until China had recovered from her internal confusion, there was nothing to be gained and much to be lost by protracted resistance to the peoples of the West. Whatever could be retained by tact and finesse were to form part of the natural rights of China: but the privileges only to be asserted in face of Armstrong guns and rifles were to be abandoned with as good a grace as the injured feeling of a nation can ever display.

CHAPTER XX.

THE TAEPING REBELLION.

WE left the Taepings supreme at Nankin, but maintaining themselves there with some difficulty against two Imperial armies raised by the loyal efforts of the inhabitants of the central provinces. This was at the beginning of 1857, and there is no doubt that if the Government had avoided a conflict with the Europeans, and concentrated its efforts and power on the contest with the Taeping rebels they would have speedily annihilated the tottering fabric of Tien Wang's authority. But the respite of four years secured by the attention of the central government being monopolised by the foreign question enabled the Taepings to consolidate their position, augment their fighting forces, and present a more formidable front to the Imperial authorities. When Prince Kung learnt from Lord Elgin the full extent of the success of the Taepings on the Yangtse, of which the officials at Pekin seemed to possess a very imperfect and inaccurate knowledge, the Manchu authorities realised that it was a vital question for them to reassert their authority without further delay, but on beginning to put their new resolve into practice they soon experienced that the position of the Taepings in 1861 differed materially from what it was in 1857.

The course of events during that period must be briefly summarised. In 1858 the Imperialists under Tseng Kwofan and Chang Kwoliang renewed the siege of Nankin, but as the city was well supplied with provisions, and as the Imperialists were well known to have no intention of delivering an assault, the Taepings did not feel any apprehension. After the investment had continued for nearly a year, Chung Wang, who had now risen to the supreme place among the rebels, insisted on quitting the city before it was completely surrounded, with the object of beating up levies and generally relieving the pressure caused by the besiegers. In this endeavour he more than once experienced the unkindness of fortune, for when he had collected 5,000 good troops he was defeated in a vigorous attempt to cut his way through a far larger Imperial force. Such, however, was his reputation that the Imperial commanders before Nankin sent many of their men to assist the officers operating against him, and Chung Wang, seizing the opportunity, made his way by forced marches back to Nankin, overcoming such resistance as the enfeebled besiegers were able to offer. The whole of the year 1859 was passed in practical inaction, but at its close the Taepings only retained possession of four towns, besides Nankin, on the Yangtse. It again became necessary for Chung Wang to sally forth and assume the offensive in the rear and on the line of supplies of the beleaguering Imperialists. His main difficulty was in obtaining the consent of Tien Wang, who was at this time given over to religious pursuits or private excesses, and Chung Wang states that he only consented when he found that he could not stop him. In January, 1860, Chung Wang began what proved to be a very remarkable campaign. He put his men in good humour by distributing a large sum of money among them, and he succeeded in eluding the Imperial commanders, and in misleading them as to his intentions. While they thought he had gone off to relieve Ganking, he had really hastened to attack the important city of Hangchow, where much spoil and material for carrying on the war might be secured by the victor. He captured the city with little or no loss, on 19th March, 1860, but the Tartar city held out until relieved by Chang Kwoliang, who hastened from Nankin for the purpose. Once again the Imperial commanders in their anxiety to crush Chung Wang had reduced their force in front of Nankin to an excessively low condition, and the Taeping leader, placed in a desperate position, seized the only chance of safety by hastening from Hangchow to Nankin at full speed, and attacking the Imperial lines. This battle was fought early in the morning of a cold snowy day— 3 May, 1860—and resulted in the loss of 5,000 Imperialists, and the compulsory raising of the siege. The Taeping cause might have been resuscitated by this signal victory if Tien Wang had only shown himself able to act up to the great part he assumed, but not merely was he incapable of playing the part of either a warrior or a statesman, but his petty jealousy prevented his making use of the undoubted ability of his lieutenant Chung Wang, who after the greatest and most opportune of his successes was forbidden to re-enter Nankin.

The energy and spirit of Chung Wang impelled him to fresh enterprises, and seeing the hopelessness of Tien Wang, he determined to secure a base of operations for himself, which should enable him to hold his own in the warring strife of the realm, and perhaps to achieve the triumph of the cause with which he was associated. It says much for his military energy and skill that he was able to impart new vigour to the Taeping system, and to sustain on a new field his position single-handed against the main forces of the Empire. He determined to obtain possession of the important city of Soochow, on the Grand Canal, and not very far distant from Shanghai. On his way to effect this object he gained a great victory over Chang Kwoliang, who was himself killed in the battle. As the ex-Triad chief possessed great energy, his loss was a considerable one for the government, but his troops continued to oppose the advance of the Taepings, and fought and lost three battles before Chung Wang reached Soochow. That place was too large to be successfully defended by a small force, and the Imperialists hastily abandoned it. At this critical moment— May, 1860—Ho Kweitsin, the Viceroy of the Two Kiang, implored the aid of the English and French, who were at this moment completing their arrangements for the march on Pekin, against these rebels, and the French were so far favourable to the suggestion that they offered to render the assistance provided the English would combine with them. Mr. Bruce, however, declined the adventure, which is not surprising, considering that we were then engaged in serious hostilities with the Chinese, but the incident remains unique of a country asking another for assistance during the progress of a bitter and doubtful war. The utmost that Mr. Bruce would do was to issue a notification that Shanghai would not be allowed to again fall into the hands of an insurgent force. The Viceroy who solicited the aid was at least consistent. He memorialised the Throne, praying that the demands of the Europeans should be promptly granted, and that they should then be employed against the Taepings. His memorial was ill-timed. He was summoned to Pekin and executed for his very prudent advice. With the possession of Soochow, Chung Wang obtained fresh supplies of money, material, and men, and once more it was impossible to say to what height of success the Taepings might not attain. But Chung Wang was not satisfied with Soochow alone; he wished to gain possession of Shanghai.

Unfortunately for the realisation of his project, the Europeans had determined to defend Shanghai at all hazards, but Chung Wang believed either that they would not, or that their army being absent in the north they had not the power to carry out this resolve. The necessity of capturing Shanghai was rendered the greater in the eyes of Chung Wang by its being the base of hostile measures against himself, and by a measure which threatened him with a new peril. The wealthy Chinese merchants of Shanghai had formed a kind of patriotic association, and provided the funds for raising an European contingent. Two Americans, Ward and Burgevine, were taken into their pay, and in July, 1860, they, having raised a force of 100 Europeans and 200 Manilla men, began operations with an attack on Sunkiang, a large walled town about 20 miles from Shanghai. This first attack was repulsed with some loss, but Ward, afraid of losing the large reward he was promised for its capture, renewed the attack, and with better success, for he gained possession of a gate, and held it until the whole Imperial army had come up and stormed the town. After this success Ward was requested to attack Tsingpu, which was a far stronger place than Sunkiang, and where the Taepings had the benefit of the advice and leading of several Englishmen who had joined them. Ward attacked Tsingpu on 2 August, 1860, but he was repulsed with heavy loss. He returned to Shanghai for the purpose of raising another force and two larger guns, and then renewed the attack. It is impossible to say whether the place would have held out or not, but after seven days' bombardment Chung Wang suddenly appeared to the rescue, and, surprising Ward's force, drove it away in utter confusion, and with the loss of all its guns and stores. Encouraged by this success, Chung Wang then thought the time opportune for attacking Shanghai, and he accordingly marched against it, burning and plundering the villages along the road. The Imperialists had established a camp or stockade outside the western gate, and Chung Wang carried this without any difficulty, but when he reached the walls of the town he found a very different opponent in his path. The walls were lined with English and French troops, and when the Taepings attempted to enter the city they were received with a warm fire, which quickly sent them to the rightabout. Chung Wang renewed the attack at different points during the next four or five days, but he was then obliged to retreat. Before doing so, however, he sent a boasting message that he had come at the invitation of the French, who were traitors, and that he would have taken the city but for the foreigners, as "there was no city which his men could not storm." At this moment the attention of Chung Wang was called off to Nankin, which the Imperialists were investing for a sixth time, under Tseng Kwofan, who had been elevated to the Viceroyalty of the Two Kiang. Tien Wang, in despair, sent off an urgent summons to Chung Wang to come to his assistance, and although he went with reluctance he felt that he had no course but to obey.

Chung Wang found matters in great confusion at Nankin, and the chief Wangs quite incapable of following a wise course under the critical circumstances of the hour. When they enunciated such ridiculous statements that Tien Wang, as the lord of Heaven, had only to say the word and there would be peace, he curtly admonished them to buy rice and prepare for a siege. Having done what he could to place Nankin in an efficient state of defence, Chung Wang hastened back to Soochow to resume active preparations. It is unnecessary to describe these in detail; but although Chung Wang was twice defeated by a Manchu general named Paochiaou, he succeeded, by rapidity of movement, in holding his own against his more numerous adversaries. In the meantime an important change had taken place in the situation. The peace between China and the foreign Powers compelled a revision of the position at Shanghai. Admiral Hope sailed up to Nankin, interviewed the Wangs, and exacted from them a pledge that Shanghai should not be attacked for twelve months, and that the Taeping forces should not advance within a radius of thirty miles of that place. In consequence of this arrangement Ward and Burgevine were compelled to desist from recruiting Europeans; but after a brief interval they were taken into the Chinese service for the purpose of drilling Chinese soldiers, a measure from which the most important consequences were to flow, for it proved to be the origin of the Ever Victorious Army. These preparations were not far advanced when Chung Wang, elated by his capture of Ningpo and Hangchow, resolved to disregard Tien Wang's promise, and make a second attack on Shanghai, the possession of which he saw to be indispensable if his cause was to attain any brilliant triumph. He issued a proclamation that "the hour of the Manchus had come! Shanghai is a little place, and we have nothing to fear from it. We must take Shanghai to complete our dominions." The death of Hienfung seems to have encouraged Chung Wang to take what he hoped would prove a decisive step.

On the 14th January, 1862, the Taepings reached the immediate vicinity of the town and foreign settlement. The surrounding country was concealed by the smoke of the burning villages, which they had ruthlessly destroyed. The foreign settlement was crowded with thousands of fugitives, imploring the aid of the Europeans to save their houses and property. Their sufferings, which would at the best have been great, were aggravated by the exceptional severity of the winter. The English garrison of two native regiments and some artillery, even when supported by the volunteers, was far too weak to attempt more than the defence of the place; but this it was fortunately able to perform. The rebels, during the first week after their reappearance, plundered and burned in all directions, threatening even to make an attack on Woosung, the port at the mouth of the river, where they were repulsed by the French. Sir John Michel arrived at Shanghai with a small reinforcement of English troops, and Ward, having succeeded in disciplining two Chinese regiments of about one thousand strong in all, sallied forth from Sunkiang for the purpose of operating on the rear of the Taeping forces. Ward's capture of Quanfuling, with several hundred rebel boats which were frozen up in the river, should have warned the Taepings that it was nearly time for them to retire. However, they did not act as prudence would have dictated, and, during the whole of February their raids continued round Shanghai. The suburbs suffered from their attacks, the foreign factories and boats were not secure, and several outrages on the persons of foreigners remained unatoned for. It was impossible to tolerate any longer their enormities. The English and French commanders came to the determination to attack the rebels, to enforce the original agreement with Tien Wang, and to clear the country round Shanghai of the presence of the Taepings for the space of thirty miles.

On the 21st of February, therefore, a joint force composed of 336 English sailors and marines, 160 French seamen, and 600 men from Ward's contingent, accompanied by their respective commanders, with Admiral Hope in chief charge, advanced upon the village of Kachiaou, where the Taepings had strengthened their position, and placed guns on the walls. After a sharp engagement the place was stormed, Ward's men leading the attack with Burgevine at their head. The drilled Chinese behaved with great steadiness, but the Taepings were not to be dismayed by a single defeat. They even resumed their attacks on the Europeans. On one occasion Admiral Hope himself was compelled to retire before their superior numbers, and to summon fresh troops to his assistance. The reinforcements consisted of 450 Europeans and 700 of Ward's force, besides seven howitzers. With these it was determined to attack Tseedong, a place of great strength, surrounded by stone walls and ditches seven feet deep. The Taepings stood to their guns with great spirit, receiving the advancing troops with a very heavy fire. When, however, Ward's contingent, making a detour, appeared in the rear of the place, they hastily evacuated their positions, but the English sailors had carried the walls, and, caught between two fires, they offered a stubborn but futile resistance. More than seven hundred were killed and three hundred were taken prisoners. The favourable opinion formed of "the Ever Victorious Army" by the action at Kachiaou was confirmed by the more serious affair at Tseedong; and Mr. Bruce at Pekin brought it under the favourable notice of Prince Kung and the Chinese government. Having taken these hostile steps against the rebels, it necessarily followed that no advantage would accrue from any further hesitation with regard to allowing Europeans to enter the Imperial service for the purpose of opposing them. Ward was officially recognised, and allowed to purchase weapons and to engage officers. An Englishman contracted to convey nine thousand of the troops who had stormed Ganking from the Yangtse to Shanghai. These men were Honan braves, who had seen considerable service in the interior of China, and it was proposed that they should garrison the towns of Kiangsu accordingly as they were taken from the rebels. The arrival of General Staveley from Tientsin at the end of March, with portions of two English regiments (the 31st and 67th) put a new face on affairs, and showed that the time was at hand when it would be possible to carry out the threat of clearing the country round Shanghai for the space of thirty miles.

The first place to be attacked towards the realisation of this plan was the village of Wongkadza, about twelve miles west of Shanghai. Here the Taepings offered only a brief resistance, retiring to some stronger stockades four miles further west. General Staveley, considering that his men had done enough work for that day, halted them, intending to renew the attack the next morning. Unfortunately Ward was carried away by his impetuosity, and attacked this inner position with some five hundred of his own men. Admiral Hope accompanied him. The Taepings met them with a tremendous fire, and after several attempts to scale the works they were repulsed with heavy loss. Admiral Hope was wounded in the leg, seven officers were wounded, and seventy men killed and wounded. The attack was repeated in force on the following day, and after some fighting the Taepings evacuated their stockades. The next place attacked was the village of Tsipoo; and, notwithstanding their strong earthworks and three wide ditches, the rebels were driven out in a few hours. It was then determined to attack Kahding, Tsingpu, Nanjao, and Cholin, at which places the Taepings were known to have mustered in considerable strength.

The first place was taken with little resistance, and its capture was followed by preparations for the attack on Tsingpu, which were hastened rather than delayed by a desperate attempt to set fire to Shanghai. The plot was fortunately discovered in time, and the culprits captured and summarily executed to the number of two hundred. Early in May a strong force was assembled at Sunkiang, and proceeded by boat, on account of the difficulties of locomotion, to Tsingpu. The fire of the guns, in which the expedition was exceptionally strong, proved most destructive, and two breaches being pronounced practicable the place was carried by assault. The rebels fought well and up to the last, when they found flight impossible. The Chinese troops slew every man found in the place with arms in his hands. A few days later Nanjao was captured, but in the attack the French commander, Admiral Protet, a gallant officer who had been to the front during the whole of these operations, was shot dead. The rebels, disheartened by these successive defeats, rallied at Cholin, where they prepared to make a final stand. The allied force attacked Cholin on the 20th of May, and an English detachment carried it almost at the point of the bayonet. With this achievement the operations of the English troops came for the moment to an end, for a disaster to the imperial arms in their rear necessitated their turning their attention to a different quarter.

The troops summoned from Ganking had at last arrived to the number of five or six thousand men; and the Futai Sieh, who was on the point of being superseded to make room for Li Hung Chang, thought to employ them before his departure on some enterprise which should redound to his credit and restore his sinking fortunes. The operation was as hazardous as it was ambitious. The resolution he came to was to attack the city and forts of Taitsan, a place north-west of Shanghai, and not very distant from Chung Wang's headquarters at Soochow. The imperialist force reached Taitsan on the 12th of May, but less than two days later Chung Wang arrived in person at the head of ten thousand chosen troops to relieve the garrison. A battle ensued on the day following, when, notwithstanding their great superiority in numbers, the Taepings failed to obtain any success. In this extremity Chung Wang resorted to a stratagem. Two thousand of his men shaved their heads and pretended to desert to the Imperialists. When the battle was renewed at sunrise on the following morning this band threw aside their assumed character and turned upon the Imperialists. A dreadful slaughter ensued. Of the seven thousand Honan braves and the Tartars from Shanghai, five thousand fell on the field. The consequences of this disaster were to undo most of the good accomplished by General Staveley and his force. The Imperialists were for the moment dismayed, and the Taepings correspondingly encouraged.

General Staveley's communications were threatened, one detachment was cut off, and the General had to abandon his intended plan and retrace his steps to Shanghai.

Chung Wang then laid regular siege to Sunkiang, where Ward was in person, and he very nearly succeeded in carrying the place by escalade. The attempt was fortunately discovered by an English sailor just in time, and repulsed with a loss to the rebels of one hundred men. The Taepings continued to show great daring and activity before both Sunkiang and Tsingpu; and although the latter place was bravely defended, it became clear that the wisest course would be to evacuate it. A body of troops was therefore sent from Shanghai to form a junction with Ward at Sunkiang, and to effect the safe retreat of the Tsingpu garrison. The earlier proceedings were satisfactorily arranged, but the last act of all was grossly mismanaged and resulted in a catastrophe. Ward caused the place to be set on fire, when the Taepings, realising what was being done, hastened into the town, and assailed the retiring garrison. A scene of great confusion followed; many lives were lost, and the Commandant who had held it so courageously was taken prisoner. Chung Wang could therefore appeal to some facts to support his contention that he had got the better of the Europeans and the Imperialists in the province of Kiangsu.

From the scene of his successes Chung Wang was once more called away by the timidity or peril of Tien Wang, who was barely able to maintain his position at Nankin, but when he hastened off to assist the chief of the Taepings he found that he was out of favour, and that the jealousy or fear of his colleagues brought about his temporary disgrace and loss of title. Shortly after Chung Wang's departure Ward was killed in action and Burgevine succeeded to the command, but it soon became apparent that his relations with the Chinese authorities would not be smooth. General Ching was jealous of the Ever-Victorious Army and wished to have all the credit for himself. Li Hung Chang who had been appointed Futai or Governor of Kiangsu entertained doubts of the loyalty of this adventurer, and a feud broke out between them at an early stage of their relations. Burgevine was a man of high temper and strong passions, who was disposed to treat his Chinese colleagues with lofty superciliousness, and who met the wiles of the Futai with peremptory demands to recognise the claims of himself and his band. Nor was this all. Burgevine had designs of his own. Although the project had not taken definite form in his mind—for an unsubdued enemy was still in possession of the greater part of the province—the inclination was strong within him to play the part of military dictator with the Chinese; or failing that, to found an independent authority on some convenient spot of Celestial territory. Burgevine's character was described at a later period as being that of "a man of large promises and few works." "His popularity was great among a certain class. He was extravagant in his generosity, and as long as he had anything would divide it with his so-called friends, but never was a man of any administrative or military talent; and latterly, through the irritation caused by his unhealed wound and other causes, he was subject to violent paroxysms of anger, which rendered precarious the safety of any man who tendered to him advice that might be distasteful. He was extremely sensitive of his dignity, and held a higher position in Soochow than any foreigner did before." The Futai anticipated, perhaps, more than divined his wishes. In Burgevine he saw, very shortly after their coming into contact, not merely a man whom he disliked and distrusted, but one who, if allowed to pursue his plans unchecked, would in the end form a greater danger to the Imperial authority than even the Taepings. It is not possible to deny Li's shrewdness in reading the character of the man with whom he had to deal.

Although Burgevine had succeeded to Ward's command, he had not acquired the intimacy and confidence of the great Chinese merchant, Takee and his colleagues, at Shanghai, which had been the main cause of his predecessor's influence and position. In Ward they felt implicit faith; Burgevine was comparatively unknown, and where known only regarded with suspicion. The patriotism of the Shanghai merchants consisted in protecting their own possessions. Having succeeded in this they began to consider whether it was necessary to expend any longer the large sums voluntarily raised for the support of the contingent.

The Futai Li, in order to test his obedience, proposed that Burgevine and his men should be sent round by sea to Nankin to take part in the siege of that city. The ships were actually prepared for their conveyance, and the Taotai Wou, who had first fitted out a fleet against the rebels, was in readiness to accompany Burgevine, when Li and his colleague, as suspicious of Burgevine's compliance as they would have been indignant at his refusal, changed their plans and countermanded the expedition. Instead of carrying out this project, therefore, they laid a number of formal complaints before General Staveley as to Burgevine's conduct, and requested the English Government to remove him from his command, and to appoint an English officer in his place. The charges against Burgevine did not at this time amount to more than a certain laxness in regard to the expenditure of the force, a disregard for the wishes and prejudices of the Chinese Government, and the want of tact, or of the desire to conciliate, in his personal relations with the Futai. If Burgevine had resigned, all would have been well, but he regarded the position from the stand-point of the adventurer who believes that his own interests form a supreme law and are the highest good. As commander of the Ever-Victorious Army he was a personage to be considered even by foreign governments. He would not voluntarily surrender the position which alone preserved him from obscurity. Having come to this decision it was clear that even the partial execution of his plans must draw him into many errors of judgment which could not but embitter the conflict. The reply of the English commander was to the effect that personally he could not interfere, but that he would refer the matter to London as well as to Mr. Bruce at Pekin. In consequence of the delay thus caused the project of removing the force to Nankin was revived, and, the steamers having been chartered, Burgevine was requested to bring down his force from Sunkiang and to embark it at Shanghai. This he expressed his willingness to do on payment of his men who were two months in arrear, and on the settlement of all outstanding claims. Burgevine was supported by his troops. Whatever his dislike to the proposed move, theirs was immeasurably greater. They refused to move without the payment of all arrears; and on the 2nd of January they even went so far as to openly mutiny. Two days later Burgevine went to Shanghai, and had an interview with Takee. The meeting was stormy. Burgevine used personal violence towards the Shanghai merchant, whose attitude was at first overbearing, and he returned to his exasperated troops with the money, which he carried off by force. The Futai Li, on hearing of the assault on Takee, hastened to General Staveley to complain of Burgevine's gross insubordination in striking a mandarin, which by the law of China was punishable with death. Burgevine was dismissed the Chinese service, and the notice of this removal was forwarded by the English General, with a recommendation to him to give up his command without disturbance. This Burgevine did, for the advice of the English general was equivalent to a command, and on the 6th of January, 1863, Burgevine was back at Shanghai. Captain Holland was then placed in temporary command, while the answer of the Home Government was awaited to General Staveley's proposition to entrust the force to the care of a young captain of engineers, named Charles Gordon. Chung Wang returned at this moment to Soochow, and in Kiangsu the cause of the Taepings again revived through his energy. In February a detachment of Holland's force attacked Fushan, but met with a check, when the news of a serious defeat at Taitsan, where the former Futai Sieh had been defeated, compelled its speedy retreat to Sunkiang. Li had some reason to believe that Taitsan would surrender on the approach of the Imperialists, and he accordingly sent a large army, including 2,500 of the contingent, to attack it. The affair was badly managed. The assaulting party was stopped by a wide ditch; neither boats nor ladders arrived. The Taepings fired furiously on the exposed party, several officers were killed, and the men broke into confusion. The heavy guns stuck in the soft ground and had to be abandoned; and despite the good conduct of the contingent the Taepings achieved a decisive success (13th February). Chung Wang was able to feel that his old luck had not deserted him, and the Taepings of Kiangsu recovered all their former confidence in themselves and their leader. This disaster inflicted a rude blow on the confidence of Li and his assistants; and it was resolved that nothing should be attempted until the English officer, at last appointed, had assumed the active command.

Such was the position of affairs when on 24th March, 1863, Major Gordon took over the command of the Ever-Victorious Army. At that moment it was not merely discouraged by its recent reverses, but it was discontented with its position, and when Major Gordon assumed the command at Sunkiang there was some fear of an immediate mutiny. The new commander succeeded in allaying their discontent, and believing that active employment was the best cure for insubordination resolved to relieve Chanzu without delay. The Taepings were pressing the seige hard and would probably have captured the place before many days when Major Gordon attacked them in their stockades and drove them out with no inconsiderable loss. Having thus gained the confidence of his men and the approbation of the Chinese authorities Major Gordon returned to Sunkiang where he employed himself in energetically restoring the discipline of his force, and in preparing for his next move which at the request of Li Hung Chang was to be the capture of Quinsan. On the 24th April the force left Sunkiang to attack Quinsan, but it had not proceeded far when its course had to be altered to Taitsan, where, through an act of treachery, a force of 1,500 Imperialists had been annihilated. It became necessary to retrieve this disaster without delay, more especially as all hope of taking Quinsan had for the moment to be abandoned. Major Gordon at once altered the direction of his march, and joining *en route* General Ching, who had, on the news, broken up his camp before Quinsan, hastened as rapidly as possible to Taitsan, where he arrived on the 29th of April. Bad weather obliged the attack to be deferred until the 1st of May, when two stockades on the west side were carried, and their defenders compelled to flee, not into the town as they would have wished, but away from it towards Chanzu. On the following day, the attack was resumed on the north side, while the armed boats proceeded to assault the place from the creek. The firing continued from nine in the morning until five in the evening, when a breach seemed to be practicable, and two regiments were ordered to the assault. The rebels showed great courage and fortitude, swarming in the breach and pouring a heavy and well-directed fire upon the troops. The attack was momentarily checked; but while the stormers remained under such cover as they could find, the shells of two howitzers were playing over their heads and causing frightful havoc among the Taepings in the breach. But for these guns, Major Gordon did not think that the place would have been carried at all; but after some minutes of this firing at such close quarters, the rebels began to show signs of wavering. A party of troops gained the wall, a fresh regiment advanced towards the breach, and the disappearance of the snake flag showed that the Taeping leaders had given up the fight. Taitsan was thus captured, and the three previous disasters before it retrieved.

On the 4th of May the victorious force appeared before Quinsan, a place of considerable strength and possessing a formidable artillery directed by an European. The town was evidently too strong to be carried by an immediate attack, and Major Gordon's movements were further hampered by the conduct of his own men, who, upon their arrival at Quinsan, hurried off in detachments to Sunkiang for the purpose of disposing of their spoil. Ammunition had also fallen short, and the commander was consequently obliged to return to refit and to rally his men. At Sunkiang worse confusion followed, for the men, or rather the officers, broke out into mutiny on the occasion of Major Gordon appointing an English officer with the rank of lieutenant-colonel to the control of the commissariat, which had been completely neglected. The men who had served with Ward and Burgevine objected to this, and openly refused to obey orders. Fortunately the stores and ammunition were collected, and Major Gordon announced that he would march on the following morning, with or without the mutineers. Those who did not answer to their names at the end of the first half-march would be dismissed, and he spoke with the authority of one in complete accord with the Chinese authorities themselves. The soldiers obeyed him as a Chinese official, because he had been made a tsungping or brigadier-general, and the officers feared to disobey him as they would have liked on account of his commanding the source whence they were paid. The mutineers fell in, and a force of nearly 3,000 men, well-equipped and anxious for the fray, returned to Quinsan, where General Ching had, in the meanwhile, kept the rebels closely watched from a strong position defended by several stockades, and supported by the *Hyson* steamer. Immediately after his arrival, Major Gordon moved out his force to attack the stockades which the rebels had constructed on their right wing. These were strongly built; but as soon as the defenders perceived that the assailants had gained their flank they precipitately withdrew into Quinsan itself. General Ching wished the attack to be made on the Eastern Gate, opposite to which he had raised his own intrenchments, and by which he had announced his intention of forcing his way; but a brief inspection showed Major Gordon that that was the strongest point of the town, and that a direct attack upon it could only succeed, if at all, by a very considerable sacrifice of men. Like a prudent commander Major Gordon determined to reconnoitre; and, after much grumbling on the part of General Ching, he decided that the most hopeful plan was to carry some stockades situated seven miles west of the town, and thence assail Quinsan on the Soochow side, which was weaker than the others. These stockades were at a village called Chumze. On the 30th of May the force detailed for this work proceeded to carry it out. The *Hyson* and fifty imperial gun-boats conveyed the land force, which consisted of one regiment, some guns, and a large body of Imperialists. The rebels at Chumze offered hardly the least resistance; whether it was that they were dismayed at the sudden appearance of the enemy, or, as was stated at the time, because they considered themselves illtreated by their comrades in Quinsan. The *Hyson* vigorously pursued those who fled towards Soochow, and completed the effect of this success by the capture of a very strong and well-built fort covering a bridge at Ta Edin. An Imperialist garrison was installed there, and the *Hyson* continued the pursuit to within a mile of Soochow itself.

The defenders of Quinsan itself were terribly alarmed at the cutting off of their communications. They saw themselves on the point of being surrounded, and they yielded to the uncontrollable impulse of panic. During the night, after having suffered severely from the *Hyson* fire, the garrison evacuated the place, which might easily have held out; and General Ching had the personal satisfaction, on learning from some deserters of the flight of the garrison, of leading his men over the eastern walls which he had wished to assault. The importance of Quinsan was realised on its capture. Major Gordon pronounced it to be the key of Soochow, and at once resolved to establish his headquarters there, partly because of its natural advantages, but also and not less on account of its enabling him to gradually destroy the evil associations which the men had contracted at Sunkiang.

The change was not acceptable, however, to the force itself; and the artillery in particular refused to obey orders, and threatened to shoot their officers. Discipline was, however, promptly reasserted by the energy of the commander, who ordered the principal ringleader to be shot and "the Ever-Victorious Army" became gradually reconciled to its new position at Quinsan. After the capture of Quinsan there was a cessation of active operations for nearly two months. It was the height of summer and the new troops had to be drilled. The difficulty with Ching, who took all the credit for the capture of Quinsan to himself, was arranged through the mediation of Dr. Macartney, who had just left the English army to become Li's right-hand man. Two other circumstances occurred to embarrass the young commander. There were rumours of some meditated movement on the part of Burgevine, who had returned from Pekin with letters exculpating him and who endeavoured to recover the command in spite of Li Hung Chang, and there was a further manifestation of insubordination in the force, which, as Gordon said, bore more resemblance to a rabble than the magnificent army it was popularly supposed to be. The artillery had been cowed by Major Gordon's vigour, but its efficiency remained more doubtful than could be satisfactory to the general responsible for its condition, and also relying upon it as the most potent arm of his force. He resolved to remove the old commander, and to appoint an English officer, Major

Tapp, in his place. On carrying his determination into effect the officers sent in "a round robin," refusing to accept a new officer. This was on the 25th of July, and the expedition which had been decided upon against Wokong had consequently to set out the following morning without a single artillery officer. In face of the inflexible resolve of the leader, however, the officers repented, and appeared in a body at the camp begging to be taken back, and expressing their willingness to accept " Major Tapp or anyone else " as their colonel.

With these troops, part of whom had only just returned to a proper sense of discipline, Gordon proceeded to attack Kahpoo, a place on the Grand Canal south of Soochow, where the rebels held two strongly-built stone forts. The force had been strengthened by the addition of another steamer, the *Firefly*, a sister vessel to the *Hyson*. Major Gordon arrived before Kahpoo on the 27th of July; and the garrison, evidently taken by surprise, made scarcely the least resistance. The capture of Kahpoo placed Gordon's force between Soochow and Wokong, the next object of attack. At Wokong the rebels were equally unprepared. The garrison at Kahpoo, thinking only of its own safety, had fled to Soochow, leaving their comrades at Wokong unwarned and to their fate. So heedless were the Taepings at this place of all danger from the north, that they had even neglected to occupy a strong stone fort situated about 1,000 yards north of the walls. The Taepings attempted too late to repair their error, and the loss of this fort caused them that of all their other stockades. Wokong itself was too weak to offer any effectual resistance : and the garrison on the eve of the assault ordered for the 29th of July sent out a request for quarter, which was granted, and the place surrendered without further fighting. Meanwhile an event of far greater importance had happened than even the capture of these towns, although they formed the necessary preliminary to the investment of Soochow. Burgevine had come to the decision to join the Taepings.

Disappointed in his hope of receiving the command, Burgevine remained on at Shanghai, employing his time in watching the varying phases of a campaign in which he longed to take part, and of which he believed that it was only his due to have the direction, but still hesitating as to what decision it behoved him to take. His contempt for all Chinese officials became hatred of the bitterest kind of the Futai, by whom he had been not merely thwarted but over-reached, and predisposed him to regard with no unfavourable eye the idea of joining his fortunes to those of the rebel Taepings. To him in this frame of mind came some of the dismissed officers and men of the Ward force, appealing to his vanity by declaring that his soldiers remembered him with affection, and that he had only to hoist his flag for most of his old followers to rally round him. There was little to marvel at if he also was not free from some feeling of jealousy at the success and growing fame of Major Gordon, for whom he simulated a warm friendship. The combination of motives proved altogether irresistible as soon as he found that several hundred European adventurers were ready to accompany him into the ranks of the Taepings, and to endeavour to do for them what they had failed to perform for the Imperialists. On the 15th of July, Dr. Macartney wrote to Major Gordon stating that he had positive information that Burgevine was enlisting men for some enterprise, that he had already collected about 300 Europeans, and that he had even gone so far as to choose a special flag, a white diamond on a red ground, and containing a black star in the centre of the diamond. On the 21st of the same month Burgevine wrote to Major Gordon saying that there would be many rumours about him, but that he was not to believe any of them, and that he would come and see him shortly. This letter was written as a blind, and, unfortunately, Major Gordon attached greater value to Burgevine's word than he did to the precise information of Dr. Macartney. He was too much disposed to think that, as the officer who had to a certain extent superseded Burgevine in the command, he was bound to take the most favourable view of all his actions, and to trust implicitly in his good faith. Major Gordon, trusting to his word, made himself personally responsible to the Chinese authorities for his good faith, and thus Burgevine escaped arrest. Burgevine's plans had been deeply laid. He had been long in correspondence with the Taepings, and his terms had been accepted. He proclaimed his hostility to the Government by seizing one of their new steamers.

At this very moment Major Gordon came to the decision to resign, and he hastened back to Shanghai in order to place his withdrawal from the force in the hands of the Futai. He arrived there on the very day that Burgevine seized the *Kajow* steamer at Sunkiang, and on hearing the news he at once withdrew his resignation, which had been made partly from irritation at the irregular payment of his men, and also on account of the cruelty of General Ching. Not merely did he withdraw his resignation, but he hastened back to Quinsan, into which he rode on the night of the very same day that had witnessed his departure. The immediate and most pressing danger was from the possible defection of the force to its old leader, when, with the large stores of artillery and ammunition at Quinsan in their possession, not even Shanghai, with its very weak foreign garrison, could be considered safe from attack. As a measure of precaution Major Gordon sent some of his heavy guns and stores back to Taitsan, where the English commander, General Brown, consented to guard them, while he hastened off to Kahpoo, now threatened both by the Soochow force and by the foreign adventurers acting under Burgevine. He arrived at a most critical moment. The garrison was hard pressed. General Ching had gone back to Shanghai, and only the presence of the *Hyson* prevented the rebels, who were well-armed and possessed an efficient artillery, from carrying the fort by a rush. The arrival of Major Gordon with 150 men on board his third steamer, the *Cricket*, restored the confidence of the defenders, but there was no doubt that Burgevine had lost a most favourable opportunity, for if he had attacked this place instead of proceeding to Soochow it must have fallen.

General Ching, who was a man of almost extraordinary energy and restlessness, resolved to signalise his return to the field by some striking act while Major Gordon was completing his preparations at Quinsan for a fresh effort. His head-quarters were at the strong fort of Ta Edin, on the creek leading from Quinsan to Soochow, and having the *Hyson* with him, he determined to make a dash to some point nearer the great rebel stronghold. On the 30th of August he had seized the position of Waiquaidong, where, in three days, he threw up stockades, admirably constructed, and which could not have been carried save by a great effort on the part of the whole of the Soochow garrison. Towards the end of September, Major Gordon, fearing lest the rebels, who had now the supposed advantage of Burgevine's presence and advice, might make some attempt to cut off

General Ching's lengthy communications, moved forward to Waiquaidong to support him; but when he arrived, he found that the impatient mandarin encouraged either by the news of his approach or at the inaction of the Taepings in Soochow, had made a still further advance of two miles, so that he was only 1,000 yards distant from the rebel stockades in front of the East Gate. Major Gordon had at this time been reinforced by the Franco-Chinese corps, which had been well disciplined, under the command of Captain Bonnefoy, while the necessity of leaving any strong garrison at Quinsan had been obviated by the loan of 200 Belooches from General Brown's force. The rebel position having been carefully reconnoitred, both on the east and on the south, Major Gordon determined that the first step necessary for its proper beleaguerment was to seize and fortify the village of Patachiaou, about one mile south of the city wall. The village, although strongly stockaded, was evacuated by the garrison after a feeble resistance, and an attempt to recover it a few hours later by Mow Wang in person resulted in a rude repulse chiefly on account of the effective fire of the *Hyson*. Burgevine, instead of fighting the battles of the failing cause he had adopted, was travelling about the country: at one moment in the capital interviewing Tien Wang and his ministers, at another going about in disguise even in the streets of Shanghai. But during the weeks when General Ching might have been taken at a disadvantage, and when it was quite possible to recover some of the places which had been lost, he was absent from the scene of military operations. After the capture of Patachiaou most of the troops and the steamers that had taken it were sent back to Waiquaidong, but Major Gordon remained there with a select body of his men and three howitzers. The rebels had not resigned themselves to the loss of Patachiaou, and on the 1st of October they made a regular attempt to recover it. They brought the *Kajow* into action, and, as it had found a daring commander in a man named Jones, its assistance proved very considerable. They had also a 32-pounder gun on board a junk, and this enabled them to overcome the fire of Gordon's howitzers and also of the *Hyson*, which arrived from Waiquaidong during the engagement. But notwithstanding the superiority of their artillery, the rebels hesitated to come to close quarters, and when Major Gordon and Captain Bonnefoy led a sortie against them at the end of the day they retired precipitately.

At this stage Burgevine wrote to Major Gordon two letters—the first exalting the Taepings, and the second written two days later asking for an interview, whereupon he expressed his desire to surrender on the provision of personal safety. He assigned the state of his health as the cause of this change, but there was never the least doubt that the true reason of this altered view was dissatisfaction with his treatment by the Taeping leaders and a conviction of the impossibility of success. Inside Soochow, and at Nankin, it was possible to see with clearer eyes than at Shanghai that the Taeping cause was one that could not be resuscitated. But although Burgevine soon and very clearly saw the hopelessness of the Taeping movement, he had by no means made up his mind to go over to the Imperialists. With a considerable number of European followers at his beck and call, and with a profound and ineradicable contempt for the whole Chinese official world, he was loth to lose or surrender the position which gave him a certain importance. He vacillated between a number of suggestions, and the last he came to was the most remarkable, at the same time that it revealed more clearly than any other the vain and meretricious character of the man. In his second interview with Major Gordon he proposed that that officer should join him, and combining the whole force of the Europeans and the disciplined Chinese, seize Soochow, and establish an independent authority of their own. It was the old filibustering idea, revived under the most unfavourable circumstances, of fighting for their own hand, dragging the European name in the dirt, and founding an independent authority of some vague, undefinable and transitory character. Major Gordon listened to the unfolding of this scheme of miserable treachery, and only his strong sense of the utter impossibility, and indeed the ridiculousness of the project, prevented his contempt and indignation finding forcible expression. Burgevine, the traitor to the imperial cause, the man whose health would not allow him to do his duty to his new masters in Soochow, thus revealed his plan for defying all parties, and for deciding the fate of the Dragon Throne. The only reply he received was the cold one that it would be better and wiser to confine his attention to the question of whether he intended to yield or not, instead of discussing idle schemes of "vaulting ambition."

Meantime, Chung Wang had come down from Nankin to superintend the defence of Soochow; and in face of a more capable opponent he still did not despair of success, or at the least of making a good fight of it. He formed the plan of assuming the offensive against Chanzu whilst General Ching was employed in erecting his stockades step by step nearer to the eastern wall of Soochow. In order to prevent the realisation of this project Major Gordon made several demonstrations on the western side of Soochow, which had the effect of inducing Chung Wang to defer his departure. At this conjuncture serious news arrived from the south. A large rebel force, assembled from Chekiang and the silk districts south of the Taho lake, had moved up the Grand Canal and held the garrison of Wokong in close leaguer. On the 10th of October the Imperialists stationed there made a sortie, but were driven back with the loss of several hundred men killed and wounded. Their provisions were almost exhausted, and it was evident that unless relieved they could not hold out many days longer. On the 12th of October Major Gordon therefore hastened to their succour. The rebels held a position south of Wokong, and, as they felt sure of a safe retreat, they fought with great determination. The battle lasted three hours; the guns had to be brought up to within fifty yards of the stockade, and the whole affair is described as one of the hardest fought actions of the war. On the return of the contingent to Patachiaou, about thirty Europeans deserted the rebels, but Burgevine and one or two others were not with them. Chung Wang had seized the opportunity of Gordon's departure for the relief of Wokong to carry out his scheme against Chanzu. Taking the *Kajow* with him, and a considerable number of the foreign adventurers, he reached Monding, where the Imperialists were strongly intrenched at the junction of the main creek from Chanzu with the canal. He attacked them, and a severely contested struggle ensued, in which at first the Taepings carried everything before them. But the fortune of the day soon veered round. The *Kajow* was sunk by a lucky shot, great havoc was wrought by the explosion of a powder-boat, and the Imperialists remained masters of a hard-fought field. The defection of the Europeans placed Burgevine in serious peril, and only Major Gordon's urgent representations and acts of courtesy to the Mow Wang saved his life. The Taeping leader, struck by the gallantry and fair dealing of the English officer, set Burgevine free, and the American consul thanked Major Gordon for his great kindness to that misguided officer. Burgevine came out of the whole complication with a reputation in every way tarnished. He had not even the most common courage which would have impelled him to stay in Soochow and take the chances of the party to which he had attached himself. Whatever his natural talents might have been, his vanity and weakness obscured them all. With the inclination to create an infinity of mischief, it must be considered fortunate that his ability was so small, for his opportunities were abundant.

The conclusion of the Burgevine incident removed a weight from Major Gordon's mind. Established on the east and south of Soochow, he determined to secure a similar position on its western side, when he would be able to intercept the communications still held by the garrison across the Taho lake. In order to attain this object it was necessary, in the first place, to carry the stockades at Wuliungchow, a village two miles west of Patachiaou. The place was captured at the first attack and successfully held, notwithstanding a fierce attempt to recover it under the personal direction of Chung Wang, who returned for the express purpose. This success was followed by others. Another large body of rebels had come up from the south and assailed the garrison of Wokong. On the 26th of October one of Gordon's lieutenants, Major Kirkham, inflicted a severe defeat upon them, and vigorously pursued them for several miles. The next operation undertaken was the capture of the village of Leeku, three miles north of Soochow, as the preliminary to investing the city on the north. Here Major Gordon resorted to his usual flanking tactics, and with conspicuous success. The rebels fought well; one officer was killed at Gordon's side, and the men in the stockade were cut down with the exception of about forty, who were made prisoners. Soochow was then assailed on the northern as well as on the other sides, but Chung Wang's army still served to keep open communications by means of the Grand Canal. That army had its principal quarters at Wusieh, where it was kept in check by a large Imperialist force under Santajin, Li's brother, who had advanced from Kongyin on the Yangtse. Major Gordon's main difficulty now arose from the insufficiency of his force to hold so wide an extent of country; and in order to procure a reinforcement from Santajin, he agreed to assist that commander against his able opponent Chung Wang. With a view to accomplishing this the Taeping position at Wanti, two miles north of Leeku, was attacked and captured.

At this stage of the campaign there were 13,500 men round Soochow, and of these, 8,500 were fully occupied in the defence of the stockades, leaving the very small number of 5,000 men available for active measures in the field. On the other hand, Santajin had not fewer than 20,000, and possibly as many as 30,000 men under his orders. But the Taepings still enjoyed the numerical superiority. They had 40,000 men in Soochow, 20,000 at Wusieh, and Chung Wang occupied a camp, half-way between these places, with 18,000 followers. The presence of Chung Wang was also estimated to be worth a corps of 5,000 soldiers. Had Gordon been free to act, his plan of campaign would have been simple and decisive. He would have effected a junction of his forces with Santajin, he would have overwhelmed Chung Wang's 18,000 with his combined army of double that strength, and he would have appeared at the head of his victorious troops before the bewildered garrison of Wusieh. It would probably have terminated the campaign at a stroke. Even the decisive defeat of Chung Wang alone might have entailed the collapse of the cause now tottering to its fall. But Major Gordon had to consider not merely the military quality of his allies, but also their jealousies and differences. General Ching hated Santajin on private grounds as well as on public. He desired a monopoly of the profit and honour of the campaign. His own reputation would be made by the capture of Soochow. It would be diminished and cast into the shade were another imperial commander to defeat Chung Wang and close the line of the Grand Canal. Were Gordon to detach himself from General Ching he could not feel sure what that jealous and impulsive commander would do. He would certainly not preserve the vigilant defensive before Soochow necessary to ensure the safety of the army operating to the north. The commander of the Ever-Victorious Army had consequently to abandon the tempting idea of crushing Chung Wang and to have recourse to slower methods.

On the 19th of November Major Gordon collected the whole of his available force to attack Fusaiquan, a place on the Grand Canal six miles north of Soochow. Here the rebels had barred the canal at three different points, while on the banks they occupied eight earthworks, which were fortunately in a very incomplete state. A desperate resistance was expected from the rebels at this advantageous spot, but they preferred their safety to their duty, and retreated to Wusieh with hardly any loss. In consequence of this reverse Chung Wang withdrew his forces from his camp in face of Santajin, and concentrated his men at Monding and Wusieh for the defence of the Grand Canal. The investment of Soochow being now as complete as the number of troops under the imperial standard would allow of, Major Gordon returned to General Ching's stockades in front of that place, with the view of resuming the attack on the eastern gate. General Ching and Captain Bonnefoy had met with a slight repulse there on the 14th of October. The stockade in front of the east gate was known by the name of the Low Mun, and had been strengthened to the best knowledge of the Taeping engineers. Their position was exceedingly formidable, consisting of a line of breastwork defended at intervals with circular stockades. Major Gordon decided upon making a night attack, and he arranged his plans from the information provided by the European and other deserters who had been inside. The Taepings were not without their spies and sympathisers also, and the intended attempt was revealed to them. The attack was made at two in the morning of the 27th of November, but the rebels had mustered in force and received Major Gordon's men with tremendous volleys. Even then the disciplined troops would not give way, and encouraged by the example of their leader, who seemed to be at the front and at every point at the same moment, fairly held their own on the edge of the enemy's position. Unfortunately the troops in support behaved badly, and got confused from the heavy fire of the Taepings which never slackened. Some of them absolutely retired and others were landed at the wrong places. Major Gordon had to hasten to the rear to restore order, and during his absence the advanced guard were expelled from their position by a forward movement led by Mow Wang in person. The attack had failed, and there was nothing to do save to draw off the troops with as little further loss as possible. This was Major Gordon's first defeat, but it was so evidently due to the accidents inseparable from a night attempt, and to the fact that the surprise had been revealed, that it produced a less discouraging effect on officers and men than might have seemed probable. Up to this day Major Gordon had obtained thirteen distinct victories besides the advantage in many minor skirmishes.

Undismayed by this reverse Major Gordon collected all his troops and artillery from the other stockades, and resolved to attack the Low Mun position with his whole force. He also collected all his heavy guns and mortars and cannonaded the rebel stockade for some time; but on an advance being ordered the assailants were compelled to retire by the fire which the Taepings brought to bear on them from every available point. Chung Wang had hastened down from Wusieh to take part in the defence of what was rightly regarded as the key of the position at Soochow, and both he and Mow Wang superintended in person the defence of the Low Mun stockade. After a further cannonade the advance was again sounded, but this second attack would also have failed had not the officers and men boldly plunged into the moat or creek and swum across. The whole of the stockades and a stone fort were then carried, and the imperial forces firmly established at a point only 900 yards from the inner wall of Soochow. Six officers and fifty men were killed, and three officers, five Europeans, and 128 men were wounded in this successful attack. The capture of the Low Mun stockades meant practically the fall of Soochow. Chung Wang then left it to its fate, and all the other Wangs except Mow Wang were in favour of coming to terms with the Imperialists. Even before this defeat Lar Wang had entered into communications with General Ching for coming over, and as he had the majority of the troops at Soochow under his orders Mow Wang was practically powerless, although resolute to defend the place to the last. Several interviews took place between the Wangs and General Ching and Li Hung Chang. Major Gordon also saw the former, and had one interview with Lar Wang in person. The English officer proposed as the most feasible plan his surrendering one of the gates. During all this period Major Gordon had impressed on both of his Chinese colleagues the imperative necessity there was, for reasons of both policy and prudence, to deal leniently and honourably by the rebel chiefs. All seemed to be going well. General Ching took an oath of brotherhood with Lar Wang, Li Hung Chang agreed with everything that fell from Gordon's lips. The only one exempted from this tacit understanding was Mow Wang, always in favour of fighting it out and defending the town; and his name was not mentioned for the simple reason that he had nothing to do with the negotiations. For Mow Wang Major Gordon had formed the esteem due to a gallant enemy, and he resolved to spare no effort to save his life. His benevolent intentions were thwarted by the events that had occurred within Soochow. Mow Wang had been murdered by the other Wangs, who feared that he might detect their plans and prevent their being carried out. The death of Mow Wang removed the only leader who was heartily opposed to the surrender of Soochow, and on the day after this chief's murder the Imperialists received possession of one of the gates. The inside of the city had been the scene of the most dreadful confusion. Mow Wang's men had sought to avenge their leader's death, and on the other hand the followers of Lar Wang had shaved their heads in token of their adhesion to the Imperialist cause. Some of the more prudent of the Wangs, not knowing what turn events might take amid the prevailing discord, secured their safety by a timely flight. Major Gordon kept his force well in hand, and refused to allow any of the men to enter the city, where they would certainly have exercised the privileges of a mercenary force in respect of pillage. Instead of this Major Gordon endeavoured to obtain for them two months' pay from the Futai, which that official stated his inability to procure. Major Gordon thereupon resigned in disgust, and on succeeding in obtaining one month's pay for his men, he sent them back to Quinsan without a disturbance.

The departure of the Ever-Victorious Army for its headquarters was regarded by the Chinese officials with great satisfaction and for several reasons. In the flush of the success at Soochow both that force and its commander seemed in the way of the Futai, and to diminish the extent of his triumph. Neither Li nor Ching also had the least wish for any of the ex-rebel chiefs, men of ability and accustomed to command, to be taken into the service of the Government. Of men of that kind there were already enough. General Ching himself was a sufficiently formidable rival to the Futai, without any assistance and encouragement from Lar Wang and the others. Li had no wish to save them from the fate of rebels; and although he had promised, and General Ching had sworn to, their personal safety, he was bent on getting rid of them in one way or another. He feared Major Gordon, but he also thought that the time had arrived when he could dispense with him and the foreign-drilled legion in the same way as he had got rid of Sherard Osborn and his fleet. The departure of the Quinsan force left him free to follow his own inclination. The Wangs were invited to an entertainment at the Futai's boat, and Major Gordon saw them both in the city and subsequently when on their way to Li Hung Chang. The exact circumstances of their fate were never known; but nine headless bodies were discovered on the opposite side of the creek, and not far distant from the Futai's quarters. It then became evident that Lar Wang and his fellow Wangs had been brutally murdered. Major Gordon was disposed to take the office of their avenger into his own hands, but the opportunity of doing so fortunately did not present itself. He hastened back to Quinsan, where he refused to act any longer with such false and dishonourable colleagues. The matter was reported to Pekin. Both the mandarins sought to clear themselves by accusing the other; and a special decree came from Pekin conferring on the English officer a very high order and the sum of 10,000 taels. Major Gordon returned the money, and expressed his regret at being unable to accept any token of honour from the Emperor in consequence of the Soochow affair.

A variety of reasons, all equally creditable to Major Gordon's judgment and single-mindedness, induced him after two months' retirement to abandon his inaction and to sink his difference with the Futai. He saw very clearly that the sluggishness of the imperial commanders would result in the prolongation of the struggle with all its attendant evils, whereas, if he took the field, he would be able to bring it to a conclusion within two months. Moreover, the Quinsan force, never very amenable to discipline, shook off all restraint when in quarters, and promised to become as dangerous to the government in whose pay it was as to the enemy against whom it was engaged to fight. Major Gordon, in view of these facts, came to the prompt decision that it was his duty, and the course most calculated to do good for him to retake the field, and strive as energetically as possible to expel the rebels from the small part of Kiangsu still remaining in their possession. On the 18th of February, 1864, he accordingly left Quinsan at the head of his men who showed great satisfaction at the return to active campaigning. Wusieh had been evacuated on the fall of Soochow, and Chung Wang's force retired to Changchow, while that chief himself returned to Nankin. A few weeks later General Ching had seized Pingwang, thus obtaining the command of another entrance into the Taho lake. Santajin established his force in a camp not far distant from Changchow, and engaged the rebels in almost daily skirmishes. This was the position of affairs when Major Gordon took the field towards the end of February, and he at once resolved to carry the war into a new country by crossing the Taho lake and attacking the town of Yesing on its western shores. By seizing this and the adjoining towns he hoped to cut the rebellion in two, and to be able to attack Changchow in the rear. The operations at Yesing occupied two days; but at last the rebel stockades were carried with tremendous loss, not only to the defenders but also to a relieving force sent from Liyang. Five thousand prisoners were also taken. Liyang itself was the next place to be attacked; but the intricacy of the country, which was intersected by creeks and canals, added to the fact that the whole region had been desolated by famine, and that the rebels had broken all the bridges, rendered this undertaking one of great difficulty and some risk. However, Major Gordon's fortitude vanquished all obstacles, and when he appeared before Liyang he found that the rebel leaders in possession of the town had come to the decision to surrender. At this place Major Gordon came into communication with the general Paochiaou, who was covering the siege operations against Nankin which Tseng Kwofan was pressing with ever-increasing vigour. The surrender of Liyang proved the more important, as the fortifications were found to be admirably constructed, and as it contained a garrison of fifteen thousand men and a plentiful supply of provisions. From Liyang Major Gordon marched on Kintang, a town due north of Liyang, and about half-way between Changchow and Nankin. The capture of Kintang, by placing Gordon's force within striking distance of Changchow and its communications, would have compelled the rebels to suspend these operations and recall their forces. Unfortunately the attack on Kintang revealed unexpected difficulties. The garrison showed extraordinary determination; and although the wall was breached by the heavy fire, two attempts to assault were repulsed with heavy loss, the more serious inasmuch as Major Gordon was himself wounded below the knee, and compelled to retire to his boat. This was the second defeat Gordon had experienced.

In consequence of this reverse, which dashed the cup of success from Gordon's hands when he seemed on the point of bringing the campaign to a close in the most brilliant manner, the force had to retreat to Liyang, whence the commander hastened back with one thousand men to Wusieh. He reached Wusieh on the 25th March, four days after the repulse at Kintang, and he there learnt that Fushan had been taken and that Chanzu was being closely attacked. The Imperialists had fared better in the south. General Ching had captured Kashingfoo, a strong place in Chekiang, and on the very same day as the repulse at Kintang Tso Tsung Tang had recovered Hangchow. Major Gordon, although still incapacitated by his wound from taking his usual foremost place in the battle, directed all operations from his boat. He succeeded, after numerous skirmishes, in compelling the Taepings to quit their position before Chanzu; but they drew up in force at the village of Waisso, where they offered him battle. Most unfortunately Major Gordon had to entrust the conduct of the attack to his lieutenants, Colonels Howard and Rhodes, while he superintended the advance of the gunboats up the creek. Finding the banks were too high to admit of these being usefully employed, and failing to establish communications with the infantry, he discreetly returned to his camp, where he found everything in the most dreadful confusion owing to a terrible disaster. The infantry in fact had been out-manœuvred and routed with tremendous loss. Seven officers and 265 men had been killed, and one officer and sixty-two men wounded. Such an overwhelming disaster would have crushed any ordinary commander, particularly when coming so soon after such a rude defeat as that at Kintang. It only roused Major Gordon to increased activity. He at once took energetic measures to retrieve this disaster. He sent his wounded to Quinsan, collected fresh troops, and, having allowed his own wound to recover by a week's rest, resumed in person the attack on Waisso. On the 10th of April Major Gordon pitched his camp within a mile of Waisso, and paid his men as the preliminary to the resumption of the offensive. The attack commenced on the following morning, and promised to prove of an arduous nature; but by a skilful flank movement Major Gordon carried two stockades in person, and rendered the whole place no longer tenable. The rebels evacuated their position and retreated, closely pursued by the Imperialists. The villagers who had suffered from their exactions, rose upon them, and very few rebels escaped. The pursuit was continued for a week, and the lately victorious army of Waisso was practically annihilated. The capture of Changchow was to be the next and crowning success of the campaign. For this enterprise the whole of the Ever-Victorious Army was concentrated, including the ex-rebel contingent of Liyang. On the 23rd of April Major Gordon carried the stockades near the west gate. In their capture the Liyang men, although led only by Chinese, showed conspicuous gallantry, thus justifying Major Gordon's belief that the Chinese would fight as well under their own countrymen as when led by foreigners. Batteries were then constructed for the bombardment of the town itself. Before these were completed the Imperialists assaulted, but were repulsed with loss. On the following day (April 27th) the batteries opened fire, and two pontoon bridges were thrown across, when Major Gordon led his men to the assault. The first attack was repulsed, and a second one, made in conjunction with the Imperialists, fared not less badly. The pontoons were lost, and the force suffered a greater loss than at any time during the war, with the exception of Waisso. The Taepings also lost heavily; and their valour could not alter the inevitable result. Changchow had consequently to be approached systematically by trenches, in the construction of which the Chinese showed themselves very skilful. The loss of the pontoons compelled the formation of a cask-bridge; and, during the extensive preparations for renewing the attack, several hundred of the garrison came over, reporting that it was only the Cantonese who wished to fight to the bitter end. On the 11th of May, the fourth anniversary of its capture by Chung Wang, Li requested Major Gordon to act in concert with him for carrying the place by storm. The attack was made in the middle of the day, to the intense surprise of the garrison, who made only a feeble resistance, and the town was at last carried with little loss. The commandant, Hoo Wang, was made prisoner and executed. This proved to be the last action of the Ever Victorious Army, which then returned to Quinsan, and was quietly disbanded by its commander before the 1st of June.

To sum up the closing incidents of the Taeping war. Tayan was evacuated two days after the fall of Changchow, leaving Nankin alone in their hands. Inside that city there were the greatest misery and suffering. Tien Wang had refused to take any of the steps pressed on him by Chung Wang, and when he heard the people were suffering from want, all he said was, "Let them eat the sweet dew." Tseng Kwofan drew up his lines on all sides of the city, and gradually drove the despairing rebels behind the walls. Chung Wang sent out the old women and children; and let it be recorded to the credit of Tseng Kwotsiuen that he did not drive them back, but charitably provided for their wants, and despatched them to a place of shelter. In June Major Gordon visited Tseng's camp, and found his works covering twenty-four to thirty miles, and constructed in the most elaborate fashion. The Imperialists numbered eighty thousand men, but were badly armed. Although their pay was very much in arrear, they were well fed, and had great confidence in their leader, Tseng Kwofan. On the 30th of June, Tien Wang, despairing of success, committed suicide by swallowing golden leaf. Thus died the Hungtsiuen who had erected the standard of revolt in Kwangsi thirteen years before. His son was proclaimed Tien Wang on his death becoming known, but his reign was brief. The last act of all had now arrived. On the 19th of July the Imperialists had run a gallery under the wall of Nankin, and charged it with forty thousand pounds of powder. The explosion destroyed fifty yards of the walls, and the Imperialists, attacking on all sides, poured in through the breach. Chung Wang made a desperate resistance in the interior, holding his own and the Tien Wang's palace to the last. He made a further stand with a thousand men at the southern gate, but his band was overwhelmed, and he and the young Tien Wang fled into the surrounding country. In this supreme moment of danger Chung Wang thought more of the safety of his young chief than of himself, and he gave him an exceptionally good pony to escape on, while he himself took a very inferior animal. As the consequence Tien Wang the Second escaped, while Chung Wang was captured in the hills a few days later. Chung Wang, who had certainly been the hero of the Taeping movement, was beheaded on the 7th of August, and the young Tien Wang was eventually captured and executed also, by Shen Paochen. For this decisive victory, which extinguished the Taeping rebellion, Tseng Kwofan, whom Gordon called "generous, fair, honest and patriotic," was made a Hou, or Marquis, and his brother Tseng Kwotsiuen an Earl.

Although Gordon took no direct part in the closing scene of Taeping power at Nankin, everybody felt, and history accepts the view, that the triumphant and speedy suppression of the rebellion was due to his extraordinary military successes. He himself, with characteristic modesty, was disposed to minimise the importance of his services; and he often declared that the Imperialists were certain to have overcome the Taepings eventually, although their caution and military inexperience might have prolonged the struggle. Another opinion to which he strongly adhered was, that the Chinese did not require European leading, that they were very good under their own officers, and that the inevitable consequence of their being placed under Europeans was that they became rebels to their government. These opinions show the disinterested spirit in which he served the Chinese. He fought the Taepings not for any empty or vainglorious desire to make a military reputation, but because he saw an opportunity of rendering a great service to a suffering people, among whom the horrors of a civil war had spread death and disease. It is impossible to exaggerate the impression made by his disinterestedness on the Chinese people, who elevated him for his courage and military prowess to the pedestal of a national god of war. The cane which he carried when leading his men to the charge became known as "Gordon's wand of victory"; and the troops whom he trained, and converted by success from a rabble into an army, formed the nucleus of China's modern army. The service he rendered his adopted country was, therefore, lasting as well as striking, and the gratitude of the Chinese has, to their credit, proved not less durable. The name of Gordon is still one to conjure with among the Chinese, and if ever China were placed in the same straits, she would be the more willing, from his example, to entrust her cause to an English officer. As to the military achievements of General Gordon in China, nothing fresh can be said. They speak indeed for themselves, and they form the most solid portion of the reputation which he gained as a leader of men. In the history of the Manchu dynasty he will be known as "Chinese Gordon"; although for us his earlier soubriquet must needs give place, from his heroic and ever-regrettable death, to that of "Gordon of Khartoum."

CHAPTER XXI

THE REGENCY.

WHILE the suppression of the Taeping rebellion was in progress, events of great interest and importance happened at Pekin. It will be recollected that when the allied forces approached that city in 1860, the Emperor Hienfung fled to Jehol, and kept himself aloof from all the peace negotiations which were conducted to a successful conclusion by his brother, Prince Kung. After the signature of the convention in Pekin, ratifying the Treaty of Tientsin, he refused to return to his capital; and he even seems to have hoped that he might, by asserting his Imperial prerogative, transfer the capital from Pekin to Jehol, and thus evade one of the principal concessions to the foreigners. But if this was impossible, he was quite determined, for himself, to have nothing to do with them, and during the short remainder of his life he kept his Court at Jehol. While his brother was engaged in meeting the difficulties of diplomacy, and in arrranging the conditions of a nove'˯ ˒˖ion, Hienfung, by collecting round his person the most bigoted me   ˙˙ showed that he preferred those counsellors who had lear   .ı recent events, and who would support him in his claims   ‚hed superiority and inaccessibility. Prominent among the   confidence was Prince Tsai, who had taken so discreditable a   . ın the arrest of Parkes and his companions at Tungchow, and among his other advisers were several inexperienced and impetuous members of the Manchu family. They were all agreed in the policy of recovering, at the earliest possible moment, what they considered to be the natural and prescriptive right of the occupant of the Dragon Throne to treat all other potentates as in no degree equal to himself. No respect for treaties would have deterred them from reasserting what had solemnly been signed away, and the permanent success of the faction at Jehol would have entailed, within a comparatively short period, the outbreak of another foreign war. But the continued residence of the Emperor at Jehol was not popular with either his own family or the inhabitants of Pekin. The members of the Manchu clan, who received a regular allowance during the Emperor's residence at Pekin, were reduced to the greatest straits, and even to the verge of starvation, while the Chinese naturally resented the attempt to remove the capital to any other place. This abnegation of authority by Hienfung, for his absence meant nothing short of that, could not have been prolonged indefinitely, for a Chinese Emperor has many religious and secular duties to perform which no one else can discharge, and which, if not discharged, would reduce the office of Emperor to a nonentity. The only sign that Hienfung gave of his realising that there wer: foreigners in his capital, and that a treaty had been signed with them, was his listening to all the information he could procure about England; but the only appreciable result of his study is contained in the declaration that "the English were always at war, or preparing to go to war, with someone." Prince Tsai and his associates had no difficulty in working upon the fears of this prince, who held the most exalted idea of his own majesty, at the same time that he had not the power or knowledge to vindicate it.

While such were the views prevailing in the Imperial circle at Jehol, arrangements were in progress for the taking up of his residence at Pekin of the British minister. After Lord Elgin's departure, his brother, Sir Frederick Bruce, who was knighted for his share in the negotiations, was appointed first occupant of the post of Minister in the Chinese capital, and on 22nd March, 1861, he left Tientsin for Pekin, where the palace of the Duke of Leang, a member of the Manchu family, had been leased in perpetuity to the English government at a rent of 1,500 taels a year, and had been prepared for the reception of the British legation. Mr.—now Sir Thomas—Wade accompanied Sir Frederick as principal secretary, and the staff included six student interpreters, whose ranks, constantly recruited, have given many able men to the public service. Before Sir Frederick reached the capital, the Chinese minister had taken a step to facilitate the transaction of business with the foreign representatives. Prince Kung —and the credit of the measure belongs exclusively to him—will always be gratefully remembered by any foreign writer on modern China as the founder of the department known as the Tsungli Yamen, which he instituted in January, 1861. This department, during the thirty years of its existence, has very fully answered all the expectations formed of it; and, although it is erroneous to represent it as in any sense identical with the Chinese government, or as the originating source of Chinese policy, it has proved a convenient and well-managed vehicle for the despatch of international business. Prince Kung became its first president, and acted in that capacity until his fall from power in 1884. Before Sir Frederick Bruce had been in Pekin a month, reports began to be spread of the serious illness of the Emperor, and a pamphlet which enjoyed considerable circulation stated that "his doctors declared his case to be hopeless, and that, even if he promptly abandoned some pernicious habits, he could not hope to live beyond six months." All the available evidence went to show that he did not take any precautions, but during the summer nothing definite was stated as to his health, although rumours of the gravity of Hienfung's complaint continued to circulate so freely that the announcement of his death at any moment would not have caused surprise. The superstitious were the more disposed to believe that something extraordinary might happen, because a comet appeared in the sky and remained some weeks; for in China, as in mediæval Europe, it was held—

> "When beggars die there are no comets seen,
> The heavens themselves blaze forth the death of princes."

In August Prince Kung hastened to Jehol, the object of his journey, and indeed the journey itself, being kept secret. The members of the Tsungli Yamen were observed by the foreign officials to be pre-occupied, and even the genial Wansiang could not conceal that they were passing through a crisis. Not merely was Hienfung dying, but it had become known to Prince Kung and his friends that he had left the governing authority during the minority of his son, a child of less than six years of age, to a Board of

THE REGENCY.

Regency composed of eight of the least intelligent and most arrogant and self-seeking members of the Imperial family, with Prince Tsai at their head. The Emperor died on the 22nd of August. A few hours later the Imperial decree notifying the last wishes of the ruler as to the mode of government was promulgated. The Board of Regency assumed the nominal control of affairs, and Hienfung's son was proclaimed Emperor under the style of Chiseang. In all of these arrangements neither Prince Kung nor his brothers, nor the responsible ministers at the capital, had had the smallest part. It was an intrigue among certain members of the Imperial clan to possess themselves of the ruling power, and for a time it seemed as if their intrigue would be only too successful. Nothing happened during the months of September and October to disturb their confidence, for they remained at Jehol, and at Pekin the routine of government continued to be performed by Prince Kung. That statesman and his colleagues employed the interval in arranging their own plan of action, and in making sure of the fidelity of a certain number of troops. Throughout these preparations Prince Kung was ably and energetically supported by his brother, Prince Chun, by his colleague, Wansiang, and by his aged father-in-law, the minister Kweiliang. But the conspirators could not keep the young Emperor at Jehol indefinitely, and when, at the end of October, it became known that he was on the point of returning to Pekin, it was clear that the hour of conflict had arrived. At Jehol the Board of Regency could do little harm; but once its pretensions and legality were admitted at the capital, all the ministers would have to take their orders from it, and to resign the functions which they had retained. The main issue was whether Prince Kung or Prince Tsai was to be supreme. On the 1st of November the young Emperor entered his capital in state. It was said that he was driven through the streets in a carriage, sitting on his mother's lap, while the Empress Dowager, or the principal widow of Hienfung, occupied another seat in the same carriage; but no European actually saw the *cortége*, because Prince Kung had asked the ministers as a favour to keep their suites at home until the procession reached the palace. A large number of soldiers, still dressed in their white mourning, accompanied their Sovereign from Jehol; but Shengpao's garrison was infinitely more numerous, and thoroughly loyal to the cause of Prince Kung. The majority of the Regents had arrived with the reigning prince; those who had not yet come were on the road, escorting the dead body of Hienfung towards its resting-place. If a blow was to be struck at all, now was the time to strike it. The Regents had not merely placed themselves in the power of their opponent, but they had actually brought with them the young Emperor, without whose person Prince Kung could have accomplished little. Prince Kung had spared no effort to secure, and had fortunately succeeded in obtaining, the assistance and co-operation of the Empress Dowager, Hienfung's principal widow, named Tsi An. Her assent had been obtained to the proposed plot before the arrival in Pekin, and it now only remained to carry it out. On the day following the entry into the capital, Prince Kung hastened to the palace, and, producing before the astonished Regents an Imperial Edict ordering their dismissal, he asked them whether they obeyed the decree of their Sovereign, or whether he must call in his soldiers to compel them. Prince Tsai and his companions had no choice save to signify their acquiescence in what they could not prevent; but, on leaving the chamber in which this scene took place, they hastened towards the Emperor's apartment in order to remonstrate against their dismissal, or to obtain from him some counter-edict reinstating them in their positions. They were prevented from carrying out their purpose, but this proof of contumacy sealed their fate. They were promptly arrested, and a second decree was issued ordering their degradation from their official and hereditary rank. To Prince Kung and his allies was entrusted the charge of trying and punishing the offenders.

The next step was the proclamation of a new Regency, composed of the two empresses, Tsi An, principal widow of Hienfung, and Tsi Thsi, mother of the young Emperor. Two precedents for the administration being entrusted to an empress were easily found by the Hanlin doctors during the Ming dynasty, when the Emperors Chitsong and Wanleh were minors. Special edicts were issued and arrangements made for the transaction of business during the continuance of the Regency, and as neither of the empresses knew Manchu it was specially provided that papers and documents, which were always presented in that language, should be translated into Chinese. Concurrently with these measures for the settlement of the Regency happened the closing scenes in the drama of conspiracy which began so successfully at Jehol and ended so dramatically at Pekin. For complete success and security it was necessary that all the ringleaders should be captured, and some of them were still free.

The bravest, if not the ablest, of the late Board of Regency, Sushuen, remained at large. He had been charged with the high and honourable duty of escorting the remains of Hienfung to the capital. It was most important that he should be seized before he became aware of the fate that had befallen his colleagues. Prince Chun volunteered to capture the last, and in a sense the most formidable, of the intriguers himself, and on the very day that the events described happened at Pekin he rode out of the capital at the head of a body of Tartar cavalry. On the following night Prince Chun reached the spot where he was encamped, and, breaking into the house, arrested him whilst in bed. Sushuen did not restrain his indignation, and betrayed the ulterior plans entertained by himself and his associates by declaring that Prince Chun had been only just in time to prevent a similar fate befalling himself. He was at once placed on his trial with the other prisoners, and on the 10th of November the order was given in the Emperor's name for their execution. Sushuen was executed on the public ground set apart for that purpose; but to the others, as a special favour from their connection with the Imperial family, was sent the silken cord, with which they were permitted to put an end to their existence. In the fate of Prince Tsai may be seen a well merited retribution for his treachery and cruelty to Sir Harry Parkes and his companions.

Another important step which had to be taken was the alteration of the style given to the young Emperor's reign. It was felt to be impolitic that the deposed ministers should retain any connection whatever in history with the young ruler. Were Hienfung's son to be handed down to posterity as Chiseang there would be no possibility of excluding their names and their brief and feverish ambition from the national annals. After due deliberation, therefore, the name of Tungche was substituted for that of Chiseang, and, meaning as it does "the union of law and order," it will be allowed that the name was selected with some proper regard for the circumstances of the occasion. Prince Kung was rewarded with many high offices and sounding titles in addition to the post of Chief Minister under the two empresses. He was made president of the Imperial Clan Court in the room of Prince Tsai, and the title of Iching Wang, or Prince Minister, was conferred upon him. His staunch friends and supporters, Wansiang, Paukwen, and Kweiliang, were appointed to the Supreme Council. Prince Chun, to whose skill and bravery in arresting Sushuen Prince Kung felt very much indebted, was also rewarded. With these incidents closed what might have proved a grave and perilous complication for the Chinese government. Had Prince Kung prematurely revealed his plans there is every reason to suppose that he would have alarmed and forewarned his rivals, and that they, with the person of the Emperor in their possession, would have obtained the advantage. His patience during the two months of doubt and anxiety while the Emperor remained at Jehol was matched by the vigour and promptitude that he displayed on the eventful 2nd of November. That his success was beneficial to his country will not be disputed by anyone, and Prince Kung's name must be permanently remembered both for having commenced, and for having ensured the continuance of, diplomatic relations with England and the other foreign Powers.

The increased intercourse with Europeans not merely led to greater diplomatic confidence and to the extension of trade, but it also induced many foreigners to offer their services and assistance to the Pekin government during the embarrassment arising from internal dissension. At first these persons were, as has been seen, encouraged and employed more in consequence of local opinion in the treaty-ports than as a matter of State policy. But already the suggestion had been brought forward in more than one form for the employment of foreigners, with the view of increasing the resources of the Government by calling in the assistance of the very agency which had reduced them. A precedent had been established for this at an earlier period—before, in fact, the commencement of hostilities—by the appointment of Mr. Horatio N. Lay to direct and assist the local authorities in the collection of customs in the Shanghai district. Mr. Lay's experience had proved most useful in drawing up the tariff of the Treaty of Tientsin, and his assistance had been suitably acknowledged. In 1862, when the advantages to be derived from the military experience of foreigners had been practically recognised by the appointment of Europeans to command a portion of the army of China, and in pursuance of a suggestion made by the present Sir Robert Hart in the previous year, it was thought desirable for many reasons that something should also be done to increase the naval resources of the Empire, and Mr. Lay was entrusted with a commission for purchasing and collecting in Europe a fleet of gunboats of small draught, which could be usefully employed for all the purposes of the Pekin government on the rivers and shallow estuaries of the country. Mr. Lay, who undertook the commission, said, "This force was intended for the protection of the treaty-ports, for the suppression of piracy then rife, and for the relief of this country from the burden of 'policing' the Chinese waters"; but its first use in the eyes of Prince Kung was to be employed against the rebels and their European supporters of whom Burgevine was the most prominent. Captain Sherard Osborn, a distinguished English naval officer, was associated with Mr. Lay in the undertaking. An Order of Council was issued on the 30th of August, 1862, empowering both of these officers to act in the matter as delegates of the Chinese. Captain Osborn and Mr. Lay came to England to collect the vessels of this fleet, and the former afterwards returned with them to

China in the capacity of their commodore. The transaction was not well managed from the very commencement. Mr. Lay wrote in August, 1862, to say that he had chosen as the national ensign of the Chinese navy "a green flag, bearing a yellow diagonal cross," and he wrote again to request that an official notification should appear in the *Gazette*. Had his request been complied with, there would have been very strong reason for assuming that the English government was prepared to support and facilitate every scheme for forcing the Chinese to accept and submit to the exact method of progress approved of and desired by the European servants of their government, without their taking any part in the transaction save to ratify terms that might be harsh and exorbitant. Fortunately, the instinctive caution of our Foreign Office was not laid aside on this occasion. Mr. Lay was informed that no notice could appear in the *London Gazette* except after the approval of the Pekin authorities had been expressed; and Prince Kung wrote on the 22nd of October to say that the Chinese ensign would be of "yellow ground, and on it will be designed a dragon with his head toward the upper part of the flag." Mr. Lay preceded the vessels—seven gun-boats and one store-ship—and arrived at Pekin in May, 1863. At the capital he found two opinions prevailing, which did not promise to contribute to the harmony of the new arrangement. In the first place, he found Sir Frederick Bruce resolved not to take any active part in the affair at all, without instructions to do so from his government. But if the attitude of Sir Frederick Bruce was embarrassing, that of the Chinese themselves was far more discouraging. Their fears had been already aroused as to the possibly independent attitude these foreign commanders might assume when affairs had settled down. The views of Prince Kung and Mr. Lay were distinctly opposed on the point of the position of the new ships as part of the external defences of China. The former considered that the fleet purchased in Europe out of Chinese treasure should form an integral portion of the warlike resources of the Empire, and be as subservient to the orders of the local authorities as if it were one of the old fleets of war-junks. Mr. Lay could not bring himself to take the same view. The fleet was to be virtually independent. Captain Sherard Osborn would, by his personal arrangement with Mr. Lay, act only upon "orders of the Emperor which may be conveyed direct to Lay," and, moreover, he refused to act on any orders conveyed through any different channel. To the unprejudiced observer it would seem that the proper persons to decide by whom the orders should be given were the Chinese themselves, and not their foreign officers and servants. When it is realised how much the originators of this scheme took the whole arrangement out of the hands of Prince Kung and his colleagues, there will not be much surprise at the scheme coming to the abortive and unfortunate end that it did.

Prince Kung had been most anxious for the speedy arrival of the flotilla; and the doubtful fortune of the campaign in Kiangsu, where the gun-boats would have been invaluable, rendered him extremely desirous that they should commence active operations immediately on arrival. But he found, in the first place, that Mr. Lay was not prepared to accept the appointment of a Chinese official as joint-commander, and in the second place, that he would not receive orders from any of the provincial authorities. Such a decision was manifestly attended with the greatest inconvenience to China; for only the provincial authorities knew what the interests of the state demanded, and where the fleet might co-operate with advantage in the attacks on the Taepings. Unless Captain Sherard Osborn were to act on the orders of Tseng Kwofan, and particularly of Li Hung Chang, it was difficult to see what possible use he or his flotilla could be to China. The founders of the new Chinese navy claimed practically all the privileges of an ally, and declined the duties devolving on them as directing a department of the Chinese administration. Of course, it was more convenient and more dignified for the foreign officers to draw their instructions and their salaries direct from the fountain head; but if the flotilla was not to be of any practical use to China it might just as well never have been created. The fleet arrived in safety, but remained inactive. The whole summer and autumn of 1863, with its critical state of affairs round Soochow, passed away without anything being done to show what a powerful auxiliary Mr. Lay's ships might be. The ultimate success of those operations without the smallest co-operation on the part of Captain Osborn or his flotilla virtually sealed its fate. In October, Wansiang, in the name of the Foreign Office, declared that the Chinese could not recognise or ratify the private arrangement between Mr. Lay and his naval officer, and that it was essential for Captain Osborn to submit to receive his instructions from the provincial authorities. In the following month Mr. Lay was summarily dismissed from the Chinese service, and it was determined, after some delay and various counter suggestions, to send back the ships to Europe, there to be disposed of. Sir Frederick Bruce recorded his opinion in a dispatch dated 19th of November, 1863: "I do not think the Chinese government open to the charge of bad faith, as the conditions they were called upon to ratify are not such as the authority given to Mr. Lay entitled him to assent to in their name. Mr. Lay mistook his position and overrated his influence when he resolved on starting this flotilla, without having previously ascertained that the terms agreed upon with Captain Osborn would be accepted." The radical fault in the whole arrangement had been Mr. Lay's wanting to take upon himself the responsibility not merely of Inspector-General of Customs, but also of supreme adviser on all matters connected with foreign questions. His views were of the largest scope and most benevolent character so far as the progress of China was concerned. But then it was all to be effected under his own direction. The Chinese themselves were to take quite a subordinate part in their realisation, and were to be treated, in short, as if they did not know how to manage their own affairs. Mr. Lay's dreams were suddenly dispelled, and his philanthropic schemes fell to the ground. Neither Prince Kung nor his colleagues had any intention to pave the way for their own effacement. And similar will be the fate of those who ever again assume that the Chinese may be induced to surrender the direction of their own affairs into the hands of foreigners. General Gordon alone adopted the just tone on this matter, as in everything else. He saw what were the true views of the Chinese on the subject, and he impressed upon them the advisability of carrying out reforms and improvements in their own way. Mr. Lay was amply compensated by the Chinese. Sir Frederick Bruce wrote: "The Chinese have acted fairly by him. I do not think that more could have been demanded of them."

After Mr. Lay's departure the Maritime Customs were placed under the control of Mr. Robert Hart, who had acted during Mr. Lay's absence in Europe, and who still holds the post which he has filled for thirty years with conspicuous ability. This appointment was accompanied by the transfer of the official residence from Pekin to Shanghai, which was attended with much practical advantage. Already the customs revenue had risen to three millions, and trade was steadily expanding as the rebels were gradually driven back, and as the Yangtsekiang and the coasts became safer for navigation. Numerous schemes were suggested for the opening up of China by railways and the telegraph; but they all very soon ended in nothing, for the simple reason that the Chinese did not want them. They were more sincere and energetic in their adoption of military improvements. English officers drilled Chinese troops in their permanent camp at Fungwang, and Dr. Macartney constructed and organised a great arsenal at Soochow, which was afterwards removed to Nankin as a town more conveniently situated.

The anxieties of Prince Kung on the subject of the dynasty, and with regard to the undue pretensions and expectations of the foreign officials who looked on the Chinese merely as the instruments of their self-aggrandisement, were further increased during this period by the depredations of the Nienfei rebels in the province of Shantung. During these operations Sankolinsin died, leaving Tseng Kwofan in undisputed possession of the first place among Chinese officials. Sankolinsin, when retreating after a reverse, was treacherously murdered by some villagers whose hospitality he had claimed. The career of the great Mongol prince, who had unsuccessfully opposed the allied forces during the Pekin campaign, terminated thus ignominiously; but his constant activity, when he was to a certain extent in disgrace, showed that he was unremitting in his fidelity to the Tartar ruler. The Nienfei rebellion continued to alarm and agitate the provinces on the northern bank of the Yellow River, and the task of suppressing it was rendered more difficult by the mutinous state of the soldiery. However, the Nienfei never became formidable in the sense of being a national danger; and although they continued for several years longer to be a source of trouble and disturbance, they owed their own safety as much to the celerity of their movements, being mounted rebels, as to their military power.

The events of this introductory period may be appropriately concluded with the strange stroke of misfortune that befell Prince Kung in the spring of 1865, and which seemed to show that he had indulged some views of personal ambition. The affair had probably a secret history, but if so the truth is hardly likely to be ever known. The known facts were as follows: On the 2nd of April, 1865, there appeared an edict degrading the Prince in the name of the two Regent-Empresses. The charge made against him was of having grown arrogant and assumed privileges to which he had no right. He was at first "diligent and circumspect," but he has now become disposed "to overrate his own importance." In consequence, he was deprived of all his appointments and dismissed from the scene of public affairs. There was not much likelihood that a man who had taken so decisive a share in arranging the accession of the ruling prince, and in the appointment of the Regents during his minority, would tamely acquiesce in being set on one side by the decree of two women. All his friends on the Imperial Council petitioned the Throne, representing in the plainest terms the great inconvenience that would be entailed by the withdrawal of Prince Kung from the control of public affairs. It was significantly observed in one of these memorials that "if the Imperial household be the first to begin misunderstandings" there was no telling where the excitement would not extend. These representations could not fail to produce their due effect. Five weeks after his fall Prince Kung was reinstated, on the 8th of May, in all his offices, with the exception of that of President of the Council. This episode, which might have produced grave complications, closed with a return to almost the precise state of things previously existing. There was one important difference. The two empresses had asserted their predominance. Prince Kung had hoped to be supreme, and to rule uncontrolled. From this time forth he was content to be their minister and adviser, on terms similar to those that would have applied to any other official.

The year 1865, which witnessed this very interesting event in the history of the Chinese government, beheld before its close the departure of Sir Frederick Bruce from Pekin, and the appointment of Sir Rutherford Alcock, who had been the first British minister to Japan during the critical period of the introduction of foreign intercourse with that country, to fill the post of Resident Minister at Pekin. Sir Frederick Bruce could claim the distinction of being the first English official to recognise the inherent claims to respect of the Chinese government, and he left an example to his successors of how the dignity of the English Crown, in dealing with a government which was also a great one, was to be sustained without making undue or uncalled for demands. Sir Rutherford Alcock then found the opportunity to put in practice some of the honourable sentiments to which he had given expression twenty years before at Shanghai. When Sir Rutherford left Yeddo for Pekin, the post of Minister in Japan was conferred on Sir Harry Parkes, who had been acting as Consul at Shanghai since the conclusion of the war. The relations between the countries were gradually settling down on a satisfactory basis, and the appointment of a Supreme Court for China and Japan at Shanghai, with Sir Edmund Hornby as Chief Judge, promised to enforce obedience to the law among even the unsettled adventurers of different nationalities left by the conclusion of the Taeping rebellion and the cessation of piracy without a profitable pursuit.

While the events which have been set forth were happening in the heart of China, other misfortunes yet had befallen the executive in the more remote quarters of the realm, but resulting none the less in the loss and ruin of provinces, and in the subversion of the Emperor's authority. Two great uprisings of the people occurred in opposite directions, both commencing while the Taeping rebellion was in full force, and continuing to disturb the country for many years after its suppression. The one had for its scene the great south-western province of Yunnan; the other the two provinces of the north-west, Shensi and Kansuh, and extending thence westwards to the Pamir. They resembled each other in one point, and that was that they were instigated and sustained by the Mahomedan population alone. The Panthays and the Tungani were either indigenous tribes or foreign immigrants who had adopted or imported the tenets of Islam. Their sympathies with the Pekin government were probably never very great, but they were impelled in both cases to revolt more by local tyranny than by any distinct desire to cast off the authority of the Chinese; but, of course, the obvious embarrassment of the central executive encouraged by simplifying the task of rebellion. The Panthay rising calls for description in the first place, because it began at an earlier period than the other, and also because the details have been preserved with greater fidelity. Mahomedanism is believed to have been introduced into Yunnan in or about the year 1275, and it made most progress among the so-called aboriginal tribes, the Lolos and the Mantzu. The officials were mostly Chinese or Tartars, and, left practically free from control, they more often abused their power than sought to employ it for the benefit of the people they governed. In the very first year of Hienfung's reign (1851) a petition reached the capital from a Mahomedan land proprietor in Yunnan named Ma Wenchu, accusing the Emperor's officials of the gravest crimes, and praying that "a just and honest man" might be sent to redress the wrongs of an injured and long-suffering people. The petition was carefully read and favourably considered at the capital; but beyond a gracious answer the Emperor was at the time powerless to apply a remedy to the evil. Four years passed away without any open manifestation of the deep discontent smouldering below the surface. But in 1855 the Chinese and the Mahomedan labourers quarrelled in one of the principal mines of the province, which is covered with mines of gold, iron, and copper. It seems that the greater success of the Mahomedans in the uncertain pursuit of mining had roused the displeasure of the Chinese. Disputes ensued, in which the Mussulmans added success in combat to success in mining; and the official appointed to superintend the mines, instead of remaining with a view to the restoration of order, sought his personal safety by precipitate flight to the town of Yunnan. During his absence the Chinese population raised a levy *en masse*, attacked the Mahomedans who had gained a momentary triumph, and compelled them by sheer weight of numbers to beat a hasty retreat to their own homes in a different part of the province. This success was the signal for a general outcry against the Mahomedans, who had long been the object of the secret ill-will of the other inhabitants. Massacres took place in several parts of Yunnan, and the followers of the Prophet had to flee for their lives.

Among those who were slain during these popular disorders was a young chief named Ma Sucheng; and when the news of his murder reached his native village, his younger brother, Ma Sien, who had just received a small military command, declared his intention to avenge him, and fled to join the Mahomedan fugitives in the mountains. In this secure retreat they rallied their forces, and, driven to desperation by the promptings of want, they left their fastnesses with the view of regaining what they had lost. In this they succeeded better than they could have hoped for. The Chinese population experienced in their turn the bitterness of defeat; and the mandarins had the less difficulty in concluding a temporary understanding between the exhausted combatants. Tranquillity was restored, and the miners resumed their occupations. But the peace was deceptive, and in a little time the struggle was renewed with increased fury. In this emergency the idea occurred to some of the officials that an easy and efficacious remedy of the difficulty in which they found themselves would be provided by the massacre of the whole Mussulman population. In this plot the foremost part was taken by Hwang Chung, an official who bitterly hated the Mahomedans. He succeeded in obtaining the acquiescence of all his colleagues with the exception of the Viceroy of the province, who exposed the iniquity of the design, but who, destitute of all support, was powerless to prevent its execution. At the least he resolved to save his honour and reputation by committing suicide, and he and his wife were found one morning hanging up in the hall of the yamen. His death simplified the execution of the project which his refusal might possibly have prevented. The 19th of May, 1856, was the date fixed for the celebration of this Chinese St. Bartholomew. But the secret had not been well kept. The Mahomedans, whether warned or suspicious, distrusted the authorities and their neighbours, and stood vigilantly on their guard. At this time they looked chiefly to a high priest named Ma Tesing for guidance and instruction. But although on the alert they were, after all, taken to some extent by surprise, and many of them were massacred after a more or less unavailing resistance. But if many of the Mussulmans were slain, the survivors were inspired with a desperation which the mandarins had never contemplated. From one end of Yunnan to the other the Mahomedans, in face of great personal peril, rose by a common and spontaneous impulse, and the Chinese population was compelled to take a hasty refuge in the towns. At Talifoo, where the Mahomedans formed a considerable portion of the population, the most desperate fighting occurred, and after three days' carnage the Mussulmans, under Tu Wensiu, were left in possession of the city. Their success inspired them with the hope of retaining the freedom they had won, and, impressed with the conviction that nothing would atone for their acts of rebellion in the eyes of the government, they had no choice save to exert themselves for the retention of their independence. The rebels did not remain without leaders, whom they willingly recognised and obeyed; for the kwanshihs, or chiefs, who had accepted titles of authority from the Chinese, cast off their allegiance and placed themselves at the head of the popular movement. The priest Ma Tesing was raised to the highest post of all as Dictator, but Tu Wensiu admitted no higher authority than his own within the walls of Talifoo. Ma Tesing had performed the pilgrimage to Mecca, he had resided at Constantinople for two years, and his reputation for knowledge and saintliness stood highest among his co-religionists.

While Ma Tesing exercised the supremacy due to his age and attainments, the young chief Ma Sien led the rebels in the field. His energy was most conspicuous, and in the year 1858 he thought he was sufficiently strong to make an attack upon the city of Yunnan itself. His attack was baffled by the resolute defence of an officer named Lin Tzuchin, who had shown great courage as a partizan leader against the insurgents before he was entrusted with the defence of the provincial capital. Ma Sien was compelled to beat a retreat, and to devote himself to the organisation of the many thousand Ijen or Lolos recruits who signified their attachment to his cause. For the successful defence of Yunnan Lin was made a Titu, and gradually collected into his own hands such authority as still remained to the Emperor's lieutenants. On both sides preparations were made for the renewal of the struggle, but before the year 1858 ended Ma Sien met with a second repulse at the town of Linan. The year 1859 was not marked by any event of signal importance, although the balance of success inclined on the whole to the Mussulmans. But in the following year the Mahomedans drew up a large force, computed to exceed 50,000 men, round Yunnanfoo, to which they laid vigorous siege. The Imperialists were taken at a disadvantage, and the large number of people who had fled for shelter into the town rendered the small store of provisions less sufficient for a protracted defence. Yunnanfoo was on the point of surrender when an event occurred which not merely relieved it from its predicament, but altered the whole complexion of the struggle. The garrison had made up its mind to yield. Even the brave Lin had accepted the inevitable, and begun to negotiate with the two rebel leaders, Ma Sien and the priest Ma Tesing. Those chiefs, with victory in their grasp, manifested an unexpected and surprising moderation. Instead of demanding from Lin a complete and unconditional surrender, they began to discuss with him what terms could be agreed upon for the cessation of the war and for the restoration of tranquillity to the province. At first it was thought that these propositions concealed some intended treachery, but their sincerity was placed beyond dispute by the suicide of the mandarin Hwang Chung, who had first instigated the people to massacre their Mahomedan brethren. The terms of peace were promptly arranged, and a request was forwarded to Pekin for the ratification of a convention concluded under the pressure of necessity with some of the rebel leaders. The better to conceal the fact that this arrangement had been made with the principal leader of the disaffected, Ma Sien changed his name to Ma Julung, and received the rank of general in the Chinese service; while the high priest accepted as his share the not inconsiderable pension of two hundred taels a month. It is impossible to divine the true reasons which actuated these instigators of rebellion in their decision to go over to the side of the government. They probably thought that they had done sufficient to secure all practical advantages, and that any persistence in hostilities would only result in the increased misery and impoverishment of the province. They thought that their kinsmen and followers would obtain justice and security; and, as for themselves, no moment would be more opportune for securing the largest possible personal advantage with the minimum of risk. But they were also influenced by other considerations. Powerful as they were, there were other Mahomedan leaders seeking to acquire the supreme position among their co-religionists; and foremost among these was Tu Wensiu, who had reduced the whole of Western Yunnan to his sway, and reigned at Talifoo. The Mahomedan cause, important as it was, did not afford scope for the ambitions of two such men as Ma Julung and Tu Wensiu. The former availed himself of the favourable opportunity to settle this difficulty in a practical and, as he shrewdly anticipated, the most profitable manner for himself personally, by giving in his adhesion to the government.

This important defection did not bring in its train any certainty of tranquillity. Incited by the example of their leaders, every petty officer and chief thought himself deserving of the highest honours, and resolved to fight for his own hand. Ma Julung left Yunnanfoo for the purpose of seizing a neighbouring town which had revolted, and during his absence one of his lieutenants seized the capital, murdered the Viceroy, and threatened to plunder the inhabitants. Ma Julung was summoned to return in hot haste, and as a temporary expedient the priest Ma Tesing was elected Viceroy. When Ma Julung returned with his army he had to lay siege to Yunnanfoo, and although he promptly effected an entrance into the city, it took five days' hard fighting in the streets before the force in occupation was expelled. The insurgent officer was captured, exposed to the public gaze for one month in an iron cage, and then executed in a cruel manner. Ma Tesing was deposed from the elevated position which he had held for so short a time, and a new Chinese Viceroy arrived from Kweichow. The year 1863 opened with the first active operations against Tu Wensiu, who, during these years of disorder in central Yunnan, had been governing the western districts with some prudence. It would have been better if they had not been undertaken, for they only resulted in the defeat of the detachments sent by Ma Julung to engage the despot of Talifoo. Force having failed, they had recourse to diplomacy, and Ma Tesing was sent to sound Tu Wensiu as to whether he would not imitate their example and make his peace with the authorities. These overtures were rejected with disdain, and Tu Wensiu proclaimed his intention of holding out to the last, and refused to recognise the wisdom or the necessity of coming to terms with the government. The embarrassment of Ma Julung and the Yunnan officials, already sufficiently acute, was at this conjuncture further aggravated by an outbreak in their rear among the Miaotze and some other mountain tribes in the province of Kweichow. To the difficulty of coping with a strongly placed enemy in front was thus added that of maintaining communications through a hostile and difficult region. A third independent party had also come into existence in Yunnan, where an ex-Chinese official named Liang Shihmei had set up his own authority at Linan, mainly, it was said, through jealousy of the Mahomedans taken into the service of the government. The greatest difficulty of all was to reconcile the pretensions of the different commanders, for the Chinese officials, and the Futai Tsen Yuying in particular, regarded Ma Julung with no friendly eye. With the year 1867, both sides having collected their strength, more active operations were commenced, and Ma Julung proceeded in person, at the head of the best troops he could collect, to engage Tu Wensiu. It was at this time that the Imperialists adopted the red flag as their standard in contradistinction to the white flag of the insurgents. A desultory campaign ensued, but although Ma Julung evinced both courage and capacity, the result was on the whole unfavourable to him; and he had to retreat to the capital, where events of some importance had occurred during his absence in the field. The Viceroy, who had been staunchly attached to Ma Julung, died suddenly and under such circumstances as to suggest a suspicion of foul play; and Tsen Yuying had by virtue of his rank of Futai assumed the temporary discharge of his duties. The retreat of Ma Julung left the insurgents free to follow up their successes; and in the course of 1868, the authority of the Emperor had disappeared from every other part of the province except the prefectural city of Yunnanfoo. This bad fortune led the Mussulmans who had followed the advice and fortunes of Ma Julung to consider whether it would not be wise to rejoin their co-religionists, and to at once finish the contest by the destruction of the government. Had Ma Julung wavered in his fidelity for a moment they would have all joined the standard of Tu Wensiu, and the rule of the Sultan of Talifoo would have been established from one end of Yunnan to the other, but he stood firm and arrested the movement in a summary manner.

Tu Wensiu, having established the security of his communications with Burmah, whence he obtained supplies of arms and munitions of war, devoted his efforts to the capture of Yunnanfoo, which he completely invested. The garrison was reduced to the lowest straits before Tsen Yuying resolved to come to the aid of his distressed colleague. The loss of the prefectural town would not merely entail serious consequences to the Imperialist cause, but he felt it would personally compromise him as the

Futai at Pekin. In the early part of 1869, therefore, he threw himself into the town with three thousand men, and the forces of Tu Wensiu found themselves obliged to withdraw from the eastern side of the city. A long period of inaction followed, but during this time the most important events happened with regard to the ultimate result. Ma Julung employed all his artifice and arguments to show the rebel chiefs the utter hopelessness of their succeeding against the whole power of the Chinese Empire, which, from the suppression of the Taeping rebellion, would soon be able to be employed against them. They felt the force of his representations, and they were also oppressed by a sense of the slow progress they had made towards the capture of Yunnanfoo. Some months after Tsen Yuying's arrival, those of the rebels who were encamped to the north of the city hoisted the red flag and gave in their adhesion to the government. Then Ma Julung resumed active operations against the other rebels, and obtained several small successes. A wound received during one of the skirmishes put an end to his activity, and the campaign resumed its desultory character. But Ma Julung's illness had other unfortunate consequences; for during it Tsen Yuying broke faith with those of the rebel leaders who had come over, and put them all to a cruel death. The natural consequence of this foolish and ferocious act was that the Mahomedans again reverted to their desperate resolve to stand firmly by the side of Tu Wensiu. The war again passed into a more active phase. Ma Julung had recovered from his wounds. A new Viceroy, and a man of some energy, was sent from Pekin. Lin Yuchow had attracted the notice of Tseng Kwofan among those of his native province who had responded to his appeal to defend Hoonan against the Taepings sixteen years before; and shortly before the death of the last Viceroy of Yunnan, he had been made Governor of Kweichow. To the same patron at Pekin he now owed his elevation to the Viceroyalty. It is said that he had lost the energy which once characterised him; but he brought with him several thousand Hoonan braves, whose courage and military experience made them invaluable auxiliaries to the embarrassed authorities in Yunnan. A still more important circumstance as contributing towards the establishment of peace was the order sent from Pekin that the treasuries of six provinces should send to Yunnanfoo every month the total sum of 70,000 taels, until tranquillity had been restored. Although the whole of this amount was never received, still the officials in the south-west were thus provided with an invaluable source of revenue in which they were more deficient than in any other of the elements of war. The details of the campaign that followed would fail to be instructive, and the mention of names that are not merely uncouth but unpronounceable would only repel the reader. The result is the principal, or indeed the single, fact worthy of our consideration. In the course of the year 1870 most of the towns in the south and the north of Yunnan were recovered, and communications were re-opened with Szchuen. As soon as the inhabitants perceived that the government had recovered its strength, they hastened to express their joy at the change by repudiating the white flag which Tu Wensiu had compelled them to adopt. The Imperialists even to the last increased the difficulty of their work of pacification by exhibiting a relentless cruelty; and while the inhabitants thought to secure their safety by a speedy surrender, the Mussulmans were rendered more desperate in their resolve to resist. The chances of a Mahomedan success were steadily diminishing when Yang Yuko, a mandarin of some military capacity, who had begun his career in the most approved manner as a rebel, succeeded in capturing the whole of the salt-producing district which had been the main source of their strength. In the year 1872 all the preliminary arrangements were made for attacking Talifoo itself. A supply of rifles had been received from Canton or Shanghai, and a few pieces of artillery had also arrived. With these improved weapons the troops of Ma Julung and Tsen Yuying enjoyed a distinct advantage over the rebels of Talifoo. The horrors of war were at this point increased by those of pestilence, for the plague broke out at Puerh on the southern frontier, and, before it disappeared, devastated the whole of the province, completing the effect of the civil war, and ruining the few districts which had escaped from its ravages. The direct command of the siege operations at Talifoo was entrusted to Yang Yuko, a hunchback general, who had obtained a reputation for invincibility ; and when Tsen Yuying had completed his own operations he also proceeded to the camp before the Mahomedan capital for the purpose of taking part in the crowning operation of the war.

Tu Wensiu and the garrison of Talifoo, although driven to desperation, could not discover any issue from their difficulties. They were reduced to the last stage of destitution, and starvation stared them in the face. In this extremity Tu Wensiu, although there was every reason to believe that the Imperialists would not fulfil their pledges, and that surrender simply meant yielding to a cruel death, resolved to open negotiations with Yang Yuko for giving up the town. The Emperor's generals signified their desire for the speedy termination of the siege, at the same time expressing acquiescence in the general proposition of the garrison being admitted to terms. Although the Futai and Yang Yuko had promptly come to the mutual understanding to celebrate the fall of Talifoo by a wholesale massacre, they expressed their intention to spare the other rebels on the surrender of Tu Wensiu for execution and on the payment of an indemnity. The terms were accepted, although the more experienced of the rebels warned their comrades that they would not be complied with. On the 15th of January, 1873, Tu Wensiu, the original of the mythical Sultan Suliman, the fame of whose power reached England, and who had been an object of the solicitude of the Indian government, accepted the decision of his craven followers as expressing the will of Heaven, and gave himself up for execution. He attired himself in his best and choicest garments, and seated himself in the yellow palanquin which he had adopted as one of the few marks of royal state that his opportunities allowed him to secure. Accompanied by the men who had negotiated the surrender, he drove through the streets receiving for the last time the homage of his people, and out beyond the gates to Yang Yuko's camp. Those who saw the cortège marvelled at the calm indifference of the fallen despot. He seemed to have as little fear of his fate as consciousness of his surroundings. The truth soon became evident. He had baffled his enemies by taking slow poison. Before he reached the presence of the Futai, who had wished to gloat over the possession of his prisoner, the opium had done its work, and Tu Wensiu was no more. It seemed but an inadequate triumph to sever the head from the dead body, and to send it preserved in honey as the proof of victory to Pekin. Four days after Tu Wensiu's death, the Imperialists were in complete possession of the town, and a week later they had taken all their measures for the execution of the fell plan upon which they had decided. A great feast was given for the celebration of the convention, and the most important of the Mahomedan commanders, including those who had negotiated the truce, were present. At a given signal they were attacked and murdered by soldiers concealed in the gallery for the purpose, while six cannon shots announced to the soldiery that the hour had arrived for them to break loose on the defenceless townspeople. The scenes that followed are stated to have surpassed description. It was computed that 30,000 men alone perished after the fall of the old Panthay capital, and the Futai sent to Yunnanfoo twenty-four large baskets full of human ears, as well as the heads of the seventeen chiefs.

With the capture of Talifoo the great Mahomedan rebellion in the south-west, to which the Burmese gave the name of Panthay, closed, after a desultory struggle of nearly eighteen years. The war was conducted with exceptional ferocity on both sides, and witnessed more than the usual amount of falseness and breach of faith common to Oriental struggles. Nobody benefited by the contest, and the prosperity of Yunnan, which at one time had been far from inconsiderable, sank to the lowest possible point. A new class of officials came to the front during this period of disorder, and fidelity was a sufficient passport to a certain rank. Ma Julung, the Marshal Ma of European travellers, gained a still higher station; and notwithstanding the jealousy of his colleagues, acquired practical supremacy in the province. The high priest, Ma Tesing, who may be considered as the prime instigator of the movement, was executed or poisoned in 1874 at the instigation of some of the Chinese officials. Yang Yuko, the most successful of all the generals, only enjoyed a brief tenure of power. It was said that he was dissatisfied with his position as commander-in-chief, and aspired to a higher rank. He also was summoned to Pekin, but never got further than Shanghai, where he died, or was removed. But although quiet gradually descended upon this part of China, it was long before prosperity followed in its train.

About six years after the first mutterings of discontent among the Mahomedans in the south-west, disturbances occurred in the north-west provinces of Shensi and Kansuh, where there had been many thousand followers of Islam since an early period of Chinese history. They were generally obedient subjects and sedulous cultivators of the soil; but they were always liable to sudden ebullitions of fanaticism or of turbulence, and it was said that during the later years of his reign Keen Lung had meditated a wholesale execution of the male population above the age of fifteen. The threat, if ever made, was never carried out, but the report suffices to show the extent to which danger was apprehended from the Tungan population. The true origin of the great outbreak in 1862 in Shensi seems to have been a quarrel between the Chinese and the Mahomedan militia as to their share of the spoil derived from the defeat and overthrow of a brigand leader. After some bloodshed, two Imperial Commissioners were sent from Pekin to restore order. The principal Mahomedan leader formed a plot to murder the Commissioners, and on their arrival he rushed into their presence and slew one of them with his own hand. His co-religionists deplored the rash act, and voluntarily seized and surrendered him for the purpose of undergoing a cruel death. But although he was torn to pieces, that fact did not satisfy the outraged dignity of the Emperor. A command was issued in Tungche's name to the effect that all those who persisted in following the creed of Islam should perish by the sword. From Shensi the outbreak spread into the adjoining province of Kansuh; and the local garrisons were vanquished in a pitched battle at Tara Ussu, beyond the regular frontier. The insurgents did not succeed, however, in taking any of the larger towns of Shensi, and after threatening with capture the once famous city of Singan, they were gradually expelled from that province. The Mahomedan rebellion within the limits of China proper would not, therefore, have possessed more than local importance, but for the fact that it encouraged a similar outbreak in the country further west, and that it resulted in the severance of the Central Asian provinces from China for a period of many years.

The uprising of the Mahomedans in the frontier provinces appealed to the secret fears as well as to the longings of the Tungan settlers and soldiers in all the towns and military stations between Souchow and Kashgar. The sense of a common peril, more perhaps than the desire to attain the same object, led to revolts at Hami, Barkul, Urumtsi, and Turfan, towns which formed a group of industrious communities half-way between the prosperous districts of Kansuh on the one side, and Kashgar on the other. The Tungani at these towns revolted under the leading of their priests, and imitated the example of their co-religionists within the settled borders of China by murdering all who did not accept their creed. After a brief interval, which we may attribute to the greatness of the distance, to the vigilance of the Chinese garrison, or to the apathy of the population, the movement spread to the three towns immediately west of Turfan, Karashar, Kucha, and Aksu, where it came into contact with, and was stopped by, another insurrectionary movement under Mahomedan, but totally distinct, auspices. West of Aksu the Tungan rebellion never extended south of the Tian Shan range. The defection of the Tungani, who had formed a large proportion, if not the majority, of the Chinese garrisons, paralysed the strength of the Celestials in Central Asia. Both in the districts dependent on Ili, and in those ruled from Kashgar and Yarkand, the Chinese were beset by many great and permanent difficulties. They were with united strength a minority, and now that they were divided among themselves almost a hopeless minority. The peoples they governed were fanatical, false, and fickle. The ruler of Khokand and the refugees living on his bounty were always on the alert to take the most advantage of the least slip or act of weakness on the part of the governing classes. Their machinations had been hitherto baffled, but never before had so favourable an opportunity presented itself for attaining their wishes as when it became known that the whole Mahomedan population was up in arms against the Emperor, and that communications were severed between Kashgar and Pekin. The attempts made at earlier periods on the part of the members of the old ruling family in Kashgar to regain their own by expelling the Chinese, have been described. In 1857 Wali Khan, one of the sons of Jehangir, had succeeded in gaining temporary possession of the city of Kashgar, and seemed for a moment to be likely to capture Yarkand also. He fell by his vices. The people soon detested the presence of the man to whom they had accorded a too hasty welcome. After a rule of four months he fled the country, vanquished in the field by the Chinese garrison, and followed by the execrations of the population he had come to deliver. The invasion of Wali Khan further embittered the relations between the Chinese and their subjects; and a succession of governors bore heavily on the Mahomedans. Popular dissatisfaction and the apprehension in the minds of the governing officials that their lives might be forfeited at any moment to a popular outbreak added to the dangers of the situation in Kashgar itself, when the news arrived of the Tungan revolt, and of the many other complications which hampered the action of the Pekin ruler. We cannot narrate here the details of the rebellion in Kashgar. Its influence on the history of China would not sanction such close exactitude. But in the year 1863 the Chinese officials had become so alarmed at their isolated position that they resolved to adopt the desperate expedient of massacreing all the Mahomedans or Tungani in their own garrisons. The amban and his officers were divided in council, and dilatory in execution. The Tungani heard of the plot while the governor was summoning the nerve to carry it out. They resolved to anticipate him. The Mahomedans at Yarkand, the largest and most important garrison in the country, rose in August, 1863, and massacred all the Buddhist Chinese. Seven thousand men are computed to have fallen. A small band fled to the citadel, which they held for a short time; but at length, overwhelmed by numbers, they preferred death to dishonour, and destroyed themselves by exploding the fort with the magazine. The defection of the Tungani thus lost Kashgaria for the Chinese, as the other garrisons and towns promptly followed the example of Yarkand; but they could not keep it for themselves. The spectacle of this internal dissension proved irresistible for the adventurers of Khokand, and Buzurg. The last surviving son of Jehangir, resolved to make another bid for power and for the recovery of the position for which his father and kinsmen had striven in vain. The wish might possibly have been no more attained than theirs had he not secured the support of the most capable soldier in Khokand, Mahomed Yakoob, the defender of Ak Musjid against the Russians. It was not until the early part of the year 1865 that this Khoja pretender, with his small body of Khokandian officers, and a considerable number of Kirghiz allies, appeared upon the scene. Then, however, their success was rapid. The Tungan revolt in Altyshahr resolved itself into a movement for the restoration of the Khoja dynasty. In a short time Buzurg was established as ruler, while his energetic lieutenant was employed in the task of crushing the few remaining Chinese garrisons, and also in cowing his Tungan allies, who already regarded their new ruler with a doubtful eye. By the month of September in the same year that witnessed the passage of the invading force through the Terek defile, the triumph of the Khoja's arms was assured. A few weeks later Mahomed Yakoob deposed his master, and caused himself to be proclaimed ruler in his stead. The voice of the people ratified the success of the man; and in 1866 Mahomed Yakoob, or Yakoob Beg, received at the hands of the Ameer of Bokhara the proud title of Athalik Ghazi, by which he was long known. The Mahomedan rising spread still further within the limits of Chinese authority in Central Asia. While the events which have been briefly sketched were happening in the region south of the great Tian Shan range, others of not less importance had taken place in Ili or Kuldja, which, under Chinese rule, had enjoyed uninterrupted peace for a century. It was this fact which marked the essential difference between the Tungan rebellion and all the disturbances that had preceded it. The revolution in the metropolitan province was complicated by the presence of different races just as it had been in Kashgaria by the pretensions of the Khoja family. A large portion of the population consisted of those Tarantchis who were the descendants of the Kashgarians deported on more than one occasion by the Chinese from their own homes to the banks of the Ili; and they had inherited a legacy of ill-will against their rulers which only required the opportunity to display itself. The Tungan—or Dungan, as the Russians spell it—element was also very strong, and colonies of the Sobo and Solon tribes, who had been emancipated from their subjection to the Mongols by the Emperor Kanghi for their bravery, further added to the variety of the nationalities dwelling in this province. It had been said with some truth that the Chinese ruled in this quarter of their dominions on the old principle of commanding by the division of the subjected; and it had been predicted that they would fall whenever any two of the dependent populations combined against them. There is little difficulty in showing that the misfortunes of the Chinese were due to their own faults. They neglected the plainest military precautions, and the mandarins thought only of enriching themselves. But the principal cause of the destruction of their power was the cessation of the supplies which they used to receive from Pekin. The government of these dependencies was only possible by an annual gift from the Imperial treasury. When the funds placed at the disposal of the Ili authorities were diverted to other uses, it was no longer possible to maintain the old efficiency of the service. Discontent was provided with a stronger argument at the same time that the executive found itself embarrassed in grappling with it

The news of the Mahomedan outbreak in China warned the Tungani in Ili that their opportunity had come. But although there were disturbances as early as January, 1863, these were suppressed, and the vigilance of the authorities sufficed to keep things quiet for another year. Their subsequent incapacity, or hesitation to strike a prompt blow, enabled the Mahomedans to husband their resources and to complete their plans. A temporary alliance was concluded between the Tungani and the Tarantchis and they hastened to attack the Chinese troops and officials. The year 1865 was marked by the progress of a sanguinary struggle, during which the Chinese lost their principal towns, and some of their garrisons were ruthlessly slaughtered after surrender. The usual scenes of civil war followed. When the Chinese were completely vanquished and their garrisons exterminated, the victors quarrelled among themselves. The Tungani and the Tarantchis met in mortal encounter, and the former were vanquished and their chief slain. When they renewed the contest, some months later, they were, after another sanguinary struggle, again overthrown. The Tarantchis then ruled the state by themselves, but the example they set of native rule was, to say the least, not encouraging One chief after another was deposed and murdered. The same year witnessed no fewer than five leaders in the supreme place of power; and when Abul Oghlan assumed the title of Sultan the cup of their iniquities was already full. In the year 1871 an end was at last put to these enormities by the occupation of the province by a Russian force, and the installation of a Russian governor. Although it is probable that they were only induced to take this step by the fear that if they did not do so Yakoob Beg would, the fact remains that the Russian government did a good thing in the cause of order by interfering for the restoration of tranquillity in the valley of the Ili.

The Mahomedan outbreaks in south-western and north-western China resulted, therefore, in the gradual suppression of the Panthay rebellion, which was completed in the twelfth year of Tungche's reign, while the

Tungan rising, so far as the Central Asian territories were concerned, remained unquelled for a longer period. The latter led to the establishment of an independent Tungan confederacy beyond Kansuh, and also of the kingdom of Kashgaria ruled by Yakoob Beg. The revolt in Ili, after several alternations of fortune, resulted in the brief independence of the Tarantchis, who were in turn displaced by the Russians under a pledge of restoring the province to the Chinese whenever they should return. Judged by the extent of territory involved, the Mahomedan rebellion might be said to be not less important than the Taeping; but the comparison on that ground alone would be really delusive, as the numerical inferiority of the Mahomedans rendered it always a question only of time for the central power to be restored.

The young Emperor Tungche, therefore, grew up amidst continual difficulties, although the successes of his principal lieutenants afforded good reason to believe that, so far as they arose from rebels, it was only a question of time before they would be finally removed. The foreign intercourse still gave cause for much anxiety, although there was no apprehension of war. It would have been unreasonable to suppose that the relations between the foreign merchants and residents and the Chinese could become, after the suspicion and dangers of generations, absolutely cordial. The commercial and missionary bodies, into which the foreign community was naturally divided, had objects of trade or religion to advance, which rendered them apt to take an unfavourable view of the progress made by the Chinese government in the paths of civilisation, and to be ever sceptical even of its good faith. The main object with the foreign diplomatic representatives became not more to obtain justice for their countrymen than to restrain their eagerness, and to confine their pretensions to the rights conceded by the treaties. A clear distinction had to be drawn between undue coercion of the Chinese government on the one hand, and the effectual compulsion of the people to evince respect towards foreigners and to comply with the obligations of the treaty on the other. Instances repeatedly occurred in reference to the latter matter, when it would have been foolish to have shown weakness, especially as there was not the least room to suppose that the government possessed at that time the power and the capacity to secure reparation for, or to prevent the repetition of, attacks on foreigners. Under this category came the riot at Yangchow in the year 1868, when some missionaries had their houses burnt down, and were otherwise maltreated. A similar outrage was perpetrated in Formosa; but the fullest redress was always tendered as soon as the Executive realised that the European representatives attached importance to the occurrence. The recurrence of these local dangers and disputes served to bring more clearly than ever before the minds of the Chinese Ministers the advisability of taking some step on their own part towards an understanding with European governments and peoples. The proposal to depute a Chinese ambassador to the West could hardly be said to be new, seeing that it had been projected after the Treaty of Nankin, and that the minister Keying had manifested some desire to be the first mandarin to serve in that novel capacity. But when the Tsungli Yamen took up the question it was decided that in this as in other matters it would be expedient to avail themselves in the first place of foreign mediation. The favourable opportunity of doing so presented itself when Mr. Burlinghame retired from his post as Minister of the United States at

Pekin. In the winter of 1867-68 Mr. Burlinghame accepted an appointment as accredited representative of the Chinese government to eleven of the principal countries of the world, and two Chinese mandarins and a certain number of Chinese students were appointed to accompany him on his tour. The importance of the Burlinghame Mission was certainly exaggerated at the time, and the speculations to which it gave rise as to the part China was about to take in the movement of the world were no doubt based on erroneous data; but still it would be a mistake to say that it failed to produce any of the beneficial effect which had been expected. It was something for the outer world to learn in those days that the Chinese represented a great power. Mr. Burlinghame was sanguine as to the future development of China and the intention of her Executive, and the expectations of his audiences both in America and in Europe overleapt all difficulties and spanned at a step the growth of years; but only shallow-minded observers will deny that Mr. Burlinghame's widest stretches of fancy were supported by an amount of truth which events are making clearer every year. Of course those who only looked on the surface, who saw the difficulties under which China staggered, and the dogged pride with which she refused the remedy forced upon her by foreigners, who had at least as much their own interests as hers in view, declared that Mr. Burlinghame's statements were "enthusiastic fictions." The Chinese themselves did not attach as much importance as they might have done to his efforts, and Mr. Burlinghame's Mission will be remembered more as an educational process for foreigners than as signifying any decided change in Chinese policy. His death at St. Petersburg, in March, 1870, put a sudden and unexpected close to his tour, but it cannot be said that he could have done more towards the elucidation of Chinese questions than he had already accomplished, while his bold and optimistic statements, after awakening public attention, had already begun to produce the inevitable reaction.

In 1869 Sir Rutherford Alcock retired, and was succeeded in the difficult post of English representative in China by Mr. Thomas Wade, whose services have been more than once referred to. In the very first year of his holding the post an event occurred which cast all the minor aggressive acts that had preceded it into the shade. It may perhaps be surmised that this was the Tientsin massacre—an event which threatened to re-open the whole of the China question, and which brought France and China to the verge of war. It was in June, 1870, on the eve of the outbreak of the Franco-Prussian war, that the foreign settlements were startled by the report of a great popular outbreak against foreigners in the important town of Tientsin. At that city there was a large and energetic colony of Roman Catholic priests, and their success in the task of conversion, small as it might be held, was still sufficient to excite the ire and fears of the literary and official classes. The origin of mob violence is ever difficult to discover, for a trifle suffices to set it in motion. But at Tientsin specific charges of the most horrible and, it need not be said, the most baseless character were spread about as to the cruelties and evil practices of those devoted to the service of religion. These rumours were diligently circulated, and it need not cause wonder if, when the mere cry of "Fanquai"—Foreign Devil— sufficied to raise a disturbance, these allegations resulted in a vigorous agitation against the missionaries, who were already the mark of popular execration. It was well known beforehand that an attack on the missionaries would take place unless the authorities adopted very efficient measures of protection. The foreign residents and the consulates were warned of the coming outburst, and a very heavy responsibility will always rest on those who might, by the display of greater vigour, have prevented the unfortunate occurrences that ensued. At the same time, allowing for the prejudices of the Chinese, it must be allowed that not only must the efforts of all foreign missionaries be attended with the gravest peril, but that the acts of the French priests and nuns at Tientsin were, if not indiscreet, at least peculiarly calculated to arouse the anger and offend the superstitious predilections of the Chinese. That the wrong was not altogether on the side of the Chinese may be gathered from an official despatch of the United States Minister, describing the originating causes of the outrage : " At many of the principal places in China open to foreign residence, the Sisters of Charity have established institutions, each of which appears to combine in itself a foundling hospital and orphan asylum. Finding that the Chinese were averse to placing children in their charge, the managers of these institutions offered a certain sum per head for all the children placed under their control, to be given to them ; it being understood that a child once in their asylum no parent, relative, or guardian could claim or exercise any control over it. It has for some time been asserted by the Chinese, and believed by most of the non-Catholic foreigners residing here, that the system of paying bounties induced the kidnapping of children for these institutions for the sake of the reward. It is also asserted that the priests or sisters, or both, have been in the habit of holding out inducements to have children brought to them in the last stages of illness for the purpose of being baptised *in articulo mortis*. In this way many children have been taken to these establishments in the last stages of disease, baptised there, and soon after taken away dead. All these acts, together with the secrecy and seclusion which appear to be a part and parcel of the regulations which govern institutions of this character everywhere, have created suspicions in the minds of the Chinese, and these suspicions have engendered an intense hatred against the Sisters."

Had the officials in the town acted with promptitude and instituted an official inquiry with the view of demonstrating the falseness of these charges, it is probable that the outbreak might have been averted. Such a course had proved availing on equally critical occasions in some of the towns along the Yangtse ; and the responsibility of not taking it rested in equal proportions between the Chinese officials and the French Consul. At that time Chung How, the Superintendent of Trade for the three Northern Ports, was the principal official in Tientsin ; but although some representations, not as forcible however as the occasion demanded, were made to him by M. Fontanier, the French Consul, on the 18th of June, three days before the massacre, no reply was given, and no precautions were taken. On the 21st a large crowd assembled outside the Mission House. They very soon assumed an attitude of hostility, and it was clear that at any moment the attack might begin. M. Fontanier hastened off in person to Chung How, but his threats seem to have been as unavailing as his arguments. On his return he found the attack on the point of commencing. He made use of menaces, and he fired a shot from his revolver, whether in self-defence or in the heat of indignation at some official treachery will never be known. The mob turned upon him, and he was murdered. The Chinese then hastened to complete the work they had begun. Chung How, like Surajah Dowlah, was not to be disturbed, and the attack on the Mission House and Consulate proceeded, while the officials responsible for order remained inactive. Twenty-one foreigners in all were brutally murdered under circumstances of the greatest barbarity, while the number of native converts who fell at the same time can never be ascertained. This event naturally produced the greatest feeling of alarm, and for the moment it was feared that the rioters would proceed to attack the rest of the foreign settlement. The mandarins still refrained from intervention, and as there happened to be no gun-boat at Tientsin, the foreign residents were for the moment placed in an extremely dangerous predicament. They, of course, took all the measures they could to defend themselves, but it was said at the time that if the mob had only attacked at once they would probably have overcome such resistance as the Europeans could then have offered. They did not do so, however, chiefly because they distrusted or failed to realise their strength; and the massacre of Tientsin did not assume the larger proportions that were at one moment feared.

The Tientsin massacre was followed by a wave of anti-foreign feeling over the whole country; but although an official brought out a work—entitled "Death-blow to Corrupt Doctrine"—which obtained more than a passing notoriety, and notwithstanding that some members of the Imperial Family, and notably, as it was stated, Prince Chun, regarded the movement with favour, the arguments of Prince Kung and the more moderate ministers carried the day, and it was resolved to make every concession in the power of the government for the pacific settlement of the dispute that had arisen with France. The outbreak of the war between France and Germany, while it contributed to a peaceful settlement of the question, rendered the process of diplomacy slow and dubious. The Tsungli Yamen, as soon as it realised that nothing short of the despatch of a mission of apology to Europe would salve the injured honour of France, determined that none other than Chung How himself should go to Paris to assure the French that the government deplored the popular ebullition and had taken no part in it. The untoward result of the great war for France embarrassed her action in China. Chung How's assurances were accepted, the proffered compensation was received; but the Chinese were informed that in recognition of France's moderation, and in return for the reception of their envoy by M. Thiers, the right of audience should be conceded to the French Minister resident at Pekin. The Audience question naturally aroused the greatest interest at Pekin, where it agitated the official mind not merely because it signified another concession to force, but also because it promised to produce a disturbing effect on the mind of the people. The young Emperor was growing up, and might be expected to take a direct share in the administration at an early date. It was not an idle apprehension that filled the minds of his ministers lest he might lay the blame on them for having cast upon him the obligation of receiving ministers of foreign states in a manner such as they had never before been allowed to appear in the presence of the occupant of the Dragon Throne. The youth of the sovereign served to postpone the question for a short space of time, but it was no longer doubtful that the assumption of personal authority by the young Emperor Tungche would be accompanied by the re-introduction, and probably by the settlement, of the Audience Question. It was typical of the progress Chinese statesmen were making that none of them seemed to consider the possibility of distinctly refusing this privilege. Its concession was only postponed until after the celebration of the young Emperor's marriage.

It had been known for some time that the young ruler had fixed his affections on Ahluta, a Manchu lady of good family, daughter of Duke Chung, and that the Empresses had decided that she was worthy of the high rank to which she was to be raised. The marriage ceremony was deferred on more than one plea until after the Emperor had reached his sixteenth birthday, but in October, 1872, there was thought to be no longer any excuse for postponement, and it was celebrated with great splendour on the 16th of that month. The arrangements were made in strict accordance with the precedent of the Emperor Kanghi's marriage in 1674, that ruler having also married when in occupation of the throne, and before he had attained his majority. It was stated that the ceremonial was imposing, that the incidental expenses were enormous, and that the people were very favourably impressed by the demeanour of their young sovereign. Four months after the celebration of his marriage the formal act of conferring upon Tungche the personal control of his dominions was performed. In a special decree issued from the Board of Rites the Emperor said that he had received "the commands of their Majesties the two Empresses to assume the superintendence of business." This edict was directed to the Foreign Ministers, who in return presented a collective request to be received in audience. Prince Kung was requested "to take his Imperial Majesty's orders with reference to their reception." The question being thus brought to a crucial point, it was not unnatural that the Chinese Ministers should make the most vigorous resistance they could to those details which seemed to and did encroach upon the prerogative of the Emperor as he had been accustomed to exercise it. For, in the first place, they were no longer free agents, and Tungche had himself to be considered in any arrangement for the reception of foreign envoys. The discussion of the question assumed a controversial character, in which stress was laid on the one side upon the necessity of the kotow even in a modified form, while on the other it was pointed out that the least concession was as objectionable as the greatest, and that China would benefit by the complete settlement of the question. It says a great deal for the fairness and moderation of Prince Kung and the ministers with him that, although they knew that the Foreign governments were not prepared to make the Audience Question one of war, or even of the suspension of diplomatic relations, they determined to settle the matter in the way most distasteful to themselves and most agreeable to foreigners. On the 29th of June, 1873, Tungche received in audience the ministers of the principal Powers at Pekin, and thus gave completeness to the many rights and concessions obtained from his father and grandfather by the treaties of Tientsin and Nankin. The privilege thus secured caused lively gratification in the minds of all foreign residents, to whom it signified the great surrender of the inherent right to superiority claimed by the Chinese Emperors, and we have recently seen that it has been accepted as a precedent.

The sudden death of Tseng Kwofan in the summer of 1872 removed unquestionably the foremost public man in China. After the fall of Nankin he had occupied the highest posts in the Empire, both at that city and in the metropolis. He was not merely powerful from his own position, but from his having placed his friends and dependents in many of the principal offices throughout the Empire. At first prejudiced against foreigners, he had gradually brought himself to recognise that some advantage might be derived from their knowledge. But the change came at too late a period to admit of his conferring any distinct benefit on his country from the more liberal policy he felt disposed to pursue with regard to the training of Chinese youths in the science and learning of the West. It was said that had he been personally ambitious he might have succeeded in displacing the Tartar regime. But such a thought never assumed any practical shape in his mind, and to the end of his days Tseng Kwofan was satisfied to remain the steadfast supporter and adherent of the Manchus. In this respect he has been closely imitated by his most distinguished lieutenant. Li Hung Chang, who succeeded to some of his dignities and much of his power.

Another of Tseng's protégés, Tso Tsung Tang, had been raised from the Vice-royalty of Chekiang and Fuhkien to that of Shensi and Kansuh. The promotion was of the more doubtful value, seeing that both those provinces were in the actual possession of the rebels; but Tso threw himself into the task of reconquering them with remarkable energy, and within two years of his arrival he was able to report that he had cleared the province of Shensi of all insurgents. He then devoted his attention to the pacification of Kansuh; and after many desultory engagements proceeded to lay siege to the town of Souchow, where the Mahomedans had massed their strength. At the end of the year 1872 the Imperial army was drawn up in front of this place, but Tso does not seem to have considered himself strong enough to deliver an attack, and confined his operations to preventing the introduction of supplies and fresh troops into the town. Even in this he was only partially successful, as a considerable body of men made their way in in January, 1873. In the following month he succeeded in capturing, by a night attack, a temple outside the walls, upon which the Mahomedans placed considerable value. The siege continued during the whole of the summer, and it was not until the month of October that the garrison was reduced to such extremities as to surrender. The chiefs were hacked to pieces, and about four thousand men perished by the sword. The women, children, and old men were spared, and the spoil of the place was handed over to the soldiery. It was Tso's distinctive merit that, far from being carried away by these successes, he neglected no military precaution, and devoted his main efforts to the reorganisation of the province. In that operation he may be left employed for the brief remainder of Tungche's reign; but it may be said that in 1874 the campaign against Kashgaria had been fully decided upon. A thousand Manchu cavalry were sent to Souchow. Sheep-skins, horses, and ammunition in large quantities were also despatched to the far west, and General Kinshun, the Manchu general, was entrusted with the command of the army in the field.

The year 1874 witnessed an event that claims notice. There never has been much good-will between China and her neighbours in Japan. The latter are too independent in their bearing to please the advocates of Chinese predominance, at the same time that their insular position has left them safe from the attack of the Pekin government. The attempt made by the Mongol, Kublai Khan, to subdue these islanders had been too disastrous to invite repetition. In Corea the pretensions of the ruler of Yeddo had been repelled, if not crushed; but wherever the sea intervened the advantage rested more or less decisively with him. The island of Formosa is dependent upon China, and the western districts are governed by officials duly appointed by the Viceroy of Fuhkien. But the eastern half of the island, separated from the cultivated districts by a range of mountains covered with dense if not impenetrable forests, is held by tribes who own no one's authority, and who act as they deem fit. In the year 1868 or 1869 a junk from Loochoo was wrecked on this coast, and the crew were murdered by the islanders. The civil war in Japan prevented any prompt claim for reparation, but in 1873 the affair was revived, and a demand made at Pekin for compensation. The demand was refused, whereupon the Japanese, taking the law into their own hands, sent an expedition to Formosa. China replied with a counter-demonstration, and war seemed inevitable. In this crisis Mr. Wade offered his good services in the interests of peace, and after considerable controversy he succeeded in bringing the two governments to reason, and in inducing them to agree to as equitable terms as could be obtained without having recourse to arms. The Chinese paid an indemnity of half a million taels, and the Japanese evacuated the island.

In all countries governed by an absolute sovereign it is as interesting as it is difficult to obtain some accurate knowledge of the character of the autocrat. A most important change had been effected in the government of China, yet it is impossible to discover what its precise significance was, or to say how far it influenced the fortunes of the country. The Empresses had retired into private life, and for a time their Regency came to an end. Prince Kung was only the minister of a young prince who had it in his power to guide affairs exactly as he might feel personally disposed. Prince Kung might be either the real governor of the state or only the courtier of his nephew. It depended solely on that prince's character. There were not wanting signs that Tungche had the consciousness, if not the capacity, of supreme power and that he wished his will to be paramount. Such evidence as was obtainable agreed in stating that he was impatient of restraint, and that the prudent reflections of his uncle were not over much to his fancy. On the 10th of September the young ruler took the world into his confidence by announcing in a Vermilion Edict that he had degraded Prince Kung and his son in their hereditary rank as princes of the Empire for using "language in very many respects unbecoming." Whether Tungche took this very decided step in a moment of pique or because he perceived that there was a plan among his chief relatives to keep him in leading-strings, must remain a matter of opinion. At the least he must have refused to personally retract what he had done, for on the very following day (September 11th) a Decree appeared from the Two Empresses reinstating Prince Kung and his son in their hereditary rank and dignity, and thus reasserting the power of the ex-Regents over the sovereign.

Not long after this disturbance in the interior of the palace, of which only the ripple reached the surface of publicity, there were rumours that the Emperor's health was in a precarious state, and in the month of December it became known that Tungche was seriously ill with an attack of small-pox. The disease seemed to be making satisfactory progress, for the doctors were rewarded; but on the 18th of December an edict appeared ordering or requesting the Empresses Dowager to assume the personal charge of the administration. Six days later another edict appeared which strengthened the impression that the Emperor was making good progress towards recovery. But appearances were deceptive, for, after several weeks' uncertainty, it became known that the Emperor's death was inevitable. On the 12th of January, 1875, Tungche "ascended upon the Dragon, to be a guest on high," without leaving any offspring to succeed him. There were rumours that his illness was only a plausible excuse and that he was really the victim of foul play ; but it is not likely that the truth on that point will ever be revealed. Whether he was the victim of an intrigue similar to that which had marked his accession to power, or whether he only died from the neglect or incompetence of his medical attendants, the consequences were equally favourable to the personal views of the two Empresses and Prince Kung. They resumed the exercise of that supreme authority which they had resigned little more than twelve months. The most suspicious circumstance in connection with this event was the treatment of the young Empress Ahluta, who, it was well known, was pregnant at the time of her husband's death. Instead of waiting to decide as to the succession until it was known whether Tungche's posthumous child would prove to be a son or a daughter, the Empresses Dowager hastened to make another selection and to place the young widow of the deceased sovereign in a state of honourable confinement. Their motive was plain. Had Ahluta's child happened to be a son, he would have been the legal Emperor, as well as the heir by direct descent, and she herself could not have been excluded from a prominent share in the Government. To the Empresses Dowagers one child on the throne mattered no more than another ; but it was a question of the first importance that Ahluta should be set on one side. In such an atmosphere there is often grievous peril to the lives of inconvenient personages. Ahluta sickened and died. Her child was never born. The charitable gave her credit for having refused food through grief for her husband, Tungche. The sceptical listened to the details of her illness with scorn for the vain efforts to obscure the dark deeds of ambition. In their extreme anxiety to realise their own designs and at the same time not to injure the constitution, the two Empresses had been obliged to resort to a plan that could only have been suggested by desperation. For the first time since the Manchu dynasty occupied the throne, it was necessary to depart from the due line of succession, and to make the election of the sovereign a matter of individual fancy or favour instead of one of inheritance. The range of choice was limited ; for the son of Prince Kung himself, who seemed to enjoy the prior right to the throne, was a young man of sufficient age to govern for himself ; and moreover his promotion would mean the compulsory retirement from public life of Prince Kung, for it was not possible in China for a father to serve under his son, until Prince Chun, the father of the present reigning Emperor, established quite recently a precedent to the contrary. The name of Prince Kung's son, if mentioned at all, was only mentioned to be dismissed. The choice of the Empresses fell upon Tsai Tien, the son of Prince Chun or the Seventh Prince, who on the 13th of January was proclaimed Emperor. As he was of too tender an age to rule for himself, his nomination served the purposes of the two Empresses and their ally Prince Kung, who thus entered upon a second lease of undisputed power.

CHAPTER XXII.

THE REIGN OF KWANGSU.

THUS after a very brief interval the governing power again passed into the hands of the Regents who had ruled the state so well for the twelve years following the death of Hienfung. The nominal Emperor was a child of little more than three years of age, to whom was given the style of "Kwangsu," or "illustrious succession," and the Empresses could look forward to many years of authority in the name of so young a sovereign. The only opposition to their return to power seems to have come from the Palace eunuchs, who had asserted themselves during the brief reign of Tungche and hoped to gain predominance in the Imperial councils. But they found a determined mistress in the person of Tse An, the Eastern Empress, as she was also called, who took vigorous action against them, punishing their leaders with death and effectually nipping all their projects for making themselves supreme in the bud.

The return of the Empresses to power was followed by a great catastrophe in the relations between England and China. For the moment it threw every other matter into the shade, and seemed to render the outbreak of war between the two countries almost inevitable. In the year 1874 the government of India, repenting of its brief infatuation for the Panthay cause, yet still reluctant to lose the advantages it had promised itself from the opening of Yunnan to trade, resolved upon sending a formal mission of explory under Colonel Horace Browne, an officer of distinction, through Burmah to that province. The difficulties in the way of the undertaking seemed comparatively few, as the King of Burmah was friendly and appeared disposed at that time to accept his natural position as the dependent of Calcutta. The Pekin authorities also were outwardly not opposed to the journey; and the only opposition to be apprehended was from the Yunnan officials and people.

It was thought desirable, with the view of preparing the way for the appearance of this foreign mission, that a representative of the English embassy at Pekin, having a knowledge of the language and of the ceremonial etiquette of the country, should be deputed to proceed across China and meet Colonel Browne on the Burmese frontier. The officer selected for this delicate and difficult mission was Mr. Raymond Augustus Margary, who to the singular aptitude he had displayed in the study of Chinese added a buoyant spirit and a vigorous frame that peculiarly fitted him for the long and lonely journey he had undertaken across China. His reception throughout was encouraging. The orders of the Tsungli Yamen, specially drawn up by the Grand Secretary Wansiang, were explicit, and not to be lightly ignored. Mr. Margary performed his journey in safety;

and, on the 26th January, 1875, only one fortnight after Kwangsu's accession, he joined Colonel Browne at Bhamo. A delay of more than three weeks ensued at Bhamo, which was certainly unfortunate. Time was given for the circulation of rumours as to the approach of a foreign invader along a disturbed frontier held by tribes almost independent, and whose predatory instincts were excited by the prospect of rich plunder at the same time that their leaders urged them to oppose a change which threatened to destroy their hold on the caravan route between Bhamo and Talifoo. When on the 17th of February Colonel Browne and his companions approached the limits of Burmese territory, they found themselves in face of a totally different state of affairs from what had existed when Mr. Margary passed safely through three weeks before. The preparations for opposing the English had been made under the direct encouragement, and probably the personal direction, of Lisitai, a man who had been a brigand and then a rebel, but who at this time held a military command on the frontier.

As Colonel Browne advanced he was met with rumours of the opposition that awaited him. At first these were discredited, but on the renewed statements that a large Chinese force had been collected to bar his way, Mr. Margary rode forward to ascertain what truth there was in these rumours. The first town on this route within the Chinese border is Momein, which, under the name of Tengyue, was once a military station of importance, and some distance east of it again is another town, called Manwein. Mr. Margary set out on the 19th of February, and it was arranged that only in the event of his finding everything satisfactory at Momein was he to proceed to Manwein ; and on the first suspicious occurrence he was to retreat at once to the main body.

Mr. Margary reached Momein in safety, and reported in a letter to Colonel Browne that all was quiet at that place, and that there were no signs of any resistance. That letter was the last news ever received from Mr. Margary. On the 19th of February he started from Momein, and the information subsequently obtained left no doubt that he was treacherously murdered on that or the following day at Manwein. An ominous silence followed, and Colonel Browne's party delayed its advance until some definite news should arrive as to what had occurred in front, although the silence was sufficient to justify the worst apprehensions. Three days later the rumour spread that Mr. Margary and his attendants had been murdered. It was also stated that an army was advancing to attack the English expedition ; and on the 22nd of February a large Chinese force did make its appearance on the neighbouring heights. There was no longer any room to doubt that the worst had happened, and it only remained to secure the safety of the expedition. The Chinese numbered several thousand men under Lisitai in person, while to oppose them there were only four Europeans and fifteen Sikhs. Yet superior weapons and steadfastness carried the day against greater numbers. The Sikhs fought as they retired, and the Chinese, unable to make any impression on them, abandoned an attack which was both perilous and useless.

The news of this outrage did not reach Pekin until a month later, when Mr. Wade at once took the most energetic measures to obtain the amplest reparation in the power of the Pekin government to concede. The first and most necessary point in order to ensure not merely the punishment of the guilty, but also that the people of China should not have cause to suppose that their rulers secretly sympathised with the authors of the attack, was that no punitive measures should be undertaken, or, if undertaken, recognised, until a special Commission of Inquiry had been appointed to investigate the circumstances on the spot. Mr. Margary was an officer of the English government travelling under the special permission and protection of the Tsungli Yamen. The Chinese government could not expect to receive consideration if it failed to enforce respect for its own commands, and the English government had an obligation which it could not shirk in exacting reparation for the murder of its representative. The treacherous killing of Mr. Margary was evidently not an occurrence for which it could be considered a sufficient atonement that some miserable criminals under sentence of death, or some desperate individuals anxious to secure the worldly prosperity of their families, should undergo painful torture and public execution in order to shield official falseness and infamy. Although no one ever suspected the Pekin government of having directly instigated the outrage, the delay in instituting an impartial and searching inquiry into the affair strengthened an impression that it felt reluctant to inflict punishment on those who had committed the act of violence. Nearly three months elapsed before any step was taken towards appointing a Chinese official to proceed to the scene of the outrage in company with the officers named by the English minister; but on the 19th of June an edict appeared in the *Pekin Gazette* ordering Li Han Chang, Governor-General of Houkwang, to temporarily vacate his post, and "repair with all speed to Yunnan to investigate and deal with certain matters." Even then the matter dragged along but slowly. Li Han Chang, who, as the brother of Li Hung Chang, was an exceptionally well-qualified and highly-placed official for the task, and whose appointment was in itself some evidence of sincerity, did not leave Hankow until August, and the English Commissioners, Messrs. Grosvenor, Davenport, and Colborne Baber, did not set out from the same place before the commencement of October. The intervening months had been employed by Mr. Wade in delicate and fluctuating negotiation with Li Hung Chang (who had succeeded Tseng Kwofan as Viceroy of Pechihli and who had now come to the front as the chief official in the Chinese service) at Tientsin and with the Tsungli Yamen at Pekin. It was not till the end of the year that the Commission to ascertain the fate of Mr. Margary began its active work on the spot. The result was unexpectedly disappointing. The mandarins supported one another. The responsibility was thrown on several minor officials, and on the border-tribes or savages. Several of the latter were seized, and their lives were offered as atonement for an offence they had not committed. The furthest act of concession which the Chinese Commissioner gave was to temporarily suspend Tsen Yuying the Futai for remissness; but even this measure was never enforced with rigour. The English officers soon found that it was impossible to obtain any proper reparation on the spot.

Sir Thomas Wade, who was knighted during the negotiations, refused to accept the lives of the men offered, whose complicity in the offence was known to be none at all, while its real instigators escaped without any punishment. When the new year, 1876, opened, the question was still unsettled, and it was clear that no solution could be discovered on the spot. Sir Thomas Wade again called upon the Chinese in the most emphatic language allowed by diplomacy to conform with the spirit and letter of their engagements, and he informed the Tsungli Yamen that unless they proffered full redress for Mr. Margary's murder it would be impossible to continue diplomatic relations. To show that this was no meaningless expression, Sir Thomas Wade left Pekin, while a strong reinforcement to the English fleet demonstrated that the Government was resolved to support its representative. In consequence of these steps, Li Hung Chang was, in August, 1876, or more than eighteen months after the outrage, entrusted with full powers for the arrangement of the difficulty; and the small seaport of Chefoo was fixed upon as the scene for the forthcoming negotiations. Even then the Chinese sought to secure a sentimental advantage by requesting that Sir Thomas Wade would change the scene of discussion to Tientsin, or at least that he would consent to pay Li Hung Chang a visit there. This final effort to conceal the fact that the English demanded redress as an equal and not as a suppliant having been baffled, there was no further attempt at delay. The Chefoo Convention was signed in that town, to which the Viceroy proceeded from Tientsin. Li Hung Chang entertained the Foreign Ministers at a great banquet; and the final arrangements were hurried forward for the departure to Europe of the Chinese Ambassador, whose dispatch had been decided upon in the previous year. When the secret history of this transaction is revealed it will be seen how sincere were Li Hung Chang's wishes for a pacific result, and how much his advice contributed to this end.

The most important passage in the Chefoo Convention was unquestionably that commanding the different viceroys and governors to respect, and afford every protection to, all foreigners provided with the necessary passport from the Tsungli Yamen, and warning them that they would be held responsible in the event of any such travellers meeting with injury or maltreatment. The next most important passage was that arranging for the despatch of an Embassy to London bearing a letter of regret for the murder of the English official. The official selected for this duty was Kwo Sungtao, a mandarin of high rank and unexceptionable character. The letter was submitted to Sir Thomas Wade in order that its terms should be exactly in accordance with Chinese etiquette, and that no phrase should be used showing that the Chinese government attached less importance to the mission than the occasion demanded. The Embassy proceeded to Europe, and, whatever may be thought of its immediate effect, it must be allowed that it established a precedent of friendly intercourse with this country, which promises to prove an additional guarantee of peace. Kwo Sungtao was accompanied by the present Sir Halliday Macartney, who had rendered such good service to China, his adopted country, during the Taeping war and afterwards, and who, during the last sixteen years, has taught the Chinese government how to make itself listened to by the most powerful States of Europe.

A curious incident arising from the passion of gambling which is so prevalent in China, and bearing incidentally upon the national character, may be briefly referred to. The attention of the Pekin government was attracted to this subject by a novel form of gambling, which not merely attained enormous dimensions, but which threatened to bring the system of public examination into disrepute. This latter fact created a profound impression at Pekin, and roused the mandarins to take unusually prompt measures. Canton was the headquarters of the gambling confederacy which established the lotteries known as the Weising, but its ramifications extended throughout the whole of the province of Kwantung. The

Weising, or examination sweepstakes, were based on the principle of drawing the names of the successful candidates at the official examinations. They appealed, therefore, to every poor villager, and every father of a family, as well as to the aspirants themselves. The subscribers to the Weising lists were numbered by hundreds of thousands. It became a matter of almost as much importance to draw a successful number or name in the lottery as to take the degree. The practice could not have been allowed to go on without introducing serious abuses into the system of public examination. The profits to the owners of the lottery were so enormous that they were able to pay not less than eight hundred thousand dollars as hush-money to the Viceroy and the other high officials of Canton. In order to shield his own participation in the profits, the Viceroy declared that he devoted this new source of revenue to the completion of the river defences of Canton.

In 1874 the whole system was declared illegal, and severe penalties were passed against those aiding, or participating in any way in, the Weising Company. The local officers did not, however, enforce with any stringency these new laws, and the Weising fraternity enjoyed a further but brief period of increased activity under a different name. The fraud was soon detected, and in an Edict of 11th August, 1875, it was very rightly laid down that "the maintenance of the purity of government demands that it be not allowed under any pretext to be re-established," and for their apathy in the matter the Viceroy Yinghan and several of the highest officials in Canton were disgraced and stripped of their official rank.

In China natural calamities on a colossal scale have often aggravated political troubles. The year 1876 witnessed the commencement of a dearth in the two great provinces of Honan and Shansi which has probably never been surpassed as the cause of a vast amount of human suffering. Although the provinces named suffered the most from the prevalent drought, the suffering was general over the whole of Northern China, from Shantung and Pechihli to Honan and the course of the Yellow River. At first the government, if not apathetic, was disposed to say that the evil would be met by the grant of the usual allowance made by the Provincial Governors in the event of distress; but, when one province after another was absorbed within the famine area, it became no longer possible to treat the matter as one of such limited importance, and the high ministers felt obliged to bestir themselves in face of so grave a danger. Li Hung Chang in particular was most energetic, not merely in collecting and forwarding supplies of rice and grain, but also in inviting contributions of money from all those parts of the Empire which had not been affected by famine. Allowing for the general sluggishness of popular opinion in China, and for the absence of any large amount of currency, it must be allowed that these appeals met with a large and liberal response. The foreign residents also contributed their share, and even the charity of London found a vent in sending some thousands of pounds to the scene of the famine in Northern China. This evidence of foreign sympathy in the cause of a common humanity made more than a passing impression on the minds of the Chinese people.

While the origin of the famine may be attributed to either drought or civil war, there is no doubt that its extension and the apparent inability of the authorities to grapple with it may be traced to the want of means of communication, which rendered it almost impossible to convey the needful succour into the famine districts. The evil being so obvious, it was hoped that the Chinese would be disposed to take a step forward on their own initiative in the great and needed work of the introduction of railways and other mechanical appliances. The Viceroy of the Two Kiang gave his assent to the construction of a short line between Shanghai and the port of Woosung. The great difficulty had always been to make a start; and now that a satisfactory commencement had been made the foreigners were disposed in their eagerness to overlook all obstacles, and to imagine the Flowery Land traversed in all directions by railways. But these expectations were soon shown to be premature. Half of the railway was open for use in the summer of 1876, and during some weeks the excitement among the Chinese themselves was as marked as among the Europeans. The hopes based upon this satisfactory event were destined to be soon dispelled by the animosity of the officials. They announced their intention to resort to every means in their power to prevent the completion of the undertaking. The situation revealed such dangers of mob violence that Sir Thomas Wade felt compelled to request the Company to discontinue its operations, and after some discussion it was arranged that the Chinese should buy the line. After a stipulated period the line was placed under Chinese management, when, instead of devoting themselves to the interests of the railway, and to the extension of its power of utility, they wilfully and persistently neglected it, with the express design of destroying it. At this conjuncture the Viceroy allowed the Governor of Fuhkien to remove the rails and plant to Formosa. The fate of the Woosung railway destroyed the hopes created by its construction, and postponed to a later day the great event of the introduction of railways into China. Notwithstanding such disappointments as this, and the ever present difficulty of conducting relations with an unsympathetic people controlled by suspicious officials, there was yet observable a marked improvement in the relations of the different nations with the Chinese. Increased facilities of trade, such as the opening of new ports, far from extending the area of danger, served to promote a mutual good-will. In 1876 Kiungchow, in the island of Hainan, was made a treaty port, or rather the fact of its having been included in the treaty of Tientsin was practically accepted and recognised. In the following year four new ports were added to the list. One, Pakhoi, was intended to increase trade intercourse with Southern China. Two of the three others, Ichang and Wuhu, were selected as being favourably situated for commerce on the Yangtse and its affluents, while Wenchow was chosen for the benefit of the trade on the coast. Mr. Colborne Baber, who had been a member of the Yunnan commission, was despatched to Szchuen, to take up his residence at Chungking for the purpose of facilitating trade with that great province. The successful tour of Captain Gill, not merely through South-West China into Burmah, but among some of the wilder and more remote districts of Northern Szchuen, afforded reason to believe that henceforth travelling would be safer in China, and nothing that has since happened is calculated to weaken that impression.

When Kwangsu ascended the throne the preparations for the campaign against Kashgaria were far advanced towards completion, and Kinshun had struck the first of those blows which were to ensure the overthrow of the Tungani and of Yakoob Beg. The fall of Souchow had distinguished the closing weeks of the year 1873, and in 1874 Kinshun had begun, under the direction of Tso Tsung Tang, who was described by a French writer as "very intelligent, of a bravery beyond all question, and an admirable organiser," his march across the desert to the west. He followed a circuitous line of march, with a view of avoiding the strongly placed and garrisoned town of Hami. The exact route is not certain, but he seems to have gone as far north as Uliassutai, where he was able to recruit some of the most faithful and warlike of the Mongol tribes. But early in 1875 he arrived before the walls of Barkul, a town lying to the north-west of Hami. No resistance was offered, and a few weeks later Hami was also occupied. The Tungani retreated on the approach of the Chinese, and assembled their main force for the defence of the two towns of Urumtsi and Manas, which are situated on the northern side of the eastern spurs of the Tian Shan. Once Barkul and Hami were in the possession of the Chinese, it became necessary to reopen direct communications with Souchow. This task occupied the whole of the next twelve months, and was only successfully accomplished after many difficulties had been overcome, and when halting-stations had been established across Gobi. There is nothing improbable in the statement that during this period the Chinese planted and reaped the seed which enabled them, or those who followed in their train, to march in the following season. With the year 1876 the really arduous portion of the campaign commenced. The natural difficulties to the commencement of the war from distance and desert had been all overcome. An army of about twenty-five thousand effective troops, besides a considerable number of Mongol and other tribal levies, had been placed in the field and within striking distance of the rebels. The enemies were face to face. The Tungani could retreat no further. Neither from Russia nor from Yakoob Beg could they expect a place of refuge. The Athalik Ghazi might help them to hold their own; he certainly would not welcome them within the limits of the six cities. The Tungani had, therefore, no alternative left save to make as resolute a stand as they could against the Chinese who had returned to revenge their fellow-countrymen who had been slaughtered in their thousands twelve years before. The town of Urumtsi, situated within a loop of the mountains, lies at a distance by road of more than 300 miles from Barkul. Kinshun, who had now been joined by Liu Kintang, the taotai of the Sining district and a man of proved energy and capacity, resolved to concentrate all his efforts on its capture. He moved forward his army to Guchen, 200 miles west of Barkul, where he established a fortified camp and a powder-factory, and took steps to ascertain the strength and intentions of the enemy. Towards the end of July the Chinese army resumed its march. The difficulties of the country were so great that the advanced guards of the opposing armies did not come into contact until the 10th of August. The Chinese general seems to have attempted on that date a night surprise; but although he gained some success in the encounter which ensued, the result must have been doubtful, seeing that he felt obliged to call off his men from the attack. It was only, however, to collect his forces for the delivery of a decisive blow. On the 13th of August a second battle was fought with a result favourable to the Chinese. Two days later the enemy, who held a fortified camp at Gumti, were bombarded out of it by the heavy artillery brought from the coasts of China for the purposes of the war, and after twenty-four hours' firing three breaches were declared to be practicable. The place was carried by storm at the close of four hours' fighting and slaughter, during which 6,000 men were stated to have been killed. Kinshun followed up his victory by a rapid march on

Urumtsi. That town surrendered without a blow, and many hundred fugitives were cut down by the unsparing Manchu cavalry, which pursued them along the road to Manas, their last place of shelter. As soon as the necessary measures had been taken for the military protection of Urumtsi, the Chinese army proceeded against Manas. Their activity, which was facilitated by the favourable season of the year, was also increased by the rumoured approach of Yakoob Beg with a large army to the assistance of the Tungani. At Manas the survivors of the Tungan movement proper had collected for final resistance, and all that desperation could suggest for holding the place had been done. Kinshun appeared before Manas on the 2nd of September. On the 7th his batteries were completed, and he began a heavy fire upon the north-east angle of the wall. A breach of fourteen feet having been made, the order to assault was given, but the stormers were repulsed with the loss of 100 killed. The operations of the siege were renewed with great spirit on both sides. Several assaults were subsequently delivered : but although the Chinese always gained some advantage at the beginning they never succeeded in retaining it. In one of these later attacks they admitted a loss of 200 killed alone. The Imperial army enjoyed the undisputed superiority in artillery, and the gaps in its ranks were more than filled by the constant flow of reinforcements from the rear. The siege gradually assumed a less active character. The Chinese dug trenches and erected earthworks. They approached the walls by means of galleries in readiness to deliver the attack on any symptom of discouragement among the besieged. On the 16th October a mine was sprung under the wall, making a wide breach ; but although the best portion of the Chinese army made two assaults on separate occasions, they were both repulsed with loss. Twelve days later another mine was sprung, destroying a large portion of the wall; but when the Chinese stormers endeavoured to carry the remaining works, they were again driven back with heavy loss, including two generals killed in the breach. Although thus far repulsed, the Imperialists had inflicted very heavy losses on the besieged, who, seeing that the end of their resources was at hand, that there was no hope of succour, and that the besiegers were as energetic as ever, at last arrived at the conclusion that they had no choice left save to surrender on the best terms they could obtain. On the 4th of November, after a two months' siege, Haiyen, as the Chinese named the Mahomedan leader, came out and offered to yield the town. His offer seems to have been partly accepted, and on the 6th of the month the survivors of the brave garrison, to the number of between two and three thousand men, sallied forth from the west gate. It was noticed as a ground of suspicion that all the men carried their weapons, and that they had placed their old men, women, and children, in the centre of their phalanx, as if they contemplated rather a sortie than a tame and unresisting surrender. The Chinese commanders were not indisposed to deal with the least suspicious circumstances as if they meant certain treachery. The Imperialists gradually gathered round the garrison. The Mahomedans made one bold effort to cut their way through. They failed in the attempt, and were practically annihilated on the ground. Those men who were taken by the cavalry were at once beheaded, whether in the city or among those who had gone forth, but the aged, the women, and the children, were spared by Kinshun's express orders. All the leaders taken were tortured before execution as rebels, and even the bodies of the dead chiefs were exhumed in order that they might be subjected to indignity.

The siege of Manas was interesting both for the stubbornness of the attack and defence, and also as marking the successful termination of the Chinese campaign against the Tungani. With its capture, those Mahomedans who might be said to be Chinese in ways and appearance ceased to possess any political importance. It would not be going much too far to say that they no longer existed. The movement of rebellion which began at Hochow in 1862 was thus repressed in 1876, after having involved during those fourteen years the north-western provinces of China, and much of the interior of Asia, in a struggle which, for its bitter and sanguinary character, has rarely been surpassed.

The successes of the Chinese gave their generals and army the confidence and prestige of victory, and the overthrow of the Tungani left them disengaged to deal with a more formidable antagonist. The siege of Manas had been vigorously prosecuted in order that the town might be taken before the army of Yakoob Beg should arrive. The Athalik Ghazi may have believed that Manas could hold out during the winter, for his movements in 1876 were leisurely, and betrayed a confidence that no decisive fighting would take place until the following spring. His hopes were shown to be delusive, but too late for practical remedy. Manas had fallen before he could move to its support. The Chinese had crushed the Tungani, and were in possession of the mountain passes. They were gathering their whole strength to fall upon him, and to drive him out of the state in which he had managed to set up a brief authority. While the events recorded had been in progress, Yakoob Beg had been ruling the state of Kashgaria with sufficient vigour and wisdom to attract the observation of his great neighbours the governments of England and Russia. He had shown rare skill in adapting circumstances to suit his own ends. The people passively accepted the authority which he was prepared to assert with his Khokandian soldiery, and the independent state of Kashgaria might have continued to exist for a longer period had the Chinese not returned. But in 1875 the arrival of Kinshun at Barkul showed Yakoob Beg that he would have to defend his possessions against their lawful owners, while the overthrow of the Tungani and the capture of their strongholds, in 1876, carried with them a melancholy foreboding of his own fate. The Athalik Ghazi made his preparations to take the field, but there was no certainty in his mind as to where he should make his stand. He moved his army eastwards, establishing his camp first at Korla and then moving it on to Turfan, 900 miles distant from Kashgar. The greatest efforts of this ruler only availed to place 15,000 men at the front, and the barrenness of the region compelled him to distribute them. The Ameer was at Turfan with 8,500 men and twenty guns. His second son was at Toksoun, some miles in the rear, at the head of 6,000 more and five guns. There were several smaller detachments between Korla and the front. Opposed to these was the main Chinese army under Kinshun at Urumtsi, while another force had been placed in the field at Hami by the energy of Tso, and entrusted to the direction of a general named Chang Yao. No fighting took place until the month of March, 1877, and then the campaign began with a rapid advance by Chang Yao from Hami to Turfan. The Kashgarians were driven out of Pidjam, and compelled, after a battle, to evacuate Turfan. The Chinese records do not help us to unravel the events of the month of April. The campaign contained no more striking or important episodes, and yet the reports of the generals have been mislaid or consigned to oblivion. The Athalik Ghazi fought a second battle at Toksoun, where he rejoined his son's army, but with no better fortune. He was obliged to flee back to his former camp at Korla. After the capture of Turfan the Chinese armies came to a halt. It was necessary to reorganise the vast territory which they had already recovered, and to do something to replenish their arsenals. During five months the Celestials stayed their further advance, while the cities were being re-peopled and the roads rendered once more secure. Tso Tsung Tang would leave nothing to chance. He had accomplished two of the three parts into which his commission might be naturally divided. He had pacified the North-West and overthrown the Tungani, and he would make sure of his ground before attempting the third and the most difficult of all. And while the Chinese Viceroy had, for his own reasons, come to the very sensible conclusion to refresh his army after its arduous labours in the limited productive region situated between two deserts, the stars in their courses fought on his side.

Yakoob Beg had withdrawn only to Korla. He still cherished the futile scheme of defending the eastern limits of his dominion, but with his overthrow on the field of battle the magic power which he had exercised over his subjects vanished. His camp became the scene of factious rivalry and of plots to advance some individual pretension at the cost of the better interests and even the security of the State. The exact details of the conspiracy will never be known, partly from the remoteness of the scene, but also on account of the mention of persons of whom nothing was, or is ever likely to be, known. The single fact remains clear that Yakoob Beg died at Korla on the 1st of May, 1877, of fever according to one account, of poison administered by Hakim Khan Torah according to another. Still the Chinese did not even then advance, and Yakoob's sons were left to contest with Hakim Khan Torah over the dismembered fragments of their father's realm. A bitter and protracted civil war followed close upon the disappearance of the Athalik Ghazi. On the removal of his dead body for sepulture to Kashgar his eldest son, Kuli Beg, murdered his younger brother over their father's bier. It was then that Hakim Khan came prominently forward as a rival to Kuli Beg, and that the Mahomedans, weak and numerically few as they were, divided themselves into two hostile parties. While the Chinese were recruiting their troops and repairing their losses, the enemy were exhausting themselves in vain and useless struggles. In June, 1877, Hakim Khan was signally defeated and compelled to flee into Russian territory, whence on a later occasion he returned for a short time in a vain attempt to disturb the tranquillity of Chinese rule. When, therefore, the Chinese resumed their advance much of their work had been done for them. They had only to complete the overthrow of an enemy whom they had already vanquished, and who was now exhausted by his own disunion. The Chinese army made no forward movement from Toksoun until the end of August, 1877. Liu Kintang, to whom the command of the advance had been given, did not leave until one month later; and when he arrayed his forces he found them to number about 15,000 men. It had been decided that the first advance should not be made in greater force, as the chief difficulty was to feed the army, not to defeat the enemy.

The resistance encountered was very slight, and the country was found to be almost uninhabited. Both Karashar and Korla were occupied by a Chinese garrison, and the district around them was entrusted to the administration of a local chief. The information that the rebel force was stationed at the next town, Kucha, which is as far beyond Korla as that place is from Toksoun, induced Liu Kintang to renew his march and to continue it still more rapidly. A battle was fought outside Kucha in which the Chinese were victorious, but not until they had overcome stubborn resistance. However, the Chinese success was complete, and with Kucha in their power they had simplified the process of attacking Kashgar itself. A further halt was made at this town to enable the men to recover from their fatigue, to allow fresh troops to come up, and measures to be taken for ensuring the security of communications with the places in the rear. At Kucha also the work of civil administration was entrusted to some of the local notables. The deliberation of the Chinese movements, far from weakening their effect, invested their proceedings with the aspect of being irresistible. The advance was shortly resumed. Aksu, a once flourishing city within the limits of the old kingdom of Kashgar, surrendered at the end of October. Ush Turfan yielded a few days later. The Chinese had now got within striking distance of the capital of the state. They had only to provide the means of making the blow as fatal and decisive as possible. In December they seized Maralbashi, an important position on the Kashgar Darya, commanding the principal roads to both Yarkand and Kashgar. Yarkand was the chief object of attack. It surrendered without a blow on December 21st. A second Chinese army had been sent from Maralbashi to Kashgar, which was defended by a force of several thousand men. It had been besieged nine days, when Liu Kintang arrived with his troops from Yarkand. A battle ensued, in which the Mahomedans were vanquished, and the city with the citadel outside captured. Several rebel leaders and some eleven hundred men were said to have been executed; but Kuli Beg escaped into Russian territory. The city of Kashgar was taken on the 26th of December, and one week later the town of Khoten, famous from a remote period for its jade ornaments, passed into the hands of the race who best appreciated their beauty and value. The Chinese thus brought to a triumphant conclusion the campaigns undertaken for the reassertion of their authority over the Mahomedan populations which had revolted. They had conquered in this war by the superiority of their weapons, and their organisation, and not by an overwhelming display of numbers. Although large bodies of troops were stationed at many places, it does not seem that the army which seized the cities of Yarkand and Kashgar numbered more than twenty thousand men. Having vanquished their enemy in the field, the Celestials devoted all their attention to the reorganisation of what was called the New Dominion, the capital of which after much deliberation was fixed at Urumtsi. Their rule has been described by a Mussulman as being both very fair and very just.

Having conquered Eastern Turkestan, the Chinese next took steps for the recovery of Ili. Without the metropolitan province the undertaking of Tso Tsung Tang would lack completeness, while indeed many political and military dangers would attend the situation in Central Asia. But this was evidently a matter to be effected in the first place by negotiation, and not by violence and force of arms. Russia had always been a friendly and indeed a sympathetic neighbour. In this very matter of Ili, she had originally acted with the most considerate attention for China's rights, when it seemed that they had permanently lost all definite meaning, for she had declared that she would surrender it on China sending a sufficient force to take possession, and now this had been done. It was, therefore, by diplomatic representations on the part of the Tsungli Yamen to the Russian Minister at Pekin that the recovery of Ili was expected in the first place to be achieved. At about the same time the Russian authorities at Tashkent came to the conclusion that the matter must rest with the Czar, and the Chinese official world perceived that they would have to depute a Minister Plenipotentiary to St. Petersburg.

The official selected for the difficult and, as it proved, dangerous task of negotiating at St. Petersburg, was that same Chung How who had been sent to Paris after the Tientsin massacre. He arrived at Pekin in August, 1878, and was received in several audiences by the Empresses while waiting for his full instructions from the Tsungli Yamen. He did not leave until October, about a month after the Marquis Tseng, Tseng Kwofan's eldest son, set out from Pekin to take the place of Kwo Sungtao as Minister in London and Paris. Chung How reached St. Petersburg in the early part of the following year, and the discussion of the various points in question, protracted by the removal of the Court to Livadia, occupied the whole of the summer months. At last it was announced that a treaty had been signed at Livadia, by which Russia surrendered the Kuldja valley, but retained that of the Tekes, which left in her hands the command of the passes through the Tian Shan range into Kashgar. Chung How knew nothing about frontiers or military precautions, but he thought a great deal about money. He fought the question of an indemnity with ability, and got it fixed at five million roubles, or little more than half that at which it was placed by the later treaty. There was never any reason to suppose that the Chinese government would accept the partial territorial concession obtained by Chung How. The first greeting that met Chung How on his return revealed the fate of his treaty. He had committed the indiscretion of returning without waiting for the Edict authorising his return, and as the consequence he had to accept suspension from all his offices, while his treaty was submitted to the tender mercies of the grand secretaries, the six presidents of boards, the nine chief ministers of state, and the members of the Hanlin. Three weeks later, Prince Chun was specially ordered to join the Committee of Deliberation. On the 27th of January Chung How was formally cashiered and arrested, and handed over to the Board of Punishment for correction. The fate of the treaty itself was decided a fortnight later. Chung How was then declared to have "disobeyed his instructions and exceeded his powers." On the 3rd of March an Edict appeared, sentencing the unhappy envoy to "decapitation after incarceration." This sentence was not carried out, and the reprieve of the unlucky envoy was due to the Queen's expression of a hope that the Chinese government would spare his life. To the Marquis Tseng belongs the credit of having made the representation which resulted in the realisation of the wish of the British Sovereign.

At the same time that the Chinese refused their ratification to Chung How's treaty, they expressed their desire for another pacific settlement, which would give them more complete satisfaction. The Marquis Tseng was accordingly instructed to take up the thread of negotiation, and to proceed to the Russian capital as Ambassador and Minister Plenipotentiary. Some delay ensued, as it was held to be doubtful whether Russia would consent to the reopening of the question. But owing to the cautious and well-timed approaches of the Marquis Tseng, the St. Petersburg Foreign

Office acquiesced in the recommencement of negotiations, and after six months' discussion, accepted the principle of the almost unqualified territorial concession for which the Chinese had stood firm. On the 12th February, 1881, these views were embodied in a treaty, signed at St. Petersburg, and the ratification within six months showed how differently its provisions were regarded from those of its predecessor. With the Marquis Tseng's act of successful diplomacy the final result of the long war in Central Asia was achieved. The Chinese added Ili to Kashgar and the rest of the New Dominion, which at the end of 1880 was made into a High Commissionership and placed under the care of the dashing general Liu Kintang.

The close of the great work successfully accomplished during the two periods of the Regency was followed within a few weeks by the disappearance of the most important of the personages who had carried on the government throughout these twenty years of constant war and diplomatic excitement. Before the Pekin world knew of her illness, it heard of the death of the Empress Dowager Tsi An, who as Hienfung's principal widow had enjoyed the premier place in the government, although she had never possessed a son to occupy the throne in person. In a proclamation issued in her name and possibly at her request, Tsi An described the course of her malady, the solicitude of the Emperor, and urged upon him the duty of his high place to put restraint upon his grief. Her death occurred on 18th April, from heart disease when she was only forty-five, and her funeral obsequies were as splendid as her services demanded. For herself she had always been a woman of frugal habits, and the successful course of recent Chinese history was largely due to her firmness and resolution. Her associate in the Regency, Tsi Thsi, who has always been more or less of an invalid, still survives.

The difficulty with Russia had not long been composed, when, on two opposite sides of her extensive dominion, China was called upon to face a serious condition of affairs. In Corea, "the forbidden land" of the Far East, events were forced by the eagerness and competition of European states to conclude treaties of commerce with that primitive kingdom, and perhaps also by their fear that if they delayed Russia would appropriate some port on the Corean coast. To all who had official knowledge of Russia's desire and plan for seizing Port Lazareff, this apprehension was far from chimerical, and there was reason to believe that Russia's encroachment might compel other countries to make annexations in or round Corea by way of precaution. Practical evidence of this was furnished by the English occupation of Port Hamilton, and by its subsequent evacuation when the necessity passed away, but should the occasion again arise the key of the situation will probably be found in the possession not of Port Hamilton or Quelpart, but of the Island of Tsiusima. Recourse was had to diplomacy to avert what threatened to be a grave international danger; and although the result was long doubtful, and the situation sometimes full of peril, a gratifying success was achieved in the end. In 1881 a draft commercial treaty was drawn up, approved by the Chinese authorities and the representatives of the principal powers at Pekin, and carried to the Court of Seoul for acceptance and signature by the American naval officer, Commodore Schufeldt. The Corean king made no objection to the arrangement, and it was signed with the express stipulation that the ratifications of the treaty were to be exchanged in the following year. Thus was it harmoniously arranged at Pekin that Corea was to issue from her hermit's cell, and open her ports to trading countries under the guidance and encouragement of China. There can be no doubt that if this arrangement had been carried out, the influence and the position of China in Corea would have been very greatly increased and strengthened. But, unfortunately, the policy of Li Hung Chang—for if he did not originate, he took the most important part in directing it—aroused the jealousy of Japan, which has long asserted the right to have an equal voice with China in the control of Corean affairs; and the government of Tokio, on hearing of the Schufeldt treaty, at once took steps not merely to obtain all the rights to be conferred by that document, to which no one would have objected, but also to assert its claim to control equally with China the policy of the Corean Court. With that object, a Japanese fleet and army were sent to the Seoul river, and when the diplomatists returned for the ratification of the treaty, they found the Japanese in a strong position close to the Corean capital. The Chinese were not to be set on one side in so open a manner, and a powerful fleet of gunboats, with 5,000 troops, were sent to the Seoul river to uphold their rights. Under other circumstances, more especially as the Chinese expedition was believed to be the superior, a hostile collision must have ensued, and the war which has so often seemed near between the Chinese and Japanese would have become an accomplished fact; but fortunately the presence of the foreign diplomatists moderated the ardour of both sides, and a rupture was averted. By a stroke of judgment the Chinese seized Tai Wang Kun, the father of the young king, and the leader of the anti-foreign party, and carried him off to Pekin, where he was kept in imprisonment for some time, until matters had settled down in his own country. The opening of Corea to the Treaty Powers has not put an end to the old rivalry of China and Japan in that country, of which history contains so many examples; and, before the Corean question is definitively settled, it may again become obtrusive. Such evidence as is obtainable points to the conclusion that Chinese influence is gradually getting the better of Japanese in the country, and the attack on the Japanese legation in 1884 was a striking revelation of popular antipathy or of an elaborate anti-Japanese plot headed by the released Chinese prisoner, Tai Wang Kun.

At the opposite point of the frontier China was brought face to face with a danger which threatened to develop into a peril of the first magnitude, and in meeting which she was undoubtedly hampered by her treaties with the general body of foreign Powers and her own peculiar place in the family of nations. It is the special misfortune of China that she cannot engage in any, even a defensive, war with a maritime power without incurring the grave risk, or indeed the practical certainty that, if such a war be continued for any length of time, she must find herself involved with every other foreign country through the impossibility of confining the hostility of her own subjects to one race of foreigners in particular. In considering the last war with a European country in which China was engaged, due allowance must be made for these facts, and also for the anomalous character of that contest when active hostilities were carried on without any formal declaration of war—a state of things which gave the French many advantages. Towards the end of the year 1882, the French government came to the decision to establish a "definite protectorate" over Tonquin. Events had for some time been shaping themselves in this direction, and the colonial ambition of France had long fixed on Indo-China as a field in which it might aggrandise itself with comparatively little risk and a wide margin of advantage. The weakness of the kingdom of Annam was a strong enough temptation in itself to assert the protectorate over it which France had, more or less, claimed for forty years; but when the reports of several French explorers came to promote the conviction that France might acquire the control of a convenient and perhaps the best route into some of the richest provinces of interior China without much difficulty, the temptation became irresistible. French activity in Indo-China was heightened by the declaration of Garnier, Rocher, and others, that the Songcoi, or Red River, furnished the best means of communicating with Yunnan, and tapping the wealth of the richest mineral province in China. The apathy of England in her relations with Burmah, which presented, under its arrogant and obstructive rulers, what may have seemed an insuperable obstacle to trade intercourse between India and China, afforded additional inducement to the French to act quickly; and, as they felt confident of their ability and power to coerce the Court of Hué, the initial difficulties of their undertaking did not seem very formidable. That undertaking was, in the first place, defined to be a protectorate of China, and, as the first step in the enterprise, the town of Hanoi, in the delta of the Red River, and the nominal capital of Tonquin, was captured before the end of the year 1882.

Tonquin stood in very much the same relationship to China as Corea; and, although the enforcement of the suzerain tie was lax, there was no doubt that at Pekin the opinion was held very strongly that the action of France was an encroachment on the rights of China. But if such was the secret opinion of the Chinese authorities, they took no immediate steps to arrest the development of French policy in Tonquin by proclaiming it a Chinese dependency, and also their intention to defend it. It is by no means certain that the prompt and vigorous assertion of their rights would have induced the French to withdraw from their enterprise, for its difficulties were not revealed at first; but if China is to make good her hold over such dependencies, she must be prepared to show that she thinks them worth fighting for. While Li Hung Chang and the other members of the Chinese government were deliberating as to the course they should pursue, the French were acting with great vigour in Tonquin, and committing their military reputation to a task from which they could not in honour draw back. During the whole of the year 1883 they were engaged in military operations with the Black Flag irregulars, a force half piratical and half patriotic, who represented the national army of the country. It was believed at the time, but quite erroneously, that the Black Flags were paid and incited by the Chinese. Subsequent evidence showed that the Chinese authorities did not take even an indirect part in the contest until a much later period. After the capture of Hanoi, the French were constantly engaged with the Black Flags, from whom they captured the important town of Sontay, which was reported to be held by Imperial Chinese troops, but on its capture this statement was found to be untrue. The French were in the full belief that the conquest of Tonquin would be easily effected, when a serious reverse obliged them to realise the gravity of their task. A considerable detachment, under the command of Captain Henri Rivière, who was one of the pioneers of French enterprise on the Songcoi, was surprised and defeated near Hanoi. Rivière was killed, and it became necessary to make a great effort to recover the ground that had been lost. Fresh troops were sent from Europe, but before they arrived the French received another check at Phukai, which the Black Flags claimed as a victory because the French were obliged to retreat.

Before this happened the French had taken extreme measures against the King of Annam, of which state Tonquin is the northern province. The King of that country, by name Tuduc, who had become submissive to the French, died in July, 1883, and after his death the Annamese, perhaps encouraged by the difficulties of the French in Tonquin, became so hostile that it was determined to read them a severe lesson. Hué was attacked and occupied a month after the death of Tuduc, and a treaty was extracted from the new king which made him the dependent of France. When the cold season began in Tonquin, the French forces largely increased, and, commanded by Admiral Courbet, renewed operations, and on 11th December attacked the main body of the Black Flags at Sontay, which they had reoccupied and strengthened. They offered a desperate and well sustained resistance, and it was only with heavy loss that the French succeeded in carrying the town. The victors were somewhat recompensed for their hardships and loss by the magnitude of the spoil, which included a large sum of money. Desultory fighting continued without intermission; Admiral Courbet was superseded by General Millot, who determined to signalise his assumption of the command by attacking Bacninh, which the Black Flags made their headquarters after the loss of Sontay. On 8th March, he attacked this place at the head of 12,000 men, but so formidable were its defences that he would not risk an attack in front, and by a circuitous march of four days he gained the flank of the position, and thus taken at a disadvantage, the Black Flags abandoned their formidable lines, and retreated without much loss, leaving their artillery, including some Krupp guns, in the hands of the victors. At this stage of the question diplomacy intervened, and on 11th May a treaty of peace was signed by Commander Fournier, during the ministry of M. Jules Ferry, with the Chinese government. One of the principal stipulations of this treaty was that the French should be allowed to occupy Langson and other places in Tonquin. When the French commander in Tonquin sent a force under Colonel Dugenne to occupy Langson it was opposed in the Bacle defile and repulsed with some loss. The Chinese exonerated themselves from all responsibility by declaring that the French advance was premature, because no date was fixed by the Fournier convention, and because there had not been time to transmit the necessary orders. On the other hand, M. Fournier declared on his honour that the dates in his draft were named in the original convention. The French government at once demanded an apology, and an indemnity fixed by M. Jules Ferry, in a moment of mental excitement, at the ridiculous figure of ten millions sterling. An apology was offered, but such an indemnity was refused, and eventually France obtained one of only £160,000.

After the Bacle affair hostilities were at once resumed, and for the first time the French carried them on not only against the Black Flags, but against the Chinese. M. Jules Ferry did not, however, make any formal declaration of war against China, and he thus gained an advantage of position for his attack on the Chinese which it was not creditable to French chivalry to have asserted. The most striking instance of this occurred at Foochow, where the French fleet, as representing a friendly power, was at anchor above the formidable defences of the Min river. In accordance with instructions telegraphed to him, the French admiral attacked those places in reverse and destroyed the forts on the Min without much difficulty or loss, thanks exclusively to his having been allowed past them as a friend. The French also endeavoured to derive all possible advantage from there being no formal declaration of war, and to make use of Hongkong as a base for their fleet against China. But this unfairness could not be tolerated, and the British minister at Pekin, where Sir Harry Parkes had in the autumn of 1883 succeeded Sir Thomas Wade, issued a proclamation that the hostilities between France and China were tantamount to a state of war, and that the laws of neutrality must be strictly observed. The French resented this step, and showed some inclination to retaliate by instituting a right to search for rice, but fortunately this pretension was not pushed to extremities, and the war was closed before it could produce any serious consequences. The French devoted much of their attention to an attack on the Chinese possessions in Formosa, and the occupation of Kelung; a fort in the northern part of that island was captured, but the subsequent success of the French was small. The Chinese displayed great energy and resource in forming defences against any advance inland from Kelung or Tamsui, and the French government was brought to face the fact that there was nothing to be gained by carrying on these desultory operations, and that unless they were prepared to send a large expedition, it was computed of not less than 50,000 men, to attack Pekin, there was no alternative to coming to terms with China. How strong this conviction had become may be gathered from the fact that the compulsory retreat, in March, 1885, of the French from before Langson, where some of the Chinese regular troops were drawn up with a large force of Black and Yellow Flags—the latter of whom were in Chinese pay—did not imperil the negotiations which were then far advanced towards completion. On 9th June of the same year a treaty of peace was signed by M. Patenotre and Li Hung Chang which gave France nothing more than the Fournier convention.

The military lessons of this war must be pronounced inconclusive, for the new forces which China had organized since the Pekin campaign were never fully engaged, and the struggle ended before the regular regiments sent to Langson had any opportunity of showing their quality. But the impression conveyed by the fighting in Formosa and the northern districts of Tonquin was that China had made considerable progress in the military art, and that she possessed the nucleus of an army that might become formidable. But while the soldiers had made no inconsiderable improvement, as much could not be said of the officers, and among the commanders there seemed no grasp of the situation, and a complete inability to conduct a campaign. Probably these deficiencies will long remain the really weak spot in the Chinese war organisation, and although they have men who will fight well, the only capacity their commanders showed in Tonquin and Formosa was in selecting strong positions and in fortifying them with consummate art. But as the strongest position can be turned and avoided, and as the Chinese, like all Asiatics, become demoralised when their rear is threatened, it cannot be denied that, considerable progress as the Chinese have made in the military art, they have not yet mastered some of its rudiments. All that can be said is that the war between France and China was calculated to teach the advisability of caution in fixing a quarrel upon China. Under some special difficulties from the character of the war and with divided councils at Pekin, the Chinese still gave a very good account of themselves against one of the greatest Powers of Europe.

During the progress of this struggle a *coup d'état* was effected at Pekin of which at the time it was impossible to measure the whole significance. In July, 1884, the Chinese world was startled by the sudden fall and disgrace of Prince Kung, who had been the most powerful man in China since the Treaty of Pekin. A decree of the Empress Regent appeared dismissing him from all his posts and consigning him to an obscurity from which after nine years he has not yet succeeded in emerging. The causes of his fall are not clear, but they were probably of several distinct kinds. While he was the leader of the peace party and the advocate of a prompt arrangement with France, he was also an opponent of Prince Chun's desire to have a share in the practical administration of the state, or, at least, an obstacle in the way of its realisation. Prince Chun, who was a man of an imperious will, and who, on the death of the Eastern Empress, became the most important personage in the palace and supreme Council of the Empire, was undoubtedly the leader of the attack on Prince Kung, and the immediate cause of his downfall. Prince Kung, who was an amiable and well intentioned man rather than an able statesman, yielded without resistance, and indeed he had no alternative, for he had no following at Pekin, and his influence was very slight except among Europeans. Prince Chun then came to the front, taking an active and prominent part in the government, making himself President of a new Board of National Defence and taking up the command of the Pekin Field Force, a specially trained body of troops for the defence of the capital. He retained possession of these posts after his son assumed the government in person, notwithstanding the law forbidding a father serving under his son, which has already been cited, and he remained the real controller of Chinese policy until his sudden and unexpected death in the first days of 1891. Some months earlier in April, 1890, China had suffered a great loss in the Marquis Tseng, whose diplomatic experience and knowledge of Europe might have rendered his country infinite service in the future. He was the chosen colleague of Prince Chun, and he is said to have gained the ear of his young sovereign. While willing to admit the superiority of European inventions, he was also an implicit believer in China's destiny and in her firmly holding her place among the greatest Powers of the world. In December, 1890, also died Tseng Kwo Tsiuen, uncle of the Marquis, and a man who had taken a prominent and honourable part in the suppression of the Taeping rebellion.

In 1885 an important and delicate negotiation between England and China was brought to a successful issue by the joint efforts of Lord Salisbury and the Marquis Tseng. The levy of the lekin or barrier tax on opium had led to many exactions in the interior which was injurious to the foreign trade and also to the Chinese government, which obtained only the customs duty raised in the port. After the subject had been thoroughly discussed in all its bearings a convention was signed in London, on 19th July, 1885, by which the lekin was fixed at eighty taels a chest, in addition to the customs due of thirty taels, and also that the whole of this sum should be paid in the treaty port before the opium was taken out of bond. This arrangement was greatly to the advantage of the Chinese government, which came into possession of a large revenue that had previously been frittered away in the provinces, and much of which had gone into the pockets of the mandarins. This subject affords the most appropriate place for calling attention to the conspicuous services rendered, as Director-General of Chinese Customs during more than thirty years, by Sir Robert Hart, who, on the premature death of Sir Harry Parkes, was appointed British Minister at Pekin, which post, for weighty reasons, he almost immediately resigned. It is impossible to measure the consequences and important effect of his conduct and personal influence upon the policy and opinion of China, while his work in the interests of that country has been both striking and palpable. To his efforts the central government mainly owes its large and increasing cash revenue, and when some candid Chinese historian sums up the work done for his country by foreigners, he will admit that, what Gordon did in war and Macartney in diplomacy, Hart accomplished in those revenue departments which are an essential element of strength, and we must hope that this truthful chronicler will also not forget to record that all these loyal servants were English, members of a race which, after fighting China fairly, frankly held out the hand of friendship and alliance. In connection with this subject it may be noted that the Emperor issued an edict in 1890 formally legalising the cultivation of opium, which, although practically carried on, was nominally illegal. An immediate consequence of this step was a great increase in the area under cultivation, particularly in Manchuria, and so great is the production of native opium now becoming that that of India may yet be driven from the field as a practical revenge for the loss inflicted on China by the competition of Indian tea. But at all events these measures debar China from ever again posing as an injured party in the matter of the opium traffic. She has very rightly determined to make the best of the situation and to derive all the profit she can by taxing an article in such very general use and consumption; but there is an end to all representations like those made by prominent officials from Commissioner Lin to Prince Kung and Li Hung Chang, that the opium traffic was iniquitous, and constituted the sole cause of disagreement between China and England.

During these years the young Emperor Kwangsu was growing up. In February, 1887, in which month falls the Chinese New Year, it was announced that his marriage was postponed in consequence of his delicate health, and it was not until the new year of 1889, when Kwangsu was well advanced in his eighteenth year, that he was married to Yeh-ho-na-la, daughter of a Manchu general named Knei Hsiang, who had been specially selected for this great honour out of many hundred candidates. The marriage was celebrated with the usual state, and more than a million sterling is said to have been expended on the attendant ceremonies. At the same time the Empress Regent issued her farewell edict and passed into retirement, but there is reason to believe that she has continued to exercise no inconsiderable influence over the young Emperor.

The marriage and assumption of governing power by the Emperor Kwangsu brought to the front the very important question of the right of audience by the foreign ministers resident at Pekin. This privilege had been conceded by China at the time of the Tientsin massacre, and it had been put into force on one occasion during the brief reign of Tungche. The time had again arrived for giving it effect, and, after long discussions as to the place of audience and the forms to be observed, Kwangsu issued in December, 1890, an edict appointing a day soon after the commencement of the Chinese New Year, for the audience, and also arranging that it should be repeated annually on the same date. In March, 1891, Kwangsu gave his first reception to the foreign ministers, but after it was over some criticism and dissatisfaction were aroused by the fact that the ceremony had been held in the Tse Kung Ko, or Hall of Tributary Nations. As this was the first occasion on which Europeans saw the young Emperor, the fact that he made a favourable impression on them is not without interest, and the following personal description of the master of so many millions may well be quoted. "Whatever the impression 'the Barbarians' made on him the idea which they carried away of the Emperor Kwangsu was pleasing and almost pathetic. His air is one of exceeding intelligence and gentleness, somewhat frightened and melancholy looking. His face is pale, and though it is distinguished by refinement and quiet dignity it has none of the force of his martial ancestors, nothing commanding or imperial, but is altogether mild, delicate, sad and kind. He is essentially Manchu in features, his skin is strangely pallid in hue, which is, no doubt, accounted for by the confinement of his life inside these forbidding walls and the absence of the ordinary pleasures and pursuits of youth, with the constant discharge of onerous, complicated and difficult duties of state which, it must be remembered, are, according to Imperial Chinese etiquette, mostly transacted between the hours of two and six in the morning. His face is oval shaped with a very long narrow chin and a sensitive mouth with thin nervous lips; his nose is well shaped and straight, his eyebrows regular and very arched, while the eyes are unusually large and sorrowful in expression. The forehead is well shaped and broad, and the head is large beyond the average."

Owing to the dissatisfaction felt at the place of audience, which seemed to put the Treaty Powers on the same footing as tributary states, the foreign ministers have endeavoured to force from the Tsungli Yamen the formal admission that a more appropriate part of the Imperial city should be assigned for the ceremony, but as the Powers themselves were not disposed to lay too much stress on this point, no definite concession has yet been made, and the Chinese ministers have held out against the pressure of some of the foreign representatives. But, although no concise alteration has been made in the place of audience, the question has been practically settled by a courteous concession to the new English minister, Mr. O'Conor, who succeeded Sir John Walsham last year, and it is gratifying to feel that this advantage was gained more by tact than by coercion. When Mr. O'Conor wished to present his credentials to the Emperor, it was arranged that the Emperor should receive him in the Cheng Kuan Tien Palace, which is part of the imperial residence of Peace and Plenty within the Forbidden City. The British representative, accompanied by his secretaries and suite in accordance with arrangement, proceeded to this palace on 13th December, 1892, and was received in a specially honourable way at the principal or imperial entrance by the officials of the Court. Such a mark of distinction was considered quite unique in the annals of foreign diplomacy in China, and has since been a standing grievance with the other ministers at Pekin. It was noticed by those present that the Emperor took a much greater interest in the ceremony than on previous occasions, and that he showed special attention as Prince Ching, the President of the Yamen, translated the letter from Queen Victoria. This audience, which lasted a considerable time, was certainly the most satisfactory and encouraging yet held with the Emperor Kwangsu by any foreign envoy, and it also afforded opportunity of confirming the favourable impression which the intelligence and dignified demeanour of the Emperor Kwangsu have made on all who have had the honour of coming into his presence. One incident in the progress of the audience question deserves notice, and that was the Emperor's refusal, in 1891, to receive Mr. Blair, the United States Minister, in consequence of the hostile legislation of that country against China. The anti-foreign outbreak along the Yangtsekiang, in the summer of 1891, was an unpleasant incident, from which at one time it looked as if serious consequences might follow; but the ebullition fortunately passed away without an international crisis, and it may be hoped that the improved means of exercising diplomatic pressure at Pekin will render these attacks less frequent, and their settlement and redress more rapid.

During the last ten years events in Central Asia and Burmah have drawn England and China much more closely together, and have laid the basis of what it must be hoped will prove a firm and durable alliance. If suspicion was laid aside and candid relations established on the frontier, it should not be difficult to maintain an excellent understanding with China, and at the present moment every difficulty has been smoothed over with the exception of that on the Burmese frontier. It is to be hoped that not less success will be obtained in this quarter than in Sikhim and Hunza, and Mr. O'Conor's convention of Pekin in July, 1886, recognising China's right to receive a tribute mission from Burmah once in ten years went far to prove the extent of concession England would make to China. It is divulging what cannot long be kept secret, to explain the circumstances under which Mr. O'Conor's convention was signed, and the unusual concession made by a British government of admitting its liability to send a tribute mission. The Chefoo Convention, closing the Yunnan incident, contained a promise from the Chinese government to allow an English mission to pass through Tibet. Years passed without any attempt to give effect to this stipulation, but at last, in 1884, Mr. Colman Macaulay, a member of the Indian Civil Service, obtained the assent of his government to requesting the permission of the Chinese government to visit Lhasa. He went to Pekin and he came to London, and he obtained the necessary permission, and the formal passport of the Tsungli Yamen; and there is no doubt that if he had set off for Tibet with a small party, he would have been honourably received, and passed safely through Tibet to India. On the other hand there is no doubt that such a visit would have presented no feature of special or striking importance. It would have been an interesting individual experience, but scarcely an international landmark. This modest character for his long-cherished project did not suit Mr. Macaulay, and unmindful of the adage that there may be a slip betwixt the cup and the lip, he not merely delayed the execution of his visit, but he made ostentatious preparations for an elaborate mission, and he engaged many persons with scientific qualifications to accompany him, with the view of examining the mineral resources of Tibet. The Chinese themselves did not like, and had never contemplated, such a mission, but their dissatisfaction was slight in comparison with the storm it raised in Tibet; and the Chinese government was thus brought face to face with a position in which it must either employ its military power to coerce the Tibetans, who made preparations to oppose the Macaulay mission by force of arms, or acquiesce in the Tibetans ignoring its official passports, and thus provoke a serious complication with this country. Such was the position of the Tibetan question when Burmah was annexed in January, 1886, and negotiations followed with China for the adjustment of her claims in the country. Negotiations were carried on, in the first place by Lord Salisbury, and in the second by Lord Rosebery, with the Chinese minister in London, and the draft of more than one convention was prepared. Among such contemplated arrangements were the despatch of a mission from Burmah to China, and of a return one from China; the appointment of the Head Priest of Mandalay as the person to send the mission, thus making it a purely native matter, outside the participation of the British Government; and the concession of material advantages on the Irrawaddy and in the Shan country, as the equivalent for the surrender of the tribute. It is probable that one of these three arrangements would have been carried out, but that, on certain points being referred to Pekin, the knowledge came to the ears of the British government that if the Tibetan mission were withdrawn, the Chinese would be content with the formal admission of their claim to receive the tribute mission from Burmah in accordance with established usage. As both governments wanted a speedy settlement of the question, the Chinese, with the view of allaying the rising agitation in Tibet and getting rid of a troublesome question, and the English not less anxious to have the claims of China in Burmah defined in diplomatic language, the convention which bears Mr. O'Conor's name was drawn up and signed with quite remarkable despatch. For the abandonment of the Macaulay mission, and the recognition of their right to receive the tribute mission from Burmah, the authorities at Pekin were quite, at the moment, willing to forego material claims such as a port on the Irrawaddy. Diplomacy has not yet said the last word on this matter, and the exact frontier between Burmah and China has still to be delimited, but the fixing of a definite date for the despatch of the first mission from Mandalay to Pekin, which is timed to set out in January, 1894, is in itself of hopeful augury for the settlement of all difficulties. When this matter is composed there will be no cloud in the sky of Anglo-Chinese relations, and that such an auspicious result will be obtained is not open to serious doubt. The most gratifying fact in the history of China during the last ten years is the increasing sympathy and tacit understanding between the two great Empires of England and China in Asia, which must in time constitute an effective alliance against any common danger in that continent, and the aggressive policy of Russia.

HOW CHINA IS GOVERNED.*

The recent marriage of the young Emperor of China has invested the subject of how China is governed with new interest. The new reign may be considered to have fairly begun under auspicious circumstances. Were the attempt to explain the inner mechanism of Chinese government made for the benefit of French readers, it would suffice to enlist their attention to say that the system of administration related to several hundred millions of people, and that it had existed for several thousand years. But the ear of English readers must be gained by more worldly considerations, such as our increasing commercial intercourse with China, the newly-established contact between the Chinese and ourselves on the extensive frontiers of the Indian Empire, and the larger place assigned by public opinion generally to China in the affairs of the world. Both theoretically and practically there is much reason to justify inquiry as to how the task of government is carried on in the great country of the Far East on strictly Oriental principles. China, we must remember, owes nothing to the West in her political constitution, although her vigour and vitality are unlike anything that Asia elsewhere has produced. The system of administration is quite original, and has been devised by native wit and ingenuity to meet Chinese requirements, and to stand successfully the one unimpeachable test of time. Whether we accept the modern scientific view that Chinese government only acquired its present form after Confucius, or about 2,300 years ago, or cling to the older belief that Chinese life had reached an advanced stage of civilisation before the Assyrian and Egyptian monarchies were in their prime, there remains an ample margin of time to show that the Chinese government is not merely the oldest existing administration in the world, but that at the least it was contemporary with, and at the same time totally independent of, the systems of Greece and Rome, upon which European culture and freedom are equally modelled. If it has stood triumphantly the test of time, it has also met the requirements of the Chinese themselves so admirably that change of dynasty and even of dominant race has produced little or no alteration in the form of government. China has been conquered by the rude barbarians of the desert and the mountain, by the Mongol and the Manchu, but each and all have adopted the Chinese system and the Confucian ethics as they found them, and proclaimed them to be, by imitation, the sincerest form of flattery, super-excellent and incapable of improvement. Such qualities of endurance command attention, and if they do not excite envy, they certainly stimulate curiosity to see the secret springs that have kept ancient machinery from becoming useless, and that have made the Chinese system not unsuitable to even modern exigencies.

* I am indebted to the Proprietors of the *Times* for permission to reproduce this article, which appeared in that paper on September 27th and 30th, 1889.

The subject covers so wide a field, and includes so many various departments, executive, judicial, and political, that for the sake of clearness each division must be separately considered. The most important branches of the question fall under such heads as the Emperor, the central and provincial administrations, the recruiting of the public services, the dispensation of justice, including the police, the revenue and expenditure of the Empire, and, lastly, the army and navy.

It is singular, but true, that the most important personage in the Chinese Constitution—the man on whose will and superior judgment everything is supposed to turn as on a pivot—the Emperor, who is popularly described as "the father and mother of his people," has been a cipher for more than twenty-seven years, with one brief and unimportant interval. Since the death of the Emperor Hienfung, at the end of 1861, China has been governed by a Regency, with the exception of Tungche's brief tenure of power in 1873-4, and it has only just passed again under the personal rule of its autocrat, the youthful Emperor Kwangsu. The great energy and ability shown by the two Empresses, widows of Hienfung, of whom one still survives, rendered it less a matter of regret that the chief personage in the executive system should so long remain unrepresented, but we cannot doubt that the assumption of ruling power by Kwangsu, followed by his marriage, has satisfied many popular and national aspirations which no female Regency could meet, and revived all the traditional majesty of the occupant of the Dragon Throne. The description of the Emperor's power and duties is therefore made at a moment when the topic is suggested by passing events, and when it again possesses practical importance from the cessation of the Regency and the beginning of Kwangsu's personal reign.

The powers of a Chinese Emperor, as defined by the great jurists and constitutional authorities of the country, are, with the addition of some high-flown verbiage about a Celestial origin and a sway over the bodies of all men, such as the Pope claimed over their souls, precisely the same as those awarded to the Christian Sovereigns of Europe who ruled and still rule by "right divine." They, not less than an Emperor of China, are the dispensers of honour and the supreme centre of justice, they have the vested right in the services of the whole of the able-bodied population, and nominally the freehold of the State is theirs. This is the case in China where, instead of Parliaments and papers, the will of the ruler is checked by the accepted code of Confucius, which lays down the proper conduct for Sovereign as well as for subject, and by the vigilant and unsparing criticism of the Board of Censors, who are always comparing the acts of to-day with the precedents of the past, and who apparently need little excuse to set their pointed pens in motion. The check on a Chinese Emperor is, therefore, the very effectual one of an educated public opinion, with perfect freedom to give expression to its disapprobation and to offer advice. This brake on the impetuosity or malignity of a man intrusted with irresponsible power was not invented yesterday, and we consequently find very few cases in the long annals of China of a Chinese Emperor's whim bringing sudden calamity on any large section of his people. The bad Emperor's cruelty or bloodthirstiness was always limited in its operation to the Palace. The people generally never suffered from the personal excesses of the Emperor. Their calamities arose indirectly from misgovernment and bad policy, which entailed scarcity, insecurity, and invasion.

The power of the Emperor of China is not in any practical sense greater than that of the Czar or the Sultan. Its remarkable feature is that it finds expression in the most emphatic and commanding terms, and that the people of all classes are so instilled with the duty of obedience that the behests of the ruler are at once carried out with what may be truly termed unflinching devotion. The Emperor's order, written or signed with the vermilion pencil, is useful for the necessary purposes of government as facilitating the despatch of business, and, indeed, were there not some form of compulsion—the natural right of the tyrant—in every country, whether it be our own subpœnas and mandamuses or the Chinese Emperor's writ, there would soon be an end to order and to law. The idea that the Emperor of China wielded a power upon which there was no constitutional check was probably derived from the style employed in Imperial edicts and rescripts wherein the Chinese ruler is generally designated "the Son of Heaven," and where special mention is always made of his representing the Celestial will. At the same time he exercises, even with the limitations that have been referred to, an arbitrary power not inferior to that of any absolute ruler in any civilised or semi-civilised State: and it can well be imagined that when the Emperor happens to be possessed of a strong will, and more than ordinary intelligence, he is able to impress his character and wishes on the Board of Censors and the whole of the Hanlin College. Of such rulers China has not possessed one for over one hundred years, since the death of the great Emperor Keen Lung.

There is certainly no other country in the world where such pains have been taken to convert the respect and loyalty shown to a Sovereign into the national worship of an office identified with the sway of the King of Heaven on earth, acting through his vicegerent at Pekin. These efforts have not been made in any recent time, and the originator of the whole pageantry of Chinese royalty, including both the intricate Court ceremonial and the numerous forms of obedience expressing the humiliation of the subject before the Imperial office, is forgotten in an antiquity that cannot be fathomed. Such changes as have been made in 2,000 years have been introduced imperceptibly, and the Court officials can always, and as a matter of fact do, quote precedents of centuries ago for deciding trifling points of procedure, and for the proper celebration of important events. Woe unto them if the precedent is not applicable, and some lynx-eyed Censor is sure to discover the mistake if slip there be. A case happened only this year in connexion with the marriage of the young Emperor. The Board of Ceremonies fixed the second day before the marriage for the worship of Heaven and Earth, whereas it should have been the first day, or that immediately before the august ceremony. The blunder was discovered, and by the ex-Empress Regent herself, and the delinquents, including two Senior Secretaries, were deprived of five steps of rank! One was still more unfortunate. Li-Hung-Tsao, although a near relative of the great Li-Hung-Chang, was cashiered.

In order to emphasise the wide gulf which separates sovereign and people, many articles are specially associated with the former, and, therefore, forbidden to the latter, as, for instance, the colour yellow, which is exclusively the Imperial emblem. The kotow, or form of worship, is rendered not merely to the person of the Sovereign in Pekin, but to every form in which he delegates his authority to others. It is well known that the Imperial edict is always received with the nine prostrations and the burning of incense. But it is not so generally understood that an official of even superior rank has to perform the kotow on meeting another official who has recently quitted the Imperial presence. Similar obeisances are paid during the week containing his birthday to the Emperor in the Imperial Temple to be found in every provincial capital. The fact that the Emperor's proper name is never mentioned, and that to pronounce it is a criminal offence, shows how exclusive the dynastic policy of the Chinese has always been. On ascending the throne the ruler takes what is called a *kwoh hao*, and by that name he becomes known to his people and to history. The present Emperor's real or personal name is Tsai-tien, but on being placed on the throne in 1875 he was given the style of Kwangsu, by which he will continue to be known. As Kwangsu means "illustrious succession," it will be seen that these titles are selected with some regard to the circumstances of the accession of the particular Prince to the throne, and with a strong wish to propitiate the unseen powers.

So much depends in the future on the character and capacity of the Emperor Kwangsu that much ingenuity will be displayed to obtain details, correct or misleading, as to his habits and opinions, and upon them will be built up many theories and suggestions of change, indicating, according to the bent of the writer, progress or retrogression. The absolute truth it is hopeless to expect with regard to the mental capacity of an Emperor of China, even at the present day—so little has that country altered in all the essentials of constitutional procedure and etiquette—but from the glimpses that reach the outer and profane world it does seem that the youth who dwells in the inner recesses of the Palace of Plenty and Peace has a marked individuality, and that, if he has the physical strength, he possesses the brains to assert himself in the administration of his dominions. If rumour is favourable to the intelligence of Kwangsu, it is certainly the reverse of being so to his health and strength. He is described as a puny youth, with an exceedingly large head and a melancholy countenance, combining an exceptional acquaintance, for his years, with the Chinese classics, with extreme ignorance of the outside world, and showing in all his acts and sayings that his education has been conducted in accordance with the old ideas of his race and country, and not with what we Europeans are disposed to consider their new and essential requirements. If the Imperial family at Pekin had been imbued with the idea that China's true or inevitable policy is to associate herself more closely with the West, and to approximate towards the standard of European civilisation and progress, it cannot be doubted that Kwangsu's education would have been of a different character from what it has been. It would have resembled more closely that given to the Princes of India during the last thirty years, with the special object of enabling them to understand the merits of modern culture, and of government based on justice and the interests of the people.

With regard to the new and all-powerful element introduced into Chinese life, both as regards its internal affairs and its external policy, by the Emperor's assumption of power, we have no better ground for anticipating that Kwangsu will be on the side of rational conduct and progress, than his youth and a certain infantile curiosity and anxiety to see novelties, which has already cost his staid guardians some trouble, may afford. The youth of Kwangsu—he is only just eighteen—is in itself not an unfavourable fact, for he ascends the throne at an impressionable age, and his opinions, we may hope, will be matured by his own personal observations.

An event is approaching that must have the effect of quickening his imagination on the subject of the outside nations, and that may afford some indication of his own personal feelings. The accession to power, followed by his marriage, of the Chinese Emperor has immediate and important consequences for all the Treaty Powers. It brings on the *tapis* the great audience question, which formed such a bone of contention at the time of the war of 1859-61, and which, with the exception of Tungche's brief reign, has lain dormant through all the years of the Regency. As there is the clear precedent of 1873, there is no reason to anticipate any serious difficulty on the part of the Chinese Executive in according the same privilege of personal reception by the Emperor in the present year. The important part of the subject is that Kwangsu will then be brought face to face with those representatives of foreign countries of which he may have heard much, but of which he certainly knows very little. Whether the fact is agreeable or not to the high powers at Pekin, there is no escaping from the conclusion that the affairs of China are now indissolubly interwoven with those of her civilised neighbours and all the great trading nations of the world. It will make much for the harmonious settlement of these relations if the Emperor Kwangsu is impressed by the facts that cannot be concealed from him when he is invited by his own officials to appoint the day for receiving the Ministers of the Foreign Powers.

There is a still more pressing and not less important point than Kwangsu's attitude towards the Powers about which considerable uncertainty must be felt, and that is his future relations with his father, Prince Chun. Prince Chun has only become known to Europeans generally since the final disgrace of his brother, Prince Kung, in 1884; but he has taken an active part in affairs ever since the death of his brother, Emperor Hienfung, in 1861, and the selection of his own son to ascend the vacant throne in 1875 was an unequivocal testimony to his tact and influence. The advancement of his son entailed his own retirement, for by Chinese law a father cannot serve under his own son; but in 1880 Prince Chun thought it so far safe and necessary to emerge from his obscurity as to accept the command of the Pekin field force, which comprises what may be called the Household Troops of China. In 1884 he came still more prominently forward in connexion with the circumstances that led to the deposition of Prince Kung, and there is no doubt that he was mainly instrumental in bringing about the fall of his brother. He showed no hesitation in accepting the post of President of the Grand Council, which is the most important office in China, and there is no question that during the last five years his influence has been the dominant one in Chinese affairs rather than that of the Empress Regent. Even during the twelve months which have elapsed since Kwangsu nominally took over the reins of government, Prince Chun's prominent place in the administration has remained undisturbed. Much curiosity will be felt as to whether Prince Chun can maintain his position permanently, and also as to how the sticklers for Confucian law and etiquette will regard with any tolerance so flagrant a breach of them as a father serving under his son in the highest places in the realm.

There is no evidence to show what are the feelings between the Emperor Kwangsu and Prince Chun, and it may be only due to malevolence that a report has been spread to the effect that they are the reverse of cordial, and that the young Sovereign has already shown signs of chafing at the presence of his father at the Council-board in a position which gives him practical control of the Executive. If it is little better than guesswork to speculate on the unformed opinions of a youth of eighteen, we find ourselves on surer ground when we say that the Emperor Kwangsu stands in the path of Prince Chun's ambition. For the suggestion that the present exceptional arrangement of the father being head of the Cabinet with his son on the throne may be prolonged indefinitely cannot readily be adopted, because the Chinese are far too consistent in their conservatism to tolerate a breach of custom that would expose their whole system to general ridicule and contempt. We may, therefore, assume that before very long Prince Chun's withdrawal from public affairs will be announced, when Kwangsu will be finally released from the leading-strings in which he has so long been kept. Whether this will be wholly for the young Emperor's own good, or whether Prince Chun will find his enforced seclusion too irksome to be borne, time alone can tell. Any attempt to cut short the present ruler's reign, as was suspected by many to have been the case with regard to his predecessor, Tungche, would be attended with very great risk, and it might be doubted if those who perpetrated the crime would derive any benefit from it. Prince Chun will probably have to seek his opportunities in the private influence a parent may exert over a son, even in a palace, and in impressing upon him the political maxims and advice drawn from his own long experience.

With regard to the first institution in the government of China, the most ancient and sacrosanct office of the Emperor, we find that at this very moment it has been revived in a practical form; that its old powers and privileges will henceforth be exercised by the ruler himself and not by deputy, and that the Chinese, having been safely led through the storm and stress of many years, marked by internal rebellions and external complications, by wise and capable Regents, are now rejoicing at the revival of that paternal authority which forms the pivot of their own domestic affairs as well as of their political constitution. As to the manner in which Kwangsu will dispense the unlimited authority placed in his hands there is no need to prophesy. The final settlement of Prince Chun's place in the administration and with regard to the throne will afford one indication as to the character of the new ruler of so many millions, and we must trust to the right of audience and the perspicacity of our diplomatists to provide us with an insight into his character. At the same time it has to be noted that a personal influence, omnipotent, yet unknown and, indeed, unascertainable, has now been introduced into the government of China. We and all others having relations with that country are bound to take it seriously into account, and while we hope that it may be exerted on the side of progress, it is necessary to face the other alternative—that Kwangsu, without the bitter experiences of Prince Kung and Li-Hung-Chang, may be disposed to adopt a more pronounced and, consequently, less friendly policy than China has attempted to follow since the Anglo-French expedition to Pekin.

A subject connected more with the dynasty than with the government presents itself for brief notice in the regulation of the Imperial clan. The Manchu dynasty now ruling in China is officially designated the Ta Tsing, or Sublimely Pure, but the name of the family is really Gioro, or Golden. To compare the state of things in China with what obtains among ourselves, Ta Tsing stands for House of Brunswick and Gioro for Guelph.

The Manchus took the name of Gioro from Aisin Gioro, their chief in the early years of the fifteenth century, and the direct ancestor of the great conqueror, Noorhachu, and the present line of Emperors. The name has not altogether fallen into desuetude, for, as will be seen, it continues to be employed as marking one section of the Manchu princes. As the Manchus adopted from the first the principle that every member of the family had a right to share in the fortunes of its head, it is not surprising to find that the Imperial clan has in the course of 250 years become exceedingly numerous, and that an Imperial Clan Court (Tsung-jin-fu) has had to be formed for their special regulation. The careful registration of the names of the members of the clan is the most important of the many functions devolving upon this institution. The members themselves are divided into two sections, the Tsung-shih, or Imperial kindred, and the Gioro, or descendants of the Manchu chiefs before they assumed the title of Chinese Emperor. The Tsung-shih are restricted to the direct descendants of Noorhachu. The Gioro are the descendants of Noorhachu's uncles and brothers. The former wear a yellow girdle to show their Imperial origin, the latter are only entitled to a red.

The allowance paid to each member of the clan varies with the degree of the remoteness of his relationship to the Emperor as head of the family. There are twelve different grades, and the pay of the lowest is described as a miserable pittance, barely sufficient to purchase the necessary food for subsistence. They are also granted a sum of about £26 when they marry, and £30 for funeral expenses for themselves or their wives. Let us hope that generally most accurate writer on China, the late Mr. Wells Williams, was unintentionally led into committing a libel when he wrote that these grants "induce some of them to maltreat their wives to death in order to receive the allowance and dowry as often as possible." Although an absolutely complete list is kept, no total has been published of the members of the Imperial clan, which is known, however, to number several thousands, and which is the most Tartar-like and original feature connected with the Manchu dynasty. In every other particular the regime is Chinese. Whether the total cost of maintaining these scions of the reigning family is excessive or not may be left for the ingenuity of some Chinese Radical when the Middle Kingdom possesses the European invention of representative institutions. But a matter which is injurious to both the dynasty and the country, particularly the former—namely, the enforced idleness and disability for active employment of these Manchu princelets—is well worthy the prompt attention of Kwangsu and his advisers. Originally these members of the Imperial House were assigned a place in this honourable prison and abode of idleness because it was feared that they might give the Emperor trouble by aspiring to the throne. The fear was an intelligible one, and the remedy has proved complete and without a flaw. In 250 years no Manchu ruler has been troubled with a rival in his own house, and a disputed succession has been unknown. But the danger is now passed, and it is a mistake to perpetually surrender the possible services and source of strength which might be derived from the ability of these members of the dominant race. The unknown descendants of the Emperors of the seventeenth and eighteenth centuries could not possibly advance any serious pretensions to the Chinese throne, and they at least might be released from their bondage and compelled to perform some useful work in the State.

The central administration of China under the Emperor consists of what may be called two inner Cabinets and a number of nominally subsidiary Boards controlling separate departments of State. The two Cabinets are the Grand Secretariat and the General Council. The former, termed in Chinese Niu Koh, is nominally the more important, and has always existed under the Chinese Emperors. It is composed of four Grand Secretaries, two Manchu and two Chinese, and two assistants. As, however, these officials always hold other posts, requiring their presence elsewhere, they are not constantly resident in Pekin, with the consequence that their collective influence is not as great as theoretically it should be. It was always considered necessary that the Senior Grand Secretary should be a Manchu, and Li Hung Chang enjoys the distinction of being the first Chinese accorded that pre-eminence. To assist the secretaries and their assistants are ten learned men (hioh-sy), who are generally doctors of the Hanlin College. In this grade the Manchus have a preponderance and number six. The staff of the Secretariat numbers about 200 officials altogether. The duties of the Niu Koh are many and varied. They are in the closest contact with the Sovereign, to whom they submit all papers, and from whom they receive the replies and instructions upon which the official edicts are drawn up. The officers of the Secretariat also keep the Imperial seals, of which there are twenty-five forms, used for different documents and departments. If the Niu Koh cannot be strictly termed a Cabinet, it answers the same purposes as our Treasury.

The Kiun Ki Chu, or General Council, is a comparatively new institution, but notwithstanding its want of antiquity, it has become, so far as there is such a thing, the real depository of power in China. It was founded by the Emperor Yung Ching in 1730, and the right of nominating its members was not merely left to the Sovereign, but was loosely defined. It was essentially a council at which the heads of departments and others could be brought together for consultative purposes by the will of the Emperor. Less ornamental than the Grand Secretariat, it has met more practical requirements, and to it also has fallen the privilege of framing edicts for the Imperial signature. Although the original idea was that this Council should be fairly numerous, such has not been the case of recent years, and its influence is probably enhanced by the fact that its four members speak with one voice. Prince Kung used to be the chief of this Council; his place is now occupied by Prince Chun. Both these Councils or bodies have the right of audience with the Sovereign, and, indeed, it is the understood routine that they should meet him in conclave every day for the transaction of the affairs of his vast Empire. The papers which are treated and passed by the General Council are handed over by it to the *Pekin Gazette* for publication. That paper, which is the oldest official journal in the world, having existed for more than 1,000 years, provides the only means of acquainting the people with the acts and motives as they would be officially represented of the government. Thousands of the *literati* gain a living by extracting and copying those passages that are of local or exceptional interest for the information of the many millions of their countrymen who cannot buy for themselves a copy of the Pekin paper. The General Council are assigned a room in the interior of the Forbidden Palace for their deliberations, which are supposed to be carried on at the early hour of five to six in the morning.

Under these two Councils come the six administrative Boards. They are the Civil Office, the Boards of Revenue, of Rites, of War, of Punishment, and of Public Works. Their names indicate with comparative completeness their respective functions. Each Board has two presidents and four vice-presidents (again divided equally between Manchus and Chinese), while the three important sections of War, Revenue, and Punishment form the special care of superintendents as well, who are generally members of one of the Councils. Each Board possesses a thoroughly organised office, with a large staff of clerks, and for the arrangement and despatch of business no system could possibly work better. To briefly record the respective duties of these Boards, the Civil Office controls the members of the mandarinate both as regards pay and promotion, the grant of leave, and the assignment of work. It has also to distribute rewards, including posthumous rewards, among which the most curious, according to our ideas, is the conferring of honour upon deceased ancestors because their living descendants have gained fame or earned public applause. This is not done, however, with the view of conveying pleasure to the shades of the departed, but of gratifying the feelings of the living. The motive is similar to that which sends the *nouveau riche* to Sir Bernard Burke or some more complaisant genealogist for an illustrious ancestor, or association with some ancient family. The Chinese, having long ago sounded the depths of human weakness, have simplified the search, and at the same time made the ennobling of a grandfather who has gone over to the majority one of the highest rewards of meritorious service.

None of the other Boards can pretend to the same degree of general interest as the Civil Office. The Board of Revenue (Hu Pu), in addition to the task of receiving the contributions from the Provinces and disbursing the payments of the administration, is, however, intrusted as a minor duty with making out the lists of the Manchu maidens who are deemed eligible for admission into the Imperial harem. The Board of Rites (Li Pu) controls all ceremonies and ritual observances which make up so large a part of Chinese life, and which illustrate some of the most distinguishing features of the national character. It performs both the religious duties which devolve among us on archbishops and bishops, and also the secular functions discharged by the Lord Chamberlain. To regulate the ceremony of a feast-day and to define the cut of a Court jacket appertain equally to its office. As China is essentially the land of ceremony, and as ceremony is regulated by the Book of Rites, which in fourteen volumes forms the statutes of this Board, it can easily be understood how powerful this department is and how perilous it is to give it offence.

The Board of War (Ping Pu) has less authority over military matters than its name would imply. For instance, it has no control over the large Banner army of the Manchus and Mongols, or over the garrison of Pekin, which forms a distinct organisation. The Board of Punishment, or Hing Pu, corresponds to our Home Office and Court of Appeal combined. At certain periods of the year it associates with itself the Censors—individuals of unlimited power in respect of criticism, who are constantly employed in the task of examining and commenting upon the work of the different departments and of the highest persons in the State—and a Court of Revision, known as the Tali Sz', when the three combined form a supreme court for the trial of capital offences. At another time of the year these three chief courts meet, with six minor courts, thus forming the complete judicial bench of Pekin, for the purpose of revising the punishments ordered throughout all the provinces before placing them before the Emperor for his sanction. The yamen of the Hing Pu is also a prison, and it was in this building that the late Sir Harry Parkes and Sir Henry Loch were confined in 1860. It is said that few of those who enter ever leave it alive. Executions are numerous, and there is an iron door in the back wall through which the dead bodies are cast, so that they may be carted away by the scavengers of Pekin. All the writings of the Chinese inculcate a love of justice, and an elaborate system of revising judgments and imposing checks on official error or tyranny has been adopted; but it is much to be feared that injustice is not infrequent, and that the innocent suffer more than the guilty through the venality of the mandarins. The last of the Boards is that of Works (Kung Pu), and its duties are multitudinous. It is a transport department and the Public Works Office. It coins money and makes gunpowder. If it performs its other work no better than it cleans out the sewers of Pekin—the worst smelling capital in the world—which are placed under this Board, its efficiency cannot be very great, and its members cannot be complimented on the discharge of their duties.

There are some other public offices at Pekin which call for notice. The Colonial Office (Li Fan Yuen) is the old department to which used to be intrusted the direction of all foreigners, but since the treaties gave outside nations a *locus standi*, its authority has been limited to the control of the dependents and tributaries outside China proper. It is remarkable as being the one department from which Chinese are strictly excluded. This office controls all matters relating to the Mongols and also to Tibet. The Governor of the New Dominion (Ili and Eastern Turkestan) also reports to it. In January, 1861, the Tsung-li-Yamen, or Chinese Foreign Office, was formed by Prince Kung for the purpose of transacting business with the ministers of the foreign Powers resident in Pekin. It has answered the purpose for which it was formed, and although it possesses no real executive authority, its usefulness as a vehicle for the issue of the orders necessary to the maintenance of harmonious relations between China and foreign Powers has been fully established. The Astronomical Office and other minor bureaus may be passed over, but the celebrated Hanlin College requires a few words of description. This Imperial Academy was very appropriately compared by Sir John Davis to the Sorbonne, and in a literary country to be a doctor of the Hanlin is synonymous with the highest distinction. The college is governed by two life presidents, and below them are twenty subordinates of different grades. The number of ordinary members is unlimited, but periodical examinations are held to prevent their knowledge getting rusty, and those who fail to pass are dismissed from the college. One of the chief duties of the Hanlin Yuen is to supervise and correct the language used in all official documents, so that it may be most elegant and in the purest style. The historiographer's department is perhaps the most interesting branch of this Imperial Academy. It is composed of twenty-two members, who wait constantly on the Emperor to take down his words and to record the acts of his government. What they write is preserved as an inviolable secret so long as the same dynasty remains on the throne. The official history of the Manchu family will only be given to the world when in the course of time it has ceased to reign, and when the duty of publishing it shall have devolved as a sacred charge upon its successor. For this apparently we shall have to wait a long time, but we may strengthen our patience with the reflection that when it appears it may tell us little of interest that was not already known from less authentic but more accommodating sources.

In all these Boards, departments, and offices at Pekin, it is computed that there are not fewer than 20,000 officials employed in their respective grades. They are arrayed in strict order of seniority, and their names adorn the pages of an official Red-book, which is issued periodically. With regard to nationality, there are about three Chinese to one Manchu. The members of this civil service are actively employed and subject to close supervision. The least neglect or slip is visited with condign punishment in the loss of steps of seniority affecting pay, position, and pension. The last-named is only granted in cases of old age, when deserving officials are physically unable to work any longer. China possesses at the seat of Empire all the bureaucratic machinery required by the vastness of her affairs. The organisation is admirable, and, if the administration is not as successful as it ought to be, the sole cause is the presence of an all-pervading corruption. In that respect alone China reveals the canker-worm of Asiatic decay.

The provincial administration of China is not less carefully organised than the central, which was described in our previous article. China proper is divided into eighteen provinces, and Manchuria, which, as the native home of the Tartars, long enjoyed an exceptional form of administration, has from a comparatively recent date ranked as the nineteenth. The Viceroy, Tsungtuh or Chetai, is the highest rank in the service, but there are only two single provinces rejoicing in a ruler of that grade. They are Pechihli and Szchuen. Thirteen provinces are grouped into the following six viceroyalties :—Liang or Two Kwang (Kwantung and Kwangsi), Liang or Two Kiang (Kiangsi Kiangsu and Anhwui), Min Cheh (Chekiang and Fuhkien), Yunnan, including Kweichow, Houkwang (Hupeh and Hunan), and last Kansuh and Shensi. The three remaining provinces, Shansi, Honan, and Shantung, are administered by the inferior grade of Futai, or Governor, and Formosa has lately been placed under an officer of the same rank. The eight Viceroys are assisted by twelve Futais, so that the head administration of the eighteen provinces is composed in all of twenty-four officials. With regard to Manchuria, which has now its own Viceroy, not included in the preceding list, the organisation has always been, and is still to a great extent, different from the rest of the Empire.

When the Manchus conquered China they adopted the régime of the conquered, but in their own native country they left the organisation undisturbed. Moukden, its capital, was declared twin seat of the Government with Pekin; the chief departments were compelled to keep branch offices there, and the executive power was entrusted to a military governor of the rank of Tsiangkun. In China civil authority was supreme, in Manchuria the Tartars clung to their simple military habits. The system worked sufficiently well until recent reigns, although the friction between rude Manchu officers and lettered Chinese scribes was constant. At last a commission of enquiry was appointed by the late Emperor Tungche, and Chung Shih, brother of Chung How, notorious for the Treaty of Livadia, was placed at its head. He reported in favour of converting Manchuria into a Viceroyalty, and as his reward, or punishment, he was appointed the first Viceroy. The pay is nominally £6,000 a year, but he has only been allowed to draw one-third of it—at least, so says Mr. James. Notwithstanding the investing of the Tsiangkun with the higher and civilian title of

Tsungtuh, the governors of the different divisions of Manchuria are at present military men and not civilians.

The regular provincial administration is very much weaker in numbers than the central bureaucracy, and not more than 2,000 officials are enrolled on the official list and receive a fixed salary. The hordes of expectant officials who hang round every yamen, and who form a sort of bodyguard for every taotai and magistrate, have to feed themselves. By right of success at the stipulated examinations, they await their turn for an appointment which may never be conferred, and while waiting for the favourable turn in Fortune's wheel they levy blackmail by bullying and extortion from the mass of the people. The imprudent litigant, the unfortunate merchant, and, in fact, all who become marked as possessing wealth, furnish these expectant officials with the harvest upon which they exist and, indeed, flourish. There is no greater evil in China at the present day than this—the open and unchecked exactions of the unscrupulous and unpaid minor grades of the provincial service. The central Government shrinks from applying the real remedy to the sore, because it does not see its way to promising and fulfilling its promise of regular payment to the great body of its employés throughout the provinces. In this matter it lies under a constant reproach, and exposes itself to the danger of popular discontent and revolt against the tyranny of the mandarins.

Nominally, at least, if not so in reality, the system of recruiting the service by universal competitive examination, open to all subjects of the Emperor, enhances the difficulty of providing employment for all those who have qualified for the lower grades of official rank, or, at all events, of paying them when appointed. Something of the same difficulty already besets us in India, where our system of education has only been at work for fifty years, whereas China has pursued the same course for countless centuries. In China, as a matter of sheer necessity, steps have had to be taken to convert universal into limited competition, and to place as many hindrances as possible in the way of the successful candidate at the first of the periodical and essential examinations. This is for the degree of *siutsai* (flowering talent), which is held once a year in all the prefectural towns. Thousands come forward in each district for the preliminary examination, but only tens succeed in passing. Mr. Wells Williams mentions a case of twenty-seven successful candidates out of 4,000 aspirants. A second and more severe examination has to be passed by those who succeed at the "little go," before the coveted degree of *siutsai* is obtained, and even then the privileges do not include official employment. For that a further examination, held once in three years, for the higher degree of *ku jin* has to be undergone. This takes place in September in every provincial capital. The numbers that present themselves at each town vary from 3,000 to 8,000. To strike a fair average, 90,000 young men who have already qualified present themselves every three years for an examination which would entitle them to an appointment in a service that at the very outside does not contain more than 22,000 paid members. The examination hall, or rather encampment, at Pekin is provided with cells for 10,000 candidates—each candidate being shut up in one of them during examination. Another original feature is the absence of limitation as to age—at one examination there were successful candidates from the ages of twenty-five to eighty-three!

It is difficult to ascertain the average of successful candidates at this second examination, but it does not seem to much exceed 1 per cent. The average number of *ku jin* certificates granted every three years is stated to be not more than 1,300. A further degree of *tsin sz* is competed for at Pekin every three years, also by those *ku jin* who have not been fortunate enough to get official employment. This is a hazardous ordeal, for those who fail may lose the degree they hold and be forbidden to present themselves again. The fourth examination is for the highest degree of *hanlin*, which secures a name on the roll of the Imperial Academy and a fixed salary. The number that reaches this final stage is, as can be imagined, very small and select. It will thus be seen that the supply of raw material for the service of the administration is abundant and ever increasing The number of *siutsai* far exceeds any possible requirements of the Executive, and these aspirants to office have to exist as best they can, and at the expense of the country and very often of the good name of the government. Even the *ku jin* cannot be provided for, although the examiners show such severity in eliminating the incapable or unlucky. The system of competitive examination in China, which has been so much belauded and imitated by ourselves, has from absolute need evolved another system, that of sweeping and, it cannot be doubted, intentional rejection. The Chinese government would not exist for a year if the average of successful candidates were based on the true merits of the competitors. Its reputation has been impaired and its position sapped by the indiscipline prevailing among the thousands and tens of thousands of *siutsai* who never have had and never can have any definite official employment. If China had a Press or a Parliament the disappointment of these men would find expression, and their personal chagrin would speedily develop into active disloyalty.

If the government of China is carried on to a great extent by the unpaid or self-paid services of the lower grades of the provincial civil service, it makes a still greater convenience of these individuals for the police of the realm. In the strict sense of the term, China has no police organisation at all. What this means may be gathered from the fact that in India, with a considerably smaller population, there are 150,000 policemen fully organised and regularly paid. China has to intrust the work to the unpaid voluntary runners of the yamen, and to the loafers who have known how to attach themselves to the fortunes of some particular mandarin. These very inefficient guardians of the peace are in any emergency reinforced by the soldiers of the local army. All these forces taken together supply a very inefficient body for the maintenance of order in great cities like Canton and Hankow. If the people themselves were not among the most law-abiding in the world, disorders and riot would be ceaseless and unending. In Pekin itself, where the security of the Court necessitates the most strenuous measures, the result, although sufficiently satisfactory, is secured by a scratch corps of policemen—the Banner Army being invested with the requisite authority and whips to impress the citizens of Pekin with respect for constituted authority. There is no subject on which the *Pekin Gazette* contains more frequent and more persistent petitions than the rapacity and tyranny of the police; but a remedy has never been forthcoming, and the evil is as crying to-day as it was sixty years ago, when the incapacity and exactions of this branch of the executive were the chief causes of the formation of the Triad and Water Lily secret societies, which led up to the Taeping rebellion.

With regard to the dispensation of justice, it is difficult to assume that it can be pure and efficient where essential administration for insuring an impartial hearing and verdict is so lacking in vigour and integrity. At the same time there is no reason to dispute the desire or intention of the statutes of China to promote justice and equity. The litigation is so vast, the number of criminal cases so great, in a country populated like China, that rapidity in disposing of them becomes a merit, and perhaps the greatest merit, in a judge. It is no unusual thing to see honourable mention made of a judge who has decided a thousand cases in a year. In theory nothing can be more admirable than the system of judicature existing in China. The courts are open at all hours, and the person who wishes to make an appeal has only to strike a drum that is supposed to be placed at the entrance of every court. Whether this is universally done may be doubted, but the idea shows how easy Chinese lawgivers intended recourse to the protection of the laws to be. Every litigant or person suffering from an alleged injustice who could not obtain reparation in the provincial courts was allowed the right of appeal to Pekin. That right can, however, be only exercised by the rich, and it is said to have the lamentable result of leaving them poor.

The two most common forms of punishment in China are whipping and the wearing of the cangue, a heavy wooden case, into an aperture of which the head of an offender is inserted, and which bears a resemblance to our stocks. Capital punishment is of various kinds; decapitation and "the slow and painful process," which means being hacked to pieces, are the most common. Several thousand people suffer every year at the hands of the public executioner, but it is believed that their numbers are few in comparison with those who die from the effects of torture and confinement in unhealthy prisons. Although slavery does not exist, properly speaking, in China, it is curious to know that in the eyes of the law the large boating population and actors fill the position of slaves. They are only relieved from that disqualification by taking the *siutsai* degree, which never happens with regard to the former, and rarely in the case of the latter. Another curious feature of law which also sheds a strange light on national character is connected with the honourable opinion held of suicides. The motives of suicides are various, but to all Chinese law extends the most lenient consideration. Very frequently they are prompted by motives of revenge, for the householder on whose premises the dead body is found has always to provide the funeral expenses and to compensate the relatives of deceased. Some more unfortunate are indicted for murder and fleeced by the officials until they are reduced to beggary. In China suicide has been made a fine art, and finds many devotees because it provides the means of rescuing one's relatives from poverty. It need hardly be added after this that there is seldom much difficulty in procuring a substitute when one has to be decapitated, provided a sufficient sum is put down for the benefit of the sufferer's family. In China life is cheap, and their heads rest securely on the shoulders of men who have a sufficient supply of money, and who will not hesitate to expend it to prolong their own existence.

With regard to the military organisation and resources of China much might be written, but, to summarise the chief facts, it may be said that the military organisation on paper is only slightly less elaborate than the civil administration, and that the Emperor controls forces of nearly one million armed men—only to a large degree the arms are out of date and the men untrained. Although events have compelled the authorities to show greater activity and to increase the number of troops by the formation of fresh corps, such as Li Hung Chang's trained regiments and the garrison in Manchuria and Central Asia, the division of the army remains unchanged and goes back to the date of the Manchu conquest, when it became necessary to organise the permanent forces of the Empire. They were then divided into three separate bodies, composed of the races to which they belonged—Manchu, Mongol, and Chinese. The Manchus number 678 companies of 100 men each, or nearly seventy thousand fighting men. The Mongols furnish about 80,000 men; and the two combined give what has been generally called the Tartar Army. The Chinese or Green Flag army numbers between six and seven hundred thousand men, but no attempt has yet been made to organise this force for modern war. China is strong in numbers even with respect to her army, which has always been delegated to an inferior position in her community, priding itself on the pre-eminence of the educated civilian, but she is lamentably deficient in organisation.

Of late years strenuous efforts have been made to render efficient those portions of the Chinese army which are intrusted with duties that are considered of exceptional importance. The army of Li Hung Chang, garrisoning the metropolitan province of Pechihli, has for twenty years been subjected to a stricter discipline than the rest, caused as much by Li's experience of war, gained against the Taeping rebels in co-operation with General Gordon, as by the desire to save the capital. This force, known as the model corps or Black Flag army, numbers about 50,000 men, and is intrusted with the special duty of garrisoning Port Arthur, the forts at Taku and on the Peiho, and Tientsin. If China posseses such a thing as an efficient *corps d'armée*, it is to be found in this force, which is mainly recruited from the Chinese population. The men are well-armed, and there are many foreign instructors, among whom Germans are the most numerous. The late General Prjevalsky was sceptical of the military value of even this force, but other and equally competent critics entertain no doubt that it is a fairly efficient body of troops, and that the work to be done—namely, the defence of forts—is peculiarly suited to their temperament.

The garrison of Pekin is still composed exclusively of the Tartar or Banner army. The Pekin field force is always commanded by a Manchu of high rank, and latterly it was under the personal orders of Prince Chun himself. The organisation of this force is backward, and only feeble attempts have been made to bring up its armament to the exigencies of modern war. On the other hand, the raw material is the best in China. It consists of the *élite* of the Manchu and Mongol Banners, men of fine physique, who, unlike the Chinese, believe that the sword is better than the pen, and that courage is superior to chicane. If their training were taken seriously in hand China would possess in her northern province an army which could safeguard Pekin against any conceivable invasion. Greater progress has been made with regard to the Tartar army garrisoning the all important province of Manchuria. Twenty years ago the garrison of that part of the Empire consisted of the tribal levies, armed with bows and arrows and spears. A flintlock appeared an engine of destruction. To-day there are nearly 200,000 Bannermen on the rolls of Manchuria alone, and of these it is confidently stated that one-third are armed with Winchester and other rifles, and are performing garrison duties at Moukden.

Kirin, and on the Ussuri. It is not contended that these troops are yet as carefully trained as the model corps of Li, but they probably possess superior fighting qualities. Leaving a wide margin for exaggeration, there is the important fact that China now has one strong army to defend her capital against attack from the sea, and another to oppose any assault by land from the Amour and Russian Manchuria. This really means a complete revolution in the military position of China. It is unnecessary to go into details on the subject of the garrisons in Central Asia and on the southern frontiers. In both quarters China has important interests to consider and defend, but they are not to be compared with those in the north. She has rightly commenced her task of improvement where it was most needed, and although she has not done all that she could have done, and will yet have to accomplish, she is already strong where she was weak, and could now render a good account of herself against a first-class opponent. The desire to reform the army is keenly and honestly felt in the highest circles of Chinese life, but the difficulty in adapting the old organisations of the Banner and Green Flag armies to modern requirements is very great and perhaps insuperable. In some things China has made great progress, and in others she has hardly advanced at all. It is much to be feared that she has few competent and honest officers, and that she does not possess even one general. That China should enjoy a superior organisation and a more formidable military force than she does will be admitted when it is stated on good authority that her total war expenditure, including the pay of the provincial garrisons, does not fall short of twenty millions sterling.

With regard to her navy, China has in less than twenty years made enormous progress. She has purchased some excellent vessels, she has built some useful arsenals and repairing docks, her guns have not burst, and her navy in tonnage, armament, and being generally up to date, comes sixth among the fleets of the world. The weak point is connected with her officers and the fighting capacity of their crews. If they will do their duty, China possesses a navy which completes the defensive power of the country, and would give it besides opportunities of assuming the offensive in more than one quarter. When it is remembered how short a period has elapsed since China only possessed antiquated sailing junks, it will be allowed that the progress made has been little short of marvellous.

The revenue of the Empire is the last branch of the great subject of the government of this curious country and people that need claim our attention. There is great difficulty in arriving at any conclusion as to what the gross total may be. In the first place the bulk of the revenue raised in each province is spent on local administration, and only a small portion is sent to Pekin for the requirements of the central government. Much of the revenue also is raised in grain, and much of the proportion handed over to the Pekin Treasury is in kind. It is not surprising to find that the estimates vary from twenty to one hundred millions sterling. A recent return states that the revenue received at Pekin now amounts to twenty-two millions sterling in silver and between four and five millions in grain. With this sum the Emperor has to pay his Court, the Pekin administration, the navy, the disciplined troops (not the Green Flag or local Bannermen), and to purchase arms, as well as to provide for special contingencies. Accepting this figure as correct, there seems no valid reason to summarily reject the higher sum of one hundred millions as the total contribution of the people of China to their government. There need also be no hesitation in saying that neither the people nor their government get the value of this large sum of money. Much of it is wasted for want of system, a great deal more is devoted to the benefit of corrupt officials, and even the balance is assigned to many purposes that are no longer suitable to the age or the national requirements.

The revenue derived from foreign customs, which are collected by a large staff of European officials, first organised thirty years ago, and ably controlled from almost the beginning by Sir Robert Hart, exceeds five millions sterling now that the *lekin* is paid as part of the import duty. It provides the central government with a certain and increasing source of income, which enables it to meet pressing liabilities and to offer a specific guarantee for the payment of interest on any loans that it may raise in the European markets. Let it be noted to her credit that China has not turned her opportunities of borrowing money to undue account, like her neighbour Japan. Her pride, or perhaps a shrewd perception that the time will come when she can borrow money at a very much lower interest than is now expected, has prevented her incurring permanent liabilities for the sake of a temporary gain. A single year's income from customs alone would wipe out the total indebtedness of China, whereas the debt of Japan is several times as great as its whole revenue. The financial strength of China arises from the magnitude of its revenues and its freedom from indebtedness. Its financial weakness consists in the want of system with regard to the provincial revenue, and in the fact that the central executive has to defray all the substantial burdens of the Empire out of that portion of the taxes which reaches Pekin. It is not to be expected that any material improvement in these points can be effected until the means of communication have been greatly improved between the capital and the provincial seats of government.

The facts that have been recorded will perhaps have the effect of showing that the larger place which has been conceded to China in the family of nations of recent years is deserved on the whole by the condition of that country and the character of its government. Whether the work is satisfactorily performed in every department of the administration or not, the rulers of China have at all times set themselves in earnest to the task of governing that vast country, and they have fairly faced the many problems arising from it. In China the *raison d'être* of the government is the benefit of the people. The daily work of the Emperor and his advisers is the discharge of the complicated and overwhelming business of the realm, which is mainly decided within the walls of the Imperial Palace at Pekin. Everything is conducted in an orderly manner and in strict accordance with what experience has shown to be politic and expedient. The meanest offender in China receives the same consideration as an accused viceroy at the hands of the whole hierarchy of Chinese judges until his sentence is finally pronounced or approved by the Emperor on the throne. In the busy hive of Chinese life none work harder than the bureaucrats at Pekin, and it must not be supposed that the drier duties of administration are not enlivened by discussions on *la haute politique* and diplomatic finesse. A service that has in our time produced such subtle minds as Li Hung Chang and the Marquis Tseng is not to be assigned a low place among the official systems of the age. This is not the place to discuss the bearings of Chinese policy in its relations with foreign countries, but it may be said that that policy will be based on the same solid facts as underlie the structure of its government. It will be only a transitory phase, due to some passing apprehension, if it loses the national characteristics of confidence, persistency, and indifference to external opinion. The policy of China can never be one altogether agreeable to the contemplation of the interested foreigner. There must always be something in its nature akin to the Monroe doctrine, which, if enforced, would make the United States an unpleasant neighbour. But if we on our side are willing to make allowances for the position and traditions of the Chinese Emperor and his executive, there should be no difficulty in maintaining harmonious relations between England and China. In dealing with China we have some assurance that we are treating with a strong and stable government, for the weakness of China is more on the surface than at the core, and there is always a guarantee of durability when the institutions of a country are seen to be performing their expected functions. To this much credit the government of China can, without exaggeration, lay claim, and on that ground alone it is entitled to our respect.

CHRONOLOGICAL TABLE.

Dynasty.	Emperor.	Year of Accession. B.C.	Year of Death,&c. B.C.	Length of Reign.
Semi-Mythical Period	Hwangti	2637	2577	60
	Chaohow	2577	2457	120
	Chwenhio	2457	2397	60
	Tikou	2397	2366	31
	Tichi	2366	2357	9
	Yao	2357	2257	100
	Chun, associated with Yao	2285		(reigned in all)
	Chun	2257	2208	77
	Yu, associated with Chun	2224		(in all)
The Hia	Yu	2208	2197	27
	Tiki	2197	2188	9
	Taikang	2188	2159	29
	Chungkang	2159	2118	41
	Siang	2146	2118	28
	Chaokang	2118	2057	61
	Chou	2057	2040	17
	Hoai	2040	2014	26
	Mang	2014	1996	18
	Lie	1996	1980	16
	Poukiang	1980	1921	59
	Kiung	1921	1900	21
	Kin	1900	1879	21
	Kungkia	1879	1848	31
	Kao	1848	1837	11
	Fa	1837	1818	19
	Kia	1818	1776	42

Dynasty.	Emperor.	Year of Accession. B.C.	Year of Death, &c. B.C.	Length of Reign.
The Chang	Ching Tang	1776	1753	23
	Taikia	1753	1720	33
	Wouting	1720	1691	29
	Taikeng	1691	1666	25
	Siaokia	1666	1649	17
	Yungki	1649	1637	12
	Taiwou	1637	1562	75
	Chungting	1562	1549	13
	Waijen	1549	1534	15
	Hotankia	1534	1525	9
	Tsouy	1525	1506	19
	Tsousin	1506	1490	16
	Woukia	1490	1465	25
	Tsouting	1465	1433	32
	Nankeng	1433	1408	25
	Yangkia	1408	1401	7
	Pankeng	1401	1373	28
	Siaosin	1373	1352	21
	Siaoy	1352	1324	28
	Wouting	1324	1265	59
	Tsoukeng	1265	1258	7
	Tsoukia	1258	1225	33
	Linsin	1225	1219	6
	Kengting	1219	1198	21
	Wouy	1198	1194	4
	Taiting	1194	1191	3
	Tiy	1191	1154	37
	Chousin	1154	1122	32
The Chow	Wou Wang	1122	1115	7
	Ching Wang	1115	1078	37
	Kang Wang	1078	1052	26
	Chao Wang	1052	1001	51
	Mou Wang	1001	946	55
	Kung Wang	946	934	12
	Y Wang	934	909	25
	Hiao Wang	909	894	15
	I Wang	894	878	16
	Li Wang	878	827	51
	Siuan Wang	827	781	46
	Yeou Wang	781	770	11
	Ping Wang	770	719	51
	Hing Wang	719	696	23
	Chwang Wang	696	681	15
	Li Wang	681	676	5
	Hwei Wang	676	651	25
	Siang Wang	651	618	33
	King Wang	618	612	6
	Kwang Wang	612	606	6

CHRONOLOGICAL TABLE.

Dynasty.	Emperor.	Year of Accession. B.C.	Year of Death, &c. B.C.	Length of Reign.
The Chow	Ting Wang	606	585	21
	Kien Wang	585	571	14
	Ling Wang	571	544	27
	King Wang	544	519	25
	Keng Wang	519	475	44
	Youan Wang	475	468	7
	Chingting Wang	468	440	28
	Kao Wang	440	425	15
	Weili Wang	425	401	24
	Gan Wang	401	375	26
	Lie Wang	375	368	7
	Hien Wang	368	320	48
	Chintsen Wang	320	314	6
	Nan Wang	314	255	59
The Tsin	Chow Siang	255	250	5
	Hiao Wang	250	249	1
	Chwang Siang Wang	249	246	3
	Wang Ching	246	221	25
	Tsin Chi Hwangti	221	209	12
	Eulchi Hwangti	209	206	3
	Tsoupa Wang	206	202	4
The Han	Kaotsou	202	194	8
	Hiao Hweiti	194	187	7
	Kaohwang	187	179	8
	(Regency of Empress Liuchi.)			
	Wenti	179	156	23
	Kingti	156	140	16
	Vouti	140	86	54
	Chaoti	86	73	13
	Hieunti	73	48	25
	Yuenti	48	32	16
	Chingti	32	6	26
			A.D.	
	Gaiti	6	1	7
		A.D.		
	Pingti	1	6	5
	Usurper, Wang Mang	6	23	17
	Ti Yuen	23	25	2
	Kwang Vouti	25	58	23
	Mingti	58	76	18
	Changti	76	89	13
	Hoti	89	106	17
	Changti II.	106	107	1
	Ganti	107	126	19
	Chunti	126	145	19

Dynasty	Emperor	Year of Accession. A.D.	Year of Death, &c. A.D.	Length of Reign
The Han	Chungti	145	146	1
	Chiti	146	147	1
	Hiuenti	147	168	21
	Lingti	168	190	22
	Hienti	190	220	30
The Period of the Sankoue, or Three Kingdoms	Various minor Princes of Wei and the two Hans	from 220	to 265	45
The Later Tsin	Vouti	265	290	25
	Hweiti	290	307	17
	Hoaiti	307	313	6
	Mingti	313	317	4
	Yuanti	317	323	6
	Mingti	323	326	3
	Chingti	326	343	17
	Kangti	343	345	2
	Mouti	345	362	17
	Gaiti	362	366	4
	Tiy	366	371	5
	Kian Wenti	371	373	2
	Hiao Vouti	373	397	24
	Ganti	397	419	22
	Kungti	419	420	1
The Song	Vouti	420	423	3
	Ying Wang	423	424	1
	Wenti	424	454	30
	Vouti	454	465	11
	Mingti	465	473	8
	Gou Wang	473	477	4
	Chunti	477	479	2
The Tsi	Kaoti	479	483	4
	Vouti	483	494	11
	Mingti	494	499	5
	Paokwen	499	501	2
	Hoti	501	502	1
The Leang	Vouti	502	550	48
	Wenti	550	552	2
	Yuenti	552	555	3
	Kingti	555	556	1
The Chin	Vouti	556	564	8
	Wenti	564	567	3
	Petsong	567	569	2
	Suenti	569	580	11
The Soui	Wenti	580	601	21
	Vouti	601	605	4
	Yangti	605	617	12
	Kungti	617	618	1

CHRONOLOGICAL TABLE.

Dynasty.	Emperor.	Year of Accession. A.D.	Year of Death,&c. A.D.	Length of Reign.
The Tang	Kaotsou	618	627	9
	Taitsong	627	650	23
	Kaotsong	650	684	34
	Chungtsong	684	710	26
	Jouitsong	710	712	2
	Mingti	712	756	44
	Soutsung	756	763	7
	Taitsong II.	763	780	17
	Tetsong	780	805	25
	Chuntsong	805	806	1
	Hientsung	806	821	15
	Moutsung	821	825	4
	Kingtsung	825	827	2
	Wentsung	827	841	14
	Woutsung	841	847	6
	Hiuentsung	847	860	13
	Ytsong	860	874	14
	Hitsong	874	889	15
	Chaotsung	889	905	16
	Chao Hiuenti	905	907	2
Five small Dynasties. The Later Leangs (1)	Taitsou	907	913	6
	Chouching	913	915	2
	Ching	915	923	8
The Later Tangs (2)	Chwangtsong	923	926	3
	Mingtsong	926	934	8
	Minti	934	934	A few mths.
	Lou Wang	934	936	2
The Later Tsin (3)	Kaotsou	936	943	7
	Tsi Wang	943	947	4
The Later Han (4)	Kaotsou	947	948	1
	Ynti	948	951	3
The Later Chow (5)	Taitsou	951	954	3
	Chitsong	954	960	6
The Sung	Taitsou	960	976	16
	Taitsong	976	998	22
	Chintsong I.	998	1023	25
	Jintsong	1023	1064	41
	Yngtsong	1064	1068	4
In 1115 the Kin Dynasty began to rule in Northern China concurrently with the Sung in Southern. For list of Rulers see further on.	Chitsong II.	1068	1086	18
	Chutsong	1086	1101	15
	Hweitsong	1101	1126	25
	Kingtsong	1126	1127	1
	Kaotsong	1127	1163	36
	Hiaotsong	1163	1190	27
	Kwangtsong	1190	1195	5
	Ningtsong	1195	1225	30

Dynasty.	Emperor.	Year of Accession. A.D.	Year of Death,&c. A.D.	Length of Reign.
The Sung	Litsong	1225	1265	40
	Toutsong	1265	1275	10
	Tihien	1275	1276	1
	Touantsong	1276	1278	2
	Tiping	1278	1279	1
The Kin	Taitsou	1115	1123	8
	Taitsong	1123	1135	12
	Hitsong	1135	1149	14
	Chuliang	1149	1161	12
	Chitsong	1161	1190	29
	Changtsong	1190	1209	19
	Choo Yungki	1209	1213	4
	Hiuentsong	1213	1224	11
	Gaitsong	1224	1234	10
The Mongol or Yuen	Chitsou (Kublai Khan)	1260	1295	35
	Chingtsong	1295	1308	13
	Woutsong	1308	1312	4
	Jintsong	1312	1321	9
	Yngtsong	1321	1324	3
	Taitingti	1324	1328	4
	Wentsong	1328	1333	5
	Chunti	1333	1368	35
The Ming	Hongwou	1368	1398	30
	Kien Wenti	1398	1403	5 deposed
	Yonglo	1403	1425	22
	Gintsong	1425	1426	1
	Suentsong	1426	1435	9
	Yngtsong	1435	1450	15
	Chinwang or Kingti	1450	1458	8
	Yngtsong (restored)	1458	1465	7
	Hientsong	1465	1488	23
	Hiaotsong	1488	1506	18
	Woutsong	1506	1522	16
	Chitsoug	1522	1567	45
	Moutsong	1567	1573	6
	Wanleh	1573	1620	47
	Kwantsong	1620	1621	1
	Chiti	1621	1624	3
	Hitsong	1624	1628	4
	Hoaitsong	1628	1644	16
The Manchu or Tatsing (still ruling)	Chuntche or Chitsou	1644	1661	17
	Kanghi	1661	1722	61
	Yung Ching	1722	1735	13

Dynasty.	Emperor.	Year of Accession. A.D.	Year of Death, &c. A.D.	Length of Reign.
The Manchu or Tatsing (still ruling)	Keen Lung	1735	1796 abdctd. / 1799 died.	61
	Kiaking	1796	1821	25
	Taoukwang	1821	1850	29
	Hienfung	1850	1861	11
	Tungche	1861	1875	14
	Kwangsu	1875	still reigning.	

APPENDIX.

Treaty between Her Majesty and the Emperor of China, signed, in the English and Chinese Languages, at Nankin, August 29, 1842. (Ratifications exchanged at Hong Kong, June 26, 1843.)

HER MAJESTY the Queen of the United Kingdom of Great Britain and Ireland, and His Majesty the Emperor of China, being desirous of putting an end to the misunderstandings and consequent hostilities which have arisen between the two countries, have resolved to conclude a Treaty for that purpose, and have therefore named as their Plenipotentiaries, that is to say:

Her Majesty the Queen of Great Britain and Ireland, Sir Henry Pottinger, Bart., a Major-General in the employ of the East India Company, &c.;

And His Imperial Majesty the Emperor of China, the High Commissioners Keying, a Member of the Imperial House, a guardian of the Crown Prince, and General of the garrison of Canton; and Elepoo, of the Imperial Kindred, graciously permitted to wear the insignia of the first rank and the distinction of a peacock's feather, lately Minister and Governor-General, &c., and now Lieutenant-General commanding at Chapoo;[*]

Who, after having communicated to each other their respective full powers, and found them to be in good and due form, have agreed upon and concluded the following Articles:—

ARTICLE I.

There shall henceforward be Peace and Friendship between Her Majesty the Queen of the United Kingdom of Great Britain and Ireland and His Majesty the Emperor of China, and between their respective subjects, who shall enjoy full security and protection for their persons and property within the dominions of the other.

ARTICLE II.

His Majesty the Emperor of China agrees, that British subjects, with their families and their establishments, shall be allowed to reside, for the purpose of carrying on their mercantile pursuits, without molestation or restraint, at the cities and towns of Canton, Amoy, Foo-chow-foo, Ningpo, and Shanghai; and Her Majesty the Queen of Great Britain. &c., will appoint Superintendents, or Consular officers, to reside at each of the

[*] Although only two Chinese Plenipotentiaries are here named, the treaty was in fact signed by three.

above-named cities or towns, to be the medium of communication between the Chinese authorities and the said merchants, and to see that the just duties and other dues of the Chinese Government, as hereafter provided for, are duly discharged by Her Britannic Majesty's subjects.

ARTICLE III.

It being obviously necessary and desirable that British subjects should have some port whereat they may careen and refit their ships when required, and keep stores for that purpose, His Majesty the Emperor of China cedes to Her Majesty the Queen of Great Britain, &c., the Island of Hong Kong, to be possessed in perpetuity by Her Britannic Majesty, her heirs and successors, and to be governed by such laws and regulations as Her Majesty the Queen of Great Britain, &c., shall see fit to direct.

ARTICLE IV.

The Emperor of China agrees to pay the sum of six millions of dollars, as the value of the opium which was delivered up at Canton in the month of March, 1839, as a ransom for the lives of Her Britannic Majesty's Superintendent and subjects, who had been imprisoned and threatened with death by the Chinese high officers.

ARTICLE V.

The Government of China having compelled the British merchants trading at Canton to deal exclusively with certain Chinese merchants, called Hong Merchants (or Co Hong), who had been licensed by the Chinese Government for that purpose, the Emperor of China agrees to abolish that practice in future at all ports where British merchants may reside, and to permit them to carry on their mercantile transactions with whatever persons they please; and His Imperial Majesty further agrees to pay to the British Government the sum of three millions of dollars, on account of debts due to British subjects by some of the said Hong merchants, or Co-Hong, who have become insolvent, and who owe very large sums of money to subjects of Her Britannic Majesty.

ARTICLE VI.

The Government of Her Britannic Majesty having been obliged to send out an expedition to demand and obtain redress for the violent and unjust proceedings of the Chinese high authorities towards Her Britannic Majesty's Officer and subjects, the Emperor of China agrees to pay the sum of twelve millions of dollars, on account of the expenses incurred; and Her Britannic Majesty's Plenipotentiary voluntary agrees, on behalf of Her Majesty, to deduct from the said amount of twelve millions of dollars, any sums which may have been received by Her Majesty's combined forces, as ransom for cities and towns in China, subsequent to the 1st day of August, 1841.

ARTICLE VII.

It is agreed, that the total amount of twenty-one millions of dollars described in the three preceding Articles, shall be paid as follows :—
    Six millions immediately.

Six millions in 1843; that is, three millions on or before the 30th of the month of June, and three millions on or before the 31st of December.

Five millions in 1844; that is two millions and a half on or before the 30th of June, and two millions and a half on or before the 31st December.

Four millions in 1845; that is, two millions on or before the 30th of June, and two millions on or before the 31st of December.

And it is further stipulated, that interest, at the rate of 5 per cent. per annum, shall be paid by the Government of China on any portion of the above sums that are not punctually discharged at the periods fixed.

ARTICLE VIII.

The Emperor of China agrees to release, unconditionally, all subjects of Her Britannic Majesty (whether natives of Europe or India), who may be in confinement at this moment in any part of the Chinese Empire.

ARTICLE IX.

The Emperor of China agrees to publish and promulgate, under His Imperial Sign Manual and Seal, a full and entire amnesty and act of indemnity to all subjects of China, on account of their having resided under, or having had dealings and intercourse with, or having entered the service of, Her Britannic Majesty, or of Her Majesty's officers; and His Imperial Majesty further engages to release all Chinese subjects who may be at this moment in confinement for similar reasons.

ARTICLE X.

His Majesty the Emperor of China agrees to establish at all the ports which are, by Article II. of this Treaty, to be thrown open for the resort of British merchants, a fair and regular Tariff of export and import Customs and other dues, which Tariff shall be publicly notified and promulgated for general information; and the Emperor further engages, that when British merchandise shall have been once paid at any of the said ports the regulated customs and dues, agreeable to the Tariff to be hereafter fixed, such merchandise may be conveyed by Chinese merchants to any province or city in the interior of the Empire of China, on paying a further amount as transit duties, which shall not exceed*   per cent. on the tariff value of such goods.

ARTICLE XI.

It is agreed that Her Britannic Majesty's Chief High Officer in China shall correspond with the Chinese High Officers, both at the capital and in the Provinces, under the term "communication"; the subordinate British Officers and Chinese High Officers in the Provinces, under the terms "statement" on the part of the former, and on the part of the latter, "declaration"; and the subordinates of both countries on a footing of perfect equality; merchants and others not holding official situations, and therefore not included in the above, on both sides, to use the term "repre-

* See declaration on this subject, which follows the Treaty.

sentation" in all papers addressed to, or intended for the notice of, the respective Governments.

ARTICLE XII.

On the assent of the Emperor of China to this Treaty being received, and the discharge of the first instalment of money, Her Britannic Majesty's forces will retire from Nankin and the Grand Canal, and will no longer molest or stop the trade of China. The military post at Chinhai will also be withdrawn; but the Islands of Koolangsoo, and that of Chusan, will continue to be held by Her Majesty's forces until the money payments, and the arrangements for opening the ports to British merchants, be completed.

ARTICLE XIII

The ratification of this Treaty by Her Majesty the Queen of Great Britain, &c., and His Majesty the Emperor of China, shall be exchanged as soon as the great distance which separates England from China will admit; but in the meantime, counterpart copies of it, signed and sealed by the Plenipotentiaries on behalf of their respective Sovereigns, shall be mutually delivered, and all its provisions and arrangements shall take effect.

Done at Nankin, and signed and sealed by the Plenipotentiaries on board Her Majesty's ship "Cornwallis," this twenty-ninth day of August, one thousand eight hundred and forty-two; corresponding with the Chinese date, twenty-fourth day of the seventh month, in the twenty-second year of Taoukwang.

(L.S.)   HENRY POTTINGER,
Her Majesty's Plenipotentiary.

Seal of the Chinese High Commissioner.
Signature of 3rd Chinese Plenipotentiary.
Signature of 2nd Chinese Plenipotentiary.
Signature of 1st Chinese Plenipotentiary.

Supplementary Treaty between Her Majesty and the Emperor of China, signed at Hoomun-Chae, October 8, 1843.

WHEREAS a Treaty of perpetual Peace and Friendship between Her Majesty the Queen of the United Kingdom of Great Britain and Ireland, and His Majesty the Emperor of China, was concluded at Nankin, and signed on board Her said Majesty's ship "Cornwallis" on the 29th day of August, A.D. 1842, corresponding with the Chinese date of the 24th day of the 7th month, of the 22nd year of Taoukwang, of which said Treaty of perpetual Peace and Friendship, the ratifications, under the respective Seals and Signs Manual of the Queen of Great Britain, &c., and the Emperor of China, were duly exchanged at Hong Kong on the 26th day of June, A.D. 1843, corresponding with the Chinese date the 29th day of the 5th month, in the 23rd year of Taoukwang; and whereas in the said Treaty it was provided (amongst other things), that the five ports of Canton, Foo-chow-foo, Amoy, Ningpo, and Shanghai, should be thrown open for the resort and residence of British merchants, and that a fair and regular tariff of export and import duties, and other dues, should be established at such ports; and whereas various other matters of detail, connected with, and bearing relation to, the said Treaty of perpetual Peace and Friendship, have been since under the mutual discussion and consideration of the Plenipotentiary and accredited Commissioners of the High Contracting Parties; and the said tariff and details having been now finally examined into, adjusted, and agreed upon, it has been determined to arrange and record them in the form of a Supplementary Treaty of Articles, which Articles shall be held to be as binding, and of the same efficacy, as though they had been inserted in the original Treaty of perpetual Peace and Friendship.

Article I.

The Tariff of Export and Import Duties, which is hereunto attached, under the seals and signatures of the respective Plenipotentiary and Commissioners, shall henceforward be in force at the five ports of Canton, Foochow-foo, Amoy, Ningpo, and Shanghai.

Article II.

The General Regulations of Trade, which are hereunto attached, under the seals and signatures of the respective Plenipotentiary and Commissioners, shall henceforward be in force at the five aforenamed ports.

Article III.

All penalties enforced or confiscations made under the third clause of the said General Regulations of Trade, shall belong and be appropriated to the public service of the Government of China.

Article IV.

After the five ports of Canton, Foo-chow-foo, Amoy, Ningpo, and Shanghai, shall be thrown open, English merchants shall be allowed to trade only at those five ports. Neither shall they repair to any other ports or places, nor will the Chinese people at any other ports or places be permitted to trade with them. If English merchant-vessels shall, in contravention of this agreement, and of a Proclamation to the same purport, to be issued by the British Plenipotentiary, repair to any other ports or places, the Chinese Government officers shall be at liberty to seize and confiscate both vessels and cargoes; and should Chinese people be discovered clandestinely dealing with English merchants at any other ports or places, they shall be punished by the Chinese Government in such manner as the law may direct.

Article V.

The fourth clause of the General Regulations of Trade, on the subject of commercial dealings and debts between English and Chinese merchants, is to be clearly understood to be applicable to both parties.

Article VI.

It is agreed that English merchants and others residing at, or resorting to, the five ports to be opened, shall not go into the surrounding country beyond certain short distances to be named by the local authorities, in concert with the British Consul, and on no pretence for purposes of traffic. Seamen and persons belonging to the ships shall only be allowed to land under authority and rules which will be fixed by the Consul, in communication with the local officers; and should any persons whatever infringe the stipulations of this Article, and wander away into the country, they shall be seized and handed over to the British Consul for suitable punishment.

Article VII.

The Treaty of perpetual Peace and Friendship provides for British subjects and their families residing at the cities and towns of Canton, Foochow-foo, Amoy, Ningpo, and Shanghai, without molestation or restraint. It is accordingly determined that ground and houses, the rent or price of which is to be fairly and equitably arranged for, according to the rates prevailing amongst the people, without exaction on either side, shall be set apart by the local officers, in communication with the Consul, and the number of houses built, or rented, will be reported annually to the said local officers by the Consul, for the information of their respective Viceroys and Governors; but the number cannot be limited, seeing that it will be greater or less according to the resort of merchants.

Article VIII.

The Emperor of China having been graciously pleased to grant to all foreign countries whose subjects or citizens have hitherto traded at Canton, the privilege of resorting for purposes of trade to the other four ports of Foochow-foo, Amoy, Ningpo, and Shanghai, on the same terms as the English, it is further agreed, that should the Emperor hereafter, from any cause whatever, be pleased to grant additional privileges or immunities to any of the subjects or citizens of such foreign countries, the same privileges and immunities will be extended to, and enjoyed by, British subjects; but it is to be understood that demands or requests are not on this plea to be unnecessarily brought forward.

Article IX.

If lawless natives of China, having committed crimes or offences against their own Government, shall flee to Hong Kong, or to the English ships of war, or English merchant ships, for refuge, they shall, if discovered by the English officers, be handed over at once to the Chinese officers for trial and punishment; or if, before such discovery be made by the English officers, it should be ascertained or suspected by the officers of the Government of China, whither such criminals and offenders have fled, a communication shall be made to the proper English officer, in order that the said criminals and offenders may be rigidly searched for, seized, and, on proof or admission of their guilt, delivered up. In like manner, if any soldier or sailor, or any other person, whatever his caste or country, who is a subject of the Crown of England, shall, from any cause or on any pretence, desert, fly, or escape into the Chinese territory, such soldier or sailor, or other person, shall be apprehended and confined by the Chinese authorities, and sent to the nearest British Consular or other Government officer. In neither case shall concealment or refuge be afforded.

Article X.

At each of the five ports to be opened to British merchants, one English cruiser will be stationed to enforce good order and discipline amongst the crews of merchant shipping, and to support the necessary authority of the Consul over British subjects. The crew of such ship of war will be carefully restrained by the officer commanding the vessel, and they will be subject to all the rules regarding going on shore, and straying into the country, that are already laid down for the crews of merchant-vessels. Whenever it may be necessary to relieve such ships of war by another, intimation of that intention will be communicated by the Consul, or by the British Superintendent of Trade, where circumstances will permit, to the local Chinese authorities, lest the appearance of an additional ship should excite misgivings amongst the people; and the Chinese cruisers are to offer no hindrance to such relieving ship, nor is she to be considered liable to any port-charges, or other rules laid down in the General Regulations of Trade, seeing that British ships of war never trade in any shape.

Article XI.

The post of Chusan and Koolangsoo will be withdrawn, as provided for in the Treaty of Perpetual Peace and Friendship, the moment all the monies stipulated for in that Treaty shall be paid; and the British Plenipotentiary distinctly and voluntarily agrees, that all dwelling-houses, store-houses, barracks, and other buildings that the British troops or people may have occupied, or intermediately built or repaired, shall be handed over, on the evacuation of the posts, exactly as they stand, to the Chinese Authorities, so as to prevent any pretence for delay, or the slightest occasion for discussion or dispute on those points.

Article XII.

A fair and regular Tariff of duties and other dues having now been established, it is to be hoped that the system of smuggling which has heretofore been carried on between English and Chinese merchants—in many cases with the open connivance and collusion of the Chinese Custom-house officers—will entirely cease; and the most peremptory Proclamation to all English merchants has been already issued on this subject by the British Plenipotentiary, who will also instruct the different Consuls to strictly watch over, and carefully scrutinise, the conduct of all persons, being British subjects, trading under his superintendence. In any positive instance of smuggling transactions coming to the Consul's knowledge, he will instantly apprise the Chinese Authorities of the fact, and they will proceed to seize and confiscate all goods, whatever their value or nature, that may have been so smuggled, and will also be at liberty, if they see fit, to prohibit the ship from which the smuggled goods were landed from trading further, and to send her away, as soon as her accounts are adjusted and paid. The Chinese Government officers will, at the same time, adopt whatever measures they may think fit with regard to the Chinese merchants and Custom-house officers who may be discovered to be concerned in smuggling.

Article XIII.

All persons, whether natives of China or otherwise, who may wish to convey goods from any one of the five ports of Canton, Foo-chow-foo, Amoy, Ningpo, and Shanghai, to Hong Kong, for sale or consumption, shall be at full and perfect liberty to do so, on paying the duties on such goods, and obtaining a pass, or port-clearance, from the Chinese Custom-house at one of the said ports. Should natives of China wish to repair to Hong Kong to purchase goods, they shall have free and full permission to do so; and should they require a Chinese vessel to carry away their purchases, they must obtain a pass, or port-clearance, for her at the custom-house of the port whence the vessel may sail for Hong Kong. It is further settled, that in all cases these passes are to be returned to the officers of the Chinese Government, as soon as the trip for which they may be granted shall be completed.

Article XIV.

An English officer will be appointed at Hong Kong, one part of whose duty will be to examine the registers and passes of all Chinese vessels that may repair to that port to buy or sell goods; and should such officer at any time find that any Chinese merchant-vessel has not a pass, or register, from one of the five ports, she is to be considered as an unauthorised or smuggling vessel, and is not to be allowed to trade, whilst a report of the circumstance is to be made to the Chinese authorities. By this arrangement, it is to be hoped that piracy and illegal traffic will be effectually prevented.

Article XV.

Should natives of India who may repair to Hong Kong to trade, incur debts there, the recovery of such debts must be arranged for by the English Courts of Justice on the spot; but if the Chinese debtor shall abscond, and be known to have property, real or personal, within the Chinese territory, the rule laid down in the fourth clause of the General Regulations for Trade shall be applied to the case; and it will be the duty of the Chinese Authorities, on application by, and in concert with, the British Consuls, to do their utmost to see justice done between the parties. On the same principle, should a British merchant incur debts at any of the five ports, and fly to Hong Kong, the British Authorities will, on receiving an application from the Chinese Government officers, accompanied by statements and full proofs of the debts, institute an investigation into the claims, and, when established, oblige the defaulter or debtor to settle them to the utmost of his means.

Article XVI.

It is agreed that the Custom-house officers at the five ports shall make a monthly return to Canton, of the passes granted to vessels proceeding to Hong Kong, together with the nature of their cargoes; and a copy of these returns will be embodied in one return, and communicated once a month to the proper English officer at Hong Kong. The said English officer will, on his part, make a similar return or communication to the Chinese Authorities at Canton, showing the names of Chinese vessels arrived at Hong Kong, or departed from that port, with the nature of their cargoes: and the Canton Authorities will apprise the Custom-houses at the five ports, in order that, by these arrangements and precautions, all clandestine and illegal trade, under the cover of passes, may be averted.

XVII., or Additional Article.
Relating to British Small Craft.

Various small vessels belonging to the English nation, called schooners, cutters, lorchas, &c., &c., have not hitherto been chargeable with tonnage dues. It is now agreed, in relation to this class of vessels, which ply between Hong Kong and the city, and the city and Macao, that if they only carry passengers, letters, and baggage, they shall, as heretofore, pay no tonnage dues; but if these small craft carry any dutiable articles, no matter how small the quantity may be, they ought, in principle, to pay their full tonnage dues. But this class of small craft are not like the large ships which are engaged in foreign trade; they are constantly coming and going; they make several trips a month, and are not like the large foreign ships, which, on entering the port, cast anchor at Whampoa. If we were to place them on the same footing as the large foreign ships, the charge would fall unequally; therefore, after this, the smallest of these craft shall be rated at 75 tons, and the largest not to exceed 150 tons; whenever they enter the port (or leave the port with cargo), they shall pay tonnage dues at the rate of one mace per ton register. If not so large as 75 tons, they shall still be considered and charged as of 75 tons; and if they exceed 150 tons, they shall be considered as large foreign ships, and, like them, charged tonnage dues, at the rate of five mace per register ton. Foo-chow-foo and the other ports having none of this kind of intercourse, and none of this kind of small craft, it would be unnecessary to make any arrangement as regards them.

The following are the rules by which they are to be regulated:—

1st. Every British schooner, cutter, lorcha, &c., shall have a sailing letter or register in Chinese and English, under the seal and signature of the Chief Superintendent of Trade, describing her appearance, burthen, &c., &c.

2nd. Every schooner, lorcha, and such vessel, shall report herself, as large vessels are required to do, at the Bocca Tigris; and when she carries cargo, she shall also report herself at Whampoa, and shall, on reaching Canton, deliver up her sailing letter or register to the British Consul, who will obtain permission from the Hoppo for her to discharge her cargo, which she is not to do without such permission, under the forfeiture of the penalties laid down in the 3rd clause of the General Regulations of Trade.

3rd. When the inward cargo is discharged, and an outward one (if intended) taken on board, and the duties on both arranged and paid, the Consul will restore the register or sailing letter, and allow the vessel to depart.

This Supplementary Treaty, to be attached to the original Treaty of Peace, consisting of sixteen Articles, and one Additional Article relating to small vessels, is now written out, forming, with its accompaniments, four pamphlets, and is formally signed and sealed by their Excellencies the British Plenipotentiary and the Chinese Imperial Commissioner, who, in the first instance, take two copies each, and exchange them, that their provisions may be immediately carried into effect. At the same time, each of these high functionaries, having taken his two copies, shall duly memorialise the Sovereign of his nation; but the two countries are differently situated as respects distance, so that the will of the one Sovereign can be known sooner than the will of the other. It is now therefore agreed, that on receiving the gracious assent of the Emperor in the Vermilion Pencil, the Imperial Commissioner will deliver the very document containing it into the hands of His Excellency Hwang, Judge of Canton, who will proceed to such place as the Plenipotentiary may appoint, and deliver it to the English Plenipotentiary, to have and to hold. Afterwards, the Sign

Manual of the Sovereign of England having been received at Hong Kong, likewise graciously assenting to and confirming the Treaty, the English Plenipotentiary will despatch a specially appointed officer to Canton, who will deliver the copy containing the Royal Sign Manual to his Excellency Hwang, who will forward it to the Imperial Commissioner, as a rule and a guide to both nations for ever, and as a solemn confirmation of our peace and friendship.

A most important Supplementary Treaty.

Signed and sealed at Hoomun-Chae, on the eighth day of October, 1843, corresponding with the Chinese date of the fifteenth day of the eighth moon, of the twenty-third year of Taoukwang.

(L.S.) HENRY POTTINGER.
Seal and Signature of the Chinese Plenipotentiary.

Convention signed at Bocca Tigris, April 4, 1846.

HER Majesty the Queen of the United Kingdom of Great Britain and Ireland, and His Majesty the Emperor of China, having, with a view to the settlement of all questions between the two countries, and for the preservation of mutual harmony and good understanding, appointed as their Plenipotentiaries, that is to say, Her Majesty the Queen of Great Britain and Ireland, Sir John Francis Davis, a Baronet of the United Kingdom, Governor and Commander-in-chief of Her Majesty's Colony of Hong Kong, &c., and His Majesty the Emperor of China, the High Commissioner Keying, a Member of the Imperial House, a Cabinet Councillor, a Guardian of the Crown Prince, and Governor-General of the Two Kwang Provinces;

The said Plenipotentiaries respectively have, in pursuance of the above-mentioned ends, and after communicating to each other their respective full powers, and finding them to be in good and due form, agreed upon and concluded the following Articles:—

1. His Majesty the Emperor of China having, on his own part, distinctly stated that when in the course of time mutual tranquillity shall have been insured, it will be safe and right to admit foreigners into the city of Canton, and the local authorities being for the present unable to coerce the people of that city, the Plenipotentiaries on either side mutually agree that the execution of the above measure shall be postponed to a more favourable period; but the claim of right is by no means yielded or abandoned on the part of Her Britannic Majesty.

2. British subjects shall in the meanwhile enjoy full liberty and protection in the neighbourhood, on the outside of the city of Canton, within certain limits fixed according to previous Treaty, comprising seventy localities of which the names were communicated by the district magistrates to the British Consul on the 21st November, 1845. They may likewise make excursions on the two sides of the river where there are not numerous villages.

3. It is stipulated, on the part of His Majesty the Emperor of China, that on the evacuation of Chusan by Her Britannic Majesty's forces, the said island shall never be ceded to any other foreign Power.

4. Her Britannic Majesty consents, upon her part, in case of the attack of an invader, to protect Chusan and its dependencies, and to restore it to the possession of China as of old; but as this stipulation proceeds from the

friendly alliance between the two nations, no pecuniary subsidies are to be due from China on this account.

5. Upon the receipt of the sign-manual of His Majesty the Emperor of China to these presents, it is agreed, on account of the distance which separates the two countries, that the Island of Chusan shall be immediately delivered over to the Chinese authorities; and on the ratification of the present Convention by Her Britannic Majesty, it shall be mutually binding on the High Contracting Powers.

Done at Bocca Tigris, and signed and sealed by the Plenipotentiaries, this fourth day of April 1846, corresponding with the Chinese date, Taoukwang twenty-sixth year, third moon, ninth day.

Inclosure in No. 181.
Treaty between Her Majesty and the Emperor of China. Signed, in the English and Chinese languages, at Tien-tsin, June 26, 1858.

HER Majesty the Queen of the United Kingdom of Great Britain and Ireland, and His Majesty the Emperor of China, being desirous to put an end to the existing misunderstanding between the two countries, and to place their relations on a more satisfactory footing in future, have resolved to proceed to a revision and improvement of the Treaties existing between them; and, for that purpose, have named as their Plenipotentiaries, that is to say:—

"Her Majesty the Queen of Great Britain and Ireland, the Right Honourable the Earl of Elgin and Kincardine, a Peer of the United Kingdom, and Knight of the Most Ancient and Most Noble Order of the Thistle;

And His Majesty the Emperor of China, the High Commissioner Kweiliang, a Senior Chief Secretary of State, styled of the East Cabinet, Captain-General of the Plain White Banner of the Manchu Banner Force, Superintendent-General of the administration of Criminal Law; and Hwashana, one of His Imperial Majesty's Expositors of the Classics, Manchu President of the Office for the Regulation of the Civil Establishment, Captain-General of the Bordered Blue Banner of the Chinese Banner Force, and Visitor of the Office of Interpretation;

Who, after having communicated to each other their respective full powers, and found them to be in good and due form, have agreed upon and concluded the following Articles:—

ARTICLE I.

The Treaty of Peace and Amity between the two nations, signed at Nankin on the twenty-ninth day of August, in the year one thousand eight hundred and forty-two, is hereby renewed and confirmed.

The Supplementary Treaty and General Regulations of Trade having been amended and improved, and the substance of their provisions having been incorporated in this Treaty, the said Supplementary Treaty and General Regulations of Trade are hereby abrogated.

ARTICLE II.

For the better preservation of harmony in future, Her Majesty the Queen of Great Britain and His Majesty the Emperor of China mutually agree that, in accordance with the universal practice of great and friendly nations, Her Majesty the Queen may, if She see fit, appoint Ambassadors, Ministers, or other Diplomatic Agents to the Court of Pekin; and His Majesty the Emperor of China may, in like manner, if He see fit, appoint Ambassadors, Ministers, or other Diplomatic Agents to the Court of St. James.

ARTICLE III.

His Majesty the Emperor of China hereby agrees that the Ambassador, Minister, or other Diplomatic Agent, so appointed by Her Majesty the Queen of Great Britain, may reside, with his family and establishment, permanently at the capital, or may visit it occasionally, at the option of the British Government. He shall not be called upon to perform any ceremony derogatory to him as representing the Sovereign of an independent nation on a footing of equality with that of China. On the other hand, he shall use the same forms of ceremony and respect to His Majesty the Emperor as are employed by the Ambassadors, Ministers, or Diplomatic Agents of Her Majesty towards the Sovereigns of independent and equal European nations.

It is further agreed, that Her Majesty's Government may acquire at Pekin a site for building, or may hire houses for the accommodation of Her Majesty's Mission, and that the Chinese Government will assist it in so doing.

Her Majesty's Representative shall be at liberty to choose his own servants and attendants, who shall not be subjected to any kind of molestation whatever.

Any person guilty of disrespect or violence to Her Majesty's Representative, or to any member of his family or establishment, in deed or word, shall be severely punished.

ARTICLE IV.

It is further agreed, that no obstacle or difficulty shall be made to the free movements of Her Majesty's Representative, and that he, and the persons of his suite, may come and go, and travel at their pleasure. He shall, moreover, have full liberty to send and receive his correspondence, to and from any point on the sea-coast that he may select; and his letters and effects shall be held sacred and inviolable. He may employ, for their transmission, special couriers, who shall meet with the same protection and facilities for travelling as the persons employed in carrying despatches for the Imperial Government; and, generally, he shall enjoy the same privileges as are accorded to officers of the same rank by the usage and consent of Western nations.

All expenses attending the Diplomatic Mission of Great Britain shall be borne by the British Government.

ARTICLE V.

His Majesty the Emperor of China agrees to nominate one of the Secretaries of State, or a President of one of the Boards, as the high officer with whom the Ambassador, Minister, or other Diplomatic Agent of Her Majesty the Queen shall transact business, either personally or in writing, on a footing of perfect equality.

ARTICLE VI.

Her Majesty the Queen of Great Britain agrees that the privileges hereby secured shall be enjoyed in Her dominions by the Ambassadors, Ministers, or Diplomatic Agents of the Emperor of China accredited to the Court of Her Majesty.

Article VII.

Her Majesty the Queen may appoint one or more Consuls in the dominions of the Emperor of China; and such Consul or Consuls shall be at liberty to reside in any of the open ports or cities of China, as Her Majesty the Queen may consider most expedient for the interests of British commerce. They shall be treated with due respect by the Chinese authorities, and enjoy the same privileges and immunities as the Consular Officers of the most favoured nation.

Consuls and Vice-Consuls in charge shall rank with Intendants of Circuits; Vice-Consuls, Acting Vice-Consuls, and Interpreters, with Prefects. They shall have access to the official residences of these officers, and communicate with them, either personally or in writing, on a footing of equality, as the interests of the public service may require.

Article VIII.

The Christian religion, as professed by Protestants and Roman Catholics, inculcates the practice of virtue, and teaches man to do as he would be done by. Persons teaching it or professing it, therefore, shall alike be entitled to the protection of the Chinese authorities, nor shall any such, peaceably pursuing their calling, and not offending against the laws, be persecuted or interfered with.

Article IX.

British subjects are hereby authorised to travel, for their pleasure or for purposes of trade, to all parts of the interior, under passports which will be issued by their Consuls, and countersigned by the local authorities. These passports, if demanded, must be produced for examination in the localities passed through. If the passport be not irregular, the bearer will be allowed to proceed, and no opposition shall be offered to his hiring persons, or hiring vessels for the carriage of his baggage or merchandise. If he be without a passport, or if he commit any offence against the law, he shall be handed over to the nearest Consul for punishment, but he must not be subjected to any ill-usage in excess of necessary restraint. No passport need be applied for by persons going on excursions from the ports open to trade to a distance not exceeding 100 *li*, and for a period not exceeding five days.

The provisions of this Article do not apply to crews of ships, for the due restraint of whom regulations will be drawn up by the Consul and the local authorities.

To Nankin, and other cities disturbed by persons in arms against the Government, no pass shall be given, until they shall have been recaptured.

Article X.

British merchant-ships shall have authority to trade upon the Great River (Yang-tsz). The Upper and Lower Valley of the river being, however, disturbed by outlaws, no port shall be for the present opened to trade, with the exception of Chin-kiang, which shall be opened in a year from the date of the signing of this Treaty.

So soon as peace shall have been restored, British vessels shall also be admitted to trade at such ports as far as Han-kow, not exceeding three in number, as the British Minister, after consultation with the Chinese Secretary of State, may determine shall be ports of entry and discharge.

Article XI.

In addition to the towns and cities of Canton, Amoy, Foo-chow-foo, Ningpo, and Shanghai, opened by the Treaty of Nankin, it is agreed that British subjects may frequent the cities and ports of New-Chwang, Tang-Chow, Tai-Wan (Formosa), Chau-Chow (Swatoa), and Kiung-Chow (Hainin).

They are permitted to carry on trade with whomsoever they please, and to proceed to and fro at pleasure with their vessels and merchandise.

They shall enjoy the same privileges, advantages, and immunities, at the said towns and ports, as they enjoy at the ports already opened to trade, including the right of residence, of buying or renting houses, of leasing land therein, and of building churches, hospitals, and cemeteries.

Article XII.

British subjects, whether at the ports or at other places, desiring to build or open houses, warehouses, churches, hospitals, or burial-grounds, shall make their agreement for the land or buildings they require, at the rates prevailing among the people, equitably, and without exaction on either side.

Article XIII.

The Chinese Government will place no restrictions whatever upon the employment, by British subjects, of Chinese subjects in any lawful capacity.

Article XIV.

British subjects may hire whatever boats they please for the transport of goods or passengers, and the sum to be paid for such boats shall be settled between the parties themselves, without the interference of the Chinese Government. The number of these boats shall not be limited, nor shall a monopoly in respect either of the boats, or of the porters or coolies engaged in carrying the goods, be granted to any parties. If any smuggling takes place in them, the offenders will, of course, be punished according to law.

Article XV.

All questions in regard to rights, whether of property or person, arising between British subjects, shall be subject to the jurisdiction of the British authorities.

Article XVI.

Chinese subjects who may be guilty of any criminal act towards British subjects, shall be arrested and punished by the Chinese authorities, according to the laws of China.

British subjects who may commit any crime in China shall be tried and punished by the Consul, or other public functionary authorised thereto, according to the laws of Great Britain.

Justice shall be equitably and impartially administered on both sides.

Article XVII.

A British subject having reason to complain of a Chinese must proceed to the Consulate, and state his grievance. The Consul will inquire into the merits of the case, and do his utmost to arrange it amicably. In like manner, if a Chinese have reason to complain of a British subject, the Consul shall no less listen to his complaint, and endeavour to settle it in a friendly manner. If disputes take place of such a nature that the Consul cannot arrange them amicably, then he shall request the assistance of the Chinese authorities, that they may together examine into the merits of the case, and decide it equitably.

Article XVIII.

The Chinese authorities shall, at all times, afford the fullest protection to the persons and property of British subjects, whenever these shall have been subjected to insult or violence. In all cases of incendiarism or robbery, the local authorities shall at once take the necessary steps for the recovery of the stolen property, the suppression of disorder, and the arrest of the guilty parties, whom they will punish according to law.

Article XIX.

If any British merchant vessel, while within Chinese waters be plundered by robbers or pirates, it shall be the duty of the Chinese authorities to use every endeavour to capture and punish the said robbers or pirates, and to recover the stolen property, that it may be handed over to the Consul for restoration to the owner.

Article XX.

If any British vessel be at any time wrecked or stranded on the coast of China, or be compelled to take refuge in any port within the dominions of the Emperor of China, the Chinese authorities, on being apprised of the fact, shall immediately adopt measures for its relief and security; the persons on board shall receive friendly treatment, and shall be furnished, if necessary, with the means of conveyance to the nearest Consular station.

Article XXI.

If criminals, subjects of China, shall take refuge in Hong Kong, or on board the British ships there, they shall, upon due requisition by the Chinese authorities, be searched for, and, on proof of their guilt, be delivered up.

In like manner, if Chinese offenders take refuge in the houses or on board the vessels of British subjects at the open ports, they shall not be harboured or concealed, but shall be delivered up, on due requisition by the Chinese authorities, addressed to the British Consul.

Article XXII.

Should any subject fail to discharge debts incurred to a British subject, or should he fraudently abscond, the Chinese authorities will do their utmost to affect his arrest, and enforce recovery of the debts. The British authorities will likewise do their utmost to bring to justice any British subject fraudulently absconding or failing to discharge debts incurred by him to a Chinese subject.

Article XXIII.

Should natives of China who may repair to Hong Kong to trade incur debts there, the recovery of such debts must be arranged for by the English Courts of Justice on the spot; but should the Chinese debtor abscond, and be known to have property, real or personal, within the Chinese territory, it shall be the duty of the Chinese authorities, on application by, and in concert with, the British Consul, to do their utmost to see justice done between the parties.

Article XXIV.

It is agreed that British subjects shall pay, on all merchandise imported or exported by them, the duties prescribed by the Tariff; but in no case shall they be called upon to pay other or higher duties than are required of the subjects of any other foreign nation.

Article XXV.

Import duties shall be considered payable on the landing of the goods, and duties of export on shipment of the same.

Article XXVI.

Whereas the Tariff fixed by Article X. of the Treaty of Nankin, and which was estimated so as to impose on imports and exports a duty at about the rate of five per cent. *ad valorem*, has been found, by reason of the fall in value of various articles of merchandise therein enumerated, to impose a duty upon these, considerably in excess of the rate originally assumed as above to be a fair rate, it is agreed that the said Tariff shall be revised, and that as soon as the Treaty shall have been signed, application shall be made to the Emperor of China to depute a high officer of the Board of Revenue to meet, at Shanghai, officers to be deputed on behalf of the British Government, to consider its revision together, so that the Tariff, as revised, may come into operation immediately after the ratification of this Treaty.

Article XXVII.

It is agreed that either of the High Contracting Parties to this Treaty may demand a further revision of the Tariff, and of the Commercial Articles of this Treaty, at the end of ten years, but if no demand be made on either side within six months after the end of the first ten years, then the Tariff shall remain in force for ten years more, reckoned from the end of the preceding ten years; and so it shall be, at the end of each successive ten years.

Article XXVIII.

Whereas it was agreed in Article X. of the Treaty of Nankin, that British imports, having paid the tariff duties, should be conveyed into the interior free of all further charges, except a transit duty, the amount whereof was not to exceed a certain percentage on tariff value; and whereas no accurate information having been furnished of the amount of such duty, British merchants have constantly complained that charges are suddenly and arbitrarily imposed by the provincial authorities as transit duties upon produce on its way to the foreign market, and on imports on their way into the interior, to the detriment of trade; it is agreed that within four months from the signing of this Treaty, at all ports now open to British trade, and within a similar period at all ports that may hereafter be opened, the authority appointed to superintend the collection of duties shall be obliged, upon application of the Consul, to declare the amount of duties leviable on produce between the places of production and the port of shipment, and upon imports between the Consular port in question and the inland markets named by the Consul; and that a notification thereof shall be published in English and Chinese for general information.

But it shall be at the option of any British subject, desiring to convey produce purchased inland to a port, or to convey imports from a port to an inland market, to clear his goods of all transit duties, by payment of a single charge. The amount of this charge shall be leviable on exports at the first barrier they may have to pass, or, on imports, at the port at which they are landed; and, on payment thereof, a certificate shall be issued, which shall exempt the goods from all further inland charges whatsoever.

It is further agreed, that the amount of this charge shall be calculated as nearly as possible, at the rate of two-and-a-half per cent. *ad valorem*, and that it shall be fixed for each article at the Conference to be held at Shanghai for the revision of the Tariff.

It is distinctly understood that the payment of transit dues, by commutation or otherwise, shall in no way affect the tariff duties on imports or exports, which will continue to be levied separately and in full.

Article XXIX.

British merchant-vessels of more than one hundred and fifty tons burden shall be charged tonnage dues at the rate of four mace per ton; if of one hundred and fifty tons and under, they shall be charged at the rate of one mace per ton.

Any vessel clearing from any of the open ports of China for any other of the open ports or for Hong Kong, shall be entitled, on application of the master, to a special certificate from the Customs, on exhibition of which she shall be exempt from all further payment of tonnage-dues in any open port of China, for a period of four months, to be reckoned from the date of her port-clearance.

Article XXX.

The master of any British merchant-vessel may, within forty-eight hours after the arrival of his vessel, but not later, decide to depart without breaking bulk, in which case he will not be subject to pay tonnage-dues. But tonnage-dues shall be held due after the expiration of the said forty-eight hours. No other fees or charges upon entry or departure shall be levied.

Article XXXI.

No tonnage-dues shall be payable on boats employed by British subjects in the conveyance of passengers, baggage, letters, articles of provision, or other articles not subject to duty, between any of the open ports. All cargo-boats, however, conveying merchandise subject to duty shall pay tonnage-dues, once in six months, at the rate of four mace per register ton.

Article XXXII.

The Consuls and Superintendents of Customs shall consult together regarding the erection of beacons or light-houses, and the distribution of buoys and light-ships, as occasion may demand.

Article XXXIII.

Duties shall be paid to the bankers authorised by the Chinese Government to receive the same in its behalf, either in sycee or in foreign money, according to the assay made at Canton, on the thirteenth of July, one thousand eight hundred and forty-three

Article XXXIV.

Sets of standard weights and measures, prepared according to the standard issued to the Canton Custom-house by the Board of Revenue, shall be delivered by the Superintendent of Customs to the Consul at each port, to secure uniformity and prevent confusion..

Article XXXV.

Any British merchant-vessel arriving at one of the open ports shall be at liberty to engage the services of a pilot to take her into port. In like manner, after she has discharged all legal dues and duties, and is ready to take her departure, she shall be allowed to select a pilot to conduct her out of port.

Article XXXVI.

Whenever a British merchant-vessel shall arrive off one of the open ports, the Superintendent of Customs shall depute one or more Customs officers to guard the ship. They shall either live in a boat of their own, or stay on board the ship, as may best suit their convenience. Their food and expenses shall be supplied them from the Custom-house, and they shall not be entitled to any fees whatever from the master or consignee. Should they violate this regulation, they shall be punished proportionately to the amount exacted.

Article XXXVII.

Within twenty-four hours after arrival, the ship's papers, bills of lading, &c., shall be lodged in the hands of the Consul, who will, within a further period of twenty-four hours, report to the Superintendent of Customs the name of the ship, her register tonnage, and the nature of her cargo. If, owing to neglect on the part of the master, the above rule is not complied with within forty-eight hours after the ship's arrival, he shall be liable to a fine of fifty taels for every day's delay: the total amount of penalty, however, shall not exceed two hundred taels.

The master will be responsible for the correctness of the manifest, which shall contain a full and true account of the particulars of the cargo on board. For presenting a false manifest he will subject himself to a fine of five hundred taels; but he will be allowed to correct, within twenty-four hours after delivery of it to the Customs officers, any mistake he may discover in his manifest, without incurring this penalty.

Article XXXVIII.

After receiving from the Consul the report in due form, the Superintendent of Customs shall grant the vessel a permit to open hatches. If the master shall open hatches and begin to discharge any goods without such permission, he shall be fined five hundred taels, and the goods discharged shall be confiscated wholly.

Article XXXIX.

Any British merchant who has a cargo to land or ship, must apply to the Superintendent of Customs for a special permit. Cargo landed or shipped without such permit will be liable to confiscation.

Article XL.

No transhipment from one vessel to another can be made without special permission, under pain of confiscation of the goods so transhipped.

Article XLI.

When all dues and duties shall have been paid, the Superintendent of Customs shall give a port-clearance, and the Consul shall then return the ship's papers, so that she may depart on her voyage.

Article XLII.

With respect to articles subject, according to the Tariff, to an *ad valorem* duty, if the British merchant cannot agree with the Chinese officer in affixing a value, then each party shall call two or three merchants to look at the goods, and the highest price at which any of these merchants would be willing to purchase them shall be assumed as the value of the goods.

Article XLIII.

Duties shall be charged upon the net weight of each article, making a deduction for the tare weight of congee, &c. To fix the tare on any article, such as tea, if the British merchant cannot agree with the Customhouse officer, then each party shall choose so many chests out of every hundred, which being first weighed in gross, shall afterwards be tared, and the average tare upon these chests shall be assumed as the tare upon the whole, and upon this principle shall the tare be fixed upon all other goods and packages. If there should be any other points in dispute which cannot be settled, the British merchant may appeal to his Consul, who will communicate the particulars of the case to the Superintendent of Customs, that it may be equitably arranged. But the appeal must be made within twenty-four hours, or it will not be attended to. While such points are still unsettled, the Superintendent of Customs shall postpone the insertion of the same in his books.

Article XLIV.

Upon all damaged goods a fair reduction of duty shall be allowed, proportionate to their deterioration. If any disputes arise, they shall be settled in the manner pointed out in the clause of this Treaty having reference to articles which pay duty *ad valorem*.

Article XLV.

British merchants who may have imported merchandise into any of the open ports and paid the duty thereon, if they desire to re-export the same shall be entitled to make application to the Superintendent of customs, who, in order to prevent fraud on the revenue, shall cause examination to be made by suitable officers, to see that the duties paid on such goods, as entered in the Custom-house books, correspond with the representation made, and that the goods remain with their original marks unchanged. He shall then make a memorandum on the port-clearance of the goods and of the amount of duties paid, and deliver the same to the merchant; and shall also certify the facts to the officers of Customs of the other ports. All which being done, on the arrival in port of the vessel in which the goods are laden, everything being found on examination there to correspond, she shall be permitted to break bulk, and land the said goods, without being subject to the payment of any additional duty thereon. But if, on such examination, the Superintendent of Customs shall detect any fraud on the revenue in the case, then the goods shall be subject to confiscation by the Chinese Government.

British merchants desiring to re-export duty-paid imports to a foreign country, shall be entitled, on complying with the same conditions as in the case of re-exportation to another port in China, to a drawback-certificate, which shall be a valid tender to the Customs in payment of import or export duties.

Foreign grain brought into any port of China in a British ship, if no part thereof has been landed, may be re-exported without hindrance.

Article XLVI.

The Chinese authorities at each port shall adopt the means they may judge most proper to prevent the revenue suffering from fraud or smuggling.

Article XLVII.

British merchant-vessels are not entitled to resort to other than the ports of trade declared open by this Treaty. They are not unlawfully to enter other ports in China, or to carry on clandestine trade along the coasts thereof. Any vessel violating this provision, shall, with her cargo, be subject to confiscation by the Chinese Government.

Article XLVIII.

If any British merchant-vessel be concerned in smuggling, the goods, whatever their value or nature, shall be subject to confiscation by the Chinese authorities, and the ship may be prohibited from trading further and sent away, as soon as her accounts shall have been adjusted and paid.

Article XLIX.

All penalties enforced, or confiscations made, under this Treaty, shall belong and be appropriated to the public service of the Government of China.

Article L.

All official communications addressed by the Diplomatic and Consular Agents of Her Majesty the Queen to the Chinese authorities shall, henceforth, be written in English. They will for the present be accompanied by a Chinese version, but it is understood that, in the event of there being any difference of meaning between the English and Chinese text, the English Government will hold the sense as expressed in the English text to be the correct sense. This provision is to apply to the Treaty now negotiated, the Chinese text of which has been carefully corrected by the English original.

Article LI.

It is agreed, that henceforward the character " I " (barbarian) shall not be applied to the Government or subjects of Her Britannic Majesty, in any Chinese official document issued by the Chinese authorities, either in the capital or in the provinces.

Article LII.

British ships of war coming for no hostile purpose, or being engaged in the pursuit of pirates, shall be at liberty to visit all ports within the dominions of the Emperor of China, and shall receive every facility for the purchase of provisions, procuring water, and, if occasion require, for the making of repairs. The Commanders of such ships shall hold intercourse with the Chinese authorities on terms of equality and courtesy.

Article LIII.

In consideration of the injury sustained by native and foreign commerce from the prevalence of piracy in the seas of China, the High Contracting Parties agree to concert measures for its suppression.

Article LIV.

The British Government and its subjects are hereby confirmed in all privileges, immunities, and advantages conferred on them by previous Treaties; and it is hereby expressly stipulated that the British Government and its subjects will be allowed free and equal participation in all privileges, immunities, and advantages that may have been, or may be hereafter, granted by His Majesty the Emperor of China to the Government or subjects of any other nation.

Article LV.

In evidence of Her desire for the continuance of a friendly understanding, Her Majesty the Queen of Great Britain consents to include in a Separate Article, which shall be in every respect of equal validity with the Articles of this Treaty, the conditions affecting indemnity for expenses incurred and losses sustained in the matter of the Canton question.

Article LVI.

The ratifications of this Treaty, under the hand of Her Majesty the Queen of Great Britain and Ireland and His Majesty the Emperor of China, respectively, shall be exchanged at Pekin, within a year from this day of signature.

In token whereof, the respective Plenipotentiaries have signed and sealed this Treaty.

Done at Tien-tsin, this twenty-sixth day of June, in the year of our Lord one thousand eight hundred and fifty-eight; corresponding with the

Chinese date, the sixteenth day, fifth moon, of the eighth year of Hien Fung.

(L.S.) ELGIN AND KINCARDINE.
Signature of First Chinese Plenipotentiary.
Signature of Second Chinese Plenipotentiary.
Seal of the Chinese Plenipotentiaries.

Separate Article annexed to the Treaty concluded between Great Britain and China, on the twenty-sixth day of June, in the year one thousand eight hundred and fifty-eight.

It is hereby agreed that a sum of two millions of taels, on account of the losses sustained by British subjects through the misconduct of the Chinese authorities at Canton ; and a further sum of two millions of taels on account of the military expenses of the expedition which Her Majesty the Queen has been compelled to send out for the purpose of obtaining redress, and of enforcing the due observance of Treaty provisions ; shall be paid to Her Majesty's Representatives in China by the authorities of the Kwang-tung province.

The necessary arrangements with respect to the time and mode of effecting these payments, shall be determined by Her Majesty's Representative, in concert with the Chinese authorities of Kwang-tung.

When the above amount shall have been discharged in full, the British forces will be withdrawn from the city of Canton.

Done at Tien-tsin, this twenty-sixth day of June, in the year of our Lord one thousand eight hundred and fifty-eight, corresponding with the Chinese date, the sixteenth day, fifth moon, of the eighth year of Hien Fung.

(L.S.) ELGIN AND KINCARDINE.
Signature of First Chinese Plenipotentiary.
Signature of Second Chinese Plenipotentiary.
Seal of the Chinese Plenipotentiaries.

CONVENTION OF PEACE BETWEEN HER MAJESTY AND THE EMPEROR OF CHINA.

Signed at Peking, 24th October, 1860.

Her Majesty the Queen of Great Britain and Ireland, and his Imperial Majesty the Emperor of China, being alike desirous to bring to an end the misunderstanding at present existing between their respective Governments, and to secure their relations against further interruption, have for this purpose appointed Plenipotentiaries, that is to say :—

Her Majesty the Queen of Great Britain and Ireland, the Earl of Elgin and Kincardine; and His Imperial Majesty the Emperor of China, His Imperial Highness the Prince of Kung ; who having met and communicated to each other their full powers, and finding these to be in proper form, have agreed upon the following Convention, in Nine Articles :—

ART. I.—A breach of friendly relations having been occasioned by the act of the Garrison of Taku, which obstructed Her Britannic Majesty's

Representative when on his way to Peking, for the purpose of exchanging the ratifications of the Treaty of Peace, concluded at Tientsin in the month of June, one thousand eight hundred and fifty-eight, His Imperial Majesty the Emperor of China expresses his deep regret at the misunderstanding so occasioned.

Art. II.—It is further expressly declared, that the arrangement entered into at Shanghai, in the month of October, one thousand eight hundred and fifty-eight, between Her Britannic Majesty's Ambassador the Earl of Elgin and Kincardine, and His Imperial Majesty's Commissioners Kweiliang and Hwashana, regarding the residence of Her Britannic Majesty's Representative in China, is hereby cancelled, and that, in accordance with Article III. of the Treaty of one thousand eight hundred and fifty-eight, Her Britannic Majesty's Representative will henceforward reside, permanently or occasionally, at Peking, as Her Britannic Majesty shall be pleased to decide.

Art. III.—It is agreed that the separate Article of the Treaty of one thousand eight hundred and fifty-eight is hereby annulled, and that in lieu of the amount of indemnity therein specified, His Imperial Majesty the Emperor of China shall pay the sum of eight millions of taels, in the following proportions or instalments, namely,—at Tientsin, on or before the 30th day of November, the sum of five hundred thousands taels; at Canton, on or before the first day of December, one thousand eight hundred and sixty, three hundred and thirty-three thousand and thirty-three taels, less the sum which shall have been advanced by the Canton authorities towards the completion of the British Factory site of Shameen; and the remainder at the ports open to foreign trade, in quarterly payments, which shall consist of one-fifth of the gross revenue from Customs there collected; the first of the said payments being due on the thirty-first day of December, one thousand eight hundred and sixty, for the quarter terminating on that day.

It is further agreed that these monies shall be paid into the hands of an officer whom her Britannic Majesty's Representative shall specially appoint to receive them, and that the accuracy of the amounts shall, before payment, be duly ascertained by British and Chinese officers appointed to discharge this duty.

In order to prevent future discussion, it is moreover declared that of the eight millions of taels herein guaranteed, two millions will be appropriated to the indemnification of the British Mercantile Community at Canton, for losses sustained by them; and the remaining six millions to the liquidation of war expenses.

Art. IV.—It is agreed that on the day on which this Convention is signed, His Imperial Majesty the Emperor of China shall open the port of Tientsin to trade, and that it shall be thereafter competent to British subjects to reside and trade there, under the same conditions as at any other port of China by Treaty open to trade.

Art. V.—As soon as the ratifications of the Treaty of one thousand eight hundred and fifty-eight shall have been exchanged, His Imperial Majesty the Emperor of China, will, by decree, command the high authorities of every province to proclaim throughout their jurisdictions, that' Chinese, in choosing to take service in British Colonies or other parts beyond sea, are at perfect liberty to enter into engagements with British subjects for that purpose, and to ship themselves and their families on board any British vessels at the open ports of China; also that the high authorities aforesaid shall, in concert with Her Britannic Majesty's Representative in China, frame such regulations for the protection of Chinese emigrating as above as the circumstances of the different open ports may demand.

ART. VI.—With a view to the maintenance of law and order in and about the harbour of Hongkong, His Imperial Majesty the Emperor of China agrees to cede to Her Majesty the Queen of Great Britain and Ireland Her heirs and successors, to have and to hold as a dependency of Her Britannic Majesty's Colony of Hongkong, that portion of the township of Cowloon, in the province of Kwang-Tung, of which a lease was granted in perpetuity to Harry Smith Parkes, Esquire, Companion of the Bath, a Member of the Allied Commission at Canton, on behalf of Her Britannic Majesty's Government, by Lau T'sung-kwang, Governor-General of the Two Kwang.

It is further declared that the lease in question is hereby cancelled, that the claims of any Chinese to property on the said portion of Cowloon shall be duly investigated by a mixed Commission of British and Chinese officers, and that compensation shall be awarded by the British Government to any Chinese whose claim shall be by that said Commission established, should his removal be deemed necessary by the British Government.

ART. VII.—It is agreed that the provisions of the Treaty of one thousand eight hundred and fifty-eight, except in so far as these are modified by the present Convention, shall without delay come into operation as soon as the ratifications of the Treaty aforesaid shall have been exchanged. It is further agreed, that no separate ratification of the present Convention shall be necessary, but that it shall take effect from the date of its signature, and be equally binding with the Treaty above-mentioned on the high contracting parties.

ART. VIII.—It is agreed that, as soon as the ratifications of the Treaty of the year one thousand eight hundred and fifty-eight shall have been exchanged, His Imperial Majesty the Emperor of China shall, by decree, command the high authorities in the capital, and in the provinces, to print, and publish, the aforesaid Treaty and the present Convention, for general information.

ART. IX.—It is agreed that, as soon as the Convention shall have been signed, the ratification of the Treaty of the year one thousand eight hundred and fifty-eight shall have been exchanged, and an Imperial Decree respecting the publication of the said Convention and Treaty shall have been promulgated, as provided for by Article VIII. of this Convention, Chusan shall be evacuated by Her Britannic Majesty's troops there stationed, and Her Britannic Majesty's force now before Peking shall commence its march towards the city of Tientsin, the forts of Taku, the north coast of Shantung, and city of Canton, at each or all of which places, it shall be at the option of Her Majesty the Queen of Great Britain and Ireland to retain a force, until the indemnity of eight millions of taels, guaranteed in Article III., shall have been paid.

Done at Peking, in the Court of the Board of Ceremonies, on the twenty-fourth day of October, in the year of our Lord one thousand eight hundred and sixty.

    [L.S.]   (Signed) ELGIN AND KINCARDINE.
Seal of Chinese Plenipotentiary.
Signature of Chinese Plenipotentiary.

APPENDIX.

AGREEMENT BETWEEN THE MINISTERS PLENIPOTENTIARY OF THE GOVERNMENTS OF GREAT BRITAIN AND CHINA.

Signed, in the English and Chinese Languages, at Chefoo,
13th September, 1876.
Ratified by the Emperor of China, 17th September, 1876.

Agreement negotiated between Sir Thomas Wade, K.C.B., Her Britannic Majesty's Envoy Extraordinary and Minister Plenipotentiary at the Court of China, and Li, Minister Plenipotentiary of His Majesty the Emperor of China, Senior Grand Secretary, Governor-General of the Province of Chih Li, of the First-Class of the Third Order of Nobility.

The negotiation between the Ministers above-named has its origin in a despatch received by Sir Thomas Wade, in the spring of the present year, from the Earl of Derby, Principal Secretary of State for Foreign Affairs, dated 1st January, 1876. This contained instructions regarding the disposal of three questions; first, a satisfactory settlement of the Yün Nan affair; secondly, a faithful fulfilment of engagements of last year respecting intercourse between the high officers of the two Governments; thirdly, the adoption of a uniform system in satisfaction of the understanding arrived at in the month of September, 1875 (8th moon of the first year of the reign Kwang Sü), on the subject of rectification of conditions of trade. It is to this despatch that Sir Thomas Wade has referred himself in discussions on these questions with the Tsung-li Yamên, farther reference to which is here omitted as superfluous. The conditions now agreed to between Sir Thomas Wade and the Grand Secretary are as follows :—

SECTION I.—*Settlement of the Yün Nan Case.*

(i.) A Memorial is to be presented to the Throne, whether by the Tsung-li Yamên or by the Grand Secretary Li is immaterial, in the sense of the memorandum prepared by Sir Thomas Wade. Before presentation, the Chinese text of the Memorial is to be shown to Sir Thomas Wade.

(ii.) The Memorial having been presented to the Throne, and the Imperial Decree in reply received, the Tsung-li Yamên will communicate copies of the Memorial and Imperial Decree to Sir Thomas Wade, together with copy of a letter from the Tsung-li Yamên to the Provincial Governments, instructing them to issue a proclamation that shall embody at length the above Memorial and Decree. Sir Thomas Wade will thereon reply to the effect that for two years to come officers will be sent, by the British Minister, to different places in the provinces, to see that the proclamation is posted. On application from the British Minister, or the Consul of any port instructed by him to make application, the high officers of the provinces will depute competent officers to accompany those so sent to the places which they go to observe.

(iii.) In order to the framing of such regulations as will be needed for the conduct of the frontier trade between Burma and Yün Nan, the Memorial, submitting the proposed settlement of the Yün Nan affair, will contain a request that an Imperial Decree be issued, directing the Governor-General and Governor, whenever the British Government shall send officers to Yün Nan, to select a competent officer of rank to confer with them and to conclude a satisfactory arrangement.

(iv.) The British Government will be free for five years, from the first of January next, being the 17th day of the 11th moon of the 2nd year of the reign of Kwang Sü, to station officers at Ta-li Fu, or at some other suitable place in Yün Nan, to observe the conditions of trade; to the end that they may have information upon which to base the regulations of trade when these have to be discussed. For the consideration and adjustment of any matter affecting British officers or subjects, these officers will be free to address themselves to the authorities of the province. The opening of the trade may be proposed by the British Government, as it may find best, at any time within the term of five years, or upon expiry of the term of five years.

Passports having been obtained last year for a Mission from India into Yün Nan, it is open to the Viceroy of India to send such Mission at any time he may see fit.

(v.) The amount of indemnity to be paid on account of the families of the officers and others killed in Yün Nan; on account of the expenses which the Yün Nan case has occasioned; and on account of claims of British merchants arising out of the action of officers of the Chinese Government up to the commencement of the present year, Sir Thomas Wade takes upon himself to fix at two hundred thousand taels, payable on demand.

(vi.) When the case is closed, an Imperial Letter will be written, expressing regret for what has occurred in Yün Nan. The Mission bearing the Imperial Letter will proceed to England immediately. Sir Thomas Wade is to be informed of the constitution of this Mission, for the information of his Government. The text of the Imperial Letter is also to be communicated to Sir Thomas Wade by the Tsung-li Yamên.

SECTION II.—*Official Intercourse.*

Under this heading are included the conditions of intercourse between high officers in the capital and the provinces, and between Consular officers and Chinese officials at the ports; also the conduct of judicial proceedings in mixed cases.

(i.) In the Tsung-li Yamên's Memorial of the 28th September, 1875, the Prince of Kung and the Ministers stated that their object in presenting it had not been simply the transaction of business in which Chinese and Foreigners might be concerned; missions abroad and the question of diplomatic intercourse lay equally within their prayer.

To the prevention of farther misunderstanding upon the subject of intercourse and correspondence, the present conditions of both having caused complaint in the capital and in the provinces, it is agreed that the Tsung-li Yamên shall address a circular to the Legations, inviting Foreign Representatives to consider with them a code of etiquette, to the end that foreign officials in China, whether at the ports or elsewhere, may be treated with the same regard as is shown them when serving abroad in other countries, and as would be shown to Chinese Agents so serving abroad.

The fact that China is about to establish Missions and Consulates abroad renders an understanding on these points essential.

(ii.) The British Treaty of 1858, Article XVI., lays down that "Chinese subjects who may be guilty of any criminal act towards British subjects shall be arrested and punished by Chinese authorities according to the laws of China.

"British subjects who may commit any crime in China shall be tried and punished by the Consul, or any other public functionary authorised thereto, according to the laws of Great Britain.

"Justice shall be equitably and impartially administered on both sides."
The words "functionary authorised thereto" are translated in the Chinese text "British Government."

In order to the fulfilment of its Treaty obligations, the British Government has established a Supreme Court at Shanghai, with a special code of rules, which it is now about to revise. The Chinese Government has established at Shanghai a Mixed Court; but the officer presiding over it, either from lack of power, or dread of unpopularity, constantly fails to enforce his judgments.

It is now understood that the Tsung-li Yamên will write a circular to the Legations, inviting Foreign Representatives at once to consider with the Tsung-li Yamên the measures needed for the more effective administration of justice at the ports open to trade.

(iii.) It is agreed that, whenever a crime is committed affecting the person or property of a British subject, whether in the interior or at the open ports, the British Minister shall be free to send officers to the spot to be present at the investigation.

To the prevention of misunderstanding on this point, Sir Thomas Wade will write a Note to the above effect, to which the Tsung-li Yamên will reply, affirming that this is the course of proceeding to be adhered to for the time to come.

It is farther understood that so long as the laws of the two countries differ from each other, there can be but one principle to guide judicial proceedings in mixed cases in China, namely, that the case is tried by the official of the defendant's nationality; the official of the plaintiff's nationality merely attending to watch the proceedings in the interests of justice. If the officer so attending be dissatisfied with the proceedings, it will be in his power to protest against them in detail. The law administered will be the law of the nationality of the officer trying the case. This is the meaning of the words *hui t'ung*, indicating combined action in judicial proceedings, in Article XVI. of the Treaty of Tientsin; and this is the course to be respectively followed by the officers of either nationality.

SECTION III.—*Trade*.

(i.) With reference to the area within which, according to the treaties in force, *likin* ought not to be collected on foreign goods at the open ports, Sir Thomas Wade agrees to move his Government to allow the ground rented by foreigners (the so-called Concessions) at the different ports, to be regarded as the area of exemption from *likin*; and the Government of China will thereupon allow I-ch'ang in the province of Hu-Pei, Wu-hu in An-Hui, Wên-chow in Che-Kiang, and Pei-hai (Pak-hoi) in Kwang-Tung, to be added to the number of ports open to trade, and to become Consular stations. The British Government will farther be free to send officers to reside at Ch'ung K'ing, to watch the conditions of British trade in Ssu-Ch'uen. British merchants will not be allowed to reside at Ch'ung K'ing, or to open establishments or warehouses there, so long as no steamers have access to the port. When steamers have succeeded in ascending the river so far, farther arrangements can be taken into consideration.

It is farther proposed as a measure of compromise that at certain points on the shore of the Great River, namely Ta-t'ung, and Ngan-Ching, in the province of An-Hui; Hu-K'ou, in Kiang-Si; Wu-sueh, Lu-chi-k'ou, and Sha-shih, in Hu Kuang; these being all places of trade in the interior, at which, as they are not open ports, foreign merchants are not legally authorised* to land or ship goods, steamers shall be allowed to touch for the purpose of landing or shipping passengers or goods; but in all instances by means of native boats only, and subject to the regulations in force affecting native trade.

Produce accompanied by a half-duty certificate may be shipped at such points by the steamers, but may not be landed by them for sale. And at all such points, except in the case of imports accompanied by a transit duty certificate, or exports similarly certificated, which will be severally passed free of *likin* on exhibition of such certificates, *likin* will be duly collected on all goods whatever by the native authorities. Foreign merchants will not be authorised to reside or open houses of business or warehouses at the places enumerated as ports of call.

(ii.) At all ports open to trade, whether by earlier or later agreement, at which no settlement area has been previously defined, it will be the duty of the British Consul, acting in concert with his colleagues, the Consuls of other Powers, to come to an understanding with the local authorities regarding the definition of the foreign settlement area.

(iii.) On opium, Sir Thomas Wade will move his Government to sanction an arrangement different from that affecting other imports. British merchants, when opium is brought into port, will be obliged to have it taken cognisance of by the Customs, and deposited in bond, either in a warehouse or in a receiving hulk, until such time as there is a sale for it. The importer will then pay the tariff duty upon it, and the purchasers the *likin*; in order to the prevention of the evasion of the duty. The amount of *likin* to be collected will be decided by the different Provincial Governments, according to the circumstances of each.

(iv.) The Chinese Government agrees that Transit Duty certificates shall be framed under one rule at all ports, no difference being made in the conditions set forth therein; and that so far as imports are concerned, the nationality of the person possessing and carrying these is immaterial. Native produce carried from an Inland Centre to a Port of Shipment, if *bonâ fide* intended for shipment to a foreign port, may be, by treaty, certificated by the British subject interested, and exempted by payment of the half-duty from all charges demanded upon it *en route*. If produce be not the property of a British subject, or is being carried to a port not for exportation, it is not entitled to the exemption that would be secured it by the exhibition of a Transit Duty Certificate. The British Minister is prepared to agree with the Tsung-li Yamên upon rules that will secure the Chinese Government against abuse of the privilege as affecting produce.

The words *nei ti*, inland, in the clause of Article VII. of the Rules appended to the Tariff, regarding carriage of imports inland, and of native produce purchased inland, apply as much to places on the sea coasts and river shores, as to places in the interior not open to foreign trade; the Chinese Government having the right to make arrangements for the prevention of abuses thereat.

(v.) Article XLV. of the Treaty of 1858 prescribes no limit to the term within which a drawback may be claimed upon duty paid Imports. The British Minister agrees to a term of three years, after expiry of which no drawback shall be claimed.

(vi.) The foregoing stipulation, that certain points are to be opened to

* N.B.—In the Chinese text, this sentence reads: . . . are not authorised, *according to the Yangtsze Regulations* to land and ship, &c.

foreign trade, and that landing and shipping of goods at six places on the Great River is to be sanctioned, shall be given effect to within six months after receipt of the Imperial Decree approving the Memorial of the Grand Secretary Li. The date for giving effect to the stipulations affecting exemption of imports from *likin* taxation within the foreign settlements, and the collection of *likin* upon opium by the Customs' Inspectorate at the same time as the Tariff duty upon it, will be fixed as soon as the British Government has arrived at an understanding on the subject with other foreign Governments.

(vii.) The Governor of Hongkong having long complained of the interference of the Canton Customs' Revenue Cruisers with the junk trade of that Colony, the Chinese Government agrees to the appointment of a Commission, to consist of a British Consul, an officer of the Hongkong Government, and a Chinese official of equal rank, in order to the establishment of some system that shall enable the Chinese Government to protect its revenue, without prejudice to the interest of the Colony.

SEPARATE ARTICLE.

Her Majesty's Government having it in contemplation to send a Mission of exploration next year by way of Peking through Kan-Su and Koko-Nor, or by way of Ssu-Ch'uen to Thibet, and thence to India, the Tsung-li Yamên, having due regard to the circumstances, will, when the time arrives, issue the necessary passports, and will address letters to the high provincial authorities, and to the Resident in Thibet. If the Mission should not be sent by these routes, but should be proceeding across the Indian frontier to Thibet, the Tsung-li Yamên, on receipt of a communication to the above effect from the British Minister, will write to the Chinese Resident in Thibet, and the Resident, with due regard to the circumstances, will send officers to take due care of the Mission; and passports for the Mission will be issued by the Tsung-li Yamên, that its passage be not obstructed.

Done at Chefoo, in the Province of Shan Tung, this thirteenth day of September, in the year of our Lord One Thousand Eight Hundred and Seventy-Six.

[L.S.] (Signed) THOMAS FRANCIS WADE.
[L.S.] (Signed) CHINESE PLENIPOTENTIARY.

Treaty between Russia and China concerning the Re-establishment of the Authority of the Chinese Government in Ili.

His Majesty the Emperor and Autocrat of All the Russias and His Majesty the Emperor of China, being desirous of settling certain frontier questions concerning the interests of both Empires, and of drawing closer the friendly relations between the two countries, have named as their Plenipotentiaries, in order to arrive at an understanding on these questions:—

His Majesty the Emperor of All the Russias, his Secretary of State, Nicolas de Giers, Senator, Actual Privy Councillor, in charge of the Imperial Ministry for Foreign Affairs; and his Envoy Extraordinary and Minister Plenipotentiary at the Court of China, Eugene de Butzow, Actual Councillor of State;

And His Majesty the Emperor of China, Tsêng, Marquis of Neyoung, Vice-President of the High Court of Justice, his Envoy Extraordinary and Minister Plenipotentiary at the Court of Russia, intrusted with special powers to sign the present Treaty as Ambassador Extraordinary.

The aforesaid Plenipotentiaries, intrusted with full powers, which have been found sufficient, have agreed to the following stipulations:—

Article I.

His Majesty the Emperor of All the Russias consents to the re-establishment of the Chinese Government in the country of Ili, which has been temporarily occupied, since 1871, by the Russian forces.

Russia remains in possession of the western part of that country, within the limits indicated by Article VII. of the present Treaty.

Article II.

His Majesty the Emperor of China undertakes to issue the necessary Decrees, in order that the inhabitants of Ili, to whatever race or religion they may belong, may be freed from all liability, whether as concerns their persons or their property, for acts committed during or after the disorders which have taken place in that country.

A Proclamation in conformity with this undertaking will be addressed by the Chinese authorities, in the name of His Majesty the Emperor of China, to the people of Ili, before that country is made over to the said authorities.

Article III.

The Inhabitants of Ili will be at liberty to remain in the places where they at present reside as Chinese subjects, or to emigrate to Russia and to adopt Russian nationality. They will be called upon for a decision on the subject before Chinese authority is re-established in Ili, and a term of one year, to be reckoned from the date of the restoration of the country to the Chinese authorities, will be granted to those who express a wish to emigrate to Russia. The Chinese authorities will place no obstacles in the way of their emigration and of the removal of their personal property.

Article IV.

Russian subjects holding land in Ili will retain their rights of ownership, even after the re-establishment of the authority of the Chinese Government in that country.

This arrangement does not apply to those inhabitants of Ili who adopt Russian nationality at the time of the re-establishment of Chinese authority in that country.

Russian subjects whose lands are situated outside the areas assigned for Russian factories, in virtue of Article XIII. of the Kuldja Treaty of 1851, will pay the same taxes and contributions as Chinese subjects.

Article V.

The two Governments will send to Kuldja Commissioners, who will proceed on the one part to cede and on the other part to resume the administration of the Province of Ili, and to whom will be confided, in general, the execution of the stipulations of the present Treaty which relate to the re-establishment in that country of the authority of the Chinese Government.

The said Commissioners will carry out their instructions in accordance with the understanding to be arrived at as to the manner of ceding on the one part, and of resuming on the other, the administration of Ili, between the Governor-General of Turkestan and the Governor-General of the Provinces of Chan-si* and Kan-sou, to whom the management of this business has been intrusted by the two Governments.

The transfer of the administration of Ili should be concluded within a term of three months or earlier, if possible, to date from the day of the arrival at Tashkend of the official delegated by the Governor-General of Chan-si and Kan-sou to the Governor General of Turkestan to notify to him the ratification and promulgation of the present Treaty by His Majesty the Emperor of China,

Article VI.

The Government of His Majesty the Emperor of China will pay to the Government of Russia the sum of 9,000,000 metallic roubles, to meet the expenses of the occupation of Ili by Russian troops since 1871, to satisfy all pecuniary claims which have been brought forward up to this date for losses of Russian subjects whose goods have been plundered in Chinese territory, and to assist the families of Russian subjects killed in armed attacks of which they have been the victims in Chinese territory.

The above-mentioned sum of 9,000,000 metallic roubles is to be paid within a term of two years from the date of the exchange of the ratifications of the present Treaty, in the order and in accordance with the conditions agreed to by the two Governments in the special Protocol annexed to the present Treaty.

Article VII.

The western part of Ili is incorporated with Russia, to serve as a place for the establishment of the inhabitants of that country who adopt Russian nationality, and who will therefore have had to abandon the lands they possessed.

The frontier between the Russian possessions and the Chinese Province of Ili, starting from the Bedjin-Taou Mountains, will follow the course of the Khorgos River as far as the spot where it falls into the River Ili, and, crossing this last river, will take a southerly direction, towards the Ouzontaou Mountains, leaving the village of Koldjat on the west. From this point it will follow in a southerly direction the line laid down by the Protocol signed at Tchougoutchak in 1864.

Article VIII.

A portion of the frontier-line to the east of Lake Zaïsan, as laid down by the Protocol signed at Tchougoutchak in 1864 having been found incorrect, the two Governments will nominate Commissioners, who will jointly modify the former line in such a manner as to correct the errors

---

* So printed in the Blue Book, but beyond question a mistake for Shensi. Kan-suh and Shensi form the same Viceroyalty.

pointed out, and to establish a sufficient separation between the Kirghiz tribes subject to the two Empires.

The new line shall, as far as possible, take a direction intermediate between the old frontier and a straight line starting from the Kouïtoun Mountains towards the Saour Mountains, and crossing the Tcherni-Irtych.

Article IX.

The two Contracting Parties will name Commissioners for erecting boundary posts upon the line fixed by Articles VII. and VIII., as well as upon that portion of the frontier where no posts have been erected. The time and place of meeting of these Commissioners will be settled by an understanding between the two Governments.

The two Governments will also name Commissioners to examine the frontier, and to erect boundary posts between the Russian Province of Ferganah and the Western part of the Chinese Province of Kachgar. These Commissioners will take the present frontier as the basis of their labours.

Article X.

The recognised Treaty right of the Russian Government to appoint Consuls at Ili, at Tarbagataï, at Kachgar, and at Ourga, is henceforth extended to the towns of Sou-Tcheou (Tsia-yu-kouan) and Tourfan. In the following towns: Kobdo, Ouliassoutai, Khami, Ousoumtsi, and Goutchen, the Russian Government will establish Consulates accordingly as they are called for by the development of commerce, and after coming to an understanding with the Chinese Government.

The Consuls at Sou-Tcheou (Tsia-yu-kouan) and Tourfan will exercise Consular functions in the neighbouring districts, where the interests of Russian subjects may call for their presence.

The Provisions of Articles V. and VI. of the Treaty concluded at Peking in 1860, relating to the concession of lands for Consular dwellings, for cemeteries, and for pasturage, will be in like manner applicable to the towns of Sou Tcheou (Tsia-yu-kouan) and Tourfan. The local authorities will assist the Consuls in finding temporary residences until the Consular houses are built.

The Russian Consuls in Mongolia and the districts situated on the two slopes of the Tian-chan will, for travelling purposes and for forwarding their correspondence, make use of the Government postal establishments, according to the stipulations of Article XI. of the Treaty of Tien-tsin and Article XII. of the Treaty of Peking. The Chinese Authorities, when called upon by them for this purpose, will afford them their aid and assistance.

The town of Tourfan not being a place open for foreign trade, the right of establishing a Consulate there shall not serve as a precedent upon which to rest a similar right with respect to the ports of China, to the internal provinces, and to Manchouria.

Article XI.

, Russian Consuls in China will communicate on business matters, either with the local authorities of their place of residence or with the superior authorities of the district or province, accordingly as the nature of the interests respectively intrusted to them and the importance or urgency of the business to be transacted may require. The correspondence between them will take the shape of official letters. As to the rules of etiquette to be observed in their interviews, they will be based upon the consideration which the officers of friendly Powers owe to one another.

All questions arising on Chinese territory with regard to commercial or other matters between the dependents of the two States will be examined and settled by common consent by the Consuls and the Chinese authorities.

In disputes concerning commercial matters the parties may settle their differences amicably by means of arbitrators chosen by both sides. If by this course an understanding cannot be arrived at, the question will be examined and settled by the authorities of the two States.

Written engagements between Russian and Chinese subjects concerning orders for goods or their carriage, the hire of shops, houses, and other places, or relating to other similar transactions, may be presented for the legalisation of the Consulates and of the higher local administrations whose duty it is to legalise documents presented to them. In case of the non-fulfilment of engagements contracted, the Consuls and the Chinese Authorities will consider as to measures calculated to insure the execution of such obligations.

ARTICLE XII.

Russian subjects are authorised, as heretofore, to carry on trade free of duty in Chinese Mongolia, in those localities or aimaks where there are Chinese authorities, as well as in those where there are none.

Russian subjects may likewise carry on trade free of duty in the towns and other localities of the Provinces of Ili, Tarbagatai, Kachgar, Ouroumtsi, and others, situated on the northern and southern slopes of the Tian-chan range, as far as the Great Wall. This privilege will be withdrawn when the development of trade necessitates the enactment of a Customs Tariff, in accordance with an understanding to be arrived at between the two Governments.

Russian subjects may import into and export from the aforesaid provinces of China, products of every kind, no matter what their origin may be. They may effect purchases and sales either for cash or by barter; they will be entitled to make payments in merchandise of all kinds.

ARTICLE XIII.

In the localities where the Russian Government is entitled to establish Consulates, as in the town of Kalgan, Russian subjects may construct houses, shops, store-houses, and other buildings on the land they may acquire by purchase, or which may be granted to them by the local authorities, in accordance with what is laid down for Ili and Tarbagatai by Article XIII. of the Kuldja Treaty of 1851.

Privileges granted to Russian subjects in the town of Kalgan, where there will be no Consulate, constitute an exception which cannot be extended to any other locality in the internal provinces.

ARTICLE XIV.

Russian merchants wishing to send from Russia by land goods for the inner provinces of China, may, as formerly, send them by the towns of

Kalgan and Toun-Tcheou to the port of Tien-tsin, and thence to other ports and inner markets, and sell them in those different localities.

Merchants will use the same route to export to Russia goods purchased in the towns and ports above mentioned, or in the inner markets.

They will likewise be entitled to proceed on commercial business to Sou-Tcheou (Tsia-yu-kouan), the terminus of Russian caravans, and will there enjoy all the rights granted to Russian commerce at Tien-tsin.

Article XV.

Trade carried on by land by Russian subjects in the inner and outer provinces of China will be governed by the Regulations annexed to the present Treaty.

The commercial stipulations of the present Treaty, as well as the Regulations which serve as its complement, may be revised after the lapse of ten years, to date from the day of the exchange of the ratifications of the Treaty; but if, within the course of six months before that term expires, neither of the Contracting Parties should manifest a desire to proceed to its revision, the commercial stipulations, as well as the Regulations, will remain in force for a further term of ten years.

Trade by sea carried on by Russian subjects in China will come under the general Regulations established for foreign maritime commerce with China. Should it become necessary to modify these Regulations, the two Governments will come to an understanding on the subject.

Article XVI.

Should the development of Russian trade by land call for the enactment of a Customs Tariff applicable to goods exported from and imported into China, which shall harmonise better with the necessities of that trade than the existing Tariffs, the Governments of Russia and China will come to an understanding on the subject, taking as a basis for fixing the export and import duties an *ad valorem* rate of 5 per cent.

Pending the enactment of this Tariff, the export duties levied on certain kinds of teas of inferior quality which are at present subject to the rates established for teas of high quality will be lowered in proportion to value. The settlement of those duties for each kind of tea will be sought for by means of an understanding between the Chinese Government and the Russian Envoy at Peking, within the term of one year, at the outside, from the date of the exchange of the ratifications of the present Treaty.

Article XVII.

Differences of opinion having heretofore arisen as to the application of Article X. of the Treaty concluded at Peking in 1860, it is hereby agreed that the stipulations of the aforesaid Article concerning the settlement of claims arising out of the theft or driving of cattle across the frontier will in future be interpreted to mean that parties found guilty of theft or driving astray will be condemned to pay the real value of the cattle not restored to the owners. It is understood that, in case of the insolvency of the guilty parties, the idemnity to be paid for the missing cattle shall not fall upon the local authorities.

The frontier authorities of both States will prosecute with the full rigour of the laws of their country parties guilty of driving astray or stealing cattle, and will take such measures as may lie in their power to restore to the rightful owners cattle which has been driven astray or which has crossed the frontier.

The tracks of cattle driven astray, or which have crossed the frontier, may be pointed out not only to the frontier guards, but also to the elder of the nearest villages.

Article XVIII.

The stipulations of the Treaty concluded at Aïgoun on the 16th May, 1858, concerning the rights of the subjects of the two Empires to navigate the Amour, the Soungari, and the Oussouri, and to trade with the inhabitants of riverain places, are and remain confirmed.

Both Governments will proceed to the establishment of an understanding concerning the mode of applying the said stipulations.

Article XIX.

The provisions of former Treaties between Russia and China, not modified by the present Treaty, remain in full force.

Article XX.

The present Treaty, after having been ratified by the two Emperors, will be promulgated in either Empire for the information and guidance of all persons concerned. The ratifications will be exchanged at St. Petersburgh within six months from the date of the signature of the Treaty.

Having settled the aforesaid Articles, the Plenipotentiaries of the two Contracting Parties have signed and sealed two copies of the present Treaty in the Russian, Chinese, and French languages. Of the three texts duly collated and found to correspond, the French text shall be held to be authoritative for the interpretation of the present Treaty.

Done at St. Petersburgh the 12th February, 1881.

(Signed) NICOLAS DE GIERS. (Signed) TSENG.
(L.S.) (L.S.)

(Signed) EUGENE BUTZOW.
(L.S.)

Protocol.

In virtue of the VIth Article of the Treaty signed this day by the Plenipotentiaries of the Russian and Chinese Governments, the Chinese Government will pay to the Russian Government the sum of 9,000,000 metallic roubles to meet the expenses of the occupation of Ili by Russian troops, and to satisfy divers pecuniary claims of Russian subjects. This sum is to be paid within a term of two years from the date of the exchange of the ratifications of the Treaty.

In order to fix the mode of payment of the aforesaid sum, the Undersigned have agreed as follows:—

. The Chinese Government will pay the equivalent of the sum of 9,000,000 roubles in pounds sterling, viz, £1,431,664 2s., to Messrs. Baring Brothers and Co., of London, in six equal parts of £238,610 13s. 8d. each, less the usual banking charges incurred by the transfer of these payments to London.

A space of four months shall intervene between the payments, the first being effected four months after the exchange of the ratifications of the Treaty signed this day, and the last after the completion of two years from the date of that exchange.

The present Protocol will have the same force and value as if it had been inserted word for word in the Treaty signed this day.

In token of which the Plenipotentiaries of the two Governments have signed the present Protocol and have affixed their seals to it.

Done at St. Petersburgh the 12th February, 1881.

    (Signed) NICOLAS DE GIERS. (Signed) TSENG.
       (L.S.)   (L.S.)
    (Signed) EUGENE BUTZOW.
       (L.S.)

English Text of Convention between great Britain and China relating to Burmah and Thibet. Signed at Peking, July 24, 1886.

WHEREAS Her Majesty the Queen of Great Britain and Ireland, Empress of India, and His Majesty the Emperor of China, being sincerely desirous to maintain and perpetuate the relations of friendship and good understanding which now exist between their respective Empires, and to promote and extend the commercial intercourse between their subjects and dominions, the following Convention has been agreed upon and concluded:—

On the part of Great Britain by Nicholas Roderick O'Conor, Esquire, Her Majesty's Secretary of Legation at Washington, and lately Her Majesty's Chargé d'Affaires in China, Companion of the Most Distinguished Order of St. Michael and St. George, duly empowered thereunto:

And on the part of China by his Highness Prince of Ch'ing, President of the Tsung-li Yamên, and his Excellency Sun, Minister of the Tsung-li Yamên, Senior Vice-President of the Board of Works.

ARTICLE I.

Inasmuch as it has been the practice of Burmah to send decennial Missions to present articles of local produce, England agrees that the highest authority in Burmah shall send the customary decennial Missions, the Members of the Missions to be of Burmese race.

ARTICLE II.

China agrees that, in all matters whatsoever appertaining to the authority and rule which England is now exercising in Burmah, England shall be free to do whatever she deems fit and proper.

ARTICLE III.

The frontier between Burmah and China to be marked by a Delimitation Commission, and the conditions of frontier trade to be settled by a

Frontier Trade Convention, both countries agreeing to protect and encourage trade between China and Burmah.

ARTICLE IV.

Inasmuch as inquiry into the circumstances by the Chinese Government has shown the existence of many obstacles to the Mission to Thibet provided for in the Separate Article of the Chefoo Agreement, England consents to countermand the Mission forthwith.

With regard to the desire of the British Government to consider arrangements for frontier trade between India and Thibet, it will be the duty of the Chinese Government, after careful inquiry into the circumstances, to adopt measures to exhort and encourage the people with a view to the promotion and development of trade. Should it be practicable, the Chinese Government shall then proceed carefully to consider Trade Regulations; but, if insuperable obstacles should be found to exist, the British Government will not press the matter unduly.

ARTICLE V.

The present Convention shall be ratified, and the ratifications shall be exchanged in London as soon as possible after the date of the signature thereof.

In witness whereof the respective negotiators have signed the same and affixed thereunto the seals of their arms.

Done in triplicate at Peking this twenty-fourth day of July, in the year of our Lord one thousand eight hundred and eighty-six, corresponding with the Chinese date the twenty-third day of the sixth moon of the twelfth year of Kuang Hsu.

    (L.S.)   NICHOLAS RODERICK O'CONOR.
         (L.S.)
    (Monogram) CH'ING.
    (Monogram) SUN YU-WEN.

INDEX.

Abul Oghlan, 325.
Adams, J Q., 230.
Adoption, right of, not accepted in China, 24.
Afghanistan, war in, arrests China expedition, 222.
Ahluta, 330; death of, 333.
Aisin Gioro, 102.
Aiyuli Palipata, 78.
Ak Musjid, 324.
Akoui, 170, 171, 179.
Akouta, 41; changes name from Niuche to Kin, 41; defeats Khitans, 42.
Aksakals, 199.
Aksu, 323, 344.
Albazin, 141.
Alcock, Sir Rutherford, 245, 253, 315, 327.
Alihaya, 65.
Alikouen, Count, 169.
Alompra, 169.
Alouhiya, 79.
Altyshahr, 324.
Ama Wang, 121, 122, 126; takes field against Kiangtsai, 127; death of, 129.
Amherst, Lord, 188; his mission, *ibid.*; discourteous reception of, *ibid.*; failure of his mission, 189; some special considerations about, *ibid.*
Amien, 74.
Amiens, Treaty of, 184.
Amiot, Pere, 177, 185.
Amour, 47, 141.
Amoy, 177, 215, 221, 229; disturbance at, 244-5, 247.
Amursana, 163, 164, 165, 166, 167.
Anderson, Lieut., 273 n., 280.
Andrade, Don F. P. d', 93, 94.
Annam, 75, 78, 349.
Anshu, 30.
Anson, Major, 270.
Antchar, 36.
Anting, Gate, 281.
Anunghoy, 217.
Apachi, 75.
Apaoki, 41.
Arabs, the, 32.
Arikbuka, 60, 61, 62, 71, 76.
Army, Chinese, 351.

Arrow, the lorcha, 253; seizure of, *ibid.*; its nationality, 254; history of ownership, *ibid.*; its seizure not the sole cause of war, 255, 257.
Artchu, 66, 67.
Artillery, Flying, 145.
Ashburnham, General, 260.
Athalik Ghazi, 324. *See* Yakoob Beg
Attila, 18.
Attiret, 160.
Audience, right of, 329, 330; question of, 352.
Australia, 250.
Ava, 169.
Ayouka, 168.

Baber, Mr. Colborne, 336, 339.
Bacle, 349.
Bacninh, 349.
Bactria, kingdom of, 13.
Badakshan, 167.
Baiju, 78.
Balfour, Captain G., 247.
Banners, the Manchu, 113; the Mongol, 143.
Barhanuddin Khoja, 164, 167, 199.
Barkul, 323, 340.
Batu, 58.
Baturu, 50.
Baturu Kong, 133.
Bayan, 66, 67; his military axiom, *ibid.*; final triumph of, 68, 70, 71 75; last successes of, *ibid.*; averts dynastic crisis, 77.
Bayan, the second, 78-9.
Beira, 111, *passim.*
Bell, Mr., 150.
Bengala, 73.
Bert, Paul, 75.
Bhamo, 169, 335.
Bhutan, 147.
Black Crows, the, 34.
Black Flags, the, 348, 349.
Bogdo Khan, the, 140, 168.
Bogue, the, 176, 234.
Bogue Forts, 185, 209, 212, 216, 249,1 256.
Bonham, Sir George, 242, 243, 250, 252.
Bonnefoy, Captain, 297, 300.

Boojai, 103, 104.
Books, burning of the, 7.
Bowlby, Mr., 273 n., 280.
Bowring, Sir John, 251; expresses his views of the situation, *ibid.*; his official letter to Yeh, 252; proceeds to Shanghai, 252; further correspondence with Yeh, 253.
Brabazon, Captain, 275, 280.
Bremer, Sir Gordon, 214.
Brown, General, 296, 297.
Browne, Colonel, 334, 335.
Bruce, Sir Frederick, 266; appointed Minister at Pekin, *ibid.*; reaches Peiho, *ibid.*; sends ultimatum to Pekin, 267; 281, 285, 288, 308, 312, 313, 315.
Budantsar, 47.
Buddha, bone of, 33.
Buddhism in China, 17; Kublai's relations with, 63.
Burgevine, 286, 287, 288; appointed to command EverVictorious Army, 290; his relations with Chinese, *ibid.*; his views, 291; dismissed Chinese service, 292; returns from Pekin, 294; joins Taepings, 295; deceives Gordon, 296; movements of, 297; his vacillation, *ibid.*; his proposal to Gordon, 298; owes his life to Gordon, 298; character of, 299.
Burlinghame, Mr., 326; mission of, 327; death of, *ibid.*
Burmah, 60, 73, 74, 77, 78; Chinese war with, 169; signs peace with China, *ibid.*; 319; English relations with, 348; negotiations about, 354-5.
Buzurg, 324; deposed by Yaboob Beg, *ibid.*

Calcutta, 261, 263.
Calendar, Chinese, 101.
California, 250.
Cambaluc, 61, 70. *See* Pekin.
Campbell, Sir Colin, 224.
Canals in China, 26, 93.
Canning, Lord, 258.
Canton, 68, 80; first European to reach by sea, 93; 100, 124, 129, 131, 150, 177, 184; abortive attack on, 185; 187, 204, 205, 206, 211, 212; British expedition arrives at, 214; negotiation transferred to, 215; advance on, 216; defences captured, 217; Chinese hostility at, 218; attacked, 219; Convention of, 220; 229, 239, 246; turbulent population of, 247; question of opening gates of, 248-9; date fixed for opening, 249; date postponed, 250; foreign settlement at destroyed, 256; attack on, 261-2; capture of, 262; governed by foreign commission, 263.

Carpino, 58.
Caspian, 168.
Castiglione, 160.
Cathcart, Colonel, 177.
Catherine, Empress, 176.
Censors, Board of, 184, 208.
Census of China, 32, 38, 86, 195.
Central Asia, Chinese in, 18, 29, 32.
Chahan Timour, 79.
Chamuka, 49, 50.
Changchi, Empress, 90, 91, 94.
Chang Chikia, 67, 68.
Changchow, 67, 303, 304, 305.
Changchun, 65.
Chang dynasty, 3.
Chan-chia-wan, 272, 273, 274, 275; battle of, 275-7.
Changkoua, 65.
Chang Keen, 13.
Chang, General, 200.
Chang Kwoliang, 239, 240, 243, 244, 284, 285.
Changte, 21.
Changtu, 95.
Changsunchi, 30.
Changtsiun, 44, 45.
Changsha, 239.
Changti, 18.
Chang Yao, 342.
Chanyang, Prince of, 19.
Chanzu, 292, 293, 298, 303.
Chao Maofa, 67.
Chao Siuenti, 34.
Chaoti, 14, 15.
Chao Yuen, 38, 39.
Chapoo, 223; battle of, 224.
Chato, supposed ancestors of Tungani, 34.
Chefoo, 337; Convention of, *ibid.*
Chentu, 128.
Chepe Noyan, 51.
Cheng Kuan Tien, 353.
Chepsuntanpa, 142.
Chetsong (Sung), 40.
Chetsong (Ming), 110.
Chichi, 15.
Chichow, 67.
China, isolation of, 1; first division of, 2; stability of, 9; military power of, 174; first signs of disaffection in, 190; opening of trade with, 204.
Chinese people, no materials for history of, 94-5; claim right to punish Europeans, 185-6; as a nation, 194; as opponents in war, 226; emigration, 250.
Ching, Prince, 353.
Ching, son of Koshinga, 135, 137.
Ching Chelong, 123; imprisoned by Manchus, 124.
Ching, General, 290, 292, 293, 296, 297, 298, 299, 300, 301, 302, 303.
Ching Tang, Prince of Chang, 3.
Chingti, 16.

INDEX. 423

Chingtse, 17.
Chingtsong, 77. See Timour.
Chinhai, 222, 223.
Chinkiang, 243.
Chinkiangfoo, battle of, 224-5; heroism of Manchus at, ibid.; pestilence at, 225-6; occupied by Taepings, 241.
Chinkin, 77.
Chinpasien, 25.
Chintsong (Sung), 38, 39, 40.
Chinyong, 88.
Chiseang, 309. See Tungche.
Chitsong (Ming), 94, 95, 96.
Chitsou, 70. See Kublai.
Cholin, 289.
Choo Yuen Chang, early career of, 79; overthrows Mongols, 80. See Hongwou.
Chorcha. See Niuche.
Chonghei, 51. See Madacou.
Chongtsong, 32.
Chousin, 3.
Chow dynasty, 3.
Chow, principality of, 21.
Chowki, 64.
Chow Kwang Yn, 35. See Taitsou Sung.
Chowmodo, 145.
Chow Pow, 19.
Chow Siang Wang, 4.
Chowti (Song), 23.
Christianity, edict about, 179; agitation against, 132-3; native converts sent to Ili, 180.
Chu Changlo, 101, 108.
Chuenpee, 210; action at, 212, 216.
Chuen Gaisoowun, 30.
Chumze, 294.
Chun, 2.
Chun, Prince, 236, 310, 311, 329, 333, 345, 351; comes to the front, ibid.; death of, ibid.
Chung How, 328, 329; sent to Paris, ibid.; sent to St. Petersburg, 345; signs Treaty of Livadia, ibid.; disgrace of, ibid.
Chungwan, 110, 111, 112, 113.
Chung Wang, Taeping leader, 243; his campaign with Imperialists, 244; efforts of, 284; remarkable campaign of, 285; captures Soochow, 286; gains a victory, ibid.; places Nankin in state of defence, 287; attacks Shanghai, ibid.; relieves Taitsan, 289; besieges Sunkiang, 290; his successes, ibid.; recalled to Nankin, ibid.; returns to Soochow, 292; disposition of his forces, 299; arrives at Soochow, 298; repulsed at Chanzu, ibid.; takes part in defence of Soochow, 301; his valiant conduct, 305; fate of, ibid.
Chuntche, 121; speech of, ibid.; 126; assumes personal authority, 130;
creates Dalai Lama, ibid.; death of 131, 132; anecdote of, 152.
Chunti (Han), 18.
Chunti (Yuen), 78, 79, 82.
Chusan, 177; occupied, 214, 215; evacuation of, 217; re-captured, 221; 223, 229, 247; provision about its occupation, ibid.
Chutepala, 78.
Chuwen, 34, 87. See Kien Wenti.
Clarendon Lord, 252, 254.
Cochin China, 95.
Colbert, 176.
Confucius, 3-4, passim; opinion of, 30; proclaimed king of literature, 32; family title of, 59, 78.
Coolie corps, Chinese, 261; gallantry of, 270.
Corea, 29; war with, 30, 31.
Corea, King of, warns Sungs against Kins, 42; acknowledges Mongol supremacy, 53; relations with, 62, 63, 72; change of ruling family in, 86, 98; invaded by Japan, ibid.; 99, 114, 115; affairs in, 346-7.
Cornwallis, the, 228, 229.
Council, the Imperial, 314, 315.
Couplet, P., 131.
Courbet, Admiral, 349.
Cricket, the, 296.
Crimson Eyebrows, the, 16, 17.
Customs, Inspector General of, 313.
Cycle, Chinese, 180.

Dalai Lama, the first, 130; 140, 142, 144, 147, 171.
Dangan Pass, 113.
Daniel, 158.
Dardsha, 163.
Davatsi, 163, 164.
Davenport, Mr., 336.
David of Georgia, 58.
Davis, Sir John, 204, 247, 238; precipitate action of, ibid.; his convention with Keying, 249, 250.
Death blow to Corrupt Doctrine, 329.
Degarchi, 172.
De Luc, Abbé, 280.
Dilun Boldak, 48.
D'Ohsson, quoted, 58.
Dolonor, 143.
Dorgun, Prince, 121. See Ama Wang.
Drury, Admiral, 184; proceedings of 184-5.
Dugenne, Col., 349.
Du Halde, quoted, 17, 177.
Dutch, the, 100, 130; in Formosa, 132; relation with China, 176.
Dutch Folly, 217.

Earthquake, terrible, in China, 158.
Eastern Empress, 346. See Tsi An.
Eastern Turkestan, 167. See Kashgaria.

East India Company, its monopoly, 204.
Eclipses in China, 234.
Eleung, 217, 252.
Elepoo, 198; begins negotiation for peace, 226; courtesy of, 227, 229.
Eleuths, the, 140, 141, 142, 145, 146, 147, 148, 163, 165, 167.
Elgin, Earl of, appointed ambassador to China, 257; his instructions, 258; receives Lord Canning's letter about Indian Mutiny, *ibid.*; reaches Hong Kong, 260; uncertainty of his plans, *ibid*; proceeds to Calcutta, 261; returns to Hong Kong, *ibid.*; writes to Yeh, *ibid.*; proceeds to Shanghai, 263; sails for the Peiho *ibid.*; difference of opinion with Admiral, *ibid.*; arrives at Tientsin, 264; negotiates with Commissioners, *ibid.*; signs Treaty of Tientsin, 265; proceeds to China a second time, 268; refuses to negotiate, 270; enters Tientsin, 271; names terms of peace, *ibid.*; leaves Tientsin, 272; joins army, 278; replies to Prince Kung, *ibid.*; demands release of Parkes, 279; desire for peace but orders destruction of Summer Palace, 280; enters Pekin, 281.
Ellenborough, Lord, valuable suggestion of, 223.
Elliot, Capt., 207; succeeds Lord Napier, *ibid.*; relations with local authorities, 208; hauls down his flag and leaves Canton, 209; issues notice on opium traffic, *ibid.*; surrenders opium, 210; orders English to leave Canton, 211; removes to Hongkong, 212; review of his proceedings, 213; negotiates with Keshen, 215; hostile reception of, 218; grants suspension of arms, 219; receives indemnity, 220.
Elliott, Commodore, 259.
Ellis, Mr. H., 183, 188, 189.
Empress, as regent, precedents for, 310.
Empresses-Regent, 314, 315, 330; retire into private life, 332; reinstate Prince Kung, *ibid.*; resume power, 333.
English, the, early relations with China, 177; necessity for an embassy to Pekin, *ibid.*; second embassy to China, 187; circumstances leading up to it, *ibid.*
Erchu Jong, 25.
Escape Creek, 259.
Eulchi, 8.
Eulogy of Moukden, 177.
Eunuchs, as a powerful body in the Palace, 19; a Grand Council of, 92; the, 334.

European, first to reach China by sea, 93; 93-4, 100.
Ever Victorious Army, 288, 290, 291, 294.
Examinations, important regulation under, 90.
Ex-territorial rights asserted, 186.
Eye, a barbarian, 205.

Famine, great, 338.
Fanching, 64, 65.
Fanchong, 16, 17, 91.
Fane's Horse, 277.
Fangkue Chin, 79.
Fanquai, 327.
Fanyang, 108.
Fashiba, 98; rises to power in Japan, *ibid.*; invades Corea, *ibid.*; war with China, 99.
Fatshan, 248, attack on English party at, *ibid.*; 259; Chineseat, *ibid.*; English attack on, 259-60.
Feast of Lanterns, 145.
Ferry, M. Jules, 349.
Feyanku, 145, 146.
Firefly, the, 249.
Flag, Chinese, 312.
Fleet, Chinese, 311, 312.
Flying bridges, 10.
Fohi, 2.
Foley Colonel, charge of, 277.
Fongsian, 56.
Fongy, 17.
Fontanier, M. 328.
Foochow, 229, 234, 250, 349.
Fooshun, 105, 106.
"Foreigners, insults to," 255.
Foreign relations with China, 282-3.
Formosa, 100, 132, 173, 174; present state of, *ibid.*; 200, 229, 326, 332, 350.
Formosa Channel, 221.
Fournier, Commander, 349.
Fouta, 166, 167, 171.
Fou Wang, 101, 122, 123.
French, the, relations with China, 176-7; French, the, at Shanghai, 245; repulsed, 245-6; join England against China, 261, 267; in Indo-China, 347-50; attack Min forts, 350; attack Formosa, *ibid.*
French Folly fort, 256.
Fu, Prince, 236.
Fuhkien, 160.
Fung Shui, 248.
Fusaiquan, 300.
Fushan, 98, 99, 292.
Fuyuta, 82; heroism of, 85, 86.

Gaiti, 16.
Galdan, early career of, 140; sends mission to China, *ibid.*; attacks Khalkas, 141; receives Kanghi's envoys, *ibid.*; war with China, 142; attacked by nephew, *ibid.*; seeks Russian alliance,

ibid.; attacked by Kanghi, 143; defeated at Oulan Poutong, *ibid.*; becomes a Mahomedan, 144; retreats before Chinese army, 145; defeated at **Chowmodo**, *ibid.*; death of, 146.
Galdan **Chereng**, 158, 162.
Gangwa, 115.
Ganking, 240, 285, 288, 289.
Ganlochan, 32.
Ganpangyen, 110.
Ganti (Han), 18.
Garnier, 348.
Genghis Khan, claims kinship with Attila, 47; birth of, 48; repudiated by his clan, *ibid.*; named **Temujin**, *ibid.*; his early struggles, 49; first success *ibid.*; defeats Naimans, 50; takes name of Genghis, *ibid.*; meaning of name, *ibid.*; war with Hia, *ibid.*; attacks Kins, 52; massacres his prisoners, *ibid.*; captures Pekin, *ibid.*; entrusts to Muhula conquest of China, 53; his campaign in Western Asia, 54; his second war with Hia, *ibid.*; death of, *ibid.*; his character and career, 55.
Gensing, 235.
Gerbillon, 145.
Gill, Captain, 339.
Ginching, 24.
Gintsong (Ming), 90.
Gobi, 340.
Gold in China, 92.
Golden mirror, the, 30.
Golden River district, Great, 170.
Golden River district, Little, 170.
Goloyken, Count, 186, 187.
Goolo, 103, 104.
Goorkhas, invade Tibet, 172; retreat before Chinese, *ibid.*; defeated by Chinese in second battle, 172-3; sign peace, 173; pay tribute to China, *ibid.*; request aid from China, 188.
Gordon Major Charles, 292; takes over command of Ever Victorious Army, *ibid.*; relieves Chanzu, *ibid.*; captures Taitsan, 293; his difficulties, *ibid.*; made a brigadier-general, *ibid.*; captures Quinsan, 294; suppresses mutiny, *ibid.*; captures Kahpoo, 295; warned about Burgevine, *ibid.*; trusts his word, 296; resigns and resumes command, *ibid.*; relieves Kahpoo, *ibid.*; captures and defends Patachiaou, 297; beats Taepings at Wokong, 298; saves Burgevine, 299; co-operates with General Ching, *ibid.*; attacks Fusaiquan, 300; first repulse, *ibid.*; carries Low Mun stockades, 301; arranges surrender of Soochow, *ibid.*; his indignation at murder of Wangs, 302; rejects Imperial presents, *ibid.*; resumes command, *ibid.*; his second cam-

paign, 303; wounded, *ibid.*; serious defeat, 304; restores fortune of war, *ibid.*; captures Changchow, *ibid.*; disbands Ever Victorious army, 305; visits Tseng's camp, *ibid.*; closing remarks on, 305-6, referred to, 313.
Gough, Sir H., assumes command, 217; at Hongkong, 218; attacks Canton, 219; attack on camp of, 220; threatens to bombard Canton, *ibid.*; wins battle of Chinkiangfoo, 224, 240; opinion of, 225; his plan of attack on Nankin, 226, 240.
Grand Canal, 224, 285.
Grand Council, institution of, 130.
Grant, Sir Hope, appointed to command of English expedition, 267; strength of his force, 268; turns Taku forts, *ibid.*; captures Taku forts, 270-1; advances beyond Tientsin, 272; advances on Tungchow, 274; warned by Parkes and Loch, *ibid.*; attacks Chinese, 277; calls up Napier's brigade, 278; forms plan of attacking Pekin, 279; enters Pekin, 281.
Granville, Lord, 251.
Great Wall, the, 5, 51; repaired, 93; keeps out Manchus, 115.
Green Water Lily, 232.
Grey, Lord, 249.
Gribble, Mr., 212, 247.
Gros, Baron, 261, 268, 281.
Grosvenor, Mr., 336.
Guchen, 240.
Gulbagh, 198.
Gumti, 340.
Gunpowder Plot, a Chinese, 135.
Gutzlaff, Mr., 213.
Gyalpo, 171.

Haft Khojagan, 233.
Haida, 102, 103.
Haidsu, 113, 152.
Haichan, 78.
Hailing, 48.
Hailing, General, 225.
Hainan, 93, 200, 201, 339.
Haiyen, 341.
Hakim Beg, the, 168.
Hakim Khan Torah, 343.
Hakkas, the, 237.
Hall of Ceremonies, 281.
Hamar, 79.
Hami, 93, 148, 162, 325, 340, 342.
Han dynasty. See ch. ii. and *passim*; its place in Chinese estimation, 19, 20.
Han, Prince of, 36.
Hang, 270, 271.
Hangchow, 66, 123, 225, 285, 303.
Hankow, 240, 241, 242.
Hanlin College, the, 32, 78, 81, 151, 209, 236.

Hanoi, 348.
Hanyang, 66, 240.
Hart, Sir R., 311: appointed Inspector-General, 313; his services to China, 352.
Hates, the seven, 104-5.
Hay, Capt., 234.
Heang Yung, 244.
Hengan, 198, 201, 202.
Henry the Fourth, 176.
Herbert, Sir T., 216.
Hermes, the, 243.
Hia dynasty, 3.
Hia, 38, 42, 50, 54; becomes a Mongol prince, 54; king of, 85.
Hiangmas, 93.
Hiaotsong (Sung), 45.
Hiaotsong (Ming), 93.
Hideyoshi, 98. See Fashiba.
Hienfung, 236; his action in face of internal rebellion, 237; his danger from Taepings, 242; flees to Jehol, 279; sanctions Treaty, 281; retires to Jehol, 307; wishes to make it capital, ibid.; opinion of English, 308; illness of, ibid.; death and will of, 309; funeral of, 310.
Hienti (Han), 19.
Hientsong (Tang), 33.
Hientsong (Ming), 92; grants estates to his kinsmen, ibid.; death of, 93;
Hienyang, 6, 7.
Hingchang, 99.
Hingking, 106.
Hiongnou, 5, 11. See Huns.
Hitsong (Tang), 34.
Hiung Tingbi, 107, 108, 110.
Hoangho, 17; bridging of, 22; 82, 97, 116; great floods of, 157; 179, engineering opportunity, ibid.
Hochan, 61.
Hochow, 84, 342.
Hochun, 243.
Hociti (Han), 12.
Hoeitsong (Sung), 40, 42, 43
Hohien, 15.
Ho Koong Yay, 189.
Hokwan, 183; his fate, ibid., 184.
Ho Kwang, 15.
Ho Kweitsin, 285; executed, 286.
Hola, 44, 47, 48.
Holland, Captain, 292.
Honan, important province, 44; a bone of contention, 57; 121; famine in, 338.
Honan (town), 116.
Honan (island), 261.
Honanta, 78.
Hong, the, 204.
Hongkong, 212; cession of, 216-7; 218, 228, 230, 231, 254; attempt to poison Europeans at, 256; 258, 260, 261, 268.
Hongwou founds Ming dynasty, 81;
erects hall to generals, ibid.; endows Hanlin, ibid.; his literary works, ibid.; his frugality, 81-2; his later campaigns, 82; his magnanimity, 84; conquers southern provinces, 85; his relations with Corea, 86; death and character of, 86-7.
Honkilachi, 77.
Hoonan, 239; braves of, 230.
Hootooala, 102, 103.
Hoo Wang, 304.
Hope, Admiral, 266; repulsed at Taku forts, 267; 268, 287, 288, 289.
Hoppo, 184, 185, 187, 204, 205.
Hornby, Sir E., 315.
Hosiwu, 272, 278.
Hoti (Han), 18.
Hotsin, 19.
Hou, title, 305.
Houchi, 25.
Houkwang, 336.
Houlieoupi, 34.
Howard, Colonel, 304.
Howqua's Folly, 217.
Hué, 348, 349.
Huen, 102, 103.
Hung-tsiuen, 237. See Tien Wang.
Huns, the, 5, 8, 11, 13, 14, 16, 18.
Hushahu, 48, 52.
Hwaiking, 241.
Hwaiti (Later Tsin), 22.
Hwang, 265.
Hwang Chao, 34.
Hwang Chung, 316, 318.
Hwangti, 2; as title of Emperor, passim.
Hwanti (Han), 19.
Hwashana, 264, 265, 266.
Hwun, 102, 106.
Hwuy, Wang, 196, 201, 236.
Hyacinth Island, 259.
Hyson, the, 293, 294, 296, 297.

Ichang, 242, 339.
Iching Wang, 311.
Ijen, 317.
Ili, 140, 164, 166, 167, 200, 323, 324. See Kuldja.
Imperial Clan Court, 310.
Imperial Dictionary, Chinese, 151.
Imperial Guard, the, 223.
Indian Mutiny, causes diversion of China expedition, 258
Ing Wang, 1.
Irish Regiment, Royal, 219.
Irmak, 130.
Ismaloff, Leon, 150, 151.
Issik Kul, 200.

Jade, 344.
Japanese, 31; war with Mongols, 72, 73, 95; a military nation, ibid.; relations with China, 95-6; their invasion of Corea, 98; seven years' war

with China, 99-100; 315; in Corea, 347; dispute with, 331, 332.
Jats, the, 13.
Jehangir, 199, 200.
Jehol, 161, 178, 197, 279, 281, 307, 308, 309, 310.
Jesuits, the, 150, 155.
Jicfan, 106.
Jinsin, Packhouse, 252.
Jintsong (Sung), 38, 39; promotes education, 39.
Jones, Mr., 297.
Jungaria, 147, 162, 163, 167.
Juriats, 49.

Kabul Khan, 47; proclaimed Emperor of Mongols, 48.
Kachiaou, 288.
Kahpoo, 295, 296.
Kaifong, 43, 44, 52, 56, 57, 116, 117, 241.
Kaiyuen, 107.
Kaidu, 76, 77.
Kajow, 297, 298.
Kalgan, 41, 186.
Kanchang, 242.
Kanchow, 124.
Kanghi, selected heir by Chuntche, 131; his youth, *ibid.*; regents govern for him, 131-2; assumes personal government, 133; resolves to coerce Wou Sankwei, 134; summons him to Pekin, *ibid.*; suppresses Mongol rising, 136; conquers Yunnan, 137; invades Formosa, *ibid.*; consolidates Manchu authority, 139; his central Asian policy, *ibid.*; his relations with Galdan, 141; war with Russia, *ibid.*; assists Khalkas, 142; declares war against Galdan, *ibid.*; vanquishes him, 143; his letter to Galdan, 143-4; denounces Galdan, 144; his great campaign in Central Asia, 144-5; assumes personal command of army, 145; returns to Pekin, 146; corresponds with Tse Wang Rabdan, *ibid.*; defeats Tse Wang Rabdan, 148; his relations with Catholic missionaries, 148-9; receives Russian ambassador, 150; his domestic trouble, 151; anecdote of, 152; dies of a chill, *ibid.*; his early precocity, *ibid.*; character and different opinions of, 152-3; his place among Chinese rulers, 153; 325.
Kang Wang preserves Sung dynasty, 43; becomes Emperor Kaotsong, *ibid.*; improves his army, *ibid.*, 44; abdicates, 45.
Kanmala, 76.
Kansuh, 82, 83, 322.
Kaochi, 17.
Kaochun, 38.

Kaoleang, 37.
Kaoli, 30.
Kaou Meaou Temple, 279.
Kaoti, 24.
Kaotsong, 31, 32.
Kaotsou (Han), 10, 11, 12.
Karai, 170.
Kara Khitay, 42.
Karakoram, 51, 52, 57, 58, 59, 60, 61, 62.
Kara Tau, 169.
Karashar, 323, 343.
Kashgar, 164, 167, 199, 200, 323, 324, 342, 344, 345.
Kashgaria, 140, 158, 162, 197; administration of, 198-9; Khokand intrigues in, 199; Khoja rising in, 232; campaign against, 339.
Kashingfoo, 303.
Keen Lung, history of Mings, 87; placed on throne, 159; his studiousness, *ibid.*; appoints four regents, *ibid.*; reverses several of Yung Ching's measures, 159-60; his early policy towards Christians, 160; domestic afflictions of, 161; not a general but organises victory, 162; receives Amursana, 163; takes up Central Asian question, 163; his energy, 165; his political consistency, 166; action in Central Asia, 167; mode of governing Central Asia, 167; annexes Kashgaria, 167; welcomes the Tourguts, 168; character of his new frontier, 168-9; his war with Burmah, 169; his campaign against Miaotze, 170-1; his policy in Tibet, 171; his war with the Goorkhas, 172-3; his war in Formosa, 173-4; his project of massacreing the Tungani, 174; his relations with Russia, 176; his literary works, 177; welcomes project of English embassy, 177; his honourable reception of Lord Macartney, 178; takes up difficulty of Hoangho, 179; abdication of, 180; personal appearance, 180; death of, 181; his character and achievements, 181-2, 183.
Kelung, 350.
Keo, General, 222.
Keppel, Commodore Harry, gallantry of, 260.
Keraits, 49, 50.
Kerulon, 47, 90.
Keshen, 198, 215; arrives at Canton, 216; agrees with Lin, *ibid.*; delays of, *ibid.*; requests suspension of hostilities, *ibid.*; his promises, 217; removed for his candour, *ibid.*; banished to Tibet, 218.
Key, Captain Cooper, 262.
Keying, 198, 227; advice to Emperor, 228; appointed Commissioner for

drafting tariff, 229; signs convention, 230; 236, 248, 249, 250, 252; his attempt to delude Lord Elgin, 264; his fate, *ibid.*, 326.
Khalkas, the. 139, 141, 142, 143, 144.
Khatmandu, 173.
Khitans in Leaoutung, 37, 39, 40, 42.
Khokand pays tribute to China, 168, 199, 323, 324.
Khoten, 344.
Khudayar, 233.
Khwaresm, 53.
Kia (Hia ruler), 3.
Kiachta, 176, 187.
Kiaking. 180; his father's opinion of him, 183; his letter to George III., 186; refuses to receive Russian ambassador, *ibid.*; his attitude towards Lord Amherst, 189; letter to Prince Regent, *ibid.*; attack on, 190; his will, 193; death, 195.
Kiangnan, dual province of, 36, 37.
Kiangtsai, 126, 127; killed, 128.
Kiangsu, 263, 312.
Kiaochi, 73.
Kiassetao, 64, 66, 67.
Kia-yu-kwan, 83.
Kien Kang, 67.
Kien Wenti (Ming), 87; defeated and flees to Yunnan, 88-9; death of, 89.
Kinchakiang, 60.
Kincsay, 66, 67, 223.
Kingchow, 115.
Kingti (Ming), 91.
Kingti (Han), 13.
Kingyang, 83.
Kins, meaning of name, 41; conquer northern provinces, 42; carry off Emperor, 43; reverses of, 44; retreat of, 45; last success of, 46; unprepared to oppose Mongols, 52, 56; overthrow of, 57.
Kinshun, General. 331.
Kiungchow, 339.
Kiukiang, 240.
Kirkham, Major, 299.
Kirong, 142, 172, 173.
Kintang, 303, 304.
Kinshun, 339, 340, 341, 342.
Kintsong, 43.
Kirghiz, 62, 146, 165, 166.
Kiuchessa, 129.
Knei Hsiang, 352.
Kobdo, 145.
Koko, 78.
Kokonar, 38.
Kok Robat, 233.
Kongtsong (Sung), 68.
Kongyin, 299.
Kongyuta, 114.
Koria, 342, 343, 344.
Kortsin Mongols. 112, 144.
Koshinga, 124, 131, 132.
Kotao ceremony, 130, *passim.*

Kowlun, 268.
Krusenstern, 187.
Kublai Khan, 59; entrusted with conquest of China, *ibid.*; adopts a temperate policy, *ibid.*; invades Yunnan, 60; deprived of posts by his brother, *ibid.*; holds kuriltai at Pekin, 61; rivalry with Arikbuka, *ibid.*; overcomes him, 62; resumes conquest of China, *ibid.*; treaty with Litsong, *ibid.*; skilful treatment of Corea, 63; his relations with Chinese, *ibid.*; his action in Tibet, *ibid.*; resumes war with Sungs, 64; besieges Sianyang, *ibid.*, 68; consolidates his authority, 70; gives name to his dynasty, *ibid.*; embellishes his capital, *ibid.*; his policy, 71; his religion, *ibid.*; personal appearance of, 71-2; his expedition against Japan, 72-73; his relations with Tonquin, 73; his war with Burmah, 73-4; receives foreign embassies, 75; never overcame Chinese dislike, 76; war with other Mongol chiefs, *ibid.*; death and character of, 77.
Kucha, 323, 344.
Kuchu, 58.
Kuku Khoten, 51.
Kuku Timour, 83, 84, 85, 86.
Kuldja, 324, 325; revolt in, *ibid.*; Russia occupies, 325; 344, 345, 346.
Kulangsu, 221, 229, 247.
Kuli Beg, 343, 344.
Kuti, 172.
Kutula or Kublai, 48.
Kuriltai, a, 50, 57, 58.
Kung, Prince, 236; writes to Lord Elgin, 278; resolves to make all concessions, 279; releases Parkes, *ibid.*; returns Sikhs, 280; signs treaty in Pekin, 281; learns from Lord Elgin extent of Taeping success, 284, 288, 307, 308, 309; his great achievement, 310; merit of his success, 311; selects Chinese flag, 312, 314; disgraced. *ibid.*; restored, 314-15, 329, 330, 332; helps Empresses, 333; disgraced, 351.
Kutan, 58.
Kutuktoo, 142.
Kuyuk, 58, 59.
Kwangsi, 238, 246.
Kwangsu, 333; meaning of name, 334; marriage of, 352; gives first audience, 352-3; personal appearance of, 353; receives Mr. O'Conor, *ibid.*
Kwangtsong (Sung), 46.
Kwangtsong (Ming), 108.
Kweichow, 110, 170, 318, 319, 320.
Kwei Wang, 133.
Kweiling, 238, 239.
Kweiliang, 264, 265, 266, 271, 272, 309, 311.
Kwanshihs, 317.

Kwo Sungtao, 337, 345.
Kwo Tsey, 32, 33.

Laguerre, Admiral, 245.
Lanchefoo, 83.
Lanessan, De, 75.
Lange, M. de, 150.
Langson, 349, 350.
Lao Chang, 13.
Laos, 77.
Laoutse, 3-4, *passim*.
Lar Wang, 301.
Later Tsin, dynasty, 22.
Latsan Khan, 147, 171.
Lay, Mr. G. T., 247.
Lay, Mr. H. N., 311, 312, 313.
Leang dynasty, 24.
Leang, Duke of, 308.
Leangki, 19.
Leaoutung, kingdom of, 36. 37 ; successes of, 38. 41 ; end of, 42 : 103, 104, 105, 106, 108, 109, 111.
Leaouyang, 109.
Leeku, 299.
Lekin, 351.
Leseen, 54.
Lessihin, 155.
Lhasa, 131, 140, 147, 188.
Liang Shihinei, 319.
Libraries in China, 81.
Lichi, Empress, 46.
Lichimin, 26, 27 ; takes title of Taitsong, *ibid*.
Li Chitsao, 101.
Lichitsi, 29.
Li Chongsin, 36.
Li Chungwei, 86.
Lieuchow, 201.
Li Han Chang, 336.
Li Hung Chang, 289 ; suspects Burgevine, 290-1 ; causes Burgevine to be dismissed, 292; suspends action, *ibid.*; opposes Burgevine's return, 294 ; feud with Burgevine, 295 ; interview with Wangs, 301 ; his dealings with them, 302 ; relations with Gordon, *ibid*. ; 313, 331; succeeds Tseng as Viceroy, 336 ; entrusted with full power in Yunnan question, 337 ; energy of, 338 ; his Corean policy, 347 ; and Tonquin, 348 ; signs treaty with France, 350 ; and opium, 352 ;
Li Jusong, 97, 98, 99.
Likeyong, 34.
Likimao, 89.
Li Kwangli, 14.
Li Kweiching, 119.
Liling, 14.
Lin, family of Huns, 22.
Linan 317, 319.
Ling, 174.
Lingan, 66.
Lin's fort, 261, 262.
Lintin, 184.

Lin Tsihseu, Commissioner, 208; arrives at Canton, 209 ; his programme, 210 : demands surrender of opium, *ibid* ; demands persons of merchants, 211 ; rewarded by Emperor, *ibid.* : demands surrender of a sailor, 211 : review of his proceedings 213 ; places reward on Englishmen, 214 ; disgraced, 215.
Lin Linming Pass, 241.
Linsong, 22.
Lintao, 82, 83.
Lintsing, 242.
Lin Tzuchin, 317, 318.
Linyu, 23.
Lin Yuchow. 320.
Lipan, 98, 99.
Lisitai, 335.
Lossechi 82, 83.
Lisseh, 5, 7, 8.
Litan, 64.
Li Tsecbing, 115 ; his successes, *ibid.* : takes name of Emperor, 117 ; captures Pekin, 118 ; his relations with Wou Sankwei, 119; his overthrow, 120 ; death of, 121.
Litsong (Sung), 57, 58, 59, 62, 64.
Litsunhiu, 34.
Little Bokhara, 167. *See* Kashgaria
Liuchi, Empress, 12.
Liuchi, 25.
Liucho, 15.
Liu Hiuen, 16.
Liukin, 93.
Liu Kintang, 340, 343, 344. 346.
Liu Pang, 10.
Liu Sieou ; Kwang Vouti, 16, 17.
Liuwen Hoan, 64, 65, 66.
Liuyen, 107.
Livadia, Treaty of, 345.
Liyang, 303, 304.
Liyuen, 26.
Lobsang Kalsang, 171.
Loch, Sir Henry, 272 n., 273 n., 274; gallantry of, *ibid.*, 276, 279-80, 281.
Lolos, 315, 317.
London, Convention of, 351
"London Gazette," the, 312.
Loo, Viceroy, 207.
Loochoo, 332.
Lorcha, meaning of name, 253.
Lousionfoo, 68.
Low Mun, 300, 301.
Loyang, 10, 16.
Loyang, 22.
Luwenti, 61.
Ly Wenchong, 84.

Ma, Marshal, 322
Macartney, Sir Halliday 294 ; warns Gordon of Burgevine, 295-6; founds a great Chinese arsenal, 314 ; services of, 337, 352.
Macartney, Lord, 172 ; sails from

INDEX.

Portsmouth for China, 178; his honourable reception, *ibid.*; success of his embassy, *ibid.*
Macao, 100, 150, 175; tenure of, 184; British occupation of, *ibid.*; evacuated, 185, 205, 206, 209, 212, 215; Macao passage, 255.
Macaulay, Mr. Colman, 354.
Machi, 18.
Madacou, 46, 49, 51.
Magay, 244.
Magazine Hill, 262.
Mahomed Ali, of Khokand, 199; refuses to pay tribute, *ibid.*; 200, 233.
Mahomedans in North-west China, 322; Keen Lung's project, *ibid.*
Mailla quoted, 41, 152, 177.
Maitilipala, 84, 85.
Ma Julung, 318, 319, 320.
Malacca, 93.
Malin, 106, 107.
Malmesbury, Lord, 251, 266.
Manas, 340, 341, 342.
Manchus, the, 101; meaning of name, 102; early history of, *ibid.*; their connection with Kins, *ibid.*; their first chief, *ibid.*; feuds with China, 103; their division and union, 103; comparison with Prussia, 105, 107; discover jade seal of Mongols, 114; build Tartar citadels in China, 124; their conquest of China, 124-5.
Manchu family, the, 191.
Mangonels, 65.
Manila, 176.
Manwein, 335.
Mangu, 59, 60, 61; death of, 61; last of the Great Khans, 62
Manzu, 315.
Maralbashi, 344.
Marco Polo, 67, 70, 77, 93.
Margary, Mr. R. A., 334; sent to Yunnan, *ibid.*; murdered at Manwein, *ibid.*, 336.
Ma Sien, 316, 317, 318. *See* Ma Julung.
Ma Sucheng, 316.
Ma Tesing, 317, 318.
Mati, 143.
Matow, 272.
Ma Wenchu, 316.
Mayuen, 17, 18.
Mecca, 317.
Meenning, Prince, 191, 193.
Meha, 11, 12, 13.
Mencius, 3, 4, *passim*
Meta. *See* Meha.
Miaotze, 107, 170; prisoners executed, 171; 198, 201, 319.
Michel, Sir J., 268, 287.
Mien, 73. *See* Burmah.
Millot, General, 349.
Min river, 350.
Mines in Yunnan, 316.

Ming dynasty, meaning of name, 81. *See* Chapters VII., VIII., and IX., *passim*.
Mingti (Han), 17.
Mingti (Later Tsin), 23.
Mingti, 32.
Minister, Resident, at Pekin, 264-5, 266, 272.
Missionaries, 101, 148-9, 156-7; proceedings of, in China, 328.
Momein, 335.
Monding, 298, 300.
Mongchi, 24, 43
Mongkong, 56, 57, 59.
Mongkwan, 22.
Mongols, the; meaning of name, 47; early history of *ibid.*; growth of power, 48; cause of their success, 51; triumphs of, 54-5; final Ming campaigns with, 83-6; rising of, 136.
Mongtsin, 22.
Montauban, General, 268, 270, 277.
Morrison, Mr., 225.
Moukden, 102, 108, 109, 115.
Moungtien, 8, 11.
Moutsong (Tang), 33
Moutsong (Ming), 96, 97.
Mow Wang, northern king, 243, 298, 300; murdered, 301.
Muchangah, 236.
Muhula, 50, 53; death of, 54.

Naimans, 49, 50.
Nalsing, 276.
Nanhai, 11.
Nanjao, 289.
Nankin, 23, 26, 44, 67, 79, 80, 82, 86, 87, 89, 117, 122, 123, 131, 132, 211, 223, 225; English fleet arrives at, *ibid.*, 227; treaty of, 228-9: captured by Taepings, 240; re-fortified by Taepings, 241, 284; sixth siege of, 286; affairs at, 287, 290, 303, 305; recaptured from Taepings, *ibid.*, 314, 330.
Nanning, 238.
Nan Wang, 4, 5.
Napier, Lord, 204; his instructions, 205; inauspicious beginning, *ibid.*; his efforts, 206; death of, *ibid.*
Napier, Sir R. (Lord Napier of Magdala), 268, 269, 272.
Nasiuddin, 74.
National Defence, Board of, 351.
Nayakot, 173.
Nayan, 76.
Nepaul, 171; Goorkha conquest of, 172.
Nerchinsk, treaty of, 141, 175-6.
Nestorian Christians, 33.
Neutrals in China, 349-50.
New Dominion, the, 344, 346.
New Year's Day, 234.
Nienfei, 314.

Nieuhoff, 130.
Ninghia, 83, 84, 85, 97.
Ningpo, 215, 221, 222; attack on, 223, 229.
Ningtsong, 46.
Ningtsong (Sung), 53, 57.
Ningyuen, 110, 111, 112, 113, 115, 119.
Ninkiassu, 54, 56; suicide of, 57.
Niuche Tartars, 41; description of their army, 41-2, 101, 102, 103, 106, 107.
Niu Kien, 227; letters from, *ibid.*
Niyamoho, 44.
Noorhachu, birth of, 102; his first military experience, 103; his oath, *ibid.*; unites Niuche tribes, *ibid.*; victory of, 104; his army, *ibid.*; his denunciation of China, *ibid.*; dramatic proceeding of, 105; compared with House of Brandenburg, *ibid.*; defeats Chinese armies, 106; captures Moukden, 108-9; consolidates his position, 110; siege of Ningyuen, 110; repulsed at, 111; dies of chagrin, *ibid.*; his character, *ibid.*
Normann De, 273 n., 280.

Ochterloney, Sir D., 173.
O'Conor, Mr., received in audience, 353; signs Convention of Pekin, 355.
Ogelen Eke, 48, 49.
Ogotai, 55, 56, 58.
Ohto, 44.
Ongut, 51.
Onon, 47, 48, 49.
Opium, its increased import, 184; Manchu princes degraded for using, 208, 210; question of, 212-3; discussion about, 229; to be legalised or not, 230; left contraband, *ibid.*; not the real cause of war, *ibid.*; legalisation of, 265, 351, 352; cultivation legalised, *ibid.*
Opossum, the, 267.
Ordus, the, 95.
Orenburg, 168.
Osborn, Captain, Sherard, 261, 311, 312, 313.
Ou, principality of, 21.
Oubacha, 168.
Oukiai, 44.
Oukimai, 42, 44, 48.
Oulo, 45.
Ourga, 49, 142, 145.

Pakba Lama, 63, 71.
Pakhoi, 339.
Palikao bridge, 278, 280.
Palmerston, Lord, 205, 215, 250.
Pamir, 167.
Panchow, 17; his campaign against Huns, 18.
Pandects of Yunglo, 81.
Pang Wanching, 267.

Panthays, 315, 322.
Panti, 164, 165.
Paochiaou, 287, 303.
Papesifu, 77.
Parker, Dr., 257.
Parker, Sir W., 223.
Parkes, Sir Harry, 247; consul at Canton, 253; reports *Arrow* case, 253; enters Canton, 256, 261; discovers and captures Yeh, 262; sent to arrange advance of army, etc., 272-3; reaches Tungchow, 273; interview with commissioners, *ibid.*; finds Chinese army in position, *ibid.*; realises danger, 274; returns to Commissioners, *ibid.*; interview with Prince Tsai, 275; attempts to reach English army, *ibid.*; confidence in his judgment, 276; seized by Sankolinsin, *ibid.*; place of confinement, 279; released, *ibid.*; his sufferings and chivalry, 279-80; sent into Pekin, 281; minister in Japan, 315; minister at Pekin, 350; death of, 352.
Patachiaou, 298, 299.
Patenotre, M., 350.
Paukwen, 311.
Pears, Captain, 224.
Pechihli, 93, 115, 120.
Pechihli, Gulf of, 178, 263.
Pegu, 169.
Pehtang, 268; plot at, 263.
Peiho, 178, 188, 215, 263, 264, 265, 266, 278.
Pekin, 61, 80, 108, 113, 114, 120, 121; Russian colony at, 141, 142; convention of, 169, 178, 187, 242, 265, 267, 272; strength of, 279; north-east gate surrendered to English, 280; expedition returns from, 281; treaty of, *ibid.*; significance of treaty, 282-3; 307-308, plot at, 309; 312, 314, 320, 321, 322, 330, 346, 347; *coup d'état* at, 351.
Pekin Gazette, the, 32, 336.
Pekin field force, 351.
Pe-leen-keaou, 192.
Perestralo Raphael, 93.
Pescadore Islands, 132, 137.
Peter the Great, embassy from, 150.
Philippines, 100; massacre in, *ibid.*; 150.
Phipps, 274.
Phukai, 348.
Pidjam, 342.
Pienkiao, 28, 29.
Pigtail, the, doubtful origin of, 109.
Pihkwei, 262.
Pingching, 11, 24.
Pingsiuki, 98. *See* Fashiha.
Ping-si-Wang, 121.
Pingti, 16.
Pingtseuen, 201.
Pingyang, 23, 99.

Pintici, 41.
Pirates on Canton river, 234.
Poki, 154.
Polo Timour, 79.
Ponghu, 137.
Popai, 97.
Porcelain Tower, outrage on, 229.
Porshu, 50.
Port Hamilton, 346.
Port Lazareff, 346.
Portuguese, outrages of, 94; offer help to China, 108-9, 100; injure European reputation, *ibid.*; their relations with China, 175, 177.
Pottinger, Sir Henry, arrives as plenipotentiary, 220; sails north, 221; issues a proclamation, 222, 227; states terms of negotiation, *ibid.*; receives Chinese Commissioners, 228; signs treaty, 229; drafts tariff, 229-30, 247; opinion of opium, 265.
Probyn's Horse, 277.
Protet, Admiral, 289.
Puerh, 321.

Quelpart, 346.
Quemoy, 221.
Quinsan, 292, 293, 294, 296, 297, 302, 304.

Railway, first in China, 339.
Rassoa, 173.
Red Caps, the, 147.
Red Girdles, 171.
Red River, 348. *See* Songcoi.
Regulo or Prince, 157.
Ricci, Matthew, 101.
Rites, tribunal of, 149.
Rhodes, Colonel, 304.
Rivière Capt. Henri, 75, 348.
Rocher, 348.
Roger, Michel, 101.
Roman Catholics, the, 148.
Russell, Lord John, 214.
Russians, the, 130, 139, 141; relations with China, 176; in Kuldja, 344.

St. Petersburg, 327, 345; treaty of, 346.
Sacæ, the, 13.
Saichangah, 238.
Sakya Muni, 17.
Salisbury, Marquis of, 351.
Saltoun, Lord, 224.
Samuka, 53.
Sanchuen, 39.
Sankoue, 21.
Sankolinsin, 242, 267, 272, 275; offers indignity to Parkes, 276, 277; murdered, 314.
Santajin, 299, 300.
Sanpou, the, 63; chief of Tibet, 29, 31.
Sapsu, 145.
Sarhoo Hill, 106.
Sarimsak, 167, 199.

Satchar, 136, 139.
Schaal, Adam, 130, 132, 133.
Schufeldt, Commodore, 346, 347.
Scythians, the, 13.
Secret Societies, the, 192; objects of, *ibid.*; their organisation, 193.
Segaou Hills, 223.
Selinga river, 76.
Sembuen, 169.
Seoul, 99, 347.
Sessaka, 154, 155.
Seymour, Sir Michael, captures Barrier Forts, 255; arrives at Canton, *ibid.*; enters Canton, 256; requests 5,000 troops, *ibid.*; resumes active operations, 258; attacks Chinese in Fatshan Channel, 259-60; differences with Lord Elgin, 263; captures Taku Forts, 264.
Shanghai, 224, 229, 245; seized by rebels, *ibid.*; invested by Imperialists, *ibid.*; Chinese re-capture, 246, 266, 267, 285; Europeans' guarantee, *ibid.*; attack on, 287; thirty miles round to be cleared of rebels, 288; attempt to set fire to, 289; 295, 314, 322, 339.
Shanhaikwan, 110, 115, 119, 198.
Shantung, 242, 314.
Shansi, 82, 114, 115, 120, 121, 126; famine in, 338.
Shapuntsai, 234, 235.
Shektsin, 265, 266.
Shen Paochen, 305.
Shensi, 82, 121, 126, 322, 323.
Shu Kofa, 122; refuses to flood country, 123.
Shun, Prince, 236.
Siangkong, Prince of Tsin, 3.
Sianyang, 64; heroic episode at, 65.
Siaotaoching, 24.
Siberia, conquest of, 130, 151.
Sieh Futai, 289, 292.
Sienpi, 18, 19.
Sikhs, some gallant, 273, 274, 275; cruel fate of, 280.
Silver, export of, 205, 207.
Sinching, 21.
Singapore, 258.
Singtur, 74.
Singanfoo, 10, 16; triumph at, 26, 29; stone at, 33, 117, 323.
Sinho, 269.
Sining, 147, 171, 340.
Sinlo, 30, 31.
Siuenti (Han), 15.
Si Wang, 128; his cruelties, *ibid.*; massacres women, 129; killed, *ibid.*
Sobo, 325.
Solon contingent, the, 163, 325.
Song dynasty, 23.
Songcoi, 348.
Songshan, 115.
Sonom, 170, 171.
Sontay, 348, 349.

Sony, 132, 133.
Soochow, 123, 285, 286, 292, 294, 295, 298, 299, 300, 301, 303, 313, 314.
Soodsu, 102.
Soponomo, 14.
Souchow, 83, 323, 331, 340.
Soui dynasty, 25, 26.
Sourniama, 155.
Soutsong, 32.
Spaniards, the, 100; massacre Chinese, *ibid.*, 160; relations with China, 176.
Ssemachong, 22.
Ssemachow, 21, 22.
Ssemachu, 22.
Ssemakwang, 39.
Ssematsien, 14.
Stanton, Mr. Vincent, 215.
Staunton, Sir George, 177, 178, 188.
Staveley, General, 288, 289, 291, 292.
Stonecutter Island, 268.
Subutai, 56, 59.
Suentsong (Ming), 90; rearranges civil service, *ibid.*
Sultan Suliman, 321.
Summer Palace. *See* Yuen Min Yuen.
Sund Fo, 172, 173, 178.
Sungs, the national dynasty of their time, 47; folly of their policy in regard to Mongols, 57; reduced to extremities, 66; their struggle with Mongols begins, 58, 59.
Sung Tajin, 186, 187, 189, 197.
Sunghen, 23.
Sunhow, 22.
Sunkiang, 286, 289, 290, 292, 293.
Sunkiuen, 21.
Supreme Court for China and Japan, 315.
Sushuen, 310, 311.
Suta, 80, 82; defeats Mongols of the West, 83; desert campaign, 85; death and eulogy of. 86.
Szchuen. 85, 86, 93, 109, 110, 128, 129, 170, 174, 320.

Tadi, 173.
Ta Chereng, 162, 163.
Tachun, 117.
Ta Edin, 294, 296.
Taepings, 237, 238; meaning of name, 238-9; capture Nankin, 240, 241; most northern point of advance, *ibid.*; campaigns of, 242; foreign views of, *ibid.*; their degree of success, 246; growth of power, 284; their confidence, 288, 292, 293; disposition of their troops, 299, 300, 301; their Wangs murdered, 302.
Taho Lake, 298, 299, 303
Tai, Prince of (Han), 12.
Tai (island), 68.
Taikok, 216.
Taiko Sama, 98. *See* Fashiba.

Taitong, 51, 52, 117, 126, 127, 128.
Taitsan, 289, 292, 293.
Taitsong (Sung), 37.
Taitsong the Great, 27-31.
Taitsong the Second, 32.
Taipe, 72.
Taitsong (Manchu), 111; letter of, 111-12; resolved to continue Noorhachu's work, 112; his brilliant plan, 112-13; divides army into Banners, 113; appeals to Chinese opinion, 113; besieges Pekin, *ibid.*; again invades China, 114; assumes title of Emperor, *ibid.*; conquers Corea, 115; death and character of, *ibid.*
Taitsou Hwangti, 111. *See* Noorhachu.
Taitsou founds Sung dynasty, 35; his military reforms, 35-6; deprives governors of powers of life and death, 36; conquers Szchuen, 36; annexes Kiangnan, 37; death of, *ibid.*
Taiwan, 132.
Tai Wang Kun, 347.
Taiyuen, 32, 36, 37, 38, 95, 117.
Taku Forts, capture of, 263-4, 265; second attack on, 267; English repulse at, *ibid.*; turned by Sir Hope Grant, 268; fighting at, 270; capture of 270-1.
Takee, 291.
Talifoo, 60, 317, 319; massacre of, 321-2.
Tamerlane, 90.
Tamsui, 350.
Tangku, 269, 270.
Tangut, 38. *See* Hia, 83.
Taoukwang, meaning of name, 196; appearance of, *ibid.*; his first acts, 197; his clemency, 197; tranquillity of early years probably deceptive, 198; kills his son, 201; his position and possibilities, 202; dismisses Portuguese astronomers, 204; issues regulations for trade, 206; edict of, 207; rewards Lin, 211; adopts anti-foreign policy, 212; letter to, 215; appoints a High Commissioner, *ibid.*; orders up troops, *ibid.*; denounces the English, 217; his obstinacy, *ibid.*; sends fresh Commissioners, 218; still hostile, 221; his military preparations, 222; admits necessity of peace, 226; replies to Keying, 228; ratifies Treaty, 229; his character as Chinese ruler, 232; his superstitious act, 234; appoints his heir, 235; death and character of, 235-6; admission of about Christianity, 248.
Taouism, 3.
Tapp, Major, 295.
Taranath Lama, 142.
Tarantchis, 200, 324-5, 326.
Tara Ussu, 323.

Tashkent, 168.
Tayan, 305.
Tchaohoei, 166, 167.
Tea, ode on, 177.
Techow, 88.
Tefei, 40.
Tehshun Gate, 279.
Tekes Valley, 345.
Temujin, 48.
Tengai, 21.
Tengyue, 333.
Terek Pass, 324.
Teshu Lama, 172.
Teshu Lumbo, 172.
Tetsong, 32, 33.
Theen-te-Hwuy, 192.
Thiers, M., 329.
Thom, Mr. R., 247.
Thotho Timour, 91.
Thsin, the Great, 18.
Tian Shan, 323.
Tibet, 29, 31, 32, 63; Grand Lama of, visits Pekin, 78, 130; Eleuth policy in, 146-7; Chinese position in, *ibid.*; garrisoned by China, 148; situation in, 171; Chinese policy in, 171-2, 218; opposes Macaulay's mission, 354.
Ticounai, 44, 45; defeat of, *ibid.*
Tienki, 108, 110, 112.
Tientsin, 178, 188, 241; treaty of, 263, 264, 265, 266, 267, 271, and Appendix; massacre of, 327-9; events leading up to it, 328; consequence of, 329; 337.
Tien Wang, 237, 238; his proclamation, *ibid.*: marches north, 239; captures Nankin, 240; proclaims Nankin his capital, 241; his relations with his lieutenants, 243; 284, 285, 286, 290; commits suicide, 305.
Tiki, 3.
Timour. Yuen Emperor, 77, 78.
Times, The, correspondent of, 272.
Tingan, 89.
Tinghai, 214, 221.
Tipa, the, 147.
Togan, 74, 75.
Tohan Timour, 78.
Tokio, 347.
Toksoun, 342, 343.
Tonquin, 68, 74, 75; French in, 75, 89, 90, 347.
Toolun, 103.
Topatao, 24.
Toto, 79.
Toufan, 29. *See* Tibet.
Toukinei, 28.
Toula, 91.
Toupo, 29. *See* Tibet.
Toumon, 91.
Tourguts, flee from Tse Wang Rabdan, 168; reside in Russian territory, *ibid.*; return on Chinese re-conquest, *ibid.*

Tousong, 106.
Tou Timour, 78.
Toutsong (Sung), 64, 66.
Treaty Ports, 229.
Triads, the, 192, 237, 239; abandon Taepings, *ibid.*; at Shanghai, 245; at Canton, 246.
Tsai, Prince of I, 272, 275, 278, 281, 307, 309; fate of, 310.
Tsaichan, 56, 57.
Tsai Tien, 333. *See* Kwangsu.
Tse Kung Ko, 353.
Tseng Kwofan, 239, 240, 284, 286, 303, 305, 313, death of, 314, 320, 330-1.
Tseng Kwotsiuen, 305, 351.
Tseng, Marquis, 345; sent to Russia, *ibid.*; death of, 351; loss to China, *ibid.*
Tsenka, 142, 146.
Tsen Yuying, 319, 320, 321, 336.
Tse Wang Rabdan, 142, 143; becomes chief of the Eleuths, 146; remonstrates with Kanghi, 146; his action in Tibet, 146-7; death of, 158.
Tseedong, 288.
Tsi An, Empress, 309; vigorous action of *ibid.*; appointed Regent, 310; 334, 346; her death and achievements, 346.
Tsi Hiwen, 88.
Tsi Thsi, Empress, 310, 346; decree of, 351; retires, 352.
Tsin dynasty, 5, 8.
Tsin Chi Hwangti, Emperor, 5; builds Great Wall of China, *ibid.*; constructs roads, 6; his public works, *ibid.*; strife with literary classes, 6-8; his death, 8; burial of, *ibid.*
Tsing, 102, 241.
Tsinan, 88.
Tsinghai, 242.
Tsingho, 106.
Tsingpu, 286, 289, 290.
Tsinliang, 110.
Tsin-yuen, 82.
Tsiusima 72, 346.
Tsipoo, 289.
Tsongching (Ming), 112; his hard position, 117; speech of, 117-18; commits suicide, 118, 119.
Tsong-ming, 131.
Tsongtse, 44.
Tso Tsung Tang, 303; made Viceroy of N.W. provinces, 331; organises Central Asian campaign, *ibid.*, 339; character of, 340; energy of, 342; his caution, 343; his work, 344.
Tsowpi, 19, 21.
Tsow Tsow, 19.
Tsungli Yamen, creation of, 308 326, 334, 336, 337, 345.
Tszeki, 223.
Tuduc, 349.
Tuli, 56, 57.

INDEX.

Tungani, 116, 174, 315, 322; beginning of their revolt, *ibid.*; its extent, 323; in Kuldja, 325; defend Urumtsi, 340; their last stand, *ibid.*; massacre of, 341; end of rising, 342.
Tungche, 310; difficulties during his reign, 326; marriage of, 330; receives foreign ministers in audience, *ibid.*; relations with Prince Kung, 332; ill health of, 332; his death, 333.
Tungchow, 272, 273, 274, 275, 278.
Tungking, 32.
Tungting, 240.
Tunkwan, 53, 56, 117.
Tung Wang, Eastern King, the, 243, 244.
Turakina, 58.
Turfan, 148, 162, 323, 342.
Tu Wensiu, 317, 318, 319, 320, 321; original of Sultan Suliman, 321.
Twan Kang, 19.
Ty, Prince of Yen, 87, 88; triumph of, 88; becomes Emperor, 89; death of, 90.

Uliassutai, 340.
Uriangkadai, 59, 60, 61, 62, 73.
Urtish, Upper, 158.
Urumsit, 323, 340, 341, 344.
Ush Turfan, 344.
Utubu, 52, 53, 54.

Verbiest, Father, 133.
Vermilion Edict, 235.
Victoria, Queen, and Chinese problem, 210; intercedes for Chung How, 345.
Volga, 168.
Voltaire, 177.
Volunteer Corps at Canton, 209.
Vouti (Han), 13, 14.
Vouti (Song), 24.
Voutsong (Tang), 33.

Wade, Sir Thomas, 247, 261, 278, 308, 327, 332, 335; receives news of Yunnan outrage, 335; demands special Commission of Inquiry, 336; demands satisfaction, *ibid.*; leaves Pekin, 337; signs Chefoo Convention, *ibid.*; action in Woosung railway, 339; leaves China, 350.
Waiquaidong, 296, 297.
Waisso, 303, 304.
Wali Khan, 323.
Walker, Colonel, 273, 276.
Walipou, 43.
Walsham, Sir J., 353.
Wang (title), 2.
Wanganchi, socialist statesman, 39, 40.
Wangchin, 90, 91.
Wang Khan, Kerait chief, 49.
Wangkien, 61.

Wang Kua, 13.
Wang Mang, 16, 17.
Wangtien, 62, 63.
Wanleh, 96; his long reign, 97; speech of, *ibid.*; helps Corea, 99; war with Japan, 99, 100; employs Europeans, 101; selects an heir, *ibid.*; death of, *ibid.*, 107.
Wansiang, 308, 309, 311, 313, 334.
Wansin Hill, 118.
Wanti, 299.
Ward, 286, 287, 288, 290; death of, *ibid.*
Water Lily Society, 192.
Weddell, Captain, 100.
Wei, principality of, 21.
Weijoui, 25.
Weising lotteries, 337-8.
Wei Tsing, 13.
Wenchow, 339.
Wenti (Han), 12, 13.
Wenti (Song), 23.
Wentsong (Tang), 33.
Whampoa, 176, 217.
Willis, Captain, 269.
Wokong, 295, 298, 299.
Wolseley, Lord, 269.
Wongkadza, 288.
Woosung, 227, 287, 339.
Wou, Empress, 31, 32.
Wou, Taotai, 291.
Wouchang, 62, 240.
Wou Sankwei entrusted with defence of frontier, 115; evacuates Ningyuen to march on Pekin, 119; invites aid of Manchus, *ibid.*; defeats Li, 120; gains decisive battle, 121; really conquers China for Manchus, 124-5; governs south-west China, 133: an object of suspicion to Manchus, 134; summoned to Pekin, *ibid.*; refuses to go, 135; war with Kanghi, *ibid.*; final struggles, 136; death and character, 136-7; plot of son of, 134-5.
Wou Shufan, 137.
Woutsong (Ming), 93.
Wou Wang, Prince of Chow, 3.
Wuhlahai, 50.
Wuhu, 339.
Wuliungchow, 229.
Wusieh, 299, 300, 303.

Xanadu, 82. *See* Changtu.

Yaik, 168.
Yakoob Beg, early career of, 324; deposes Buzurg, *ibid.*; 339, 340, 341; marches to meet Chinese army, 342; defeated, 343; death of, *ibid.*
Yalookiang, 103.
Yangabad, 200.
Yangchow, 44, 123, 241, 326.
Yang Moulong, 39.
Yangti, 25.
Yangtsekiang, 223, *passim.*

Yangyeh, 38.
Yangyshahrs, 233.
Yang Yuko, 320, 321, 322.
Yao, 2.
Yaochu, 59, 60, 70.
Yaoujin, 202.
Yarkand, 164, 167, 233, 324; massacre at, *ibid*.; 344.
Yaroslaf of Russia, 58.
Yeddo, 315.
Yeh, Commissioner, 252; refuses interview, *ibid*.; applies to English for assistance, *ibid*.; rejects all overtures, 253; action in *Arrow* case, 253-5; arrogance of, 255; his defiant attitude, 256; offers reward for Englishmen, *ibid*.; encouraged by delayed arrival of English expedition, 258; replies to Lord Elgin, 261; capture of, 262; sent to Calcutta, 263.
Yeho, 104, 106, 107.
Yeh-ho-na-la, 352.
Yeke Yilatu, 48.
Yeliu Chutsia, 56, 58.
Yeliu Hiuco, 38.
Yeliu Liuko, 51, 52, 53.
Yellow Caps, the, 147.
Yellow Flags, the, 350.
Yellow Girdles, 171; revolt of, 191.
Yenking, now Pekin, 52, 53.
Yenta, 95, 96.
Yeoutou, now Pekin, 35.
Yesien, 90.
Yesing, 303.
Yesun Timour, 78.
Yihchoo, 235. *See* Hienfung.
Yinghan, 338.
Yissugei, father of Genghis, 48.
Yngtsong, Sung, 39..
Yngtsong, Ming, 90, 91; captured by Mongols, *ibid*.; restored to throne, *ibid*.
Yochow, 240.
Yongchi, 67.
Yongchang, 117.
Yonglo, 89. *See* Ty, Prince of Yen.
Yu, 2, 3.
Yuchi, the, 13.
Yuchi, 18.
Yuching, 263.
Yuchow, 56.
Yuen dynasty, 70, 77; fall of, 80.
Yuen Min Yuen, 158, 188, 189; sack of, 279; destruction of, 280-1.
Yuenti (Han), 15.
Yukien, 91, 92.
Yukwang, Chinese d'Assas, 83.
Yuen Yingtai, 109.
Yungan, 239.
Yungchang, 74.
Yung Ching, 154; his relations with his kinsmen, 154-5; prejudiced against Christians, 155; his speech on Christianity in China, 156-7; dispels Christian illusions, 157; foreign policy of, 158; death of, *ibid*.; character of, 159.
Yungping, 120.
Yunnan, Mongol invasion of, 60-1, 73, 85, 86, 110; first Mahomedan rising in, 232, 348; Mahomedan rising in, 315-21.
Yunnanfoo, 317, 318, 320, 322.
Yusuf, 199
Yu Tsing Wang, 143.

Zanho, 120.
Zealand, Fort, 132.
Zeren Donduk 147, 148.
Zuhuruddin, 233.

www.ingramcontent.com/pod-product-compliance
Lightning Source LLC
Chambersburg PA
CBHW022142300426
44115CB00006B/309